Using Q&A® 4

David P. Ewing
Bill Langenes

Revised by
George R. Beinhorn

Publisher: Lloyd J. Short

Associate Publisher: Karen A. Bluestein

Acquisitions Manager: Terrie Lynn Solomon

Product Developement Manager: Mary Bednarek

Managing Editor: Paul Boger

Production Team: Scott Boucher, Claudia Bell, Sandy Grieshop, Bob LaRoche, Howard Peirce, Cindy L. Phipps, Tad Ringo, Johnna VanHoose, Lisa A. Wilson, Sue VandeWalle

DEDICATION

To the Ewing clan—Bob, Mark, Kathy, Bill,
Mary Beth, Rita, Janet, and Tom

D.E.

To Marie, my best friend

B.L.

Production Editor
Lori A. Lyons

Editors
Kelly Currie
Leigh Davis
Daniel Schnake

Technical Editors
William Coy Hatfield
Andrew R. Young

*Composed in Garamond and Macmillan
by Que Corporation.*

David P. Ewing

David P. Ewing is President/Publisher of New Riders Publishing Company, a division of Macmillan Computer Publishing Company. Prior to this position, he was the Publishing Director for Que Corporation. Mr. Ewing is the author of Que's *1-2-3 Macro Library*, *Using 1-2-3 Workbook and Disk*, and *Using 1-2-3 Workbook Instructor's Guide*; coauthor of Que's *Using Symphony*, *Using Q&A*, *Using Javelin*, and *1-2-3 Macro Workbook*; and contributing author to *Using 1-2-3*, Special Edition, *1-2-3 QuickStart*, and *Upgrading to 1-2-3 Release 3*. Over the past five years, in addition to authoring and coauthoring a number of Que titles, Ewing has served as Product Development Director for many of Que's applications software and DOS titles. He has directed the development of such Que series as the Que workbooks and instructor's guides, QueCards, and QuickStart books.

Bill Langenes

Bill Langenes is the Director of Marketing for Microware Distributors, a major multiregional hardware distributor. He has more than 20 years' experience in marketing and communications, the last 14 years of which have been spent in the personal computer industry. Mr. Langenes received his B.S. degree from the University of North Dakota. He now lives in Portland, Oregon, with his wife.

TRADEMARK
ACKNOWLEDGMENTS

Que Corporation has made every effort to supply trademark information about company names, products, and services mentioned in this book. Trademarks indicated below were derived from various sources. Que Corporation cannot attest to the accuracy of this information.

1-2-3, Lotus, Symphony, and Visicalc are registered trademarks of Lotus Development Corporation.

3Com is a registered trademark of 3Com Corporation.

Apple, LaserWriter, and Macintosh are registered trademarks, and AppleShare is a trademark of Apple Computer, Inc.

COMPAQ is a registered trademark and COMPAQ DeskPro 386 is a registered trademark of COMPAQ Computer Corporation.

dBASE, dBASE II, dBASE III, dBASE III Plus, and MultiMate are registered trademarks of Ashton-Tate Corporation.

IBM and PS/2 are registered trademarks and IBM PC XT and IBM Writing Assistant are trademarks of International Business Machines Corporation.

LaserJet is a registered trademark of Hewlett-Packard Co.

Microsoft and MS-DOS are registered trademarks of Microsoft Corporation.

NetWare is a registered trademark of Novell, Inc.

PFS, PFS:FILE, PFS:GRAPH, PFS: Professional Write, and PFS:REPORT are registered trademarks of Software Publishing Corporation.

PostScript is a registered trademark of Adobe Systems Incorporated.

Q&A is a registered trademark of Symantec Corporation.

R:BASE is a registered trademark of Microrim, Inc.

SmartKey is a trademark of Software Research Technologies.

WordPerfect is a registered trademark of WordPerfect Corporation.

WordStar is a registered trademark of WordStar International Incorporated.

Z80 is a registered trademark of Zilog, Inc.

Trademarks of other products mentioned in this book are held by the companies producing them.

CONTENTS AT A GLANCE

Part VI Advanced Q&A's Applications

TABLE OF CONTENTS ▼

II   Using Q&A File

III Using Q&A Write

IV Using Q&A Report

14 Q&A Report Quick Start

V   Using Q&A's Intelligent Assistant and Query Guide

18 Using the Intelligent Assistant and Query Guide

IV Advanced Q&A Applications

Introduction

What Is Q&A and What Can It Do for You?

Q&A is an easy-to-use data filing program that combines word processing, report generation, and artificial intelligence in a tightly integrated package. The first microcomputer software to use artificial-intelligence technology, Q&A is suitable for a wide range of business and personal applications.

Q&A's Intelligent Assistant, a natural-language processor, responds to queries in English. The program's integrated design automatically uses data from the File module in the Write and Report modules. Q&A is consistent; similar menus and screens appear in each module, so the user is always on familiar ground.

The Evolution of Q&A

Because Q&A was the first integrated program on the market to provide a user-friendly interface and artificial-intelligence capabilities, Q&A has a lead on the software industry. The makers of Q&A used knowledge gleaned from tests and competitors' programs to develop a highly functional and competitive product.

Q&A first was introduced in 1985 with Version 1.0. Q&A was a flexible and powerful program, but as is common with any software, the program has evolved.

1

Version 1.1, released in January, 1986, added features and enhancements, including a Spell module to help check spelling in Write documents, an extended and more flexible search and replace capability, and the capacity to draw double lines and mix double and single lines.

Version 2.0, released in September, 1986, was an upgraded edition of Version 1.1. The system became easier to use on dual disk systems, and overall program speed was increased. Users could print text in columns from the Write module and could print mailing labels directly from Write. File no longer accepted blank forms, preventing accidental entry of empty forms in files. Report became more flexible, and this version expanded macro and report-formatting capabilities. Import and export capabilities were enhanced greatly. Version 2.0 could integrate worksheet and graph files into Q&A documents and read Lotus 1-2-3 worksheets into Q&A databases. The Intelligent Assistant ran four times faster and corrected Version 1.1's database recovery problems.

In early 1988, the company released Version 3.0. Available commands and functions were expanded, and an external LOOKUP feature was added to permit linking of external files to the current file. This addition moved Q&A toward a relational database that provided significant improvements to the program.

Version 3.0 supports networking for multiuser access and uses the PostScript printing standard. More date and time functions were added, and additions were made to the Report and Write modules. The Intelligent Assistant and Write modules are faster than in Version 2.0. The program is available on 3.5-inch diskettes.

Version 4.0, release 1991, adds dozens of refinements and conveniences to Q&A's already burgeoning package of features, a few of which are: a new Query Guide that assists the user in performing Intelligent Assistant requests; cross-tab reports for automated data analysis; expanded document conversion options; custom application menus; fonts and character enhancements; and the ability to look up data from multiple fields in an external file.

A Hardware History

The personal computer was conceived in 1974 by Intel Corporation, not as the I/O box, monitor, and keyboard now used but as a silicon chip containing electronic circuits powerful enough to run applications performed previously on room-sized mainframe computers. Called the 8008 microprocessor, the chip, less than one-inch square, soon was used by hobbyists in the first homemade personal computers.

About the same time, a more powerful chip was developed by MOS Technologies (later acquired by Commodore Business Machines). This chip, the 6502, was used in the early generation of microcomputers when computer kits weren't user-friendly. Kit computers usually had flashing lights and switches used by creators to program machines. The first personal computers, therefore, were used only by people who could build and program computers.

The Apple I arrived in 1977, thanks to developers Steve Wozniak and Steve Jobs. Originally sold as a kit, the Apple I sold 500 units before being upgraded to the Apple II. Unlike its predecessors, the Apple II was preassembled and included a disk drive and disk operating system.

Tandy/Radio Shack joined the market with the Z80 chip and TRS-80 computer, and a new generation of computing began. Each of these computers had expansion slots so that users could attach printers, additional disk drives, and modems. Nontechnical people with no knowledge of mainframes or programming languages could join the microcomputer revolution.

The IBM Personal Computer, which used the 8088 microprocessor, was introduced in 1981. The IBM PC quickly dominated the market, setting the standard for computers that followed. As the need for more powerful computers arose, researchers worked on a nonremovable disk that could store larger amounts of information and increase the computer's execution speed. IBM responded in early 1983 by introducing the IBM PC XT—the first mass-market personal computer with a hard disk drive. The hard disk and expanded memory capacity enabled developers to create complex programs such as Q&A.

In the industry's quest for faster and more powerful machines, the IBM Personal Computer AT was introduced in 1984. This microcomputer was the first computer to have Intel's 80286 microprocessor, which was three to five times faster than the 8088 of the IBM PC.

Another advance was made when COMPAQ introduced the COMPAQ Deskpro 386 in the fall of 1986. This computer was one of the first on the market with the 80386 microprocessor, which is up to 18 times faster than the 80286. Computer hardware technology has taken the fast track in recent years, and software development has followed a similar trail.

Today, high performance microcomputers using 80286, 80386, and 80486 chips are commonplace. IBM's PS/2 line and computers from COMPAQ and other vendors have brought minicomputer performance to the desktop. Increasingly powerful and functional software is evolving with the development of hardware platforms to support them.

The Software Story

The need for an easy-to-use programming language was discovered soon after the Apple microcomputer was introduced. A programming language called BASIC (Beginner's All-purpose Symbolic Instruction Code) was included with the new computers. Because BASIC was much easier to use than machine or assembly language, users could write their own programs.

Developers soon came out with "canned" software, programs written to answer specific needs such as spreadsheet or accounting applications. The first software program to make it big was VisiCalc, a spreadsheet applications program introduced in 1978. During the next five years, VisiCalc sold more than 500,000 copies, making it the most popular software program of its time.

As software needs were recognized and answered, programs were developed for different applications. Word processing programs threatened to make typewriters obsolete; data management programs began to replace metal file cabinets and manila file folders. Researchers worked on developing a microcomputer alternative to minicomputer and mainframe database systems.

In 1979, Software Publishing introduced the Personal Filing System (PFS:FILE), a program used to store, sort, and retrieve data. Because PFS:FILE has limited report capabilities, PFS:REPORT soon was introduced. The programs were slow, and storage space was limited, but they were the first to use menu selections instead of a complex command structure. PFS:FILE is considered the forerunner of Q&A.

Each program improved its predecessor. Software developers took what they learned from previous successes and failures and streamlined products. Software became more powerful and could perform more tasks in less time. Software for microcomputers was easier to use than their mainframe counterparts, but one problem remained: the more powerful the program, the more the user had to learn. If the user needed more than one powerful program, the microcomputer was no longer as easy to use as advertisements promised.

As software evolved, software designers created different types of programs. If your office used VisiCalc for accounting, PFS:FILE for personnel files, and

WordStar for writing letters and reports, you had to use three separate programs. Integrated software was introduced to solve the compatibility problem.

Lotus 1-2-3, the first integrated software program, combined graphics and data management capabilities in a strong spreadsheet environment. The data-management aspect of 1-2-3 is its well-known weakness, however—a fact that makes compatibility with Q&A an attractive aspect of both programs.

The designers of Q&A understood the need for an integrated program that would work easily with an existing spreadsheet program like 1-2-3. Going a step further, they made the program as easy to use as possible by including artificial intelligence; the Intelligent Assistant is a user-friendly interface that makes it possible to use the computer without having to learn the computer's language.

The Development of Artificial Intelligence

You probably recognize the term *artificial intelligence*. If your computer is artificially intelligent, it can't think, but it can make decisions when given necessary information. Artificial intelligence was designed so that you can communicate with the computer in your own language. Instead of learning command sequences or selecting menu options, you can use Q&A's artificial intelligence to interpret and respond to sentence-style requests. Artificial intelligence also enables Q&A to "learn" about your database and provides a way of asking questions so that you can build on the base of knowledge programmed into the Intelligent Assistant.

In the mid-1970s, Gary Hendrix and a team of researchers developed the first artificial-intelligence program for the U.S. government. An improved version of the program appeared in 1978. The program was powerful, but the software was slow, could be run only on a million-dollar computer, and could be operated only by people trained in computational linguistics.

Hendrix also developed a natural-language technology that could be used in a database for less-experienced users. In 1982, he and coworker Norman Haas founded Symantec Corporation and began creating prototype English systems for personal computers. Q&A was introduced in 1985 and was the first microcomputer program that could adapt to any database, "learn" about the database, understand requests in the English language, and be used by people with varying degrees of expertise.

A Note on the Versions of Q&A

As this book is written, Version 4.0 is the latest release of Q&A and provides significant enhancements over previous versions. Q&A is a rich and dynamic product that has undergone several significant enhancements during its life. If you are using an earlier version of Q&A, you may want to upgrade to the latest release. Refer to your user's manual for details.

Upgrading: Getting the Latest Features

If you are happy with the product you have, the expense of upgrading to a later software release may not seem warranted, but there are good reasons for upgrading.

You obviously receive new documentation and all upgrades and additions to the software. Any minor bugs or problems probably have been fixed. One advantage to upgrading, therefore, is that you always have all the latest features available in a given software package. The advantage to vendors is that they have to support only a single software version, because all customers are using the latest release of the product.

If your application is a casual one and you are satisfied with the operation of the software version you have, you may see little reason to upgrade. However, popular software products tend to gather third-party support that provides additional functionality. Add-on products and training guides usually are designed around the latest software version and are upgraded to reflect changes in the target product.

Finally, as a software package gains popularity, users frequently wish to exchange design information, software templates, and even data files. If everybody is using the same version of the software, this process is much easier.

If you keep your software up-to-date, you will get better service from the software and the company that supports the software.

About This Book

Using Q&A 4 will help you get the most out of Symantec's software. Like the product it describes, this book is dynamic. As the first edition was being prepared for publishing in 1986, Symantec released an updated version of its software, and the original text had to be modified to reflect these changes.

Again in 1988 and 1991, Symantec released enhanced versions of Q&A. In the third edition of this book, Q&A is covered from the perspective of Version 4.0. Earlier versions are fully compatible with Version 4.0, but if you are using an earlier release of the software, some of the advanced functions won't work. You also should be aware that after a document or database is converted for use with Q&A 4.0, it no longer can be used with earlier Q&A versions. No matter which release of Q&A you have, *Using Q&A 4* will be a valuable addition to your reference library.

Conventions Used in This Book

Q&A is an integrated, microcomputer-based, software application that includes facilities for creating data files to manage most kinds of information and for manipulating that information with reporting, word processing, and artificial-intelligence querying.

For convenience, and to conform to microcomputer-industry conventions, the term *database* is used to refer to the Q&A software and the pool of information files the program creates and maintains.

In this book, the term *File* means the group of programs within Q&A that perform data management functions. Write is the word processor and its associated formatting and output functions, and Report is the database reporting tool. Generally, the Intelligent Assistant is referred to as the IA.

Who Should Use This Book?

If you own Q&A, you should own this book. *Using Q&A 4* is not meant to replace the program documentation; the manual provided in the package serves as a useful reference tool. The Instruction Manual divides the information about each module into sections in two books, so you easily can look up information on a specific area. *Using Q&A 4* is an applications-oriented guide that teaches you how to use Q&A through examples and tutorial-style text.

Whether you are a first-time user or an old hand at composing data-filing programs, *Using Q&A 4* introduces you to the unique features of the Intelligent Assistant and shows you how to streamline your applications to minimize time and effort. If you currently use 1-2-3, Symphony, PFS:FILE, the IBM Filing Assistant, Paradox, or any of the dBASE products, you can learn how to import files into Q&A by reading Chapter 20.

If you still are trying to decide whether to buy Q&A, *Using Q&A 4* will help you investigate the program's full range of capabilities. By reading through sample applications and procedures, you will see how easy it is to create and use a Q&A data system. You then can decide for yourself whether Q&A answers your business needs.

How Do You Use This Book?

Using Q&A 4 will help you learn to use this innovative program to your best advantage. We demonstrate, through examples and discussions, how to create, customize, and implement a Q&A system.

We view this book as a direct-access reference. Although you certainly can begin with Chapter 1 and read through to the end, we anticipate that most readers will select portions of interest and go directly to them.

If you need additional help installing the software, refer to Appendix A. After Q&A is installed, each section of this book should stand alone to provide quick reference information or detailed step-by-step procedures.

Notice the "Quick Start" Chapters 4, 9, and 14. These sections are designed to teach you quickly how to use software features. The material following each chapter expands on the Quick Start topics, providing increasingly detailed information as you are ready.

What Is in This Book?

This book is divided into parts that reflect the various Q&A modules and applications. If you plan to use the data-filing features of Q&A, we recommend you read *Using Q&A 4* in the order presented. If word processing is what you're after, however, you may want to start reading in Part III, "Using Q&A Write." Remember that before you can use the Intelligent Assistant feature or print reports, you must create a data file in the File module.

Part I

The information in Part I focuses on teaching you the basics of Q&A. Chapter 1, "A Quick Tour of Q&A," introduces you to Q&A's features and provides some detail on individual Q&A modules. You also will learn when to use Q&A. This chapter can be a general Q&A reference as you read the remainder of the book.

Chapter 2, "Database Concepts," introduces you to database design and terminology that will help you understand other material in this book. Database design philosophy will be introduced.

Chapter 3, "Q&A Basics," shows you how to start and end a Q&A session and provides additional detail on specific program features, such as the menu system, on-line help, the tutorial, and error messages.

Part II

From the quick start chapter through customizing and printing a document, Part II focuses on Q&A File. Chapter 4, "Q&A File Quick Start," is the first of several quick start sessions that provide detailed instructions for Q&A procedures. The quick start chapters are a good place to start when you are trying new operations and a good memory refresher for later in your experience.

Chapter 5, "Setting Up a File," guides you through the Q&A File design process, providing step-by-step instructions and offering suggestions on how to get the most from Q&A File. You will learn the procedures for designing, formatting, and selecting options for a data-entry form as well as ways to modify and redesign the data file.

Chapter 6, "Using File," discusses ways to enter data and build the database file. In this chapter, you will learn to edit forms, add information, search and update forms, copy files, and delete information from the database.

Chapter 7, "Customizing and Programming a File," teaches you how to make data manipulation easy by using Q&A custom features. You also will learn how to use calculation and programming statements to have Q&A File perform tasks automatically.

Chapter 8, "Printing from File," explains how to move your data file information from disk to paper. We provide step-by-step procedures for creating print specifications, including Q&A's special features such as printing mailing labels.

Part III

In Part III, detailed instructions are given for using Q&A Write. Chapter 9, "Q&A Write Quick Start," shows you how to use the Write module. Use this chapter when you first start experimenting with Q&A Write and refer to it often to refresh your memory.

Chapter 10, "Creating a Write Document," explains Write's capabilities and guides you through the steps to produce a document. Editing, moving, copying, deleting, and formatting are just a few of the topics discussed in this chapter.

Chapter 11, "Enhancing a Write Document," discusses text enhancements and formatting, including tabs, margins, and fonts. This chapter also shows you how to customize Write features and how to use special operations, such as WordStar control characters and Q&A math functions.

Chapter 12, "Merging Documents with Q&A Write," teaches you to use Write to merge data from the Q&A File module with documents such as form letters, memos, and reports. This chapter also includes the procedures necessary for merging ASCII documents into Write documents.

Chapter 13, "Printing a Write Document," details printing procedures within Write. The print menus are explained along with special print operations, including PostScript and other font operations.

Part IV

Using Q&A Report is detailed in Part IV. Chapter 14, "Q&A Report Quick Start," is an initial introduction to Q&A's report features. Use this chapter to familiarize yourself with the basic operations and as a reference chapter.

Chapter 15, "Creating a Report," expands on the information in Chapter 14. In this chapter, you learn about the various features of this module so that you can create formatted columnar and cross-tab reports with custom features.

Chapter 16, "Printing a Report," shows you in detail how to use the print features of the Report module. Menus, print specification changes, and report previewing are a few of the topics.

Part V

Part V focuses on understanding and using the Q&A Intelligent Assistant and the closely related Query Guide. Chapter 17, "Understanding the Intelligent Assistant and Query Guide," introduces you to the concept of Q&A's natural-language interface and teaches you to enter queries and requests that will be understood by the Intelligent Assistant. The Query Guide, also described in Chapter 17, makes entering Intelligent Assistant requests a simple matter of choosing from menus and responding to prompts.

Chapter 18, "Using the Intelligent Assistant and Query Guide," shows you how to expand the Intelligent Assistant's programmed "knowledge." You learn to teach the Intelligent Assistant facts and relationships that pertain to your particular database.

Part VI

Part VI shows you how to get the most from Q&A by introducing advanced applications such as networking. Chapter 19, "Creating and Using Q&A Macros and Custom Menus," teaches you to use macros and menus to streamline your data-management and data-entry tasks. You learn to record often-used sequences to execute a series of commands with one keystroke, and you learn to combine macros with menus to create customized applications.

Chapter 20, "Importing and Exporting Data in Q&A," walks you through the processes of importing and exporting data from popular programs such as 1-2-3, Symphony, PFS:FILE, IBM Filing Assistant, Paradox, and dBASE products.

Chapter 21, "Networking: Using Q&A in a Multiuser Environment," shows how to design files for shared access, discusses general network terms and concepts, and provides information on setting file and field security parameters.

Appendix A, "Installing and Starting Q&A," shows you how to install the software for operation with your systems. Printer and font installation specifics also are provided.

What Is Not in This Book

Using Q&A 4 will not replace the Symantec user's manual. *Using Q&A 4* is a reference and tutorial guide designed to supplement the material supplied with the software.

This book is not a tutorial on database structures and design, although we include some information in this area. You will find many examples to illustrate Q&A features, but we do not show you how to create a comprehensive inventory and billing system, for example. However, you can use the concepts illustrated to help you design such applications on your own.

This book is not a programming text. We show you how to customize Q&A applications with standard software features at the beginner and intermediate levels, but we do not try to cover advanced programming procedures.

Whether you're a die-hard database user who needs a sophisticated data-management tool or a novice who needs nurturing, the chapters that follow will introduce you to the power and unique capabilities of Q&A.

Part I

Learning the Basics of Q&A

Includes

A Quick Tour of Q&A

Understanding Database Concepts

Getting Started

A Quick Tour of Q&A

I f you think of the phrase "question and answer" when you see the name Q&A, you already are aware of a major feature of the Q&A program. Q&A is defined as a sophisticated data manager, report writer, and word processor, but a special element called the Intelligent Assistant (IA) makes using the program as easy as entering a question and receiving an answer.

Unlike many other database programs, Q&A gives you the option of changing, querying, sorting, or reporting database information by simply typing English sentences and phrases. The type of answer you receive depends on your application. Whether you want the Intelligent Assistant to sort a list of company names or display a financial report, you simply enter the question and Q&A supplies the answer. The Query Guide, introduced with Q&A Release 4.0, makes communicating with the Intelligent Assistant a simple matter of choosing menu items and responding to program prompts. You can use the Intelligent Assistant and/or the Query Guide to change, query, or sort the data in a database that you created in the File module. And you don't have to remember multiple menu commands and function keys.

Sound easy? It is. But even when you use the individual modules (File, Write, and Report) instead of the Intelligent Assistant, you don't need to be a computer specialist to perform data-management tasks, create documents, and print reports. Q&A makes data management, word processing, and report writing easy. The program includes similar screen layouts, function keys, and command menu systems in each of the three modules so that you know where you are in the program no matter which module you use most.

In this chapter, you learn to think of Q&A as an information-management tool and learn what the makers of Q&A had in mind when they designed the program. The range of Q&A capabilities and features is introduced in this chapter. Additionally, references to other sections point you toward more detailed information on the topics covered here.

Deciding Where and When To Use Q&A

Different users respond differently to the issues of where and when to use a feature-rich program such as Q&A. Suppose that someone asks, "What do you do with a car?" Your answer can be simple: "I drive it to work." On the other hand, you may reply, "I use it for work, vacations, racing, and customizing." You also may use a car for more activities, depending on your needs and experience. The answer, however, is based on your basic understanding of what an automobile is and on your experience in applying that understanding. This same concept applies to Q&A.

If you have used other computer-based information-management software, you can appreciate the value of a product such as Q&A. Q&A provides a nonthreatening, quick-to-learn user interface that also includes powerful and versatile features. If this is your first experience with such a product, you may need guidance. Either way, Q&A can solve many —if not most—of your data-management requirements.

At the low end of the applications scale, you may want to use Q&A File to maintain a simple name-and-address file of family members or business contacts. The Write module offers sophisticated word processing features, but Write works just fine as a simple electronic typewriter to help make your letter- and memo-typing tasks easier.

At the high end of the applications scale, you can use the integrated features of the Q&A package for a comprehensive patient-tracking, appointments-scheduling, or medical-billing system. You can design an inventory, purchase order, and billing system for a wholesale business. You also can use Q&A as a card catalog reference system for a personal, corporate, or public library.

Consider using Q&A as a travel-expense tracker and report writer. Use Q&A for project management and scheduling to prepare form letters for advertising, surveys, and billing. Use some of the IA features for statistical analysis of survey results or employee performance. Q&A is an excellent tool for maintaining organization membership records, such as records for a church.

Although Q&A basically is not designed for textual databases, the IA component can help you keep short notes and ideas so that you can find random thoughts later.

Q&A is an information tool. To say "use your imagination" in applying this tool seems trite, but most users do just that after making most software purchases. These customers usually have one or two specific needs in mind or are responding to an intuitive belief that they should use such a tool. After the software is installed and the initial applications are in place, users begin thinking in terms of computer-based solutions to business and personal information-handling needs. Each application then builds on what was accomplished previously.

Accept Q&A as a tool in much the same way that you accept a screwdriver, wheelbarrow, food processor, or microwave oven. Each of these tools has one or more obvious applications, but new opportunities present themselves as the tools become comfortable in your hands.

At the same time, be cognizant of the design parameters of each tool that you use. You don't use a screwdriver as a hammer or a chisel. Although a screwdriver may serve the purpose, the results probably wouldn't be satisfactory.

The same applications concept applies to a software tool. Q&A is a microcomputer-based product with excellent and powerful features. The program is not intended for on-line transaction processing, however, in which millions of records must be manipulated in real time. Q&A doesn't serve well for highly customized applications in which the user must be insulated from the database by applications-specific menus and procedures. Don't use Q&A for linked applications that require a database back-end called from conventional programming languages.

Q&A will not be your only database program if you intend to construct a true database of information for networked applications, if you expect the number of entries to be large, and if you want maximum flexibility in applying the data. If you truly are serious about database applications, however, Q&A *will* be one of your data-management software packages.

A number of applications do not require relational structure. Many applications in an office or even in a programming shop need to be brought on-line quickly, perhaps by the end user. Q&A can be an excellent choice for these applications.

Don't limit your horizons unnecessarily by your own preconceived notions or by the limitations suggested in this book. Be reasonable, but be creative. You then will get the most out of any software tool.

Understanding the Design Philosophy of Q&A

One big headache that you often get when using many new software programs is caused by the "setup and discovery" stage. You spend time mulling over the documentation, designing the forms and fields that you will use, and experimenting with the various features of the program. Often, by trial and error, you discover that the setup stage is more complex than you originally thought.

The developers of Q&A designed the program to require a minimum amount of time for you to set up and discover. With Q&A, you can set up a file, enter data, and produce a report from the Query Guide in minutes. You don't need to learn complicated programming languages or sophisticated menu structures. Whether you want to use the Intelligent Assistant, the Query Guide, or the File, Write, and Report modules, you can learn how to use Q&A by just sitting down and getting to work.

In designing Q&A, the developers also considered the need for easy integration. Because Q&A is meant to be used for a variety of applications, the three separate modules (File, Write, and Report) were designed to be used together (see fig. 1.1). The data from File, for example, can be incorporated into a letter that you compose in Write or into a printout from Report. You can move quickly from one module to another without switching from program to program, as you would with individual programs. For business users, this "seamless" integration is an important selling point. Major stand-alone programs, such as WordStar or dBASE IV, often are difficult or impossible to integrate. Depending on your application and the size of your database, some data-management tasks may be faster with Q&A than they would be with a more powerful database program.

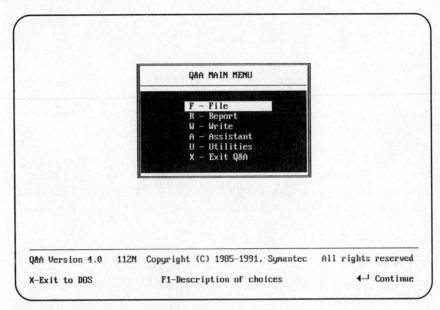

```
                    ┌─────────────────────────────┐
                    │        Q&A MAIN MENU         │
                    ├─────────────────────────────┤
                    │      F - File               │
                    │      R - Report             │
                    │      W - Write              │
                    │      A - Assistant          │
                    │      U - Utilities          │
                    │      X - Exit Q&A           │
                    │                             │
                    └─────────────────────────────┘


 Q&A Version 4.0   112N  Copyright (C) 1985-1991, Symantec   All rights reserved

 X-Exit to DOS           F1-Description of choices              ↵ Continue
```

Fig. 1.1.   *The Q&A Main menu.*

Q&A also offers an import/export feature that transfers data with a minimum of user effort. Importing and exporting data from other programs such as 1-2-3, PFS:FILE, or the IBM Filing Assistant is almost as easy as copying a file. Similarly, you can import data from the Paradox or dBASE products into a Q&A file with just a few simple keystrokes. If you currently use any of these database programs, or if you use 1-2-3 for your spreadsheet needs, you can begin building your Q&A data system right away. (For more information on Q&A's import/export capabilities, see Chapter 20.)

Because Q&A is used in many different environments, the program must be flexible enough to meet the needs of persons with varying degrees of computer experience. In a small business, for example, the person responsible for designing database applications requires a package with the range of capabilities available in powerful programs such as dBASE or R:BASE. At the same time, Q&A must be easy to use so that an employee with no previous computer experience can enter data and produce reports.

Q&A can be used by people who are familiar with programming and applications and by people who have no computer experience. Creating a database form in File is as simple as entering text in the Write module. When you design a report, you can use the database form that you created in File. Although the focus of Q&A is on front-end, easy-to-use features, don't be fooled. Q&A is powerful enough to perform a wide range of data-management, word processing, and report-generating tasks.

Looking Inside Q&A

Before you begin exploring the capabilities of Q&A, you need to investigate the Q&A package. When you open the package, you find seven 5.25-inch disks. The software is available optionally on a 3.5-inch format; in this case, you find only four disks. A swap form is included so that you can exchange the disks you have for the ones you want, directly from Symantec. Currently, Symantec doesn't charge for this service.

You also have a user's manual, a "getting started" manual, an applications programming tools manual, a number of compact quick-reference guides, and order forms for Symantec and third-party support products such as keyboard templates.

The Q&A disks contain all the programs you need to create, change, sort, and query database files; to design and print reports; and to enter and edit word processing text. Table 1.1 gives you an overview of the Q&A program.

Table 1.1
Q&A Version 4.0 Vital Statistics

Description: A personal-computer program that integrates a file manager and report writer with artificial intelligence, a word processor, and a spelling checker.

Package Contents: Four program disks, a dictionary disk, a tutorial disk, a sample disk, quick-reference booklets and other references, an application programming tools manual, a user's manual and a "getting started" manual.

System Requirements:

- An IBM PC, PC XT, Personal Computer AT, or other compatible personal computer

- A hard disk drive

- An 80-column color or monochrome monitor

- 512K RAM (640K required for DOS 4.0 and network use, and 484K for each local computer on a network)

- MS-DOS or PC DOS Version 2.1 or above; DOS 3.1 is required to use Q&A on a network

- A printer

Suggested Retail Price: $399 and $499 for Q&A Network pack.

Availability: Version 1.0, November, 1985; Version 2.0, October, 1986; Version 3.0, February, 1988; Version 4.0, 1991.

Software Publisher:

Symantec Corporation
10201 Torre Avenue
Cupertino, California, USA 95014
(408) 253-9600

Module Overview:

File	Used to store, organize, and analyze information in database form
Report	Used to retrieve data from File to produce reports
Write	Used to create letters, memos, and reports
Spell	Used to find misspellings in Write documents and to offer alternative spellings from a 100,000-word vocabulary
Thesaurus	Used to look up synonyms in a 60,000-word dictionary
Intelligent Assistant	A natural-language artificial-intelligence interface used to enter sentence-style requests for managing data and producing reports

Using Q&A File

The File module is probably the flagship portion of Q&A for most users. File is the data-storage module in which you create data files for names and addresses, inventory, personnel, accounting, or other information. Although other Q&A modules can use information from File for an integrated application, the File module also can stand alone. File actually is a series of complex programs that work together so that you can define the database, design data presentation screens, enter and edit information, and produce reports.

File Structures and Capacities

Q&A File uses two basic file structures to store all the information about your data file. The DTF file stores the main database definition and information. The IDX file contains the database index information (see Chapter 3 for additional information on database and index concepts). Embedded in these files is additional information about your data, including search and report formats. You ordinarily do not need to know much more about how Q&A handles the information that you supply. If you move or copy a database from inside Q&A, the program knows to move or copy DTF and IDX files. If you use DOS to back up or move an application, however, you must remember to copy all files associated with the application.

Q&A can accept up to 16 million records per file. This storage capacity is so great that you probably will never face program limitations when you use File for personal or business data management. Table 1.2 lists the File module statistics.

Table 1.2
File Module Statistics

Item	Capacity
Records	16 million
Record size	65,536 characters
Pages per form	10
Fields per record	2,045
Fields per page	248
Characters per field	32,768
Indexed fields	115
Lookup table size	64K characters
Data types	7
Decimal accuracy	15 digits
File size	1,024 megabytes
File report width	1,000 characters
File report columns	5 0
Sort limits	Up to 512 levels, ascending or descending

File versus Other Databases

Some notable differences exist between Q&A File and other popular database programs. Q&A has more capacity than many other database programs. In addition, the Intelligent Assistant sets Q&A apart from the majority of offerings.

With Version 4.0 of Q&A File, you can relate multiple external files to the current application through the File and Report modules. You can have a name-and-address file that includes a company ID, for example, but no more information on that company. A separate company file can store the detailed company information, including the address and main telephone number. However, you cannot construct logical views of the database that are independent of the physical structure of the file currently displayed.

You can construct a report that combines information from both files, and you can use the company-ID file as a lookup source to fill in information in the CONTACTS file. However, the external file information must reside in one or more fields on a displayed form.

Packages with full programming support give you access to screen design in such a way that you can construct custom display screens by combining information from multiple files. You then can write the information directly to the screen wherever you want. With Q&A, however, information retrieved from a linked file can be placed only on a database form.

This limitation is minor and probably will not cause problems for most Q&A users, if they understand the design philosophy of the product before using Q&A.

Other differences are in Q&A's favor. The modules contain user-oriented features available in a relatively limited number of higher performance products.

The reporting capabilities of Q&A, for example, are extremely easy to use. Even inexperienced users can retrieve the information they need with minimal training. The menu system and on-line help system keep the learning time to a minimum. Q&A is powerful enough that experienced database users will find its features useful.

Q&A also is an integrated product, providing word processing and merging facilities in addition to the basic database functions. The macro features permit you to construct complicated command sequences that you can execute later with a simple key sequence.

File Screen-Design Features

Among the strengths of the File module is its capability to custom-design data input and update screens. The procedure is as simple as using Q&A File's built-in word processor to place the field names and record labels where you want them on-screen. This easy-to-use feature permits you to specify a basic database structure without having to learn much beyond how to access the menu and how to use simple editing procedures (see Chapter 5 for more detailed information on designing File databases).

File Reporting Features

Q&A includes a separate and versatile Report module, but File also can produce printed or on-screen reports directly. A Print menu selection from within the File module accesses these reporting facilities.

You can use File's reporting features to design output for preprinted forms (Symantec calls this technique *coordinate* printing) or to custom-design a tabular report (*free-form* printing).

As with most Q&A operations, you use QBE (query by example) or QBF (query by form) procedures to design the reports. You are presented with the screen form designed when the database was created, and you enter information into individual fields to construct the report. If your computer monitor supports graphics, you can preview an accurate image of a report before sending the report to the printer. See Chapter 8 for additional information on printing from the File module.

Using Q&A Write

Like File, Q&A Write is a collection of sophisticated programs that you can use to perform full-screen editing, text formatting, printing, report writing, and data-merging functions. Although Write's word processing functions are not nearly as diverse as Microsoft Word's or WordPerfect's, Write is a versatile package that can provide all the power most word processing users need. The following section introduces you to the Write module's capabilities. For additional details, see Part III, "Using Q&A Write."

Write Features

Write is a full-featured word processor with some useful enhancements that result from close integration with the File database module.

The usual editing features are supported, including search and replace operations, block operations, and bold, underline, and other font selections. Write also has an integral spelling checker and thesaurus. In addition, Write supports row and column math with an interesting twist—you can place the results of a math operation anywhere in the document.

Write's mail-merge features are particularly strong, for example. With the mail-merge feature, you can write letters, mailing labels, invoices, memos, and other customized material that uses information (in a fill-in-the-blank fashion) from a File database during printing. You even can import data into the document from multiple fields in one or more external database files at print time. The printing specification is as simple as surrounding the proper File field labels with asterisks inside the Write document. To print a different name and address at the top of each letter, for example, you can place the following header at the top of the letter:

```
*First Name* *Last Name*
*Title*
*Address*
*City*, *State* *Zip*

Dear *First Name*,
```

In addition to supporting merges with File, the Q&A Write module can import 1-2-3 worksheets or named ranges from within worksheets. The Write module can insert bit-mapped images or 1-2-3 PIC files into a document, and Write supports document joins at printing. The Write module also supports data import and export with other text processors.

With Version 4.0, Write's printing features are enhanced significantly. The program now supports well over 100 printers, PostScript output specifications, and versatile font selection and management. You now can print up to nine fonts in a document.

Write provides an almost WYSIWYG (What You See Is What You Get) screen display, although you don't see accurate representations of proportional spacing typefaces. If your monitor can display graphics, however, you can preview an image of a document that very closely resembles the final, printed copy. An on-screen ruler shows you your location in the document, and a horizontal menu is displayed continuously at the bottom of the screen.

Table 1.3 lists the Write module specifications.

Table 1.3
Write Module Specifications

Item	Capacity
Document size	80 pages (with 640K RAM)
Document width	250 characters
Header/Footer	18 lines total
Spelling checker	100,000 words
Thesaurus	60,000 words
Laser printers	HP LaserJet, Apple LaserWriter, others
Columns	Up to eight columns (printout only)
Line drawing	Single or double lines
Math	Column/row total, average, count, multiply, divide

Write versus Other Word Processors

Q&A Write is a full-featured word processor and can serve for many, if not all, of your text-editing operations. Support for fonts, as well as PostScript and bit-mapped files, increases Write's functionality with laser technology and other modern printers. The Write module's close integration with the File module offsets some of the program's limitations. Together, File and Write are much more powerful than Write would be as a stand-alone word processor.

Write, however, is not designed for true electronic publishing and will not serve in word-processing operations that require very large documents. Because Write documents are stored entirely in RAM, the maximum document size is about 80 pages with 640K of memory. You can, of course, use the join feature to print combined files for larger documents (see Chapter 13 for more information on using the join feature).

Write does not support such formatting enhancements as automatic list preparation (indexes and tables of contents), parallel columns, split screens, simultaneous editing of multiple documents, footnotes, or sorting (you can print multiple snaking columns, but you cannot display them as such on-screen).

Many users find that Write is the only word processor they ever need. Others don't use Write at all and prefer a separate word processor. Some users apply Write for operations that benefit from the File connection and apply a stand-alone product for word processing-only functions. As with any software product, you should assess your needs carefully before deciding on a single product.

Write Reporting Features

The ultimate reason for maintaining any computer-based data is so that you can access the data in a useful form. Write's reporting features are versatile and functional. With the mailing-label print routine, for example, you easily can print labels from a File database by using Write's mail-merge facility.

The standard document print routine includes many formatting and merging functions that you can use to add additional flexibility to Write reporting. A routine also is included that you can use to print an address on an envelope from information in a letter document. By combining this routine with embedded printer-control codes, you can use a dual-bin printer to prepare letters and envelopes simultaneously.

You can select single or multiple copies of a document as it is printed. Right margin justification is supported, and you can print a document in multiple columns. Print queues, special fonts, and document merge are among the other supported print operations.

PostScript print command support provides a wide range of output options. Write supports font descriptions for several popular laser printers. You also can load additional font descriptions from the Symantec bulletin board, and you can design your own font description files.

Chapter 13 provides detailed information on formatting and printing Write documents.

Using Q&A Report

Report is another of the integrated modules of the Q&A package. Report supplements the output features of the File module by providing extensive preprogrammed capabilities. With Report, for example, control breaks are automatic. A control break occurs when data in one of the report fields changes. Suppose that you are listing names and addresses, sorted by city. Without control-break capability, a program must repeat the city with each record. Q&A, however, can print the city the first time the city appears and then show blanks in that column as long as the city does not change:

CITY	NAME	SALESMAN	TELEPHONE
Atlanta	Franklyn McCormic	SJ	404-552-7722
	Likado Tango	JJ	404-526-6677
	Jordan Wills	JJ	404-723-5511
Boston	Martha Eden	SJ	617-426-5645
	John Thomas	SJ	617-584-2323

Report uses query by form (QBF) for easy report generation. The report process therefore uses the record forms with which you already are familiar because you designed the record forms during database design. For the simplest report, specify which records you want to retrieve and the order that you want the fields to appear. Q&A does the rest.

Flexible sorting capabilities enable you to arrange data in just about any way. In fact, you probably can sort every field in the report, and you can choose ascending or descending order for individual fields. Report can produce listings up to 1,000 characters wide, assuming that your printer can support that number. You can send the printer special control codes from within Report, and you have good control over character and line spacing. Table 1.4 lists the Report module specifications.

Table 1.4
Report Module Specifications

Item	Capacity
Columns	50
Width	1,000 characters
Sort levels	50
Derived columns	16
Invisible columns	49
Saved formats	100 per database file

You can find more detailed information on Report in Part IV, "Using Q&A Report."

Using the Intelligent Assistant and Query Guide

The idea of an English-language query came when the first computer drew power. But faster CPUs, larger disks, and huge memory were needed to make the idea possible. When Q&A first was released, the program was the only microcomputer database product to include this kind of artificial intelligence query. The concept is so popular that a number of database programs now have some kind of conversational query capability.

The Q&A IA probably will not replace conventional reporting with the Report module, but the IA is an excellent supplement. In addition, the IA can provide database tools to people who can benefit from database access but do not want to be involved in the design process. Beginning with Q&A Version 4.0, a helpful Query Guide enables you to fill in Intelligent Assistant requests by choosing menu items and responding to program prompts.

Because you can "teach" the Intelligent Assistant to recognize various words and phrases relating to your database, you can query, change, and add data by entering simple English phrases and sentences. After you have designed a database with File, you can rely entirely on the IA for your data-management needs, bypassing the program's command menu completely. For example, if you enter the request *Display the Chicago leads*, the Intelligent Assistant retrieves the appropriate records from the File module and displays the records in a columnar report (see fig. 1.2). You then can opt to print the report or ask another question.

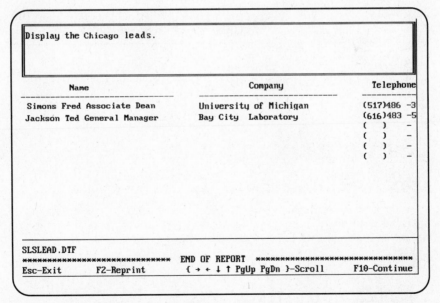

Fig. 1.2. *The results of a simple request.*

The IA has a built-in vocabulary that enables the IA to recognize standard queries without any training from you. The IA can respond to date, time, and math questions, for example, without additional training. When you start the

IA with each database, the IA first scans the file to learn about field names and database contents. Beyond that, you must spend some time training the IA about the terms you want to use in asking questions. You can teach the IA synonyms for the information in your database, and you can add new vocabulary to its basic knowledge. This process can be time-consuming, depending on how large and complicated your database is, but the rewards can be great. The Query Guide provides a much simpler way to work with the Intelligent Assistant, requiring virtually no setup time and with no risk of asking a question that the program may not understand.

The IA/QG are excellent tools for ad hoc queries as a supplement to stored, macro-driven conventional reports. Table 1.5 lists the IA/QG specifications.

Table 1.5
Intelligent Assistant Specifications

Item	Capacity
Built-in vocabulary	650 words
User-defined vocabulary	Unlimited (up to disk capacity)
Sort levels	50
Intrinsic queries	Math, time, and date questions
Query Guide queries	Retrieval, columnar and cross-tab report, count, statistics, stored operations

For additional information about the Q&A IA/QG, see Part V, "Using Q&A's Intelligent Assistant and Query Guide."

Learning about Other Q&A Features

Q&A has a number of additional features in addition to those already mentioned. The next sections introduce you to these features.

Integrated Features

As an integrated product, Q&A performs more than one software function, and the functions are tied together closely. Mail-merge is one example of this integration. You can select database information to be included in printed Write documents. This information can include not only names and addresses for letters, but also invoice and billing information, inventory and personnel data, or anything else you have stored in a File database.

Data integration in Q&A flows the other way too. When you design a database file screen, use QBE searching, and enter or edit database information, you are using Write-compatible editing functions. In addition, the menu structures across Q&A modules are consistent, enhancing the integrated feel of the product and reducing learning time.

Macros, Menus, and Applications

A *macro* is a single command that combines a sequence of software functions. Suppose, for example, that you want to enter new information into the CONTACTS file. You must perform the following sequence of functions. First, you select File from the Main menu and then select Add Data from the File menu. Next, you specify the name of the file to edit. This process can be reduced to a two-key combination. You can create a macro labeled Alt-E (for Edit) that enters the File module and calls up a blank form from the CONTACTS file. Up to six macros can be installed on the Q&A Main menu to become part of the on-screen menu structure. However, you can define many more macros that can be accessed directly from the keyboard. Best of all, you can assign macros to custom menus that supplement or even replace Q&A's program menus.

To define a keyboard macro, perform the following steps:

1. Press Shift-F2 to display the Macro menu box from within any Q&A screen.

2. Choose Define Macro and enter the key combination that you want to use for this macro identifier.

   A flashing block appears in the lower right corner of the screen to remind you that a macro definition is in process.

From that point, everything you type is saved in a special macro file to be played back when you enter the specified Alt-key combination.

3. After you enter all the keystrokes for this particular macro, press Shift-F2 again to turn off the macro recorder.

Q&A displays a Macro Options dialog box in which you can give your macro a name of up to 31 characters, choose to allow or suppress screen displays during macro playback, and name a custom menu, if any, for Q&A to display when the macro ends.

4. Press F10, and you are asked which file to use to store the macro (accept the default QAMACRO.ASC).

With Q&A 4.0, you can give your macros descriptive names, then run the macros by picking them from a menu. You also can create custom menus that pop up over Q&A screens, and run your macros by simply choosing menu items. Finally, you even can link menus together in dedicated applications that supplement or even replace Q&A's menu system.

You can do about anything that you want with macros, but one caution needs to be mentioned: don't use special key combinations that Q&A already uses for other operations. The software warns you if you try.

Multiuser Applications

One interesting aspect of the evolution of powerful desktop computers is the trend toward connecting computers in Local Area Networks (LANs). This trend is interesting particularly because early microcomputer users generally purchased their machines in a rebellion of sorts against restrictions imposed by minicomputer and mainframe connections. As individual users have developed databases of information and applications, they have returned to central server connections for information sharing.

Symantec responded to this trend with the release of Q&A Version 3.0, which included some multiuser features. Q&A is compatible with virtually any popular network products, including products from 3Com, Novell, and IBM.

Software for a multiuser environment has to be different because, just as with physical matter, two pieces of database information cannot be at the same place at the same time. If two or more users access the same record, update it, and then try to save the record back to disk, somebody gets short-circuited. Only the last version of the record to be saved is retained.

In addition, when more than one user has access to the information in a database, some security mechanisms must be implemented to limit access to authorized users. Some data files may exist that everyone should have access to; but sensitive company data, such as payroll information, obviously should be limited in distribution.

Q&A handles these problems by providing password-controlled access and by providing information-sharing features, called *locking*. With Q&A 4.0, the program acquired a field-locking feature that allows selective access to sensitive information within a file.

In Q&A and other shared products, certain facilities of the software are locked as soon as one user gains access to them. With Q&A 4.0, all users viewing the same database record see changes as soon as they're made.

Multiuser operation obviously opens up application possibilities. Multiuser operation also imposes some user restrictions. For additional information on getting the most out of Q&A's multiuser features, see Chapter 21.

Chapter Summary

This chapter was designed to introduce you to the features of Q&A. You learned about general software capabilities and some ways to apply Q&A. And you were introduced to the Q&A design philosophy.

The information in this chapter should help you start thinking about Q&A as a data-management tool for your individual needs. Refer to specific chapters for more detailed information on each Q&A topic.

2

Understanding
Database Concepts

T he term *database* means different things to different computer users. If
you ask a minicomputer or mainframe user to describe a database, you
probably will get a different answer than you will from most microcomputer
users. The microcomputer world's database has become such a pervasive part
of computer jargon, however, that this chapter holds to that definition: a
program that enables a user to store and retrieve information in an orderly
fashion from a floppy or hard disk.

In this chapter, you learn the basics of what a database is, how databases are
structured, what types of databases are available, what types of data are stored
in databases, and how databases are designed. All this material is covered in
more detail in subsequent chapters, but this database introduction can help
you get a handle on the necessary concepts.

Defining a Database

Generally, a microcomputer database program includes all the user-
interface logic required to design files, add new information, edit
existing data, and create reports. Modern database software usually
consists of at least two distinctly separate entities. One is the data
storage and retrieval logic—sometimes called a database engine—and the
other is the support software, which presents user menus, displays
input and edit screens, supports input and edit operations, and writes
reports.

Information in a database can be quite diverse. A database may contain many different files for individual names and addresses, company names and addresses, inventory records, employee information, accounts receivable, accounts payable, a check register, a general ledger, sales-lead tracking, project management, and much more.

Physically, each class of information is stored in a separate file. Logically, information from any or all of these files can be linked to show relationships and form comparisons. These views are independent of the physical structure of the database. For example, you can combine data from the individual names and addresses file, the company names and addresses file, and the sales-lead tracking file so that on-screen the information appears to be coming from a single file.

Storing the various types of information in different files provides flexibility in database design and operations. Combining selected pieces of information in an orderly way on-screen makes the data more useful to the user. Various files in a database system also can be distributed to many computers and storage devices that are linked by some kind of networking system.

With Version 3.0 of Q&A, this microcomputer package moved another step closer to a conventional database management system (DBMS) by providing network support and rudimentary file linking through the @XLOOKUP function (see Chapter 7 for information on @XLOOKUP).

Examining Database Components

Text editors and word processing applications store and retrieve random information in blocks perhaps thousands of characters long. When you retrieve the information from a disk, you pull the data into your computer's memory as one large block. Although you can search for specific characters or word patterns in these files, output options are rather limited. Without a great deal of manual work, your only option is to print all or a portion of the file in the order in which the data is stored.

Most database applications, on the other hand, break up the data into smaller, more manageable units called *fields* and *records*. The data is stored together in a large file, but you can retrieve the units one at a time or in groups, sort the units, relate them in various ways, and print them in almost any order you choose.

Databases nearly always include three logical structures—fields, records, and files—which are discussed in the following sections.

Database Fields

A database *field* is the smallest piece of information the user identifies. This smallest database unit consists of at least two components: the field label and the field data. Other field information, such as data attributes, also may be part of the field description. As the name suggests, the *field label* describes the contents of the field. The *field data* is the piece of information you want to store and track as an individual unit. *Attribute data* defines the type of information each field can hold: text, numbers, dates, and money amounts.

Common field labels are as follows:

Name
Company
Address
City
Invoice No.
Account No.
Description
Purchase Order No.

In most database systems, field labels and attributes are stored only once for each file description. This label and attribute information forms an overlay to describe, or define, raw data as it is entered and retrieved. Consider the following items of raw data:

PF432-688-Y
Idler Retainer Ring
Franklyn Engine Concepts
880615
B-423567-00015
12
16B
33
166-C
6 6
20
183
244

Although some of this information can be deciphered, you have no way to know for sure what some of these numbers mean without field labels and attributes. When Q&A combines this raw data with separate label and attribute overlays, the user is presented with the following:

Part No:	P F 4 3 2 - 6 8 8 - Y
Description:	Idler Retainer Ring
Manufacturer:	Franklyn Engine Concepts
Date of Mfg:	06/15/1988
Serial No:	B-423567-00015
Quality Ctrl Chk:	12
Lot:	16B
Warehouse:	33
Bin:	166-C
Qty in Stock:	66
Reorder Qty:	20
Wholesale Cost:	$1.83
Retail Price:	$2.44

In Q&A, you specify field labels on an editor screen by typing each label followed by a colon to separate the label from the field contents. A greater-than symbol (>) marks the end of the field on-screen, as shown in the following collection of fields:

```
  Last Name:              >
 First Name:           >
      Title:                    >
 Company ID:        >
       Keys:                           >
```

This collection of fields describes a database record, a subject that is covered fully in Part II of this book.

Database Records

A database *record* is composed of all the fields that refer to a single item. A complete name and address is one record. The part number, description, price, and other data that describes a unique inventory part form one record. Figure 2.1 illustrates a sample contacts database record showing field labels and field contents (data).

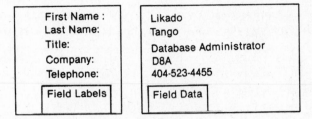

Fig. 2.1. *Structure of a database record.*

Just as individual fields combine to form a database record, all the records in a group form a database file (see fig. 2.2).

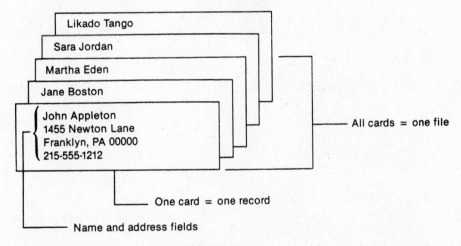

Fig. 2.2. *The field, record, and file relationship.*

Database Files

File is a term with which most computer users are at least slightly familiar. Although many kinds of files exist, the two most common basic types are program files and data files. *Program files* store the instructions that make the computer perform word processing, database management, graphics, communications, printing, and other functions. *Data files* store the information you provide for these programs to use.

A *database data file* consists of all the records about a specific topic. Usually, but not always, a database contains separate files for inventory, names and addresses, accounting, and the like. The inventory file contains only inventory records, the company file contains only company records, and so on.

In some database programs, data files also hold other information besides just data records. Somewhere in the file may be information that describes how reports will be structured, for example. Also, as mentioned earlier, field attribute information may be part of the file information.

Examining Database Types

Among the many database structures in use today are hierarchical, extended network, relational, and flat files. Within these basic structures are many implementations. Today's microcomputer users most commonly use flat file and relational databases. *Flat files* are stand-alone data structures that cannot be connected to any other file. *Relational files* may include structures that are similar to flat files, but relational files can be related to each other in various ways.

Flat Files

A flat file stands alone. It may contain all the field and record information described in the preceding paragraphs, but the database management software that supports the file is not capable of tying information from one file to information in another file. For many applications, flat file storage is sufficient. A simple name and address application used to track individuals and their companies, perhaps to print telephone directories or Rolodex cards, may require nothing more sophisticated than a flat file.

Obviously, you can create many flat files with the same software, but you cannot link information in different files with a program that supports only flat file structures.

The advantage of this type of program is its simplicity. It is usually menu driven, requires little time to learn, is probably more storage efficient than a relational program, and is low in cost.

The disadvantage is that repetitious data must be stored more than once. Suppose that your name and address file has only 300 individual companies but 1,000 individuals. That factor means that each company name and address is being stored, on the average, at least three times.

Not only is this structure wasteful of storage space, but you cannot modify the structure without rewriting the entire file. To add a field of information, for example, you have to change the basic structure of the file.

Relational Files

The data structures in a relational system are more efficient than structures in flat files. The difference is in the supporting software and other features that permit information in individual files to be linked. This operation is sometimes called a *join*.

To continue the name and address example, with a relational system, you build separate name and company files. The name file contains the individual's name, company ID, and whatever other information you want about that person. The company file contains the company ID, company name, address, telephone number, and any other information you need about the company.

The two files are linked through the common Company ID field. A relational program looks at the company identifier in the name file and then finds a matching entry in the company file. Assuming that the entry operator has not made an error, you can find out detailed information about the company for which this individual works (see fig. 2.3).

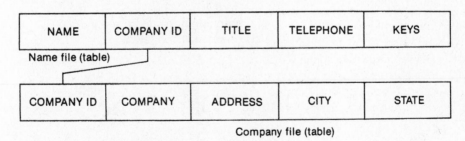

Fig. 2.3   Sample relational file join.

With a relational structure, you store the company information only once. Records about employees for each company can be stored in the name file. Storage space is conserved because the company data does not have to be repeated with each employee record.

In addition, if you discover that you need to track additional information about individuals or their companies after the basic name and company files have been in use for awhile, you don't necessarily have to redesign either file.

You can add a transaction file, for example, to track each contact you make with individuals or companies. As long as you include a company ID in the file structure, the new transaction file can be linked to companies. And, with a unique Name or Contact Number field, you can track transactions against individuals in the name file.

The main disadvantage of relational database programs is the increased complexity. The software is harder to program, so the user must learn more about the database structure in order to apply the software successfully. Nevertheless, the trend toward relational databases is clear in the database industry. Increasingly, databases for microcomputers, minicomputers, and mainframes use some form of relational structure. In addition, user-friendly front ends—software that presents menus, graphics screens, on-line help, and other user aids—are designed for easy application development. As a result, just about anybody can use these new products.

Q&A File falls somewhere between true relational and flat files. With the @XLOOKUP and XLOOKUP commands introduced in Version 3.0, File can link the current active file with information stored in other files. With Version 4.0 and later versions, @XLOOKUP and XLOOKUP can draw information from multiple fields in a single external database record. As a result, you easily can include additional data in the active file or in printed reports. You can maintain separate name and company files, as suggested, and then merge information from the two files to print a comprehensive contacts directory, complete with both company and name information.

See Chapter 7, "Customizing and Programming a File," for more information on @XLOOKUP and its associated commands and functions.

Examining Field Data Types

Most people think of data as being of two types: text and numbers. On the surface, this concept seems simple: numbers are numbers, and text is anything that isn't numbers. That distinction is partially true, but most computer programs divide data types beyond these two.

In Q&A File, for example, you can assign to each field one of seven data types: text, number, money, date, hours, yes/no (logical), and keywords. (Q&A also refers to these types as information types.) Within several of these field types, you have formatting options, which control the way the data is displayed and printed. This feature helps ensure that proper information is entered into each field and can make searching for data more precise.

Text Type

Text fields contain alphanumeric data, which is precisely what the name implies: information that includes both text and numbers. Text, however, is broader in definition than just the letters of the alphabet. In alphanumeric data types, special nonnumeric characters that are not strictly alphabetic also are allowed: hyphens, for example, or slash marks (/), percent signs (%), asterisks (*), tildes (~), and anything else that appears on the standard computer keyboard. Depending on the application, alphanumeric also may include graphics characters, such as line draw characters (|), happy faces, or other symbols.

The *text* data type is used for names, descriptions, cities, and states. In addition, although the fact may seem strange, you probably will use the text data type for ZIP codes because the hyphen (-) commonly used to separate the first five and the last four numbers in some ZIP codes is not a numeric character. You can enter the ZIP code in a numeric ZIP field, but Q&A asks every time whether you are sure that this entry is a valid number. For the same reason, telephone numbers are considered text, whether you use the 123-456-7890 or the (123)456-7890 form. The hyphens and parentheses in these examples disqualify them for treatment as numbers, leaving them as text. Telephone numbers also are treated as text because they will not be used in mathematical functions.

Number and Money Types

Basic numeric data is a little simpler. It includes the digits from 0 to 9, in any combination, perhaps preceded by a negative sign or other indicator to show a below-zero value.

Any database field that contains only numerical values, such as price, quantity sold, number in stock, and total sales to date, should be entered as a number because you can perform mathematical calculations on *number* data type fields. Text fields, on the other hand, cannot be used in any math calculations.

When you designate a field as the *money* data type, numeric values entered into the field are displayed with a dollar sign and two decimal places. The number 12.50, for example, becomes $12.50, and 12 becomes $12.00 in a Q&A money type field.

You also can specify certain formats that change the way numeric data is displayed. A global format is one that applies to all fields in the database as opposed to only one specific field. You can have field-level as well as global formats in Q&A. For example, you can have numbers shown with a comma rather than a decimal point (12,50 rather than 12.50).

In money type fields, you can change the currency symbol to something other than a dollar sign, and you can specify how many decimal places should appear after the decimal point or comma. When you make some of these changes, you also must modify the operation of other features, such as the formats for some programming statements used to customize database forms. For example, if you replace the U.S. decimal point with a European comma, you must replace the comma separator in multistatement program lines with a semicolon.

Date Type

Q&A supports 20 different formats for *date* type fields (see table 2.1). You choose a global date format by choosing the number beside the format you want. When you designate a field as a date type field, you must enter the date in one of these 20 formats. The on-screen display automatically changes to display the date in the format you have specified as the global default.

Table 2.1
Q&A Date Formats

1 - Mar 19, 1968	11 - March 19, 1968
2 - 19 Mar 1968	12 - 19 March 1968
3 - 3/19/68	13 - 3-19-68
4 - 19/3/68	14 - 3-19-1968
5 - 3/19/1968	15 - 03-19-1968
6 - 19/3/1968	16 - 03-19-1968
7 - 03/19/68	17 - 19.03.68
8 - 19/03/68	18 - 19.03.1968
9 - 03/19/1968	19 - 1968-03-19
10 - 19/03/1968	20 - 1968/03/19

Unless you change the default, dates are displayed in the form mmm dd, yyyy. If you enter a date such as 05.24.88 or 24.05.88 or 05/24/88—or any of the other supported date formats—Q&A displays May 24, 1988. If you enter information that does not conform to Q&A's supported date formats, you are asked to confirm the information. You then can leave the entry the way it is or change it to an accepted format.

Hours Type

Hours (time) formatting in Q&A is similar to date formatting. Three hours formats are supported (4:55 pm, 16:55, 16.55). You can enter data in any of the formats, and Q&A displays the information accordingly. An improper entry brings a prompt for verification from Q&A.

Q&A supports both 12- and 24-hour time formats, using either a colon or a period to separate hours and minutes. For example, you can use 13:42 or 13.42 in a time field. If you specify a 12-hour format, Q&A adds the a.m. identifier to numbers below 12 and the p.m. format to numbers above 12. If you enter *13:42*, for example, Q&A displays 1:42 pm.

Yes/No (Logical) Type

At times, you need to enter a simple yes or no answer to a field prompt. Some examples of the questions a logical field can ask are

> Is this an active record?
> Discount applied?
> Follow-up call made?
> Payment received?
> Full-time employee?

You can design a text field and enter *Y* or *N*, or you can specify a *yes/no* (also called logical or Boolean) field. Logical fields have a length of one, and they work with yes/no, 1/0, or true/false. You can enter data in such a field as Y(es), T(rue), or 1 (logical true). Lowercase letters also work.

The advantage of using a logical data type is that you can perform certain logical operations (AND, OR, NOT) that may be helpful in producing reports from the data in the field.

Keywords Type

The *keywords* data type is not a common structure. With the keywords type, you enter text information in a field with the words or topics separated by semicolons. You then can conduct database searches and produce reports based on the items in the keyword field. For example, in your contacts file you may want to enter random keywords to designate each contact by type:

    Advertising;Computers;Storage;Workstations

When you specify a keyword search, Q&A looks for the specified word pattern in that field in every record. You can search for more than one entry in a keyword field—for example, computers;workstations.

Exploring Database Design Concepts

Designing a database is a little like programming an application. The difference in products such as Q&A is that the job of specifying the database structure is much easier than with a conventional programming language.

Moreover, with Q&A you aren't stuck with the initial design. You easily can modify an existing data file if you discover, after bringing it on-line, that changes have to be made.

Nevertheless, some basic database design principles can make your job easier, reduce the number of later modifications, and produce reports that better satisfy your data-management requirements.

Everybody has a different approach to any task, and you should use procedures that work for you. Keep these basic design principles in mind, however, as you work through database design:

- Design the output first.
- Identify the field labels.
- Select reasonable field lengths.
- Design a workable entry screen.
- Automate processes.

Designing the Output First

The best place to start a database design is to spend some time designing the output. After all, the reason for storing data on a computer in the first place is to be able to look at the information in some specific way. If you start the design by deciding what output you want, you are sure to put into the database the information you need in order to get the reports you need.

Try to be imaginative at this stage. You probably are building the database for one or two specific reasons, but a general rule of computer use is that your information needs expand with your capability to process information. That is, you can do things with a computer that were impossible or too cumbersome to do by hand. Likewise, an easy-to-use product such as Q&A can make possible things that were too difficult or time-consuming with most programming languages. For these reasons, try to imagine applications that you haven't identified before.

Identifying the Field Labels

After you know how the output from the database should look, you are ready to specify the field labels. Use Q&A's Write module or another word processor as a scratch pad to help you identify which fields should appear in each database record.

Experiment with field labels. Don't necessarily use the first label that comes to mind. Remember that you want to be as descriptive as possible, but you don't want to end up with unwieldy labels, either. Although a label like *Date of Last Contact* certainly is descriptive, and Q&A supports such labels, they take up a great deal of room on reports. The label *Contacted* with a date type field serves the same purpose.

Consider issues such as whether you may need to sort the information by, for example, a last name. If you think this need may ever occur, you need individual last name and first name fields. If you enter names in one long field, producing reports sorted by last name will be difficult—or impossible.

Will it be important for you to know when each record was entered or when it was last updated? If so, include one or more date fields so that you can track this information. Q&A supports autotype entry so that when you display a record or move the cursor to a field, Q&A automatically enters the current date.

Will you probably include foreign addresses in your database? Remember that Canadian and other foreign addresses aren't formatted precisely like those in the U.S. A two-digit state field is of little use in entering these addresses, for example. How will you enter foreign addresses? Collect several examples to see what information you need to include. Ask some of the contacts themselves how they format their name and address files on their own computers. Add extra fields to cover unforeseen contingencies.

Selecting Reasonable Field Lengths

Give some thought to how long each field should be. You need fields that are long enough to accommodate the longest entry you regularly have. If you make fields too long, however, you waste disk and screen space.

With some information, the field length is obvious. ZIP codes, for example, require nine or ten spaces, depending on whether or not you use a hyphen to separate the last four digits from the first five. You should use no more than two characters for state entries (but remember to add fields for foreign addresses if you require them). The post office prefers the two-letter state abbreviations, most people recognize them, and the abbreviations save storage and screen space.

Name, company, and address fields are a little more difficult. The best answer here is to experiment with representative entries of your own in order to find out how large these fields should be. A length of 25 to 35 characters seems to be a good average for such fields. You probably will not find many entries that exceed the upper limit of that range. The few that do can be abbreviated in some way to make them fit.

If you separate first name and last name fields to give more flexibility in sorting and report generation, experiment with reasonable lengths for both fields.

Designing a Workable Entry Screen

Q&A is suited particularly to good screen design because you use a full-screen editor to tell the software what the database will look like. Don't hesitate to redo this input/update screen several times.

Think about the sequence in which you normally enter the data into the database. What is the source of this information? In what order is the data presented to you or your operator? For example, using a Last Name, First Name, Company, Title sequence may be difficult if the source document lists First Name, then Last Name, then Title, and then Company.

Isolate fields that are updated rarely—for example, social security numbers, part numbers, employee start dates, or birth dates. You can put these fields together on the right side of the screen and enclose them in a box. After the information is entered, you may not have to open these fields again. The best practice is not to have to step through these fields each time you want to make a simple change to another database field.

Automating Database Processes

Q&A File is a powerful data-management tool that provides a number of end-user programming features to make database maintenance easier. Study the customizing and programming sections of this book and of the Q&A manual to learn how to reduce or eliminate redundant effort.

Consider the Ditto command, for one thing. This useful Q&A tool copies information from the preceding form to the current form so that you enter certain information only once. Suppose that you are working with payroll information grouped by department. You do not need to reenter the department ID or number until it changes. The Ditto command carries over the department information from the preceding form, and you have to type new data in this field only when you process the first employee from the next department.

Likewise, why type the city and state every time when you are entering similar address records? Particularly if you are working with regional data, such as an employee file, identifying the major cities and towns where your employees reside should be fairly simple. Enter the cities, along with the ZIP codes for these locations, into a Q&A lookup table. Then, during record entry, you enter only the ZIP codes. Q&A looks up each city and state and inserts them into the proper fields of the database. If you are dealing with a large number of records, the extra time spent building the ZIP code lookup table can be returned many times during data entry.

See Chapter 7 for more information about using lookup tables and customizing and programming a Q&A File database.

Chapter Summary

Some basic database terms and concepts have been introduced in this chapter—terms that you will see in many other places throughout this book. This chapter has defined a database, discussed some of the different database structures, and presented the concept of data types. You also have been given a brief introduction to database design concepts. These ideas are expanded in later sections of the book.

If this chapter leaves you with one basic idea, it should be that Q&A is a versatile, user-friendly package. You should approach Q&A accordingly: use your imagination, experiment, test, redo, redesign. Your approach to getting the most out of Q&A database design should be a hands-on approach from the beginning.

3

Getting Started

Now that you understand the basic concepts and principles of databases, you are ready to begin using Q&A. In this chapter, you first find a detailed explanation of how to begin the program and how to exit safely without losing data. You learn about the Q&A keyboard, the screen displays, the menu system, and how to get help from Q&A. You also learn the basics of entering and editing text and of working with database and document files.

Starting and Ending a Q&A Session

After the installation is complete (see Appendix A for details), you are ready to use Q&A. The following paragraphs describe how to get started and how to exit when you're done.

Starting Q&A

To start Q&A, follow these steps:

1. Turn on the computer.

2. If prompted by DOS, enter the date and time. If your system has a clock/calendar, the system fills in the date and time.

3. At the DOS prompt (C> in most cases), change to the directory in which you installed Q&A. Type

   CD\QA

   or

   CD*directory name*

   If you have installed Q&A in the root directory, disregard this step.

4. Type *qa* to start the program. A large QA is displayed while the program is being loaded; then the Q&A Main menu screen appears (see fig. 3.1).

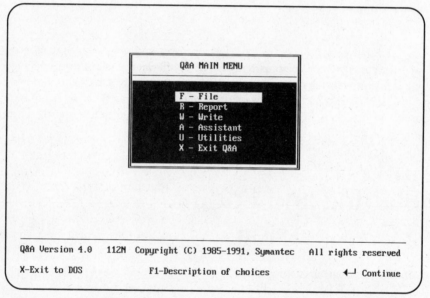

Fig. 3.1.   *The Q&A Main menu.*

Exiting Q&A

You have more than one way to exit Q&A, depending on where you want to be when you exit. The important thing to remember is to protect your data so that it isn't destroyed when you exit.

To leave Q&A and return to DOS, move to the Q&A Main menu (which you can reach in most cases just by pressing the Esc key several times); then press X (for

Exit Q&A). You also can exit from the Main menu by pressing the number 6. When the DOS prompt is displayed, you can start another program or quit by turning off the computer.

Do not turn off the computer while you are working on a document or database file in any Q&A module. If you do, you may lose important information.

Do not, under any circumstances, turn off the power or reboot your computer when you are at any point in the program other than the following menus:

- Q&A Main menu

- File menu

- Report menu

- Write menu

- Intelligent Assistant menu

- Utilities menu

If you turn off your computer from any other place, you risk destruction of some or all of the file in which you are working. (*Note:* If you are using Version 1.0, you may safely shut down at the Main menu only.) If you are careful about how you shut down, your data should be safe. As an additional safeguard, however, you should make regular backups of database and document files. For help with this procedure, refer to your DOS manual. If a file becomes damaged, select Recover Database from the File Utilities menu. Some data may be lost, but the file will be restored so that you can access it.

Understanding the Q&A Keyboard and Screen

The three most commonly used keyboards on IBM and IBM-compatible personal computers are shown in figure 3.2. The keyboards are divided into three sections: the alphanumeric keyboard in the center, the numeric keypad on the right, and the function key section on the left or across the top. The Enhanced Keyboard, which is used by the IBM Personal System/2 family of computers and some AT-compatible computers, also has a separate group of cursor-movement keys.

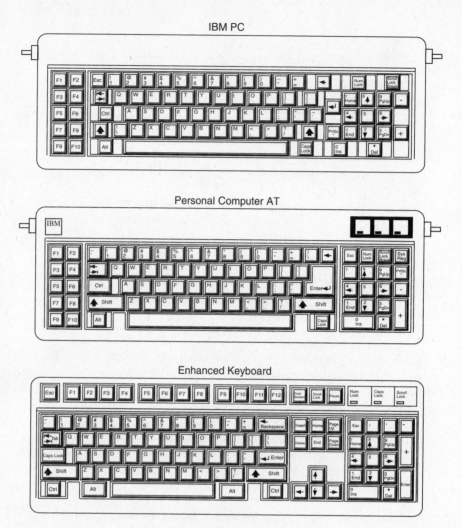

Fig. 3.2.   *The three personal computer keyboards.*

Using the Alphanumeric Keys

Most of the keys in the alphanumeric section at the center of the keyboard are
the same ones you find on a typewriter, and they maintain their customary
functions in Q&A. As table 3.1 illustrates, however, several keys on the
alphanumeric keyboard (Esc, Tab, Shift, and Alt) take on new functions or are
different from typewriter keys. As you become accustomed to these keys, you
will find them helpful and easy to use.

Table 3.1
Using Alphanumeric Keys in Q&A

Key	Function
Enter	Accepts an entry and continues; moves the cursor to the start of the next line
Esc	Cancels the current operation; exits the current screen and returns to the menu; leaves the current menu and moves to the preceding menu
Tab	Jumps the cursor to the next tab stop in a document; jumps the cursor to the start of the next field in a database form
Shift-Tab	Jumps the cursor to the start of the preceding field in a database form (reverse tab)
Alt	Used simultaneously with function keys for special functions (see table 3.2)
Shift	Used simultaneously with other keys: changes the central section of the keyboard to uppercase letters and characters; activates a temporary Num Lock enabling you to enter numbers by using the numeric keypad on the right of the keyboard
Backspace	Erases the characters to the left of the cursor

Using the Function Keys

The function keys F1 through F10 are used for special situations in Q&A. Notice the difference in the location of the function keys on the two types of keyboards; the keys are on the far left of the PC and AT keyboards but across the top of the Enhanced Keyboard. The Enhanced Keyboard also has two more function keys, F11 and F12. Q&A, like many current programs, does not use these two keys.

The function keys are explained in table 3.2. Notice that most keys have multiple actions, activated when the key is pressed with the Shift, Ctrl, or Alt key. Although Q&A is well designed for continuity across the modules, some function keys perform different operations in different modules.

Table 3.2
Using Function Keys in Q&A

Key	Action in Write	Action in File	Action in Report
F1	Get help screen	Get help screen	Get help screen
Alt-F1	Thesaurus		
Shift-F1	Check spelling in document		
Ctrl-F1	Check spelling of word		
F2	Print document	Print current form	
Shift-F2	Use macros	Use macros	
Ctrl-F2	Print text block	Print to end of stack	
F3	Delete block	Delete current form or clear spec	Clear spec
Ctrl-F3	Document specs		
F4	Delete to end of word	Delete to end of word	Delete to end of word
Shift-F4	Delete line	Delete to end of field	Delete to end of field
Ctrl-F4	Delete to end of line		
F5	Copy block	Ditto field (copy value)	
Shift-F5	Move block	Ditto form	
Ctrl-F5	Copy block to file	Insert system date	Insert system date
Alt-F5	Move block to file	Insert system time	Insert system time
F6	Set temporary margins	Edit field value	Expand field
Shift-F6	Enhance text	Define table view	Enhance text
Ctrl-F6	Define page	GoTo Add Forms (from Edit)	
Alt-F6	Hyphenate	Table view (when updating)	

Key	Action in Write	Action in File	Action in Report
F7	Search and replace	Search (retrieve spec)	
Shift-F7	Restore text/ make multiple copies	Undo Editing	
Ctrl-F7	GoTo Page/Line		
Alt-F7	List fields	List restricted values	
F8	Options menu	Calc	Derived columns
Shift-F8	Save document	Set Calc mode	
Ctrl-F8	Export document	Reset @Number	
Alt-F8			List stored specs
F9	Scroll screen up	Save form and get preceding form	Go back to preceding operation
Shift-F9	Scroll screen down	Customize specs	Customize specs
Ctrl-F9	Make font assignments		
Alt-F9	Calculate		
F10	Continue	Save form and get next form	Continue
Shift-F10		Save record and exit	

The use of each function key is explained more completely as the key is introduced in the appropriate chapter, but some general aids and guides are given here.

Q&A provides two references and reminders of what the keys do: a key assignment line and a key usage help screen. The key assignment line appears at the bottom of the screen and identifies the functions of keys in the current situation (see fig. 3.3). The key usage help screen is displayed at data-entry points in the program when you press F1, the Help function key (see fig. 3.4). Note that F1 is the Help key throughout Q&A, even though the bottom-of-screen prompt for F1 changes with different modules. You can purchase an optional function-key template to fit over the function keys of the IBM PC. This template provides an instant guide to the functions of the keys in Q&A.

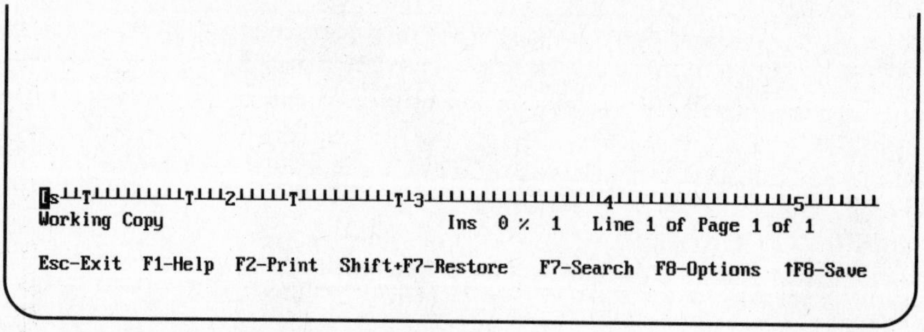

```
|s 1 1 T 1 1 1 1 1 1 1 1 1 T 1 1 2 1 1 1 1 T 1 1 1 1 1 1 1 1 T 1 3 1 1 1 1 1 1 1 1 1 1 1 1 1 1 4 1 1 1 1 1 1 1 1 1 1 1 1 1 5 1 1 1 1 1
Working Copy                               Ins  0 %  1   Line 1 of Page 1 of 1

Esc-Exit  F1-Help  F2-Print  Shift+F7-Restore    F7-Search  F8-Options  ↑F8-Save
```

Fig. 3.3.   *The function key assignment line.*

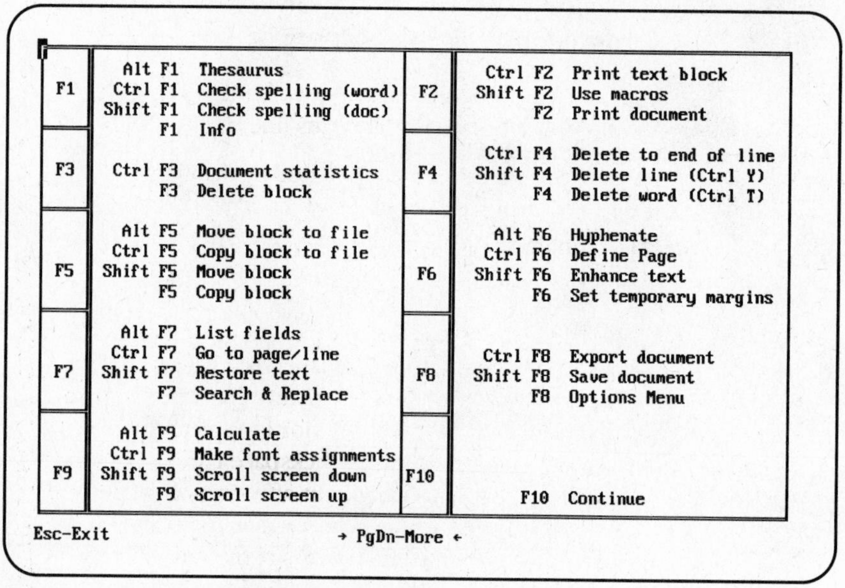

```
      ┌───┬──────────────────────────────┬───┬──────────────────────────────┐
      │   │  Alt F1   Thesaurus          │   │  Ctrl F2   Print text block   │
      │F1 │  Ctrl F1  Check spelling (word)│F2│ Shift F2   Use macros         │
      │   │  Shift F1 Check spelling (doc)│   │     F2     Print document     │
      │   │     F1    Info               │   │                               │
      │   │                              │   │  Ctrl F4   Delete to end of line│
      │F3 │  Ctrl F3  Document statistics│F4 │  Shift F4  Delete line (Ctrl Y) │
      │   │     F3    Delete block       │   │     F4     Delete word (Ctrl T) │
      │   │  Alt F5   Move block to file │   │  Alt F6    Hyphenate          │
      │   │  Ctrl F5  Copy block to file │   │  Ctrl F6   Define Page        │
      │F5 │  Shift F5 Move block         │F6 │  Shift F6  Enhance text       │
      │   │     F5    Copy block         │   │     F6     Set temporary margins│
      │   │  Alt F7   List fields        │   │                               │
      │   │  Ctrl F7  Go to page/line    │   │  Ctrl F8   Export document    │
      │F7 │  Shift F7 Restore text       │F8 │  Shift F8  Save document       │
      │   │     F7    Search & Replace   │   │     F8     Options Menu        │
      │   │  Alt F9   Calculate          │   │                               │
      │   │  Ctrl F9  Make font assignments│   │                             │
      │F9 │  Shift F9 Scroll screen down │F10│                               │
      │   │     F9    Scroll screen up   │   │     F10    Continue           │
      └───┴──────────────────────────────┴───┴──────────────────────────────┘
       Esc-Exit                       → PgDn-More ←
```

Fig. 3.4.   *The key usage help screen in Write.*

Using the Numeric Keypad

On the IBM PC and AT keyboards, the numeric keypad, situated on the right side of the keyboard, has to do double duty. The keypad functions as both a numeric-entry pad and a cursor-movement pad. The Enhanced Keyboard duplicates this functionality for those who want it but also provides separate cursor-movement keys in the keypad section between the numeric keypad and the alphanumeric keypad.

You use the numeric keypad mostly for cursor movement. The keypad holds the arrow keys, the Home key, the End key, and the PgUp and PgDn keys. The cursor-movement keys are described in detail in this chapter's section on "Using the Cursor-Movement Keys." Table 3.3 explains the operation of the numeric-keypad keys that are not used for cursor movement.

Table 3.3
Using the Numeric Keypad in Q&A

Key	Function
Num Lock	A toggle (on/off) key that affects the keys in the numeric keypad. When Num Lock is on, pressing a key creates a number; when Num Lock is off, pressing a key moves the cursor (or has no effect if the key is number 5). When the Num Lock key is on in Write, Q&A displays Num on the status line of the screen.
Del	Deletes the character highlighted by the cursor
Scroll Lock/ Break	Not used by Q&A
Ins	A toggle key that changes the typing mode from Overwrite to Insert. When Ins is on, entered characters are inserted at the cursor location; when Ins is off, entered characters replace existing characters. The Backspace key changes behavior in Insert mode. In Overwrite mode, pressing Backspace replaces characters with blank spaces without affecting the rest of the line, but in Insert mode, the key deletes characters to the left of the cursor and shifts the remainder of the line to the left.

To use the numeric keypad to enter numbers, you can do one of two things: Press the Num Lock key to turn on numbers before entering the numbers, and press the key again to turn off numbers; or hold down the Shift key while you press the number keys.

If you press a cursor-movement key and a number appears on-screen, the Num Lock key is on. Press the Num Lock key to turn it off; then use the cursor-movement keys.

Using the Cursor-Movement Keys

To move around the screen and from screen to screen, use the cursor-movement keys. If you use the arrow keys on the numeric keypad, make certain that Num Lock is disengaged.

You can use the cursor-movement keys alone or with the Tab and Ctrl keys. Generally, the cursor-movement keys are consistent from one module to the next, as you can see in tables 3.4 and 3.5. This consistency makes learning to use the keys easy.

Table 3.4
Using Cursor-Movement Keys in Q&A

Key	Movement in a Write document	Movement during form design	Movement within a form
↑	Up one line	Up one line	Up one line
↓	Down one line	Down one line	Down one line
→	Next character to right	Next character to right	Next character to right
Ctrl-→	Next word to right	Next word to right	Next word to right
←	Next character to left	Next character to left	Next character to left
Ctrl-←	Next word to left	Next word to left	Next word to left
PgUp	To first character of preceding screen	To first character of preceding page	To first character of preceding page
Ctrl-PgUp	To first character of preceding page		
PgDn	To first character of next screen	To first character of next page	To next page
Ctrl-PgDn	To first character of next page		
Tab	To next tab stop to right	To next tab stop to right	To next field

Key	Movement in a Write document	Movement during form design	Movement within a form
Shift-Tab	To next tab stop to left	To next tab stop to left	To preceding field
F9	Scroll up		
Shift-F9	Scroll down		

Table 3.5
Using the Home and End Keys in Q&A

Key	Movement in a Write document	Movement during form design	Movement within a form
Home			
First press	To first character of line	To first character of line	To first character of field
Second press	To first character of screen	To first character of page	To first character of first field of current page
Third press	To first character of page	To first character of form	To first character of first field of form
Fourth press	To first character of document		
Ctrl-Home			
	To first character of document		To first form in database stack
End			
First press	To last character of line	To last character of line	To last character of current field

continues

Table 3.5 *(continued)*

Key	Movement in a Write document	Movement during form design	Movement within a form
Second press	To last character of screen	To last character of page	To last character of last field of current page
Third press	To last character of page	To last character of form	To last character of last field of form
Fourth press	To last character of document		
Ctrl-End	To last character of document		To last form in database stack

Q&A uses certain keys to move the cursor in relation to the markings on the ruler line, which appears in the Write module and at the bottom of the blank File Forms Design screen. The following keys make moving back and forth on the ruler easier:

Key	Cursor moves to
Home	First space to the right of the left margin
End	First space to the left of the right margin
Ctrl- ←	Five spaces to the left
Ctrl- →	Five spaces to the right
Tab	Next tab marker to the right
Shift-Tab	Closest tab marker to the left

Using a Mouse with Q&A

If you have a Microsoft-compatible mouse, you can choose menu items or function key assignments displayed on the status line by clicking or double-clicking the left mouse button. (Double-clicking means quickly pressing the button twice in succession.) To select an item (the equivalent of highlighting it with the cursor and pressing Enter), point to the item with the mouse cursor and double-click. To back out of a menu or prompt (the equivalent of pressing Esc), move the mouse cursor outside the menu or prompt box and click the left button.

You also can select text blocks with the mouse in Q&A Write. To select text, place the mouse cursor on the first letter of the block you want to select. Press and hold down the left button while you move the cursor to the end of the block. Release the button, and the block remains highlighted. You then can use the mouse to perform block functions. For example, to apply a text enhancement, click the Shift-F6 (Enhance Text) item on the status line. Q&A displays the Text Enhancements and Fonts menu. To select an enhancement for the highlighted block of text, point to the enhancement with the mouse cursor and double-click the left button. The menu disappears, and the enhancement is applied to the block.

No special installation is required to use a mouse with Q&A. You simply need to load the mouse driver (MOUSE.COM, or the equivalent if you are using a Microsoft-compatible mouse not manufactured by Microsoft). Q&A recognizes the presence of the mouse and displays the mouse cursor on-screen at the Main menu.

Examining the Q&A Screen Display

Q&A's screen display places all program information on the bottom four lines, leaving the remainder of the screen available for you to use. Figure 3.5 shows this information on the Q&A File Design screen; figure 3.6 shows how Write displays function key assignments. (The screens displayed while you are working in the Intelligent Assistant, however, vary in layout; see Chapters 17 and 18 for examples.) On the left side of the status line is the file name of the database or document you are using. Q&A also displays the cursor position, the current form or page, and the total number of forms or pages.

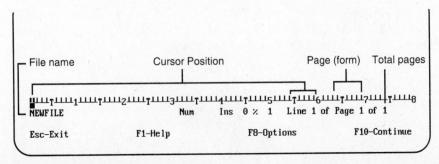

Fig. 3.5. *The Q&A File screen display.*

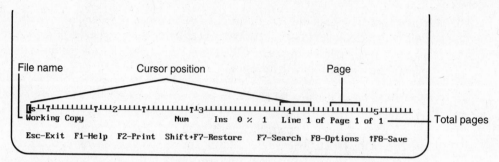

Fig. 3.6. *The Q&A Write screen display.*

The status line also shows information about the status of the toggle keys. Q&A has three of these on/off keys: Caps Lock, Num Lock, and Ins. On the status line in figure 3.7, the toggle-key indicators show that the three keys are on. When the Caps Lock key is on, all alphanumeric keys create uppercase characters. When the Num Lock key is on, all keypad number keys produce numbers rather than move the cursor. When the Ins key is on, characters to the right of the cursor move to the right as you enter new text. Notice also that when you are in Insert mode, the cursor shape changes from a single thin horizontal line to a solid rectangular box. In Overwrite mode (no Ins indicator on the status line), new characters type over or replace existing characters.

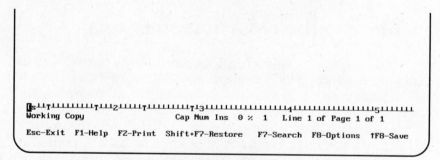

Fig. 3.7. *The on-off key indicators on the status line.*

In Q&A Write, you can change the program's Overwrite mode default to Insert. To make this change, choose Utilities from the Write menu, select Global Options, and choose Set Editing Options from the Global Options screen.

Learning the Q&A Menu System

Because of its simplicity and consistency, the Q&A menu system is one of the program's strongest features. The menu system is easy to use even though it has more than 20 screens, each offering at least two options.

Using Basic Menus

The system begins with the Q&A Main menu. Figure 3.8 shows the options available from the Main menu.

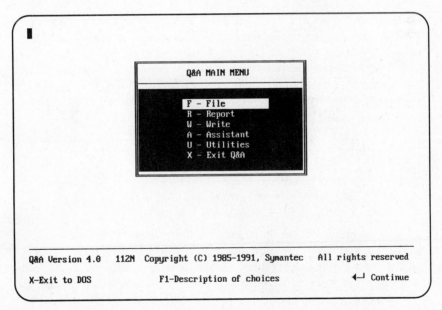

```
                          Q&A MAIN MENU

                        F - File
                        R - Report
                        W - Write
                        A - Assistant
                        U - Utilities
                        X - Exit Q&A




Q&A Version 4.0   112N  Copyright (C) 1985-1991, Symantec   All rights reserved

X-Exit to DOS          F1-Description of choices            ◄┘ Continue
```

Fig. 3.8. *The Q&A Main menu.*

On the key assignment line, beneath the heavy horizontal line, Q&A points out three keys as helpful or necessary. You can press X to leave the program, press Enter to continue with the chosen menu option, or press F1 to access the Main menu help screen, which explains the five menu options and displays a caution notice about safeguarding your data (see fig. 3.9). Press Esc to return to the Main menu from the help screen. (Help screens are explained fully in this chapter's subsequent section on "Getting Help from Q&A.") The special keys highlighted on the key assignment line are different for each menu or Q&A screen you access.

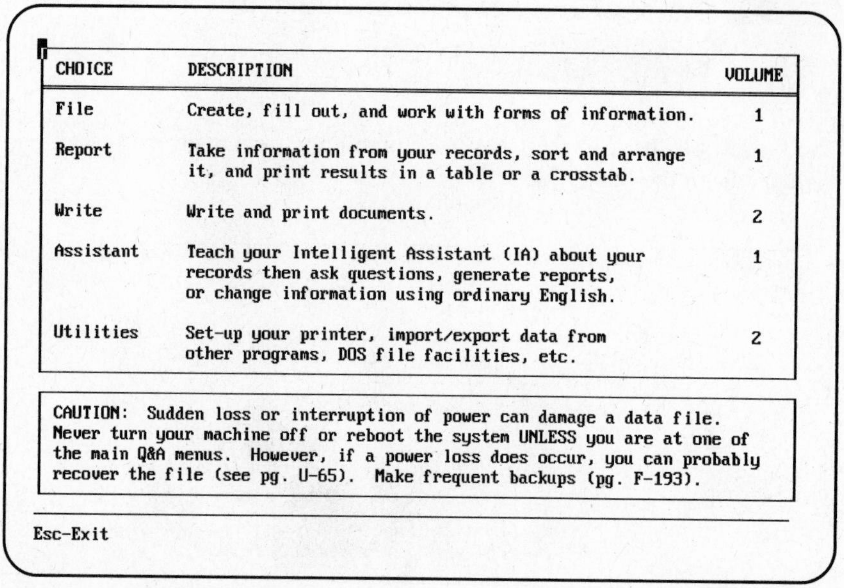

CHOICE	DESCRIPTION	VOLUME
File	Create, fill out, and work with forms of information.	1
Report	Take information from your records, sort and arrange it, and print results in a table or a crosstab.	1
Write	Write and print documents.	2
Assistant	Teach your Intelligent Assistant (IA) about your records then ask questions, generate reports, or change information using ordinary English.	1
Utilities	Set-up your printer, import/export data from other programs, DOS file facilities, etc.	2

CAUTION: Sudden loss or interruption of power can damage a data file. Never turn your machine off or reboot the system UNLESS you are at one of the main Q&A menus. However, if a power loss does occur, you can probably recover the file (see pg. U-65). Make frequent backups (pg. F-193).

Esc-Exit

Fig. 3.9.   The Q&A Main menu help screen.

You select a menu option by typing the single letter at the beginning of the option and then pressing the Enter key. Use a lowercase or an uppercase letter—it doesn't matter. For most options, the single letter is also the first letter of the menu choice—for example, F for File and R for Report.

Press F to go to the File module. If you have not configured Q&A for single-key response (see Appendix A and the following discussion for more information on single-keystroke configuration), press Enter after the F, and the File menu appears (see fig. 3.10). Notice in the key assignment line that pressing the Esc key now returns the program to the Main menu.

Q&A also uses single-key menu selection. As easy as it is to choose a menu option by typing a single letter and pressing Enter, Q&A provides an easier and quicker way—just pressing a number.

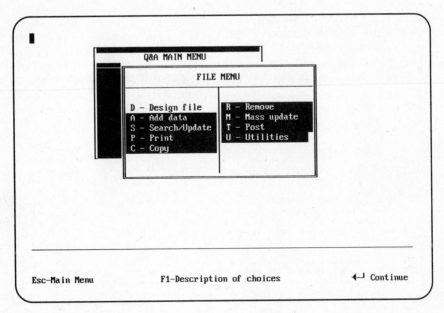

Fig. 3.10. *The File menu.*

Imagine a number in front of each option; start with 1 at the top left option, and number consecutively from top to bottom and left to right. The following list is how the Main menu would be numbered according to that scheme:

(1) F - File

(2) R - Report

(3) W - Write

(4) A - Assistant

(5) U - Utilities

(6) X - Exit Q&A

To select a menu option, press its imaginary number—no need to press Enter. Every menu can be numbered according to the same imaginary scheme and therefore can provide the same ease of choice.

You also can configure Q&A to respond instantly to the first letter in the menu choice without having to press Enter. Select Utilities from the Q&A Main menu, choose Set Global Defaults, and specify Yes under Automatic Execution. In this mode, when you press a letter to select a menu, the menu appears immediately. For example, if you press F from the Main menu, the File menu appears immediately.

Using Menu Paths

This book at times refers to a series of menu selections as a *menu path*. A menu path is a quick way to show how to get to a particular function. The path usually starts from the Main menu, with the menu selections separated by backslashes (\). For example, the path taken to the File Set Initial Values function is

File\Design File\Customize a File\Type File Name\Set Initial Values

Table 3.6 summarizes the Q&A menu structure.

Table 3.6
The Q&A Main Menu and Its Subordinate Menus

Q&A Main Menu

F-File	R-Report	W-Write	A-Assistant	U-Utilities	X-Exit Q&A
File menu	*Report menu*	*Write menu*	*Assistant menu*	*Utilities menu*	
D-Design File	D-Design/ Redesign a Report	T-Type/ Edit	G-Get Acquainted	P-Install Printer	
A-Add Data	P-Print a Report	D-Define Page	T-Teach Me about Your Database	M-Modify Font File	
S-Search/ Update	S-Set Global Options	P-Print	A-Ask Me To Do Something	D-DOS File Facilities	
P-Print	R-Rename/ Delete/ Copy	C-Clear	Q-Query Guide	S-Set Global Defaults	
C-Copy		G-Get	L-Teach Query Guide	S-Set Alternate Programs	
R-Remove		S-Save			
M-Mass Update		U-Utilities			
P-Post		M-Mailing Labels			
U-Utilities					

Getting Help from Q&A

After you become familiar with the Q&A keyboard, screen, and menu system, you may be able to begin using Q&A without further instruction. This is possible because of the thorough Q&A help screens.

Q&A provides context-sensitive help. You can reach a help screen from virtually every point in the program by pressing the F1 key. The help screen displays instructions specific to the functions available from the current screen. In most cases, the F1 key is a toggle switch: press F1 once and the help screen appears; press F1 again and the screen disappears. The Esc key provides an alternative exit from a help screen. In addition to context-sensitive and concurrent help screens, Q&A File has a custom help capability so that you can create personalized help screens.

Depending on where you are in the program when you press F1, Q&A presents one of four different help screens: menu, feature, concurrent, or two-level. Each screen offers a different kind of assistance.

Using Menu Help Screens

When you are at a menu, pressing F1 displays an explanation of that menu's options. When you press F1 at the Write menu, for example, you see the Q&A Write menu help screen illustrated in figure 3.11. Note that the screen refers you to the page in the *Q&A Instruction Manual* where you can find more information about that menu option. Press Esc to return to the Write menu.

Using Context-Sensitive Help Screens

Whatever you are doing in Q&A, you press F1 to display a help screen that has instructions specific to your environment: context-sensitive help. Suppose that you are adding data to a file form. To get help, press F1; Q&A displays the screen illustrated in figure 3.12. This help screen outlines the steps for adding or updating a form and lists function keys that are especially useful.

CHOICE	DESCRIPTION	VOLUME 2, PAGE:
Type/Edit	Edit the current document (the "working copy").	W-11
Define page	Set page size, margins, characters per inch, etc.	W-73
Print	Choose print options, then print the document.	W-79
Clear	Clear the current document from memory, and start a new one.	W-95
Get	Get a document from disk; make it the current one.	W-97
Save	Save the current document to disk.	W-101
Utilities	Set global options; export document;DOS facilities; set editing options; change Print and Define Page screen defaults;	W-159
Mailing labels	Create/edit and print mailing labels	W-119

Esc-Exit

Fig. 3.11. *The Write menu help screen.*

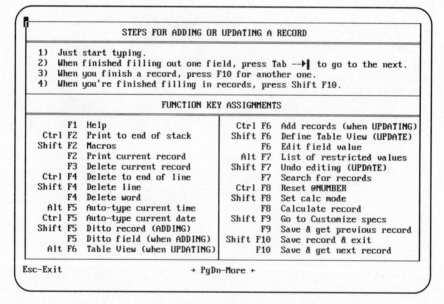

```
         STEPS FOR ADDING OR UPDATING A RECORD

1)  Just start typing.
2)  When finished filling out one field, press Tab --▶| to go to the next.
3)  When you finish a record, press F10 for another one.
4)  When you're finished filling in records, press Shift F10.

              FUNCTION KEY ASSIGNMENTS

         F1  Help                      Ctrl F6  Add records (when UPDATING)
   Ctrl F2  Print to end of stack     Shift F6  Define Table View (UPDATE)
  Shift F2  Macros                         F6  Edit field value
         F2  Print current record       Alt F7  List of restricted values
         F3  Delete current record    Shift F7  Undo editing (UPDATE)
   Ctrl F4  Delete to end of line          F7  Search for records
  Shift F4  Delete line                Ctrl F8  Reset @NUMBER
         F4  Delete word              Shift F8  Set calc mode
    Alt F5  Auto-type current time         F8  Calculate record
   Ctrl F5  Auto-type current date   Shift F9  Go to Customize specs
  Shift F5  Ditto record (ADDING)         F9  Save & get previous record
         F5  Ditto field (when ADDING) Shift F10  Save record & exit
    Alt F6  Table View (when UPDATING)    F10  Save & get next record

Esc-Exit              → PgDn-More ←
```

Fig. 3.12. *The help screen for adding or updating a file form.*

Using Concurrent Help Screens

One of Q&A's many innovations is the use of concurrent help screens, which are displayed simultaneously with your work. In figure 3.13, the box in the lower half of the screen is a help screen; the top half is the file form. With a concurrent help screen, you can work on one half of the screen and keep the instructions displayed on the other half.

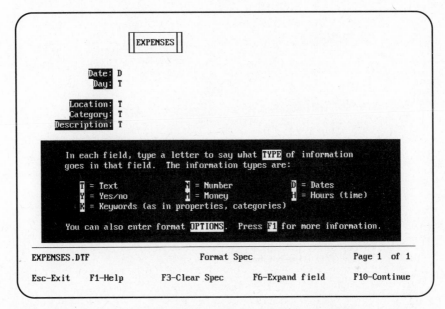

Fig. 3.13. *A concurrent help screen on the lower part of the screen.*

But what if your work is on the bottom half? The help box moves to the top half of the screen when you move the cursor to the bottom half (see fig. 3.14).

Using Two-Level Help Screens

If the program feature or operation is complex, or if all the instructions cannot fit on one screen, Q&A provides a two-level help screen. Look again at figure 3.14; notice the key assignment line reference to F1 (Help). This reference indicates a second-level help screen. Pressing F1 from this help screen displays the second level (see fig. 3.15). If the help text is long, Q&A prompts you to press the PgDn key for additional information.

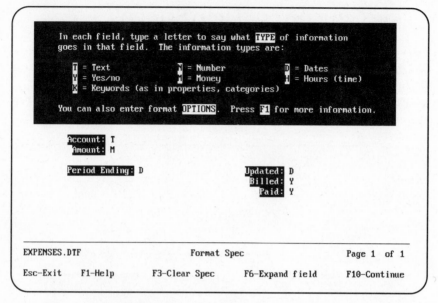

Fig. 3.14. *A concurrent help screen on the top part of the screen.*

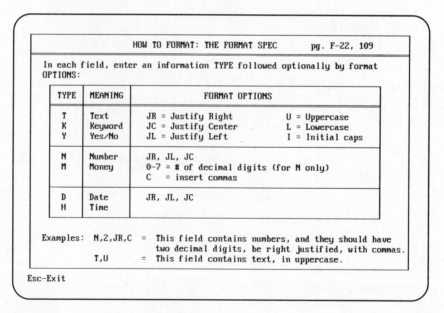

Fig. 3.15. *A second-level help screen.*

Using Custom Help Screens

A custom help screen is one that is created by the user rather than by Q&A programmers. You can create custom help screens when you first design a file or after you determine where help is needed. You can create a custom help screen for each field in a database, although the possibility that every field will need a help screen is unlikely.

Each screen can instruct the user about what information should be entered in the field. Figure 3.16, for example, shows a help screen listing the acceptable entries for the Category field of the database. Custom help screens also can help users by displaying reference material, documenting the field's formula, providing reminders for database users, or holding any other information or instructions you choose.

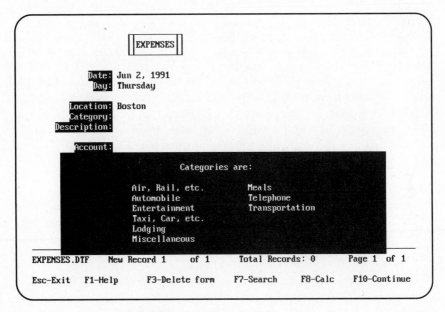

Fig. 3.16.   *A custom help screen.*

Custom help screens for a File database help everyone who uses the database. For people designing the database, custom help screens can facilitate the training of new users. For people using the database, custom help screens can be an aid in learning to use the database faster and getting work done sooner—because help is available, as needed, at the press of a key. See Chapter 7 for information on how to create custom help screens.

Entering and Editing Text in Q&A

A major reason for Q&A's ease of use is the availability of most of the word processing functions in all modules: File, Report, Intelligent Assistant, and Write. You use the word processing functions, which work the same in all the modules, to enter and edit text.

Entering Text

To enter text in any Q&A module, move the cursor to the appropriate screen location and type the text. If you have questions about what the function keys do, press F1 to display the key usage help screen.

Q&A uses *wordwrap*; when the entered text continues beyond the end of a line, the sentence wraps around to continue on the next line. Allowing text to wrap to the next line keeps text connected from line to line. This feature is important for editing and formatting the text. To stop wordwrap, press Enter at the end of each line. This procedure disconnects the lines so that you can enter information that must remain on separate lines, as in tables or addresses.

As mentioned previously, word processors operate in two modes: Insert and Overwrite. Q&A operates in Overwrite unless you change the mode to Insert. In Overwrite mode, new text writes over any characters on the screen. In Insert mode, new text is inserted into the text; existing text is pushed to the right.

To experience the difference between Overwrite and Insert modes, go from the Main menu to the Type/Edit screen in Q&A Write by pressing W and then, at the Write menu, pressing T. Type the following text:

Q&A is easy to use.

Suppose that you want to change *easy to use* to *powerful*. Use the left-arrow key to move the cursor to the first letter of *easy*. Type *powerful.* and then press the space bar four times to delete the remaining letters and period. The sentence should look like this:

Q&A is powerful.

Now suppose that you want to insert *and easy to use* after *powerful*. Switch to Insert mode by pressing the Ins key. Note that the cursor changes from the thin horizontal line to a rectangle, which is the insert cursor. Move the cursor to highlight the period after *powerful*. Press the space bar once and type

 and easy to use

The sentence then should look like this:

 Q&A is powerful and easy to use.

The Ins key is a toggle switch. To return to Overwrite mode from Insert mode, press Ins again.

To change Q&A Write's default mode from Overwrite to Insert, first choose Utilities from the Write menu. Next, select Set Global Options, select Set Editing Options, and, at the Default Editing Mode prompt, choose Insert.

Marking and Deleting Text

You can delete unwanted text one character at a time or in a block of characters: single words, groups of words, sentences, paragraphs, or any size block.

To delete a character, position the cursor under the character to be deleted and press the Del key, or position the cursor to the right of the character to be deleted and press the Backspace key. To delete the character you just typed, press the Backspace key.

To delete a word, move the cursor to the word's first letter and press F4 once. The word and the space after it are deleted. Positioning the cursor on any other letter of the word deletes from the cursor to the end of the word but does not delete the space that follows the word.

To delete a line, position the cursor anywhere in the line and press Shift-F4. In Q&A File, Shift-F4 deletes an entire field line.

To delete a block of words—including phrases, sentences, and paragraphs—move the cursor to the first character to be deleted and press F3; Q&A marks the spot. Next, move the cursor to the end of the block to be deleted. As you move the cursor, Q&A highlights the area to be deleted. When the highlighted area contains the material you want to delete, press F10. Press Esc to abandon the operation.

Suppose that you want to delete the middle sentence of the following paragraph:

 Seven salesmen went to Dallas. Six made their quotas. One did not return.

Move the cursor to the first letter of the second sentence and press F3 once. Next, move the cursor to the end of the sentence by holding down the Ctrl key and pressing the right-arrow key until the entire sentence is highlighted; then press F10. The sentence is deleted, but two extra spaces remain. You can delete the spaces by pressing the Del key twice. You also can include the trailing spaces in the marked block by highlighting them with the right-arrow key while you highlight the sentence.

A quick way to get to the end of the sentence when you are marking a block is to press the period key after you press F3. Q&A immediately marks the text between the position where you pressed F3 and the first period the program finds after that position. In fact, you can mark large blocks of text easily by first positioning the cursor at the beginning of the block you want to mark, pressing F3, and then typing the last character in the block. Q&A highlights all the text from the beginning of the block to the first occurrence of the next character you type after pressing F3. For example, press F3 and Enter to mark the end of a paragraph.

Recovering Deleted Text

If you delete a block of text by mistake, you can recover it by pressing Shift-F7. However, you must use Shift-F7 *before* you delete, copy, or move another block of text. Q&A retains in memory up to one page of text deleted in a block operation; only text that has been stored in a special section of blocked-text RAM can be recovered with Shift-F7. If the block of text being deleted is larger than Q&A can store and recover, the program issues a warning before deleting the block.

Shift-F7 recovers only text deleted by F3. Text deleted by the Del or Backspace key cannot be recovered.

Responding to Error Messages

An error message may appear on your screen from time to time as a warning that an operation is incorrect. For example, an error message tells you when you enter an invalid retrieve specification in Q&A File (see fig. 3.17) or relays information that the program has its own trouble, such as a file not found (see fig. 3.18). In either of these cases, the problem is probably incorrect data entry. Correcting the problem may be as simple as reentering the information and retrying the operation.

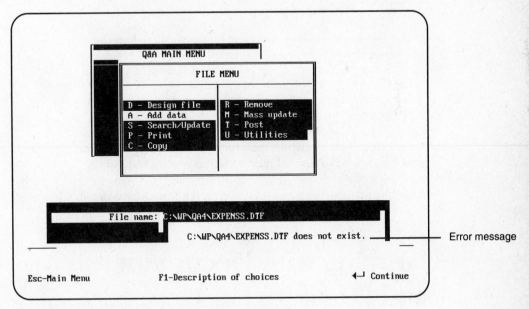

```
                TITAN TECHNOLOGY SALES LEAD TRACKING SYSTEM
                                              File Name -- SlsLead
   LastName:                        FirstName:
   Title:
   Company:                         Telephone:
   Address1:
   Address2:
   City:                            State:          Zip:
      No. of Labs:                  Annual Revenue:
      Current Customer:             Company Priority:
                            LEAD INFORMATION
      Product Interest:
      Request For:                  Lead Source:
      Months to Purchase:           Product Priority:
                             SALES ACTION
      Sales Priority:               Date Entered: All of them

   Not a valid Retrieve Spec. Press F1 for help, or see pg. F-43 of your manual.     Error message



   SLSLEAD.DTF               Retrieve Spec            Page 1 of 1

   Esc-Exit   F1-Help   F6-Expand   F8-Sort   Alt+F8-List   ↑F8-Save   F10-Continue
```

Fig. 3.17.   *An error message for operator error.*

```
            Q&A MAIN MENU
                      FILE MENU

            D - Design file      R - Remove
            A - Add data         M - Mass update
            S - Search/Update    T - Post
            P - Print            U - Utilities
            C - Copy



      File name: C:\WP\QA4\EXPENSS.DTF
                       C:\WP\QA4\EXPENSS.DTF does not exist.      Error message


   Esc-Main Menu        F1-Description of choices        ← Continue
```

Fig. 3.18.   *An error message for a program problem.*

If a program problem causes the error message, you should take immediate
steps to save your data:

1. Read the message carefully and follow any instructions it contains.

2. Refer to the "Error Messages" appendix at the end of the *Q&A Instruction Manual*.

3. Unless otherwise directed, try to save your document or database. Depending on the error condition, saving may or may not be possible. If you can save your work, use a new file name so that the old file is not erased—it may be the only good file to survive if a program malfunction has damaged the active file.

4. If an error reference number is displayed, write the number down and save it for future reference. Discuss the problem with a Symantec user-support representative; these representatives often have current information for solving and avoiding problems.

If you find no explanation of the error message in the appendix, you may have an undocumented error. Do the following:

1. Make a screen printout by turning on your printer and pressing PrtSc (or Print Screen on Enhanced Keyboards). This step prints a record of the error message and the contents of the screen.

2. Make a record of the steps you took before the message was displayed.

3. Contact a Symantec user-support representative (the telephone number is in your Q&A manual) and supply the reference number shown on the screen.

In the rare instance in which the problem resides in the Q&A program itself, there may not be an easy solution. Q&A has been tested extensively, but every program has the potential for occasional failure. If you encounter such a program error, call Symantec's user-support line to discuss possible solutions.

Working with Document and Database Files

This section introduces you to the Q&A processes you use to name, rename, save, copy, and delete Q&A documents and database files. You can perform all these functions in DOS by using the appropriate commands, but using the Q&A operations may be easier because of the way Q&A creates and handles files.

The Q&A Write and File modules create different types of files. In Write, you have full control, within the limitations of DOS, of file creation and naming. In File, Q&A creates additional files for you and supplies its own file extensions. You specify only one file name, but the program may create two files for each database. These differences between modules affect how you name, store, retrieve, copy, and delete the files. For more detailed information regarding these operations, read Chapters 6 and 10.

When you use Q&A functions to work with your database, Q&A adjusts two files: a data file (with the extension DTF), and an index file (extension IDX). If you use the corresponding DOS commands to manipulate database files, you must remember to issue the command for both files; otherwise, you may not be able to access your database. Moreover, if you have created separate subdirectories to store File and Write files, Q&A knows where the files are located, and you don't have to remember the path names. If you are familiar with the operation of DOS, however, you can freely use DOS commands to manipulate Q&A files. Using these commands may be desirable in Write because this module does not create separate files from the main document.

Naming Files

Q&A file names follow DOS naming conventions—up to eight characters in length, followed by a period (.) and a three-character extension. The format for a Q&A file name is

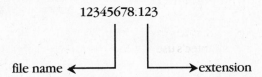

12345678.123

file name ◄————————————►extension

You can name Q&A document files according to this rule (although document files do not *require* an extension), but database files always have the extension DTF. When you name a database file, therefore, you supply a name of up to eight characters, but the program supplies the extension. For your file names, you can enter any combination of lower- and uppercase letters, but Q&A always displays file names in uppercase letters only.

The possible Q&A files and their extensions are listed in the following chart:

Type of file	Extension
Database file	DTF (for the data file) IDX (for the index)
Document file	Your choice; Q&A does not add extensions to document file names
Macro file	ASC (Q&A's default) or your choice

Because you can designate the entire file name with Write documents, you can use the extension to help you identify the file. The following list shows some examples of document file names:

Document file type	Extension	Example
Letters	LET	XMAS_88.LET
Reports	RPT	SALESOCT.RPT
Memos	MEM	STAFF.MEM
Documents	DOC	LEGAL.DOC

When you name a database file, you can use only the eight characters up to the period. The extension (DTF or IDX) is assigned by Q&A after you have defined the structure of the file.

For each database you design, Q&A File creates two files: a *data file* and an *index file*. As mentioned previously, the data file name is given the DTF extension; IDX is assigned to the index. If you create a database named CUSTOMER, for example, Q&A creates two files: CUSTOMER.DTF and CUSTOMER.IDX.

Using Long File Names

With Q&A 4.0, you can assign 72-character descriptions to your document and data file names. When Q&A lists files and you highlight the name, the high-lighted file description is displayed at the bottom of the screen.

To assign a file description, you first must save the file with a standard DOS name consisting of eight characters and a three-character extension. You then can display the file name by choosing Get from the Write menu or Add Data from the File menu. When Q&A prompts you for a file name, press Enter to display a list of files. Move the cursor to your file's DOS name and press F6. Q&A allows you to enter up to 72 characters in a box. To save the description, press F10. To change the description, repeat the process and edit by using the arrow keys, Del, and Backspace.

File-Naming Tips

Although an eight-character name doesn't give you much room to identify fully the contents of a file, you can use a few naming "tricks" to help you recognize the file later. For example, you can

- Use abbreviations (SALESRP)
- Insert an underline character to separate words (SALES_RP)
- Include a date in the name (SALE1015)
- Use the version number of the file (REPORTV2)

With a little imagination, you can come up with a variety of ways to pack information into eight-character file names.

Naming Database Reports

The Q&A Report module works differently than the File and Write modules. When you create a report for a specific database file, Q&A asks you to name that report. You can use up to 30 characters. The report name you assign is stored in the database file. To access the report, you must retrieve the database file and then specify the report name. Remember that a single database file can have many different reports, each with its own name.

Report formats are saved with the name you specify, but they are not saved the same way as document and database files. Because of this difference, you can access reports only through the Q&A Report module—not from DOS.

Naming Specs

Beginning with Version 4.0, Q&A enables you to store Retrieve, Sort, Crosstab, and other specs and recall them later from a list of saved specs. When you finish filling out a spec, press Shift-F8 to give the spec a descriptive name and save the spec. To recall a named spec, press Alt-F8 at the spec screen to display the list of saved specs. To enter the contents of the saved spec into the current spec, highlight its name with the cursor, and press Enter.

Saving Files

When you are working on a database or document file, you can easily forget to save your work, even though Q&A reminds you to do so. Until a file has been saved to disk, you risk data loss from a power failure or operator error. To avoid losing valuable time and effort, be sure to save your work regularly.

When a document is saved in Q&A Write, all contents and formatting characteristics of the document are saved in a single file. For a more detailed explanation of saving a document, see Chapter 10.

Remember to exit the database by pressing Esc or F10 and going through the menu sequence to the Main menu; never turn off your computer while your database is on-screen. Failure to follow the correct exit procedure may result in the loss of your IDX file, without which you cannot access your database. In some situations, Q&A's Recover function may be able to retrieve your database (see the earlier section, "Exiting Q&A," in this chapter).

Listing Q&A Files

You can see a list of your Q&A files in many different ways. Q&A enables you to reach a list of document files from within Q&A Write, and a list of database files from within any of the other Q&A modules, including the Intelligent Assistant. You also can list your files directly from the DOS File Facilities option of the Utilities menu. At the Q&A Main menu, press U to choose Utilities. At the Utilities menu, press D to select DOS File Facilities. At the DOS File Facilities menu, press L to select List Files. You then can list your document files, your database files, or any other data and program files in your Q&A directory or other disk or directory. Type the appropriate path, and press Enter; Q&A displays the list of files.

Using Q&A Function Keys for File Operations

This section explains some basic Q&A operations for renaming, copying, and deleting your Q&A files. Subsequent chapters explain in detail the operations available for working with documents, databases, reports, and macros.

Whenever you have a list of your document or database files on-screen, you have several options available through the function keys: F1 gets you a help screen; F3 deletes files; F5 copies files; F6 enables you to give a file a 72-character description; F7 searches for a file name; and F8 renames files. These options are available in all Q&A modules.

The F3 (Delete) key enables you to delete specified files from a displayed list. When you indicate a file and then press F3, Q&A displays the warning screen shown in figure 3.19. If you are sure that you want to delete the file, choose Yes and press Enter. Q&A then deletes the file.

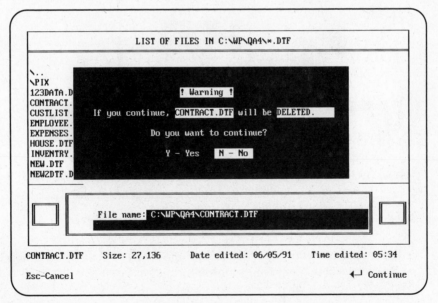

Fig. 3.19.   *Q&A's warning when you are about to delete a file.*

Remember that after a file is deleted, Q&A may not be able to bring the file back. Third-party utility programs may be capable of restoring a crucial file for you, but these programs are successful only if the areas the file occupied on the disk have not been subsequently overwritten by other files. So be careful when you delete files. A good rule of operation is always to make current file backups before conducting rename, delete, and copy operations.

The F5 (Copy) key enables you to copy specified files. If you have the list of files on your screen, you can use the arrow keys to select the file you want copied. When you press F5, you see the Copy To prompt (see fig. 3.20). Type the name of the file to which you want the file copied, and press Enter. Q&A then copies the file.

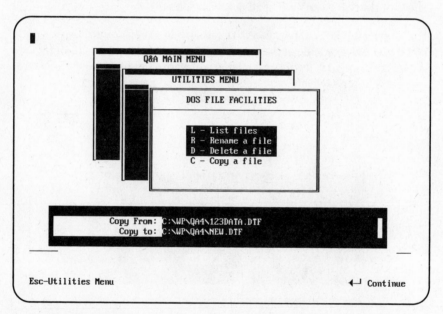

Fig. 3.20.   *The DOS Files Facilities menu showing the Copy To prompt.*

The F6 key enables you to give a file a description of up to 72 characters. When the cursor rests on the file's name, the highlighted description is displayed at the bottom of the screen.

The F7 key enables you to search through a large directory for a particular file or group of files. On the prompt line, type the first letter (or first few letters) of a file name or group of file names. Next, type two periods, and press F7. Suppose, for example, that you type the following:

SLS..

Q&A moves a highlight cursor to the first file that begins with SLS. You can press F7 to move to the next file matching the search request.

The F8 (Rename) key enables you to rename specified files from a displayed list. Highlight the file you want to rename, and press F8. Q&A shows a Rename To prompt, enabling you to rename the selected file.

Using Wild Cards in File Operations

You can use the DOS wild cards when referring to file names, except when using the special delete, copy, search, and rename function keys. The wild-card characters are the question mark (?) and asterisk (*). You use the question mark as a replacement for any single keyboard character. For example, suppose that you want to see a list of files. Type the following on the prompt line:

SALES-MO.?88

Q&A displays all file names with any character in the position where the question mark appears. For example, the program retrieves such file names as

SALES-MO.188
SALES-MO.288
SALES-MO.X88
SALES-M0.%88

The asterisk wild-card character (*) enables you to list, copy, rename, and delete multiple files with a single command; the asterisk represents a group of characters in the file names. For example, if you type

GR*.TXT

you can list, copy, or erase all files ending with a TXT extension and beginning with the letters GR. For example, if you are erasing files, you would delete such files as

GROSS.TXT
GRANT723.TXT
GROVER.TXT

All these files disappear in response to the single delete command.

Renaming Files

You can use two different methods to rename Q&A database files:

- Choose Utilities from the Main menu, DOS File Facilities from the Utilities menu, and then Rename a File.

- Rename from the List of Files screen with F8 (Rename). Display this screen by pressing Enter whenever Q&A File asks for a file name. (For more information on F8, see "Using Q&A Function Keys for File Operations" in this chapter.)

When you rename a database file, all report formats for that database are transferred to the new name.

Q&A has four different methods for renaming document files:

- Choose Utilities from the Main menu, DOS File Facilities from the Utilities menu, and then Rename a File.

- Rename from the List of Files screen with F8 (Rename). Access this screen by pressing Enter when Q&A Write asks for a file name.

- Choose the Utilities option from the Write menu and then select Rename a Document.

- Save the file under a different name. You then will have a file under the original name, and a copy of the file under the new name. (See Chapter 10 for a complete discussion of this procedure.)

Copying Files

By copying an existing database file, you can save yourself from having to create and design a new form, as well as having to enter identical data. Your options for copying a Q&A database file are as follows:

- Use Q&A's DOS File Facilities Copy command from the Utilities menu, which you select from the Main menu.

- Copy the file at the List of Files screen by using F5 (Copy). Display a list of files by pressing Enter when Q&A File asks for a file name. If a filename already is displayed, press space to remove the name and Enter to display the file list. (For more information on F5, see "Using Q&A Function Keys for File Operations" in this chapter.)

- Use the File menu's Copy option. (See Chapter 6 for a detailed explanation of this procedure.)

When you copy a database file with F5, Q&A also copies the report formats.

The three methods of copying a document file are similar to the methods of copying a database file:

- Use Q&A's DOS File Facilities Copy command, which you select from the Utilities menu under the Q&A Main menu.

- Copy the file at the List of Files screen by using F5 (Copy). Display a list of files by pressing Enter when Write asks for a file name.

- Choose the Utilities option from the Write menu, and select Copy a Document. At the prompt, type the name of the file to which you are copying and press Enter.

Deleting Files

When you delete a database file, using Q&A's facilities, both the DTF and IDX files are deleted. If you use the DOS DEL or ERASE command to delete the file, you must delete the DTF and IDX files individually. To delete database files, you can use one of these two methods:

- Use Q&A's DOS File Facilities Delete command, which you select from the Utilities menu under the Q&A Main menu.

- Delete the file at the List of Files screen by using F3 (Delete). Display a list of files by pressing Enter when Q&A asks for a file name. (For more information on F3, see "Using Q&A Function Keys for File Operations" in this chapter.)

You have three methods of deleting document files. The methods are as follows:

- Use Q&A's DOS File Facilities Delete command, which is chosen from the Utilities selection on the Q&A Main menu.

- Delete the file at the List of Files screen by using F3 (Delete). Display a list of document files by pressing Enter when Q&A asks for a document file name.

- Choose the Utilities option from the Write menu, and select Delete a Document. Use the arrow keys to select the document to be deleted, and then press Enter. Q&A displays a warning screen. If you are sure that you want to delete the document, choose Yes and press Enter. Q&A then deletes the document.

Chapter Summary

This chapter has provided information that is important to you as you begin to use Q&A. You have learned how to start the program and exit it safely, how to use the Q&A keyboard and the menu system, and how to get help from Q&A. The basics of entering and editing text have been explained, and you have learned some fundamental procedures for working with database and document files. The information provided in this chapter is enough for you to begin to work with Q&A and provides a solid foundation for the detailed information that appears in the following chapters.

Part II

Using Q&A File

Includes

Q&A File Quick Start

Setting Up a File

Using File

Customizing and Programming a File

Printing from File

4

Q&A File Quick Start

Developing and using a database with Q&A is quick and easy to do. You work in the part of the Q&A program called the File module to design and store a database. In this chapter, you learn how to design a database, customize the database for easy data entry, and use search methods for retrieving and sorting data.

To complete the database process, you need to understand some basic database terms. A *database* is an electronic filing system that stores data and enables you to retrieve that data in a variety of ways. With a Q&A database, you can print reports based on the data and merge the data with information located in Q&A's Write module.

Imagine a database as a filing cabinet. The database is the actual cabinet that holds the files. Each file within that filing cabinet is called a *form* (or *record*), and the categories of information contained within those files are called *fields*. A field consists of two parts. The first part describes what kind of data is stored in the field and is called a *field label*. The second part of a field is the actual data. You can retrieve data from any database field and sort the data in a logical manner for you to use.

Designing a Database

To understand how useful and easy a database is to work with, in this chapter you learn how to build a database for a household inventory system. Suppose that your insurance agent has requested that you keep an inventory of all covered items in your home worth more than $25.00. Your agent can use this inventory to determine whether your coverage is adequate and also as a list of your possessions in case of fire or theft.

First, you need to design the database to hold the information by performing the following steps:

1. Select File from the Q&A Main menu.

2. Select Design File from the File menu.

3. Select Design a New File from the Design menu.

You notice as you work through the system that the menu progression is displayed on the monitor. This menu progression shows you exactly where you are in the system and which menus you used to get to your current location.

After you select Design a New File, Q&A prompts you for the name of the file you want to design. The prompt for the file name includes the *drive path*, the route the computer takes to get to your file. The path begins with the drive you currently are in (C for a hard disk, and A or B for a floppy disk system). The next set of characters indicates the *directory* (the area) that holds the Q&A program. The name of that directory varies depending on how the program was copied into your computer's memory. Following the software directory should be a subdirectory separating your database files from your word processing files. These subdirectories are set using the Utilities module on the Q&A Main menu, and the file name follows the database subdirectory. Each step of the drive path is separated with a backslash (\).

4. Type the data file name of *house*.

5. Press the Enter key. Q&A adds the extension DTF to the file name, indicating that this file is a database file (see fig. 4.1).

Note: After you design your file, you can add a description to the file name. The description may contain up to 72 characters. At the Main menu, choose File, then select any item from the File menu, press Ctrl-F4 to erase the file-name prompt, and press Enter to display the file listing. Move your cursor to the file name and press F6 to add a description. You may edit the description later by pressing F6 with the cursor on the file name in any file listing.

A Q&A database file consists of two separate files. One file holds the data and has the file extension DTF. The other file consists of the index files, the form design and reports, and other files associated with the database. This file has the extension IDX. When you use the File module, Q&A combines the IDX and DTF files to form your database. When you make copies of the database using DOS, however, you should be sure to copy both files.

You now should see an almost empty screen. This is Q&A's *file form design screen* (see fig. 4.2). Near the bottom of the design screen is a *ruler line*, which shows the cursor location and tab settings. Three lines of information are displayed below the ruler line. The *status line* contains the file name, the percentage of memory the file occupies, and the line and page location of the cursor. The *message line*, usually blank, displays Q&A's messages when needed. The *key assignment line* lists frequently used function keys that you can use with this screen. The keys listed vary according to the screen. Also, not all the available function keys are displayed in the key assignment line—only those used most often. The following function keys are listed on the file form design screen:

Function key	Description
Esc (Exit)	Cancels the database design process and returns to the File menu
F1 (Help)	Accesses on-screen help and references specific pages in the instruction manual for more detail
F8 (Options)	Accesses options such as setting tabs, centering or uncentering lines, and drawing lines
F10 (Continue)	Continues the current process and proceeds to the next step

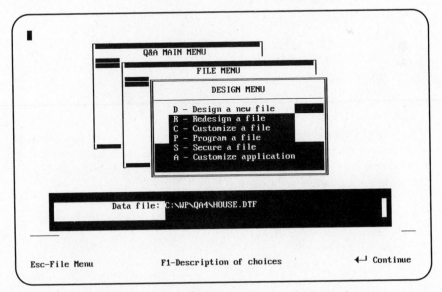

Fig. 4.1. Specifying the drive path for the file.

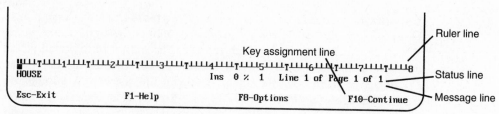

Fig. 4.2. *The file form design screen.*

You now can add a title and the field labels on the file form design screen.

6. With the cursor located in the upper left corner of the file form design screen, type the title *HOUSEHOLD INVENTORY*. Press the Enter key to move to the next line.

7. Type the following field labels as shown, following each name with a colon (:) to indicate the end of the label and the beginning of the data. After each colon, press the Enter key to move to the next line.

> Item:
>
> Quantity:
>
> Location:
>
> Date of Purchase:
>
> Amount of Purchase:
>
> Serial Number:
>
> Description:
>
> Item Number:

Your screen should look like figure 4.3.

You also can create fields without labels—for example, in the purchase description section of an invoice form. Q&A creates an invisible "internal" label for the form, which you can use to refer to the field in calculations and reports. For further information, see Chapter 7.

8. Press F10 (Continue) to save your design and proceed to the next step.

Formatting the Data

The Format Spec, a specification sheet, now appears on-screen. A letter signifying the field type appears beside each field label. Read the help screen that appears, explaining the different field types for data. By default, Q&A defines the data as text unless instructed otherwise, and all the field labels initially have the letter T. Three fields in your database use other types of data: keyword, date, and money data. You therefore need to modify these three fields.

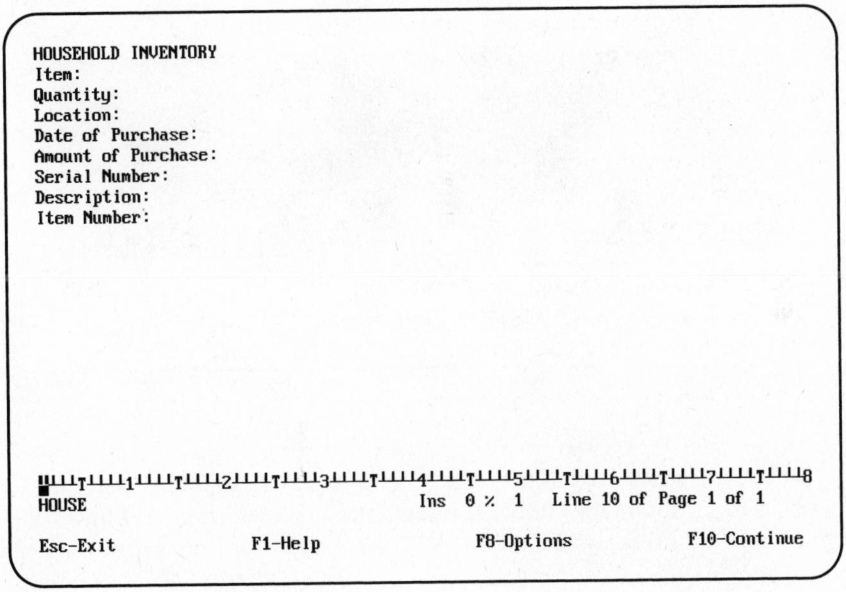

```
HOUSEHOLD INVENTORY
 Item:
 Quantity:
 Location:
 Date of Purchase:
 Amount of Purchase:
 Serial Number:
 Description:
 Item Number:




▌┅┅┊┅T┊┅┅1┅┅┅T┅┅┅2┅┅┅T┅┅┅3┅┅┅T┅┅┅4┅┅┅T┅┅┅5┅┅┅T┅┅┅6┅┅┅T┅┅┅7┅┅┅T┅┅┅8
▌HOUSE                                Ins  0 %  1    Line 10 of Page 1 of 1

Esc-Exit              F1-Help              F8-Options          F10-Continue
```

Fig. 4.3.   Entering the field labels.

1. Use the up- or down-arrow keys to move your cursor to the following fields, and type over the T to reflect the following data types:

   Location: K

   Date of Purchase: D

   Amount of Purchase: M

   Figure 4.4 shows how your screen should look.

2. Press F10 to continue to the next step.

The Global Format Options screen now appears. Use this screen to format the field types you chose on the Format Spec. You can format currency, time, and date displays for your database with this screen. Suppose that you want to change the date settings.

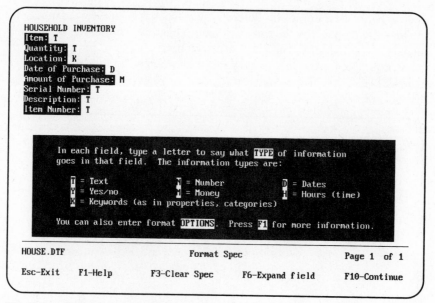

Fig. 4.4.   *Changing the data type for three fields.*

3. Use the arrow keys to move the cursor to setting number 11 in the
    Date section of the Global Format Options screen (see fig. 4.5).
    Setting 11 displays the date as Month dd, yyyy: for example,
    March 19, 1990.

4. Press F10 (Continue) to save the design and formats and return to
    the File menu.

Your design has been saved and is ready to accept data. Before you enter data,
however, you can enhance the design to make the data more agreeable to
the eye.

Redesigning Your Database

The redesign process is similar to the design process. You see the same screens
with a few modifications.

1. Select Design File from the File menu and then Redesign a File
    from the Design menu.

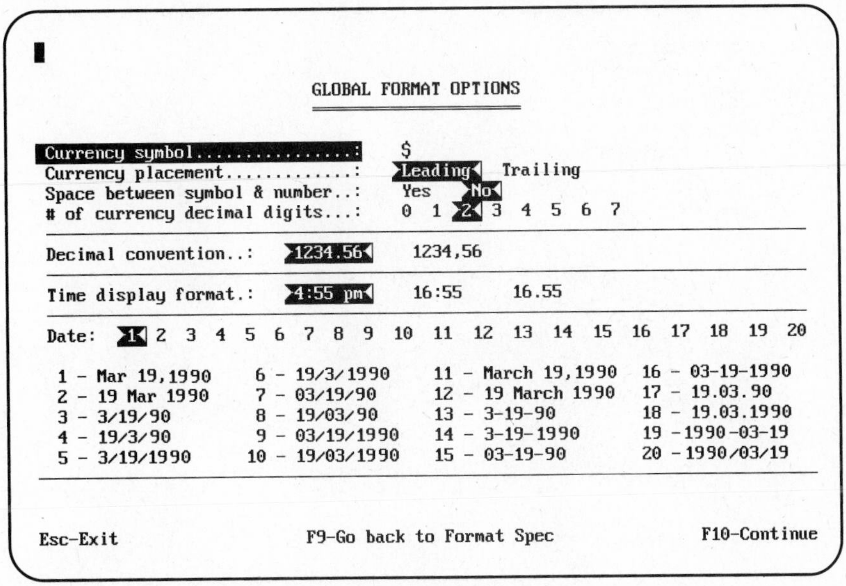

Fig. 4.5. The Global Format Options screen.

You decide to redesign the HOUSE.DTF file. This file appears automatically in the Data file prompt because HOUSE.DTF was the last file accessed in this module.

2. Select the HOUSE.DTF file by pressing the Enter key to confirm the name.

The file you just designed appears on-screen, but with one difference. Following each field label are two letters (see fig. 4.6). These characters, called *field tags*, connect the data to the field on the form. Any time a field is moved or changed, these field tags must accompany the field, or the data associated with that field will be lost.

Center the title of the database, HOUSEHOLD INVENTORY. You can use the Options menu to center and uncenter a line, draw lines on the form, or set tabs on the form.

3. Move your cursor beneath the H in HOUSEHOLD, if needed.

4. Press F8 (Options) to display the Options menu, and move the cursor to Align text. Move the cursor to the submenu that appears and select Center from that menu. The title HOUSEHOLD INVENTORY moves to the center of the screen.

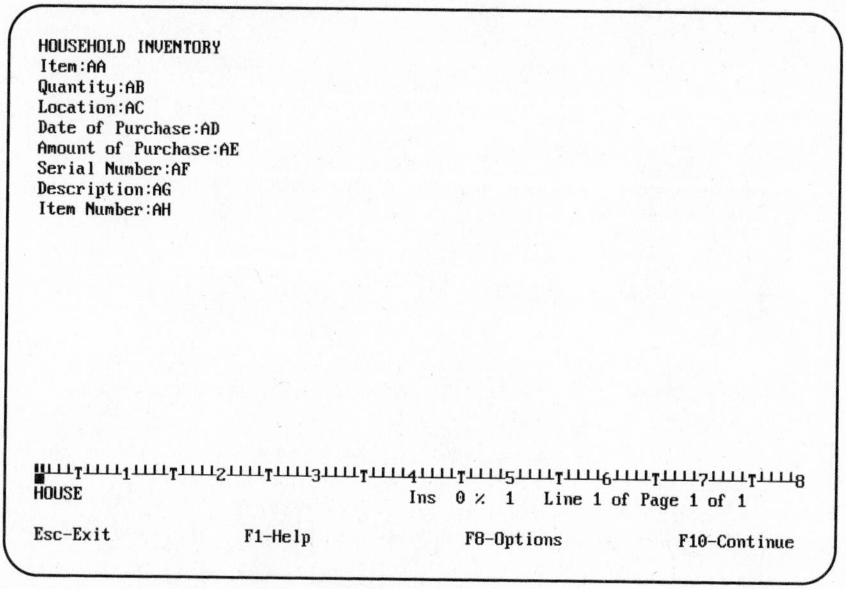

```
HOUSEHOLD INVENTORY
Item:AA
Quantity:AB
Location:AC
Date of Purchase:AD
Amount of Purchase:AE
Serial Number:AF
Description:AG
Item Number:AH




|.....T....1....T....2....T....3....T....4....T....5....T....6....T....7....T....8
HOUSE                              Ins  0 %  1    Line 1 of Page 1 of 1

Esc-Exit           F1-Help              F8-Options          F10-Continue
```

Fig. 4.6. *The field tags for the database fields.*

5. Press F10 (Continue) once to save the design, again to save the Format Spec, and again to save the global format options and automatically return to the File menu.

Customizing Your Database

Customizing provides you the ability to fine-tune your database and tailor it to fit your individual needs. To customize your database, do the following:

1. Select Design File from the File menu and then Customize a File from the Design menu to call up the Customize menu. When the file name HOUSE appears in the prompt, press the Enter key.

You use three of the features displayed on the Customize menu. First, you specify the Amount of Purchase field to display entries with commas. You then instruct Q&A to display today's date and to number the forms sequentially. Last, you develop a lookup table and program Q&A, enabling you to fill the Location field (designating the room in which the article is located) by typing just the first letter of that location.

2. Select Format Values from the Customize menu and press F1 (How to format) to review the help screen associated with this feature. Press Esc (Cancel) to clear the help screen.

3. Using the arrow keys, move the cursor to the Amount of Purchase field and insert a comma and the letter *C* after the letter *M* (as in *M,C*). The field displays entries with commas.

4. Press F10 once to get to the Global Format Options screen, and again to save the change and return to the Customize menu.

5. From the Customize menu, select Restrict values and press F1 to view the help screen. Using the arrow keys, move the cursor to the Item field and insert the characters !/=.

   These characters indicate that a value is required in the Item field. If the field is left blank during data entry, Q&A displays an error message. (By pressing Enter or Tab twice, you can make Q&A accept most nonstandard entries, but you cannot override a required field.) During data entry, you view a list of the restrictions for a required field by moving the cursor into the field and pressing Alt-F7.

6. Press F10 to return to the Customize menu.

7. From the Customize menu, select Set Initial Values and press F1 (How to set initial values) to see the help screen at the bottom of the form.

8. Move your cursor to the Date of Purchase field and type *@DATE*. This function enters the current date (see fig. 4.7).

9. Move the cursor to the Item Number field and type *@NUMBER*. This function enters sequential numbers in the field, starting with 1.

10. Press F10 to save the changes and return to the Customize menu, then press Esc to return to the Design menu.

    When you set initial values for a field, remember that you can override these values by typing over the data that appears.

11. From the Design menu, select Program a File, then specify the database name. At the Programming menu, choose Edit Lookup Table. A lookup table appears.

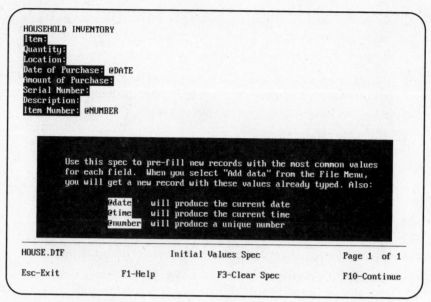

Fig. 4.7. Modifying Date of Purchase and Item Number.

Lookup tables are used to enter repetitive values in fields. They "look up" the key characters (which you enter as data in a field), match those characters in a table, and insert the appropriate information as indicated in the table into the field. Lookup tables offer two advantages: they ensure consistency of data and they assist data entry by reducing the number of keystrokes needed to enter repetitive, frequently entered data.

Lookup tables consist of five columns. The first column is the Key column, which contains the key that the program tries to match. Columns 1 through 4 contain data that is inserted after a match is found.

12. Type the following information in the table (you use only the Key column and column 1 for this exercise):

Key	1
K	Kitchen
D	Den
L	Living Room

Figure 4.8 shows your screen.

13. Press F10 to save your table and return to the Programming menu.

```
┌──────────────────────────────────────────────────────────────────┐
│       KEY              1             2            3            4    │
│  ┬                                                                 │
│  K            Kitchen                                              │
│  D            Den                                                  │
│  L            Living Room                                          │
│                                                                    │
│                                                                    │
│                                                                    │
│                                                                    │
│                                                                    │
│                                                                    │
│                                                                    │
│                                                                    │
│                                                                    │
│                                                                    │
│  HOUSE.DTF                  Lookup Table                Page 1  of 1│
│                                                                    │
│  Esc-Exit  F6-Expand field   PgUp-Previous page   PgDn-Next page   F10-Continue│
└──────────────────────────────────────────────────────────────────┘
```

Fig. 4.8. The lookup table for the database.

When the lookup table is completed, you can begin the second step of using the table: programming the form. Programming tells the form that data is stored in a lookup table and needs to be inserted into a field on the form.

14. Select Program Form from the Programming menu and review the help screens associated with this feature. This help screen is several pages long; press Enter to continue. When you have read about LOOKUP, press Esc to clear the help screen.

15. Move your cursor to the Location field and type the following:

    >#1: Lookup (#1,1,#1)

This program tells Q&A to insert data from column 1 of the lookup table in this spot. This program is made of several components, each telling Q&A to perform a separate step:

>	Executes this program when the cursor leaves this field
#1:	Identifies the field numerically
Lookup	A lookup table will be used for this program
(#1	The key that matches the table is in field #1 (the Location field)

1   The data to go in the field resides in column 1 of that Key in the lookup table

#1)   Data from column 1 is inserted into field #1

The Program Spec should look like figure 4.9.

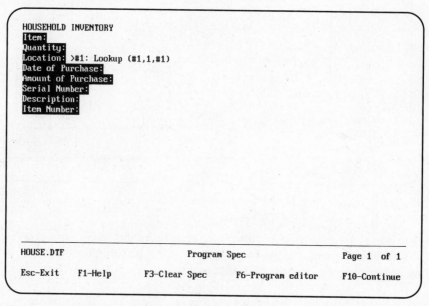

```
HOUSEHOLD INVENTORY
Item:
Quantity:
Location: >#1: Lookup (#1,1,#1)
Date of Purchase:
Amount of Purchase:
Serial Number:
Description:
Item Number:




HOUSE.DTF                    Program Spec                Page 1  of 1

Esc-Exit    F1-Help      F3-Clear Spec    F6-Program editor    F10-Continue
```

Fig. 4.9.   *Adding a program to the Location field.*

16. Press F10 to save this program and return to the Programming menu.

17. Press Esc twice to return to the File menu.

Adding Data to Your Database

Now that you have done all this work to build a database, you can enter some information and see whether the database works.

1. Select Add Data from the File menu for the file HOUSE.DTF.

You now have a blank entry form on your screen ready to receive data. Notice that today's date is entered in the Date of Purchase field. This value is added automatically as a result of Q&A's @DATE function.

You are going to fill several forms. After you type the data into the forms, you save the form by pressing F10 (Continue).

2. Fill out one form with the following information:

> Item: Radio
> Quantity: 1
> Location: D (for den)
> Date of Purchase: Sep 27, 1990 (already entered)
> Amount of Purchase: $79.95
> Serial Number: HSR260XFM
> Description: AM/FM portable radio
> Item Number: 1 (already entered)

Figure 4.10 shows how your form should look.

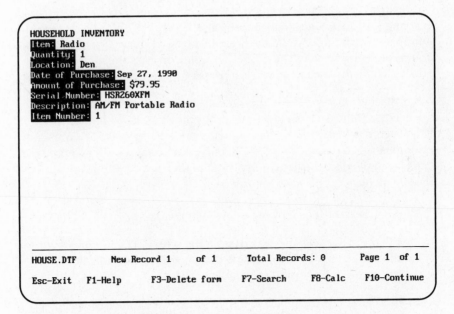

Fig. 4.10. *Entering the first record into the database.*

3. Press F10 to save this form and display a new blank form.

You can keep track of your database with the information Q&A supplies at the bottom of the screen. You can see that you are in the database HOUSE.DTF; you are looking at New Record 1 of 1 (you have one new record, and the second new form is ready to accept data); 1 record is saved; and you are on page 1 of 1. You can press F9 to view the records already entered.

When you add new forms to your database, press F5 to copy data that was entered in that particular field on the preceding form. Pressing Shift-F5 copies the entire preceding form to this form.

4. Fill out at least three more forms with one more item located in the den and two items located in the kitchen. For items in the kitchen type *K*, the symbol you entered in the lookup table for the kitchen in the Location field.

Retrieving Information from Your Database

The Search/Update function retrieves data already entered into the database, enabling you to update that information if you choose and arrange the information in the order you want. Search/Update can be accessed in two ways. You can access Search/Update on the File menu, or if you already have selected Add Data from the File menu, you can press F7 (Search) to select the function.

Note: When you press F7, you may get an error message if the field has been specified as Requested or Required data entry in the Customize menu. If Requested data entry is specified, you can press F7 again, which causes the error message to disappear and the Retrieve Spec to appear. If Required data entry is specified for the field, press Esc, and then select Search/Update from the File menu.

1. Select Search/Update by pressing F7 (Search).

   A Retrieve Spec replaces the data on the screen. The Retrieve Spec looks like a new form for adding data, but some new function keys are listed on the key assignment line.

2. Press F1 (Help) to see the first help screen. After reading that screen, press F1 again to see more retrieval parameters. Press Esc to remove the help screens and return to the Retrieve Spec.

You can search any database field for data by moving the cursor to that field and entering the correct parameters. When entering search parameters, you can type them in uppercase or lowercase; Q&A retrieves all forms matching the search parameters regardless of capitalization. Start your search by looking for items that are located in the den.

3. Move your cursor to the Location field, type *den*, and press F10 (Continue).

   The program scans the forms in the database and displays the first form that matches your retrieval specifications—in this case, the record shown in figure 4.10. To view additional forms, press F10 to page through the other forms.

4. Press F7 (Search) to return to the Retrieve Spec.

You can edit data in a retrieved form. When you exit the form by pressing F9, F10, F7, or Esc, Q&A saves your changes to your form.

Using a Wild-Card Search

You now want to retrieve the forms of items that are located in the kitchen. If you're in a hurry or are not sure how to spell kitchen, you can retrieve this information easily by doing a *wild-card* search. Wild-card searches can retrieve forms with slightly different data in the specified field. To perform a wild-card search on any group of characters, enter two periods (..) anywhere in the search parameter.

1. Move your cursor to the Location field and type the search parameter as follows:

   Location: ki..

2. Press F10 (Continue) to start the search. In this file, only the kitchen starts with *ki*, so forms for items located in the kitchen appear on-screen.

Q&A enables you to store Retrieve Specs and use them again without retyping the request. At the Retrieve Spec screen, press Shift-F8. At the prompt, type a name for the spec. To recall the stored Retrieve Spec, press Alt-F8 at the Retrieve Spec screen and choose the spec from the List of Retrieve Specs in Database. You can recall the Retrieve Spec you entered most recently in the current session. At the Retrieve Spec screen, press Shift-F7.

Sorting Retrieved Forms

When searching large databases, you sometimes may want to list the data in some order: alphabetically, or from the highest to lowest item number. You can perform this sorting by using the F8 function key.

1. Press F7 (Search) from any form on your screen to return to the Retrieve Spec. Notice that the preceding search parameters appear on the Retrieve Spec.

2. From the Retrieve Spec, press F8 (Sort Spec) to display the Sort Spec screen. Press F1 (How to sort) to review Sort Spec instructions.

3. Move your cursor to the Amount of Purchase field and type *1 AS*, indicating sort level 1 (or first sort to be done) in ascending sort order (low to high). Your Sort Spec should look like figure 4.11.

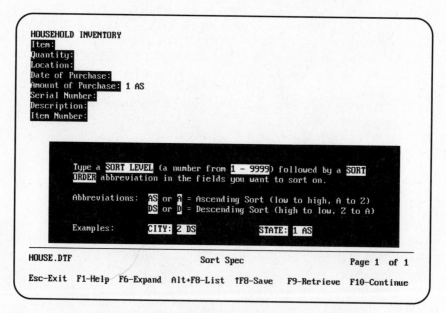

Fig. 4.11.   Specifying to sort the retrieved forms by purchase amount.

4. Press F10 to start the sort.

Q&A scans the database for forms and sorts the retrieved forms in the appropriate order. The first form, for the least expensive item, appears on-screen. Press F10 to view the other forms in order of increasing price.

You also can store and recall Sort Specs. At the Sort Spec, press Shift-F8 to name and store a spec, or Alt-F8 to recall a stored spec.

Viewing a Table of Retrieved Forms

Instead of paging through the forms one by one, you can construct a table that shows you the forms. This table can be used for display and for changing records but not for entering new records. The Alt-F6 (Table View) key controls this table.

1. Press Alt-F6 (Table View) from the current form, which displays a table with the forms. This table has five columns for the first five fields of your entry form.

   All of the keys used to display, print, and navigate through records in the single-record view are available in Table View. To scroll horizontally, use the Cursor, Tab, and Shift-Tab keys. To scroll vertically, use the Arrow, Home/End, Page Up, and Page Down keys. To exit Table View, press F10 or Alt-F6.

You can change the display to see other data in the table.

2. Press Shift-F6 from the table view screen. A Table View Spec appears, as shown in figure 4.12. As you can see, the first fields are numbered 10 through 80.

Suppose that you also want to display the serial numbers. You cannot increase or decrease the number of columns displayed, but you can change the fields displayed in those columns by renumbering the fields.

3. Move the cursor to the Location field and press the space bar, deleting the number 30.

4. Move the cursor to the Serial Number field, type *30* in that field, and press F10 (Table View). You have changed the table view. Figure 4.13 shows the new table display.

5. Return to the Retrieve Spec by pressing F7.

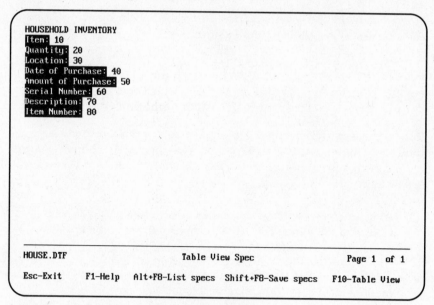

```
HOUSEHOLD INVENTORY
Item: 10
Quantity: 20
Location: 30
Date of Purchase: 40
Amount of Purchase: 50
Serial Number: 60
Description: 70
Item Number: 80




HOUSE.DTF              Table View Spec              Page 1 of 1

Esc-Exit     F1-Help    Alt+F8-List specs   Shift+F8-Save specs   F10-Table View
```

Fig. 4.12. *The column assignments of the fields in the table.*

```
┌─────────────┬────────────┬───────────────┬────────────────┬───────────────┐
│    Item     │  Quantity  │ Serial Number │ Date of Purchas│ Amount of Purc│
├─────────────┼────────────┼───────────────┼────────────────┼───────────────┤
│ Radio       │ 1          │ HSR260XFM     │ Sep 27, 1990   │        $79.95 │
│ Toaster     │ 1          │ Model #DS2050 │ Sep 27, 1990   │        $63.95 │
```

```
HOUSE.DTF       Retrieved record 1    of 2        Total records: 2

Esc-Exit F1-Help      { ↓ ↑ Home End PgUp PgDn }-Navigate      F10-Show form
```

Fig. 4.13. *The revised table of records.*

Using Keywords To Search

One other way to search a database is by using keywords. *Keywords* are words that are used to classify types of data consistently. You can use these classifications as criteria for searching and retrieving information. For example, the keyword *Den* classifies items located in the den rather than the family room. If you search for *Family Room*, you do not get the same search results.

You can enter multiple keywords in a keyword field, separating them with semicolons (;). When searching keyword fields, you can request that one or more criteria be met for Q&A to retrieve forms. The ability to use multiple keywords for searching is a definite advantage over search methods you used earlier. Keyword searches apply only to keyword fields. You have one keyword field in your database: the Location field.

1. Move your cursor to the Location field and type the keywords as follows:

       Location: den;kit..

2. Press F10 (Continue).

Q&A selects all items located in the den or the kitchen. If you add an ampersand (&) at the beginning of this search (&den;kit..), items must be located in *both* the kitchen and den to be retrieved.

3. Return to the File menu by pressing the Esc key.

Printing Information from Your Database

Reports containing database information can be generated in several ways using Q&A. You can print an individual form by pressing F2 while the form is displayed on-screen, or you can print information from a group of forms by selecting the Print command from the File menu. (A third method of printing data is discussed for the Report module in Chapter 14.)

1. Select Print from the File menu for HOUSE.DTF.

2. Select Design/Redesign a Spec from the Print menu.

A list of print specs for this database appears. Because you just created this database, no print specs should be associated with the database, and therefore no specs are listed on-screen.

3. Type *INVENTORY* at the `Enter name` prompt to name your print spec, and press Enter.

   A Retrieve Spec appears. You want to retrieve all forms in the database, and you want them to be sorted. If you are not sure how to perform these operations, press F1 (Help) to display the help screen. Do not press F10 until asked to do so.

4. Press F8 (Sort Spec), type *1 AS* to indicate Location as the sort level in ascending sort order, and press F10 to continue to the Fields Spec. The Fields Spec tells Q&A where you want each field to be printed and in what sequence.

5. Press F1 (How to print fields) and review the three help screens.

6. Clear the help screens by pressing the Esc key until the Fields Spec reappears.

   For this example, use Style #1 (Free-form) for your report.

7. Type the following information in the Fields Spec to arrange the printing of data:

Item: 3X	Third field to print followed by a return
Quantity: 2+	Second field to print followed by a space
Location: 6X	Sixth field to print followed by a return
Date of Purchase: 7+,5	Seventh field to print followed by five spaces
Amount of Purchase: 8X	Eighth field to print followed by a return
Serial Number: 5X	Fifth field to print followed by a return
Description: 4+,2	Fourth field to print followed by two spaces
Item Number: 1X	First field to print followed by a return

8. Press F10 to continue to the next screen, File Print Options. This screen enables you to change the settings that determine how the report prints.

9. Use the arrow keys to change the Print To setting from PtrA to SCREEN. (To print a report on paper, select the appropriate printer according to your computer configuration.) Also, verify that the setting for Print Field Labels is No, as in figure 4.14.

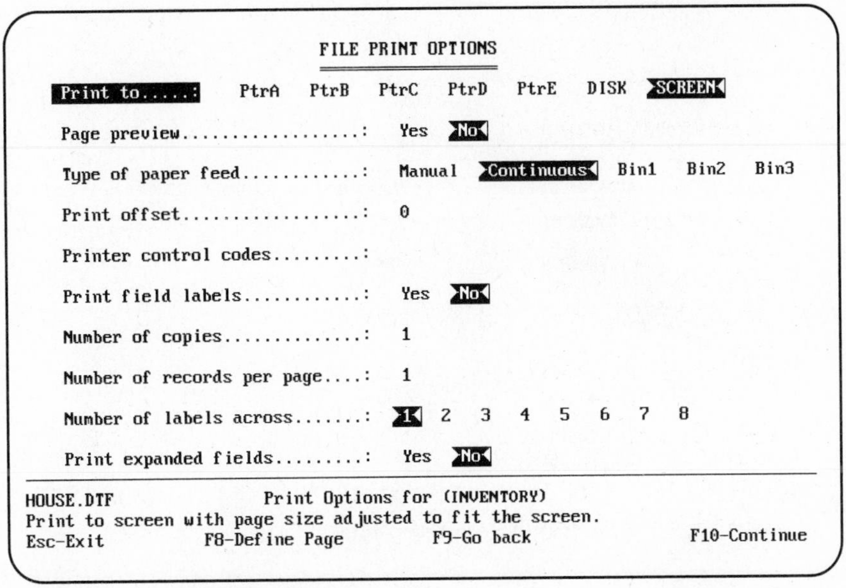

```
                        FILE PRINT OPTIONS
                        ===================
   Print to.....:   PtrA   PtrB   PtrC   PtrD   PtrE   DISK  ▶SCREEN◀

   Page preview.................:   Yes  ▶No◀

   Type of paper feed...........:   Manual  ▶Continuous◀  Bin1   Bin2   Bin3

   Print offset.................:   0

   Printer control codes........:

   Print field labels...........:   Yes  ▶No◀

   Number of copies.............:   1

   Number of records per page...:   1

   Number of labels across......:   ▶1◀  2   3   4   5   6   7   8

   Print expanded fields........:   Yes  ▶No◀
   _____
   HOUSE.DTF           Print Options for (INVENTORY)
   Print to screen with page size adjusted to fit the screen.
   Esc-Exit        F8-Define Page        F9-Go back           F10-Continue
```

Fig. 4.14. *The File Print Options screen.*

10. Press F8 (Define Page). The Define Page screen determines page
    width, length, and margins; characters per inch; and *headers* and
    footers (the text that repeats on consecutive pages).

11. Use the arrow keys to move to the page definition options, and set
    the options as follows:

Page Width : 240	Page Length.. : 66
Left Margin : 0	Right Margin : 240
Top Margin : 3	Bottom Margin : 3
Characters Per Inch :	10

    HEADER
    1: HOUSEHOLD INVENTORY as of @Date

    Your screen should look like fig. 4.15.

12. After making these changes, press F9 (Go Back to Print Options) to
    return to the File Print Options screen. If your computer can
    display graphics, choose Yes at the Page preview prompt. Press F10
    and choose Yes to view an image of your data as it will appear
    when sent to the printer.

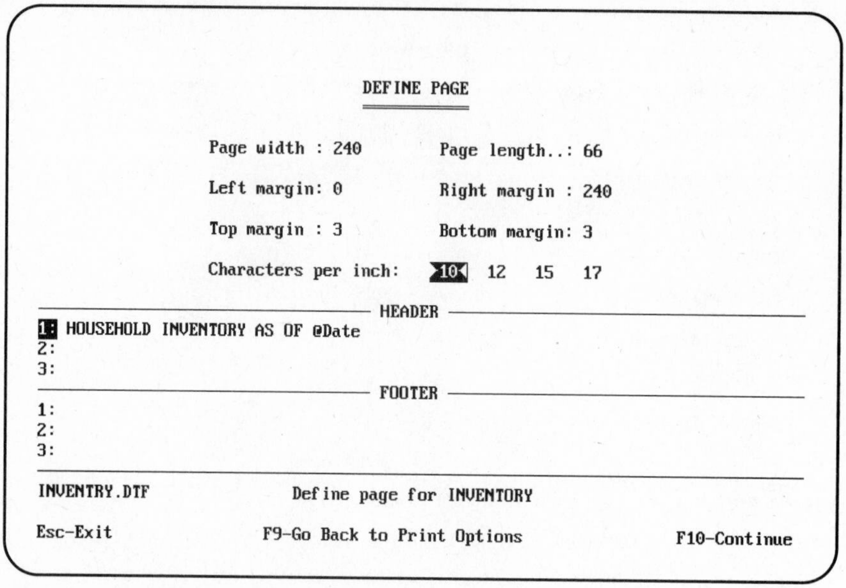

```
                              DEFINE PAGE
                              ═══════════

              Page width : 240        Page length..: 66

              Left margin: 0          Right margin : 240

              Top margin : 3          Bottom margin: 3

              Characters per inch:    ▶10◀   12   15   17

  ──────────────────────────── HEADER ────────────────────────────
  1: HOUSEHOLD INVENTORY AS OF @Date
  2:
  3:
  ──────────────────────────── FOOTER ────────────────────────────
  1:
  2:
  3:
  ─────────────────────────────────────────────────────────────────
  INVENTRY.DTF            Define page for INVENTORY

  Esc-Exit            F9-Go Back to Print Options          F10-Continue
```

Fig. 4.15.   *Adding settings to the Define Page screen.*

13. Press Esc to return to the Print menu. Return to the File Print Options menu by selecting Design/Redesign a Spec at the Print menu and Inventory at the list of print specs. Press F10 at the Retrieve and Field spec to display the File Print Options screen. Change the Page Preview prompt to No, and press F10 to continue.

    A message appears on-screen, telling you that your print specs have been saved and asking whether you want to print the forms now.

14. Respond Yes and press the Enter key. The report is printed on-screen as shown in figure 4.16.

If you want to change something in the report, you can redesign the report by pressing Shift-F9 (Redesign).

To print a report that already has been designed and saved, use the Print Forms command from the Print menu. This command enables you to bypass the design process and immediately print the report. With this command, you also can make temporary changes to a report before printing. These temporary changes are not saved. To make permanent changes to a report, you must go through the Design/Redesign process.

```
1
1 Radio
AM/FM Portable Radio
Den
Sep 27,1990 $79.95


2
1 Desk Lamp
Brass desk lamp with white lampshade
Den
Jan 24, 1990 $49.95


3
1 Microwave Oven
Microwave oven with heat sensor
Kitchen
Jun 4, 1990 $249.50




─────────────────────────────────────────

Esc-Exit     F2-Reprint    (← →)-Scroll    Shift+F9-Redesign    ↵ Continue
```

Fig. 4.16.   *The printed database report.*

Chapter Summary

In designing this database, you have learned to center, customize, format, set initial values, do sequential numbering and dating, enter data, and search for data using several methods. You also have learned how to use lookup tables to minimize data entry and program forms.

You now can modify your database to meet your particular needs and applications. Continuing with the scenario of the insurance reporting requirements, you can satisfy these requirements easily by printing a report for your agent to keep on file. You can keep a current inventory of items, updating the inventory as needed. In case of fire or theft, this inventory is easily accessible. As your needs change, you can change the database easily to fit that particular application. Before you go to the Write quick start (Chapter 9), you should look at Chapters 5 through 8 to learn more about the Q&A File module. Chapter 5 begins with setting up a file.

Setting Up a File

O ne of the most important steps in data management is setting up your file. File setup in Q&A involves several levels of file design. You must decide which fields to include in each file and how large each field should be. (Refer to Chapter 2 for help with database definitions and terms.) You must define any relationships among the fields, create an entry form (the end-user view of the data file), and define reports for the data. In Q&A, most of these processes are done at the same time, when you create the database screen form. (File\Design File\Design a New File is the path to this process from the Main menu.) You can design ad hoc reports from within the File module or use the additional reporting functions in the Report module. These separate processes are covered in later chapters.

The design of your file form determines how well your data can be organized and retrieved. A well-designed form helps other users learn to use your database. If you organize your file form so that the data can be entered in a logical order, you can save time and effort when you use the file.

The designers of Q&A understood the importance of setting up a file and designing workable input, edit, and report forms. With Q&A, you can design forms to suit your taste and fit the way you work. In addition, after you have designed one form, you can use that form to create other forms. With Q&A, you have the choice of setting up a file that is as basic or as complicated as you like. To help use the design after it is created, you can build your own custom help screens that give detailed instructions for operations on individual fields.

This chapter guides you through the Q&A File design process, providing step-by-step instructions and offering suggestions on how to get the most from Q&A File. The topics discussed in this chapter include the following:

- Laying out a file form

- Setting field lengths and formats

- Formatting the form

- Formatting the information

- Choosing global file format options

- Adding to the file form

- Redesigning a file form

What You Can Do with Q&A File

We all use databases in some way every day. Recipe boxes, filing cabinets, and phone books are like computerized databases in that they all store information. At the most basic level, Q&A File is the same as a recipe box or a file folder of expense receipts: a place to store information.

Using Q&A File is easy: you design a file and its entry form (as one operation), enter the data, and save the file. As you use Q&A File, the program quickly becomes more than just a "shoe box" of information. When you need to retrieve information from the database, Q&A can find, display, and print the data with just a few simple keystrokes. You can produce regular reports from new information in a file even though you design the report form only once. Because Q&A stores the report specifications, you can recall reports by name at any time.

You can use Q&A to store simple or relatively complex databases, including lists, personal records, expense reports, card catalogs, inventory records, customer lists, contract proposals, address lists, and personalized mailings.

Analyzing data is Q&A's forte, especially with the capabilities of the Intelligent Assistant. You can, for example, ask the Intelligent Assistant, "Which customers in Colorado have May orders greater than their April orders?" Q&A can give you the answer.

Remember, however, that the key to successful data retrieval is good file design. You cannot find information you didn't put into the file in the first place, and you cannot get information into the database if your database tool is difficult or inefficient to use—or simply lacks storage locations for critical data.

Creating the File Form

Before you start designing a file in Q&A File, you should spend some time with Q&A Write or a pad and pencil to determine informally how your database reports should appear and what information you need to capture. (Chapter 2 provides some hints on beginning file design.) If data management programs are new to you, you first may want to write the reports and the entry forms by hand (see fig. 5.1). By designing the entry form by hand, you can plan how you want the fields to appear on the form, and you can be sure to include all the fields you need for your application. You also should have a good idea about the length in characters of each field and the general order in which you will enter information most often.

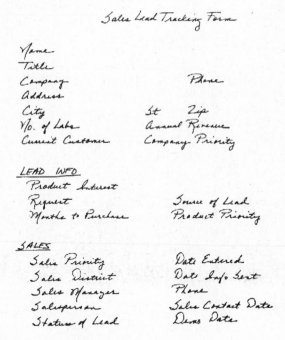

Fig. 5.1. *Planning the file form.*

The sketched form in figure 5.1 is for a sales-lead tracking file for a wholesaler of medical laboratory testing equipment. The basis for the file is a contacts' name-and-address list, which also includes other information about sales and leads for each client.

The form is organized so that related fields appear together. The most important fields (the fields that will be used most often in sort operations) appear at the top of the form; the remainder of the fields are organized into two categories: sales-lead information and sales-action information.

The next step is to bring this preliminary database design into Q&A File and design the entry form on-screen. The entry form essentially is a list of field labels with space beside each label for the user to enter the field contents. A File entry form is a picture of the database record. The form establishes how the database appears to users for data entry, editing, and report generation.

The following sections cover preliminary planning and the steps for creating your entry form.

Planning a File Form

Whether you are creating a form that only you or many people will use, take the time to make the form attractive. The form in figure 5.2 is designed so that the fields are not crowded; the space between fields makes the record easier to read. Because similar fields are together, you can skim the field names easily to find the one you need. Used in moderation, special format features—such as the lines on this form—can enhance the record. Too many special features, however, make the form look cluttered.

You want a database file to include everything required to produce the reports and queries you need. When you are laying out a form, however, you easily can get carried away. As you think of all the information you want to include, the form may grow to monstrous size. Remember that someone will have to enter all the information, and that someone may be you. To keep the form simple, include only necessary fields, and if possible, put all the fields on one page.

Before you design the form, you can determine the type of form you need by answering a few questions about the application.

How Will the Form Be Used?

When you set up the form, consider how the form will be used. Are you creating the form for a one-time project or an on-going process? For example, if the form is to be used to develop a mailing-and-attendance list for your company's twentieth-anniversary banquet, the form should be easy to create and you should not need to spend too much time on design details. If you are building a system to track maintenance and repairs for a fleet of delivery trucks, however, the form design will be more complex and used for a longer time. In this case, you need to create the form so that it can be used for regular report generation and analysis procedures and can be adapted for a variety of other uses.

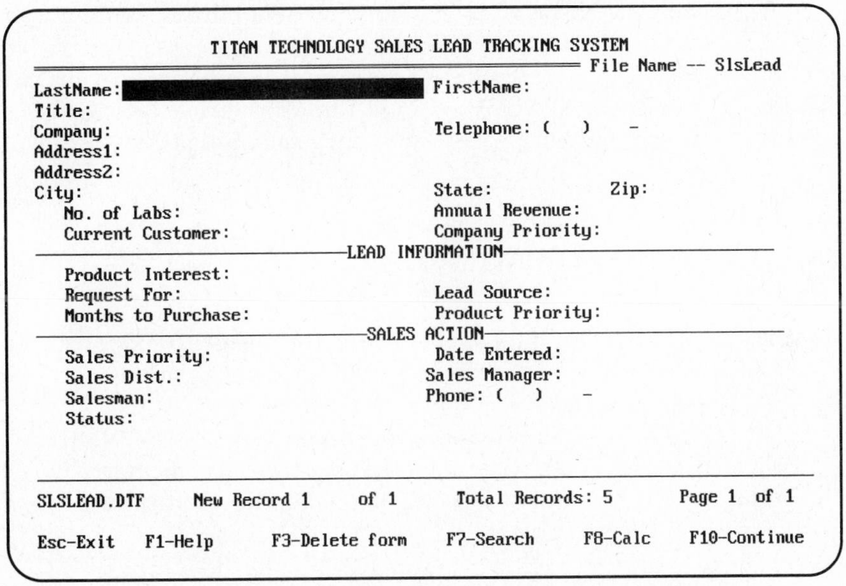

```
              TITAN TECHNOLOGY SALES LEAD TRACKING SYSTEM
========================================================= File Name -- SlsLead
LastName:█████████████████    FirstName:
Title:
Company:                      Telephone: (   )   -
Address1:
Address2:
City:                         State:           Zip:
   No. of Labs:               Annual Revenue:
   Current Customer:          Company Priority:
--------------------------LEAD INFORMATION-------------------
   Product Interest:
   Request For:               Lead Source:
   Months to Purchase:        Product Priority:
--------------------------SALES ACTION----------------------
   Sales Priority:            Date Entered:
   Sales Dist.:               Sales Manager:
   Salesman:                  Phone: (   )   -
   Status:

-------------------------------------------------------------
SLSLEAD.DTF     New Record 1    of 1     Total Records: 5     Page 1  of 1

Esc-Exit   F1-Help      F3-Delete form     F7-Search     F8-Calc    F10-Continue
```

Fig. 5.2.   *A Q&A File form on-screen.*

Data analysis and reporting capabilities are two major strengths of Q&A File. The way you design the form has a great impact on the ease, flexibility, and speed with which the program analyzes data and generates reports.

Who Will Use the Form?

You also should consider who will use the form. If you are the only user, you can design the form any way you choose. If other people will be using the form, however, the form design must be understood easily.

You can do several things to help other people use the form:

* Make the labels clear and complete. If you use abbreviations or shorthand phrases, other users may not be able to interpret them. If you have a field for the street name and you abbreviate the label as ST, for example, that field could be mistaken for the state field.

- Make the field names unique and indicative of the type of information to be entered into the field.

- Describe the information intended for a field by using a Q&A custom help screen (see Chapter 7).

- Be sure that the file name reflects the content or purpose of the file.

After you design the form on paper, you are ready to make the design with Q&A File. Don't worry about making mistakes. Q&A has a built-in safety net that gives you the option of redesigning your form at any stage without data loss.

Entering the Form Design

One major strength of Q&A is the full-screen editor you use to create data file forms. To design a form in Q&A File, perform the following steps:

1. Select File from the Main menu. (If you have configured Q&A for single-keystroke entry, you can press F. Use the Utility menu to change this configuration. See Chapter 3 for more information.) The File menu is displayed.

2. Select Design File to display the Design menu.

3. Select the Design a New File option. Q&A prompts you to enter a file name.

   The name of the file can be up to eight characters long; the first character must be a letter or number. You don't need to enter an extension with the file name; Q&A File adds the DTF extension.

4. Enter the file name *SLSLEAD* for the sales lead example, and press Enter.

   Q&A displays the File form design screen shown in figure 5.3. The cursor appears as a blinking rectangle in the top left corner of the screen. You move the cursor by pressing the cursor-movement keys.

To help you type the form design, several lines of information are displayed at the bottom of the Q&A form design screen. The first of these lines is the ruler line. The ruler is divided into 10 characters per inch (pica character spacing). As you move the cursor on the screen, the rectangular bar on the ruler line moves to correspond with the cursor position. Tab stops also appear on the ruler line. Q&A has preset tabs every inch, but you can move the tabs to the positions you choose by using F8 (Options) from the form design screen. From the Options menu, you can use submenus to set tabs, center lines, draw lines, move text, and perform other form design functions.

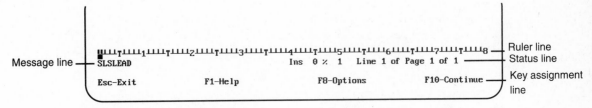

Fig. 5.3. The File form design screen.

The status line, just below the ruler line, displays information about your file. The file name is displayed on the far left side of the screen. The percentage of RAM memory used by the file is shown below the 5-inch point on the ruler. Initially, 0% is displayed because nothing has been placed in the file.

The line location of the cursor also is indicated on the status line, along with the number of the page and the total number of pages in the form. When you begin designing the form, the cursor is on the first line of the first page, and the form has only one page. The display in the status line, therefore, is Line 1 of Page 1 of 1. When you move the cursor to a different line, the display changes to show the current cursor position.

The key assignment line lists some of the function keys available when you are designing a form. Remember that you can press F1 to display help screens whenever you need assistance.

After you design the form, you can add a description to the file name. Descriptions make identifying files easier when you select the files from Q&A's List Files screen. To add a description to the file name, follow these steps:

1. Choose any item from the File menu and press Ctrl-F4 to erase the file-name prompt.

2. Press Enter to display the file listing.

3. Move the cursor to the file name and press F6 to enter a description. The description may contain up to 72 characters.

4. Press F10 twice to return to the File menu. You can edit the description later by pressing F6 at the file listing screen.

Because Q&A File is integrated with the Q&A Write word processor, entering a form design is as easy as typing. The form design has three parts: the heading, the field labels, and space for field data. As you enter the items, remember that the editing capabilities of Write are available to help you insert, copy, move, and delete text. To access these functions, use F8 (Options). You can cancel the design procedure at any time by pressing Esc.

Entering a Heading

Before you enter fields on the form, you may want to add a heading at the top of the first page of the form. The heading may include the name of the file, the date the file was created, the name of the person who created the file, and specifics about the file, such as company file number and security code. You can make the heading as complicated or as simple as you like, but remember that someone has to look at the form during data entry. Don't try to get so much information in the heading that the screen is cluttered or difficult to use. The heading appears on-screen but is not printed automatically on reports. You have to add the heading when you design the print specifications for the report. (See Chapter 8 for more information on printing File reports.)

To enter a heading, you type the text. Be careful not to use a colon (:) in the heading, however. During file design, Q&A reads any text followed by a colon as a field label.

The heading used in the sales lead example is a simple one (see fig. 5.4). As you can see, the name of the system is centered at the top of the form, and the file name is displayed on the right side of the screen. The double rule under the form heading is produced with the Draw command from the Options screen (F8).

```
                    TITAN TECHNOLOGY SALES LEAD TRACKING SYSTEM
                    ========================================= File Name -- SlsLead
        LastName:█████████████████████████  FirstName:
        Title:
        Company:                            Telephone: (   )    -
        Address1:
        Address2:
        City:                               State:          Zip:
            No. of Labs:                    Annual Revenue:
            Current Customer:               Company Priority:
```

Fig. 5.4.   A File form with a heading.

Entering Field Labels

To enter field names, move the cursor to the place where you want the first field to begin and type the label (refer to fig. 5.2 for the labels). End the field label with a colon. Figure 5.5 shows a partially completed form.

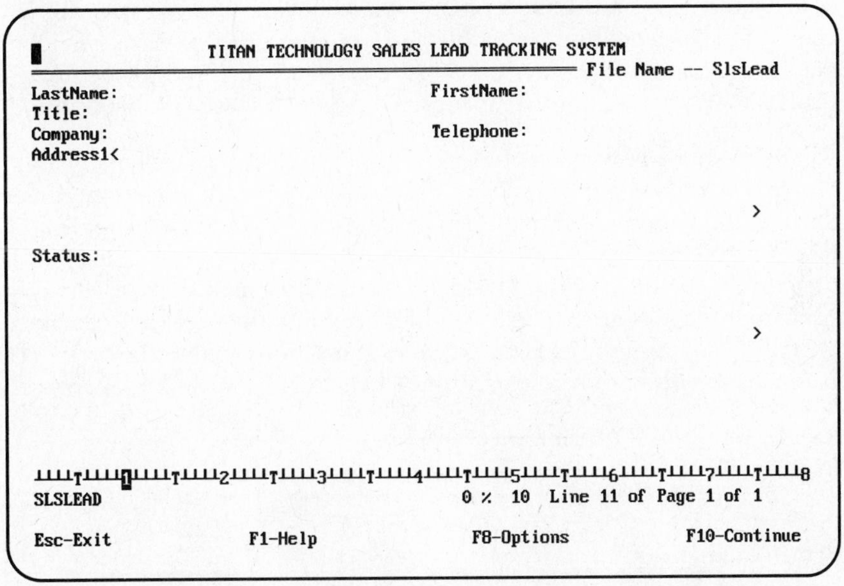

```
▌                  TITAN TECHNOLOGY SALES LEAD TRACKING SYSTEM
                    ═══════════════════════════════════ File Name -- SlsLead
LastName:                              FirstName:
Title:
Company:                               Telephone:
Address1<



                                                              >


Status:



                                                              >




⊥⊥⊥⊥T⊥⊥⊥⊥▌⊥⊥⊥⊥T⊥⊥⊥2⊥⊥⊥⊥T⊥⊥⊥3⊥⊥⊥T⊥⊥⊥⊥4⊥⊥⊥⊥T⊥⊥⊥5⊥⊥⊥T⊥⊥⊥6⊥⊥⊥⊥T⊥⊥⊥7⊥⊥⊥⊥T⊥⊥⊥8
SLSLEAD                                0 %  10  Line 11 of Page 1 of 1

Esc-Exit            F1-Help            F8-Options          F10-Continue
```

Fig. 5.5.   *Creating information blanks.*

Creating Information Blanks

Q&A File leaves space for field data next to each field name. You determine the size of the blank, of course, according to the space you need for the information. A field that accepts a true or false value, for example, requires less space than a field with comment lines. The amount of space can range from two characters to an entire screen.

During data entry or updating, Q&A enables you to override the field lengths you specified when designing the form. The Field Editor, described in Chapter 6, enables you to enter up to 32,000 characters in a text or key field. You also can enter up to 240 characters in fields of all other types (numeric, date, and so on), regardless of the length you specified for the form design.

A field is set off with a colon (:) or less-than and greater-than symbols. After you enter the label, type either a colon or a less-than symbol (<) to indicate the end of the label and mark the beginning of the field. If you want the field to extend to the end of the line, you need only the colon after the label. If you want to place another field on that same line, just enter another field label; the space for the first field stops one space before the second label begins. You use the less-than symbol when you have a blank of more than one line, and you want the left edges of the blank to line up. In this case, you insert the less-than symbol in place of the colon. To specify a field of more than one line, you enter the greater-than symbol (>) at the position on the screen where you want the blank to end.

Figure 5.5 shows how colons and greater-than symbols are used on the form design screen. In figure 5.6, you see the results of the form definition. Notice that the colons are visible but the greater-than signs are not. Q&A supplies the lines for the information, and the blank for the address field is highlighted as the current cursor position. This figure shows how multiple-line fields are handled in Q&A. Note that fields may not extend from one page to the next, although you may use the Field Editor to enter up to 32,000 characters (16 pages) of data in text or key fields. (The Field Editor is described in Chapter 6.)

```
       ■            TITAN TECHNOLOGY SALES LEAD TRACKING SYSTEM
      ══════════════════════════════════════════════════════ File Name -- SlsLead
       LastName:                              FirstName:
       Title:
       Company:                               Telephone:
       Address1

       Status:




       ──────────────────────────────────────────────────────────────────
       SLSLEAD.DTF    New Record 1     of 1     Total Records: 0      Page 1  of 1

       Esc-Exit  F1-Help     F3-Delete form   F7-Search   F8-Calc   F10-Continue
```

Fig. 5.6. *Results of the form definition.*

Formatting the Form

The Q&A Write formatting options (Set Tabs, Center Line, Uncenter Line, and Draw) also are available when you design a form. You access the Options menu by pressing F8. To choose an option, type the first letter of the option, and then select the appropriate item from the submenu that appears.

Setting Tabs

You arrange fields during the form-design process by using the Set Tabs option. The tab stops remain set for the form-design process and subsequent redesign operations, but not for data entry.

By selecting Set Tabs, you can delete existing tab stops and add new tab stops. Two types of tabs can be set: text tabs (T) align field labels flush left, and decimal tabs (D) align field labels flush right. When you begin typing above a text tab, the first character appears above the tab and the other characters are displayed to the right of the tab. When you use a decimal tab, the characters appear one space to the left of the decimal tab and move to the left until you type a period.

If you want to change the tab settings on your form, press F8 to display the Options menu. Then press L (for Lay out page) and S (for Set tabs). Q&A displays a ruler line, and the cursor appears on the ruler as a rectangular box. Notice that the ruler line has several preset text tab stops. You can move to the point on the ruler where you want to edit the tab stops by using the following keys:

Key	Cursor movement
Home	First space to the right of the left margin
End	First space to the left of the right margin
Ctrl- ←	Five spaces to the left
Ctrl- →	Five spaces to the right
Tab	Next tab marker to the right
Shift-Tab	Next tab marker to the left

To insert a tab stop, move to the position on the ruler where you want to add the tab stop. Press T for a text tab or D for a decimal tab. In figure 5.7, for example, a text tab was added in column 42 and a decimal tab in column 68. When you save the file, the new tab stop settings also are saved.

To delete a tab, move the cursor to the tab you want to delete and press either Del or the space bar. The T or D that marks the tab is erased from the ruler.

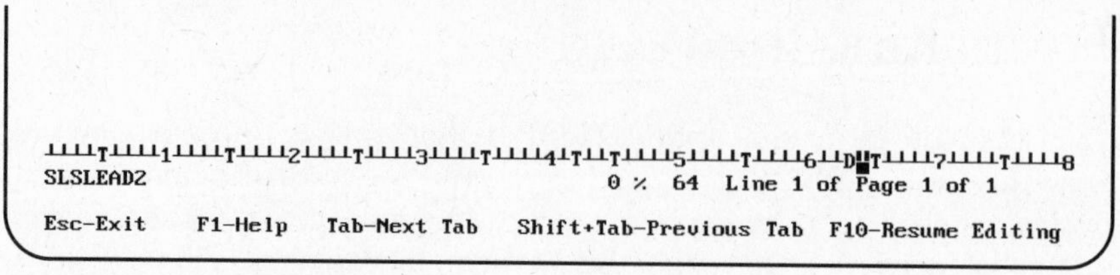

```
ЦЦЦTЦЦЦ1ЦЦЦTЦЦЦ2ЦЦЦTЦЦЦ3ЦЦЦTЦЦЦ4ЦTЦTЦЦЦ5ЦЦЦTЦЦЦ6ЦDTЦЦЦ7ЦЦЦTЦЦЦ8
SLSLEAD2                                0 % 64  Line 1 of Page 1 of 1

Esc-Exit    F1-Help    Tab-Next Tab    Shift+Tab-Previous Tab  F10-Resume Editing
```

Fig. 5.7.   *Text and decimal tabs.*

Centering Lines

To help you lay out your form, Q&A enables you to center and "uncenter" lines. To center the form heading, you position the cursor on the first line of the heading and press F8. When the Options menu is displayed, press A (for Align text) and C (for Center). Q&A centers all text on the line. Repeat the procedure for every line of the heading. Use the same option to center a line as it is entered. When you begin typing, the characters you enter are centered on the line and the cursor is kept in the center of the screen.

When you uncenter a line, you move the line back to normal left-margin alignment. To uncenter a line, move the cursor into the centered line, press F8 to bring up the Options menu, and press A (for Align text) and L (for Left). The line is realigned at the left margin.

Drawing Lines and Boxes

The Draw feature of Q&A File enables you to enhance your form design by adding lines, boxes, and illustrations. Lines and boxes often are used to group related information so that the form is easier to understand. Ambitious users can create logos and other complex illustrations with the Draw feature.

The Draw feature was used in the sales lead file form (refer to fig. 5.2). A double line separates the heading from the body of the form, and each category of information is set off by a single line.

To use Draw mode of Q&A File, place the cursor where you want the drawing to begin and press F8. When the Options menu is displayed, press L (for Lay out page) and D (for Draw). Use the cursor keys to draw the lines. When you move the cursor, Q&A draws a single line; when you press the Shift key and move the cursor, the program draws a double line. You also can draw double lines by pressing the Num Lock key and moving the cursor with the cursor-movement keys on the numeric keypad. The number keys 1, 3, 7, and 9 on the numeric keypad draw single diagonal lines. Press F10 to return to Editing mode.

You erase a line in Draw mode by pressing F8 (Erase) and moving the cursor over the lines you want to erase. When you press F8 in Draw mode, you can use any cursor-movement key to erase a line. You also can erase a line without choosing the Erase mode by pressing the Backspace key over those keystrokes. When you are ready to stop erasing and resume drawing, press F8 to return to Draw mode.

After the line is drawn and you exit Draw mode by pressing F10, the cursor can pass through the line without affecting it. If a space to the left of a line is deleted or inserted, however, the line changes positions.

Formatting the Information: The Format Spec

After you design the form, you need to fill out a format specification form to tell Q&A how the fields should be formatted. On the Format Spec screen, you enter the type of information to be included in each field and specify the data format options and global format options for each field (see fig. 5.8). At the Form Design screen, press F10 to display the Format spec.

Specifying Field Type

The first step in filling out the Format Spec is specifying the type of information to be entered in each field. Initially, each field is listed as a Text field (T), but you can change the specification to match your field types. (See Chapter 2 for a discussion of data types.)

Depending on the field type, you enter the first letter of one of the following choices: Text, Number, Yes/no, Money, Dates, Hours, or Keywords. Move the cursor from field to field by pressing the cursor keys, the Tab key, or Shift-Tab. As you move the cursor to the bottom half of the screen, the help window moves to the top so that the instructions always are visible. Figure 5.9 shows the completed Format Spec screen for the sales-lead form. You can press F1 to display a second help screen, which lists the information types and data format options (see fig. 5.10).

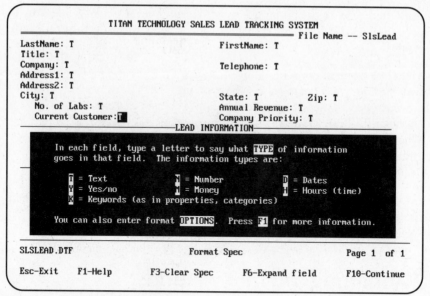

```
                TITAN TECHNOLOGY SALES LEAD TRACKING SYSTEM
                                                    ═══ File Name -- SlsLead
LastName: T                              FirstName: T
Title: T
Company: T                               Telephone: T
Address1: T
Address2: T
City: T                                  State: T        Zip: T
    No. of Labs: T                       Annual Revenue: T
    Current Customer:▓                    Company Priority: T
                            ─LEAD INFORMATION─
┌─────────────────────────────────────────────────────────────────────┐
│     In each field, type a letter to say what ▐TYPE▌ of information     │
│     goes in that field.  The information types are:                   │
│                                                                       │
│     ▐T▌ = Text          ▐N▌ = Number          ▐D▌ = Dates             │
│     ▐Y▌ = Yes/no        ▐M▌ = Money           ▐H▌ = Hours (time)       │
│     ▐K▌ = Keywords (as in properties, categories)                     │
│                                                                       │
│     You can also enter format ▐OPTIONS▌.  Press ▐F1▌ for more information.│
└─────────────────────────────────────────────────────────────────────┘
SLSLEAD.DTF               Format Spec                   Page 1  of 1

Esc-Exit    F1-Help       F3-Clear Spec    F6-Expand field    F10-Continue
```

Fig. 5.8. *The Format Spec screen.*

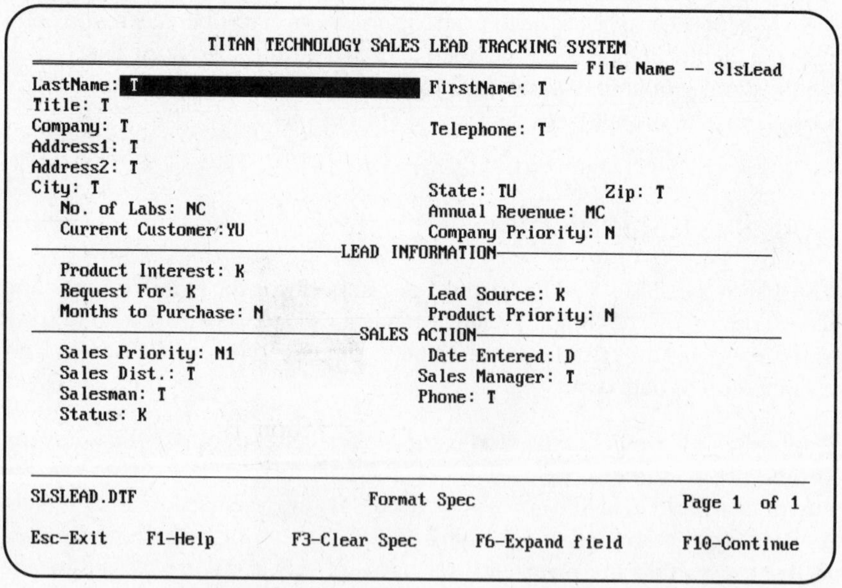

```
                TITAN TECHNOLOGY SALES LEAD TRACKING SYSTEM
                                                    ═══ File Name -- SlsLead
LastName: ▐T▌                            FirstName: T
Title: T
Company: T                               Telephone: T
Address1: T
Address2: T
City: T                                  State: TU        Zip: T
    No. of Labs: NC                       Annual Revenue: MC
    Current Customer:YU                   Company Priority: N
                            ─LEAD INFORMATION─
Product Interest: K
Request For: K                           Lead Source: K
Months to Purchase: N                    Product Priority: N
                             ─SALES ACTION─
Sales Priority: N1                       Date Entered: D
Sales Dist.: T                           Sales Manager: T
Salesman: T                              Phone: T
Status: K


SLSLEAD.DTF               Format Spec                   Page 1  of 1

Esc-Exit    F1-Help       F3-Clear Spec    F6-Expand field    F10-Continue
```

Fig. 5.9. *The completed Format Spec.*

```
┌─────────────────────────────────────────────────────────────────┐
│                                                                   │
│        HOW TO FORMAT: THE FORMAT SPEC        pg. F-22, 109         │
│  ┌──────────────────────────────────────────────────────────┐    │
│  In each field, enter an information TYPE followed optionally by format │
│  OPTIONS:                                                          │
│  ┌──────┬──────────┬────────────────────────────────────────┐    │
│  │ TYPE │ MEANING  │            FORMAT OPTIONS                │    │
│  ├──────┼──────────┼────────────────────────────────────────┤    │
│  │  T   │ Text     │  JR = Justify Right      U = Uppercase   │    │
│  │  K   │ Keyword  │  JC = Justify Center     L = Lowercase   │    │
│  │  Y   │ Yes/No   │  JL = Justify Left       I = Initial caps│    │
│  ├──────┼──────────┼────────────────────────────────────────┤    │
│  │  N   │ Number   │  JR, JL, JC                              │    │
│  │  M   │ Money    │  0-7 = # of decimal digits (for N only)  │    │
│  │      │          │  C   = insert commas                     │    │
│  ├──────┼──────────┼────────────────────────────────────────┤    │
│  │  D   │ Date     │  JR, JL, JC                              │    │
│  │  H   │ Time     │                                          │    │
│  └──────┴──────────┴────────────────────────────────────────┘    │
│                                                                   │
│  Examples:  N,2,JR,C  =  This field contains numbers, and they should have │
│                          two decimal digits, be right justified, with commas. │
│             T,U       =  This field contains text, in uppercase.  │
│                                                                   │
│  Esc-Exit                                                         │
└─────────────────────────────────────────────────────────────────┘
```

Fig. 5.10.   *Format options help screen.*

A Text field stores information that requires no special formatting features, although some are available. Fields that store both alphanumeric and numeric information—such as addresses, telephone numbers, serial numbers, or Social Security numbers—are defined as Text fields. Although you generally may think of some of these entries as numeric entries, they sometimes include non-numeric data. A telephone number, for example, can be entered as (123)456-7890; a Social Security number usually includes hyphens. Nine-digit ZIP codes frequently include a hyphen between the first group of five numbers and the last four numbers. ZIP codes beginning with zero probably will not sort as expected unless they are entered in a Text field.

Number fields store numbers only. For example, you use Number fields to store ages, quantities, and other strictly numeric data. The No. of Labs field in figure 5.9 has been designated a Number field. Only numbers, minus and plus signs, commas, and decimal points are accepted in a Number field. As an added feature, Q&A can use Number fields for mathematical operations.

A Yes/no field is shown in figure 5.9 as the Current Customer field. This type of field is used to store the answers to such questions as "Is this a preferred customer?" or "Is this customer on the mailing list?" Q&A accepts as an affirmative answer yes, Y, true, T, or 1. Negative values can be no, N, false, F, or 0.

Numbers typed in a Money field are formatted in the dollars-and-cents form—for example, $46,300.01. Q&A inserts the dollar sign and commas. You can change the currency symbol to the pound sign if you want. Calculations can be made in Money fields, as they can in Number fields.

When you specify D in a field on the Format Spec screen, Q&A recognizes the field as a Date field. The Date Entered field in figure 5.9 is an example of a Date field. Q&A's default date display is in the form mmm dd, yyyy, but you can change the format to any of 20 different options available from the Global Format Options screen, which appears after you identify field types (see the "Choosing Global Options" section later in this chapter).

An Hour field displays the time in either 12- or 24-hour format. In the 12-hour format, Q&A displays the time in the form hh:mm am/pm, such as 10:42 am or 6:40 pm. The program can correctly interpret time entered in a 24-hour format; for example, when you enter *22:05* but have chosen 12-hour format, Q&A displays the time as 10:05 pm.

The date and hour information types are helpful especially when used with Q&A File advanced programming features and the Intelligent Assistant. Using advanced programming techniques, for example, you can have Q&A notify you when a certain number of days has passed or alert you when a particular time has arrived.

Keyword fields are a special Q&A feature that programs such as dBASE III Plus and PFS:FILE don't possess. Keywords give you the freedom to enter text values in more than one way.

You can set up a Keyword field so that Q&A recognizes a set of entries for the field. For example, the sales lead sources are recorded in the Lead Source field in the database. Leads have been gained from several sources in this case, so you can designate several keywords to be accepted as entries in the field. For this example, the keywords Reference, Adv, Mailing, Salesman, and Other have been used. You can use these keywords to sort the file, produce reports, and analyze the lead-generating techniques. (For more information on specifying keywords, see Chapter 7.)

You can specify a Keyword field on a Format Spec by typing *K* in the field. In figure 5.9, the Product Interest, Request For, Lead Source, and Status fields are Keyword fields. You enter keywords by choosing the Restrict Values option from the Customize menu; you then type the keywords in the fields of the Restrict Spec, placing semicolons (;) between keywords. The specification for the preceding example appears as

   Lead Source: Reference;Adv;Mailing;Salesman;Other

Remember to make your designations consistent—Q&A does not recognize different spellings of the same keyword. For example, if you enter Reference as the keyword and later ask for References from that field, Q&A cannot process your request.

Selecting Data Format Options

Data field format specifications—Justify, Uppercase, Lowercase, Title, Decimal Digits, and Commas—are entered in the field space of the Format Spec, following the code for information type (refer to figs. 5.9 and 5.10).

When you specify *U* in a field, all text entered in that blank is displayed in uppercase letters. For example, even if you enter a value in the State field as *ca*, the value appears as CA if you marked the field as uppercase. If you specify *L* in a field, data entered into the field is formatted in all lowercase letters. If you specify *I*, the data is formatted with an initial capital letter and the rest of the data is lowercase.

You can specify up to seven decimal digits for your numeric fields, although you probably will use only two or three decimal digits for most of your fields. Figure 5.9 shows that the Sales Priority field is set to display values to one decimal place. The comma specification causes commas to be inserted in numbers containing four or more whole digits. When entering multiple specs in a field, separate the specs by using commas and no spaces. The Annual Revenue field in figure 5.9 shows you how to specify comma insertion.

You also can select the justification for your fields (refer to fig. 5.10). If you choose Justify Left (JL), the values in the field are aligned with the left edge of the field. Justify Center (JC) centers the values in the field, and Justify Right (JR) causes the values to be aligned with the right edge of the blank. To enter more than one format for a field, type the codes with or without commas. For example, Y,U or YU denotes a Yes/no field in which Q&A displays entries in uppercase.

Table 5.1 shows which data format specifications can be used with the different information types.

Figure 5.11 shows how the data in the record is displayed after the Format Spec is saved by pressing F10.

Table 5.1
Using Data Formats with Information Types

Information Type	Justify Right	Justify Center	Justify Left	Uppercase	Decimal Digits	Insert Commas
Text	Yes	Yes	Yes	Yes		
Keyword	Yes	Yes	Yes	Yes		
Yes/No	Yes	Yes	Yes	Yes		
Number	Yes	Yes	Yes		Yes	Yes
Money	Yes	Yes	Yes		Yes	
Date	Yes	Yes	Yes			
Time	Yes	Yes	Yes			

```
           TITAN TECHNOLOGY SALES LEAD TRACKING SYSTEM
                                        File Name -- SlsLead
LastName: Hope                    FirstName: Brian
Title: Vice President
Company: Hope Laboratories, Inc.  Telephone: (583) 200-0000
Address1: 413 Galmache Avenue
Address2:
City: Mobile                      State: AL        Zip: 33933
   No. of Labs: 14                Annual Revenue: $50,000,000.00
   Current Customer: Y            Company Priority: 1
─────────────────────────────LEAD INFORMATION─────────────────────
   Product Interest: 1500;1800
   Request For: Demo              Lead Source: Adv
   Months to Purchase: 3          Product Priority: 1
─────────────────────────────SALES ACTION──────────────────────────
   Sales Priority: 1.0            Date Entered: Apr 19, 1989
   Sales Dist.: Atlanta           Sales Manager: George Hall
   Salesman: Frank Alton          Phone: (583) 999-4123
   Status: Call


SLSLEAD.DTF   Retrieved form 1   of --    Total Forms: 5     Page 1  of 1

Esc-Exit   F1-Help   Alt+F6-Table   F7-Search   F8-Calc   F10-Continue
```

Fig. 5.11. *Results of data formats.*

Choosing Global Format Options

If any information type has been specified as number, money, time, or date, the Global Format Options screen is displayed as the final formatting step (see fig. 5.12). On this screen, you specify the global formats for currency, decimals, time, and date. Notice that 20 options are available for date format. By selecting Global, you are telling Q&A to use the specified format every time the program encounters data in that type of field in the current file. For example, if you change the currency symbol from the dollar sign to the pound sign on the Global Format Options menu, Q&A displays the pound sign as the currency symbol in every money field in the file on-screen and in printouts.

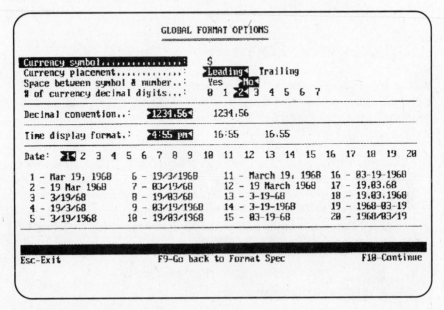

Fig. 5.12. *The Global Format Options screen.*

To select a Global Format option, use the Tab, Enter, or cursor keys to highlight a format option. When you have made your selections and saved the specifications, press F10 to continue.

Redesigning a File Form

You may think of ways to improve a form after you have used it for awhile. Perhaps your original design includes fields that you don't use, or maybe you want to change the order of the fields. In Q&A, you can change the form quickly without danger of data loss—whether you want to make a top-to-bottom overhaul or only a slight adjustment. You can delete fields, insert fields, change field lengths, or select different formats.

Most important, you can make design changes even after you have entered data into the file. Q&A accepts the changes and adjusts the data to fit the new design. If you have ever lost data in another program while trying to change the design of a database form, you will appreciate this Q&A feature.

Be sure to make a backup copy of the entire file before you redesign a database. If you decide that you like your original form better than the redesigned version, you have the original on disk.

Modifying the Form

With Q&A, you can edit the file form more extensively and more easily than you can with many programs. Because File is linked with Q&A's built-in word processor, almost all the editing features are available while you work on the form.

For example, suppose that you need to redesign the sales lead example introduced in this chapter. The original form is shown in figure 5.13. The redesigned form is shown in figure 5.14. The form has been redesigned so that the LEAD INFORMATION and SALES ACTION headings are centered. Also, several of the Date fields in the SALES ACTION section have been deleted.

```
                 TITAN TECHNOLOGY SALES LEAD TRACKING SYSTEM
                                              File Name -- SlsLead
    LastName:█████████████████████      FirstName:
    Title:
    Company:                            Telephone: (   )   -
    Address1:
    Address2:
    City:                               State:          Zip:
       No. of Labs:                     Annual Revenue:
       Current Customer:                Company Priority:
    LEAD INFORMATION───────────────────────────────────────────
       Product Interest:
       Request For:                     Lead Source:
       Months to Purchase:              Product Priority:
    SALES ACTION───────────────DATES─────────────────────────
       Sales Priority:                  Date Entered:
       Sales Dist.:                   Date Info Sent:
       Salesman:                        Sales Contact:
       Status:                            Demo Date:


    ────────────────────────────────────────────────────────────
    SLSLEAD.DTF    New Record 1    of 1    Total Records: 0    Page 1 of 1

    Esc-Exit   F1-Help     F3-Delete form   F7-Search   F8-Calc   F10-Continue
```

Fig. 5.13.   The original file form.

To redesign a form, follow these steps:

1. Select Redesign a File from the Design menu. Q&A prompts you to enter the name of the database file.

```
                    TITAN TECHNOLOGY SALES LEAD TRACKING SYSTEM
                    ============================================== File Name -- SlsLead
    LastName:▮▮▮▮▮▮▮▮▮▮▮▮▮▮▮▮▮▮    FirstName:
    Title:
    Company:                          Telephone: (   )   -
    Address1:
    Address2:
    City:                             State:          Zip:
       No. of Labs:                   Annual Revenue:
       Current Customer:              Company Priority:
    ───────────────────────────LEAD INFORMATION─────────────────────
       Product Interest:
       Request For:                   Lead Source:
       Months to Purchase:            Product Priority:
    ──────────────────────────────SALES ACTION──────────────────────
       Sales Priority:                Date Entered:
       Sales Dist.:                   Sales Manager:
       Salesman:                      Phone: (   )   -
       Status:


    ─────────────────────────────────────────────────────────────────
    SLSLEAD.DTF    New Record 1    of 1     Total Records: 5     Page 1 of 1

    Esc-Exit   F1-Help      F3-Delete form    F7-Search    F8-Calc    F10-Continue
```

Fig. 5.14.   *The redesigned file form.*

2. Type a file name, or you can select a database. Press the space bar to erase the line, if necessary.

3. Press Enter to display a list of databases.

4. Move the highlight cursor over the desired file name and press Enter to select the database you want.

    If a default file name is displayed and you want to enter a new name, just type the new name. Q&A erases the displayed file name when you type the first character.

In this example, the database selected is SLSLEAD. Each field has an identifying code supplied by Q&A (see fig. 5.15). Don't alter the codes on the form—the code for each field must stay where the code was placed by the program. The codes, also called *field tags*, are used to identify your data and to reorganize the data when the form is redesigned. If you change a code, Q&A may be unable to process your request.

If you accidentally delete a code, you can type the code as it appeared on-screen or press Esc to cancel editing. When you add fields to the form, Q&A assigns codes to the new fields.

When the database form is displayed, you are ready to make the changes to the form.

```
                    TITAN TECHNOLOGY SALES LEAD TRACKING SYSTEM
                    ═══════════════════════════════════════════ File Name -- SlsLead
    LastName:AA                           FirstName:AB
    Title:AC
    Company:AD                            Telephone:AE
    Address1:AF
    Address2:AG
    City:AH                           > State:AI  >      Zip:AJ        >
       No. of Labs:AK        >         Annual Revenue:AL              >
       Current Customer:AM>            Company Priority:AN            >
                                 ─────LEAD INFORMATION─────
       Product Interest:AO                                            >
       Request For:AP                 > Lead Source:AQ                >
       Months to Purchase:AR          > Product Priority:AS           >
                                 ─────SALES ACTION─────
       Sales Priority:AT              > Date Entered:AU               >
       Sales Dist.:AV                 > Sales Manager:AW              >
       Salesman:AX                    > Phone:AY                      >
       Status:AZ                      >


    ‖‖‖‖T‖‖‖‖1‖‖‖‖T‖‖‖‖2‖‖‖‖T‖‖‖‖3‖‖‖‖T‖‖‖‖4‖‖‖T‖‖‖‖5‖‖‖‖T‖‖‖‖6‖‖‖T‖‖‖‖7‖‖‖‖T‖‖‖‖8
    SLSLEAD                           Ins  2 %  1    Line 1 of Page 1 of 1

    Esc-Exit            F1-Help              F8-Options          F10-Continue
```

Fig. 5.15. *Q&A field identification codes.*

Changing Field Lengths

After you have designed your file form, you may find that you have allotted too much space to some fields and not enough space to others. Changing the length of a field is easy, but be careful—you can lose part of your data in the process if a field is shortened.

Note: Before you change field length, you may want to go to the Customize menu and select Change Palette. This method enables you to choose a palette that displays field lengths with highlights or lines so that the fields are easier to see and change.

To change the field length, add or delete spaces between the beginning and end of the field. Remember that colons (:) and greater-than and less-than symbols (<>) mark the area of the field. When you shorten a field, Q&A displays a warning screen telling you that you may lose data. You can cancel the process or continue.

If you plan to shorten a field, first use Search/Update to read through the forms and check the length of the data in that field. If no data extends to the end of the field, shortening the field has little or no effect. If the data fills the field, however, shortening the field may destroy some important information.

Adding a Field

You can add a field anywhere on the form. The field can be added on a new page or on a form page that has other fields. Use the PgUp and PgDn keys to move from page to page.

You may want to press the Ins key to change Q&A into Insert mode before you add a field so that you don't type over existing fields. If you want to insert a line for the new field, move the cursor to the place you want the line inserted. When you press Enter, the program inserts a new line at the cursor position, and all lines below the cursor move down one line. If a field is on the last line of the page, the field is moved to the top of the next page. To add the new field, move the cursor to the place you want the field to be and start typing.

Deleting a Field

When you delete a field, make sure that you remove the entire field—label, colon, greater-than and less-than symbols, and code. To delete a field, you can use the F4 key (or Ctrl-Y), the Backspace key, or the Del key.

Note: This occasion is the only time you should alter a code.

If your form includes calculated fields and you delete a field that is referenced in the calculation formula, the program may display a warning screen. To correct the error, you can re-enter the field, select the Program Form option from the Customize menu, and then replace the programming statement. Another way to correct the problem is to change the calculation formula. After selecting Customize a File, choose Program Form and modify the formula so that the formula no longer references the deleted field.

Moving a Field

After you begin using your file form, you may want to change the order of the fields. With Q&A, you can move and copy fields, even after data has been entered.

You can move a field in one of two ways: by copying the field and deleting the original or by moving the original. The copy-and-delete procedure is safer because if power is interrupted or a disk error occurs during the copy procedure, you still have the original intact.

Be careful when you use the Move and Copy commands. When the field is inserted in the new location, any other fields on the line shift to the right. This movement could upset the layout. You can avoid disruption by making room at the new location for the field you're about to move, perhaps by inserting an empty line.

To move a field, follow these steps:

1. Select Design File and then Redesign a File.

2. At the prompt, type *SLSLEAD* and press Enter.

3. When the Form Design screen appears for redesigning your form, position the cursor on the first character of the field label you want to move.

4. Press Shift-F5 to select Move. The cursor becomes a full-character highlight.

5. Use the right-arrow key to highlight the entire field to be moved. Make sure that you include the code and the greater-than symbol if the field has one. If you want the Title field above the LastName field, for example, you highlight that field.

6. To complete the selection, press F10.

7. Move the cursor to the new field location and press F10 again. The field is moved (see fig. 5.16).

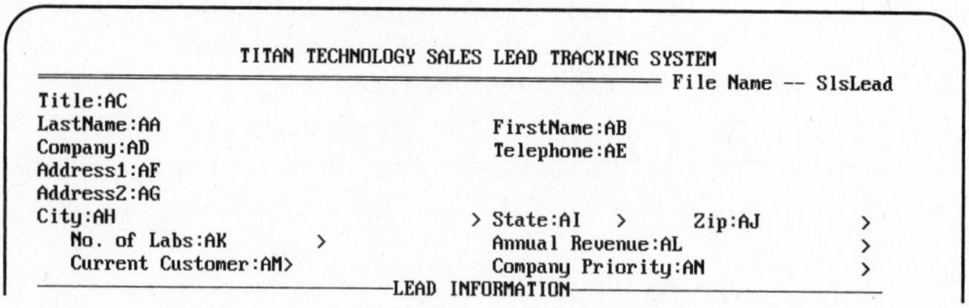

```
                  TITAN TECHNOLOGY SALES LEAD TRACKING SYSTEM
                  ═══════════════════════════════════ File Name -- SlsLead
  Title:AC
  LastName:AA                        FirstName:AB
  Company:AD                         Telephone:AE
  Address1:AF
  Address2:AG
  City:AH                          > State:AI  >    Zip:AJ          >
     No. of Labs:AK       >          Annual Revenue:AL              >
     Current Customer:AM>            Company Priority:AN            >
                          ─────────LEAD INFORMATION─────────
```

Fig. 5.16. *Moving a field.*

To copy a field and delete the original, follow these steps:

1. Move the cursor to the first character of the field label and press F5 to select Copy. The cursor becomes a full-character highlight.

2. Use the right-arrow key to highlight the material to be copied. Make sure that you include the greater-than symbol if one has been used.

3. Press F10 to complete the selection process.

4. Move the cursor to the new field location and press F10 again. The field is copied.

5. Return to the original field and delete it by moving the cursor to the first character in the field name and pressing Del as many times as required or by pressing Shift-F4 to erase the entire line.

If you forget to delete the original field, Q&A catches your mistake. When you press F10 to continue, Q&A checks the form. If the form has a duplicate field, the program moves the cursor to the copied field and displays the following warning:

```
You have a duplicate field code at the cursor. Codes must
be unique.
```

Changing Information Types and Formats

After you have moved, copied, inserted, or deleted fields, you may want to reformat some of them. You can access the Format Spec screen by pressing F10 at the completion of your changes. You then enter format codes and information types for new fields or change the format codes and information types of edited fields. When you press F10 again, the Global Format Option menu is displayed. Now press F10 to return to the File menu.

Q&A reorganizes the file. This process is part of Q&A's internal housekeeping. Depending on the size of the database and the number of changes you have made, the program may take some time to complete the task.

Chapter Summary

The design of your file form is an important part of your database. With Q&A File, you can design a form as basic or as complex as you need. This chapter has explained the steps required to get your form up and running. The next chapter teaches you how to enter and edit information with Q&A File.

If you are designing a form that will be used by other people or if you want to try out Q&A's programming features before you begin to enter information into your file, you may want to read Chapter 7 before you begin Chapter 6.

Using File

A fter you have designed and formatted your file form, you can begin entering data. For details about designing and formatting files, see Chapter 5. As you use your form, you will find that planning and preparation have saved you considerable time and effort.

If the file form you have designed uses mostly text fields and does not require automatic calculation and entry of numeric, date, or time data, you are ready to use your form by following the directions in this chapter. If your database fields use automatic calculations or require features customized to help other users, however, you may want to read Chapter 7, "Customizing and Programming a File," before you read this chapter. Chapter 7 explains programming techniques for streamlining the use of your form. This chapter explains the procedures used for the following:

- Entering and adding information

- Retrieving and updating forms

- Copying information

- Using custom help screens

- Displaying forms in a table

- Locating forms

- Deleting information from the database

Adding and Editing Information in File

Entering information in Q&A File is just as simple as in Q&A Write. The Sales Lead example used in the preceding chapter is continued here to help illustrate these operations.

You must open a file before you can add and edit information. To begin filling in forms, at the Q&A Main menu, press F for File. At the File menu, press A to choose Add Data. At the File Name prompt, type the name of a file to use, or press Enter and highlight a file name on the List of Files screen. After you select a file name, press Enter or F10 to display a blank data entry form. You now may add information, change information, and print a single form.

The number of the current form and the total number of forms in the database are displayed on the status line (see fig. 6.1). The number of new forms during a single add session is incremented with each new form. Figure 6.1 shows the first new form of this session. When you add a second form, the status line will change to show

```
New Record 2   of 2   Total Records: 19   Page 1 of 1
```

The Page 1 of 1 notation means your form has only one page and that one page is displayed. If you were on the second page of a four-part form, the Page notation would show Page 2 of 4.

```
 SLSLEAD.DTF    New Record 1    of 1    Total Records: 5    Page 1  of 1
 Esc-Exit   F1-Help     F3-Delete form   F7-Search    F8-Calc    F10-Continue
```

Fig. 6.1.   The File status line.

Using Special Keys for Entering Data and Moving through Forms

You can use various special keys to help make entering data in your form easier. When the file form is displayed, the cursor is positioned in the first field. You simply type the information for that field. If you make mistakes while typing, correct them by using the Q&A editing keys. (See "Editing Forms" in this chapter for a list of editing keys.)

After you finish entering data in the first field, press Enter or Tab to move the cursor to the next field. When you want to move to a preceding field, press Shift-Tab. When you finish entering data in all the fields on the first page of the form, you can move to the next page by pressing the PgDn key. Press PgUp to move to a preceding page.

When you have entered data in all the fields on the form, you have several options: you can press F10 to save the form and display a new one (you use this procedure when you need to fill in more than one form); you can press Shift-F10 to save the form and return to the File menu; or you can press F2 to print a quick copy of the form. (For more about printing a file, see Chapter 8.)

After you have entered and saved more than one form, you can press F9 to move through preceding forms. F10 is used to scroll forward through the forms. The procedure is similar to paging through paper forms in a file folder, but Q&A makes the process faster and easier.

Entering Data into a Form

When you enter information into Q&A File, the program checks that the information corresponds to the types you specified when you designed the form.

Entering Different Data Types

As you already know, certain types of information should be entered in certain fields. For example, numbers go in numeric fields, and dates go in date fields unless you have a good reason for overriding these restrictions.

Q&A File alerts you to mismatches so that you can correct them. Mismatches are explained in the following sections, and some additional information is given about information types and date fields. Refer also to Chapter 2 for additional information about Q&A data types.

Q&A File declares a mismatch for two reasons:

- The wrong type of information is entered into a file.

- The information doesn't conform to the restricted value.

If you specified that a field is a date field but you enter alphanumeric text, for example, Q&A notifies you that a possible mismatch has occurred. The Restrict Values feature of Q&A enables you to program individual fields for specific values or ranges of values. If information outside these limits is entered, a mismatch occurs. (See Chapters 4 and 7 for more information on entering restricted values.) If you have used the Restrict Spec to limit the range of data that can be entered in a field, you can view the list of restrictions that have been set up for that field by pressing Alt-F7 while the cursor is in the field.

Text fields accept any information, but other field types are more discriminating. If any characters other than numbers, commas, periods, plus or minus signs, and currency symbols are entered into number and money fields, Q&A does not accept the entry.

Q&A checks the information type when you try to leave date, time, and yes/no fields. If you enter mismatched information, the cursor remains in the field and an error message is displayed. You can change the entry, or you can accept it by pressing Enter and proceeding to the next field.

In figure 6.2, an attempt was made to enter the text phrase *DON'T KNOW* in the Current Customer field. Because the Current Customer field is a yes/no field, File displays a message to alert you.

```
                 TITAN TECHNOLOGY SALES LEAD TRACKING SYSTEM
                                                 File Name -- SlsLead
     LastName: Franklyn              FirstName: Albert
     Title: Vice president
     Company: Advanced Medical Associates  Telephone: 615-596-7811
     Address1: 5823 Emory Place
     Address2:
     City: Knoxville                  State: TN      Zip: 37718
        No. of Labs: 3                Annual Revenue: 5,300,623
        Current Customer: DON'T KNOW  Company Priority:  _____
     -
        This doesn't look like a yes/no value. Please verify.

     Months to Purchase:             Product Priority:
     ---------------------------SALES ACTION---------------------
```

Fig. 6.2. Warning messages for the wrong data type.

You can correct this problem in one of two ways: erase the mismatched information and enter the correct information, or accept the mismatch by pressing Enter. The information is entered if you accept the mismatch, and the cursor moves to the next field. (For this illustration, we have shown this field with a length of several characters. Normally, a yes/no field has a length of one.)

Notice that Q&A leaves the user in control. Many database products flatly refuse to accept information that does not match the specified type for a particular field for some excellent reasons. If your application depends heavily on consistent information in certain fields across the database—most successful applications do—you want to avoid mismatched data in the database.

Although you can enter incorrect information, you also can enter data that helps you find forms with missing information. Suppose that you do not know the date of some occurrence when you are entering information for a specific record. A blank date field means that the event has not occurred or has not been scheduled, so you enter something like *unknown* instead of leaving the field blank. Q&A tells you that *unknown* is not a valid date, but you can enter it anyway. Later you can search for *unknown* to enter the correct date. In the meantime, you will not get invalid data in your reports due to a wrong interpretation of a blank date field.

In many situations, being confined strictly to the format or data restrictions in a database may be inconvenient. You must consider the question carefully, however, when Q&A asks whether you are sure that you want to enter the nonconforming data. If the entry is a typo or other mistake, rather than a planned deviation from the specs, you want to correct the data instead of accepting it.

You have two options to ensure that entered information adheres to the programmed database restrictions. One option is to create carefully designed custom help for these critical fields and to instruct any data entry personnel to use custom help when Q&A returns data errors.

The second option is to program the form so that improper data simply cannot be entered. This approach is restrictive but necessary in some applications. For example, if several different people are entering data, and you want to make sure that all fields are filled consistently, you may need to restrict entry to specific data types or ranges of data. Such restrictions should be accompanied by custom help screens so that the operator doesn't get locked into one field, unable to decide what acceptable data to enter and unable to continue because the program restricts a continue or exit until certain data conditions are met.

At certain times, however, the sensible procedure is to enter information that seems to conflict with the database rules you have established. Consider an accounting database. Assume that you have imposed restrictions on account numbers during transaction entry so that expense entries are entered with account numbers between 800 and 999 only, income accounts are entered in accounts 600 to 799, and so on. (See the next section on restricted fields for more information on this concept.) To get a list of income transactions, you request all entries with account numbers between 600 and 799.

If you make a deposit and credit it to an expense account, Q&A warns you of the apparent error. However, you can use this reverse type of entry to account, in a simple way, for expenses for which you were reimbursed from your company. This example is a case in which the restrictions trap is well intended, but without having a way to override the restriction, you are forced into a more complicated form design.

Entering Long Data

While editing data in a text or key field, you can enter data that is much longer than the field length you specified during form design. With the cursor in the field, press F6 to display the Field Editor. A box appears on-screen in which you can type up to 32,000 characters (16 pages). The Field Editor provides all of the functions of Q&A's Write module, including spell checking, thesaurus, block functions, printing, and so on.

The Field Editor may be used only with text and key fields. However, you may enter up to 240 characters in fields of all other types by pressing F6 to display an extended data entry prompt at the bottom of the screen.

When printing forms, Q&A treats any long data that you have entered with the Field Editor as a long text field. The printed contents of the field are wordwrapped, beginning at the normal field printing position on the page.

Entering Data into Restricted Fields

When you customize your data entry form (see Chapter 7), you may choose to restrict some fields. Restricting fields affects the way data are entered into those fields. Restricted fields are designed to monitor and limit the data added to a field. Restricted fields are useful especially when you are using certain keywords.

Restricted fields accept specific words or phrases and alert you when unacceptable information is entered into the field. In figure 6.3, for example, *Phone* is entered into the Lead source field. However, the Lead Source field has been restricted to one of five specific words:

Mail
Telephone
Reference
Adv
Other

The word *Phone* is not one of the restricted values, so you get a warning message. In addition to demonstrating how Q&A handles information outside specified restricted ranges, this example also shows how easily you can be inconsistent in data entry.

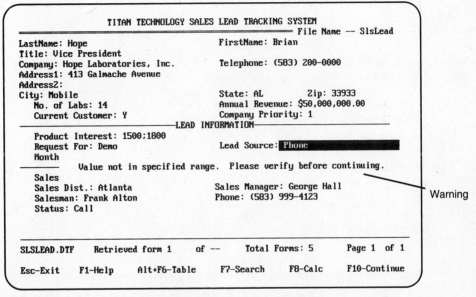

```
                   TITAN TECHNOLOGY SALES LEAD TRACKING SYSTEM
                                              ══════════ File Name -- SlsLead
LastName: Hope                      FirstName: Brian
Title: Vice President
Company: Hope Laboratories, Inc.    Telephone: (583) 200-0000
Address1: 413 Galmache Avenue
Address2:
City: Mobile                        State: AL        Zip: 33933
   No. of Labs: 14                  Annual Revenue: $50,000,000.00
   Current Customer: Y              Company Priority: 1
────────────────────────────LEAD INFORMATION───────────────────
   Product Interest: 1500;1800
   Request For: Demo                Lead Source: Phone
   Month
─────         Value not in specified range.  Please verify before continuing.
   Sales
   Sales Dist.: Atlanta             Sales Manager: George Hall
   Salesman: Frank Alton            Phone: (583) 999-4123
   Status: Call



SLSLEAD.DTF    Retrieved form 1    of --      Total Forms: 5       Page 1 of 1

Esc-Exit    F1-Help    Alt+F6-Table    F7-Search    F8-Calc    F10-Continue
```

Warning

Fig. 6.3. *Warning for unacceptable data in a restricted field.*

Good database design includes planning for many data entry situations and handling them by programming, if possible. Q&A is flexible enough to allow you to specify telephone or phone in this field so that you have more choices during data entry. You can even program the field to change the data entry to the preferred form if the operator enters something close to what is desired.

Generally, the procedure for forcing operators to enter certain data, while bypassing Q&A's built-in capability to accept information outside specified ranges, involves using a simple IF...THEN statement:

>#5: IF #5<10 OR #5>100 THEN GOTO #5

When you have this statement in a numeric or money field, you cannot exit the field if the value entered is less than 10 or greater than 100. When an incorrect value is entered and you press Enter, the cursor returns to the beginning of the field, and Q&A waits for you to enter data within the specified range. You can press Esc to exit the form, or you can press F10 to store the form and move to the next one. If you press Esc, the information already entered is not saved. If you press F10, data entered up to this point is saved and a new form is presented. The greater-than symbol (>) at the beginning of the programming statement tells Q&A to evaluate this statement when you attempt to exit the field. (See Chapter 7 for more information on programming a form.)

Entering Data into Date Fields

Q&A Version 4 offers 20 different date formats, as you can see in the following list (Version 1 accepted only 6 formats):

Mar 19, 1991	March 19, 1991
19 Mar 1991	19 March 1991
3/19/91	3-19-91
19/3/91	3-19-1991
3/19/1991	03-19-91
19/3/1991	03-19-1991
03/19/91	19.03.91
19/03/91	19.03.1991
03/19/1991	1991-03-19
19/03/1991	1991/03/19

You select a format from the Global Format Options screen when you design the form. This screen is presented automatically when you exit the Format Spec screen during form design.

When dates are entered in the forms, Q&A displays the dates in the selected format. If the form is redesigned later with a different date format, the dates in previously entered forms may not be displayed properly or may not fit the new format. If the information blank is too short for the format, the date may be cut off. For example, the longest date format requires 18 spaces (September 19, 1991), and the shortest takes 8 spaces (12/19/91).

After you specify a date format, date information is stored in that format in the file. You can enter the date information in almost any way you choose, however. For example, you may want the date stored in the format mmm dd, yyyy, but you prefer entering dates in the form mm/dd/yy. When you exit the date field, Q&A reformats the date to conform to the specified format. If the year is the same as the year in the computer's system date, you need not enter the year as part of the date. Q&A assumes that you mean the current year.

Copying Entered Data from One Form to the Next

If you are entering the same information into certain fields of consecutive forms of your database, you can use F5 (Ditto) to copy the data from one form to the same fields in the next form. Q&A File remembers the data you enter in one form when you move to the next. When you display a new form, you can move to a field and press F5 (Ditto); Q&A copies the data from the same field on the preceding form.

The Ditto feature is great to use when you're entering the same information into several consecutive forms. In figure 6.4, a sales lead from Knoxville, Tennessee, was entered. The next lead in the database is also from Knoxville, so instead of typing the information again, you can press F5 to copy the data from the City field on the last form (see fig. 6.4).

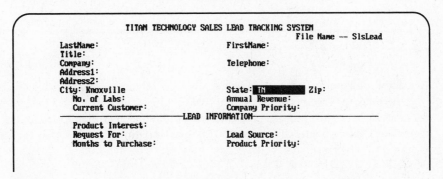

Fig. 6.4. *Using the Ditto key to enter information.*

Displaying Custom Help Screens

As you enter and edit forms, you can use custom help screens to give you specific instructions, display restricted information about particular fields, or serve as reminders about codes and abbreviations. For example, suppose that a custom help screen has been designed for the Lead Source field in the Sales Lead Tracking System. This field is restricted to one of only five words. If you cannot remember the words to use, you can press F1 to display the custom help screen. The screen is displayed as an overlay so that you can see the help information while you enter the correct value into the field (see fig. 6.5) The procedure for creating custom help screens is explained in Chapter 7.

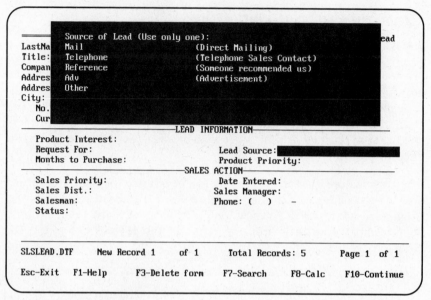

```
     ══════                                                                   ead
              Source of Lead (Use only one):
     LastNa   Mail                         (Direct Mailing)
     Title:   Telephone                    (Telephone Sales Contact)
     Compan   Reference                    (Someone recommended us)
     Addres   Adv                          (Advertisement)
     Addres   Other
     City:
        No.
        Cur
     ───────────────────────────────LEAD INFORMATION───────────────────────
        Product Interest:
        Request For:                         Lead Source:▮▮▮▮▮▮▮▮▮▮▮▮▮▮
        Months to Purchase:                  Product Priority:
                                ─────────────SALES ACTION─────────────────
        Sales Priority:                      Date Entered:
        Sales Dist.:                         Sales Manager:
        Salesman:                            Phone: (   )    −
        Status:


     ──────────────────────────────────────────────────────────────────────
     SLSLEAD.DTF      New Record 1      of 1       Total Records: 5      Page 1  of 1

     Esc-Exit   F1-Help      F3-Delete form     F7-Search     F8-Calc     F10-Continue
```

Fig. 6.5.   *A custom help screen.*

Pressing F1 during data entry displays the Adding/Updating Forms help screen. If a custom help screen is available, the first time you press F1, Q&A displays the custom help screen. If you press F1 again when the custom help screen is displayed, Q&A brings up the Steps for Adding or Updating a Form help screen.

Editing Forms

One advantage of using integrated software like Q&A is that editing and data-entry procedures can be consistent across all applications. Because File is fully integrated with Write, for example, virtually all of Write's editing features are available as you design an entry form and enter data. Table 6.1 lists the special editing and cursor-movement keys you can use to add and edit forms. (Refer to Chapter 10 for details on Q&A editing procedures.)

Table 6.1
Editing Keys Used in Q&A File

Key	Function
Enter, Tab	Moves cursor to next field
Shift-Tab	Moves cursor to previous field
↓	Moves cursor down one field

Key	Function
↑	Moves cursor up one field
→	Moves cursor to right
←	Moves cursor to left
F4	Erases data from cursor to end of field
Shift-F4	Erases contents of current line
F6	Field editor (text and key fields)
Alt-F8	Expanded field entry (all other field types)
Ins	Turns on insert mode

Entering Special Characters into a Field

At certain times, you may want to enter special characters, such as superscript or subscript numbers, in a specific field. During File and Report print operations, you can send to your printer control codes to turn on font or other characteristics for each form or report. You must, however, control field-level printing during data entry.

To use special characters in Q&A, insert ASCII codes where you want the characters to appear. The codes either turn on a specific printer characteristic or display a character that is not on your keyboard.

An ASCII (American Standard Code for Information Interchange) code is the numeric representation of a character or symbol. The letter A is represented by the decimal number 65, for example. All standard character and graphics symbols can be represented by numbers. Refer to your computer operations manual, printer manual, or display adapter instructions for a list of character and graphics symbols and their numeric equivalents.

Many people, particularly those in technical and scientific fields, use superscript and subscript characters in day-to-day database use. Superscript and subscript characters may not appear as raised or lowered characters on your screen, however, depending on your computer system. For example, the IBM monochrome adapter and display does not show raised and lowered letters. The characters are printed as raised and lowered characters only when the printer is capable of supporting the features. To find out whether your system can produce superscript or subscript characters, consult your computer and printer manuals.

You turn on superscript with some commonly used printers by pressing Alt-F10, then holding down Alt and typing *244* on the numeric keypad. (Don't use the number keys across the top of the keyboard.) You then type the characters you want to appear as superscript. To disable the superscript feature, press Alt-F10, then hold down Alt and type *245*. Note that these instructions may not control superscript printing for your particular printer. Consult your printer manual to determine the proper codes.

An example of coding for superscript is shown in figure 6.6. The special character symbols before the *V* and after the *e* in *Vice* indicate where the codes have been entered. When the form is printed, the codes will not appear.

```
               TITAN TECHNOLOGY SALES LEAD TRACKING SYSTEM
                                           File Name -- SlsLead
      LastName: Samson                 FirstName: Frank
      Title: [Vice]president      [Note: Vice prints as superscript]
      Company: ▓Prof.▓ Labs [Subscript]▓   Telephone:
      Address1:
      Address2:
      City:                        State:           Zip:
        No. of Labs:               Annual Revenue:
        Current Customer:          Company Priority:
                            ─────LEAD INFORMATION────────────────────
        Product Interest:
        Request For:               Lead Source:
```

Fig. 6.6.   *Using the superscript and subscript features.*

With many printers, you turn on the subscript feature by pressing Alt-F10, then holding down Alt and typing *246*. Again, be sure to use the numeric keypad. After you type the information you want to appear as a subscript, turn off subscript by pressing Alt-F10, then holding down Alt and typing *247*. In figure 6.6, the noncharacter subscript code used to turn on the feature appears before the first *P* in *Prof.*; the ending code is after the period. The codes will not appear on the printout. Again, the particular code for your printer may differ from these examples. Consult your printer manual for details.

With ASCII codes, you can enter virtually any character or symbol into a File database. A musical note (♪) is Alt-270, for example; the symbol pi (π) is Alt-227; a plus-or-minus sign ($\pm$) is Alt-241. Use caution with this technique, however. Some display-monitor combinations may not display the characters properly, and your printer may not be capable of handling some characters.

Calculating in Forms

The capacity to perform mathematical calculations is one of the more advanced features of Q&A File. Whether you need to calculate a simple equation or a complex financial report, chances are that at some time you will need to use the calculation features of Q&A. In an inventory application, for example, you can calculate the selling price of items based on the wholesale price and a standard percentage markup. Or you can use Q&A's calculation feature to compute late charges, interest owed, or sales tax. These calculations reduce the amount of keyboard data entry required.

Chapter 7 gives a detailed explanation of how to add calculation and programming statements to your form; this section gives only a brief overview of setting calculation modes and solving one kind of calculation error that may take place after the statements have been entered.

If your form contains arithmetic formulas or program statements, Q&A can calculate the fields manually or automatically. Q&A's default is manual calculation; you have to press F8 (Calc) each time you want to calculate a field. If you want to change the setting to automatic recalculation, press Shift-F8. Q&A then displays the calculation menu across the screen (see fig. 6.7).

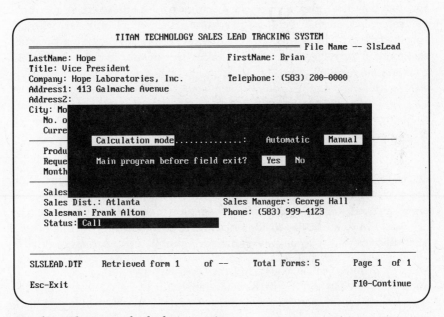

Fig. 6.7. The menu of calculation settings.

Press A to choose automatic recalculation. In automatic mode, Q&A calculates a field's program statement as soon as the cursor is moved out of that field. The process takes time and can slow your data entry. If you already have chosen the Automatic Calc setting and want to return to Manual Calc, press M.

During the calculation process, if the result of a calculation is too large for the specified field length, Q&A displays asterisks. You can eliminate the asterisks and display the number by redesigning the form so that the field can accept a number that large. Another way to solve the asterisk problem is to change the format of the field so that fewer digits are displayed after the decimal point. (Chapter 5 includes more information on redesigning a file and formatting values.)

One type of calculation error to watch for is the divide-by-zero calculation. Q&A displays an ERR message in the field when a calc statement issues a divide-by-zero calculation. Fields that refer to the ERR field interpret the ERR as a zero value. If the divide-by-zero calculation is an error in the program statement, change the statement by selecting the Program Form option from the Programming menu.

After you have entered the Program Form routine, you edit any programming statements with standard Q&A editing commands. Study any formulas to make sure that they have no explicit errors. A common mistake is to create a formula that references another field not programmed to accept only data within a specified range. The way to correct this problem is to include a program statement in the referenced field that forces the operator to enter data within a range valid for the formula.

Retrieving and Updating Forms

An electronic database is similar to a paper-filing system and is used most often to search for and update information. With Q&A's searching capability, you easily can find forms by searching for information in any field. For example, you can use Q&A to locate the customers who are covered by the Atlanta district sales office or to display a list of all the parts supplied by a certain company.

When Q&A finds the data, you can tell the program how to display the data. For example, Q&A can sort information alphabetically by company name or list parts numerically by part number. After you have located the forms you need, you can update the information.

Searching the Database

The purpose of the search and the type of information for which you're searching do not affect the search procedure; it is the same every time.

Suppose that you need to find the sales lead forms for the Atlanta sales district. To find the forms, you first select Search/Update from the File menu. Q&A then prompts you for a file name. Enter the file name (*SLSLEAD*) and press Enter. The Retrieve Spec for the Sales Lead file then is displayed (see fig. 6.8).

```
             TITAN TECHNOLOGY SALES LEAD TRACKING SYSTEM
=========================================================== File Name -- SlsLead
LastName:███████████████████████   FirstName:
Title:
Company:                           Telephone:
Address1:
Address2:
City:                              State:          Zip:
   No. of Labs:                    Annual Revenue:
   Current Customer:               Company Priority:
────────────────────────────LEAD INFORMATION────────────────────
   Product Interest:
   Request For:                    Lead Source:
   Months to Purchase:             Product Priority:
────────────────────────────SALES ACTION──────────────────────
   Sales Priority:                 Date Entered:
   Sales Dist.:                    Sales Manager:
   Salesman:                       Phone:
   Status:


─────────────────────────────────────────────────────────────────
SLSLEAD.DTF                   Retrieve Spec              Page 1  of 1

Esc-Exit   F1-Help   F6-Expand   F8-Sort   Alt+F8-List  ↑F8-Save   F10-Continue
```

Fig. 6.8.   *Retrieve Spec for the Sales Lead file.*

Q&A's search procedure sometimes is called *query by example* (QBE) or *query by form* (QBF). Instead of entering commands (LOCATE FOR SALES DIST. = ATLANTA, for example), you type the information for which you want Q&A to search in the fields you want searched. Simply move the cursor to the field you want to use in the search, and enter the search data. You can use any combination of upper-and lowercase letters. Q&A retrieves forms even when the case you type in the Retrieve Spec is different from the original. In this example, *Atlanta* is entered in the Sales Dist. field (see fig. 6.9). If you want the retrieved fields to be sorted, you have the option of accessing the Sort Spec, which is discussed later in this chapter.

You can save the filled-in Retrieve Spec and run the same search again later, without having to retype the search restrictions, by using the following steps:

1. Fill in the Retrieve Spec, then press F8 (Save).

2. At the prompt, type a name for the saved spec, and press Enter to return to the Retrieve Spec screen.

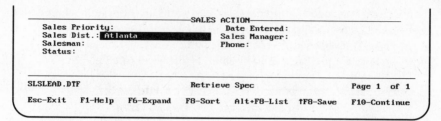

```
                          ─────SALES ACTION─────
   Sales Priority:                    Date Entered:
   Sales Dist.: Atlanta               Sales Manager:
   Salesman:                          Phone:
   Status:



   SLSLEAD.DTF                   Retrieve Spec              Page 1  of  1

   Esc-Exit    F1-Help    F6-Expand    F8-Sort    Alt+F8-List   ↑F8-Save    F10-Continue
```

Fig. 6.9.   *Filling in the Retrieve Spec.*

3. To recall the saved spec later, press Alt-F8 at the Retrieve Spec field to view the list of stored specs.

4. Move the cursor to the desired spec, and press Enter. You also can print the Retrieve Spec for reference purposes. At the Retrieve Spec screen, press F2 to display the Spec Print Options screen. Be sure to set the Print Field Labels? option to Yes.

For now, complete the Retrieve Spec as shown in figure 6.9, and press F10 to start the search procedure. Q&A searches the database, retrieves the forms that match the Retrieve Spec, and displays the first of the forms (see fig. 6.10).

```
              TITAN TECHNOLOGY SALES LEAD TRACKING SYSTEM
   ══════════════════════════════════════ File Name -- SlsLead
   LastName: Hope                    FirstName: Brian
   Title: Vice President
   Company: Hope Laboratories, Inc.  Telephone: (583) 200-0000
   Address1: 413 Galmache Avenue
   Address2:
   City: Mobile                      State: AL      Zip: 33933
      No. of Labs: 14                Annual Revenue: $50,000,000.00
      Current Customer: Y            Company Priority: 1
   ─────────────────────────LEAD INFORMATION─────────────────
      Product Interest: 1500;1800
      Request For: Demo              Lead Source: Phone
      Months to Purchase:            Product Priority:
   ─────────────────────────SALES ACTION─────────────────────
      Sales Priority: 1.0            Date Entered: Apr 19, 1989
      Sales Dist.: Atlanta           Sales Manager: George Hall
      Salesman: Frank Alton          Phone: (583) 999-4123
      Status: Call



   SLSLEAD.DTF   Retrieved form 1   of --    Total Forms: 5    Page 1  of  1

   Esc-Exit    F1-Help    Alt+F6-Table    F7-Search    F8-Calc    F10-Continue
```

Fig. 6.10.   *The form found as a result of the search operation.*

When the form has been found and displayed, you can make any changes you want. You use the function keys to perform a variety of operations, as shown in table 6.2.

Table 6.2
Function Keys in Q&A File

Key	Function
F1	Displays help screen
F2	Prints current form
F3	Deletes current form
Alt-F6	Displays (in a 5-column table) up to 17 forms
F7	Returns to Retrieve Spec for review or edit
F8	Calculates current form
F9	Displays preceding form
F10	Displays next form
Shift-F10	Saves changed form

Retrieving Forms

Q&A gives you a great deal of flexibility in finding the forms you need. By using the Retrieve Spec, you can retrieve one form, a group of forms, or all forms. You can elect to retrieve forms based on the common value of a piece of information, a range of information, or several pieces of information. You also can use calculations and programming expressions to retrieve forms.

The procedure for retrieving all forms is the easiest of the three: press F10 without entering anything on the Retrieve Spec screen. You then can look through all the forms in the database. Press F9 to show the preceding record or F10 to show the next record.

To retrieve one form, you must enter in the Retrieve Spec a piece of information only that form contains. For example, a customer's name, a part number, or the title of a book is likely to appear on only one form and therefore can help you locate a specific record.

Figure 6.11 shows how to find the form containing information about Mountain Labs. As you can see, Mountain Labs is entered in the Company field. When Q&A searches through the SLSLEAD file, the program finds only one form containing this company; therefore, only that form is retrieved (see fig. 6.12).

```
                TITAN TECHNOLOGY SALES LEAD TRACKING SYSTEM
                                          File Name -- SlsLead
     LastName:                    FirstName:
     Title:
     Company: Mountain Labs       Telephone:
     Address1:
     Address2:
     City:                        State:        Zip:
        No. of Labs:              Annual Revenue:
        Current Customer:         Company Priority:
                          ──LEAD INFORMATION──
        Product Interest:
        Request For:              Lead Source:
```

Fig. 6.11.   *The SLSLEAD file with Retrieve specification.*

```
                TITAN TECHNOLOGY SALES LEAD TRACKING SYSTEM
     ══════════════════════════════════════ File Name -- SlsLead
     LastName: Blackson             FirstName: Jeff
     Title: Operations Manager
     Company: Mountain Labs         Telephone: (803) 911-4321
     Address1: 300 10th Avenue
     Address2:
     City: Boulder                  State: CO        Zip: 80105
        No. of Labs: 3              Annual Revenue: $14,795,321.00
        Current Customer: Y         Company Priority: 1
                          ──LEAD INFORMATION──
        Product Interest: 1500;2000
        Request For: Info              Lead Source: Mailing
        Months to Purchase: 3          Product Priority: 1
                          ──SALES ACTION──
        Sales Priority: 1.0            Date Entered: Jun 6, 1988
        Sales Dist.: Denver            Sales Manager:
        Salesman: Allport              Phone: (   )   -
        Status: Sale;2000


     ──────────────────────────────────────────────────────────
     SLSLEAD.DTF    Retrieved form 1    of --    Total Forms: 5      Page 1  of 1

     Esc-Exit    F1-Help    Alt+F6-Table    F7-Search    F8-Calc    F10-Continue
```

Fig. 6.12.   *The form found as a result of the search.*

At times, you may need to specify more than one value on a Retrieve Spec. For example, suppose that you need to see all sales leads which have three or more laboratories and have annual revenues greater than $5 million. To specify these searches, you enter *>=3* in the No. of Labs field and *>5000000* in the Annual Revenue field (see fig. 6.13). When Q&A searches the file, the program selects only the forms that meet the criteria (see fig. 6.14).

Note: If you suspect mismatched data in one or more data fields of forms you want to find (text instead of a date, for example), precede the search

specification with a right (closing) bracket ( ]). This code tells Q&A to search
for this information even though a data type mismatch occurs.

Fig. 6.13. *Retrieving forms based on more than one value.*

Fig. 6.14. *The form retrieved as a result of the search.*

Using Ranges To Retrieve Forms

Although you frequently will need to find and display individual forms that
meet certain criteria, you probably will use Q&A most often to display a group
of forms that share a common value. When you retrieve forms, you can enter

a specific item in a Retrieve Spec, as previously explained, or you can enter a range that is common to a group. For example, you can have Q&A display the records for sales prospects with ZIP codes between and including 94086 and 95997 by entering *>=94086..<=95997* in the Zip field of the Retrieve Spec form.

When you tell Q&A to retrieve a group of forms that have values within a range, the range type can be specified as money, numeric, text, keyword, date, or time. With Q&A, you also have the option of selecting a range that includes all types of information.

In figure 6.15, you see an example of a numeric range. The search criterion has been entered in the Annual Revenue field; all records that have entries between $5 million and $10 million in this field will be retrieved. A numeric range is specified by separating the low and high figures by two dots. Note the difference in searching a numeric range and a text range. The ZIP code search example is for a text-formatted field. If the ZIP code field was formatted as numeric, the search criteria would be simpler: 94086..95997. However, ZIP code values with numeric formatting limit you because you cannot enter the four-digit extension common with some ZIP codes without getting a Q&A error message.

```
              TITAN TECHNOLOGY SALES LEAD TRACKING SYSTEM
                                              File Name -- SlsLead
        LastName:                    FirstName:
        Title:
        Company:                     Telephone:
        Address1:
        Address2:
        City:                        State:        Zip:
           No. of Labs:              Annual Revenue: 5000000..10000000
           Current Customer:         Company Priority:
                           LEAD INFORMATION
        Product Interest:
        Request For:                 Lead Source:
        Months to Purchase:          Product Priority:
```

Fig. 6.15. *Retrieving on a numerical range.*

Using a keyword range, you can specify the retrieval of all sales leads that have the value Mail or Telephone in the Lead Source field (see fig. 6.16). Separate multiple keyword specifications with semicolons (;).

Another example of a range is an alphabetical range. You can, for example, retrieve all sales leads that have in the Company field names beginning with the letters A through M. Specify *A..<N* indicates A through "less than" N (see fig. 6.17). Separate the alphabetical range with two dots. This example demonstrates the use of the less-than conditional operator (<) to mean "letters before N." You also can specify A..M and get the same results.

```
              TITAN TECHNOLOGY SALES LEAD TRACKING SYSTEM
                                        File Name -- SlsLead
LastName:                      FirstName:
Title:
Company:                       Telephone:
Address1:
Address2:
City:                          State:        Zip:
   No. of Labs:                Annual Revenue:
   Current Customer:           Company Priority:
LEAD INFORMATION─────────────────────────────────────────
   Product Interest:
   Request For:                Lead Source: Mail;Telephone
   Months to Purchase:         Product Priority:
SALES ACTION──────────────────────DATES──────────────────
   Sales Priority:             Date Entered:
   Sales Dist.:                Date Info Sent:
   Salesman:                   Sales Contact:
   Status:                     Demo Date:


SLSLEAD.DTF              Retrieve Spec            Page 1  of 1

Esc-Exit  F1-Help  F6-Expand  F8-Sort  Alt+F8-List  ↑F8-Save  F10-Continue
```

Fig. 6.16.   Retrieving on a keyword range.

```
              TITAN TECHNOLOGY SALES LEAD TRACKING SYSTEM
                                        File Name -- SlsLead
LastName:                      FirstName:
Title:
Company: A..<N                 Telephone:
Address1:
Address2:
City:                          State:        Zip:
   No. of Labs:                Annual Revenue:
   Current Customer:           Company Priority:
──────────────────────LEAD INFORMATION───────────────────
   Product Interest:
```

Fig. 6.17.   Retrieving on an alphabetical range.

Notice that searching for a range of values beginning with certain letters or numbers requires that you use special operators. (See the following section for lists and examples of search operators.)

Q&A gives you considerable freedom in developing your own retrieval specifications. Use your imagination. You will not damage the program or your database. If you go beyond the limitations of the program, Q&A displays a warning message and asks whether you want to check or change your specifications. Select Yes if you want to try again, and you are returned to the Retrieve Spec screen. Select No if you want to return to the File menu.

Using Wild Cards

Q&A recognizes two wild-card symbols: two dots and the question mark. As in DOS, the question mark is a substitute for any single character. The two dots (similar to the DOS asterisk) mean anything from the location of the dots to the end of the specification. For example, you can search for any date between and including the 20th and 29th of the month (05/2?/88); any last name beginning with John (John.. retrieves Johnson, Johnston, Johnstone); first names that begin with T (T.. finds Ted, Tom, Thad, Tad); or any word that begins with T and ends with m (T..m locates Tom, tam, tram, Transam).

Using wild-card searches is useful when you forget someone's exact name or when you want a narrow search range. Wild cards also reduce the number of keystrokes you have to enter if you are familiar with the database and know that you can get predictable results without entering the complete search spec. In this case, think of wild cards as abbreviations.

If you want to use wild cards in your retrieval specifications, you can use the following formats:

Wild Card	Meaning	Example
X..	Begins with X	b..
..X	Ends with X	..a
X..Y	Begins with X and ends with Y	b..a
..X..	Includes X	..n..
?	Any character	?
..X..Y..Z	Includes X and Y and Z	..b..n..a

The following list shows how you can use wild-card operators to search for keywords:

Use the operator	To find
a?	At, am, an
..a..	Bat, transamerica, aardvark
???d	Find, fond, toad
..e	Ape, mandate, George
?i..	City, hide
..i??	Mention, bring, write
h..n	Horn, Hohenzollern
P.. j..	Peggy Johnson

Q&A's range of options for retrieving data is impressive, particularly when compared with retrieval options in other databases. Q&A has another advantage over many database packages: Q&A doesn't require that you program the special conditions for retrieving data; you can enter the specifications directly on the Retrieve Spec screen.

Using Retrieval Operators

The Retrieve Spec recognizes a range of symbols, called *retrieval* (or conditional) operators. You can enter these operators to specify the forms you want to retrieve. The following text explains the retrieval operators available with Q&A. Remember, however, that in the following lists, X represents any field value—not a literal X.

Operators for Equal or Null Values. Use the following operators to locate equal or null values in a field:

Operator	Meaning	Example	Explanation
X	Equal to X	Denver	Finds exact match only
=X	Equal to X	=Denver	Finds exact match only
/X	Not X	/Denver	Finds everything except X
=	Empty	=	Finds empty fields; no value
/=	Not empty	/=	Finds any field with data

Operators for Greater- or Less-Than Values. The operators in the following list can be used to find values that are greater or less than a specification:

Operator	Meaning	Example
>X	Greater than X	>2000
<X	Less than X	<2000
>=X	Greater than or equal to X	>=2000
<=X	Less than or equal to X	<=2000
>X..<Y	Greater than X and less than Y	>2000..<4000
X..<Y	Greater than or equal to X and less than Y (numeric fields only)	2000..<4000
>=X..<Y	Greater than or equal to X and less than Y (text fields)	>=2000..<4000
>X..<=Y	Greater than X and less than or equal to Y	>2000..<=4000

Operators for And, Or, and Range of Values. The operators in this list can be used to specify either/or conditions or to determine a range of values in a field:

Operator	Meaning	Example
X;Y;Z	X or Y or Z	Chicago;New York
&X;Y;Z	X and Y and Z	& Chicago;Atlanta;New York

The & symbol can be used only in keyword fields, but x;y;z works in all fields.

Operators for Minimum and Maximum Values. Use the following operators to retrieve the highest or lowest values in a field:

Operator	Meaning	Example
MAX n	Retrieve *n* highest values	MAX5
MIN n	Retrieve *n* lowest values	MIN8

Only one of each of these specifications can be used on a Retrieval Spec. On text fields, MAX returns the highest alphabetical characters; MIN finds the lowest. These operators cannot be used on keyword fields.

Using Calculations in a Retrieval

Q&A enables you to use calculations as well as restrictions in a Retrieve Spec. You also can use programming expressions but not programming statements; you cannot enter an IF..THEN statement, for example. You can use any programming function except @NUMBER, @TOTAL, @AVERAGE, @COUNT, @MAXIMUM, @MINIMUM, @VAR, @STD, @MSG, @HELP, and @DITTO.

If you want to retrieve records in which circulation is greater than 10 percent of the population, for example, you can enter *Circulation: >{Population/10}.* Notice that all calculations and programming functions must be contained in braces ({}).

If you use a calculation in a Retrieve Spec, you can retrieve data held in separate databases by using the XLOOKUP functions. If you want to retrieve records for which Salary is greater than the Salary field in an external database called job2.dtf, and in which last names are identical, you can enter the following:

Salary: ={@XLOOKUP("job2.dtf",Last name, "Last name", "Salary")}.

If you make a mistake in formatting the retrieval statement, or if you use an expression that Q&A doesn't allow, the program displays an error message and positions the cursor at the mistake.

Retrieving Data Stored with a Template

When retrieving data stored with a template—phone numbers, for example—you should be aware that Q&A stores the data without the template formatting characters. For example, the phone number (415) 968-6502 would be stored as: 4159686502.

To retrieve data stored with a template, enter on the Retrieve Spec only the data itself and omit any formatting characters. To retrieve records containing phone numbers with a 415 area code, enter *415..* in the Retrieve Spec. Q&A displays the retrieved records with the formatting characters in place: (415) 963-6502, and so on.

Using Programming Statements in a Retrieval

Q&A Version 4.0 and later versions enable you to use programming expressions in a Retrieve Spec, which greatly increases the flexibility of database queries. For example, you can ask Q&A to look up the records for which a field's data matches the data in a field in an external file.

To retrieve records using programming statements, type the programming expressions in the appropriate fields, enclosed in braces ({}): *Salary: >={(Bonus Total*10)+10000}.*

Note that you may use only programming expressions that return a value. You cannot, for example, use such summary functions as @MIN or @SUM, which require a range of values to produce a result.

The following list shows the valid programming statements that may be used in retrievals:

Programming statement	Meaning
{@DATE}	The current date
{@TIME}	The current time
{@SUM(x,y,z)}	The sum of the values in fields x, y, and z
{@ABS(n)}	The absolute value of n
{@LOOKUP(...)}	The value returned by @LOOKUP
{@XLOOKUP(...)}	The value returned by @XLOOKUP
{Bonus Rate * 10}	The product of the field Bonus Rate times 10
{18-4}	The result of a calculation

Fields referred to in programming expressions must be referenced by name:

Current Salary: >={@SUM(Old Salary + Bonus + Comp)}

Sorting Forms before Retrieving

Q&A retrieves forms in the order they were entered. You frequently may want to sort the forms in some different order. Q&A has the capability to sort forms on one or more fields in ascending or descending alphabetical or numerical order.

When more than one field is being sorted, the first field sorted is the *primary sort*, and the other fields are the *secondary sorts*. The order in which fields are sorted makes a big difference as to how the sort turns out.

When the State field is the primary sort and the City field is the secondary sort, for example, the forms are sorted in the following order:

Form	State	City
1	Alaska	Fairbanks
2	Alaska	Nome
3	Colorado	Colorado Springs
4	Colorado	Denver
5	North Carolina	Charlotte

When the City field is the primary sort and the State field is the secondary sort, the cities are sorted first, and then the states are sorted within the cities. The resulting order is:

Form	City	State
1	Charlotte	North Carolina
2	Colorado Springs	Colorado
3	Denver	Colorado
4	Fairbanks	Alaska
5	Nome	Alaska

Suppose that you want the sales leads retrieved by the alphanumeric search in figure 6.17 to be sorted in alphabetical order. From the Retrieve Spec screen, press F8; Q&A displays the file form in the Sort Spec screen. You then move the cursor to the Company field and type *1* in the field you want to be sorted first. If you want another field sorted (the State field, for example), you enter *2* in that field. You can sort all the fields on a form if you like, and you can have up to 512 different sort levels, which is probably more sorting flexibility than you will ever need.

After you specify sort order, indicate how you want the field to be sorted: ascending or descending. Use *AS* to specify an ascending sort or *DS* to specify a descending sort.

Figure 6.18 shows how the Company and State fields are coded to specify sort order. The Company field is the primary sort and will be sorted in ascending order. The State field is the secondary sort and also will be sorted in ascending order.

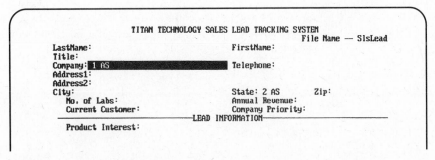

Fig. 6.18. *Filling in the Sort Spec.*

To save the current Sort Spec for later use, press Shift-F8 (Save), and type a name. To retrieve an existing stored Sort Spec, press Alt-F8, move the cursor to highlight the desired spec, and press Enter.

Press F10 when you finish with the Sort Spec. Q&A then retrieves the specified forms and displays them in the sort order you have indicated.

To print a copy of the filled-in Sort Spec, press F2 to display the Spec Print Options screen. Be sure to set Print field labels? to Yes. Press F10 to send a copy of the Print Spec to your printer.

Viewing Forms in a Table

Q&A displays forms one at a time in Search/Update mode. To display data from multiple forms simultaneously in a table, enter the Sort Spec, press F10, and press Alt-F6. You can display up to 17 forms simultaneously in Table View (see fig. 6.19). Each row in the table displays the first five fields in a form. All fields in a record are displayed, five at a time. To view fields that extend beyond the right side of the screen, use the arrow keys, Tab, and Shift-Tab to move between fields.

LastName	FirstName	Title	Company	Telephone
Hope	Brian	Vice President	Hope Laborator→	(583) 200-0000
Hamilton	Robert	Vice president	Cherry Electro→	(415) 452-4488
Blackson	Jeff	Operations Man→	Mountain Labs	(803) 911-4321
Tango	Likado	General Manager	Franklyn Lab A→	(215) 879-6435
Franklyn	Albert	Vice president	Advanced Medic→	(615) 323-7899

```
SLSLEAD.DTF      Retrieved record 1      of 5          Total records: 5

Esc-Exit  F1-Help      { ↓ ↑ Home End PgUp PgDn }-Navigate        F10-Show form
```

Fig. 6.19. *The Table View of a database.*

When you are in Table View mode, you can scroll the display of forms by pressing the up- and down-arrow keys. If you want to display an entire form, highlight the first field of the form, and press F10 or Alt-F6. Press Alt-F6 to return to Table View after you have finished examining the form. The Table View feature makes looking through forms selectively an easy procedure.

You may edit any field displayed in Table View. To change the data in a field, simply move the cursor to the field and begin typing. Note, however, that you cannot add new records in Table View. To edit a field that is longer than the 15 characters displayed on-screen, press F6 to display the Field Editor. Multiuser systems users should be aware that Q&A does not lock a record until you begin to edit.

While Table View is displayed, all customizing and programming functions that you have set up for the file remain active, including templates, restrictions, programming functions, and navigation statements that automatically move the cursor between fields. When a navigation statement moves the cursor to a field that is not included in Table View—because you haven't included the field when customizing the Table View Spec—Q&A returns you to Form View.

Customizing which fields are displayed in Table View is a straightforward process. Because of Q&A's flexibility, you can arrange the columns in any fashion you choose. While in Form View, press Shift-F6; you also can press Shift-F6 while in Table View.

You see the Table View Spec shown in figure 6.20. You can number as many fields as you want; the fields are displayed in Table View in the numerical order you have selected. (Q&A's default numbering is by tens.) In figure 6.20, the Spec is numbered to show the FirstName, LastName, Title, Company, and Telephone fields, in that order. After you set the order, press F10. Figure 6.21 shows the Table View with the columns arranged as specified in the Table View Spec.

```
                    TITAN TECHNOLOGY SALES LEAD TRACKING SYSTEM
                                                    File Name -- SlsLead
    LastName: 2                        FirstName: 1
    Title: 3
    Company: 4                         Telephone: 5
    Address1:
    Address2:
    City:                              State:          Zip:
       No. of Labs:                    Annual Revenue:
       Current Customer:               Company Priority:
    LEAD INFORMATION
       Product Interest:
       Request For:                    Lead Source:
       Months to Purchase:             Product Priority:
    SALES ACTION                DATES
       Sales Priority:          Date Entered:
       Sales Dist.:             Date Info Sent:
       Salesman:                Sales Contact:
       Status:                  Demo Date:


    SLSLEAD.DTF              Table View Spec              Page 1 of 1

    Esc-Exit    F1-Help   Alt+F8-List specs  Shift+F8-Save specs  F10-Table View
```

Fig. 6.20. *Numbering fields on the Table View Spec.*

Figure 6.22 shows a Table View for which the FirstName and LastName fields are numbered 1 and 2 on the Table View Spec. Those fields always are displayed as columns 1 and 2 when F6 is pressed in Form View. In this case, however, the highlighter was first moved to the City field to select City as the last column in the table.

When using Search/Update, you can edit the form's information blanks and change or add information. The same editing keys and functions are available as when you are adding and editing information. (See Chapter 10 for a description of editing keys and procedures.) When you finish editing a form, press F10 to save the form and display the next one.

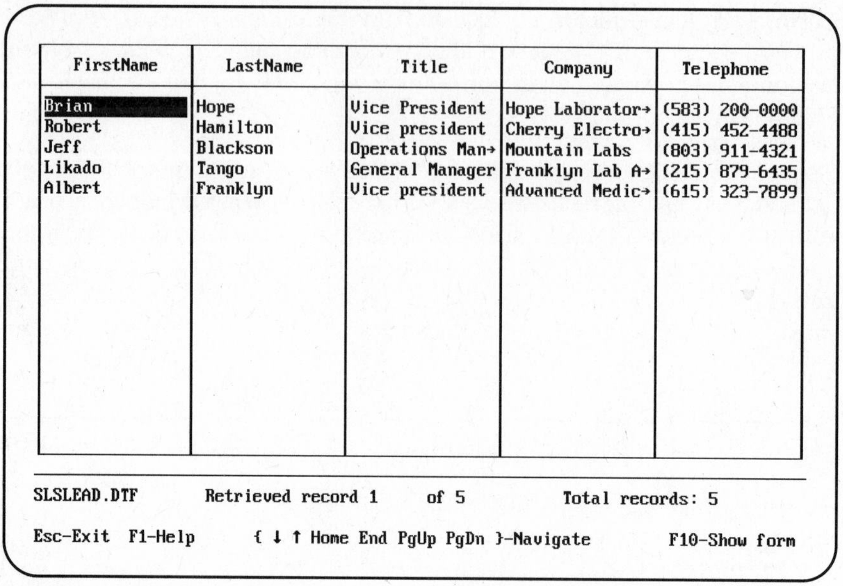

FirstName	LastName	Title	Company	Telephone
Brian	Hope	Vice President	Hope Laborator→	(583) 200-0000
Robert	Hamilton	Vice president	Cherry Electro→	(415) 452-4488
Jeff	Blackson	Operations Man→	Mountain Labs	(803) 911-4321
Likado	Tango	General Manager	Franklyn Lab A→	(215) 879-6435
Albert	Franklyn	Vice president	Advanced Medic→	(615) 323-7899

SLSLEAD.DTF   Retrieved record 1   of 5   Total records: 5

Esc-Exit F1-Help   { ↓ ↑ Home End PgUp PgDn }-Navigate   F10-Show form

Fig. 6.21.   *The Table View as specified on the Table View Spec.*

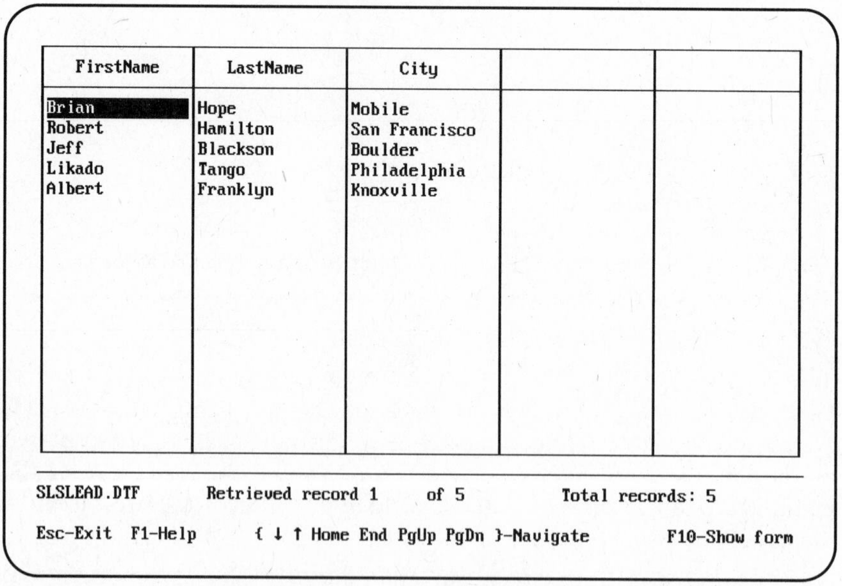

FirstName	LastName	City		
Brian	Hope	Mobile		
Robert	Hamilton	San Francisco		
Jeff	Blackson	Boulder		
Likado	Tango	Philadelphia		
Albert	Franklyn	Knoxville		

SLSLEAD.DTF   Retrieved record 1   of 5   Total records: 5

Esc-Exit F1-Help   { ↓ ↑ Home End PgUp PgDn }-Navigate   F10-Show form

Fig. 6.22.   *Displaying the City field as the final column.*

Mass-Updating Forms

Suppose that you have an inventory database that contains 250 records, and you need to update the Price field to reflect a three-percent price increase. The task would be time-consuming if you had to update each form individually. With Q&A's Mass Update command, you can update all the forms simultaneously.

Using Mass Update is a three-step process. After you select Mass Update from the File menu and indicate which database file you want to update, you use the Retrieve Spec to select the group of forms to be updated. If you want to update all forms, press F10. Q&A displays an Update Spec screen so that you can enter the information for changing or adding data. You have the option of confirming each field to be updated. After you confirm the fields, the forms are updated.

Retrieving Forms for a Mass Update

The Sales Lead example illustrates the mass-update procedure. The procedure is useful, for example, in a campaign to increase sales. Suppose that the Sales VP has designated certain sales leads as "hot" leads and plans to offer bonuses if the leads are sold. The boss considers "hot" leads to be the companies that meet two criteria:

- The company has more than three laboratories.
- The company has promised to buy within two months.

Your task is to locate and update the records for these companies. The first step is to retrieve the forms to be updated. Select the Mass Update option from the File menu. After you enter the file name and press Enter, the Retrieve Spec screen is displayed.

If all the forms will be updated, you can press F10; Q&A retrieves them all. For this example, however, you need to enter retrieve specifications. Move the cursor to the No. of Labs field and type > =3. This entry tells Q&A that you want to retrieve the leads which have three or more laboratories (see fig. 6.23).

Next, enter < =2 in the Months to Purchase field (see fig. 6.23). Q&A then retrieves the companies that have promised to make purchases within two months. When you press F10, Q&A finds the forms that meet both specifications and displays the Update Spec screen.

As with Search/Update, you can save the Retrieve Spec. Press Shift-F8 to name and save the spec. To display a list of saved specs, press Alt-F8.

```
              TITAN TECHNOLOGY SALES LEAD TRACKING SYSTEM
                                            File Name -- SlsLead
  LastName:                        FirstName:
  Title:
  Company:                         Telephone:
  Address1:
  Address2:
  City:                            State:          Zip:
     No. of Labs: >=3              Annual Revenue:
     Current Customer:             Company Priority:
  LEAD INFORMATION───────────────────────────────────────────
     Product Interest:
     Request For:                  Lead Source:
     Months to Purchase: <=2       Product Priority:
  SALES ACTION──────────────────DATES─────────────────────────
     Sales Priority:              Date Entered:
     Sales Dist.:                 Date Info Sent:
     Salesman:                    Sales Contact:
     Status:                         Demo Date:


  SLSLEAD.DTF              Retrieve Spec              Page 1  of 1

  Esc-Exit   F1-Help   F6-Expand   F8-Sort   Alt+F8-List  ↑F8-Save   F10-Continue
```

Fig. 6.23. *Filling in the Mass Update Retrieve Spec.*

Using the Update Spec for Mass Update

The Update Spec screen is used to update the fields. To enter the update specifications, move the cursor to the Sales Priority field and type *#1="Hot"*.

The pound sign and a number must be entered in every field that is to be updated or involved in calculations for the update. The pound sign indicates that a field number follows. Field numbers usually are sequential, but you may want to leave room between numbers for additions. An equal sign follows the number. Be sure to enter in quotation marks the text to be used in the update (see fig. 6.24).

```
                       ─SALES ACTION─────────────────
    Sales Priority: #1="Hot"            Date Entered:
    Sales Dist.:                        Sales Manager:
    Salesman:                           Phone:
    Status:


  SLSLEAD.DTF              Update Spec              Page 1  of 1

  Esc-Exit    F1-Help  F6-Expand  F8-Options  Alt+F8-List  ↑F8-Save  F10-Continue
```

Fig. 6.24. *Filling in the Mass Update Spec.*

If you plan to use calculations or programming functions in the update, use the format discussed in the section, "Using Calc Statements and Programming Functions," in Chapter 7. If you want to update a field that calculates sales commissions from sales, for example, you change the calculation by following the rules used for entering calculations in the Program Spec, which is accessed through the Program Form option from Q&A's Programming menu.

At the Update Spec, press Shift-F7 to the last Update Spec you filled in during the current Q&A session. (This trick doesn't work on networks.) You also can recall a stored Update Spec by pressing Alt-F8, or save the current spec by pressing Alt-F8.

After you complete the Update Spec, press F10 to begin updating the forms. Q&A displays a message that tells you the number of forms which will be updated and asks whether you want to confirm each update individually.

Selecting Yes to confirm each update usually is the better method. Select No if you want Q&A to proceed without displaying the forms to be updated. If you choose to confirm each update, Q&A displays each form so that you can update the form by pressing Shift-F10. You can continue through the forms by pressing F10. When all the selected forms have been updated, Q&A returns you to the File menu.

If you want to view the forms that have been updated, you can use the Search/Update option to retrieve them, move the cursor to the updated field, and press Alt-F6 to display the forms in Table View.

Copying Files

The File Copy command performs several functions:

- Copies a file design
- Copies a file design and IA information about the file
- Copies a file design and all or selected records
- Copies a file design and IA information and records

The Copy command helps you get extra benefits from your completed work: the file you designed, formatted, and customized, and the data you entered to build the database.

Copying File Designs and Forms

Unlike some other database products, Q&A enables designing file structure and designing forms to display file information as a single operation. When you specify field labels and field widths, you also are designing a form to view the data during entry or retrieval.

By using Copy, you can copy a file design (including the display form), give the design a new file name, make slight alterations, and have a new database—all in far less time than designing a new database takes.

Copying Form Designs

Remember that the form design includes the format of the form but not the data. You copy the form design of a customer list, for example, to create a new customer file containing some of the same fields and formats. You do not copy the data; you only use the copied form design to build a new database.

To copy a form design, you first select Copy from the File menu. Q&A prompts you for a file name. After you enter the file name and press Enter, Q&A displays the Copy menu (see fig. 6.25).

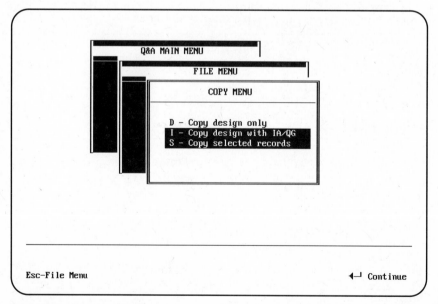

Fig. 6.25. *The Copy menu.*

Select Copy Design Only by pressing D and then pressing Enter. You again are prompted for a file name. Be sure to enter a name that is not used by another file, then press Enter. Q&A displays a message stating that the design is being copied and may take several minutes, depending on the length and complexity of the file design. When Q&A has completed the copy, the Copy menu is displayed again.

Copying a Design with Intelligent Assistant/ Query Guide Information

If you copy a design only, you do not copy any of the database information that you have taught the Intelligent Assistant/Query Guide. As you will learn in Chapters 17 and 18, you can teach the Intelligent Assistant/Query Guide (IA/QG) a great deal about your database: information about the fields, adjectives and verbs used with the fields, and ways to analyze the data and produce reports. If you copy the design only, IA/QG information is not available to the copied form.

Q&A enables you to copy the Intelligent Assistant/Query Guide information along with the file design. From the Copy menu, select the Copy Design with IA/QG option by pressing I. The procedure is the same as with the Copy Design Only option, but the IA/QG information also is copied. If you used the original design with the Intelligent Assistant/Query Guide and also want to use the copied design with the IA/QG, choose the second option on the Copy menu.

Copying Selected Records from Database to Database

The Copy command also can be used to duplicate and transfer whole or partial records from one database to another. This capability can be a significant time-saver. In the Sales Lead example, you need to transfer the company data from the sales lead file to the customer file when sales lead companies become customers. Using the Copy command is much faster than entering all the data by hand.

Two files are involved in a copy operation: the *source file* and the *destination file*. Q&A copies the data *from* the current source file *to* the destination file and places the copied records at the end of the destination database. This method means that your destination database must have at least a record (form) design (which could be copied from an existing database), although data does not need to be entered in any of the records.

In the Sales Lead application, prospects are tracked until a piece of equipment is sold; then the company becomes a customer, and the information must be copied to the customer file. Figure 6.26 shows the Customer List file form.

```
                      TITAN TECHNOLOGY CUSTOMER LIST
                  ════════════════════════════════════ File Name -- CustList
    LastName:█████████████████████████  FirstName:
    Title:
    Company:                            Telephone:
    Address1:
    Address2:
    City:                               State:        Zip:
                                                            _____

        No. of Labs:                    Annual Revenue:
        Products in Use:
        Sales Dist.:                    Salesman:
        Status:

        Notes:




    _____

    CUSTLIST.DTF                 Retrieve Spec              Page 1  of 1

    Esc-Exit   F1-Help   F6-Expand   F8-Sort   Alt+F8-List  ↑F8-Save   F10-Continue
```

Fig. 6.26. *The destination file: the customer list.*

With the Copy Selected Records option, you can copy data from database to database by copying all the data in selected records, by copying data from specified fields in all records, and by copying data from specified fields in selected records. All three copy operations can be accomplished by making slight variations in the same procedure.

To copy information from one database to another, first select Copy from the File menu. Q&A then prompts you for the file name of the source database. After you enter the source file name (SLSLEAD), press Enter; Q&A displays the Copy menu. Choose the Copy Selected Records option by pressing S; Q&A then prompts you for the destination database. Enter the name of the file to which the data will be copied (CUSTLIST) and press Enter. The Retrieve Spec for the source file is displayed.

You then can enter the specifications for the Retrieve Spec (see fig. 6.27). For this example, you want to copy the leads that have Status fields, including the keyword Sale, which indicates that equipment has been sold to those leads. To specify this choice on the Retrieve Spec, you enter *Sale* in the Status field information blank. If you want all these forms copied, you don't need to enter any other criteria on the Retrieve Spec. At this point, you can press F8 to access the Sort Spec. In this example, the forms do not need to be sorted in any particular order. To save the Retrieve Spec for later use, press Shift-F8; or to recall an existing saved spec, press Alt-F8.

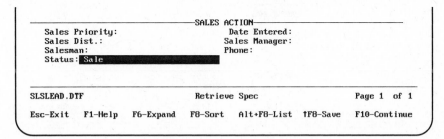

Fig. 6.27. *Filling in the Retrieve Spec for copying selected forms.*

When you have entered all the necessary specifications, press F10. Q&A displays the source database on the Merge Spec screen. If you prefer, you can skip filling out the Merge Spec. This omission causes the data in the first source field to be copied to the first destination field, the second to the second, and so on. You can use this procedure when you have two databases with identical record designs.

If you want to copy only part of the database, or if you want to copy information from a database that has a different record structure, you use the Merge Spec to specify the destination fields. Figure 6.28 shows the Merge Spec with specifications entered.

To use the Merge Spec, move the cursor to the source field that stores the data you want copied to the first field on the destination form. Type *1*. In this example, the first field on the destination form (LastName) happens to be the same as the first field on the source form. Q&A numbers the forms from left to right and from top to bottom.

Next, move the cursor to the source field for the second field and type *2*. Repeat the procedure until you have specified destination fields for all the source fields on your Merge Spec.

```
                      TITAN TECHNOLOGY SALES LEAD TRACKING SYSTEM
                     ═══════════════════════════════════ File Name -- SlsLead
   LastName: 1                         FirstName: 2
   Title: 3
   Company: 4                          Telephone: 5
   Address1: 6
   Address2: 7
   City: 8                             State: 9      Zip: 10
      No. of Labs: 11                  Annual Revenue: 12
      Current Customer:                Company Priority:
   ─────────────────────────────LEAD INFORMATION─────────────────────
      Product Interest:
      Request For:                     Lead Source:
      Months to Purchase:              Product Priority:
   ─────────────────────────────SALES ACTION──────────────────────────
      Sales Priority:                  Date Entered:
      Sales Dist.: 14                  Sales Manager:
      Salesman: 15                     Phone:
      Status:


   ────────────────────────────────────────────────────────────────
   SLSLEAD.DTF                  Merge Spec                 Page 1   of 1

   Esc-Exit   F1-Help    F3-Clear   Alt+F8-List   Shift+F8-Save  F10-Continue
```

Fig. 6.28.   *Filling in the Merge Spec.*

Note that the first 12 fields in these two files are in the same numerical positions. Field 13 in the customer list doesn't exist in the Sales Lead file. Sales Dist. and Salesman fields in the Sales Lead file fall in positions 14 and 15 in the new Customer file.

When you have completed the Merge Spec, press F10. Q&A begins the merge procedure and displays the source and destination databases in turn as each record is copied. When the records have been copied, Q&A displays a message to that effect and returns you to the File menu.

As a final step, select Search/Update from the File menu, and view the new Customer List file. This database has been created automatically by Q&A, requiring almost no time or effort on your part (see fig. 6.29).

Note: When Q&A copies data from one database field to another, the program pays no attention to labels, information types, or formats. Suppose that you tell Q&A to merge source field #1 with destination field #5, but you correctly should specify #4 as the destination. This error results in strange data in the destination file. Check labels, information types, and formats for the proper match if you get strange results after the data has been copied to the destination fields. If any factors don't match, redesign the destination form.

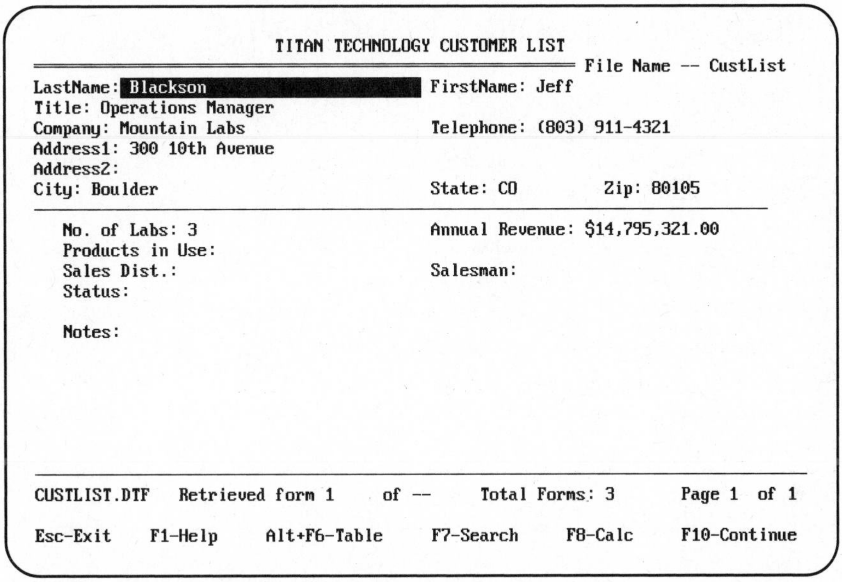

```
                    TITAN TECHNOLOGY CUSTOMER LIST
                                              File Name -- CustList
LastName: Blackson              FirstName: Jeff
Title: Operations Manager
Company: Mountain Labs          Telephone: (803) 911-4321
Address1: 300 10th Avenue
Address2:
City: Boulder                   State: CO        Zip: 80105

    No. of Labs: 3              Annual Revenue: $14,795,321.00
    Products in Use:
    Sales Dist.:               Salesman:
    Status:

    Notes:




CUSTLIST.DTF   Retrieved form 1    of --    Total Forms: 3    Page 1  of 1

Esc-Exit   F1-Help   Alt+F6-Table   F7-Search   F8-Calc   F10-Continue
```

Fig. 6.29. *The destination database with copied data.*

Deleting Data and Removing Forms from a File

With Q&A, you can delete data from a field, and you can remove forms from a file. Begin by making a backup copy of the file. To delete the contents of a field on the current form, position the cursor in the field and press Shift-F4. If you want to delete the current form, press F3. Q&A displays a window with a warning message asking whether you want to delete the form permanently. Make a selection in response to the prompt; then press Enter.

When you want to remove a group of forms from a file, you have two options. Using the Remove command is fast but risky because you aren't asked to double-check the forms that have been selected. The use of the Remove command has one restriction: all the forms must contain one or more pieces of information that are common to those forms only. If you use the Search command, however, you can press F3 to delete the form after you check it. This method is the slower but safer of the two methods.

Using the Remove Command

The Remove command makes deleting forms easy. Be careful, however; when you remove a form, it is gone forever. To delete forms with Remove, you can choose to remove selected records, remove duplicate records, or remove duplicate records and save them to an ASCII file.

For example, suppose that you want to remove from the Sales Lead file the forms that have been copied to the Customer List file. Each of these forms has the keyword Sale in the Status field. To remove these forms, select Remove from the File menu, specify a file name, choose Selected Records from the Remove Menu, and press Enter. Choose a file from the list of data files and press Enter. Q&A responds by displaying the Retrieve Spec.

Move the cursor to the field containing the information that appears in all the forms to be removed. In this case, the common field is the Status field. Next, fill in the Retrieve Spec by typing the data that is common to these forms.

If the field is a keyword field and you are entering several keywords, separate them with semicolons (;). Be sure to press F1 to display an on-screen explanation of how to retrieve the forms. Press F1 again for a table of the symbols available for your retrieval operation. Press Esc to return to the form, or press F10 to accept the Retrieve Spec, and then continue.

When Q&A displays the warning message asking you to confirm the removal of the forms, make your selection, and press Enter. Each form appears briefly on the screen just before that form is removed. After the forms have been removed, Q&A returns you to the File menu.

Removing Forms Manually

If you choose to remove the forms by using the Search option and pressing F3 (Delete Form), you first must retrieve the forms you want and then delete them manually.

From the File menu, select the Search/Update option, enter a file name, and press Enter. Q&A displays the file form in the Retrieve Spec. Move the cursor to the field containing the information that is common to the forms to be removed (the Status field, in this case).

Specify the common data items by typing them in the correct fields on the Retrieve Spec. If the field is a keyword field and you are entering several keywords, separate the keywords with semicolons (;). To save the Retrieve Spec for later use, Press F8 and enter a name for the spec. To recall a stored spec, press Alt-F8 and select from the list. Press F10 to save the Retrieve Spec and continue.

Q&A searches through the database, retrieves the forms that meet the retrieval specifications, and displays the first form that meets the criteria. When the form is displayed, you can delete it by pressing F3. Q&A asks for verification that you want to delete the form. After you make your selection, press Enter.

If you select Yes, Q&A removes the form from the database and displays the next form. You have to continue pressing F3, selecting Yes, and pressing Enter until all the forms are removed from the database. Q&A then returns you to the File menu.

Removing Duplicate Records

Duplicate records have the same data in one or more fields. Q&A can delete duplicate records permanently or remove the duplicates and store them in a separate file.

To remove duplicate records, retrieve the File menu, choose Remove, specify a file name, and choose Duplicate records. Q&A displays the Duplicate Spec. In each field that you want Q&A to check for duplicate data, press D or Del. If the fields you choose are indexed (speedy fields), the deletion procedure will be much faster. Press F10 to continue.

Saving Duplicate Records in a File

While removing duplicate records, Q&A keeps the first duplicate it finds and removes the rest. If you wish to retain certain duplicates—the records entered most recently, for example—you first can copy the database in date-sorted order, then work with the sorted file.

If you want to remove duplicates based on less clearly defined criteria, first save the duplicates in an ASCII file, then review the duplicates with Write. At the Remove menu, choose Duplicate Records to ASCII. Q&A prompts you for an ASCII file name. Fill in the Duplicate and Update Specs as described above.

Posting

The Post function saves time by taking data you enter just once and entering the same data automatically in a separate file. You can post any number of fields from the source file to the destination file in a single operation. Q&A can perform calculations on the data before entering it in the destination file and can execute programming statements in the target file.

Q&A cannot post from one file to several others. To update multiple files, you need to fill in a separate Posting Spec for each destination file and post the files separately. Before using Post, be sure that the source file already is updated with the data that you want transferred to the destination file.

To use the Post function, you must specify a key field for the source and destination files. The key fields must be the same type (text, date, etc.), and the key field in the target file must be indexed (a speedy field). To use the Post function, follow these steps:

1. Choose Post from the File menu. Q&A prompts you to enter the name of the source and target files (the files you will post from and to). If Q&A needs a password in order to open the destination file, it will request one.

2. Type the names of the files and press F10. Q&A displays the Retrieve Spec.

   Fill in the Retrieve Spec. You can recall a stored Retrieve Spec by pressing Alt-F8 and choosing a spec from the displayed list, or you can save the current Retrieve Spec by pressing F8 and giving the spec a name.

3. Press F10 to continue. Q&A displays the Posting Spec (see fig. 6.30). To recall a stored spec, press Alt-F8 and choose a spec from the list.

The Posting Spec tells Q&A which records to match in the source and target files and which field's contents in the source file should be posted to which field in the target file. The Posting Spec builds a statement of the form:

```
Post the value of field Company
...into the external field: Company
When the field: LastName
...matches the external field LastName.
```

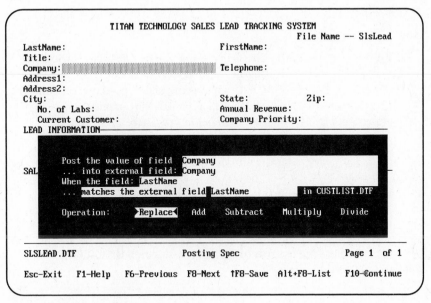

Fig. 6.30. *Filling in the Posting Spec.*

After filling in the prompts, you choose whether Q&A should replace the data in the external field with the new value, or add, subtract, multiply, or divide the data into the contents of the external field.

4. At the `Post the value of field` prompt, type the name of a field in the source file, or press Alt-F7 to display a list of fields; then move the cursor to a field, and press Enter.

5. Press F8 to move the cursor to the `...into external field:` prompt. Type the name of a field in the target file, or press Alt-F7 to view a list of fields; then move the cursor to a field name, and press Enter. To move the cursor back to the `Post the value of field` prompt, press F6.

6. Fill in the match fields (the fields that must contain exactly the same data in the source and target files). At the `When the field:` prompt, type the name of the match field in the source file. Or press Alt-F7 and choose a field name from the list.

7. At the `...matches the external field` prompt, type a field name, or press Alt-F7, and select from the list.

8. Move the cursor to the Operation: field and select Replace, Add, Subtract, Multiply, or Divide.

Repeat steps 4 through 8 for all fields you want posted to the target file.

9. Press F9 to specify the calculations that will be executed during the posting operation. These calculations will be executed in the destination file. You can have Q&A recalculate on record entry and on record exit statements, as well as calculation statements. Statements are not executed on field entry and exit.

   To save the filled-in spec for later use, press F8 and give the spec a name.

10. Press F10 to continue. Q&A displays a message: Your post spec has been saved. Do you want to execute this post now? Press Y to execute the spec or N to cancel.

11. Q&A displays the records of the source file, then displays the following message:

    Warning! 33 records will be posted. Do you want to confirm each post individually? (Press Esc to return to the Posting Spec.)

    Press Y to confirm records one at a time, or press N to have Q&A update all records without prompting.

Chapter Summary

After you have designed your Q&A database, using database files is easy for you and other users responsible for entering and updating information. Chapter 6 has introduced you to the commands and operations for using Q&A files. The Add Data command from the File menu is available for adding new forms to your database. Search/Update permits you to retrieve, sort, and change information in existing forms. The Mass Update command makes changing and adding information in a group of forms or the whole database easy. Remove helps keep your database free of duplicate records. The Copy command enables you to copy form designs and data.

Chapter 7 shows you how to customize and program File forms.

Customizing and Programming a File

The custom design features of Q&A File give you the opportunity to personalize your files with features that can save considerable time and work. The features are optional; if you are building a simple database, you may not need to use many or any of the features. On the other hand, you will benefit from Q&A's options for customizing a file if your database requires calculating numeric data from different fields or requires automatic entry of numbers, dates, and times. Custom file features also are an advantage when other users will be entering data; through the options described in this chapter, you can change the way fields and data are highlighted on-screen, design custom help screens, and program your database to accept only certain ranges of data. Q&A's customizing and programming features help you and others work more efficiently and easily.

This chapter explains how to customize a file with Q&A. In the following sections, you learn how to make data manipulation easy by adding custom features to your file form. The second part of this chapter explains a more advanced method of customizing your file—programming. With Q&A's programming features, you can program your form to perform certain tasks automatically. This capability takes Q&A far beyond many data-management programs available today.

For some of the customizing and programming examples in this chapter, a Veterinary Clinic file is used; the file tracks each pet owner's name and address and each pet's treatment history. This Veterinary Clinic file uses basic features that can be useful in many applications, including date arithmetic, money calculations, and services descriptions. In this chapter, you customize and program this file and learn some possibilities for your own file enhancement. Examples from the previous Sales Lead Tracking file also are used.

Customizing a Form

Before you can add custom features to a form, you need to call up a file. From the Design File menu, select Customize a File. Q&A then displays the Customize menu (see fig. 7.1).

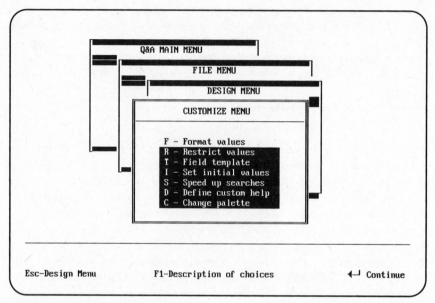

```
        ┌─────────────────────────────────────────┐
    ┌───│ Q&A MAIN MENU                            │
    ┌───│ FILE MENU                                │
    ┌───│ DESIGN MENU                              │
    │   │ CUSTOMIZE MENU                           │
    │   │                                          │
    │   │   F - Format values                      │
    │   │   R - Restrict values                    │
    │   │   T - Field template                     │
    │   │   I - Set initial values                 │
    │   │   S - Speed up searches                  │
    │   │   D - Define custom help                 │
    │   │   C - Change palette                     │
    │   └──────────────────────────────────────────┘

  Esc-Design Menu        F1-Description of choices        ↵ Continue
```

Fig. 7.1.   *The Customize menu.*

Even though a straightforward form to record only the names, addresses, and phone numbers of clients may be easy to create, the form can be difficult to use when you are entering information or when you want to review information already entered. The seven options from the Customize menu enable you to format values, restrict values, create field templates, set initial values, speed up searches, define custom help screens, and change the video display of your form. Whether you want to improve the appearance of the form or have Q&A check and format the data, this section explains how you can build on your original form to minimize your time and effort.

Changing a File's Palette

When you customize your file, you may want to begin by improving the video display of the form. By changing the file's palette (the way the form appears on-screen), you can select the different formats in which your form is displayed.

Q&A offers seven palettes. Each palette has different combinations of reverse video, underline, highlighting, color, and cursor display. (The underline capability appears only on monochrome monitors.)

To specify a palette, select Change Palette from the Customize menu. The current form is displayed. Use the F8 key to step forward through the available palettes, and the F6 key to move backward from palette to palette. As you change the palettes, the status line indicates which palette is displayed (see fig. 7.2). When a particular palette is shown on-screen, you can try out the palette by moving from field to field and entering data. The entries you make on this screen are erased when you leave the palette; the entries are for testing only. When the palette that you want to use is displayed, press F10 to select it. Each time you use the file form after that, the palette you selected is displayed.

```
                         TOP DOG VETERINARY CLINIC
                     4900 Westlake Ave., Mobile, AL 36609

   Client:                    Phone:              Date:
   Address:                   City:               St:    Zip:

   PATIENT NAME:              Breed:              Color:
   Sex:                       Weight:             Age:

   VACCINATION STATUS
       Rabies      Last vaccinated:      Next Vac:       Due Now:
       DHLP/Parvo  Last vaccinated:      Next Vac:       Due Now:
       Heartworm   Last vaccinated:      Next Vac:       Due Now:

   PATIENT SERVICES FOR:
       Office Visit:       Exam:              Amount:
       Vaccinations:                          Amount:
       Laboratory:                            Amount:
       Other Services:                        Amount:
       INVOICED:         PAID:        OVERDUE:          _____
       Statement Sent:        Client Called:       TOTAL:

   TDCLNC.DTF                     Palette 4 of 7            Page 1 of 1

   Esc-Exit        F6-Previous palette    F8-Next palette     F10-Continue
```

Fig. 7.2.   Changing the palette.

After you determine how you want the overall form to look, you can decide how to format individual data fields.

Formatting Field Information

The Format Values option from the Customize menu enables you to change field formatting on an existing file. By specifying information types, data formats, and global format options, you can make sure that data is entered in the correct format for each field. (See Chapter 5 for more information on formatting.)

When you select Format Values, Q&A displays the Format Spec screen. You can use this screen to change a field type (text, number, dates, yes/no, money, hours, and keywords) and to enter special format options for justification, case, decimal place, and forcing text data to uppercase, lowercase, or initial caps. (For more information on data types, see Chapter 2.)

Restricting Field Values

One of the best features of Q&A's customizing capabilities is the Restrict Values option on the Customize menu. By using this feature, you can have some control over the type of data that is entered in a field, thereby cutting down on data-entry errors and entry time. You simply tell Q&A what type of information to accept in a field, and the program alerts you when an incorrect entry is made.

Figure 7.3, for example, shows that the Product Interest keyword field is restricted to five entries: 700, 1500, 2000, 2400, and Other. You enter these values on the Restrict Spec screen.

```
                  TITAN TECHNOLOGY SALES LEAD TRACKING SYSTEM
                                                    File Name -- SlsLead
    LastName:                              FirstName:
    Title:
    Company:                               Telephone:
    Address1:
    Address2:
    City:                                  State:          Zip:
      No. of Labs:                         Annual Revenue:
      Current Customer:                    Company Priority:
    LEAD INFORMATION
      Product Interest: 700;1500;2000;2400;Other
      Request For: Info;Salesman;Demo;Oth→  Lead Source: Mail;Telephone;Referral→
      Months to Purchase:                  Product Priority:
    SALES ACTION                    DATES
      Sales Priority:                  Date Entered:
      Sales Dist.:                     Date Info Sent:
      Salesman:                        Sales Contact:
      Status: Sale;Postpone;700;1500;2→   Demo Date:


    SLSLEAD.DTF              Restrict Spec              Page 1  of 1

    Esc-Exit        F1-Help          F6-Expand field      F10-Continue
```

Fig. 7.3. *A field that contains restricted values.*

To enter a restricted value, select Restrict Values from the Customize menu. When the Restrict Spec screen appears, move the cursor to the field you want to restrict, and enter the restricted values. Separate individual values with a semicolon. After you finish, press F10 to return to the Customize menu.

The Restrict Values option doesn't *prevent* you—or anyone else—from entering other information into the field; Q&A just displays a warning message that the data entered is not one of the restricted values. When a warning appears, you have three options: you can change the value to meet the restrictions, press Enter to tell Q&A to accept the value, or press Alt-F7 to display a list of the possible values for the field.

If certain fields in your database should not be left blank, you can specify these fields as either *requested* or *required* fields. To *request* data input, type the following characters in the field information blank:

   /=

To *require* data in the field, type the following characters in the field information blank on the Restrict Spec screen:

   !/=

If you try to bypass a requested field without making an entry when entering information on the form, Q&A displays the prompt `This field requires a value. Please verify before continuing.` As with a restricted range specification, Q&A does not force you to place something in a requested field. If you press Enter after the warning, you can leave the field blank and go on to the next field. You may not, however, override a required field.

Requested and required fields should not contain other restrictions. For example, you may enter this field restriction:

   City: /=;Reno;Las Vegas

But North Lake Tahoe passes the /= ("not empty") restriction. A better way to format the restriction is as follows:

   City: !Reno;Las Vegas

Although this restriction format isn't given in the Q&A documentation, using this syntax prevents a blank entry and passes only the cities Reno and Las Vegas.

If you specify several restricted values on a form, you may have trouble remembering which values are restricted in which fields. To help you remember the restricted values you have specified, move the cursor into the field and press Alt-F7 to display a list of restrictions. You then can move the cursor to one of the possible field entries and press Enter, and Q&A inserts the value into the field for you.

Creating Field Templates

Field templates save you time by entering repeated formatting characters automatically. For example, if you use a telephone number field template, you can type *4159650292* and let Q&A add the formatting: (415) 965-0292.

Templates work only with text fields, but many "numerical" data types are stored most efficiently as text fields. For example, ZIP codes are sorted properly only if stored as text; and you probably would never need to sort telephone or Social Security numbers numerically.

You can use the following special template characters when you set up a template format:

Character	Function
# or 9	Specifies a single number (0 to 9)
@	Specifies a single alphabetic character (A to Z or a to z)
$	Specifies any typeable character
\	Tells Q&A that the following character is a "literal"; for example, \# tells Q&A to display a literal # on the form

To separate characters, use a space.

To set up a template, follow these steps:

1. From the Design File menu, choose Customize a File.

2. From the Customize menu, choose Field Template. Q&A displays the Field Template Spec.

3. Move the cursor to the field you want to format, and type the appropriate special template characters.

For example, to create a telephone number template, type the following:

(###) ###-####

A template can have no more than two characters separating data-entry characters. For example, 999--@@ is acceptable, but 999- - -@@ is not. Note, however, that programming functions and Mass Update override any character types you set up for templates, allowing alphabetic characters to be entered in a telephone number field, for example.

When using the Retrieve Spec to locate forms, you should enter only the raw data held in a template field. Omit the formatting characters; for example, to retrieve a telephone number, type *415..* or *4159650292*.

Setting Initial Field Values

One way to reduce your data-entry time is to have Q&A enter the data for you. By using the Set Initial Values option from the Customize menu, you can have Q&A enter preset values into any fields you want.

You use the Initial Values Spec to enter the information into the fields. Then, when you add a form to the file, that value is entered automatically in the field. You type the information once, and the information appears on every form. In the Sales Lead form, for example, an initial value has been entered in the Date Entered field (see fig. 7.4). In figure 7.5, you can see that the date has been entered automatically.

```
               TITAN TECHNOLOGY SALES LEAD TRACKING SYSTEM
                                             File Name -- SlsLead
     LastName:                  FirstName:
     Title:
     Company:                   Telephone:
     Address1:
     Address2:
     City:                      State:        Zip:
        No. of Labs:            Annual Revenue:
        Current Customer:       Company Priority:
     LEAD INFORMATION────────────────────────────────────────
        Product Interest:
        Request For:            Lead Source:
        Months to Purchase:     Product Priority:
     SALES ACTION───────────────────DATES─────────────────────
        Sales Priority:         Date Entered: @Date
        Sales Dist.:            Date Info Sent:
        Salesman:               Sales Contact:
        Status:                 Demo Date:

     SLSLEAD.DTF           Initial Values Spec        Page 1  of 1

     Esc-Exit        F1-Help        F3-Clear Spec     F10-Continue
```

Fig. 7.4.   Entering an initial value.

```
                  TITAN TECHNOLOGY SALES LEAD TRACKING SYSTEM
                                              File Name -- SlsLead
     LastName:                      FirstName:
     Title:
     Company:                       Telephone: (   )   -
     Address1:
     Address2:
     City:                          State:          Zip:
        No. of Labs:                Annual Revenue:
        Current Customer:           Company Priority:
     LEAD INFORMATION───────────────────────────────────────────
        Product Interest:
        Request For:                Lead Source:
        Months to Purchase:         Product Priority:
     SALES ACTION──────────────────────DATES───────────────────
        Sales Priority:        ,     Date Entered: Jan 1, 1992
        Sales Dist.:                 Date Info Sent:
        Salesman:                    Sales Contact:
        Status:                      Demo Date:


     ───────────────────────────────────────────────────────────
     SLSLEAD.DTF     New Record 1     of 1      Total Records: 1     Page 1  of 1

     Esc-Exit   F1-Help      F3-Delete form    F7-Search    F8-Calc   F10-Continue
```

Fig. 7.5. *The initial value entered automatically.*

To enter an initial value, select Set Initial Values from the Customize menu. Next, move the cursor to the fields you want, and enter the values. An initial value must conform to the field type of the field. Press F10 to return to the Customize menu.

You can have Q&A enter today's date, the current time, or a unique number, using the @DATE, @TIME, and @NUMBER functions. See the section on programming later in this chapter for instructions on how to use these functions.

When you enter data, if the initial value that appears is not what you want for that record, move the cursor to the field and press F4 to delete the information. You then can enter the correct information.

Speeding Search Procedures

By using Q&A's Speed-up Spec, you can decrease dramatically the time used by the program to search for records. You also can use this spec to verify that a field has a unique value.

A *speedup search* is Q&A terminology for a search through indexed fields. You create an index by extracting a field or fields from the records in a data file and storing this information in a separate location. When you retrieve records by searching these fields, the software then has to search only a portion of the record, reducing the time required to find the information you requested.

Note: Q&A suggests that you limit speedup search fields to only the minimum required to conserve time and storage space. Each time you update a record or add a new record, the speedup search field information must be extracted and stored in the proper place in the index. This procedure requires additional time and storage space.

To speed up your search procedures, select Speed Up Searches from the Customize menu. Move the cursor to the field for which you want to speed up searches, and press S. Then press F10 to return to the Customize menu.

If you want to make sure that a field accepts only a unique value (a value that has not been used in the same field on other forms), type *SU* in that field on the Speed Up spec. When you type information that has been used before into a field that has been designated unique, the following message appears:

```
This field should be unique. Please verify before continuing.
```

If you add a speedup search to one or more fields in your file, Q&A produces a special index file for these fields. The index file uses the same name as your main file but attaches an extension of IDX. Q&A uses this special file later to retrieve specified information as quickly as possible.

Creating a Custom Help Screen

In addition to the program's built-in help screens, Q&A gives you the option of defining your own custom help screens. This capability is particularly useful when the form is to be used by other people. A custom help screen can provide users with additional instructions and reminders about their data-entry tasks. For example, you can design a custom help screen to give instructions for entering data in a specific field or to remind users of restricted values that have been defined. You can define a custom help screen for each field on the form, and each screen can store six lines of up to 60 characters each.

To create a custom help screen, select Define Custom Help from the Customize menu. Q&A then displays your file form and the Help Spec. The cursor highlights the first field, indicating that a displayed help screen applies to that field.

Next, move the cursor by pressing F8 for the next field or F6 for the previous field. When the cursor is highlighting the appropriate field, type the text that you want to display on the help screen. If you want to move to another field after you finish defining the first help screen, press either F8 or F6. When you have written all the help screens that you need, press F10 to save the screens. Q&A then redisplays the Customize menu. You can return to the Help Spec at any time to create new help screens.

When you are adding or updating data, you can display a custom help screen by moving the cursor to the field and pressing F1 (see fig. 7.6). If you press F1 again, the Q&A help screen is displayed. (If no custom help screen has been assigned, the program displays the Q&A help screen the first time you press F1.) Pressing Esc removes the custom help screen from the display.

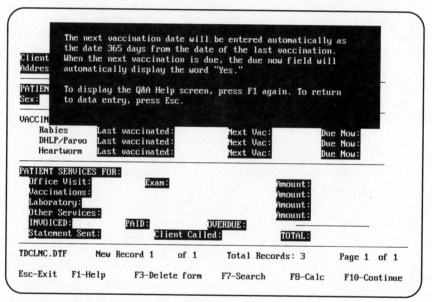

Fig. 7.6. *Displaying a custom help screen.*

Programming a Form

Programming is one of Q&A's most powerful customization features. You can program your form to retrieve and manipulate data, and can navigate through a form in accordance with special rules. The options on the Programming menu help you write programming statements to automate many routine data-entry procedures.

To display the Programming menu, follow these steps:

1. Press F at the Q&A Main menu to choose File.

2. At the File menu, press D to choose Design File.

3. At the Design menu, press P to choose Program a File.

4. At the Data file prompt, type the name of a file and press Enter, or press Enter to choose a file from the list.

Depending on the application, programming statements can be fairly simple or highly complex. The statements may involve no more than simple addition, subtraction, multiplication, or division of values from your database fields. But you also can use complex statements to test conditions, look up values from a lookup table or from one or more fields in a separate file, and automate the movement of the cursor from one field to another. Programming statements are grouped roughly into four categories of complexity, depending on the elements they contain: calculation statements, conditionals, functions, and table and form control commands.

The simplest programming statements are calculations consisting of mathematical and logical operators used in combination with numerical values, field names, or codes. The programming statement #9=(#3*Principle)/10 tells Q&A to multiply the value in field #3 by the value in the Principle field, divide the result by 10, and enter the result in field #9. Simple programming statements like this are used to calculate sales commissions, discount rates, and other data-dependent totals.

Complex programming statements can use commands for testing conditions and performing operations based on the existence of certain values. Suppose that you want Q&A to indicate in the Overdue field (which you have labeled #15) when payment is overdue on a customer account. If field TDate equals the current date and field LDate equals the date of last payment or when the obligation was made, you can use the following conditional operation in a programming statement:

   IF TDate=LDate+30 THEN #15="Yes"

A set of functions is available for use in programming statements. Functions are programming tools that usually combine many operations into a single statement or command. In procedural languages, a single function may call a program subroutine that contains hundreds of lines of code.

In Q&A, each programming function is preceded by the commercial "at" sign (@). For example, you can enter current dates and times automatically with the

@DATE and @TIME functions (#5=@DATE+30). Other types of @functions include mathematical functions (@SUM, for example), text functions (@LEFT(x,n), which extracts the leftmost *n* characters of the text string *x*, for example), and a function for numbering forms sequentially (@NUMBER).

You can use three other types of special commands in programming statements. First, a lookup command returns values from a lookup table that you have created; XLOOKUP returns values from an external file. Second, you can use less-than (<) and greater-than (>) symbols at the beginning of a programming statement to control when the statement is executed: either when the cursor moves into the field (<) or when the cursor leaves the field (>). The final programming commands move the cursor within a form (GOTO, CNEXT, and CHOME, for example).

In the following sections, you are given examples of programming statements that show how you can use all the elements available for your special applications.

Entering Program Statements

You program a form by writing programming statements, which are entered on the Program Spec screen. Q&A displays the Program Spec when you select the Program Form option from the Programming menu. You then can specify whatever programming statements you need in order to perform your calculations and automate your data-entry tasks.

On the form shown in figure 7.7, for example, most of the data is entered into fields automatically by programming statements. Very little data entry is necessary. The data in the Phone and Address fields is retrieved from a lookup table by a programming statement. (You also can use XLOOKUP to retrieve information from an external file.) The Amount field total is figured and inserted by a statement using a calculation formula.

Don't worry if you don't understand how the automatic data entry occurred in figure 7.7. The rest of this chapter explains in detail how programming statements are written and used in file forms.

The format of a programming statement is simple. Each statement contains a field name or ID number, a colon (:) or an equal sign (=), and the statement formula.

Note that you may use field names or ID numbers. Field ID numbers affect the way programming statements are executed, because Q&A always executes them in sequential, numeric order. Field names make programming statements much easier to understand. Named fields are executed in order from the top left to bottom right of the form.

A field ID number includes a pound sign (#) and an integer; the ID number identifies the field for use in programming statements. The field ID numbers are arbitrary, and a relationship doesn't exist necessarily between a number and the field position on the form. In fact, you may want to leave some numbers between sequential field IDs, to give you room to add additional programming statements later. Figure 7.8 shows a complex data-entry form with programming statements that use field numbers.

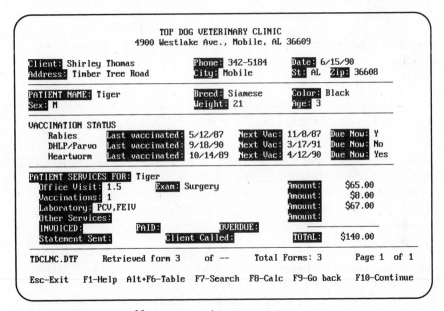

```
                    TOP DOG VETERINARY CLINIC
                4900 Westlake Ave., Mobile, AL 36609

Client: Shirley Thomas          Phone: 342-5184     Date: 6/15/90
Address: Timber Tree Road       City: Mobile         St: AL  Zip: 36608

PATIENT NAME: Tiger                  Breed: Siamese    Color: Black
Sex: M                               Weight: 21        Age: 3

VACCINATION STATUS
    Rabies      Last vaccinated: 5/12/87   Next Vac: 11/8/87  Due Now: Y
    DHLP/Parvo  Last vaccinated: 9/18/90   Next Vac: 3/17/91  Due Now: No
    Heartworm   Last vaccinated: 10/14/89  Next Vac: 4/12/90  Due Now: Yes

PATIENT SERVICES FOR: Tiger
Office Visit: 1.5       Exam: Surgery              Amount:      $65.00
Vaccinations: 1                                   Amount:       $8.00
Laboratory: PCV,FEIV                              Amount:      $67.00
Other Services:                                   Amount:
INVOICED:          PAID:           OVERDUE:
Statement Sent:        Client Called:             TOTAL:      $140.00

TDCLNC.DTF      Retrieved form 3    of --    Total Forms: 3    Page 1 of 1

Esc-Exit   F1-Help  Alt+F6-Table  F7-Search  F8-Calc  F9-Go back   F10-Continue
```

***Fig.* 7.7.** *Data entered by programming statements.*

The colon (:) separates the field ID from the statement that follows the ID. The statement can be a lookup command, a calculation that depends on logical conditions being met, or a highly complex logical statement using text and mathematical functions.

The equal sign (=) following the field ID indicates that a calculation will be made and the result entered into the field. For example, suppose that a field contains the programming statement #42=#37+22. The field ID #42 labels the field in which the statement is entered; Q&A adds 22 to the value in the field labeled #37 and enters the result in field #42.

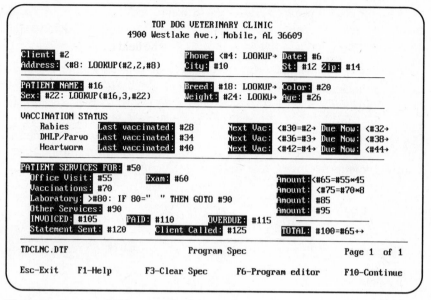

Fig. 7.8. Entering field ID numbers.

Incidentally, when programming statements become complex, printing the Program Spec gives you a convenient reference. Viewing a printed copy of the programming statements while you fill out the Navigation Spec also is helpful. Press F2 at the Program Spec to display the Spec Print Options screen. If you want to print field labels and expanded fields, be sure to set the corresponding options to Yes.

The sections that follow show you how to use Q&A's variety of programming statements.

Using Calculations in Programming Statements

For a basic form, you may have included fields that store text items (Client and Address fields, for example) and fields for numeric entries (such as charges for services). Q&A, however, can perform tasks beyond simple data-recording processes. You can include calculations in programming statements so that Q&A automatically computes and enters the results whenever you add or update a form.

Writing Calculation Statements

Each calculation statement contains three parts: the field ID number, an equal sign (=), and the formula. (The term *calculation statement* is used for convenience. A calculation statement is just a programming statement that contains a calculation.) You can add references to data in other fields in calculation statements, to save you the trouble of typing the data. For example, in the calculation statement #6=#4+14, Q&A adds 14 to the value in field #4 and then inserts the value into field #6.

Calculation statements can include operators for adding, subtracting, multiplying, and dividing data and also for comparing values. The following calculation operators are available with Q&A File:

Operator	Definition
+	Add
–	Subtract
*	Multiply
/	Divide
=	Equal to
^	Exponent
<	Less than
>	Greater than
<=	Less than or equal to
>=	Greater than or equal to
<>	Not equal to
AND	Both comparisons true
OR	Either comparison true
NOT	Reverses comparison's value

Note: This list contains the logical operators NOT, AND, and OR; these operators are explained in a later section, "Using Conditional Statements."

When you write calculation statements, you can use either upper- or lowercase letters. If the statement you are writing is too long to fit within the field width, press F6 to display the Program Editor screen (see fig. 7.9). In the Program Editor, you can use all the editing and formatting features available in Q&A's word processor. Press F10 to exit the Program Editor screen.

After you exit the Program Editor, the first part of the statement is displayed in the field, along with a right arrow indicating that the statement extends beyond the field. If you are entering the calculation statement on a field that has multiple lines, however, the statement can occupy the entire field, including the multiple lines.

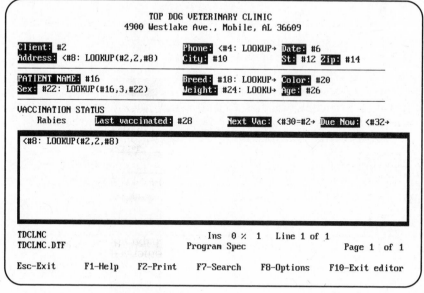

Fig. 7.9. *The Program Editor screen.*

You can include spaces in a calculation statement to make the statement more readable, but spaces are not necessary to make the calculation work.

The following examples illustrate how you can use field names, IDs, and operators in writing calculation statements:

Your Entry	*Q&A's Response*
Name=#2+#6	Add the contents of fields #2 and #6 and place the result in field Name
#9=#5/27	Divide the contents of field #5 by 27 and put the result in field #9
#10=#3	Copy the contents of field #3 into field #10

An example of a multiplication calculation statement is illustrated in the first Amount field of figure 7.10. Field #65 contains the statement #65=#55*45, which means "field #65 is equal to field #55 multiplied by 45."

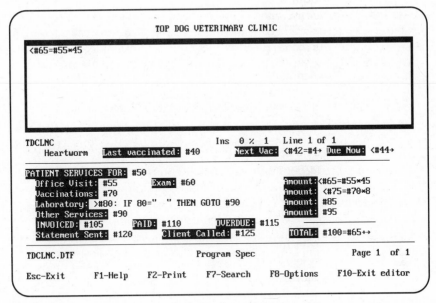

Fig. 7.10. *A multiplication calculation statement.*

Understanding the Order of Calculation in Programming Statements

Q&A calculates the operations in programming statements in a particular order, called the *order of precedence*. The following list shows the order of precedence in Q&A calculations:

Operator	Order of Calculation
( )	First
* /	Second
+ –	Third
< > <= >= <>	Fourth
NOT	Fifth
AND OR	Last

If more than one operator on the same line has the same order of precedence, Q&A calculates the statement from left to right. Calculations inside parentheses are processed according to the same rules as other statements. Q&A works inside out, beginning with the deepest set of parentheses. As a result, the structure of your statement can determine the results of your calculations; so pay careful attention to operator precedence. For example, the following formulas have the same numbers but were written differently and produce different results:

$30/5-2=4$ Q&A divides 30 by 5 and then determines that $6-2=4$.

$30/(5-2)=10$ Parentheses take precedence, so Q&A first calculates that $5-2=3$ and then determines that $30/3=10$.

Fields are calculated according to their field ID numbers. For example, field ID #1 is calculated first, field ID #2 is calculated second, and so on. When several separate statements are included in the same field, the statements are computed from left to right, regardless of the fields' locations on the form. Being able to control the order in which fields are calculated is important when you calculate fields that depend on the results of earlier calculation statements.

Solving Program-Statement Errors

Q&A fills a field with asterisks when the calculation results in a number that is longer than the field length. The asterisks are read as a zero value by calculation statements referring to the field. To solve the problem, you can redesign the form so that the field is long enough to accommodate the number. Or you can shorten the number by deleting insignificant digits after the decimal. You also can use the Format Values option from the Customize menu to reduce the number of decimal places displayed.

If you have a calculation statement that divides by zero, Q&A displays an error message in the field containing the calculation statement. Other fields that reference that particular field read the error message as a zero value.

Q&A offers you a great deal of flexibility in writing programming statements, and a wide variety of statements are possible. If you aren't sure whether you can write a statement in a certain way, try it. Q&A may display the error message Not a valid Program Spec, but you easily can correct the problem. Simply use the cursor-movement and editing keys to change the statement, and then press Enter. Q&A reevaluates the statement. If no error message is displayed, you can enter data and see whether the form works the way you had planned.

Q&A doesn't accept the Program Spec if you enter something incorrectly. An error message appears, and the program shows you where the error is by positioning the cursor under the first incorrect character.

Applying Sample Calculation Statements

In the Veterinary database, a calculation statement can be used to calculate the date of the next vaccination for each animal. This calculation involves adding one year—365 days—to the date in the Last Vaccinated field. Therefore, the calculation statement for the Next Vac field (#30) is #30=#28+365 (see fig. 7.11). This statement says, "Add the number in field #28 to 365 and put the sum in field #30." Figure 7.12 shows the result of the calculation.

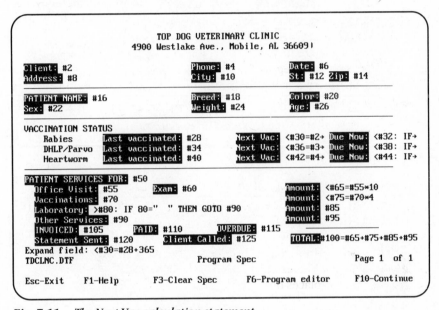

Fig. 7.11. *The Next Vac calculation statement.*

The first Amount field stores the dollar amount due for the office visit. The calculation is based on the amount of time spent on the office visit (in hours) multiplied by the doctor's hourly fee. The Amount calculation statement in the Long Value line in figure 7.13 indicates that the doctor's hourly fee is $45. The Amount calculation statement is #65=#55*45. This calculation statement says, "Multiply the number in field #55 by 45 and put the result in field #65." Figure 7.14 shows the result of the calculation.

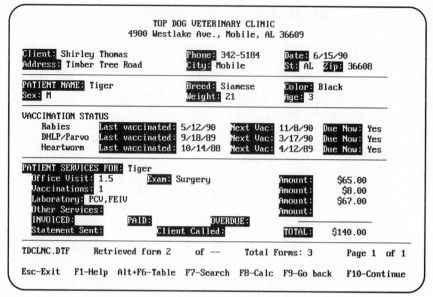

Fig. 7.12. *The result of the calculation.*

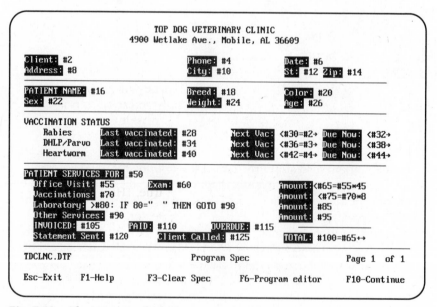

Fig. 7.13. *The Amount calculation statement.*

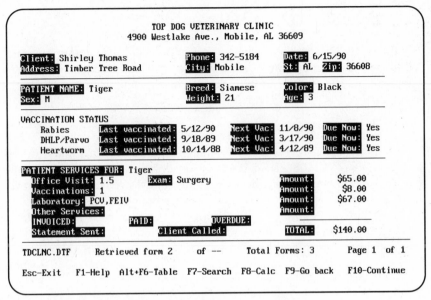

```
                    TOP DOG VETERINARY CLINIC
                  4900 Westlake Ave., Mobile, AL 36609

Client: Shirley Thomas          Phone: 342-5184     Date: 6/15/90
Address: Timber Tree Road       City: Mobile        St: AL  Zip: 36608

PATIENT NAME: Tiger             Breed: Siamese      Color: Black
Sex: M                          Weight: 21          Age: 3

VACCINATION STATUS
    Rabies      Last vaccinated: 5/12/90   Next Vac: 11/8/90  Due Now: Yes
    DHLP/Parvo  Last vaccinated: 9/18/89   Next Vac: 3/17/90  Due Now: Yes
    Heartworm   Last vaccinated: 10/14/88  Next Vac: 4/12/89  Due Now: Yes

PATIENT SERVICES FOR: Tiger
  Office Visit: 1.5      Exam: Surgery          Amount:    $65.00
  Vaccinations: 1                               Amount:     $8.00
  Laboratory: PCV,FEIV                          Amount:    $67.00
  Other Services:                               Amount:
  INVOICED:           PAID:          OVERDUE:              _____
  Statement Sent:          Client Called:       TOTAL:    $140.00

TDCLNC.DTF     Retrieved form 2      of --      Total Forms: 3      Page 1  of 1

Esc-Exit   F1-Help  Alt+F6-Table  F7-Search  F8-Calc  F9-Go back   F10-Continue
```

Fig. 7.14. *The result of the Amount calculation statement.*

Using Conditional Statements

As you learned in the preceding section, arithmetic operators are used in calculation statements to specify the operation to be performed on the data. In addition to mathematical operators, logical operators can be used in programming statements. The logical operators that you can use in Q&A's programming statements are described briefly in the following list:

Logical Operators	*Description*
IF...THEN	IF the first segment is true, THEN do the second segment.
IF...THEN...ELSE	IF the first segment is true, THEN do the second segment, ELSE do the third segment.
AND	Both the first AND second segments must be true for the third segment to occur.
OR	Either the first segment OR the second segment must be true for the third segment to occur.
NOT	NOT excludes the segment that follows from being a true condition and also negates the segment that follows by reversing its meaning.

Using the IF...THEN Statement

Use the IF...THEN statement when you need to make a programming statement conditional. For example, suppose that you want the cursor to move to field #90 if field #80 is empty. You enter the following programming statement:

    #80: IF #80="" THEN GOTO #90

Calculations such as this one can save keystrokes during data entry. In this example (refer to fig. 7.8), if no laboratory services are entered in field #80, the cursor skips the amount for that service. You can save even more time if many fields are to be skipped. Suppose that you are entering names and addresses and have only the name for some entries. When you press Enter without making an entry in the first Address field, you can have the cursor jump to the Phone field or somewhere else on the form, eliminating a number of null entries. (Cursor movements are explained in the "Navigating Fields" section later in this chapter.)

The IF...THEN statement can include a wide variety of calculations, as in the following example:

    #28: IF #28<07.15.91 THEN #32="Y"

This statement determines whether the date in field #28 is less than July 15, 1991. If the date is less than July 15, 1991, the value of field #32 is set to Y, indicating that a vaccination now is due. Field #32 is a logical field that stores true/false conditions.

Using the IF...THEN...ELSE Statement

Like the IF...THEN statement, the IF...THEN...ELSE statement is used to set up conditions in a programming statement. You can read ELSE as "or else" or "but if the first segment is not true." For example, look at this next statement:

    #32: IF #30>(#28+365) THEN #32="Yes" ELSE #32="No"

This statement says, "If field #30 is greater than the sum of field #28 plus 365, then enter the word *Yes* in field #32; or else enter the word *No* in field #32." This statement is another way you can have the program compute whether a vaccination is due.

Combining IF Statements

You can include multiple statements within an IF...THEN or IF...THEN...ELSE structure. To mark the beginning and end of the structure, use the words BEGIN and END. For example: IF statement THEN BEGIN statement 1; statement 2; statement 3; END ELSE BEGIN statement 4; statement 5; END. Q&A enables you to use curly braces ({ and }) in place of BEGIN AND END.

Using the AND Statement

When you use the AND statement, both the first and second segments must be true before the third segment is executed. For example, look at the following programming statement:

   #65: IF #60<>" " AND #55>=1 THEN #65=(#55*10)+(#60*15)

This statement says, "If field #60 is not blank and field #55 holds a value of at least 1, then field #65 is equal to the sum of field #55 times 10 and field #60 times 15." Both conditions must be true for the calculation to be conducted.

Using the OR Statement

Use the OR statement when you want either the first or the second segment to be true before the third segment is executed. An example of an OR statement follows:

   #65: IF #60<>" " OR #55>=1 THEN #65=(#55*10)+(#60*15)

This statement says, "If field #60 is not blank or field #55 holds a value of at least 1, then field #65 is equal to the sum of field #55 times 10 and field #60 times 15." In this example, the calculation is carried out if either of the conditions is true.

Using the NOT Statement

The NOT statement serves two purposes. In an IF...THEN statement, you can use NOT to exclude the truth of a value in a program statement or to search for a false condition. The following statement inserts a logical Y in field #115 if the value in field #110 is less than (NOT greater than or equal to) the amount due in #100, and the invoiced date in field #105 is more than (NOT less than or equal to) a month old:

#115: IF #110 NOT>=#100 AND @DATE−#105 NOT<=30 THEN #115="Y"

NOT also is used to indicate a false condition. For example, the following statement determines whether the value in #80 is blank. If the value is not blank, the cursor is moved to field #85; otherwise, the cursor jumps to field #90.

#80: IF #80 NOT " " THEN GOTO #85 ELSE GOTO #90

Using Functions in Programming Statements

You can use functions to automatically perform certain calculations, return certain text values, or perform other data-entry tasks. Functions save you the time and effort of writing calculation formulas or complex programming statements. When you use a function as part of a programming statement, the value returned by the function is used in the programming statement when the statement is executed. Functions offer you shortcuts when you're writing programming statements. Functions take the following form:

@function(argument)

The @ sign tells Q&A that the following word or words form a function. The *function* itself is the word that triggers a preprogrammed series of operations, and the *argument* enclosed within parentheses provides the data that the function uses to perform its calculations. Generally, an argument can be a constant, a field ID, or another calculation that returns a usable value.

Using Mathematical Functions

Q&A offers mathematical functions to perform automatically many calculations for you. If you have used spreadsheet programs, you may recognize some of the functions discussed in this section. These functions also are similar to BASIC and 1-2-3 commands that perform these kinds of operations.

Table 7.1 lists the mathematical functions available with Q&A.

Table 7.1
Mathematical Functions

Function	Example	Meaning
@ABS(n)	@ABS(#15)	Returns the absolute value of the value in field n. Strips signs so that @ABS(–10)=10.
@ASC(n)	@ASC(#15)	Returns the ASCII decimal value of the first character in field n. @ASC("Apple") is 65.
@AVG(fields)	@AVG(#1,#4,#5,#9)	Returns the average of values in listed fields.
	@AVG(#1..#9)	Returns the average of fields 1 through 9.
@EXP(n,m)	@EXP(#15,#16)	Raises n to the power of m. If n=4 and m=2, @EXP(n,m)=16.
@INT(n)	@INT(#15)	Returns the integer of the value in field n. For example, INT (10.45)=10.
@MAX(fields)	@MAX(#1,#4,#5,#9)	Returns the largest value in the listed fields.
	@MAX(#1..#9)	Returns the maximum value in range of fields 1 through 9.
@MIN(fields)	@MIN(#1,#4,#5,#9)	Returns the lowest value in the listed fields.
	@MIN(#1..#9)	Returns the lowest value in range of fields 1 through 9.
@MOD(x,y)	@MOD(14,8)	If x and y are positive numbers, @MOD(x,y) returns the remainder that results when x is divided by y. If y is zero, zero is returned.

continues

Table 7.1   *(continued)*

Function	Example	Meaning
@ROUND(n,m)	@ROUND(#15,16)	Rounds n to m number of decimal places. If n=10.45678 and m=2, @ROUND (10.45678,2)=10.46.
@SGN(x)	@SGN(#15)	Returns the sign of x. If x is a negative value, @SGN(x)=–1. If x is a positive number, @SGN(x)=1. If x is 0, @SGN(x)=0.
@SQRT(n)	@SQRT(#15)	Returns the square root of the value in field n. If #15=144, @SQRT(#15)=12.
@STD(fields)	@STD(#2,#4,#6,#8)	Calculates the standard deviation of the values in the field list. Measures how much individual items in a list vary from the average of all members. If #2=17, #4=28, #6=20, and #8=21, @STD (#2,#4,#6,#8)=4.03. Standard deviation is the square root of variance. One rule of thumb is that about 68 percent of all data points will be within one standard deviation of the average of all points.
@SUM(fields)	@SUM(#1,#4,#5,#9)	Adds the values in the listed fields and returns the total.
	@SUM(#1..#9)	Adds the values in fields 1 through 9 and returns the total.

Function	Example	Meaning
@VAR(fields)	@VAR(#2,#4,#6,#8)	Returns the variance of the values in the listed fields. Like standard deviation, variance measures how far individual data items vary from the average of all items. If #2=17, #4=28, #6=20, and #8=21, @VAR (#2,#4,#6,#8)=16.25.

Using Text Functions

In addition to the mathematical functions, Q&A provides a variety of text functions. You can use these functions to find a particular part of a text string, to extract portions of the string, or to delete selected text strings. Table 7.2 lists the text functions available with Q&A.

Table 7.2
Text-String Functions

Function	Example	Meaning
@ASC(x)	@ASC(#10)	Returns the ASCII value of the first character of x. If x is a string value, it must appear in double quotation marks. x also can be a field ID or an expression that results in a string. Abbreviation: @AS( )
@CHR(n)	@CHR(#15)	Returns the ASCII character equivalent of the value in field n. If #15=109, @CHR(#15)=m. If #15=65, @CHR(#15)=A. Abbreviation: @CH( ).

continues

Table 7.2 *(continued)*

Function	*Example*	*Meaning*
@CLEAR(fields)	@CLEAR(Salary;Bonus)	Empties the values in the listed fields.
@DEL(x,n,m)	@DEL(#9,8,5)	Deletes n characters from the text string x starting at the m character position, and returns the result. If field #9 (x) contains the text string *Old English Sheepdog*, this function deletes eight characters (n) from the fifth character position (m) (the word *English* and a space). The string *Old Sheepdog* is returned. Abbreviation: @DE().
@DITTO(fields)	@DITTO(#1,#2)	Carries values from the previous form to the current form. Useful during data entry of city, state, and other repetitive information. Abbreviation: @DI().
@FILENAME	@FILENAME	Returns the current file name. Can be used to insert name of file that provides source data for names and addresses, financial information, and other data. Can provide audit trail of data file changes. Abbreviation: @FN().
@HELP(n)	@HELP(#15)	Displays user-defined help screen for specified field. Useful during programming of a form to display help automatically for certain fields as operator prompt. Abbreviation: @HP().

Function	Example	Meaning
@INSTR(x,y)	@INSTR(#9,5)	Finds the position of the first occurrence of character y in string x. For example, finds *E* in the text string *Old English Sheepdog*. The string appears in the fifth character position, so the value 5 is returned. Abbreviation: @IN().
@LEFT(x,n)	@LEFT(#9,3)	Returns n characters from the text string x, where n is a number, a field containing a number, or an expression. For field #9=Old English Sheepdog, the word *Old* is returned. Abbreviation: @LT().
@LEN(x)	@LEN(#15)	Returns length of field x. For field #15=Old English Sheepdog, @LEN(#15)=20. Note that spaces count as characters. Abbreviation: @LN().
@MID(x,n,m)	@MID(#9,5,7)	Returns m characters from text string x starting at the nth character position. For field #9=Old English Sheepdog, the word *English* is returned. Abbreviation: @MD().
@MSG(x)	@MSG(#15)	Displays contents of field x on the message line at the bottom of the screen. Useful for operator prompting, establishing custom screens, and so on. The message may contain up to 80 characters and

continues

Table 7.2 *(continued)*

Function	Example	Meaning
		must be enclosed in double quotation marks. The argument x may be a string, a field, a field ID, or an expression.
@NUM(x)	@NUM(#15)	Converts x to text, returning a text string consisting of all the digit numbers in x in their original order.
@REPLACE (x,y, expression)	@REPLACE("LA","Los Angeles",#8)	In the specified expression, replaces each occurrence of x with y and then returns the modified expression.
@REPLFIR (x,y, expression)	@REPLFIR("LA","Los Angeles",#8)	In the specified expression, replaces only the first occurrence of x with y.
@REPLLAS (x,y, expression)	@REPLLAS("LA","Los Angeles",#8)	In the specified expression, replaces only the last occurrence of x with y.
@RIGHT(x,n)	@RIGHT(#9,3)	Returns n characters from the right side of text string x. The string *dog* is returned from the text string *Old English Sheepdog*. Abbreviation: @RT().
@TEXT(n,x)	@TEXT(5,#15)	Repeats character x a total of n times. If #15 holds a plus sign, then @TEXT (5,#15)=+++++. Abbreviation: @TXT().

Function	Example	Meaning
@WIDTH(n)	@WIDTH(#15)	Returns width of field n. This result is the numerical value that represents the total number of characters that field n can hold, not the length of the string stored in the field. Abbreviation: @WTH().

Using Conversion Functions

Conversion functions (also called *typecast functions*) change expressions from one information type to another. This capability is useful when you need to perform calculations on numbers stored in text fields, for example. Table 7.3 lists the conversion functions available in Q&A.

Table 7.3
Conversion Functions

Function	Example	Meaning
@STR(n)	@STR(#15)	Converts a number (n) to a string (text) value. Useful for including numbers in string manipulations. The number n may be a field ID, as in the example.
@TONUMBER(x)	@TONUMBER(#10)	Converts x to a number. Abbreviation: @TN().
@TOMONEY(x)	@TOMONEY(#10)	Converts x to a money value. Abbreviation: @TM().
@TODATE(x)	@TODATE(#10)	Converts x to a date value. Abbreviation: @TD().
@TOTIME(x)	@TOTIME(#10)	Converts x to a time value. Abbreviation: @TT().
@TOYESNO(x)	@TOYESNO(#10)	Converts x to a boolean (yes/no) value. Abbreviation: @TY().

Using Multiuser Functions

Q&A provides two functions, @GROUP and @USERID, that return information about the current user of a password-protected database.

The @GROUP function returns the name of the field protection group to which the user has been assigned. The following statement shows an example of using @GROUP to enter a string in field #10, depending on the field protection group to which the current user is assigned:

   IF @GROUP="Group 3" THEN #10="Protect Level B".

The @USERID function returns the user ID of the current user. The following statement shows an example of using @USERID to enter the current user's name in field #3 based on the user's password.

   IF @USERID="quark" THEN #3="John Anders".

For further information about passwords and group access functions, see Chapter 21, "Networking: Using Q&A in a Multiuser Environment."

Using the @SELECT Function

@SELECT translates between characters that you specify. For example, you can ask the user to select a character from a displayed list, and then you can translate the character to another value and insert that value in a field. The syntax of the @SELECT function is as follows:

   @SELECT(n;x;y...)

For example, suppose that you use the following statement:

   @SELECT(#3;"Sales";"Purchasing";"Order Desk")

If the user types *1* in field #3, "Sales" is returned. If #3 is 2, "Purchasing" is returned, and so on. If 3, or any value other than 1, 2, or 3 is selected, "Order Desk" is returned.

Using the @REST Function

@REST checks the contents of a field and returns Yes or No if the field's value matches or doesn't match an expression. The @REST function takes the following form:

   @REST(field;"expression")

For example, the statement @REST(#3;"Exceptional") returns Yes if field #3 holds "Exceptional" and returns No if the field contains anything else. @REST(#3;"{@DATE-30}") returns Yes only if the date in field #20 is 30 days old.

Using the @DATE and @TIME Functions

Q&A has a number of built-in functions for date and time computations. The most common of these functions are @DATE and @TIME.

@DATE

The @DATE function, abbreviated @DA, computes past and future dates by adding and subtracting whole numbers. You can use @DATE, for example, to alert you when the time comes to do something. If you need to renew some office equipment you are renting, for example, you can use the following @DATE statement:

#60: IF #15>@DATE+345 THEN #60="Time to renew"

This statement says, "If field #15 is greater than today's date plus 345 (days), then field #60 should read *Time to renew*.

The @DATE function is used frequently for date-stamping forms. If you want the current date entered automatically when you first enter information on a form, simply select Program Form from the Programming menu and move the cursor to the date field. Then, supposing that the field is #5, enter the following statement:

#5: IF #5=" " THEN #5=@DATE

This statement says, "If field #5 is empty, then field #5 should equal the current date." This statement causes the current date to be entered in all forms that have an empty date field.

@TIME

The time function is @TIME, which computes past and future time when numbers in time format (00:00) are added or subtracted. The @TIME function works like the @DATE function, except @TIME computes shorter periods. The @TIME function can be useful in a multiuser environment in which records get frequent updates. @TIME not only can report on the time of the last record change but also, like @DATE, can alert the operator if updates are too close together or too far apart when combined with some programming logic. The programming logic would be the same as for @DATE.

Working with individual portions of a composite date sometimes is convenient. Q&A File includes four functions that extract the day of the month, the year, the day, the name of the day, or the name of the month from a conventional date. These functions are discussed next.

@DOM

If you select a date format of May 28, 1991, you may want to display the day of the month separately. Or you may need to extract the value of the day for use in other calculations, such as the number of days between two dates. The @DOM function, abbreviated @DM, returns the numerical value of the day of a date:

   @DOM(date)

You usually will use @DOM to compute the day of a date stored in another field, as in @DOM(#22). For the date May 28, 1991, this function returns the number 28.

@MONTH

The @MONTH function is similar to @DOM except that @MONTH returns the numerical value for the month of a date. For example, @MONTH(#22) returns the number 5 if field #22 contains the date May 28, 1991.

@YEAR

You can isolate the year in a date for further calculations by using the @YEAR function, which takes this form:

   @YEAR(#22)

If field #22 contains the date May 28, 1991, this function returns the number 1991.

@DOW$

The @DOW$ function is convenient for automatically entering the day of the week as a word. You can use a conventional date field as the source, and @DOW$ computes the day of the week:

  @DOW$(#22)

If field #22 contains the date May 28, 1991, this function returns Tuesday.

@D(date)

Q&A's @DATE function can compute date arithmetic, as described previously. At times, you may find that employing a date constant in your calculations is useful. You know that tax returns always are due on April 15 (unless you have established another tax year), for example, and you may want to use this date in some calculation. Or you may want to base all date calculations on the beginning of your fiscal year or the date on which your business was established.

The @D function uses a fixed date for its computations. The generic form of the function is the following:

  @D(date)

If date=June 15, 1991, then the following statement stores 8/14/91 (60 days after June 15) in field #30:

  #30=@D(June 15, 1991)+60

Symantec recommends that you spell out dates in this format or use the yyyy/ mm/dd format for the greatest accuracy with this function.

@T

The @T function works like the @D function but provides a time constant for calculations. The generic format is as follows:

  @T(time)

If time=3:00 pm, then the following statement adds the value of field #5 to 3:00 pm and stores the result in field #10:

  #10=@T(3:00 pm)+#5

If field #5 contains 3 (for three hours), then #10 is set to 6:00 pm. Note that you can use 12-hour or 24-hour time formats (3:00 pm = 15:00; 6:00 pm = 18:00). If you use 12-hour formats, however, you must type *am* and *pm* in the format; otherwise, Q&A automatically uses am.

Using the @ADD and @UPDATE Functions

You can use the @ADD and @UPDATE functions to instruct Q&A to take action depending on whether forms are being added or updated. @ADD returns a True value when records are being added to the database; @UPDATE returns a True value when records are being updated. Because True/False values are returned by these functions, @ADD and @UPDATE work well in IF...THEN expressions. For example, consider the following statement:

> #15: IF @ADD THEN #15=@DATE

This statement says, "If forms are being added, then field #15 should equal the current date." These functions can be a great help in making decisions based on programming needs.

Using the @NUMBER Function

The @NUMBER function, abbreviated @NMB, enters sequential numbers (x+1) in a field. You can use this function when you need to make sure that a different number is entered in each field. @NUMBER says, "Use the previous number plus one."

When your form has fields for purchase-order numbers, ticket numbers, or any sequentially numbered set of items, your job can be made easier with the @NUMBER function.

If you want to increment numbers in a field at an interval of your choosing, use @NUMBER(*n*), in which *n* is the interval between numbers. For example, to count sales invoice numbers by 5, use the following statement:

> InvNo: @NUMBER(5)

Using Financial Functions

Like many spreadsheet programs, Q&A includes functions for financial calculations. Four such functions are compound growth rate, future value of an annuity, payment on a loan, and present value of an annuity.

Although you can construct formulas to calculate these figures from other Q&A math functions, having functions to do these tasks reduces programming time and probably will produce more accurate and consistent results. Some financial formulas can be rather complicated.

All Q&A's financial functions can accept as arguments any number, a field designator, or other formulas that result in numbers. This feature enables you to play some what-if calculation games with Q&A financial functions.

Compound Growth Rate (@CGR)

This function computes the percentage growth rate of an investment, given the present value, the future value, and the life (how long you want the investment to last).

The generic form of this function is

@CGR(pv,fv,t)

in which *pv* is present value, *fv* is future value, and *t* is term or life.

Suppose that you have $5,000 to invest now, and you want to double your money in 10 years. What interest rate will you have to find to make this plan happen? Select the field where you want the value to appear, and enter the following function:

#1=@CGR(5000,10000,10)

When the value is calculated, the number 0.0717734625 should appear in field #1, which means that your planned investment would have to earn a compound interest rate of 7.18 percent to double in 10 years.

You can use File format features to restrict the number of decimal places that are displayed as the result of such a calculation. For more readable output, select Format Values from the Customize menu, and specify two decimal places by typing *n2* in the field where the @CGR function appears.

To display in a percentage format, multiply the result by 100, as in this example:

#1=@CGR(5000,10000,10)*100

Now field #1 displays 7.18 rather than 0.07.

Future Value of an Investment (@FV)

Q&A's @FV function can tell you how much a regular investment will be worth at the end of a specified time if you know the interest rate. The generic form of this function is

@FV(pmt,in,t)

in which *pmt* is payment, *in* is periodic interest, and *t* is term.

Suppose that you can invest $1,500 a year for five years at an interest rate of 7.5 percent. How much money will you have at the end of five years? Enter the following @FV function in the field you have designated #1 (or enter the function in any other field by changing the #1 to another number):

#1=@FV(1500,.075,5)

The result is $8,712.59. Notice that you must enter the interest as *.075* rather than *7.5*. Also, the interest is the periodic rate, which means 7.5 percent per year in this example. If the payments were to be made monthly, the periodic rate would be (7.5)/12.

As with all Q&A financial functions, you can use field designators rather than numerical values for the arguments:

@FV(#6,#7,#8)

The results are based on end-of-period calculations. In other words, the regular payments are made on the last day of the period.

Payment on a Loan (@PMT)

Sometimes, showing in a Q&A File field what a loan payment would be—based on the principal, interest rate, and term of the loan—is useful. The intrinsic @PMT function can do that for you. The generic form of the function is

@PMT(pv,in,t)

in which *pv* is present value or principal, *in* is periodic interest, and *t* is term.

For example, if the present value (principal) on a loan is $50,000, at an annual interest rate of 12.5 percent, you can pay off the obligation in 30 years at a monthly rate of $533.63:

@PMT(50000,(12.5/100)/12,30*12)=$533.63

In this example,

pv = 50,000
in = 0.0104 per month
t = 360 months

Entering the formula as shown is convenient so that you have a record of how the numbers were derived. The interest rate 0.0104 wouldn't mean much after some time passes, whereas 12.5 is probably the way you normally think of interest. (12.5/100 returns the annual interest rate of 0.125. That figure is divided by 12 months to derive the monthly rate.) Also, you usually think of paying off a loan in a matter of years, not months, unless the loan is a small amount. The term therefore is shown as 30 years times 12 months per year.

As with other File financial functions, you can use field numbers for the values in @PMT calculations, as in this example:

@PMT(#1,(#2)/12,#3*12)

Again, the calculations are based on payments that occur at the end of the period.

Present Value of an Investment (@PV)

Computing present value is a way of determining how much money you can afford to borrow if you know the interest rate the lending institution is charging, you know how long you want to make payments, and you have determined the amount of the monthly payment you can afford.

The generic form of the present value function is

@PV(pmt,in,t)

in which *pmt* is payment, *in* is periodic interest, and *t* is term.

Suppose that you want to buy a new car and are willing to pay for it during a five-year span. The bank is charging you 10.5 percent for the privilege, and you calculate that you can afford $225 per month. With the @PMT function, you can determine how much you can afford to spend, as in the following example:

@PV(225,(10.5/100)/12,5*60)

The result is $10,468.09, after any down payment. As in the previous examples, enter the full values (10.5 for interest) and calculate the working values. This practice makes debugging or modifying form calculations easier. You also can use field numbers in place of numeric literals. This function uses end-of-period calculations.

Interest Rate (@IR)

Given the present value of a loan, the payment, and the number of payments, Q&A can calculate the interest rate on a loan. The generic form of the interest rate formula is

@IR(pv,pa,np)

in which *pv* is present value, *pa* is payment amount, and *np* is number of payments.

For example, suppose that field #10 contains the present value, #20 contains the payment amount, and #30 contains the number of payments. To calculate the interest rate, use this function:

@IR(#10,#20,#30)

Note that the present value must be a positive number, and the number of payments must be 1 or greater.

Using LOOKUP: Statements, Functions, and Tables

Among Q&A's more powerful programming tools are the lookup features. With LOOKUP, you can search a table that is part of the current application for matching information and automatically enter data in a form field based on data found in the table. You can program a form to accept a ZIP code from the keyboard, for example, and then look up the city and state from a table and insert this data automatically into a record.

With Q&A Version 3.0 and later, you also can use an external file to store lookup information, eliminating the size limitations of the RAM-resident table and enabling the linking of multiple files with a single application. With Version 4.0

and later, you can have Q&A fill in more than one field with data from an external file in a single operation. An *external file* is a standard Q&A database that is separate from the one you are using currently. Although the LOOKUP command uses a RAM-resident table that is part of the current database, XLOOKUP accesses a second data file to find the necessary information. Two related functions, LOOKUPR and XLOOKUPR, can retrieve data that falls within a specified range of values.

These lookup capabilities are divided between internal and external features, and programming statements and functions exist in both of these areas.

Statements form complete programming instructions, telling Q&A what information to find in a lookup table, what data to retrieve from the table, and where to put the data on the displayed form.

Functions, on the other hand, do not specify where the retrieved data should reside. You have to supply additional programming logic (field names or ID numbers) for this information, but functions are more versatile because you can include them in derived columns in reports.

Using Internal LOOKUP Commands

Internal LOOKUP commands use a table that is part of the database you are accessing currently. This internal table contains one compare (or key) column and from one to four data columns. When you use one of Q&A's internal lookup features, the software scans the key column for a specified value and then selects information from one of the data columns that is linked to the key. The data selected from the table can be placed in any of the fields on the current form, used in calculations, or applied in any way that other field data may be used.

Creating the Lookup Table

Before you can use internal LOOKUP in your form, you need to know how to create a lookup table. You can use a lookup table to store information you enter often, such as phone numbers and addresses of regular customers (see fig. 7.15). When you use the LOOKUP command, Q&A searches the first (key) column in the lookup table for the information and enters data from a corresponding column on the form.

KEY	1	2	3	4
Harlan Tompkins	342-3485	519 Juba Road		
Shirley Thomas	342-5184	Timber Tree Rd.		
Joe Crocker	342-2727	2542 14th Ave.		
Joe Carlton	342-5968	1927 Lyle St.		
Tyler Johnson	342-5811	1934 Lyle St.		
PATIENT NAME	BREED	COLOR	SEX	WEIGHT
Sheba	Cocker	Brown	F	38
Blackie	Lab	Black	M	75
Charlie	Am Husky	White	M	78
Bimbo	Cocker	Brown	M	36
Tiger	Siamese	Black	M	15
Cat	Mix Cat	Black/White	F	12
Fluffy	Mix Cat	Brown	F	18
King	Gd. Ret.	Gold	M	64
Princess	Mix Cat	Black	F	10
Sandy	Terrier	Brown	M	17
Potzie	Siamese	White	F	14

TDCLNC.DTF   Lookup Table   Page 1 of 1

Esc-Exit F6-Expand field   PgUp-Previous page   PgDn-Next page   F10-Continue

Fig. 7.15.   *A sample lookup table.*

Figure 7.16 shows how LOOKUP is used on the Veterinary Clinic form. When you enter the client's name, the LOOKUP command in the Phone field retrieves the phone number from the lookup table and enters the data into the form automatically (see fig. 7.17). The street address also is entered from the lookup table.

```
                     TOP DOG VETERINARY CLINIC
                 4900 Westlake Ave., Mobile, AL 36609

Client: #2                    Phone: <#4: LOOKUP→ Date: #6
Address: <#8: LOOKUP(#2,2,#8)  City: #10          St: #12 Zip: #14

PATIENT NAME: #16             Breed: #18: LOOKUP→ Color: #20
Sex: #22: LOOKUP(#16,3,#22)   Weight: #24: LOOKU→ Age: #26

VACCINATION STATUS
     Rabies       Last vaccinated: #28      Next Vac: <#30=#2→ Due Now: <#32→

  #24: LOOKUP(#16,4,#24)




TDCLNC                        Ins  0 %   1   Line 1 of 1
TDCLNC.DTF                    Program Spec              Page 1  of 1

Esc-Exit      F1-Help    F2-Print   F7-Search    F8-Options    F10-Exit editor
```

Fig. 7.16.   *Using LOOKUP commands.*

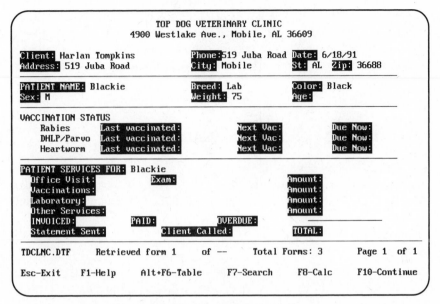

```
                    TOP DOG VETERINARY CLINIC
               4900 Westlake Ave., Mobile, AL 36609

Client: Harlan Tompkins      Phone:519 Juba Road  Date: 6/18/91
Address: 519 Juba Road       City: Mobile         St: AL  Zip: 36688

PATIENT NAME: Blackie         Breed: Lab          Color: Black
Sex: M                        Weight: 75          Age:

VACCINATION STATUS
   Rabies     Last vaccinated:       Next Vac:        Due Now:
   DHLP/Parvo Last vaccinated:       Next Vac:        Due Now:
   Heartworm  Last vaccinated:       Next Vac:        Due Now:

PATIENT SERVICES FOR: Blackie
   Office Visit:         Exam:                  Amount:
   Vaccinations:                                Amount:
   Laboratory:                                  Amount:
   Other Services:                              Amount:
   INVOICED:        PAID:          OVERDUE:
   Statement Sent:       Client Called:         TOTAL:

TDCLNC.DTF      Retrieved form 1    of --     Total Forms: 3      Page 1  of 1

Esc-Exit    F1-Help    Alt+F6-Table    F7-Search    F8-Calc    F10-Continue
```

Fig. 7.17. *The results returned by LOOKUP commands.*

In this example, then, the operator never has to type in the telephone number, the street address, the city, the state, or the ZIP code. This type of forms programming assumes that all clients live in the same city and have the same ZIP code. This design works for an application with a small area of coverage but probably will not be universally acceptable. See the section on the XLOOKUP command for a way to enter the entire address automatically, regardless of where the client resides.

To fill in a lookup table, select Edit Lookup Table from the Programming menu. When the blank table is displayed, use the Tab key to change columns and the cursor keys to select the row you want to edit. Type the data and move the cursor to the next entry location. You may want to enter column headings for each group of information so that the form will be clear to others who may use the file. Be sure to use column headings that will not be used as key values, to prevent Q&A from finding a heading during a lookup procedure and mistaking the heading for a key value. If this mishap would occur, improper data would be returned.

If you want to change something on a lookup table, move to the location you want to edit, and press F4 to delete a word or Shift-F4 to delete the entire location. Then type the new data.

A lookup table can store up to 64,000 characters, depending on the available RAM in your machine. A computer with 640K of RAM can store a lookup table with about 600 100-character lines. Each item in a lookup table can be up to 240 characters, making the maximum line length 1,200 characters.

When you enter data in the columns of a lookup table, confine each column to one set of information. For example, if the key value is a client name, you could use column 1 for phone numbers, column 2 for addresses, column 3 for cities, and so on. You can enter any type of information: text, numbers, dates, and times.

Building the LOOKUP Statement

The LOOKUP statement acts like a complete programming statement. When you write a LOOKUP command, you use a format similar to the format of programming statements. The format for a LOOKUP command, abbreviated LU, is as follows:

#*n*: LOOKUP(key, column, field ID number)

The LOOKUP statement begins with a field ID number and a colon (:). You then enter the word *LOOKUP*, along with an open parenthesis and the field ID of the key value (or the key value in quotation marks).

The key value can be any alphanumeric expression: words, numbers, or a combination of the two. The key value is the data you want Q&A to find in the first column of a lookup table. A typical key value is a ZIP code, for example. Q&A uses the ZIP code key to scan a lookup table until a matching value is found. The program then returns the city and state associated with the specified ZIP code key. Be careful to enter the key value exactly as it appears in the lookup table, or Q&A will not be able to locate the data. If the key value appears more than once, Q&A uses the first value listed.

Next, enter a comma after the key value and specify the number of the column that contains the data to be retrieved. Finally, enter the field ID of the field in which you want Q&A to enter the data, and end the statement with a closed parenthesis. For example, the following statement, typed in the Program spec, searches the lookup table for the key value stored in field #2, retrieves the data associated with it in column 1 of the LOOKUP table, and stores the retrieved information in field #4:

#4: LOOKUP(#2,1,#4)

Suppose that field #2 holds a ZIP code, for example, and the list in column 1 of the lookup table stores city names. If field #2 holds 36608, then this program statement stores Mobile in field #4.

Building the LOOKUPR Statement

The LOOKUPR statement ("look up within range"), like the other internal LOOKUP commands, uses the table resident with the data file. Unlike the LOOKUP statement, however, LOOKUPR does not have to find an exact match. If you specify a key value that LOOKUPR cannot locate, this statement returns the next lowest value in the table.

The LOOKUPR statement, abbreviated LUR, takes the following general form:

#*n*: LOOKUPR(key, column, field ID #)

The key is the value to search for in the lookup table key column, and the column is a number (1 through 4) that specifies which lookup table column holds the data to be retrieved.

Suppose that you are working with the following accounting system: account numbers from 0 to 50 are cash accounts, numbers from 51 to 100 are checking accounts, numbers from 600 to 799 are income accounts, and numbers from 800 to 999 are expense accounts. As you write reports about transactions against these accounts, you may want to show the account type on the data-entry screen. If the lookup table looked like the one in table 7.4, then as you entered detailed transactions, the appropriate category would be entered automatically in the appropriate place in the form.

Table 7.4
Sample LOOKUP Table for LOOKUPR

KEY	*1*	*2*
ACCOUNT NUMBER 1 51 600 800	TYPE ACCOUNT Cash Checking Income Expense	

Now suppose that the LOOKUPR statement contains these values:

LOOKUPR(823,1,#33)

Field #33 would be loaded with expenses from the LOOKUP table.

As with other Q&A statements, you can use formulas and field IDs for some or all of the arguments to LOOKUPR. Suppose that you are tracking inventory with Q&A. If your part-numbering scheme includes a pointer to warehouse location, you can use a formula to extract this information from the complete part number, look up the location in the table, and place the location in the Location field on the displayed form.

Consider a part number such as 1052-E4662-GE and assume that the first four digits, 1052, show the warehouse location according to the lookup table in table 7.5. If the part number is entered in field #10, and the location is entered in field #12, then the following LOOKUPR statement fills in field #12 automatically:

LOOKUPR(@LEFT(4,#10),1,#12)

The string function @LEFT removes the left four digits to use in the LOOKUPR statement, performs the lookup, and returns `Aisle 4, East` from the table for field #12.

Table 7.5
Sample LOOKUP Table for LOOKUPR

KEY	1	2
LOCATION NUMBER	WAREHOUSE LOC.	
1000	Aisle 4, East	
2000	Aisle 5, East	
3000	Aisle 1, West	
4000	Aisle 2, West	

Using the @LOOKUP Function

The @LOOKUP function, abbreviated @LU, works like the LOOKUP statement except that the @LOOKUP function does not include a target field for data retrieved from the lookup table. In addition, you can use the function in derived columns in the Report module (see Chapter 15 for more information on Report).

The generic form for @LOOKUP is as follows:

#*n*=@LOOKUP(key, column)

The key is the value to search for in the lookup table key column, and column is the lookup table data column from which information will be retrieved.

Notice that you specify where to place the information that is found by including @LOOKUP as part of a calculation formula. The preceding example shows the function used in the target field. You also can load another field, as this example shows:

    #5: #10=@LOOKUP(key,column)

In other situations, the @LOOKUP function operates like the LOOKUP statement.

Using the @LOOKUPR Function

The @LOOKUPR function, abbreviated @LUR, performs the same operations as the LOOKUPR statement except that you must include the function in a calculation formula to tell Q&A where to place the information it finds in the lookup table.

The general form of the command is as follows:

    #n=@LOOKUPR(key,column)

The key is the compare value for the lookup table's key column, and column is the table's data column from which information that is found will be retrieved.

Using External LOOKUP Commands

The external LOOKUP commands added to Q&A with Version 3.0 and expanded in Version 4.0 increase the power and flexibility of this database program. With external XLOOKUP, you are not limited to the form and size of the internal LOOKUP table. Beginning with Q&A Version 4.0, programming statements are entered on the Program Spec screen.

The external commands use another Q&A or dBASE data file as the source of retrieved information. Otherwise, the functions are similar.

The external XLOOKUP features offer relational-like functions for Q&A File; these features link key fields across multiple files. Consider the Veterinary Clinic example from the previous discussion of the internal LOOKUP statement. The internal table is a limiting factor in this application because not enough table fields are available to permit you to store the full address and telephone number.

With external XLOOKUP, however, you can build a separate name and address database and load the treatment record from this separate file.

Creating the External XLOOKUP File

The external functions depend on all the linked files being indexed on the same fields. (The speedup search must be set for the same fields. Select Speed Up Searches from the Customize menu.) Figure 7.18 shows a portion of the name and address file (NAD.DTF) and a portion of the veterinary service file (TDCLNC.DTF). The two files are linked through the indexed CLIENT field.

For this example, the clinic file is the primary file, and the name and address file is the external file. The primary file is always the one receiving the information; the external file is always the one supplying the information.

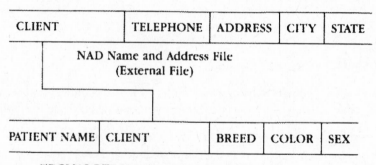

Fig. 7.18.   Sample XLOOKUP file join.

You can link a third file to TDCLNC that, for example, holds records of treatment for each patient. In that join, the common link is the indexed PATIENT NAME field. You can tie together as many files in this manner as you need. After the link is made, you can use external LOOKUP commands to fill in fields in the TDCLNC file and to construct reports on the data with the Report module. With Version 4.0 and later versions of Q&A, you can have XLOOKUP retrieve data from the external file into multiple fields, all in one operation.

Building the XLOOKUP Statement

The XLOOKUP statement functions almost identically to LOOKUP, discussed previously, except that you are using the external data file instead of the internal LOOKUP table as the reference table.

The XLOOKUP statement says: "Look into the file (fn), take the value entered in the field (key), and find the record with the matching value in the external field (xkf). From that record, retrieve the value from the lookup field (lf) in the external file and insert that value into the destination field (df)."

The generic form of the XLOOKUP statement, abbreviated XLU, follows:

XLOOKUP("fn",key,"xkf","lf",df)

The following chart defines the XLOOKUP arguments:

Argument	Definition
fn	The external file name
key	The number or name of the key field in the primary file
xkf	The name of the external key field that will link to key in the primary file
lf	The name of the field from which data will be extracted from the external file
df	The field name or number in the primary file where information from xkf should be placed

Notice that each of the named arguments in this statement is enclosed in double quotation marks; the number designations (key and df) do not take quotation marks.

If you use the files in figure 7.18, for example, the statement might take this form:

<#8: XLOOKUP("NAD",#2,"CLIENT","ADDRESS",#8)

The less-than sign at the beginning of this program statement tells Q&A to conduct the lookup procedure as soon as the cursor enters field #8. This statement uses the information in field #2 of the TDCLNC file to find a corresponding record in the NAD file. The information in the NAD ADDRESS field is copied into field #8 of the TDCLNC file. Such a statement can load addresses into the TDCLNC file automatically.

In this example, the primary field names and the external field names for client and address are the same. (Fig. 7.18 does not show the entire files. See fig. 7.16 for the complete client record.) You could, however, use CLIENT in the veterinary services file and NAME in the NAD file, and use ADDRESS in one file and STREET in the other, as long as matching data was in the two files for Q&A to find.

Building the XLOOKUPR Statement

The XLOOKUPR statement is identical to the LOOKUPR statement except that, like XLOOKUP, XLOOKUPR uses an external file for the reference table. The rules for using this statement are the same as for XLOOKUP and LOOKUPR.

The general format for the XLOOKUPR statement, abbreviated XLR, follows:

    XLOOKUPR("fn",key,"xkf","lf",df)

Again, *fn* is the external file name, *key* is the name or number of the key field in the primary file, *xkf* is the name or number of the external key field that will link to *key* in the primary file, *lf* is the name or number of the field from which data will be extracted from the external file, and *df* is the field name or number in the primary file where information from *lf* should be placed.

For examples of how to use XLOOKUPR and how to retrieve multiple fields, refer to the previous sections.

Looking up Data in Multiple Fields

You can use XLOOKUP and XLOOKUPR to complete multiple fields in the destination form with data from corresponding fields in the external file in a single operation. The format is as follows:

    XLOOKUP("fn",key,"xkf","lf",df1,lf2,df2...lf8,df8)

Again, *fn* is the external file's name (in double quotation marks), *key* is the name or number of the key field in the destination file to match, *xkf* is the key field in the external file, *lf* is a field in the external file, and *df* is a field in the destination file.

For example, to retrieve names and addresses from the file CLIENT into the file INVOICE, you can use this statement:

    XLOOKUP("CLIENT.DTF","FName","FIRSTNAME","LName",
    "LASTNAME","Address","STREET","City","CITY","State","STATE","Zip","ZIP")

Note: The field names need not agree in case; Q&A converts to uppercase when matching field labels.

Using the @XLOOKUP Function

Q&A functions add a level of flexibility that is lacking in program statements, although the user has the responsibility of writing more of the logic to make the functions work.

The @XLOOKUP function has this general structure:

@XLOOKUP("fn",key,"xkf","lf")

The argument *fn* is the external file name, *key* is the name or number of the key field in the primary file, *xkf* is the name or number of the external key field that will link to *key* in the primary file, and *lf* is the name or number of the field from which data will be extracted from the external file.

As with other Q&A functions, you must specify where the retrieved data will be placed in the primary form. If you use the Veterinary Clinic example discussed previously in this chapter, the function syntax may be the following:

#8=@XLOOKUP("NAD",#1,"CLIENT","ADDRESS")

Using XLOOKUP and @XLOOKUP with dBASE Files

You can use XLOOKUP expressions and @XLOOKUP functions to retrieve data from a dBASE file, so long as the dBASE file has not been encrypted. The commands are similar to those used with Q&A files:

XLOOKUP("fn",key,"xkf","lf",df) and @XLOOKUP("fn",key,"xkf","lf")

The following chart defines the XLOOKUP and @XLOOKUP arguments:

Argument	Definition
fn	The name of the dBASE file (in double quotation marks). dBASE data file names must have a DBF extension.
key	The matching field from the Q&A database
xkf	The matching field from the dBASE database, or the file name and path of a dBASE index file. dBASE II and III index files

Argument	Definition
	have an NDX extension. dBASE IV indexes are held in a master index file with an MDX extension. Be sure to enclose the name in double quotation marks. With dBASE II and II you must specify the NDX extension; if you don't specify an extension, Q&A looks for a dBASE IV MDX file.
lf	The lookup field in the dBASE database
df	The field in the Q&A destination file that will receive data from the dBASE source file

When you want to retrieve data from a dBASE memo file, be sure to include the DBF file extension. Note also that dBASE indexes are case-sensitive, so be sure to use XLOOKUP on fields whose case exactly matches the corresponding dBASE fields.

Using the @XLOOKUPR Function

This function is similar to @LOOKUPR except that @XLOOKUPR uses an external File database as the source of information. The general format for this function is the following:

@XLOOKUPR("fn",key,"xkf","lf")

Again, *fn* is the external file name, *key* is the name or number of the key field in the primary file, *xkf* is the name or number of the external key field that will link to *key* in the primary file, and *lf* is the name of the field from which data will be extracted from the external file.

Executing Programming Statements

Q&A executes the statements entered on the Program Spec whenever you add data to the form or update existing data on the form. Formulas are calculated and values are returned at that time. You have the option of selecting either manual or automatic calculation. Q&A's default setting is manual calculation, which means that to carry out the calculations, you must press the calculation key (F8). You also can use the less-than (<) or greater-than (>) symbols at the beginning of programming statements to have Q&A override the standard rules of execution and evaluate the statements when the cursor enters or exits a field.

If the calculation is based on data in a specific field that is entered from the keyboard, you probably will specify that the calculation should occur when the cursor exits the field. If, however, you don't want the data-entry person to add information to a field, or even to have to make a decision about entering data into a field, then you should have the value calculated when the cursor enters the field.

Using Automatic Calculation

You can have Q&A calculate the forms automatically by pressing Shift-F8 and then A while in either the Add Data or Search/Update option of the File menu. In Automatic mode, all programming statements are computed when the cursor is moved from any field that has been changed. Even if you have not changed every field on the form, each field that has a calculation statement is recalculated. That process can take quite a bit of time in a form with a dozen or more statements. Q&A remains in Automatic mode until you press Shift-F8 and then M while in either the Add Data or Search/Update option.

Overriding Standard Execution Rules

If a programming statement begins with either a greater-than or a less-than symbol, Q&A overrides the standard rules of execution. The less-than symbol causes the statement to be executed when the cursor enters the field; the greater-than symbol tells Q&A to execute the statement when the cursor is moved out of the field. Remember, however, that if you use the less-than symbol, the statement will be executed before the typist can enter data. The typist will not be able to change the data that Q&A enters. The following examples show the effect of the greater-than and less-than symbols:

Formula	How to read the formula
<#6: #6=#4+14	When the cursor enters field #6, 14 is added to the value in field #4 and the result is entered automatically in field #6.
<#4: LOOKUP(#2,1,#4)	When the cursor enters field #4, data is retrieved from the LOOKUP table and entered automatically in field #4.
>#6: #8=.05*#14	After exiting field #6, set field #8 equal to 5% of field #14.

Formula	How to read the formula
>#12: #13=@DATE	After exiting field #12, enter the date in field #13.
<#27: IF #6>(#22+245) THEN #27="Yes" ELSE #27="No"	If field #6 is greater than field #22 plus 245, field #27 displays Yes. If #6 is less than field #22 plus 245, #27 displays No. This statement is executed when the cursor enters the field.
>#17: IF #35>=(@DATE+ #30) THEN #40= "Past Due"	If field #35 is equal to or greater than the current date plus the value in field #30, then field #40 displays Past Due. This statement is executed when the cursor exits the field.

Navigating Fields

In Q&A, you use the Tab key or the Enter key to move the cursor from field to field. You can automate cursor movement with the following words, entered in the Navigation Spec, which is accessed from the Programming menu:

Word	Cursor Movement
GOTO	To specified field
GOTONP	To specified field without executing programming statements
CNEXT	To next field
CPREV	To previous field
CHOME	To first field
CEND	To last field
PGDN	To next page
PGUP	To previous page

When you use a cursor-movement command, the program statements in the form move the cursor as though you were using the Tab or Enter key. All the cursor movements happen within the same form; you cannot use cursor-movement commands to move from form to form.

Remember that fields containing any one of these cursor-movement commands do not execute according to the standard rules. Statements that contain cursor-movement commands must begin with either a greater-than (>) or a less-than (<) symbol; the statements execute as explained in the preceding section.

To create cursor-movement statements, follow these steps:

1. Select Field Navigation from the Programming menu. Q&A displays the Navigation Spec.

2. Move the cursor to the appropriate field, and type the cursor-movement statement. For example:

    #10 THEN CNEXT

    If the contents of field 2 are greater than the contents of field #10, move the cursor to the next field.

3. When you finish typing navigation statements, press F10 to return to the Programming menu.

Note that unlike programming statements, you don't have to begin cursor-movement statements with a field ID. You can, however, use field names or ID numbers to tell the cursor where to go. Note also that field IDs need not be the same in the Program and Navigation Specs. Q&A treats the two specs as completely independent.

When you have program statements in several consecutive fields, Q&A can insert initial values or enter data from a lookup table faster than the fields can be displayed on-screen. Simply use CNEXT in each field.

Q&A enables you to use only the GOTO cursor-movement command on the Program Spec, but this approach is not recommended. Having all field navigation commands referenced on the Navigation Spec is less confusing.

Writing Multiple Statements

If you need to perform several tasks at once, you can enter multiple programming statements in one field. This capability is helpful especially when the timing of data entry is important or when the other fields on the form cannot store more information.

The format for multiple statements requires that the statements be separated by a semicolon so that Q&A knows where one statement ends and another begins. For example, the following line has three statements:

```
<#65: #60=#5/15; IF #5>7 THEN #70="No";
IF #70="No" THEN GOTO #75
```

Because you can increase the number of statements when you use IF...THEN and IF...THEN...ELSE, you can execute a number of tasks with a single IF statement. The conditional statements must be set off by BEGIN and END or by braces ({ and }), where { replaces BEGIN and } replaces END. For example, consider the following statement:

IF statement THEN BEGIN statement 1; statement 2 END ELSE BEGIN statement a; statement b END

This statement says, "If the first statement is true, then do statement 1, statement 2, and other statements that follow; or else do statement a, statement b, and other statements that follow." As you can see, one IF statement can do a considerable amount of work.

Here is another example of a multiple IF statement:

```
<#140: IF #70>21500 THEN BEGIN #140="No"; #145=10000; GOTO
#150 END ELSE BEGIN #140="Yes"; #145=15000; CEND END
```

This statement says, "If field #70 is greater than 21,500, then make field #140 read No and field #145 read 10,000 and go to field #150; but if #70 is less than 21,500, then make #140 read Yes and #145 read 15,000 and go to the last field."

Multiple statements may quickly grow longer than the field space allows. To edit long programming statements, use the Program Editor. At the Program Spec, press F6. Q&A displays a word processing window in which you can use almost all the commands available in the Q&A Write module, including block functions, printing, spell-checking and thesaurus, character enhancements, and so on. You can enter up to 32,000 characters (about 16 pages) with the Program Editor, to a total of 64,000 characters for all the fields in a form.

When working in the Program Editor, pressing F8 displays the menu of word processing options. When you move the cursor to an item in the menu, its submenu is displayed to the right. Use the right-arrow key to move the cursor to the submenu, and press Enter to choose an item. To exit the Program Editor and save the programming statement, press F6 or F10. To review the program statement, move the cursor back into the field, and press F6.

Applying a Sample Programming Statement

This section describes how programming statements are used by the Veterinary Clinic employees to automate the operation of the database form.

The LOOKUP command is used in four fields that provide patient information: Breed, Color, Sex, and Weight (see fig. 7.19). When the patient name is entered, the cursor moves through these fields (because of GOTO and CNEXT commands on the Navigation Spec), and the client information is retrieved and entered automatically (see fig. 7.20). The name of the patient also is copied into the Patient Services For field because of the formula #50=#16.

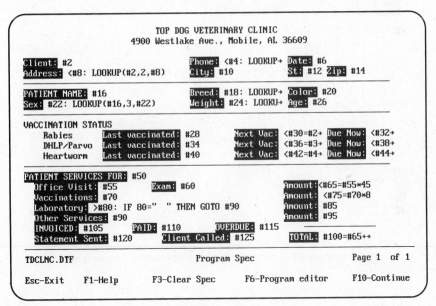

Fig. 7.19. *Using LOOKUP commands.*

The Due Now field contains a formula that displays a Yes or No value. The formula determines whether the current date is greater than or equal to the Next Vac date. If the @DATE value is greater or equal to the Next Vac date, the vaccination is due and Yes is entered in the field. If the @DATE value is not greater than or equal to the Next Vac date, No is entered in the Due Now field. The first Due Now field in figure 7.21 contains the following statement:

<#32: IF #30<=@DATE THEN (#32="Yes") ELSE (#32="No")

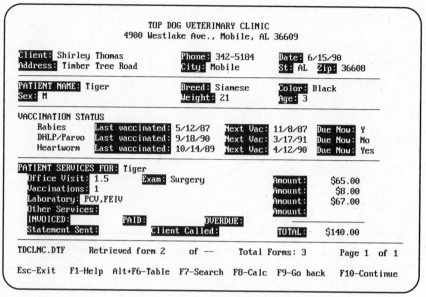

Fig. 7.20.   *Client data entered with LOOKUP commands.*

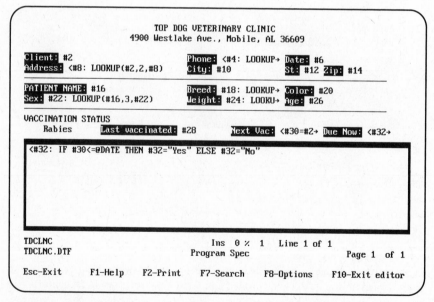

Fig. 7.21.   *Using the IF...THEN...ELSE statement in the Due Now field.*

After the formula is calculated and the result is placed in the field, the cursor is moved to the next field with a CNEXT command on the Navigation Spec (see fig. 7.22).

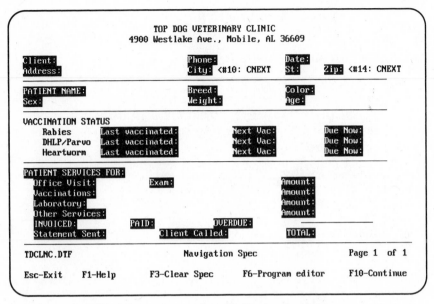

```
                    TOP DOG VETERINARY CLINIC
                  4900 Westlake Ave., Mobile, AL 36609

 Client:                         Phone:           Date:
 Address:                        City: <#10: CNEXT  St:      Zip: <#14: CNEXT

 PATIENT NAME:                   Breed:           Color:
 Sex:                            Weight:          Age:

 VACCINATION STATUS
    Rabies       Last vaccinated:     Next Vac:      Due Now:
    DHLP/Parvo   Last vaccinated:     Next Vac:      Due Now:
    Heartworm    Last vaccinated:     Next Vac:      Due Now:

 PATIENT SERVICES FOR:
    Office Visit:    Exam:                      Amount:
    Vaccinations:                               Amount:
    Laboratory:                                 Amount:
    Other Services:                             Amount:
    INVOICED:        PAID:        OVERDUE:      _____
    Statement Sent:        Client Called:       TOTAL:

 TDCLNC.DTF              Navigation Spec              Page 1  of 1

 Esc-Exit    F1-Help      F3-Clear Spec    F6-Program editor    F10-Continue
```

Fig. 7.22.   *CNEXT statements entered on the Navigation spec.*

Using Advanced Programming Functions

Q&A Version 4.0 and later versions offer commands previously available only with advanced programming languages. But don't be intimidated by the "advanced" label. Even if you're just beginning to write Q&A programs, you will find these functions valuable for the flexibility they provide.

Using Subroutines: GOSUB and RETURN

A *subroutine* is a self-contained small program contained within the larger whole. Subroutines enable you to repeat programming steps several times within the same program without rewriting the programming lines each time.

The GOSUB command tells Q&A to interrupt a program and execute a subroutine. When the subroutine has finished, the RETURN command sends control back to the main program.

All subroutines are executed when the cursor enters a field; therefore, a field that contains a GOSUB command must begin with the < (execute on-entry) symbol. Notice in the following example that subroutines also begin with a < symbol:

> <#10: #10=#30*.05;GOSUB #20
>
> <#20: IF #10>5000 THEN #40="Maximum bonus";RETURN

Q&A sets field #10 equal to 5 percent of field #30, then transfers control to the subroutine in #20. If #10 is greater than 5,000, then #40 is set to Maximum bonus, and control returns to field #10.

Each subroutine may contain many statements, including GOSUBS and RETURNS.

Using the STOP Statement

STOP halts program execution immediately. For example, take a look at this statement:

> <#50: #50=#40*.05;IF #50>5000 THEN {@MSG
> ("Too much profit!!");STOP}

If the contents of field #50 are greater than 5,000, Q&A displays the message Too much profit!! and halts all execution of programming for the form.

Using the @FIELD( ) Statement

When encountering an @FIELD( ) statement, Q&A replaces the contents of the current field with the contents of the field named within the parentheses. In programming parlance, this approach is called an *indirect field reference*. You can use this statement to transfer the contents of a field to one or more other fields in a form, depending on the contents of the first field.

For example, suppose that the user enters *March* in a field called Due Date. The following statement reads March from the Due Date field, then copies the contents of a field named Monthly Payment to a field called March:

> Due Date:>Monthly Payment: @FIELD(March) = Due Date

The @FIELD( ) statement can be abbreviated as @( ).

Chapter Summary

This chapter has explained the custom design features of Q&A File. You have learned how to highlight fields and data on your screen, create custom help screens, set initial values in your fields, create field templates, and restrict the range of data that a field will accept. You also have learned to automate data entry on your file form by including programming statements that contain calculations, functions, and commands. The features discussed in this chapter will be a continuous help to you. The more familiar you become with your routine data-entry procedures, the more you will be able to use customization and programming.

8

Printing from File

Q&A File stores information and displays records in the form you want, but frequently you also need a printed copy of the records in your database. You can print the entire database or just one record. You may, for example, want to print all the records pertaining to a certain company, person, or product. With Q&A, printing any number of records is easy.

When you print from Q&A File, you have several options:

- You can use the DOS PrtSc, or Print Screen, facility to print a single record displayed on-screen.

- You can print a single record with a Q&A print utility within File.

- You can create a print specification—called a Print Spec—to print elaborate customized reports.

You also can generate reports from Q&A files within the separate Report module. The printing features in the Report module are more flexible. (See Chapter 16 for details.) The Write module also has separate capabilities for printing information from a Q&A database file. Details on these features are in Chapters 12 and 13.

This chapter explains how to use all the printing options in Q&A File.

Printing One Complete Form

You sometimes want only a quick copy of the displayed record. The DOS Print Screen feature is a simple way to make such a copy. Use a Retrieve Spec (discussed in Chapter 6) to display the record you want to print, and press the PrtSc (Print Screen) key. The screen contents are sent to your printer. Note that the entire screen is printed with this method. In addition to the retrieved record and field names, your printout includes any on-screen Q&A prompts, messages, and function-key assignments. If the current form is longer than one page, you must scroll and print again until you get a printout of the entire form.

If you want to print information from a single record or a few selected records without also printing Q&A's on-screen messages and formatting lines, press F2 and then F10 to accept the default print specs. If your printer is installed correctly, the contents of the current record are printed with field names. If you need help installing your printer, refer to Appendix A, "Installing and Starting Q&A," for more information.

Note: Any lines or boxes on your screen may not appear properly on your printout, depending on your printer's graphics printing capabilities.

If you don't press F10 after you press F2, you can make changes to the File Print Options screen, which is slightly different from the one in the Write module. This screen does not prompt you to specify pages to print, because in File you print records, not documents.

If you plan to print a record from a database, the Print Field Labels option on the File Print Options screen is important. Unless you have changed the Global Default screen setting for this option, the default is No, in which case no labels appear when you print a record. You get a printout of "bare" data, and, depending on how many fields and different field types you defined, you may be unable to determine which labels go with which data (see fig. 8.1). To change the setting, select Yes on the Print Field Labels line.

The same record printed with labels appears in figure 8.2. As you can see, the labels make the information easier to read and understand.

If you are printing mailing labels or envelopes, however, you don't want the field labels to appear. In this case, leave the Print Field Labels option set at No.

```
        Blackson                        Jeff
   Operations Manager
      Mountain Labs                 363-254-6600
      300 18th Avenue

   Boulder                       CO              80105
            3                             5378667
              Y           .                   1

                   1500;2000
         Info                          Mailing
              2                            1

            Hot                       Jun 6, 1988
        Denver                        Bill Heist
     Allport                  303-861-4500
    Sale
```

Fig. 8.1.   *A form printed without field labels.*

```
            TITAN TECHNOLOGY SALES LEAD TRACKING SYSTEM
                                   File Name -- SlsLead
   LastName: Blackson              FirstName: Jeff
   Title: Operations Manager
   Company: Mountain Labs          Telephone: 363-254-6600
   Address1: 300 18th Avenue
   Address2:
   City: Boulder                   State: CO      Zip: 80105
      No. of Labs: 3               Annual Revenue: 5378667
      Current Customer: Y          Company Priority: 1
   --------------------------LEAD INFORMATION--------------------------
      Product Interest: 1500;2000
      Request For: Info            Lead Source: Mailing
      Months to Purchase: 2        Product Priority: 1
   ---------------------------SALES ACTION----------------------------
      Sales Priority: Hot          Date Entered: Jun 6, 1988
      Sales Dist.: Denver          Sales Manager: Bill Heist
      Salesman: Allport            Phone: 303-861-4500
      Status: Sale
```

Fig. 8.2.   *A printout with fields identified by labels.*

Creating and Using Print Specs

Printouts would be terribly boring if you always had to print the same fields on the same forms in the same typeface. Fortunately, most software packages have some flexibility for printing forms. Q&A is no exception. Through the use of Print Specs, you can pull specific data from a database to print mailing labels or fill in preprinted forms.

Before you can print from the Print menu, you must create a Print Spec to tell Q&A how you want the data to be printed. A *Print Spec* is a list of instructions that tells Q&A which fields to print in what order. Designing a Print Spec involves filling in a series of specification screens. You can save the completed Print Spec for use again later, and you also can copy an existing Print Spec or modify it to create a new one.

By using the Retrieve and Sort Specs, you designate which records to print and in what order. The following paragraphs explain how to create and use Print Specs; a later section, "Using Existing Print Specs," discusses how to use the specs you already have defined.

Designing a Print Spec

To begin creating a Print Spec, select Print from the File menu. After you choose a database, the Print menu is displayed, and you can choose one of four possibilities: design or redesign a Print Spec; start printing right away using a new or old Print Spec; set global options; or rename, delete, or copy a Print Spec.

Select Design/Redesign a Spec from the Print menu. If you already have designed other print specifications, Q&A displays a list of Print Spec names and prompts you to choose a name. If you haven't created any other Print Specs, the list is blank, but Q&A still requests a name. Enter a name that will help you identify the Print Spec you are creating. Print Spec names can be up to 30 characters long, and the names do not necessarily have to conform to DOS file-naming conventions. A name and address reference list, for example, could be called "NAD Quick Reference." A more detailed report might be named "Detailed Name/Address List."

Note: Print Specs are not DOS files, so Print Specs do not appear on a DOS file directory listing. Print specifications are stored within the database.

The following sections explain the Retrieve Spec and Sort Spec screens, which you use to select and sort the data for printouts from within the File module.

Using Retrieve Specs

After you name the Print Spec, Q&A displays the Retrieve Spec screen so that you can specify which records to select for printing (see fig. 8.3). (Notice that this Retrieve Spec screen is the same as the Retrieve Spec you fill out when you select Search/Update from the File menu.)

```
                    TITAN TECHNOLOGY SALES LEAD TRACKING SYSTEM
============================================================= File Name -- SlsLead
LastName:███████████████████████    FirstName:
Title:
Company:                                 Telephone:
Address1:
Address2:
City:                                    State:            Zip:
   No. of Labs:                          Annual Revenue:
   Current Customer:                     Company Priority:
──────────────────────────────LEAD INFORMATION──────────────────────────
   Product Interest:
   Request For:                          Lead Source:
   Months to Purchase:                   Product Priority:
──────────────────────────────SALES ACTION──────────────────────────────
   Sales Priority:                       Date Entered:
   Sales Dist.:                          Sales Manager:
   Salesman:                             Phone:
   Status:


──────────────────────────────────────────────────────────────────────
SLSLEAD.DTF                    Retrieve Spec                 Page 1  of 1

Esc-Exit   F1-Help   F6-Expand   F8-Sort   Alt+F8-List   ↑F8-Save   F10-Continue
```

Fig. 8.3. *The Retrieve Spec screen.*

For example, if you want to print fliers for your Illinois customers only, you enter the letters *IL* in the State field. You can make the set of retrieved records as selective as you like. Suppose that the mailing is for a short-term special price offering, and you want to send it to only the customers who have said they plan to purchase something within two months. You can make that specification by placing *L=2* in the Months to Purchase field. You can select records with annual sales above a certain figure or within date ranges in a similar way. After you enter the retrieve specifications, Q&A scans the database, selecting the records that meet your selection criteria and rejecting the records that do not fit the specifications.

After filling out the Retrieve Spec, you can save it and use it again later without retyping the field selection data. Before exiting the Retrieve Spec, press Shift-F8, give the spec a name, and press F10 to return to the Retrieve Spec screen. To retrieve an already defined spec, press Alt-F8 at the Retrieve Spec screen, and select the spec from the list that Q&A displays.

Keeping printed copies of the various specs while you design a Print Spec usually is helpful. To send a copy of the on-screen spec to the printer, press F2, edit the Spec Print Options screen, and press F10.

The next section shows you how to sort information within the fields.

Using the Sort Spec Screen

If you want the displayed accounts to be sorted in a particular order, such as alphabetically by last name, in ZIP code order, or by state name, press F8 at the Retrieve Spec to call up the Sort Spec screen. This screen, shown in figure 8.4, is identical to the Retrieve Spec screen, except for the name (Sort Spec) at the bottom of the screen. You can specify the sorting order by entering numbers between 1 and 999 in the fields you want to sort. Q&A recognizes the field with the number 1 as the primary sort.

```
                 TITAN TECHNOLOGY SALES LEAD TRACKING SYSTEM
                                                   File Name -- SlsLead
     LastName:                        FirstName:
     Title:
     Company:                         Telephone:
     Address1:
     Address2:
     City: 1 AS                       State:          Zip:
        No. of Labs: 2 DS             Annual Revenue:
        Current Customer:             Company Priority:
     LEAD INFORMATION————————————————————————————————————————————
        Product Interest:
        Request For:                  Lead Source:
        Months to Purchase:           Product Priority:
     SALES ACTION————————————————————————DATES————————————————————
        Sales Priority:               Date Entered:
        Sales Dist.:               Date Info Sent:
        Salesman:                     Sales Contact:
        Status:                         Demo Date:


     SLSLEAD.DTF                 Sort Spec              Page 1  of 1

     Esc-Exit  F1-Help  F6-Expand  Alt+F8-List  ↑F8-Save  F9-Retrieve  F10-Continue
```

Fig. 8.4.   *The Sort Spec screen.*

Suppose that you want to sort by city within the state of Illinois (or any other state you specify in the State field). Enter a *1* in the City field. Then enter *AS* to indicate an ascending sort, or *DS* for a descending sort. For example, a primary ascending sort by city arranges the records for the cities in the state alphabetically, starting with the letter A. The field entry is as follows:

    1 AS

If your secondary sort is to be by the number of labs, enter a *2* in that field. The secondary descending sort by number of labs ranks all the accounts in each city by showing the records with the most labs first. In the Number of Labs field, type the following:

    2 DS

You probably want a third sort, by the customer's last name. This sort should be an ascending sort so that the customers in a particular city with credit limits of $5,000, for example, are listed alphabetically within the $5,000 group for that city. In the LastName field of the Sort Spec screen, enter the following:

3 AS

You can enter the sort specs without spaces between the field number and the AS or DS specification (1AS), or you can use a comma between the two items (1, AS).

After filling out the Sort Spec, you can save it and use it again later without retyping the sort specifications. Before exiting the Sort Spec, press Shift-F8, give the spec a name, and press F10 to return to the Sort Spec screen. To retrieve an already defined spec, press Alt-F8 at the Sort Spec screen, and select the spec from the list that Q&A displays.

When you finish with the Sort Spec, press F10 to continue to the Fields Spec screen. Again, the only difference on this screen is the name displayed at the bottom of the screen. The next section explains how to use the Fields Spec screen.

Setting Field Specs: Free-Form or Coordinate

You use the Fields Spec screen to tell Q&A where to print the fields on the page (see fig. 8.5). If you press F10 when the Fields Spec screen is displayed, all fields are printed as they appear on the form design. To modify the way the fields appear on the printout, you can use the free-form or the coordinate style

The *free-form* style offers a moderate level of control over data placement on printouts. Free-form reporting is used for mailing labels and other types of printouts that can use the fields directly from the form design.

You print free-form fields by placing either an X (upper- or lowercase) or a + (plus sign) in the fields you want to print. An X tells Q&A to print the field and move down one line; a + tells the program to print the field, move to the right and skip a space, and print the next field. An E tells Q&A to print all the data in the field, even if the contents are larger than will fit in the line; if the text doesn't fit, the extra text is wrapped to subsequent lines. For example, the following entry tells Q&A to print the field called Notes in the first column, to wordwrap the contents, and then move down a line:

NOTES: IXE

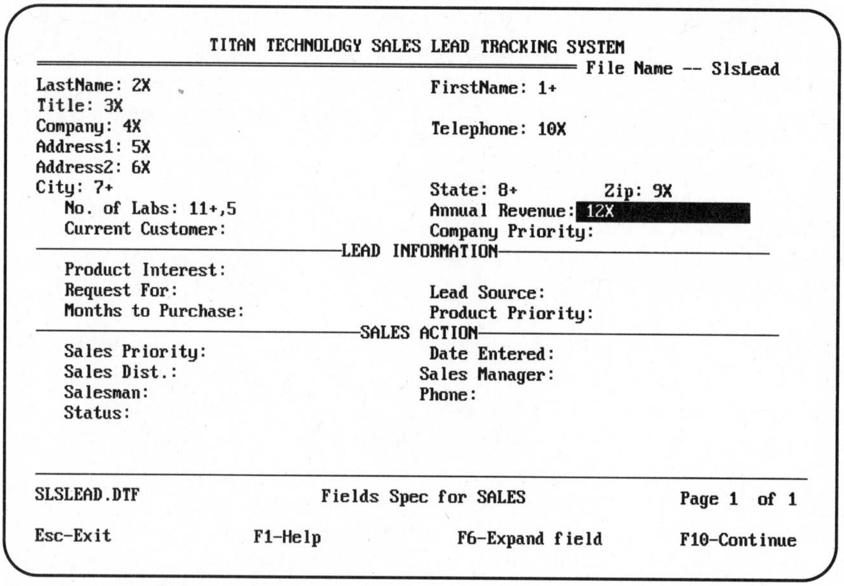

```
                  TITAN TECHNOLOGY SALES LEAD TRACKING SYSTEM
                  ==================================== File Name -- SlsLead
  LastName: 2X                           FirstName: 1+
  Title: 3X
  Company: 4X                            Telephone: 10X
  Address1: 5X
  Address2: 6X
  City: 7+                      State: 8+        Zip: 9X
      No. of Labs: 11+,5        Annual Revenue: 12X
      Current Customer:         Company Priority:
                          ----LEAD INFORMATION----
  Product Interest:
  Request For:                  Lead Source:
  Months to Purchase:           Product Priority:
                          ----SALES ACTION----
  Sales Priority:               Date Entered:
  Sales Dist.:                  Sales Manager:
  Salesman:                     Phone:
  Status:


  _____
  SLSLEAD.DTF             Fields Spec for SALES            Page 1  of 1

  Esc-Exit         F1-Help              F6-Expand field      F10-Continue
```

Fig. 8.5. *The Fields Spec screen.*

When you number the fields during free-form printing, you tell Q&A in what order to print the information. You also can specify how many lines should follow an X field and how many spaces should follow a + field. For example, if you enter *1X,3* in a field, Q&A prints that field first and moves the cursor down three lines. If you enter *2+,3* in a field, Q&A prints that field second and moves the cursor right three spaces.

Although Q&A Write includes a mailing-label routine that provides easy, flexible mailing-label preparation, you can prepare labels and similar special reports with File's free-form printing. For example, if you have a file that includes names and addresses, you can number the fields and set carriage returns (with Xs) to construct mailing labels. The field locations on the form can be in any order. Figure 8.6 shows an example of how you would format a mailing label with free-form style.

The free-form printing style basically is line-oriented because it enables you to specify where data prints only in relation to the preceding printed field. When you specify 6X, for example, you are telling Q&A to print this field sixth in line and to follow the information with a carriage return. Where field number 6 is printed depends on where field number 5 is printed.

You can use the *coordinate* style to generate custom-designed reports and to transfer information to preprinted forms. In the coordinate style, you specify

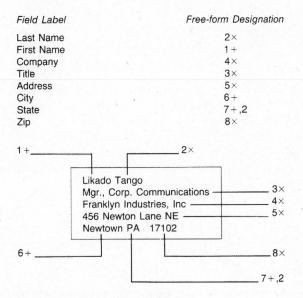

Field Label	Free-form Designation
Last Name	2×
First Name	1+
Company	4×
Title	3×
Address	5×
City	6+
State	7+,2
Zip	8×

Fig. 8.6. *A sample free-form mailing label.*

field length and the exact printing location of the fields by row and column coordinates. Unlike free-form printing, coordinate printing is page-oriented because you can print any field in the record anywhere on the page regardless of where other fields are printed. Coordinate printing is particularly useful if you are printing File output in preprinted forms and you need to have the data fit precisely in a predetermined location. You can print only one form per page with coordinate style.

The concept of coordinates assigns a unique designation to every possible printing position on the page. Two numbers are required to define any point on the page: one for the horizontal position, and another for the vertical position. You can think of coordinates as a spreadsheet's rows and columns or the coordinate positions on an XY graph. The first printing position on the upper left corner of the page is equivalent to the A1 spreadsheet location or the intersection of the X and Y axes on a graph.

This first position is designated in Q&A by the numbers 1,1—for the first row in the first column. Some other printing and screen graphics programs designate this first position as 0,0. Q&A makes understanding the concept easier by using a designation more in line with the way people think.

From this "home" position you can define any other page position by increasing the row and column numbers the proper amount. The approximate center position on the first printing line of an 8.5-inch page, for example, is 1,40. Notice that the first number is for the row, the second number is for the character column. The center printing position on the 20th printing line is 20,40. Q&A accepts these specs separated by a comma or a space.

To construct coordinate reports, you enter two or three numbers (column number, line number, and field length), separated by commas, in the fields you want to print. For example, suppose that you enter *4,6,10* in the Company field. The company name from each record prints, starting at column 6, line 4, and is truncated if the name is more than 10 characters long. The last figure is optional; you use it only if a field is too long to fit where you want it printed.

Q&A also enables you to combine coordinate and free-form print methods. You can use the coordinate method to specify the contents of one field as a heading, for example; then print the other fields with the free-form method. This combination of methods may be useful to make the design of some reports easier. Free-form reporting sometimes is less complicated because you do not have to worry about the precise location of printed data on the page, and you are concerned only with the relative positions of fields. Mixing methods, however, has no particular advantage, given the far greater flexibility of Q&A's Report module.

Remember, you can make a printed copy of the Fields Spec by pressing F2 to display the Spec Print Options screen, making changes as necessary, and pressing F10.

On the Fields Spec screen, you also can add text enhancements, as described in the next section.

Using Text Enhancements

You can improve the appearance of your printed output by applying boldface, underlining, fonts, and other enhancements to the codes on the Fields Spec. When you enter a code, simply apply the enhancement to the code itself. For example, if you enter *5X* in the Name field, you can apply a Times Roman font code and a boldface enhancement code to the X character. Use the following steps to apply text enhancement:

1. On the Fields Spec screen, press Shift-F6 to display the Enhancements menu.

2. Select the enhancement or font you want to use.

3. Use the arrow keys to highlight the part of the field to be enhanced.

To enhance only the data, highlight any portion of the field. To enhance the field label, type a comma and an *L* in the field before applying an enhancement—for example, 5X,L.

(To assign fonts to the keys, press Ctrl-F9 to display the Font Assignment screen, or press A at the Text Enhancement and Fonts Menu.)

To improve the appearance of a coordinate print spec, apply enhancements to the page coordinates. And to enhance a label, apply the enhancement to the L code or to the text in parentheses following the L code.

To enhance only the label, apply the enhancement only to the L. To enhance both data and label, apply the enhancement to the L and any other portion of the code. For example, applying fonts and/or enhancements to E,L in a field that contains the code 1XE,L enhances both data and label.

When you finish the Fields Spec screen and have added all enhancements you want to apply, press F10 to move to the File Print Options screen, shown in figure 8.7.

```
                      FILE PRINT OPTIONS

    Print to......:   PtrA   PtrB   PtrC   PtrD   PtrE   DISK  SCREEN

    Page preview.................:    Yes  No

    Type of paper feed...........:  Manual  Continuous  Bin1  Bin2  Bin3

    Print offset.................:   0

    Printer control codes........:

    Print field labels...........:   Yes  No

    Number of copies.............:   1

    Number of records per page...:   1

    Number of labels across......:   1  2  3  4  5  6  7  8

    Print expanded fields........:   Yes  No

  SLSLEAD.DTF          Print Options for SALES
  Print to screen with page size adjusted to fit the screen.
  Esc-Exit        F8-Define Page        F9-Go back        F10-Continue
```

Fig. 8.7.   The File Print Options screen.

Selecting Print Spec Options

The File Print Options screen gives you an opportunity to change some of the report output options. You can choose among five printers, a disk file, a page preview, and the screen. You also can enter print offset and printer control codes from this screen. The Print Offset option enables you to choose the default left margin for printed material. The default is 0, but you may need to change this setting to account for special paper sizes or to allow for operational peculiarities of your printer. The Printer Control Codes option enables you to send special instructions to your printer to control font selection or other features. You can turn on compressed print, for example, or send PostScript commands directly to the printer by entering the proper codes in this field.

After you specify the number of copies you want to print, you need to enter the number of forms you want printed on each page. Q&A's default for this setting is 1. If you are printing the contents of only a few fields from a small database, and your printed page is mostly blank, you may want to change this option.

One full database screen covers 21 printed lines. If each record from your database uses only one screen, you may want to set your printer page length at 66 (on the Define Page screen) and the number of forms per printed page option to 3. You then will get three records on each page and save paper. Of course, you may have good reason to print only one record per page and leave the rest of the page blank. If you need to sort the printed records, if you need to distribute parts to different locations, if you are putting the printouts into a notebook, or if you need to make handwritten notes on each record, leave one record per page.

When you have completed your choices from the File Print Options screen, you can press F8 to call up the Define Page screen in order to format the appearance of page contents. Before moving on to Define Page, however, you may find that checking the report's appearance is helpful. You can do so with the Page Preview option from the File Print Options screen.

Viewing a Page Preview

If your computer's monitor supports graphics, you can view a formatted copy of your printed data on-screen. At the File Print Options screen, set Page Preview to Yes and press F10 to display the page preview. The Page Preview feature is available from Q&A's print specs in File, Write, and Report and also can be displayed from the Intelligent Assistant.

After the page preview screen appears, you can press the + and − keys to "zoom" in and out to enlarged and reduced views of the printed data. Press F1 (Help) for the complete list of options, which include displaying side-by-side, normal, half-page, and full-page views; scrolling up and down; and viewing next and previous pages. Press F2 to return to the File Print Options screen.

Enhancing the Printout with Define Page

From the File Print Options screen, press F8 to display the Define Page screen shown in figure 8.8. On this screen, you can change margins, page width, page length, and characters per inch. You also have an opportunity to set headers and footers from this screen.

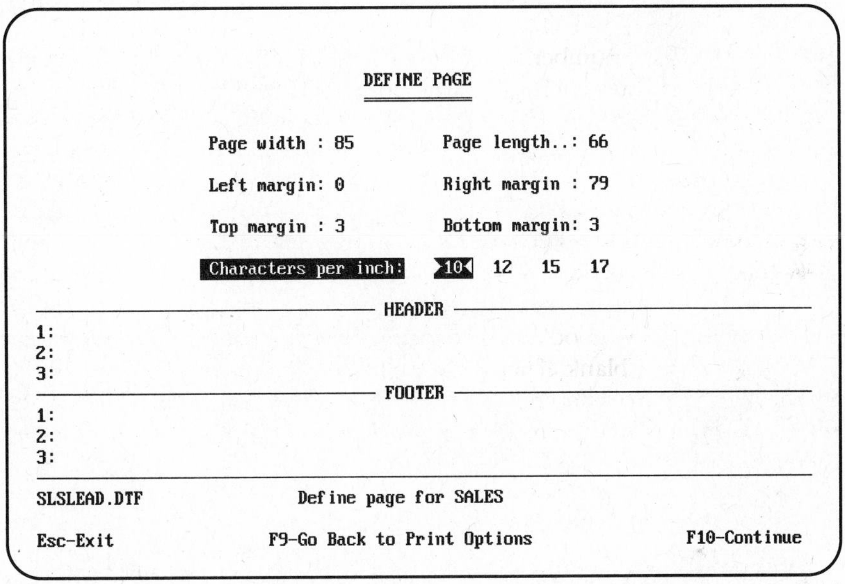

```
                           DEFINE PAGE


          Page width : 85        Page length..: 66

          Left margin: 0         Right margin : 79

          Top margin : 3         Bottom margin: 3

          Characters per inch:  ▶10◀  12   15   17
  ──────────────────────── HEADER ────────────────────────
  1:
  2:
  3:
  ──────────────────────── FOOTER ────────────────────────
  1:
  2:
  3:
  ─────────────────────────────────────────────────────────
  SLSLEAD.DTF              Define page for SALES

  Esc-Exit          F9-Go Back to Print Options      F10-Continue
```

Fig. 8.8.   *The Define Page screen.*

Changing Defaults

The default setting for page width is 85 characters, and the default page length is 66 lines. The right margin normally is set for 85 characters. You change these default settings on the Define Page screen by highlighting the option you want to change and typing the new setting in the space after that option. You can enter the new settings in inches or as the number of rows or columns. For example, if you want to specify dimensions in inches, you add the inch mark (") after each number.

In addition to controlling the page size and margins, you can change pitch (the number of characters per inch) with the Define Page screen. Ten characters per inch is used most often, but 12 pitch, which corresponds to a typewriter's elite type, is popular also. The third option, 15 pitch, may cause characters to overlap on some daisywheel or laser printers, unless you change the print wheel or font cartridge. The final option is 17 pitch, which produces condensed type on most dot-matrix printers. Some printers respond properly to this command only if they are set to print in draft mode. To change the Characters per Inch setting, use the arrow keys to highlight your choice, and then press Enter.

Using Headers and Footers

You can use the Define Page screen to customize your printouts by adding headers and footers to pages before printing. The procedure is simple. Just tab down to where the word HEADER is displayed. Position the cursor on the line below the word, and type the text you want to display at the top of each page of your printout. Handle bottom-of-page information in the same way by typing footer text below the FOOTER prompt. You may use the three available lines in the header and footer areas for anything you want. You can use one line or all three.

If you want the pages to be numbered automatically, place a pound sign (#) at the position on the line where you want the number to appear. If you put two pound signs together on a line in a header (page ##, for example), Q&A prints a pound sign with the page number. At the top of the third page, for example, you would see the following:

> page #3

In other words, when two pound signs are next to each other in a header or footer, the program interprets the first sign literally and computes and enters a page number to replace the second pound sign.

You also can have Q&A read the date and time from the system clock and enter them in a header or footer. Just type *@DATE(n)* where you want the date to appear and *@TIME(n)* where the time is to be displayed. The *n* stands for the date or time format number. For @DATE, the *n* can be a number from 1 to 20; for @TIME, the *n* can be a number from 1 to 3 (see Chapter 2 for details).

You can separate each header and footer line into three segments by using exclamation points (!) between the sections. For example, if you enter

> @DATE(1) ! WEEKLY REPORT ! Page #

Q&A prints the footer as

> August 12, 1991   WEEKLY REPORT   Page 6

Everything before the first exclamation point is left-justified, the section following the first exclamation point is centered, and the section after the second exclamation point is right-justified. Remember that Q&A treats spaces as characters, so any spaces in the information formatted with the exclamation point are included in the formatting. Unnecessary spaces may throw off centering and justification. Without the second exclamation point, everything to the right of the first exclamation point is centered.

In the following header, all the data will be right-justified because the header command is preceded by two exclamation points:

!! @DATE @TIME Page ##

As a result, the header is printed as

August 12, 1991 5:43 pm Page #6

Saving Your Print Spec and Printing

After you finish designing and customizing your Print Spec, you can save the choices by pressing F10 from the File Print Options screen or the Define Page screen. At this point, you can print your information from the specifications you have entered, or you can return to the Print menu without printing. In either case, the Print Spec you just designed is saved to disk, and you can print the spec later if you prefer. If you print, the Print menu is displayed after the printing is complete.

Using Existing Print Specs

So far in this section, you have learned to design and use a Print Spec to specify how a printed report will appear. After the Spec is created, you can reuse, rename, copy, delete, or design a new Spec. You also can make temporary changes to the Print Spec.

To use an existing Print Spec, press P from the File menu. Type the database file name if you know it. Otherwise, erase the name that appears (if any), press Enter to display a list of file names, move the highlighting to the database you want, and press Enter. When the Print menu appears, select P for Print Records. A list of existing Print Spec names is displayed. Using the cursor keys, highlight the Spec you want to use, and press Enter again.

Modifying a Print Spec

Before printing begins, a screen message asks whether you want to make any temporary changes to the design before you print. You can use this opportunity to modify the Retrieve Spec, for example, or to select a printer different from the one specified when you designed the Print Spec. If you choose to make temporary changes by selecting Y and pressing Enter, you are led through a series of screens identical to those you have seen before. On the Retrieve Spec, you specify the forms to be printed. If you want to enter sort specifications, you go to the Sort Spec screen by pressing F8. Then, from either the Retrieve or the Sort Spec, you can press F10 to get to the Fields Spec. After you have specified the field arrangement on the Fields Spec screen, press F10 to access the File Print Options screen. You can press F8 if you want to go to the Define Page options. From either File Print Options or Define Page, you then can press F10 to start the printing process.

If you press N and press Enter at the prompt that asks whether you want to make changes, the printing process begins immediately. While the document is being printed, you may see that you need to change some of the specifications. To make changes, press Shift-F9 to stop the printing. Rather than go through all the specification screens, you can directly access the screen you want to change. When you press Shift-F9, the Direct Access menu appears, as shown in figure 8.9. Press F2, choose the screen you want to edit, make the changes, and press F10 to start the printing from the beginning of the print job.

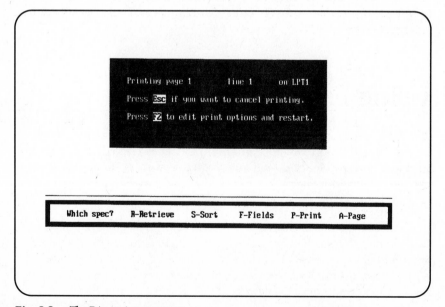

Fig. 8.9.   *The Direct Access menu.*

Renaming and Copying a Print Spec

In addition to creating a new Print Spec or modifying an existing one, you can rename or copy a print specification. The Rename/Delete/Copy menu, which you can display by selecting R at the Print menu, accesses these options.

When you select Rename a Print Spec or Copy a Print Spec from the Rename/Delete/Copy menu, Q&A asks you for the name of the Print Spec. Press Enter to see a list of defined print specifications if you cannot remember the name of the Spec you want. Use the cursor keys to highlight the name of the appropriate Print Spec, and press Enter. If you are using the Rename command, you are prompted for the new name. If you select Copy, you are asked for the name of the specification to which you want to copy.

Deleting a Print Spec

If you choose Delete a Print Spec from the Rename/Delete/Copy menu, a different prompt is displayed. After you enter a Print Spec name, Q&A asks for confirmation before the spec is deleted.

Because Print Specs are stored within the database and are not DOS files, no disk utility can restore the erased specification. If you accidentally delete a Print Spec, you cannot get it back; you have to create the specification again. If you are sure that you want to delete, select Y and press Enter at the confirmation prompt. Q&A then deletes the Print Spec.

Using Special Printing Procedures

Q&A provides several advanced printing features. You can choose from among several fonts to change the entire look of your printed document. You also can use the PostScript command language. Other commands give you increased control over your printer.

Selecting and Using Different Fonts

With Q&A Version 3.0, Symantec recognized the rising popularity of laser printers. The software now includes special files so that you can use the multiple font capabilities of laser printers.

A *font*, sometimes called a *typeface*, is a group of letters, numbers, and symbols of a particular style and size. When you change fonts, you change the size of the characters, their weight, perhaps the pitch, and certainly the overall general appearance.

Type falls into four main classes: roman, sans serif, script, and block letter. Within each class can be several hundred fonts, one for each set of characters of a particular typeface, size, and style. Some common font names are Gothic, Courier, Helvetica, and Times Roman.

Character size is measured in *points*, each point being 1/72 of an inch tall. In traditional set type, sizes range from 4-point to 144-point. Most newspapers use 8- or 9-point type. This book is set in 10-point type. A large newspaper headline may be 72-point type, or one inch tall.

Type *weight* is the relative darkness or lightness of the characters. In mechanical computer printers, such as dot-matrix or daisywheel devices, darker weight usually is achieved by hitting the paper harder and more often for each letter, sometimes with the paper offset slightly from the original position. Laser printer mechanisms achieve the same results by depositing more material at the print position instead of making multiple passes.

Using multiple fonts with Q&A requires one of Q&A's font support files and a printer with its own internal or cartridge fonts. Q&A does not supply actual fonts to the printer—only the instructions to use the fonts built into or downloaded to the printer. To change fonts at the printer level, you usually must plug in one or more electronic cartridges that store the various typefaces. Some printers support downloadable fonts. In this case, you transfer the soft font information from a floppy or hard disk, through the printer port, to the printer. If your printer uses downloadable fonts, you must load the fonts from DOS—outside Q&A—before you can use Q&A's font support. Most printers of this type have floppy disk-based utility software to help you with this procedure. Refer to your printer manual for detailed instructions.

Printing with PostScript Command Files

Different printers use different instructions to select characters and graphics. One standard instruction set that is available on many printers is PostScript, a printer-control command language used to define font and page characteristics. Because PostScript has become a printing standard, the number of printer-control languages any software or hardware manufacturer must support has been reduced. By supporting PostScript, software can output information to any PostScript-compatible printer, and the number of printers that support PostScript is growing rapidly.

If you have a PostScript printer, such as an Apple LaserWriter or an NEC LC-890, specify PostScript fonts for your File reports on the File Print Options screen (refer to fig. 8.7). On the Printer Control Codes line, you type the name of a file that stores special printer features, such as PostScript procedures or font definitions. During printing, the File print routine sends the specified control file to the printer at the beginning of each form.

An important function of PostScript support in Q&A is to reduce the number of special control files needed for a broad range of printers. Your printer may have a control language of its own; but if your printer also supports PostScript, as many do, you can use the PostScript file for almost all printer operations. Although Q&A supports many printers, with PostScript you can change printers without changing the printer definitions file.

Such computer industry standards are making life in a heterogeneous hardware and software environment much easier for users of these products.

Using Other Printer Commands

If your printer does not support PostScript, you can send the command sequences directly from the File print routine. Use the Printer Control Codes line from the File Print Options screen. Rather than specify a file name for Q&A to send to the printer (as you do to send a PostScript command file), enter a command that specifies a printer-resident font name, the point size, weight, and other features. Q&A calls this line the *On Code*, which has this format:

!Font Points (L*n* I*n* S*n*)

The exclamation point at the beginning of the line differentiates the printer command line from a PostScript command file name. *Font* is the name of any font your printer recognizes, and *Points* is the font size in 1/72-inch intervals. If you enter 4 for Points, for example, the font is 4 points high, or 4/72 of an inch. A one-inch-high font is specified as 72. To enter this point size, type *!Font 72*. The range of possible values for Points depends on your printer.

The parameters in parentheses are optional and can be used to set the following characteristics:

L*n*   Line spacing, in which *n* is the number of points between lines.
The default value for L*n* is L12, which provides the standard 6 lines
per inch (72/12 = 6).

I*n*   Control for accented characters in the IBM character set. If you
accept the default (I1), Q&A matches the IBM character set where
possible. If your printer does not support PostScript fonts, use *I0*.

S*n*   Symbol table selection. Q&A automatically matches the IBM
character set as closely as possible. Standard PostScript characters
are switched with others to match the IBM set. To disable this
feature, enter *S0*.

Creating Specific Applications

As suggested in earlier sections of this chapter, File's print features support a
variety of specialized printing capabilities, including printing labels and filling
in other printed forms. Although most stick-on labels are called mailing labels,
you can use them to print labels for inventory items or for other functions. This
section gives you two specific applications for these special printing features
accessible from Q&A File.

Printing Mailing Labels

You can use File's free-form printing option to design a print specification for
mailing labels and other special forms. Before you design a mailing label spec
in File, however, investigate the possibility of doing the job from the Write
module. Q&A Write includes some features for preparing mailing labels from
data in File, and these features could save you time. See Chapter 13 for more
information on printing mailing labels from Write.

Free-form printing from File can support label formats from one-up (one label
horizontally across the page) to eight-up (eight labels across the page). The
label becomes a custom-size form, as if you were printing on a very small piece
of paper. To specify a label size, change the print options defaults on the File
Print Options screen. The last selection on the screen is Number of Labels
Across, and you can select from 1 through 8.

The first step in designing a label Print Spec is to determine the size of your labels. How many lines at standard line spacing (6 lines per inch) will the label hold? How many characters will fit across the label? Information from the label supplier should give you these figures.

Next, decide which fields should appear on the label and in what order. Refer to the previous section on changing the order of printed fields in free-form printing. The information on sorting also applies to label printing.

To print labels from a File database, define a Print Spec for labels by placing Xs and + signs, as explained earlier, into the appropriate fields on the Fields Spec screen. For example, to print standard mailing labels from a name and address file, use the free-form style and mark the fields as shown in figure 8.10. Particularly when you have different fields for first and last names, you will want to specify field order as shown.

```
                    TITAN TECHNOLOGY SALES LEAD TRACKING SYSTEM
                                                File Name -- SlsLead
    LastName: 2X                     FirstName: 1=,10
    Title: 3X
    Company: 4X                      Telephone:
    Address1:
    Address2:
    City: 5+                         State: 6+         Zip: 7X
      No. of Labs:                   Annual Revenue:
      Current Customer:              Company Priority:
    ──────────────────────────LEAD INFORMATION──────────────
      Product Interest:
      Request For:      ▌            Lead Source:
      Months to Purchase:           Product Priority:
    ─────────────────────────SALES ACTION───────────────────
      Sales Priority:               Date Entered:
      Sales Dist.:                  Date Info Sent:
      Salesman:                     Sales Contact:
      Status:                       Demo Date:


    SLSLEAD.DTF            Retrieve Spec for SALES         Page 1  of 1

    Esc-Exit   F1-Help   F6-Expand   F8-Sort   Alt+F8-List   ↑F8-Save   F10-Continue
```

Fig. 8.10.   Free-form printing of mailing labels.

If the combined first and last name, the address field, or other label information will be longer than the width of the label, you can truncate some fields by placing at the end of that field's Print Spec a number that tells Q&A how many characters to print. The field width specification follows the spacing instructions. The sample in figure 8.10 shows the first name field shortened to 10 characters to make room for the long LastName field.

Completing Preprinted Forms

Q&A's coordinate printing, mentioned earlier in this chapter, enables you to specify precisely where File fields will be printed. You make this specification by placing coordinate numbers in the fields you want to print.

You can use coordinate printing in Q&A to print File information on preprinted forms. This capability is useful in preparing purchase orders, invoices, and other lists from the File database. The only limitation is that you can print only one record per page. Q&A has no provision for looping on fields to enable you, for example, to print a page header with information from the first record, and then fill in sequential lines with subsequent records.

You can, however, fill in forms such as employee evaluations or single-sheet product descriptions from a File database. Suppose that you are using the inventory and product description file shown in figure 8.11. This data file tracks some of the usual inventory information and, in addition, carries product specifications that might be useful in a reference catalog for an outside sales force or counter sales.

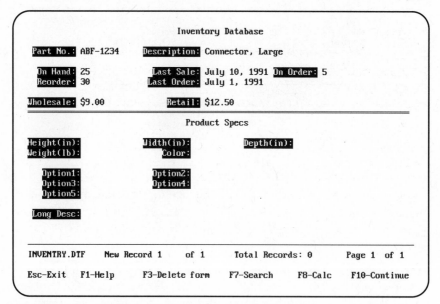

Fig. 8.11.   The inventory database record.

You can have forms printed on colored paper to present the basic information of company name and address, telephone number, and any advertising copy you want. The remainder of the form is used for information about the individual products. As the database changes, you print replacement catalog sheets for the sales force and single-sheet summary forms to mail to prospective clients for information and advertising.

If you are using preprinted forms as opposed to custom-designed forms, you should ask your supplier for a forms programming, or forms coordinate, sheet. A *forms coordinate sheet* is a reproduction of the form with print coordinates shown for each piece of information. Most suppliers have these sheets, which can greatly reduce your form setup time.

If you don't have a forms coordinate sheet, you can make one from graph paper. Use paper with an even number of squares per inch. If you use paper that has 10 squares per inch and a font that prints 10 characters per inch, for example, you can convert the number of squares directly to print positions.

First, in your File database, number the fields that will be printed on the form. Next, use a ruler to determine the coordinates on the preprinted form. Measure from the left side to get the column position and from the top to get the row number. If you find that one print position, for example, is 4.5 inches from the top and 5.25 inches from the left side, you now have the print coordinates in inches:

Row = 4.50 inches
Column = 5.25 inches

In Q&A format, these coordinates are expressed as 4.50,5.25. Q&A, however, does not use inches to position the print head on the page; the program uses print positions. Standard characters print 10 per inch, so these coordinates in Q&A are expressed as 45,52.5.

Oops! Q&A uses only whole numbers in coordinate print positions. Although today's printers can be controlled in increments smaller than one character width, this precision is not practical in a print routine like the one in File. The best you can do in this case is round the number up or down, depending on the blank you are filling. If rounding down doesn't work, round up to the nearest number. To express this measurement in Q&A terms, therefore, use 45,52 or 45,53.

Chapter Summary

In this chapter, you have learned how the File module of Q&A gives you the freedom to arrange and print your data in different forms. By designing a Print Spec, you tell the program how you want the data organized and printed. On the Retrieve Spec, you enter the fields you want the program to find. With the Sort Spec, you tell Q&A in what order you want the data sorted. Print capabilities in the Report and Write modules are explained later in this book.

The next chapter introduces you to the Write module with some quick start hints.

Part III

Using Q&A Write

Includes

Q&A Write Quick Start

Creating a Write Document

Enhancing a Write Document

Merging Documents with Q&A Write

Printing a Write Document

9

Q&A Write
Quick Start

Q &A's word-processing module is Write. Write is easy to use and offers many word-processing features:

- Search and replace text

- Check spelling

- Look up synonyms with thesaurus

- Use mailmerge (in conjunction with the File module)

- Use headers and footers

- Enhance characters by making them italic, boldface, or underlined, or use different fonts

- Print mailing labels in standard or customized formats

- Preview printed documents on-screen

- Perform calculations within a document

Many related capabilities also are available. For example, you can press F1 (Info) to access the Write module's help screens. The wordwrap feature is used while you create and edit documents. You can edit documents by using the Insert key to add text or the "strikeover" feature to type over existing text.

In this quick start chapter, you learn how to create, save, format, edit, print, and retrieve documents in Write. You apply many of Write's essential capabilities.

273

Creating a New Document

You access the Write module from the Q&A Main menu. From the Q&A Main menu, select Write. The Write menu, which has eight options, is displayed.

To create a new document, follow these steps:

1. Select Type/Edit from the Write menu.

   The screen that appears resembles the File Form Design screen in the File module. The file name displayed in the lower left corner is `Working Copy`, and several new function keys are listed on the key assignment line.

2. Press F1 (Info) and review the function key assignments. Press Esc (Exit) to return to the blank screen.

You start by typing a letter to your insurance agent, reporting a loss due to a fire in your den.

3. Move your cursor to the upper left corner of the screen and type the following letter. Press the Enter key to separate paragraphs and address lines. Do not worry about spelling errors, because you can correct them later:

   National Fire Insurance Co.
   2345 Grant Street
   Timber, CO 80459

   Dear Sirs:

   I would like to submit a claim against my homeowner's insurance policy for a radio damaged in an electrical fire. The radio was totally destroyed and cannot be repaired. Because I have no deductible amount to be satisfied on this claim, I am submitting the information on the radio along with a copy of the fire department's report on the fire.

   Thank you for your prompt attention.

Adding a Signature Block

Letters usually have a signature block at the bottom for the writer's name and signature. Before you add a signature block, you must add a tab setting to the document, using the Options menu.

To add a tab setting to your document, do the following:

1. From any location in the document, press F8 (Options) to view the Options menu. This menu is used for page layout functions, document retrieval, text alignment, block operations, print commands, and other options.

2. Select Lay Out Page from the Options menu and choose Set Tabs from the submenu. The cursor disappears from the document section of the screen and reappears on the ruler line.

3. Using the left- and right-arrow keys, move the cursor slightly more than halfway across the ruler line, type *t* for a standard tab, and press F10 to return to your document. A ⊤ appears on the ruler line to mark the tab setting.

You can set a decimal tab by typing *d* instead of *t*. You now can add the signature block two lines below the last paragraph of your document.

4. Press Enter twice to create a blank line after the last paragraph of the letter.

5. Press Tab to move to the tab you just set, and then type *Sincerely,*.

6. Press Enter three times to create two blank lines.

7. Press the Tab key to move beneath `Sincerely,` and type your name (see fig. 9.1).

```
National Fire Insurance Co.
2345 Grant Street
Timber, CO 80459

Dear Sirs:

I would like to submit a claim against my homeowner's
insurance policy for a radio damaged in an electrical
fire.  The radio was totally destroyed and cannot be
repaired.  Because I have no deductible amount to be
satisfied on this claim, I am submitting the information
on the radio along with a copy of the fire department's
report on the fire.

Thank you for your prompt attention.

                    Sincerely,


                    (Your Name)
[s⌞⌞T⌞⌞⌞⌞⌞⌞⌞⌞⌞T⌞⌞2⌞⌞⌞⌞⌞T⌞⌞⌞⌞⌞⌞⌞⌞⌞⌞T■3⌞⌞⌞⌞⌞⌞⌞⌞⌞⌞⌞⌞⌞⌞⌞⌞⌞⌞4⌞⌞⌞⌞⌞⌞⌞⌞⌞⌞⌞⌞⌞⌞⌞⌞5⌞⌞⌞⌞⌞⌞
Working Copy                      Ins  0 %  36  Line 20 of Page 1 of 1

Esc-Exit  F1-Help  F2-Print  Shift+F7-Restore   F7-Search  F8-Options  ↑F8-Save
```

Fig. 9.1. *Adding a signature block to your letter.*

Checking Your Document's Spelling

You can perform spelling checks on a single word or an entire document. Q&A uses two dictionaries for spelling checks: the main dictionary and your personal dictionary. The main dictionary is included in the software. You build your personal dictionary by adding unusual words that often appear in your writing, such as customer names or business jargon.

1. Press Ctrl-Home to move your cursor to the top left corner of the document, and press Shift-F1 to invoke the spelling checker.

You also can run the spell checker from the Options menu. Press F8 to display the Options menu, choose Other Options, and select Spellcheck Doc from the submenu. In Q&A Version 4.0 and later, you can use the Options menu to invoke many Q&A Write functions. When using the Options menu and its submenus, press the first letter of a menu item to select it. The Options submenus indicate whether a Q&A operation can be run with function keys. Using the Options menu is a great way to become familiar with Q&A Write features and their function keys.

Q&A checks the document for spelling errors (the message `Checking...` appears above the key assignment line). When Q&A finds an unknown word, the spelling menu appears. You can choose any of the following options from the spelling menu:

> List Possible Spellings
> Ignore Word & Continue
> Add to Dictionary & Continue
> Add to Dictionary & Stop
> Edit Word & Recheck

2. Proceed through the document, using the spelling menu as needed. A message on the message line tells you when the spelling check is complete, and your cursor returns to its original location.

Saving Your Document

Before you learn about some of Q&A's text-enhancement features, take a moment to save your document.

Save your documents frequently. By saving often, you will not lose your document if something happens to your computer. You can save a document by using the Shift-F8 (Save) key combination or by returning to the Write menu and selecting Save. If you try to leave a document and go into another part of the system without saving, Q&A displays a warning that the document is not saved and gives you an opportunity to save the document.

To save the letter you created, follow these steps:

1. Press Shift-F8 (Save). A prompt appears for a document name.

2. Type *fire.ltr* at the prompt and press Enter, saving the document for future use. A working copy of the document stays on-screen for you to edit further.

You can use any three-character file extension to identify a document you save. The extension LTR classifies a document as a letter. You may want to use MMO for a memo or an extension such as 191 to indicate January 1991.

This document saves quickly because it is small. With larger documents, the message Saving... shows in the message line until the process is complete. Each time you save the document, Q&A remembers the document name and fills the name in for you. You do not need to change the name unless you want to save another copy of the document under a new name.

Enhancing Text for Emphasis

By using the Shift-F6 key combination, you can improve the appearance of your letter: make text boldface, underlined, or italic; use subscript, postscript, and strikeout; select fonts; or switch settings back to regular type.

To make text boldface, follow this procedure:

1. Move your cursor to the start of the second sentence in your letter and press Shift-F6 to display the Text Enhancements and Fonts menu.

2. Type the letter of the bold enhancement. A message appears on the message line, instructing you to select the text and press F10.

3. Use the arrow keys to highlight the entire sentence, and press F10. The portion of highlighted text is displayed in a different shade depending on your particular monitor (the text doesn't appear highlighted in the figures). When printed, this portion reflects the enhancement that you requested.

You also can enhance text from the Options menu (F8) by choosing Block Operations and selecting Enhance from the submenu.

If you have a mouse, you may find that the mouse performs block operations more quickly than the keyboard. For example, to apply a text enhancement, click the Shift-F6 Enhance Text item on the status line. Q&A displays the Text Enhancements and Fonts menu. To select an enhancement for a block of text, highlight the text with the mouse cursor and double-click the left button. The menu disappears and the enhancement is applied to the block.

Using Search and Replace

Instead of referring to the damaged item as a radio, suppose you want to refer to it as an AM/FM radio. You do not have to go through the letter and retype each occurrence of radio manually, as shown in the following steps:

1. From any location in the document, press F7 (Search). A Search/ Replace box appears over your document. This dialog box has three fields: Search For, Replace With, and Method.

2. At the Search For field, type *radio* and press Enter.

3. At the Replace With field, type *AM/FM radio* and press Enter.

4. At the Method field, select the Manual option and press F10 to begin the search. Q&A stops at each occurrence of radio for you to approve the replacement.

5. Follow the prompt that appears on the message line for each occurrence of the phrase. Press F10 to replace and continue, F7 to search again, or Esc to cancel the operation. (For grammatical accuracy, you should change *a* to *an* in the first sentence.)

Figure 9.2 illustrates how your screen should look. Each occurrence of radio is now `AM/FM radio`.

You also can invoke Search by displaying the Options menu (F8), then choosing Other Options and selecting Search & Replace from the submenu.

Setting Temporary Margins

Before you have a chance to mail the letter, you discover that damage also was done to the electrical wiring in the outlet. Your electrician estimates that the rewiring will cost $275. You must add this claim to the letter. To emphasize the estimate, you want to indent the text. When starting this process, check that you are in the Insert mode—the word `Insert` should be displayed in the status line. If the indicator is missing, press the Ins key on the numeric keypad to activate this feature.

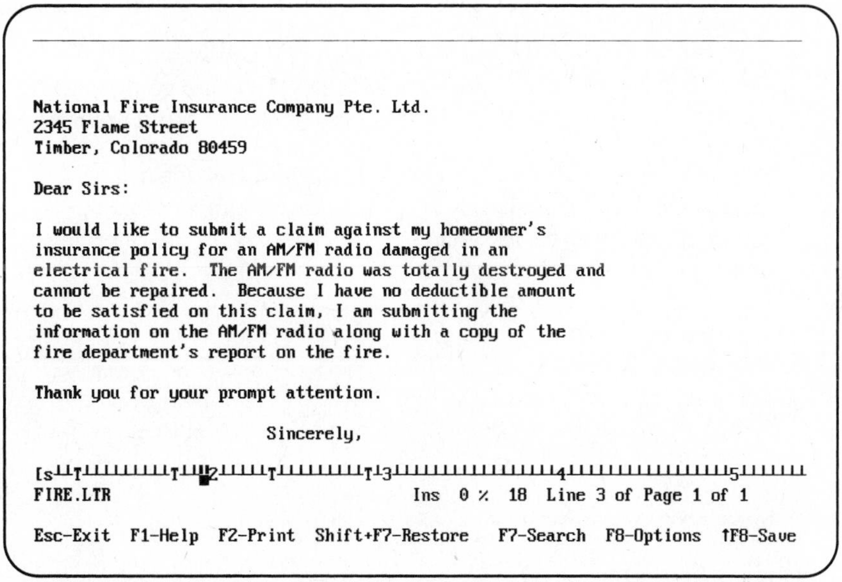

```
National Fire Insurance Company Pte. Ltd.
2345 Flame Street
Timber, Colorado 80459

Dear Sirs:

I would like to submit a claim against my homeowner's
insurance policy for an AM/FM radio damaged in an
electrical fire.  The AM/FM radio was totally destroyed and
cannot be repaired.  Because I have no deductible amount
to be satisfied on this claim, I am submitting the
information on the AM/FM radio along with a copy of the
fire department's report on the fire.

Thank you for your prompt attention.

                Sincerely,

FIRE.LTR                        Ins  0 %  18  Line 3 of Page 1 of 1

Esc-Exit  F1-Help  F2-Print  Shift+F7-Restore   F7-Search  F8-Options  ↑F8-Save
```

Fig. 9.2.   Replacing a term with another term.

To add text, follow this procedure:

1. Move the cursor to the end of the first paragraph and press the Enter key twice to create a new paragraph.

2. Add the following paragraph:

   The following electrical work must be completed to repair damaged wiring:

3. Press Enter twice and continue typing the information on the estimate:

   Replacement of the outlet and adjoining wiring and testing of the circuit. Estimate $275.00 including parts and labor.

The following steps indent the paragraph ten spaces from the left and right margins.

4. Use the arrow keys to position your cursor on the R in Replacment. Press the space bar ten times to move the line ten spaces to the right.

5. Press F6, displaying the Set Temporary Margin menu along the bottom of the screen, and select Left from that menu. The paragraph moves ten spaces to the right, and a greater-than sign (>) appears on the ruler line, indicating a temporary left margin.

6. Position your cursor ten spaces to the left of the right margin, which is indicated with a closed bracket (]). If you are going to split a word, move your cursor a few spaces to the left to avoid doing so.

7. Press F6 to display the Set Temporary Margin menu again, and then select Right from that menu. The paragraph moves in from the right margin and a less-than sign (<) appears on the ruler line, as shown in figure 9.3.

```
2345 Grant Street
Timber, CO 80459

Dear Sirs:

I would like to submit a claim against my homeowner's
insurance policy for an AM/FM radio damaged in an
electrical fire.  The radio was totally destroyed and
cannot be repaired.  Because I have no deductible amount
to be satisfied on this claim, I am submitting the
information on the radio along with a copy of the
fire department's report on the fire.

The following electrical work must be completed to
repair damaged wiring:

        Replacement of the outlet and
        adjoining wiring and testing of
        the circuit. Estimate $275.00
        including parts and labor.

[s⊥⊥T⊥⊥⊥⊥,⊥⊥⊥⊥T⊥⊥⊥2⊥⊥⊥T⊥⊥⊥⊥⊥⊥⊥⊥T▮3⊥⊥⊥<⊥⊥⊥⊥⊥⊥⊥⊥⊥⊥⊥4⊥⊥⊥⊥⊥⊥⊥⊥⊥⊥⊥⊥⊥⊥⊥5⊥⊥⊥⊥⊥⊥
FIRE.LTR                          Ins  0 %  36  Line 21 of Page 1 of 1

Esc-Exit  F1-Help  F2-Print  Shift+F7-Restore   F7-Search  F8-Options  ↑F8-Save
```

Fig. 9.3. Temporary margins appear on the ruler line.

To clear the temporary margins when you are through with them, choose Clear from the Set Temporary Margin menu.

To set temporary margins, press F8 to display the Options menu, choose Align Text, select Temp Margins from the submenu, and then select Left Margin, Right Margin, and Clear from the sub-submenu.

Deleting a Line

After reading the letter, you decide that the last sentence doesn't fit the tone you want to convey. Perhaps something milder would be appropriate. Deleting is easy in Write.

1. Move your cursor to the last sentence of the letter before the signature block (the sentence "Thank you for your prompt attention.").

2. Press Shift-F4 to delete that line.

If you want to delete only a word, press F4 (no Shift). Now you can add more information and replace the sentence.

Calculating within a Document

Just to make sure that the insurance company knows the exact amount you are expecting, include a small table with a calculation. Q&A can perform several calculations within documents: total, average, count, multiply, and divide. The following example totals a column of numbers.

1. Move your cursor to the line after the indented paragraph, press Enter to create a blank line, and type the following text (with the Insert mode active), pressing Tab at the start of each line and again to type the second column, and then pressing Enter at the end of each line:

   The total amount of my claim is as follows:

   AM/FM radio $ 79.95
   Electrical   275.00

2. To total these figures, move the cursor to the last 0 in 275.00 and press Alt-F9. The Calculation menu appears across the bottom of the screen.

3. Select Total from the Calculation menu. A message appears asking you to position your cursor where you want the result to appear and to press F10.

4. Position your cursor on the line directly below the 2 in 275.00, and press F10. Q&A inserts the total of the two numbers.

Now you need a line to separate the two figures from the total.

5. Position your cursor on the 2 in 275.00, and press Shift-F6 to display the Text Enhancements and Fonts menu.

6. Select Underline and move your cursor to highlight the entire amount of 275.00.

7. Press F10 to underline the amount. On some screens, the enhancement appears in reverse or brightened text (the text does not appear brighter in the figures). The amount prints underlined on paper.

Now add the final sentence to the letter.

8. Move your cursor one space past 354.95, and press Enter twice to create a blank line for separation.

9. Type the following sentence:

   I appreciate any help you can give me to expedite my claim.

10. Press Enter twice to create two blank lines beneath the sentence. Reposition the signature block so that `Sincerely` is even with the tab you set. Your letter should look like figure 9.4.

You also can use the Other Options submenu on the Options menu to perform calculations. Follow the instructions in step 1 above, and then press F8 (Options), press O to choose Other Options, and press C to choose Calculate.

Merging Information from the File Module

The last step you perform before printing the letter is *mailmerge*, the process of copying information from File to Write. With mailmerge, you can insert information that exists in the File module into documents. You entered information about the radio into a database called HOUSE.DTF. To import that information into the letter when printing, you must determine where you want the information to appear (in this case, between the first and second paragraphs). You then must insert the fields to be imported into the document.

```
The following electrical work must be completed to
repair damaged wiring:

        Replacement of the outlet and
        adjoining wiring and testing of
        the circuit. Estimate $275.00
        including parts and labor.

The total amount of my claim is as follows:

        AM/FM radio           $ 79.95
        Electrical             275.00
                              _____

                              $354.95

I appreciate any help you can give to expedite this
claim.

                      Sincerely,
[s⌐⌐T⌶⌶⌶⌶⌶⌶⌶⌶⌶⌶T⌶⌶2⌶⌶⌶⌶⌶T⌶⌶⌶⌶⌶⌶⌶T⌶3⌶⌶⌶⌶⌶⌶⌶⌶⌶⌶⌶⌶⌶⌶⌶⌶4⌶⌶⌶⌶⌶⌶⌶⌶⌶⌶⌶⌶⌶⌶⌶⌶5⌶⌶⌶⌶⌶
FIRE.LTR                        Ins  1 %  7   Line 30 of Page 1 of 1

Esc-Exit  F1-Help  F2-Print  Shift+F7-Restore   F7-Search  F8-Options  ↑F8-Save
```

Fig. 9.4. *Inserting a calculated total and a new closing sentence.*

To merge data from File to Write, follow this procedure:

1. Move your cursor to the end of the last sentence in the first paragraph.

2. Following fire, press the Enter key twice to create two blank lines, and then press Alt-F7.

3. When Q&A asks for the name of the database that holds the information to be merged, type *house* and press Enter. (If you are unsure of the database name, press Enter at this prompt for a list of available databases.)

   A menu appears on the right side of the screen listing field names within the HOUSE.DTF database.

4. Use the arrow keys to highlight the field name Quantity and press Enter. The field name copies into the document, including the asterisks that are necessary to complete the merge.

5. Repeat this process, separating each field by pressing the space bar once. Copy the following fields in this order: Description, Serial Number, Amount of Purchase, and Date of Purchase. Your letter should look like figure 9.5.

```
National Fire Insurance Co.
2345 Grant Street
Timber, CO 80459

Dear Sirs:

I would like to submit a claim against my homeowner's
insurance policy for an AM/FM radio damaged in an
electrical fire.  The radio was totally destroyed and
cannot be repaired.  Because I have no deductible amount
to be satisfied on this claim, I am submitting the
information on the radio along with a copy of the
fire department's report on the fire.

*Quantity* *Description* *Serial Number* *Amount of
Purchase* *Date of Purchase*

The following electrical work must be completed to
repair damaged wiring:
[s    1      2      3      4      5
FIRE.LTR                    Ins  1 %  29  Line 16 of Page 1 of 1

Esc-Exit  F1-Help  F2-Print  Shift+F7-Restore   F7-Search  F8-Options  ↑F8-Save
```

Fig. 9.5.   *Entering fields to be merged into your letter.*

You also can display the List fields box with the Options menu. Press F8 (Options), O (Other Options), and L (List Fields).

Printing Your Document

You use the Print Options screen to specify what you want printed and how. To print the letter, follow these steps:

1. Press F2 (Print) from any location in the document to begin the print operation. The first screen you see is the Print Options screen.

2. Insert a blank, formatted floppy disk in drive A.

3. Change the Print To setting to DISK, and check for the following settings on the Print Options screen:

From Page 1	To Page 1
Number of copies 1	Print Offset 0
Line Spacing .... Single	
Justify .... No	

Print to .... DISK
Page preview. .... No
Type of Paper Feed .... Continuous
Number of Columns 1
Printer Control Codes .... (blank)
Name of Merge File .... C:\QA\FILE\HOUSE.DTF

Q&A remembers the merge file from the mailmerge operation.

4. Press Ctrl-F6 (Define Pg), and check for the following settings on the Define Page screen:

Left Margin: 10   Right Margin :   68
Top Margin : 6   Bottom Margin: 6
Page Width :   78   Page Length..:   66
Characters Per Inch: 10
Begin Header/Footer on Page #...: 1
Begin Page Numbering with Page #: 1

5. Press F2 to return to the Print Options screen.

6. Press F10 (Continue) to display the Disk Print menu. Documents that are printed to disk automatically convert to a standardized code that can be read by other computers and software programs.

7. From the Disk Print menu, select IBM ASCII Format and press Enter. Write displays a prompt for the file name.

8. Type *a:fire.ltr* at the prompt and press Enter. A Retrieve Spec appears. You want to specify which form you want merged with the letter.

9. In the Item field of the Retrieve Spec, type *radio* (see fig. 9.6).

10. Press F10 (Continue) and watch the printing process.

After you press F10 (Continue), Q&A goes into the database HOUSE.DTF and scans the forms to retrieve the form for radio. When Q&A retrieves this form, the form momentarily flashes on-screen. A message indicates that Q&A is preparing to print the document. A block then appears, telling you which line and page currently are printing. The light on the front of drive A turns on, showing that the disk is in use and the document is being saved to drive A. When the process is finished, Q&A returns you to your document.

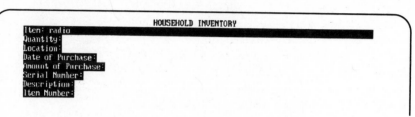

Fig. 9.6. *Entering the form to merge into the letter.*

11. After printing finishes, save your document and press Esc (Exit) to return to the Write menu. Figure 9.7 illustrates how the final letter looks with the mailmerge fields completed.

```
National Fire Insurance Co.
2345 Grant Street
Timber, CO 80459

Dear Sirs:

I would like to submit a claim against my homeowner's
insurance policy for an AM/FM radio damaged in an
electrical fire.  The radio was totally destroyed and
cannot be repaired.  Because I have no deductible amount
to be satisfied on this claim, I am submitting the
information on the radio along with a copy of the
fire department's report on the fire.

1 AM/FM portable radio HSR260XFM $79.95  Sep 27, 1990

The following electrical work must be completed to
repair damaged wiring:
[s┴┴T┴┴┴┴┴┴┴┴┴┴T┴┴2┴┴┴┴┴T┴┴┴┴┴┴┴┴┴T┴3┴┴┴┴┴┴┴┴┴┴┴┴┴┴┴┴4┴┴┴┴┴┴┴┴┴┴┴┴┴┴┴┴5┴┴┴┴┴┴
FIRE.LTR                        Ins  1 %  53  Line 15 of Page 1 of 1

Esc-Exit  F1-Help  F2-Print  Shift+F7-Restore    F7-Search  F8-Options  ↑F8-Save
```

Fig. 9.7. *Your printed letter.*

If you want to retrieve the final letter from your disk to review it, follow these steps:

1. Choose Get from the Write menu.

2. At the document name prompt, change the document name to *a:fire.ltr* and press Enter. Q&A recognizes that the document is in a different format and displays the Import Document menu.

3. Select ASCII from the Import Document menu and press Enter. The letter appears on-screen. Because this letter was converted to ASCII format, some of the text enhancements do not appear.

Mailing all the attachments with your letter requires a large envelope with a mailing label, because the attachments do not fit in an ordinary envelope. To generate mailing labels, you use the Mailing Labels command from the Write menu, the Mailing Label Print Options screen, and a Retrieve Spec. The specific steps you must take vary depending on your hardware configuration. For more information on mailing labels, see Chapter 13.

Creating Another Document

A few more features remain for you to practice. Suppose your electrician has requested a letter to authorize the required electrical repair. This letter can use the same text as the insurance letter, but the electrician's letter must be addressed to Shocky's Speedy Electrical Repair Service. Shocky's also requires a copy of the letter to send to the insurance company, as verification that the claim has been filed for payment.

Copying Text

In the following example, you copy a portion of the insurance company's letter into a new document; enter the electrical company's name, address, and salutation; and add a closing.

1. Select Type/Edit from the Write menu to return to your letter.

2. Move the cursor to the beginning of the third paragraph in the letter (The following electrical work...).

You can press F1 (Info) to find which function key copies a block to a file (Ctrl-F5). You can see from the help screen that two copy features are available. With F5 you can copy a block of text to another location in the same document. To copy a block of text into a new file or document, you use Ctrl-F5. Press Esc to clear the help screen.

3. Press Ctrl-F5. A message appears on the message line, asking you to select the text you want to copy.

4. Using the arrow keys, highlight the paragraph starting "The following electrical work" and including the next paragraph containing the estimate information (see fig. 9.8).

5. Press F10 to continue. A prompt asks you for the file name to which to copy the block of text.

```
Dear Sirs:

I would like to submit a claim against my homeowner's
insurance policy for an AM/FM radio damaged in an
electrical fire.  The radio was totally destroyed and
cannot be repaired.  Because I have no deductible amount
to be satisfied on this claim, I am submitting the
information on the radio along with a copy of the
fire department's report on the fire.

1 AM/FM portable radio HSR260XFM $79.95 Sep 27, 1990

The following electrical work must be completed to
repair damaged wiring:

        Replacement of the outlet and
        adjoining wiring and testing of
        the circuit. Estimate $275.00
        including parts and labor.
```

```
[s⌐⌐⌐⌐⌐⌐>⌐⌐⌐⌐⌐2⌐⌐⌐⌐⌐⌐⌐⌐⌐⌐3⌐⌐<⌐⌐⌐⌐⌐⌐⌐⌐⌐⌐⌐⌐4⌐⌐⌐⌐⌐⌐⌐⌐⌐⌐⌐⌐⌐⌐5⌐⌐⌐⌐⌐
FIRE.LTR                     Ins  1 %  35  Line 23 of Page 1 of 1
Use the arrow keys to select the text you want to copy, then press F10.
Esc-Exit                                                    F10-Continue
```

Fig. 9.8. Selecting the text to copy.

6. Enter the file name. Name the letter *electric.ltr*. Press the Enter key to save the text to the new document file.

Moving text is done the same way as copying text. You can move text within a document or into a new document just as you did with the copy function except that you use Shift-F5 and Alt-F5.

You also can perform block functions from the Options menu. Instead of pressing Ctrl-F3 in step 3, press F8 (Options), B (Block Operations), and C (Copy).

Adding Text

The selected information now is copied into a new document. To edit the letter to reflect the electrical company information, follow these steps:

1. Press Esc to return to the Write menu.

2. Select Get from the Write menu for the document ELECTRIC.LTR, and press Enter. The new document appears on the screen.

The letter still needs a date, address, salutation, a closing, and your name.

Your cursor should be located in the top left corner of your screen. Be sure that you are in Insert mode (if not, press the Ins key on the numeric keypad).

3. Press Enter to create a blank line. Press the up-arrow key to move your cursor to the first space of the blank line.

Instead of having the closing and signature area at the center of the page, you format the area left-aligned on the page.

4. Type today's date. Press the Enter key four times to insert four blank spaces between the date and the beginning of the address.

Now you add the name, address, and salutation to the letter.

5. Enter the name and address as shown, pressing the Enter key for each new line. Press Enter after the salutation to separate the salutation from the first paragraph of the letter:

   Shocky's Speedy Electrical Repair Service
   9054 Jolt Avenue
   (Your City, State, and ZIP code)

   Dear Mr. Shocky:

Now add the closing and your name to this letter.

6. Use the down-arrow key and the Enter key to move your cursor two lines below the last sentence of the letter.

7. Type *Thank you for your help in this matter.* Press Enter twice to put a blank line between the letter and the closing.

8. Type *Sincerely,*. Press Enter three times and then type your name. The letter to Shocky's Speedy Electrical Repair Service should look like figure 9.9 (the date scrolls past the top of the screen).

Indicating a New Page on Your Document

Shocky's requires a copy of the letter to send to the insurance company. To do this, you must add the insurance letter as a second page to this letter and reference the insurance letter as an attachment.

```
Shocky's Speedy Electrical Repair Service
9054 Jolt Avenue
(Your City, State and Zip Code)

Dear Mr. Shocky:

The following electrical work must be completed to repair damaged
wiring:

     Replacement of the outlet and adjoining wiring
     and testing of the circuit. Estimate $275.00
     including parts and labor.

Thank you for your help in this matter,

Sincerely,


(Your Name)
[s⊔⊔T⊔⊔⊔⊔⊔⊔⊔⊔T⊔⊔2⊔⊔⊔T⊔⊔⊔⊔⊔⊔⊔⊔T⊔3⊔⊔⊔⊔⊔⊔⊔⊔⊔⊔⊔⊔⊔⊔4⊔⊔⊔⊔⊔⊔⊔⊔⊔⊔⊔⊔⊔5⊔⊔⊔⊔⊔
ELECTRIC.LTR                     Ins  0 %  12  Line 19 of Page 1 of 1

Esc-Exit  F1-Help  F2-Print  Shift+F7-Restore   F7-Search  F8-Options  ↑F8-Save
```

Fig. 9.9. Your electrical company letter.

To begin, you must indicate that the current letter is page one and that you will add a second page to this document as in the following steps:

1. Move your cursor one line below your name.

2. Select F8 (Options).

3. Select Lay Out Page from the Options menu and Newpage from the submenu, and then press Enter.

Page two shows on-screen. Press the up-arrow key to view the preceding page. A character that resembles a reverse double L is on the left margin at the bottom of the page. This *page break character* tells the program that a second page follows.

Inserting a Document

To add the second page to the document, follow these steps:

1. Press the down-arrow key to move the cursor to the beginning of page two.

Because you addressed the first letter to the insurance company, you can insert that entire document on page two of Shocky's letter.

2. Press F8 (Options).

3. Select Documents from the Options menu, choose Insert a Document from the submenu, and press Enter. A prompt asks for the name of the document to be inserted. Check that the drive path displayed in the prompt is correct.

4. Type the name of the letter: *fire.ltr*. Press Enter. The letter to the insurance company appears at the top of page two of your new document.

Using Headers and Footers in Your Document

To finish the letter, you must add a header so that Mr. Shocky will know that this page is an attachment. A *header* or *footer* is a block of text that prints at the top or bottom of pages of a document. You can use the Define Page screen to specify that the header or footer begins printing on a certain page.

1. Press F8 (Options) and select Lay Out Page. Choose Edit Header from the submenu. Five blank lines and a double line appear at the top of the letter. This header editing area holds the header text.

2. Type *Attachment A* and press Enter. Your header should look like figure 9.10.

3. Press F10 to exit the header and return to the body of the document.

Headers will appear on the document when the document is printed. The header should start on page two because page one is not an attachment. The starting page number is specified on the Define Page screen. You can check this screen to verify the setting.

4. Press Ctrl-F6 (Define Pg) to see the Define Page screen.

```
Attachment A


National Fire Insurance Company Pte. Ltd.
2345 Flame Street
Timber, Colorado 12345

Dear Sirs:

I would like to submit a claim against my homeowner's insurance policy
for an AM/FM radio damaged in an electrical fire.  The radio was
totally destroyed and cannot be repaired.  Because I have no
deductible amount to be satisfied on this claim, I am submitting the
information on the radio along with a copy of the fire department's
report on the fire.

*Quantity* *Description* *Serial Number* *Amount of Purchase* *Date of
[......T....3....T....4........5........6........7........T....].....9....
ELECTRIC.LTR                         Insert   2 %   Line 2 Header

F1-Info        Shift+F6-Enhance        F8-Options          F10-Exit Header
```

Fig. 9.10.   Adding a header to your letter.

5. Adjust your settings to match the following settings:

> Left Margin: 10   Right Margin : 68
> Top Margin : 6   Bottom Margin: 6
> Page Width : 78   Page Length..: 66
> Characters Per Inch: 10
> Begin Header/Footer on Page #...: 2
> Begin Page Numbering with Page #: 1

6. Press F10 to return to your document and save the document using Shift-F8.

7. Press Esc to return to the Q&A Write menu.

Retrieving a Document That Has Been Saved

If you decide to edit your letter to the National Fire Insurance Company and select Type/Edit, you return to your ELECTRIC.LTR document. If you select

Clear, you get a blank screen. To retrieve documents that have been saved, follow these steps:

1. Select Get from the Write menu.

2. When prompted for the name of the file, type *fire.ltr* and press Enter.

Q&A retrieves the document FIRE.LTR from disk and displays the document for further editing.

If you forget the name of a document, press Enter at the Document prompt. Q&A shows a list of the files in the logged disk or subdirectory. Move the cursor to choose the correct file and press Enter to retrieve the file to the editing screen.

You also can retrieve documents from the Options menu. To do so, follow these steps:

1. Choose Type/Edit from the Write menu.

2. Press F8 (Options), and press D to open the Documents submenu.

3. Notice that in the Documents submenu Write stores the names of the last 12 documents you have edited. To recall one of these documents, move the cursor to the document's name and press Enter.

4. If the document you want isn't listed on the Document submenu, press G to choose Get a document.

You can press Enter to retrieve the document listed at the prompt. Press F4 to clear the prompt line, and then press Enter to display a complete list of files in the current subdirectory. Move the cursor to a document name and press Enter to retrieve the document.

If you want to leave Write, press Shift-F8 to save the file and press Esc until you reach the Main menu.

Chapter Summary

This quick start session has showed how to create and enhance documents with styles, such as underlining, and with options, such as headers. You printed a letter to disk and merged information residing in a database in the File module. You can set tabs, check spelling, and use temporary margins when needed. Now you have the basic tools to combine both the File module and the Write module into a database/word processor capable of sharing information between modules.

Next, you should learn about the range of Write's capabilities. Chapters 10-13 explain more about Write, including creating documents, formatting and enhancing text, and printing.

10

Creating a Write Document

Q &A Write is an easy-to-use word processor that has all the features you need for producing memos, letters, reports, and other professional documents. If you have experience with other word processors, you will find that Q&A outperforms many of them. If you have used WordStar, learning Q&A Write will be easy because of the similarities in the Ctrl-key commands. In addition to a complete toolbox for word processing features, Q&A Write includes an integrated spelling checker and thesaurus, and supports the PostScript printer definition language.

Because Q&A Write keeps the current document in RAM (random-access memory), the program is exceptionally fast. The size of your document is limited by the your computer's memory. If you use the preset page format, a typical page of your text contains about 528 6-character words, or 3,168 characters. Based on a standard 66-line page, the maximum document sizes for the standard memory sizes are as follows:

512K RAM   50-page document
640K RAM   80-page document

These limits apply if memory is not also being used by memory-resident programs, print spoolers, RAM disks, or other memory utilities.

This chapter explains Q&A Write's capabilities, from basic to advanced, and gives you tips for using them. The chapter begins with the basic operations for entering and editing text, including moving, copying, and deleting text. This chapter also explains how to add headers and footers, format the entire document page, and search text automatically for something you want to find or change. Finally, you will learn how to use the spelling checker and thesaurus and how to count the number of words in the document. When you finish this chapter, you will have a thorough understanding of how to produce a finished document. (See Chapter 11 for information on formatting text and Chapter 13 for information on printing Write documents.)

Starting the Writing Process

To start, select Write from the Q&A Main menu. Q&A displays the Write menu shown in figure 10.1.

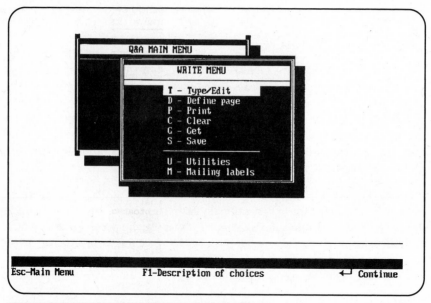

Fig. 10.1. *Selecting Type/Edit from the Write menu.*

For an explanation of each Write menu option, press F1 to view the Q&A Write help screen. The page numbers listed on the help screen indicate where to find more information in the Q&A instruction manual. Press Esc to return to the Write menu.

To begin using Write, select the Type/Edit command. You do not have to press Enter if you configured Q&A for single-key entry. (See the installation information in Appendix A.) Another way to enter commands is to use single-key number selection: instead of pressing a letter and the Enter key, you press a number that corresponds to the option. The order of menu options is numbered from upper left (1) to lower right. Using this method, you press 1 to select the Type/Edit option. You now are ready to begin a document by entering and editing text.

Entering and Editing Text

A sales lead memo shows how to prepare a document with Q&A Write, beginning with entering and editing text (see fig. 10.2). Some writers enter the entire document before they format the text; others prefer to format the text as they enter it. In this example, you enter and edit the document first. You format the document later, in Chapter 11.

```
TO:          District Sales Managers

DATE:        June 30, 1991

FROM:        Steven Hill, Marketing Support Manager

SUBJECT:     JUNE SALES LEADS

Enclosed are the sales lead forms received during June from
prospects in your sales district.  Also included is a report that
summarizes the sales leads by city, sales priority, company, and
customer request.

We are implementing a new sales tracking system that will give
you a means to keep track of sales leads and follow up. This
should help each of you unify your sales force and make sure that
each lead is pursued effectively. A Q&A disk is enclosed that
contains the sales leads for your district. Please copy these
leads into your file, and maintain them in the following manner:

     1.  When each lead is assigned, enter the name of the Sales
         Person.
     2.  Enter the date when the first sales contact was made with
         the sales lead.
     3.  Record the date of the demonstration.
     4.  Enter the status of the sale after the demonstration in
         one of the following forms:

             Sale (Model Number)        a sale was made

             Postpone                   the purchase decision was
                                        delayed

             Competitor (select one)    the prospect bought from a
                                        competitor

             Brock
             Med Sci
             Am Lab

             Other

At the end of the month, please send me a copy of this report and
the updated forms (on disk).  I will then prepare an analysis of
your district's sales activity and the effectiveness. We will be
discussing this new system more fully at our next district
meeting.
```

Fig. 10.2.   *A memo: your first writing project.*

Figure 10.3 shows the editing screen. The top portion of the screen looks like a sheet of paper; the bottom of the screen holds a ruler line indicating the location of the left ([) and right (]) margins, the tab stops (T), and the cursor. (For a detailed description of the Write Type/Edit screen, see Chapter 3.)

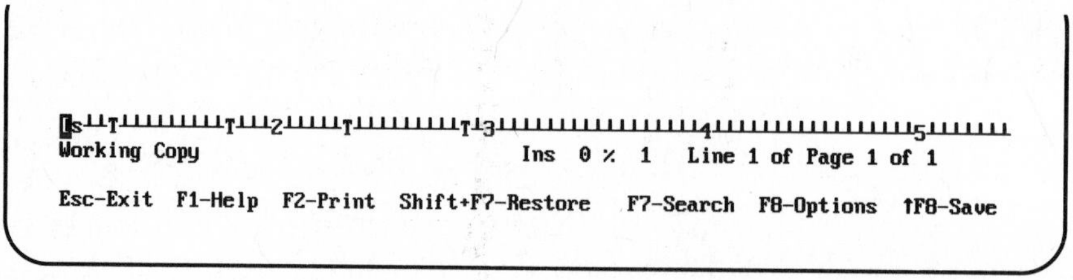

```
▮s└┴┬└┴┴┴┴┴┴┴└┬┴┴2┴┴┴┴┴└┬┴┴┴┴┴┴┴┴┴┴┬3┴┴┴┴┴┴┴┴┴┴┴┴┴┴┴4┴┴┴┴┴┴┴┴┴┴┴┴┴┴5┴┴┴┴┴┴
Working Copy                    Ins  0 %  1   Line 1 of Page 1 of 1

Esc-Exit  F1-Help  F2-Print  Shift+F7-Restore   F7-Search  F8-Options  ↑F8-Save
```

Fig. 10.3.   The Write Type/Edit screen.

To enter and edit text, you must move the cursor within the screen and around the document. When you need help, press F1 (Help) to see the key usage help screen, which lists the actions related to the function keys. Return to the Type/Edit screen by pressing the Esc key.

Entering Text

To enter text with Q&A Write, you simply type the text. Q&A Write has more power and more options than a typewriter, but entering text is similar in most respects. If you are new to computing, however, you should recognize the distinct differences between the typewriter keyboard and the computer keyboard. The following example will help you understand the special features of keys and the screen when you use Write. Begin the sample memo by entering the date and the TO and FROM information. Enter the date by typing *June 30, 1991*, then press Enter twice to move the cursor down two lines.

Begin entering the memo's address line by typing *TO:*. To make uppercase letters, you can type while holding down the Shift key or after toggling on the Caps Lock key. When you press the Caps Locks key, the indicator Cap appears in the status line to show that the key is on. Your Caps Lock key may have a light to indicate when it is on. Although the letters T and O appear in uppercase, you must press the Shift key while pressing the semicolon/colon key to enter a colon. Be sure to toggle off the Caps Lock key by pressing it again.

Press the tab key twice to move the cursor to the second tab stop (the second T on the ruler line), and type *District Sales Managers*.

Press the Enter key twice to move the cursor down two lines. To enter the FROM line, type *FROM:*, press Tab, and type *Steven Hill, Marketing Support Manager*. Press the Enter key twice to move the cursor down two more lines.

Press the Caps Lock key and type *SUBJECT:* (remembering to press the Shift key for the colon). Press the Tab key and type *JUNE SALES LEADS*. Toggle off the Caps Lock key and press the Enter key twice.

Enter the first paragraph of the memo as it appears in figure 10.4. Do not press Enter at the end of each line; Q&A Write uses wordwrap, which automatically wraps the end of one line to the beginning of the next when you type.

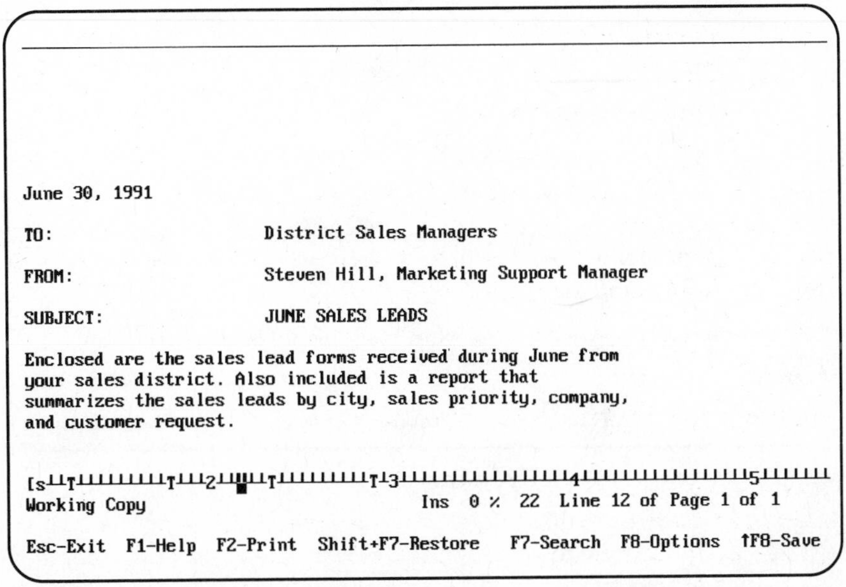

```
  June 30, 1991

  TO:                    District Sales Managers

  FROM:                  Steven Hill, Marketing Support Manager

  SUBJECT:               JUNE SALES LEADS

  Enclosed are the sales lead forms received during June from
  your sales district. Also included is a report that
  summarizes the sales leads by city, sales priority, company,
  and customer request.


  [s──T┴┴┴┴┴┴┴┴┴┴T┴┴2┴┴┴┴T┴┴┴┴┴┴┴┴┴┴┴T3┴┴┴┴┴┴┴┴┴┴┴┴┴┴┴┴4┴┴┴┴┴┴┴┴┴┴┴┴┴┴┴5┴┴┴┴┴┴┴
  Working Copy                       Ins  0 %  22  Line 12 of Page 1 of 1

  Esc-Exit  F1-Help  F2-Print  Shift+F7-Restore   F7-Search  F8-Options  ↑F8-Save
```

Fig. 10.4.   *Entering the first paragraph.*

Inserting Text

When you want to edit text by deleting or inserting characters, you can use one of two modes: Overtype or Insert. In Overtype mode (Q&A's default mode), you can change characters or add spaces directly over the text where the cursor is positioned. In Insert mode (accessed by pressing the Ins key on the numeric keypad), you can delete or insert any character or a space at the cursor position. With the typing mode set to Insert, you can type information anywhere in the text without erasing the text already there.

Notice in the memo's first paragraph that you can improve the phrase "from your sales district" by inserting words after the word *from*. To insert the new text, move the cursor to the first letter of the word *your*. Press the Ins key to change to Insert mode. Type *prospects in* and press the space bar. Finally, press the Ins key to turn off Insert mode. Your screen should look like figure 10.5. In Chapter 11, in the section on "Customizing Global Options in Q&A Write," you learn how to change Q&A Write's default from Insert off to Insert on.

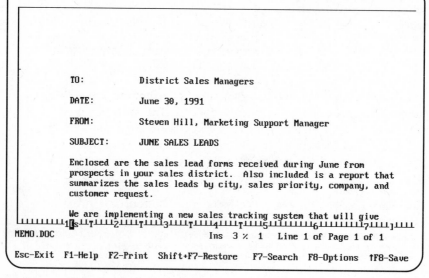

Fig. 10.5. *Inserting words in a paragraph.*

Deleting, Moving, Copying, and Printing Blocks of Text

You can work with blocks of text for eleven Write operations:

Operation	Result
Copy	Copies a block of text from one part of a document to another
Move	Moves a block of text to another part of a document
Delete	Deletes a block of text (see Restore, below)
Copy to file	Saves a copy of the block in a file
Move to file	Moves a copy of the block to a file, and deletes the block from the original location
Enhance	Formats a block with boldface, italic, underline, super-script, subscript, or fonts
Print	Prints a block of text from a document
Capitalize	Changes text within the block to uppercase
Lowercase	Changes text within the block to lowercase

Operation	Result
Title	Capitalizes the first letter of nonprepositions and acronyms in the block
Restore	Restores a deleted block and can be used to insert multiple copies of the block

A block can be as small as several words or as large as entire paragraphs or pages. Before you work with a block, you first select it. The "pivot character," central to the selection process, is the character at which the cursor is located when you start the block selection operation. The select-and-affect technique is a fast and flexible way to edit a document.

You can use a mouse to perform block operations. To select text, put the mouse cursor at the start of the text, hold down the left button, drag the cursor to the end of the block, and release the button to leave the block highlighted.

To select and work on a block of text, follow these steps:

1. Position the cursor at one end of the text block; this location becomes the pivot character.

2. Press the following function keys to affect the block:

F5	Copy
Shift-F5	Move
F3	Delete
Ctrl-F5	Copy block to file
Alt-F5	Move block to file
Shift-F6	Enhance
Ctrl-F2	Print

The preceding functions, as well as Capitalize, Lowercase, and Title, also can be selected from the Options Block Operations submenu. Using the function keys is quickest, but using the Options menu is easier for beginners. To display the Options Block Operations submenu, press F8 (Options), B (Block Operations). To choose an item from the submenu, press its first letter.

3. Select the text block by moving the cursor to the other end of the block using the cursor-movement keys; the character keys; or the Delete, Move, and Copy function keys. The text is highlighted as you select it.

4. Complete the procedure for the specified operation, as explained in the following sections.

As mentioned in step 3, three methods are available for marking a block of text. You can use the standard cursor-movement keys (the arrow keys, Home, End, PgDn, and PgUp) for selecting a text block.

You also can use character keys to select a text block. Press the following keys to select text as indicated:

Key	Function
Character key	Press a period (.), for example, to extend the block from the pivot character to the end of a sentence.
Enter	Selects text to the next carriage return
Space bar	Selects the next word
End	Selects to end of line. Press End twice to select through the last character on the screen. Press End four times to select through the end of the document.
Home	Selects to beginning of line. Press Home twice to select through the first character on the screen. Press Home four times to select through the beginning of the document.
Ctrl-End	Selects through the end of the document
Ctrl-Home	Selects through the top of the document

If you position the character at the beginning of a paragraph, press F5 to begin the Copy operation, and then type *y*. Write highlights all characters to the first *y*. If you type *y* again, the highlight continues to the next *y*. If you want to select the entire paragraph, press Enter or the period key twice (see fig. 10.6).

To cancel a selection, press Esc.

To select a block of text quickly, you can use the F3, F5, or Shift-F5 function keys (Delete, Copy, or Move, respectively). The number of times you press one of these keys determines what happens:

Pressing the key	Gives this result
Once	Activates the function (Delete, Copy, or Move)
Twice	Selects and highlights the entire word in which the cursor is located. Highlights the preceding word if the cursor is located in the single space between words or on the end-of-sentence period.

Pressing the key	Gives this result
Three times	Selects and highlights the sentence
Four times	Selects and highlights the paragraph
Five times	Selects and highlights the document

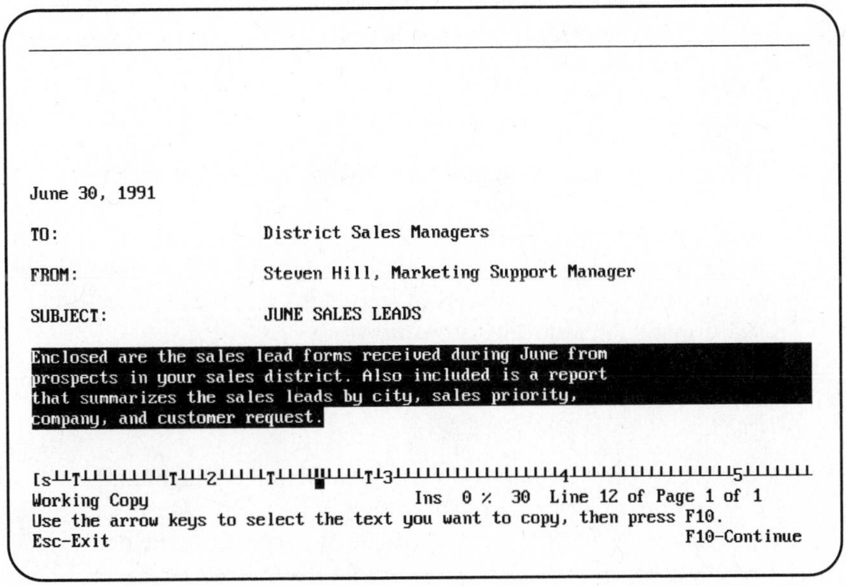

```
June 30, 1991

TO:                    District Sales Managers

FROM:                  Steven Hill, Marketing Support Manager

SUBJECT:               JUNE SALES LEADS

Enclosed are the sales lead forms received during June from
prospects in your sales district. Also included is a report
that summarizes the sales leads by city, sales priority,
company, and customer request.


[s⌐T╷╷╷╷╷╷╷╷╷╷╷T╷╷2╷╷╷╷╷T╷╷╷╷╷╷╷T³3╷╷╷╷╷╷╷╷╷╷╷╷╷╷╷╷╷4╷╷╷╷╷╷╷╷╷╷╷╷╷╷╷╷╷5╷╷╷╷╷╷
Working Copy                         Ins  0 %  30  Line 12 of Page 1 of 1
Use the arrow keys to select the text you want to copy, then press F10.
Esc-Exit                                                      F10-Continue
```

Fig. 10.6. Selecting a paragraph.

Q&A displays a message indicating what you have selected. Complete the selected operation by pressing F10 according to the procedures explained in the following sections. The following sections explain two common select-and-affect operations: moving text and copying text.

Moving Text

You can move text within a document by using the Shift-F5 key. Moving differs from copying. When you move text, you delete the text from its initial position and transfer it to a new position. When you copy text, you make a copy of the text in the new position, leaving the initial text intact.

Suppose that you decide to move the memo's date. To move the date, follow these steps:

1. Move the cursor to the line between FROM and SUBJECT, press the Ins key to turn on Insert mode, and press Enter twice to create a blank line.

2. Press the up-arrow key, type *DATE:*, and press the Tab key. Your memo, ready for the move, now has an empty DATE line.

3. Press the Home key to move the cursor to the first character of the text you want to move (in this case, the date).

4. Press Shift-F5 to begin the Move process. Q&A highlights the first character and displays the following prompt:

   ```
   Use the arrow keys to select the text you want to
   move, then press F10.
   ```

5. Select the date by pressing the down-arrow key once to select the line containing DATE: and also the first character of the blank line below. Press F10 to confirm that the highlighted text is to be moved. (If you find that the text you highlighted is not what you want moved, press Esc and repeat steps 1-3.) When you press F10, Q&A displays the following prompt:

   ```
   Move the cursor to the place you want the text
   moved, then press F10.
   ```

6. Move the cursor to where you want to move the highlighted text. To move the cursor in the memo, press the up-arrow key three times until the cursor is on the F in FROM:. Press F10. The date appears to the right of the cursor (see fig. 10.7).

```
 _____

  TO:              District Sales Managers

  DATE:            June 30, 1991

  FROM:            Steven Hill, Marketing Support Manager

  SUBJECT:         JUNE SALES LEADS

  Enclosed are the sales lead forms received during June from
  prospects in your sales district. Also included is a report
  that summarizes the sales leads by city, sales priority,
  company, and customer request.

  [s⌐T⊥⊥⊥⊥⊥⊥⊥⊥T⊥⊥2⊥⊥⊥⊥T⊥⊥⊥⊥⊥⊥⊥⊥T⊥3▪⊥⊥⊥⊥⊥⊥⊥⊥⊥⊥⊥⊥⊥⊥4⊥⊥⊥⊥⊥⊥⊥⊥⊥⊥⊥⊥⊥⊥5⊥⊥⊥⊥⊥⊥
  Working Copy                      Ins  0 %  38  Line 3 of Page 1 of 1

  Esc-Exit  F1-Help  F2-Print  Shift+F7-Restore   F7-Search  F8-Options  ↑F8-Save
```

Fig. 10.7. Moving the date.

You also can use the Options menu to move text, although the process is slower. In step 4 above, instead of pressing Shift-F5 (Move), press F8 (Options), B (Block Operations), and M (Move).

Copying Text

Copying is similar to moving: you press F5, select the text to be copied, and move to where you want to copy the text. Remember that when you copy text, the text remains in the initial location and is reproduced in the new location.

Perform the following steps to copy the first paragraph in the memo:

1. Move the cursor to the first character of the paragraph.

2. Press F5, the Copy function key. Q&A tells you to select the text to be copied and then to press F10.

3. Highlight the paragraph by moving the cursor to the end of the paragraph (remember to include the period).

   Q&A offers several ways to highlight the paragraph. An easy way is to press the period key after Block mode is turned on; Q&A moves the cursor to the next period. You also can press End to highlight the first line, press the down-arrow key three times to highlight the entire paragraph, and then press F10. Finally, you can press F5 four times to highlight the paragraph before pressing F10.

4. Use the down-arrow key to move the cursor down two lines to where you want the copied paragraph to begin; then press F10. Notice that the copied paragraph starts where the cursor is positioned.

You can review the Delete function by deleting the paragraph you just copied. Press F3 to delete this paragraph. Follow the prompts to highlight the paragraph again and press F10 to remove the text. To restore a deleted block, press Shift-F7. You can create multiple copies of the block by moving the cursor to the desired insertion point and pressing Shift-F7 several times. The Restore function does not work if you have performed another block operation since deleting the text you want to restore.

The Move and the Copy functions are powerful editing tools for creating and changing documents. Q&A Write provides an easy and flexible approach to these operations. The more you use these operations, the more you will appreciate them.

You can use the Options menu to copy text. Instead of the preceding step 2, press F8 (Options), B (Block Operations), and C (Copy).

Copying and Moving Text to a File

Q&A can save a block of text to a file. This feature enables you to save text to use again later. These *boilerplate* files save time retyping frequently used paragraphs. For example, you can save the memo heading in the sample letter and recall the heading with a few keystrokes:

1. Move the cursor to the first letter of TO:. Press Ctrl-F5 (Copy to File), and move the cursor to the letter J in June.

2. Press F10. Q&A prompts you for a file name.

3. Type *MEMO* and press F10 to save the memo header and return to the Type/Edit screen. You can recall the file later to remove the name and date information.

You can use the Options menu to copy text to a file. In step 1, instead of pressing Ctrl-F5, press F8 (Options). Press B to choose Block Operations, and use the down-arrow key to choose Copy to File. (In this case, you cannot press C to choose Copy to File, because more than one item on the submenu begins with C.)

To move the block to a file (erasing the block from the document), press Alt-F5 in step 1 above. To use the Options menu, choose Move To File at the Block submenu.

Enhancing Text

You can enhance a block of text, applying boldface, underline, italic, super-script, subscript, and fonts. Enhancing text is discussed in detail in Chapter 11, under "Enhancing Text." The following steps describe the process:

1. Move the cursor to the start or end of the text you want to en-hance, and press Shift-F6. Q&A displays the Text Enhancements and Fonts menu.

2. Type the code for the enhancement you want, and then highlight the block that you want to enhance.

3. Press F10 to apply the enhancement.

You also can enhance text with the Options menu. Instead of step 1, press F8 (Options), B (Block Operations), and E (Enhance).

Changing the Case of Text

You can convert all the text in a block to uppercase, lowercase, or initial capitalization. Unlike other block operations, these functions lack function key assignments, so they must be invoked from the Options menu.

Move the cursor to the start or end of the block you want to enhance, and press F8 (Options), B (Block Operations), and choose Capitalize, Lowercase, or Title.

Capitalize converts text to all capital letters. Lowercase converts text to all lowercase. Title capitalizes the initial letter of every word except for prepositions, articles, or conjunctions (of, a, and, the), and acronyms (NASA).

Saving and Retrieving Your Document

Computer documents are saved in files. Just as you save a paper document in a file folder with a name on the folder tab, you save a computer document by giving it a file name and storing the document on a disk. To save a document, therefore, you must know how to give it a file name.

Naming Document Files

Q&A Write file names must adhere to the rules of DOS: up to eight characters plus a three-character file extension. A period is used between the root file name and the extension, but no other punctuation or special characters are allowed. Unlike the Q&A File module, Q&A Write enables you to add your own file extension. You can take advantage of this feature by using the extension to indicate what kind of document the file contains. For example, you can use LET for letters and MEM for memos. Or you may want to use extensions to identify the category of a document, such as SLS for sales and CUS for customers. Develop an extension system that suits your documents.

Documents often evolve through several revisions. To indicate which version of a document a file contains, you can include a number in your file names. For example, you can call the first version of the sales lead memo SLSLEAD1.MEM, and the second version SLSLEAD2.MEM. This numbering system helps you to keep track of a document from first draft to final copy.

You can use this numbering system in other ways as well. For files that refer to specific months, use two digits (01 through 12) to identify the month. For example, you can use SLSTOT10.RPT as the file name for the October Sales Totals report. If documents refer to the quarters of a year, you can use Q1, Q2, Q3, and Q4 in the file name, as in FINRPT.Q1, the file name of the financial report for the first quarter.

With Q&A 4.0 and later versions, you also can give your files a 72-character description. Q&A displays this description at the bottom of the screen when the cursor rests on the file name in a file list. For details, see the section "Entering File Descriptions," later in this chapter.

Saving a Document

Write includes two ways to save Write documents: the menu method and the function key method. The function key method, Shift-F8, quickly saves a current document. To use the menu method, press the Esc key to return to the Write menu, select Save, and enter a new document name.

To save the memo using the menu, follow these steps:

1. Press Esc to leave the Type/Edit screen.

2. Choose Save from the Write menu. A prompt appears, asking for the file name.

3. Enter a document name. Type *SLSLEAD.MEM* (uppercase or lowercase) and press Enter. Q&A saves the document to the default drive and directory.

If you already have saved the document, Q&A shows the document's file name. If you want to save the document to a different file name, you can do one of three things:

- Edit the file name and then press Enter to save the document.

- Erase the existing file name (not the file itself) by pressing the space bar. Type another file name and press Enter to save the document.

- Erase the existing file name (not the file itself) by pressing the space bar. Press Enter to display the list of document names, move the cursor to the name of the file to which you want to save the document, and save the document by pressing Enter.

Q&A automatically adds the default drive and directory to the file name. You can set a different drive and directory. After saving the document, Q&A returns to the Write menu.

Use the function key method (Shift-F8) as a shortcut for saving documents. To safeguard against a sudden power outage or equipment failure, use this method frequently when you work. Shift-F8 is available only from the Type/Edit screen. When you save a document using Shift-F8, Q&A returns you to the editing screen after the save. You then can continue working with minimal interruption. To save an existing document with Shift-F8, follow these steps:

1. Press Shift-F8 at any point in Type/Edit. Q&A displays a box over the document containing the document's file name.

2. Name the document. Press Enter to confirm the current file name.

Entering File Descriptions

You can give a Q&A Write document a descriptive file name to make it easier to tell what the file contains. When Write prompts you for a file name, you can display a list of document files. When you move the cursor to a file's name, the description appears highlighted at the bottom of the screen. To assign a description to a file, follow these steps:

1. You first must save the file. To learn how to save files, refer to the preceding section on "Saving a Document."

2. At the Write menu, choose Get. Q&A prompts you for the name of a file to retrieve.

3. Press Shift-F4 to erase the prompt and press Enter to display the list of files.

4. Move the cursor to the name of the file you just saved, and press F6. Q&A displays a box in which you can type a description up to 72 characters long.

5. Press Enter to return to the list of files. Notice that the highlighted description is displayed at the bottom of the screen.

To change a file description, highlight the file's name in the list of files and press F6. You can use any of Q&A's editing keys, including the arrow keys, Delete, and Backspace.

Clearing the Type/Edit Screen

If you want to erase everything on the Type/Edit screen, press the Esc key to return to the Write menu. Select Clear and press Enter. If the contents of the Type/Edit screen have been saved already, Q&A erases whatever was on-screen and returns you to a clear screen. The saved document remains on disk; only the on-screen version is cleared in this process.

If the Type/Edit screen contains text that has not been saved, Q&A displays a warning screen when you attempt to clear the screen. To prevent erasing unsaved text, press Enter. To continue the erasing process, choose Yes and press Enter.

Retrieving a Document File

Retrieving a previously saved document, such as the sales lead memo, is easy with Q&A. From the Write menu, select Get. Q&A prompts you for the name of a document.

You can enter the document's name in two ways. You can type the name (including the extension) exactly as it was saved. You do not have to type the drive or directory unless they are different from the default drive and directory. To retrieve the sales lead memo, type *SLSLEAD.MEM*.

The other way to enter a document's name is to press Enter to display the list of documents, move the cursor to the name of the document you want to retrieve, and press Enter again.

You also can retrieve documents from the Options menu. Press F8 (Options), D (Documents), and G (Get a Document). You then can choose a file name.

In the Options Documents submenu, Q&A also lists the names of the last 12 files you edited. To recall one of those files, move the cursor to its name and press Enter.

If the file you want to retrieve is in a format that Q&A cannot recognize, Q&A displays the Import Document menu. From this menu, you can import ASCII, Special ASCII, WordStar, Lotus 1-2-3, or Symphony files. For details on importing documents, see Chapter 20.

Formatting the Page

You can set the margins, page width and length, number of characters per inch, and the appearance of headers and footers from the Define Page screen. To access the Define Page screen from the Type/Edit screen, select the Define Page command from the Write menu or press Ctrl-F6. Most page format changes show on-screen.

To set the page format, use the Tab, up-arrow, and down-arrow keys to move the cursor to the setting you want to change. Type in the new setting for all items except characters per inch (for this setting, use the space bar or the arrow keys to highlight your choice). Accept the setting by pressing Enter. Press F10 to return to your document on the editing screen.

You can change the default page format permanently so that Q&A uses your preferred settings. See Chapter 11 for further information on defining page defaults and on the last two options of the Define Page screen.

Page Size and Margins

The page size and margins determine the *document area*, which is the space available for text on the page. The preset page size and margins shown in figure 10.8 are based on an 8 1/2-by-11-inch page. Notice that the right margin, at column 68, is measured from the left edge of the page. New settings can be entered using the Define Page screen.

The document area usually is measured in columns and lines. Horizontal measurements are in columns, with each column equal to one character in the display and to one pica character when printed (pica print is 10 points per inch). Vertical measurements are in lines, usually with six lines equal to one inch.

Instead of columns and lines, you can enter measurements in inches or centimeters in the Define Page screen. You must enter " after the number of inches, or *c* for centimeters. For example, you can type *2"* for two inches or *5c* for five centimeters. Inch measurements less than one must be indicated in decimals, not fractions. Q&A converts the inch measurements to lines and columns, as shown in the following table:

Table 10.1
Inches Converted to Lines and Columns

Inches	Vertical Lines	Horizontal Columns (pica)
0"	0	0
.5"	3	5
1"	6	10
1.5"	9	15

Be careful when switching from column measurements to inches or centimeters, because Q&A measures page specifications differently for the different units. Column units measure right and left margins in characters from the left edge of the page. Inch and centimeter units measure right and left margins from the right and left edges of the page.

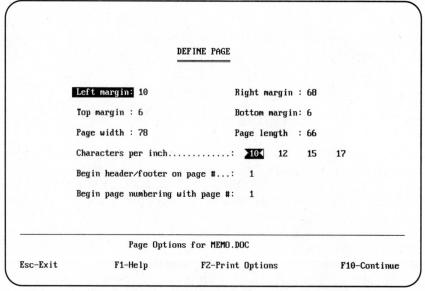

Fig. 10.8. *The Define Page screen showing preset page size and margins.*

Characters Per Inch

The width of characters is measured by the number of characters per inch (CPI). The CPI settings of 10, 12, 15, and 17 correspond to the standard measures for characters.

10 CPI	Pica (Q&A's default value)
12 CPI	Elite
15 CPI	Compressed daisywheel printing
17 CPI	Compressed dot-matrix printing

If your printer can print in varying CPI settings, you can take advantage of the capability by using the Characters Per Inch setting of the Define Page screen. Refer to your printer manual to determine your printer's capabilities. Table 10.2 lists the number of characters that can be printed on different page widths.

Table 10.2
Page Width in Pica, Elite, and Compressed Characters

Page Width	Inches	10 CPI	12 CPI	15 CPI	17 CPI
Minimum	1"	10	12	15	17
Default	7.8"	78	93	117	132
Maximum	14"	140	168	210	238
8.5"	8.5"	85	102	128	145
11"	11"	110	132	165	255

If you use a proportional font with the page width set in columns, Q&A converts the column setting to inches.

Changing Header and Footer Size

Using the Top Margin and Bottom Margin settings in the Define Page screen, you can change the size of a header or footer that contains too many or too few lines. (See Chapter 11 for more on formatting headers and footers.)

The default setting for top and bottom margins is six lines. The ordinary measurement is in lines, with six lines equal to one inch, but you also can enter a new header or footer size in inches or centimeters, adding the inch symbol (") or a *c* after the number of inches. Be sure to indicate a portion of an inch as a decimal, not as a fraction. Q&A converts the inch measurements to lines—for example:

Inches	*Vertical Lines*
0"	0
.5"	3
1"	6
1.5"	9

To change the size of headers and footers, follow these steps:

1. From the Write menu, select Define Page. From the Type/Edit screen, press Ctrl-F6 (Define Page). The Define Page screen appears.

2. Using the Tab or the down-arrow key, move the cursor to Top Margin to change the header size, or to Bottom Margin to change the footer size.

3. Type the appropriate number of lines or inches for the header or footer, and press Enter.

4. Press F10 to return to the Type/Edit screen.

Searching, Replacing, and Deleting Text

Like most other word processors, Q&A Write possesses an effective search-and-replace function. Write takes only seconds to search for, find, and replace words and phrases. Write even can delete selected words and phrases automatically.

When you want to search for something, you need only tell Q&A the word or words you want found. If you want to replace the word or phrase, you type the new word or phrase. To delete a word or phrase, you replace it with nothing.

In its default setting, Q&A finds any occurrence of a word, regardless of capitalization. If you enter sEnIoR MaNaGeR, Q&A finds senior manager, Senior Manager, or SENIOR MANAGER.

You also can tell Q&A to conduct a case-sensitive search. Press F7 and PgDn to display the Advanced Search Options screen. Change the Case setting to Sensitive. If you enter all lowercase letters when you ask Q&A to search, the program finds the item in any combination of lower- and uppercase letters. If you use any uppercase letters when you enter the search item, what Q&A finds is limited, as follows:

Searching for	*Q&A finds*
Senior manager	Senior manager, Senior Manager, SENIOR MANAGER
Senior Manager	Senior Manager, SENIOR MANAGER
SENIOR MANAGER	SENIOR MANAGER

You can begin a search anywhere in your document. Q&A searches to the end of the document and then searches from the beginning of the document to the point at which the search began. You also can tell Q&A to search from the cursor to the end or beginning of the document. From the search screen, press PgDn to display the advanced search options screen. At the Range prompt, select All to search the entire document, select To End to search from the cursor to the end of the file, and To Beginning to search the text above the cursor.

Searching for Text

To search for text in Write, press F7 (Search). The sales lead memo is addressed to District Sales Managers and refers several times to districts. Suppose that the districts are changed to areas, and you want to change the memo accordingly. To find each occurrence of district, follow these steps:

1. From the memo, press F7 (Search) to begin the search. Q&A displays the search window shown in figure 10.9.

   You also can invoke Search from the Options menu. Press F8 (Options), O (Other Options), move the cursor to Search & Replace, and press Enter.

2. At the Search for field, type the phrase you want Q&A to find and then press Enter. In this example, type *district*. Q&A accepts up to 47 characters and spaces for a search.

3. Press F10 to begin the search, skipping the other two items in the search window. Q&A finds the phrase, highlights it, and awaits your next action.

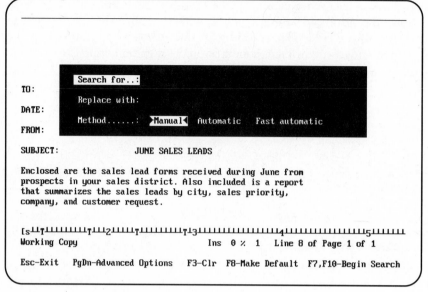

Fig. 10.9. *The search window.*

When Q&A finds the phrase you are searching for, you have three choices: edit the phrase, which cancels the search; press F7 or F10 (Begin Search) to search for the next appearance of the phrase; or press the Esc key to end the search.

If Q&A does not find the phrase, Q&A states (phrase) NOT FOUND on the message line and ends the search.

Because the search window retains your entries after you finish a search, you can repeat the search without reentering your phrase. To search for another phrase, you can erase the previous phrase by typing over it or by pressing Shift-F4.

The search options Automatic and Fast Automatic are described in the next section.

Searching with Wild Cards

What do you do if you want to search for a word or phrase that you're not sure how to spell? With Q&A, you can use a portion of a word or phrase to do a wild-card search. Q&A has two wild-card characters and two special search characters.

Character	Function
? (question mark)	Represents any single character
.. (two periods)	Represents any group of characters
\	The following character is a literal (not a wild card).
@	Finds a special function. (The special function codes are described under "Using Advanced Search Options," below.)

These characters can be used in almost any combination. Table 10.3 lists some sample search phrases; many others are possible. You can experiment with wild cards to find almost any phrase.

Table 10.3
Sample Wild-Card Search Phrases

Search word or phrase	Meaning	Examples
a?	Any two-letter word beginning with *a*	at, Al
a..	Any word beginning with *a*	ant, alpha
..m	Any word ending with *m*	am, sam, beam
???m	Any four-letter word ending with *m*	team, clam
..i??	Any word with *i* as its third-to-last character	Siam, location
Q.. W..	Two words: the first beginning with *Q*, the second beginning with *W*	Q&A Write, quit working
@UL	Underlined text	Melville's Moby Dick

Counting the Words in Your Document

Using the search function, Q&A Write can count the words in your documents. This feature helps those who must write 100 words of advertising copy, a 500-word paper, or a 3,000-word speech. To count the words in your document, follow these steps:

1. With the cursor at the beginning of your document, press F7 (Search). Q&A displays the search window.

2. At the Search For field, type .. (two dots).

3. Press Enter or Tab twice to get to the Method field. Select Automatic and press F7 or F10 to begin the count. During the process, Q&A displays `Counting...` on the message line. When the count is finished, the following phrase gives you the word count:

   ```
   Automatic search COMPLETED after (number of words)
   matches.

   The sales lead memo consists of 242 words.
   ```

You also can get a word count for your document by pressing Ctrl-F3 to display the Document Statistics screen. The Document Statistics screen shows the total word count, word count up to the cursor, and word count from the cursor to the end of the file.

When you select Fast Automatic, Q&A performs search and replace functions without showing the replacements. This feature enables the program to process the search much faster. Search and Replace is described in the next section.

Searching for and Replacing Text

If you want Q&A to find one phrase and replace it with another phrase, you must make some additional choices when you press the F7 key. Suppose that you want to replace *district* with *area* in the sales lead memo. To perform the Search and Replace, follow these steps:

1. From the memo, press F7 (Search) to begin the search. Q&A displays the search window (see fig. 10.9).

2. At the Search For field, type *district* (the phrase you want Q&A to find) and press Enter. Q&A accepts up to 47 characters and spaces.

3. At the Replace With field, type *Area* (the phrase you want Q&A to insert). Type the phrase exactly as you want it to appear, using the appropriate uppercase and lowercase letters. Press Enter.

4. Use the cursor-movement keys to highlight the method you want to use:

Manual search. Q&A flashes each change on-screen before the change happens. You can look at the phrase each time it occurs and decide whether to replace it. Manual is the best choice if the phrase occurs in different contexts—you may want to retain the phrase in some contexts and replace it in others.

Automatic search. Q&A searches for and automatically replaces the phrase each time it occurs. Q&A updates the screen display as each change is made.

Fast Automatic search. Q&A does not update the screen after each change, speeding up the process. When the search and replace operation finishes, the current screen is updated.

For this search and replace, select Manual and press F10 (Begin Search).

5. When Q&A finds the phrase, you can do one of the following:

    - Press F10 to replace the highlighted phrase, and then press F7 to continue the search or the Esc key to end the search.

    - Press F7 if you do not want to replace the current phrase, but you do want to search for the next occurrence of the phrase.

    - Edit the phrase, which cancels the search.

    - Press Esc to end the search.

To make an automatic search, choose Automatic in the Method field of the search menu and press F10. Q&A searches for a phrase, replaces it, and reports the number of replacements that occur.

Using Advanced Search Options

Q&A Write's sophisticated search-and-replace capability can find parts of words and arbitrary sequences of characters. Q&A also can search across documents united with an @JOIN command, and find and replace text marked with enhancements, such as fonts, italic, and underlining.

Using Pattern Search

Q&A can search for and replace strings of text that conform to a pattern. For example, you can replace *ed* with *ing* at the end of a word. This capability is useful when you need to make one change in several different words or phrases. Using Write, you can make these changes in one pass through the document rather than several repeated passes.

The backslash (\\) and tilde (~) are the keys to Write's extended search-and-replace capability. When you enter the backslash before and after the search characters and the replace characters, Write understands that the phrases are partial words or arbitrary sequences of characters, which will not appear as whole, separate words.

To replace *ed* with *ing* using Write's extended search-and-replace capability, follow these steps:

1. Press F7 (Search). Write displays the Search window.

2. Press PgDn to display the advanced search options. Change the Type option from Whole Words to Pattern.

3. Move the cursor back to the Search For prompt, type *ed*\\, and press Enter.

4. At the Replace With prompt, type *ing*\\ and press F7 to begin.

Use the Manual instead of the Automatic setting. Write highlights occurrences of *ed*. Notice that the Search For and Replace With prompts are repeated on the Regular and Advanced Search screens. To conduct advanced searches, you can enter search-and-replace terms at either prompt; Q&A automatically re-enters terms at the alternate prompt.

Press F10 to replace the highlighted characters. Press F7 to continue the search. Continue to press F10 or F7 until all occurrences of *ed* are found. You can edit the text at any time, but doing so cancels the search. To stop an ongoing search, press the Esc key.

Using Search Templates

You also can search or replace characters that occur in specific sequences of letters and numbers. For example, you can search for a serial number with the pattern 436-A2Q348:76BAL and replace only the letters in the position of the Q or the numerals in the positions held by 348. The following wild cards can be used to match single numbers and letters:

Wild card	Meaning	Examples
9	Matches numbers	999 matches 123 or 874
A	Matches letters	AAA matches ABC or CQJ
~	Matches nonletters and nonnumerals	~~ matches a period followed by a space (.)

To search for phone numbers, for example, you can use the template (999)~999~9999. To search and replace using templates, the search type must be set to Pattern. Press F7 (Search) and PgDn to display the Advanced Search Options screen and change the Type to Pattern.

Searching for Formatting Codes

Q&A has built-in functions for finding and replacing formatting codes. For example, you can replace underlined text in a document with italics, convert centered headlines to flush-left, or change text in the Helvetica Roman font to Avant Garde Demi. The search codes for character enhancements and formatting follow:

Code	Function
@CR	Carriage return
@NP	New page
@CT	Centered line
@RG	Regular text (removes enhancements)
@BD	Boldface
@UL	Underline
@IT	Italic
@SP	Superscript
@SB	Subscript
@XO	Strikeout
@F1	Font 1
@F2	Font 2
@F3	Font 3
@F4	Font 4
@F5	Font 5
@F6	Font 6
@F7	Font 7
@F8	Font 8

You can use the codes in the Search For and Replace With fields of the Search Dialog box. To remove text enhancements, you can replace the existing enhancement with @RG to convert the enhancement to regular (unenhanced) text.

Searching Joined Documents

Q&A can search in a single pass multiple documents that are connected with the @JOIN command. To search multiple documents, press F7 (Search) and PgDn to display the Advanced Search Options screen, and set Search Joins to Yes.

Searching for and Deleting Text

If you want to delete a certain word or phrase throughout your document, Q&A's search capability can help you make the changes. For example, if attorney Flanders leaves the law firm of Kennedy, Flanders, and Wood, you want to delete, *Flanders,* from occurrences of the firm name in a document.

To search for and delete text, you follow the same steps you follow to delete text. At the Replace With field, however, you type .. (two dots), which are a symbol for *null replace*, and then press Enter. Q&A gives you the same options that appear in the search-and-replace operation.

Using the Spelling Checker

The Write spelling checker is integrated, fast, and expandable. The spelling checker rapidly scans your documents word-by-word looking for misspellings, repeated words (such as "the the"), and typing errors. You can check one word or the entire document.

Q&A uses two dictionaries to check spelling: the main dictionary and a personal dictionary. The main dictionary contains 100,000 words. The personal dictionary can be expanded to hold as many words as will fit on your storage disk (the number virtually is unlimited if you are using a hard disk).

To use the spelling checker, press Ctrl-Home to move the cursor to the start of the document. Press Shift-F1 when your document is displayed on the

Type/Edit screen. You also can run the spelling checker from the Options menu: press F8 (Options), O (Other Options), and choose Spellcheck Doc. Q&A begins to check from the cursor to the end of the document and displays `Checking...` in the message line. To check one word only, position the cursor on or immediately after the word and press Ctrl-F1. (From the Options Other Options menu, choose Spellcheck Word.)

When performing a spelling check, Write highlights words that are not in the dictionaries (see fig. 10.10). Q&A displays the Spelling menu in the center of the screen, which offers five options. To choose an option on the Spelling menu, press the appropriate letter and then press Enter.

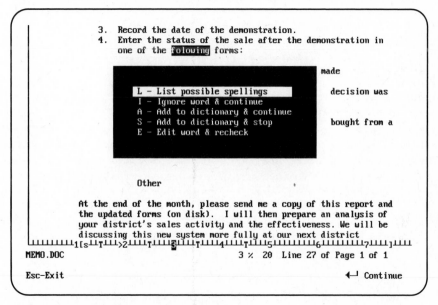

Fig. 10.10. *The spelling checker window.*

If you choose List Possible Spellings, Write displays another window containing as many as seven alternative spellings. If the correct spelling is on the list, select that word by pressing its number or by using the arrow keys to move the highlight to the word. When you press Enter, the selected word instantly replaces the misspelled word in your document.

If the correct spelling is not on the list, press the Esc key to return to the Spelling menu. Choose Edit Word & Recheck to display a box requesting the correct spelling. Type the correct spelling of the word and press F10. Q&A rechecks the word and puts the word in the document.

Choose the Ignore Word & Continue option to skip the highlighted word and continue the check. After you ignore a word, that word is skipped for the remainder of the document search. Choose this option for correctly spelled words that you do not use often enough to add to the personal dictionary, such as street addresses, proper names, cities, and so on.

Choose Add to Dictionary & Continue to add the word to the personal dictionary and continue the spelling check. Choose this option for frequently used words.

If you select Add to Dictionary & Stop, Write adds the word to the personal dictionary and ends the check.

Editing the Personal Dictionary

You cannot edit the main dictionary (the QAMAIN.DCT file), but you can put special terms, personal names, geographical names, slang terms, or any words you choose into the QAPERS.DCT file. You can fill the personal dictionary with words that are not included in the main dictionary's 100,000 words. When using the spelling checker in a normal document, select the Add to Dictionary & Continue or the Add to Dictionary & Stop option to add the new word to the personal dictionary.

To add many words to your personal dictionary, you can spell check a technical document, a glossary, or even another computer dictionary in ASCII file format.

You also can add words directly to your personal dictionary. To edit the personal dictionary file, load the file by selecting Get from the Write menu. If you are using a hard disk, the QAPERS.DCT file is stored in the same path as your Q&A program files. To access the QAPERS.DCT file for editing, you may need to indicate the correct path and the file name. When you press Enter, Q&A displays the Import Document menu, which you use to select the file format. Choose ASCII as the file format and press Enter. Q&A displays the personal dictionary (see fig. 10.11).

Now you can edit the dictionary, adding and deleting words as you would in any document. Words added to the personal dictionary, however, must be entered in alphabetical order, one word to a line. You can use uppercase or lowercase, but be sure that the words you enter are spelled correctly!

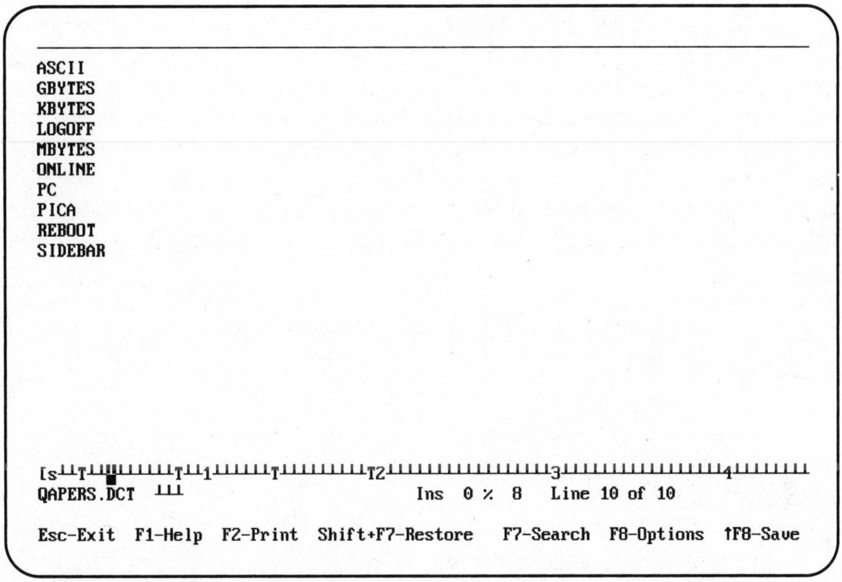

```
ASCII
GBYTES
KBYTES
LOGOFF
MBYTES
ONLINE
PC
PICA
REBOOT
SIDEBAR



                                                    [s└┴T┴┴┴┴┴┴┴T┴┴1┴┴┴┴┴┴T┴┴┴┴┴┴┴┴T2┴┴┴┴┴┴┴┴┴┴┴┴┴3┴┴┴┴┴┴┴┴┴┴┴┴┴4┴┴┴┴┴┴
QAPERS.DCT  ┴┴┴                        Ins  0 %  8   Line 10 of 10

Esc-Exit  F1-Help  F2-Print  Shift+F7-Restore    F7-Search  F8-Options  ↑F8-Save
```

Fig. 10.11. *The personal dictionary.*

Saving the Personal Dictionary

To save the personal dictionary after you have edited it, follow these steps:

1. Press the Esc key to return to the Write menu.

2. Select the Utilities command and press Enter.

3. Select Export from the Write Utilities menu.

4. Select ASCII from the Export menu. Q&A displays the file name QAPERS.DCT, along with any drive or path designation you specified. Press Enter to save the personal dictionary to disk in ASCII format.

Remember to use the Utilities menu's Export option to save the edited personal dictionary. Do not use the Save option.

Using Q&A's Thesaurus

Q&A Write's built-in thesaurus enables you to look up word alternatives from a 50,000-word synonym file. You can conduct association searches by highlighting a displayed definition and pressing Enter. Q&A shows you synonyms for the highlighted word. If you find an appropriate synonym, Q&A can replace the old word with the synonym automatically. To use the thesaurus, follow these steps:

1. Place the cursor in the word for which you need a synonym and press Alt-F1. Q&A displays the Thesaurus screen, with a selection of potential replacement words (see figure 10.12). You also can run the Thesaurus from the Options menu. Press F8 (Options), O (Other Options), and choose Thesaurus.

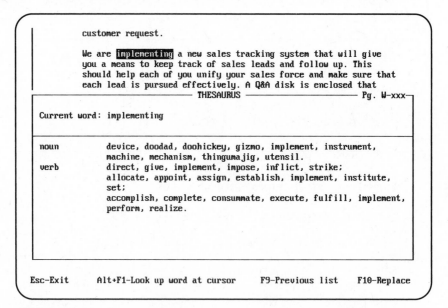

```
        customer request.

        We are implementing a new sales tracking system that will give
        you a means to keep track of sales leads and follow up. This
        should help each of you unify your sales force and make sure that
        each lead is pursued effectively. A Q&A disk is enclosed that
─────────────────────────── THESAURUS ───────────────────── Pg. W-xxx─

 Current word: implementing


 noun       device, doodad, doohickey, gizmo, implement, instrument,
            machine, mechanism, thingumajig, utensil.
 verb       direct, give, implement, impose, inflict, strike;
            allocate, appoint, assign, establish, implement, institute,
            set;
            accomplish, complete, consummate, execute, fulfill, implement,
            perform, realize.




 Esc-Exit     Alt+F1-Look up word at cursor     F9-Previous list     F10-Replace
```

Fig. 10.12.   The thesaurus window.

2. Move the cursor to the most appropriate synonym and press F10 to insert the synonym in place of the highlighted word in your text.

3. If none of the words displayed seem appropriate, you can highlight the best word and press Alt-F1. Q&A displays a set of synonyms for the highlighted synonym. You can repeat this step until you locate a good choice.

4. To move backward through the list of words you just looked up, press F9. To move forward again, press Shift-F9.

5. Press Esc at any point to return to your document.

Chapter Summary

This chapter introduces Q&A Write's capabilities and shows how to produce a document. You learned how to use the search-and-replace function of Q&A Write, and you were shown how to use the spelling checker and thesaurus. After reading this chapter, you should be able to use the word processing capabilities of Q&A Write to produce a document. Chapter 11 covers Write's formatting capabilities, including formatting text, setting tabs and margins, and setting headers and footers. You use these features to produce a polished Write document.

11

Enhancing a Write Document

Chapter 10 covered the fundamental Write capabilities of creating and saving documents and entering and searching for text. This chapter shows you how to enhance your Write document with special text features such as boldface, underline, tabs, margins, fonts, and line drawing. In addition, this chapter covers changing indentations and margins, enhancing headers and footers, and using Q&A Write's math functions.

Formatting Text

Formatting improves your documents in several ways. Formatting adds style, emphasis, and clarity to your documents; it makes documents easy to read; and it gives documents a professional appearance.

Q&A Write offers the following formatting capabilities:

- Text tabs and decimal tabs
- Temporary margins and indentations
- Boldface, italic, and underlined text
- Support for printer fonts
- Superscript and subscript characters
- Centered lines
- Single- and double-line drawing

These formatting characteristics reside in the document file with the text. When you save a document, you save not only the text but all the formatting information as well.

As with most Q&A operations, setting document formats generally involves pressing a special key combination (Shift-F6, for example) that displays a menu of possible operations. You select the enhancement you want from the list, and then highlight the text you want to format. Most text enhancements can be specified for a single character, a word, or a block of text. Centering text, however, is line-oriented. You must repeat the centering procedure for each line on the page you want to center.

The following sections describe Write's formatting features in detail.

Using and Setting Tabs

The Tab key moves the cursor to the left and right a preset number of spaces, according to tab stops set in the ruler line. Q&A Write documents can contain two kinds of tab stops: *text tabs* (marked by a T in the ruler line) and *decimal tabs* (marked by a D). You set both in the same way, but they affect text differently.

Figure 11.1 illustrates the default ruler line in a Q&A Write document: each of its four text tab stops is indicated by a T marker in the 15th, 25th, 35th, and 45th columns. These stops are relative to the left margin; if you change the left margin, the positions of the preset tab stops change.

Q&A gives you complete control over the number and kind of tab stops in every document. The following sections explain how to add and delete tab stops and then how to use them.

How To Change Tab Settings

To set tab stops, press F8 to open the Options menu, select Lay Out Page, and select Set Tabs from the Lay Out Page submenu. Using the Set Tabs option, you can delete and add standard text tab stops (T) or decimal tab stops (D). The new tab settings are saved when you save your document.

You used Write's preset tab stops when you typed the information in the various lines of the memorandum in Chapter 10. If you want less space between TO: and District Sales Managers, you can change the tab stops to change the space.

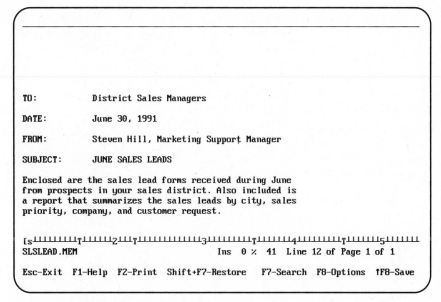

Fig. 11.1. *The ruler line's default tab stops.*

To add a tab stop from the editing screen, do the following:

1. Press F8 to go to the Options menu (see fig. 11.2).

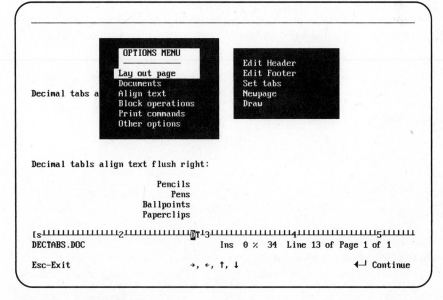

Fig. 11.2. *The Options menu.*

2. Select Lay Out Page from the Options menu and Set Tabs from the Lay Out Page submenu. The cursor appears as a rectangle on the ruler line, and a new set of key assignments is listed at the bottom of the screen:

    Esc (Exit)

    F1 (Help)

    Tab (Next Tab)

    Shift-Tab (Previous Tab)

    F10 (Resume Editing)

3. Move the cursor to the position where you want to set the new tab stop (at column 21, for example), and press T. A T appears at the ruler line's corresponding column, marking the tab setting. To set a decimal tab stop, press D instead of T.

4. Press F10 or Enter to resume editing.

Deleting a tab stop is similar to adding one. To delete a tab stop, select Set Tabs from the Options Lay Out Page submenu, move the cursor to that tab stop, and press the Del key or the space bar to delete the tab stop from the ruler line. Press F10 or Enter to resume editing.

Moving back and forth on the ruler line is easy when you use these keys:

Key(s)	Cursor movement
Home	To first space to the right of the left margin
End	To first space to the left of the right margin
Ctrl- ←	Five spaces to the left
Ctrl- →	Five spaces to the right
Tab	To next tab stop to the right
Shift-Tab	To next tab stop to the left

How To Use Tabs

The Tab key is used commonly to indent the first line of a paragraph or to indent whole sections of text. You make this indentation by pressing the Tab key once. Each subsequent press of the Tab key moves the indent to the next tab stop. To tab to the left, press the Shift and Tab keys at the same time; the cursor moves to the first tab stop to the left.

Before you type a paragraph in a Write document, you can indent a line in either Overtype or Insert mode. To indent previously entered text, however, you must use Insert mode; if you use Overtype mode, you move the cursor without changing the text.

To eliminate a tab indent, position the cursor on the first character of the line and move the character to the left margin by pressing the Backspace key repeatedly while in Insert mode.

Q&A's default is to insert spaces when you press Tab, but you can insert "real" tab characters by changing a setting on the Set Global Options menu. For details, see "Customizing Global Options in Q&A Write" later in this chapter.

A *text tab* aligns text and numbers at the tab stop, proceeding from the stop to the right. In figure 11.3, for example, one column is aligned with the left margin, and the other three columns are aligned with three text tabs. To use text tab stops to align text in this manner, you type the first column, press the Tab key once to jump to the first tab stop, type the second column, and press the Tab key again.

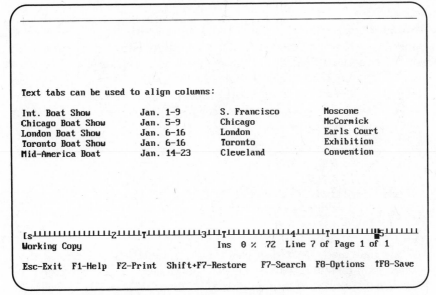

Fig. 11.3. Aligning columnar text with text tabs.

Q&A Write's *decimal tabs* can make formatting a document with numbers easy. Decimal tabs are used to align numbers on the decimal point, as shown in figure 11.4. You also can use decimal tabs as a convenient way to right-justify single lines of text for lists.

```
┌─────────────────────────────────────────────────────────────┐
│ ─────────────────────────────────────────────────────────── │
│                                                               │
│                                                               │
│                                                               │
│  Decimal tabs align numbers on the decimal point:             │
│                                                               │
│                        2,604.95                               │
│                           13.                                 │
│                            .055                               │
│                          1.58334                              │
│                                                               │
│  Decimal tabs align text flush right:                         │
│                                                               │
│                            Pencils                            │
│                               Pens                            │
│                         Ballpoints                            │
│                         Paperclips                            │
│                                                               │
│ [s⊥⊥⊥⊥⊥⊥⊥⊥⊥⊥⊥⊥2⊥⊥⊥⊥⊥⊥⊥⊥⊥⊥⊥T┃3⊥⊥⊥⊥⊥⊥⊥⊥⊥⊥⊥4⊥⊥⊥⊥⊥⊥⊥⊥⊥⊥5⊥⊥⊥⊥⊥│
│ Working Copy                      Ins  0 %  34  Line 13 of Page 1 of 1 │
│                                                               │
│ Esc-Exit  F1-Help  F2-Print  Shift+F7-Restore  F7-Search  F8-Options  ↑F8-Save │
└─────────────────────────────────────────────────────────────┘
```

Fig. 11.4. *Aligning numbers and text with decimal tabs*

To use a decimal tab stop, press the Tab key to jump to the stop; then enter your information. Note that numbers and text appear to the left of the cursor until you enter a decimal point. By moving the cursor before or during the data-entry process, you cancel the decimal tab alignment. To right-justify a text list, using decimal tabs, use the Tab key to move the cursor to the decimal tab, and enter the text (make sure that the text has no periods). The text moves to the left, ending at the decimal tab.

Changing Temporary Margins and Indentations

Left and right margins are displayed on-screen exactly as they appear when printed. You therefore are assured that the margins you set on-screen will remain the same on your printed output. Two methods are available for changing margins. You can change margins for the whole document by using the Define Page screen from the Write Editing screen, accessed by pressing Ctrl-F6 (see the "Formatting the Page" section in Chapter 10), or you can change margins temporarily for a part of your document.

How Temporary Margins Format Text

Temporary left and right margins do different things to your text depending on when and where you use the margins. When you enter new text, a temporary left margin affects the line below the cursor but does not affect the line in which the cursor is positioned. A temporary right margin affects the line that the cursor is on when you enter new text.

Q&A Write's temporary-margin and indentation capabilities are more flexible than those of many word processors, but the program is not a powerful formatter. If you decide that five paragraphs you have just typed should be indented, for example, you cannot select the five paragraphs and then set the temporary margin once. You must set a temporary margin five times, once for each paragraph. If you add text after the temporary margin has been set, however, any text added below the temporary margin adopts that margin, even if you add hard carriage returns. A lesson is evident here: Plan your document in advance (when possible) so that you can specify a temporary indent and then carry the indent with the text as you enter it.

How To Set a Temporary Margin

You can change the left and right margins by using F6, the Temporary Margin key. Setting temporary margins is a three-step process in which you move the cursor where you want to set the margin, press F6, and then press L for the left margin or R for the right margin. You can set and clear temporary margins anywhere in your document, as often as you choose.

In the sales lead memo (see fig. 11.5), the second paragraph is followed by a list of instructions that require a temporary margin. To prepare your memo, enter the second paragraph as it appears in figure 11.5; include the colon (:) at the end of the paragraph. Then press Enter twice to move the cursor two lines below the second paragraph.

To set the temporary left margin, follow these steps:

1. Move the cursor to the memo's 16th column.

2. Press F6. The Set Temporary Margin menu appears at the bottom of the screen (see fig. 11.6). The menu offers three choices:

   • To create a left margin, you choose Left. The Set Temporary Margin menu disappears, and a greater-than sign (>) marks the margin in the ruler line.

```
FROM:              Steven Hill, Marketing Support Manager

SUBJECT:           JUNE SALES LEADS

Enclosed are the sales lead forms received during June from
prospects in your sales district. Also included is a report
that summarizes the sales leads by city, sales priority,
company, and customer request.

We are implementing a new sales tracking system that will
give you a means to keep track of sales leads and follow up.
This should help each of you to unify your sales force and
make sure each lead is pursued effectively. A Q&A disk is
enclosed that contains the sales leads for your district.
Please copy these leads into your file and maintain them
in the following manner:


[s⊥⊥T⊥⊥⊥⊥⊥⊥⊥⊥⊥T⊥⊥2⊥⊥⊥⊥T⊥⊥⊥⊥⊥⊥⊥⊥T⊥3⊥⊥⊥⊥⊥⊥⊥⊥⊥⊥⊥⊥4⊥⊥⊥⊥⊥⊥⊥⊥⊥⊥⊥⊥5⊥⊥⊥⊥⊥
SLSLEAD.DOC                      Ins  0 %  1    Line 20 of Page 1 of 1

Esc-Exit  F1-Help  F2-Print  Shift+F7-Restore   F7-Search  F8-Options  ↑F8-Save
```

Fig. 11.5.   *Preparing to set temporary margins in the memo.*

```
            DATE:      June 30, 1991

            FROM:      Steven Hill, Marketing Support Manager

            SUBJECT:   JUNE SALES LEADS

            Enclosed are the sales lead forms received during June from
            prospects in your sales district.  Also included is a report that
            summarizes the sales leads by city, sales priority, company, and
            customer request.

            We are implementing a new sales tracking system that will give
            you a means to keep track of sales leads and follow up. This
            should help each of you unify your sales force and make sure that
            each lead is pursued effectively. A Q&A disk is enclosed that
            contains the sales leads for your district. Please copy these
            leads into your file, and maintain them in the following manner:


⊥⊥⊥⊥⊥⊥⊥⊥⊥1[s⊥⊥■⊥⊥⊥>2⊥⊥⊥⊥T⊥⊥⊥3⊥⊥⊥⊥T⊥⊥⊥⊥4⊥⊥T⊥⊥⊥⊥5⊥⊥⊥⊥⊥⊥⊥6⊥⊥⊥⊥⊥⊥⊥⊥7⊥⊥⊥⊥┘⊥⊥⊥⊥
┌─────────────────────────────────────────────────────────────────────┐
│    Set temporary margin:       L-Left      R-Right      C-Clear       │
└─────────────────────────────────────────────────────────────────────┘
```

Fig. 11.6.   *The Set Temporary Margin menu.*

   • To create a right margin, you choose Right. The Set Tempo-
     rary Margin menu disappears, and a less-than sign (<) marks
     the margin in the ruler line.

- To delete a temporary margin and restore the default margin settings, you move the cursor into the paragraph you want to change and choose Clear. The temporary margin marker on the ruler line is deleted.

3. For this example, select Left to set a temporary left margin for the memo's first numbered item.

After you set the temporary left margin at column 16, enter the first of the memo's numbered items (see fig. 11.7).

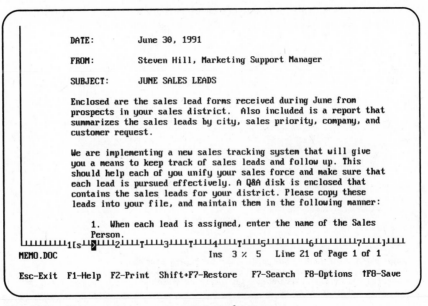

Fig. 11.7. *Using a temporary margin to indent text.*

You also can set temporary margins from the Options menu, but this process is slower. Press F8 (Options), press A (Align Text), and choose Temp Margins from the Align Text submenu. Then press L for the left margin, R for the right margin, or C to clear a temporary margin setting.

How To Create a Hanging Indent

Temporary margins are used most often to create a hanging indent format for numbered or bulleted text. (A *bullet* is a special character, usually a small circle or dot, used to mark the beginning of elements in a list.)

1. This text is an example of the hanging indent format used for numbered or bulleted paragraphs. All text "hangs" flush left, to the right of a number or bullet.

   - This text is an example of a hanging indent format using a bullet.

To create indented text, you use tab stops to position both the number or bullet and a temporary left margin for the text. To create the memo's second indented item in a hanging indent format, follow these steps:

1. Set regular tab stops at the 16th and 19th columns, as described earlier in the section "How To Change Tab Settings."

2. Press Enter to begin a new item.

3. Press the Tab key to move to the first tab stop (the 16th character on the ruler line).

4. Type *2.*, and press Tab.

5. Press F6, and select Left.

6. Type the text as shown in figure 11.8.

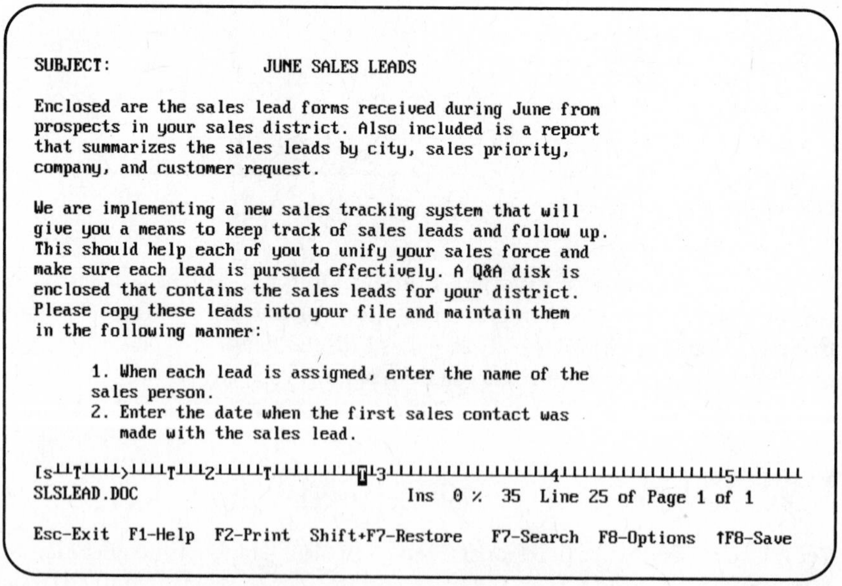

```
 SUBJECT:                JUNE SALES LEADS

 Enclosed are the sales lead forms received during June from
 prospects in your sales district. Also included is a report
 that summarizes the sales leads by city, sales priority,
 company, and customer request.

 We are implementing a new sales tracking system that will
 give you a means to keep track of sales leads and follow up.
 This should help each of you to unify your sales force and
 make sure each lead is pursued effectively. A Q&A disk is
 enclosed that contains the sales leads for your district.
 Please copy these leads into your file and maintain them
 in the following manner:

         1. When each lead is assigned, enter the name of the
         sales person.
         2. Enter the date when the first sales contact was
            made with the sales lead.

 [s⌐⌐T⌐⌐⌐⌐⟩⌐⌐⌐⌐T⌐⌐⌐2⌐⌐⌐⌐⌐⌐T⌐⌐⌐⌐⌐⌐⌐⌐⌐█⌐3⌐⌐⌐⌐⌐⌐⌐⌐⌐⌐⌐⌐⌐⌐⌐⌐⌐⌐4⌐⌐⌐⌐⌐⌐⌐⌐⌐⌐⌐⌐⌐⌐⌐⌐5⌐⌐⌐⌐⌐⌐
 SLSLEAD.DOC                        Ins  0 %  35  Line 25 of Page 1 of 1

 Esc-Exit  F1-Help  F2-Print  Shift+F7-Restore   F7-Search  F8-Options  ↑F8-Save
```

Fig. 11.8.   Entering a hanging indent paragraph.

To enter another indented item, press Enter to begin a new item, press Shift-Tab to move the cursor to the left so that you can enter a number or a bullet, and then type the text.

Compare the numbered items in figure 11.8. Notice the difference between the normal format of item 1 and the hanging indent format of item 2, in which the number juts out. You can delete tabs when you finish using them, to keep the ruler line from being cluttered with too many tabs.

To cancel a temporary margin, press F6 to display the Set Temporary Margins menu. Next, press C to select Clear.

Enhancing Text

Q&A Write includes a full range of text enhancements: boldface, underline, italic, superscript, subscript, and fonts. You can enhance text as you enter it or afterward. In either case, you press Shift-F6 to display the Text Enhancements and Fonts menu and then select the appropriate option (see fig. 11.9).

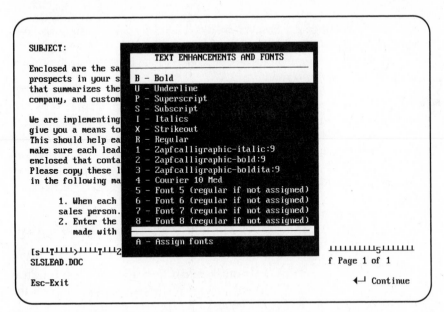

Fig. 11.9. *The Text Enhancements and Fonts menu.*

To enhance text as you type it, follow this procedure:

1. Press Shift-F6 to display the Text Enhancements and Fonts menu.

2. Choose an enhancement from the menu.

3. Press F10 twice to continue.

4. Press the Ins key to turn on Insert mode.

5. Enter the text.

You can use one of several methods to turn off the enhancement: press the Ins key to turn off Insert mode; return to the Text Enhancements and Fonts menu and select Regular; or press the right-arrow key.

To enhance text that already has been entered, press Shift-F6 to display the Text Enhancements and Fonts menu, select an enhancement, highlight the text to be enhanced, and press F10. (You can use a macro to automate the procedure for turning on an enhancement. For information about macros, see Chapter 19.) You can repeat the process to add multiple enhancements to the same text (for example, bold and underline).

You also can enhance existing text by using the Options menu. Press F8 to display the Options menu, press B to choose Block and E to select Enhance, then follow the preceding procedure described for highlighting a block of text and applying an enhancement.

Your computer system determines whether you see the enhancements on-screen or only on the printout. Most displays and printers show boldface; underline is visible on monochrome displays but is shown as a change in color on most color displays. With displays that cannot show text enhancements, you have another way to tell whether text has been enhanced. As the cursor moves through enhanced text, the name of the enhancement or font appears on the status line.

You edit enhanced text as you do any other text. Characters added within enhanced text also are enhanced.

If you have a mouse, you may find it quicker than the keyboard for applying text enhancements. First highlight a block of text with the mouse, and then click the Shift-F6 Enhance Text item on the status line. Q&A displays the Text Enhancements and Fonts menu. To select an enhancement for the highlighted block of text, highlight the enhancement with the mouse cursor, and double-click the left button. The menu disappears, and the enhancement is applied to the block.

Creating Boldface Text

Boldface text usually prints as especially dark text. In the memo example, suppose that you want to boldface JUNE SALES LEADS. To boldface text that has been entered, follow these steps:

1. Move the cursor to the first character you want to boldface (the J of JUNE in this example).

2. Press Shift-F6. Q&A displays the Text Enhancements and Fonts menu.

3. Choose Bold from the Text Enhancements and Fonts menu. The menu disappears, and Q&A prompts you to select the text to boldface.

4. Move the cursor to highlight the text you want to boldface (JUNE SALES LEADS).

5. Press F10. The text you selected is now boldface. Notice that the Bold indicator appears in the status line when the cursor is positioned within the boldface text.

Creating Underlined Text

Underlining text that already has been entered requires a slightly different procedure than for typing underlined text. In the example, the memo's second paragraph asks district sales managers to copy and maintain their files. Because busy sales managers may not read the memo carefully, you may want to underline this sentence for emphasis:

> Please copy these leads into your file, and maintain them in the following manner:

To underline existing text, follow this procedure:

1. Move the cursor to the first character you want to underline. (In the memo, that character is the P in Please.)

2. Press Shift-F6. Q&A displays the Text Enhancements and Fonts menu at the bottom of the screen.

3. Select Underline. The menu disappears, and Q&A prompts you to select the text to be underlined.

4. Move the cursor to highlight the text you want underlined.

5. Press F10.

The text you selected now will print underlined. Notice that the status line includes the Undl indicator when the cursor is positioned within the underlined text. How the underlined text appears on-screen depends on the type of display adapter and monitor you are using.

Underlining a blank line presents special problems. If you are creating a form, you may want a line such as the following:

Name _

You cannot use underlining in completely empty spaces. The line may be displayed on your screen but probably will not print on your printer. To get around this obstacle, put an insignificant character (like a period) at the end of the series of blanks to be underlined.

You can try to use the Q&A Draw features (explained later in this chapter) to create an underlined blank space. The Draw line, however, is a midline that appears in the middle of the character space, whereas an underline appears under the character space. Compare the preceding underline with the following line created with Draw:

Name———————————————————————————————

Creating Italic Text

Q&A Write also supports italic text. You can use this enhancement if your printer supports italic type. Most printers do. Refer to your printer manual for the specific codes necessary to initiate italic text with your printer. The standard IBM monochrome and color graphic adapters do not display italics. Instead, italicized text is marked with boldface and the status line indicates Ital when the cursor is in the italic text.

Suppose that you want to italicize the term "sales person" in step 1 of the sales lead memo. To italicize text that has been entered previously, do the following:

1. Move the cursor to the first character you want to italicize. (In the sales lead memo, that character is the first *s* in sales.)

2. Press Shift-F6. Q&A displays the Text Enhancements and Fonts menu at the bottom of the screen.

3. Select Italic from the menu. The menu disappears, and Q&A prompts you to select the text to be italicized.

4. Move the cursor to highlight the text you want italicized (the words "sales person" in the memo).

5. Press F10.

The text you selected is now italic. Notice that the status line includes the `Ital` indicator when the cursor is in the italic text.

Creating Superscript and Subscript Text

Superscript and *subscript* text is printed above and below the base printing line, respectively, and usually is smaller than surrounding text. Documents that include scientific terms or footnotes may use superscript or subscript text. A superscript frequently is used to point to a footnote or other document note:

...is the smallest of the subatomic particles.[1]

Superscripts also are used in measurement or other special designations:

ft^3
yd^2

Subscripts are useful in scientific and engineering applications:

...Enter the number $A5_{16}$ and press Enter.
H_2O

As with other text enhancements, superscript and subscript may not be available for your printer and they most likely will not show up on your screen.

To superscript or subscript existing text, follow these steps:

1. Move the cursor to the first character you want to enhance.

2. Press Shift-F6. Q&A displays the Text Enhancements and Fonts menu at the bottom of the screen.

3. Choose Sup (superscript) or Sub (subscript) from the menu. The menu disappears, and Q&A prompts you to select the text to be enhanced.

4. Move the cursor to highlight the text you want enhanced.

5. Press F10.

The text you select now will print as superscript or subscript (assuming that your printer supports the enhancement). Note that Q&A cannot display these special text enhancements on-screen. The status line includes the Subs indicator when the cursor is in subscript text. When the cursor is in superscript text, the Sups indicator is displayed.

Using Fonts

Changing fonts is as easy as applying a character enhancement—you select fonts by number from the Text Enhancements and Fonts menu. Your printer may support many fonts, but Q&A does not recognize the fonts until you install them for use with Write.

Installing Fonts

You install fonts from the Font Assignments screen (see fig. 11.10).

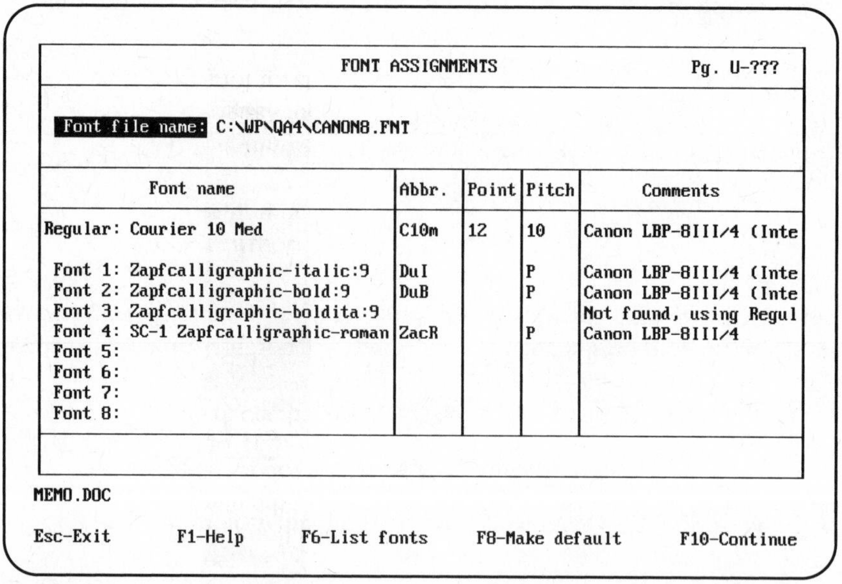

```
                        FONT ASSIGNMENTS                    Pg. U-???

   Font file name: C:\WP\QA4\CANON8.FNT

          Font name              Abbr.  Point Pitch      Comments

   Regular: Courier 10 Med       C10m   12    10     Canon LBP-8III/4 (Inte

   Font 1: Zapfcalligraphic-italic:9    DuI        P   Canon LBP-8III/4 (Inte
   Font 2: Zapfcalligraphic-bold:9      DuB        P   Canon LBP-8III/4 (Inte
   Font 3: Zapfcalligraphic-boldita:9               Not found, using Regul
   Font 4: SC-1 Zapfcalligraphic-roman ZacR        P   Canon LBP-8III/4
   Font 5:
   Font 6:
   Font 7:
   Font 8:


   MEMO.DOC

   Esc-Exit      F1-Help      F6-List fonts      F8-Make default      F10-Continue
```

Fig. 11.10. *The Font Assignments screen.*

Q&A offers three ways to display the Font Assignments screen. From the Type/Edit screen, you can press Ctrl-F9. Or, from the Type/Edit screen, you can press Shift-F6 to display the Text Enhancements and Fonts menu, and then press A to display the Font Assignments screen. You also can use the Options menu: press F8 (Options), O (Other Options), and A (Assign Fonts).

From the Font Assignments screen, follow these steps to assign fonts:

1. Press F6 to display a list of the font description files that are available for your printer. You chose these files when you set up Q&A. (See Appendix A, "Installing and Starting Q&A.")

2. At the List of Files screen, move the cursor to a printer description file, and press Enter. Q&A returns you to the Font Assignments screen.

3. Move the cursor to the Regular field to choose the font that Q&A should use for unenhanced text.

4. Press F6 to list the font descriptions for the description file you chose in step 1.

5. Move the cursor to a font name, and press Enter. Q&A returns you to the Font Assignments screen and inserts the name in the Regular field. If the font is scalable, Q&A prompts you for a point size.

6. Move the cursor into the fields for fonts 1 through 8, and repeat steps 4 through 5 for any other fonts you want to assign.

7. To make this Font Assignments screen the default for all new documents you create with Q&A Write, and for text enhancements you use in File, press F8.

8. Press F10 to return to the Text Enhancements and Fonts menu.

Pressing F10 does not make the current Font Assignments screen the default. To choose a default, you must press F8 at the Font Assignments screen. If you don't choose a default, Q&A displays blank fields for fonts 1 through 9 in the Text Enhancements and Fonts menu whenever you create a new document.

Applying Fonts

The procedure for applying fonts is exactly the same as for applying character enhancements. Follow these steps:

1. Place the cursor on the first character of the text to which you want to apply a font. Press Shift-F6 to display the Text Enhancements and Fonts menu.

2. Press a number from 1 to 9 to choose a font, or press R to use the regular (unenhanced) font.

3. Move the cursor to the end of the block of text to which you want the font to apply, and press F10.

You can mix fonts and enhancements. For example, you can choose a Times Roman font and then apply an italic enhancement.

Centering and Uncentering a Line

Q&A Write offers an easy way to center text on a page. With the Center Line command from the Align Text submenu on the Options menu, you can center a line of text instantly between the left and right margins. With the Left command on the Align Text submenu, you quickly can uncenter a centered line.

As with other formatting commands, you can use Center Line to center existing text or to center text as you enter it. To see how this feature works, type the word *INSTRUCTIONS* at the left margin, between the first and second paragraphs of the memo. To center the word as shown in figure 11.11, follow these steps:

1. Move the cursor to the line you want to center.

2. Press F8 (Options).

3. Select Align Text, and choose Center from the Align Text submenu. Q&A instantly moves the text to the center of the page.

To uncenter the line, move the cursor to the centered line, and press F8 (Options), A (Align Text), and L (Left). Q&A moves the text back to the left margin.

Drawing Lines and Boxes

Q&A's drawing capability is a formatting feature that enables you to create single or double lines with ease. Using the Draw feature, you can add lines, boxes, and even simple illustrations to your documents, reports, and forms. Figures 11.12 and 11.13 demonstrate some of the possibilities.

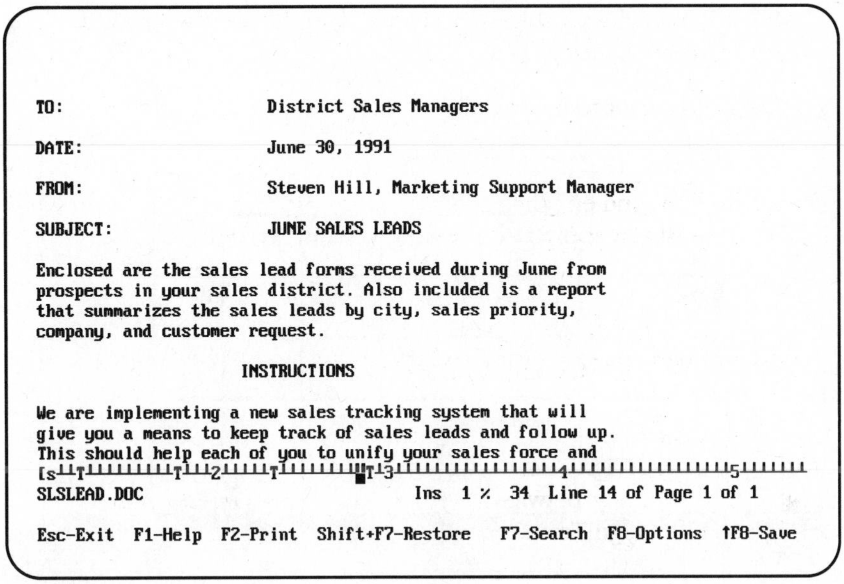

```
TO:                  District Sales Managers

DATE:                June 30, 1991

FROM:                Steven Hill, Marketing Support Manager

SUBJECT:             JUNE SALES LEADS

Enclosed are the sales lead forms received during June from
prospects in your sales district. Also included is a report
that summarizes the sales leads by city, sales priority,
company, and customer request.

                     INSTRUCTIONS

We are implementing a new sales tracking system that will
give you a means to keep track of sales leads and follow up.
This should help each of you to unify your sales force and
[s⌐⌐⌐T⌐⌐⌐⌐⌐⌐⌐⌐⌐⌐T⌐⌐2⌐⌐⌐⌐⌐T⌐⌐⌐⌐⌐⌐⌐⌐⌐█⌐⌐T3⌐⌐⌐⌐⌐⌐⌐⌐⌐⌐⌐⌐⌐⌐4⌐⌐⌐⌐⌐⌐⌐⌐⌐⌐⌐⌐⌐⌐⌐⌐5⌐⌐⌐⌐⌐⌐
SLSLEAD.DOC                        Ins  1 %  34  Line 14 of Page 1 of 1

Esc-Exit  F1-Help  F2-Print  Shift+F7-Restore   F7-Search  F8-Options  ↑F8-Save
```

Fig. 11.11.   Centering a line.

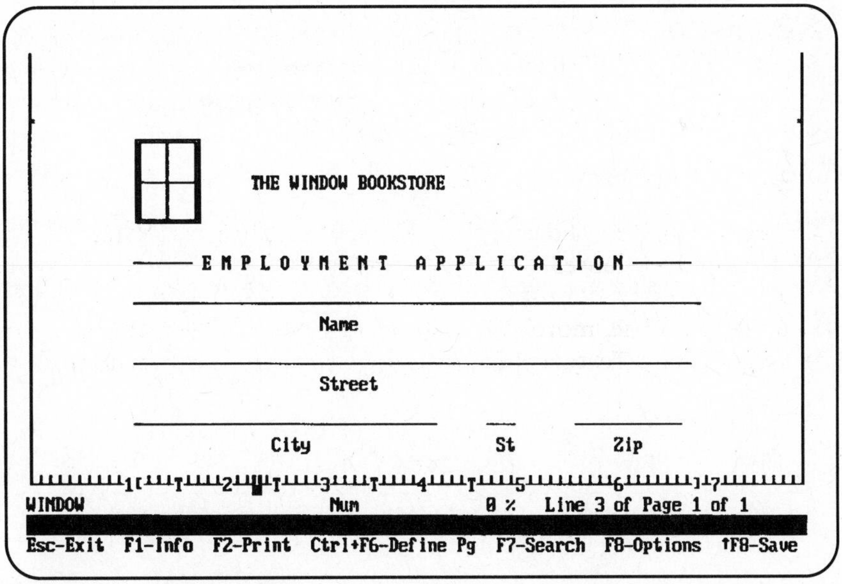

```
        ┌─┬─┐
        ├─┼─┤        THE WINDOW BOOKSTORE
        └─┴─┘


          ──── E M P L O Y M E N T   A P P L I C A T I O N ────


          _____
                         Name

          _____
                         Street

          _____
              City              St          Zip
⌐⌐⌐⌐⌐⌐⌐⌐⌐⌐1[⌐⌐⌐T⌐T⌐⌐2█⌐T⌐⌐⌐3⌐⌐⌐T⌐⌐⌐⌐4⌐⌐⌐T⌐⌐5⌐⌐⌐⌐⌐⌐⌐⌐⌐6⌐⌐⌐⌐⌐⌐⌐⌐⌐]7⌐⌐⌐⌐⌐⌐⌐
WINDOW                        Num            0 %   Line 3 of Page 1 of 1
Esc-Exit  F1-Info  F2-Print  Ctrl+F6-Define Pg  F7-Search  F8-Options  ↑F8-Save
```

Fig. 11.12.   Creating business forms with Draw.

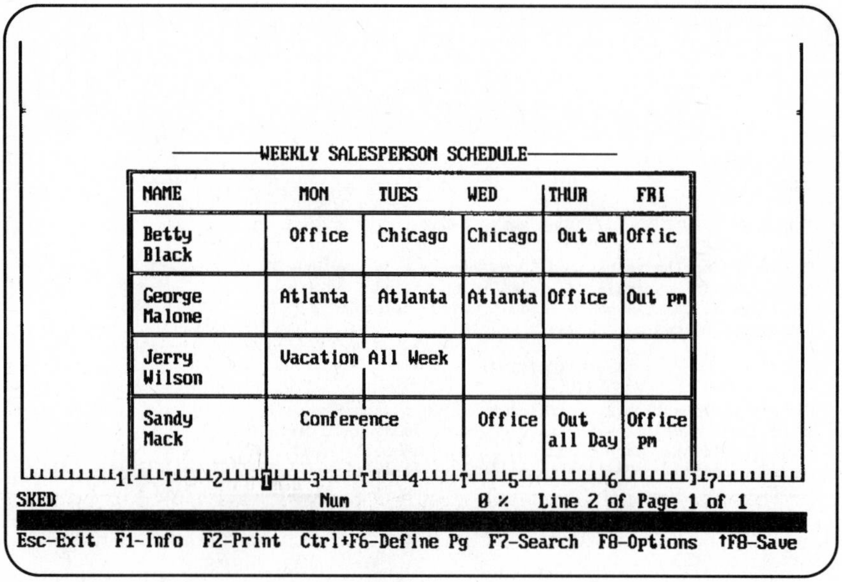

Fig. 11.13. Making a form with Draw.

To use the Draw feature, you first enter and edit the text, leaving room for the lines; then you draw the lines. You must work in this order because inserting and deleting characters can move sections of lines, leaving distorted illustrations. As you enter the text, imagine where you will put the lines. Be sure to leave enough space to ensure a pleasing layout.

You can use a line to box a section of a document (see fig. 11.14). To box the text, set temporary margins to indent the text and make room for the box. Then draw the box, using the cursor drawing keys shown in figure 11.15 and following these steps:

1. Place the cursor where you want to start drawing the corner of the box.

2. Press F8 (Options).

3. Select Lay Out Page and choose Draw from the submenu. Q&A displays drawing instructions in the message line.

4. To draw single lines, press the cursor drawing keys to move the cursor. To draw double lines, hold down the Shift key and then move the cursor, or press Num Lock (the Num indicator appears) and then move the cursor. (As illustrated in fig. 11.15, draw diagonal lines by pressing the 1, 3, 7, and 9 keys.)

5. Press F10 to exit Draw mode.

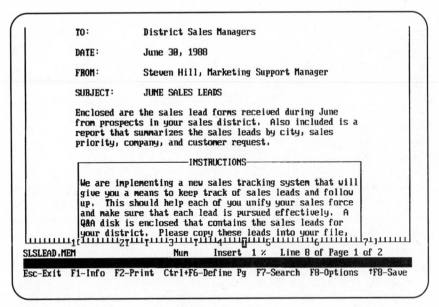

```
        TO:        District Sales Managers

        DATE:      June 30, 1988

        FROM:      Steven Hill, Marketing Support Manager

        SUBJECT:   JUNE SALES LEADS

        Enclosed are the sales lead forms received during June
        from prospects in your sales district.  Also included is a
        report that summarizes the sales leads by city, sales
        priority, company, and customer request.

        ┌─────────────────────INSTRUCTIONS────────────────────┐
        │We are implementing a new sales tracking system that will│
        │give you a means to keep track of sales leads and follow│
        │up.  This should help each of you unify your sales force│
        │and make sure that each lead is pursued effectively.  A │
        │Q&A disk is enclosed that contains the sales leads for  │
        │your district.  Please copy these leads into your file, │
```

```
SLSLEAD.MEM                    Num       Insert  1 %   Line 8 of Page 1 of 2

Esc-Exit  F1-Info  F2-Print  Ctrl+F6-Define Pg  F7-Search  F8-Options  ↑F8-Save
```

Fig. 11.14.   *Using the Draw feature to create a box.*

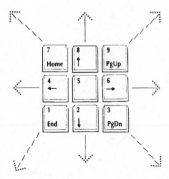

Fig. 11.15.   *The cursor drawing keys.*

Note: If you have a keyboard with separate cursor-control keys as well as cursor controls on the numeric keypad (such as on the IBM Enhanced Keyboard), you need to work a little differently. You can use the separate cursor-control keys to draw single lines, but you must use the numeric keypad's cursor controls to draw double lines.

While in Draw mode, you can create more than one drawing in the same document. Do this by pressing F6 (Pen Up) and moving the cursor to the location of the next drawing. Notice that when you press F6, the description of F6 in the key assignment line changes to Pen Down. F6 is a toggle. If the pen is down, F6 raises it; if the pen is up, F6 lowers it.

If you make a mistake while drawing with Q&A, you can erase the error. Press F8 to put Q&A in Erase mode. When you move the cursor, you erase both lines and text—so be careful. When you are ready to begin drawing again, press F8 to return to Draw mode. To erase part of a line while you are drawing it, you also can use the Backspace key. After you enter the line or box, you can erase at the Editing screen after exiting Drawing mode by using the Backspace key.

Be careful with your drawing. After you return to Type/Edit mode, you can ruin the drawing by typing over it, deleting part of it, inserting new text, or moving a line out of place.

Drawing anything more than fairly simple shapes requires some real concentration and probably a little frustration. Even in Draw mode, Q&A moves the cursor by character spaces, so you may envision exactly the drawing you want but be unable to get the cursor to go there precisely. Also, the quality of the lines depends on the graphic capabilities of your printer. A little testing, and some flexibility on your part about how the finished drawing should look, will result in attractively enhanced documents.

Starting a New Page

When you want to begin a section of a document on a new page, you can insert a page break at that spot in the document. The text following the break begins at the top of the next page. To start a new page, move the cursor to the line on which you want to start the next page, press F8 for the Options menu, choose Lay Out Page, and select Newpage from the Lay Out Page submenu.

To start the sales memo's INSTRUCTIONS box on a new page, for example, follow these steps:

1. Position the cursor on what will be the first line of the new page.

2. Press F8 (Options).

3. Select Lay Out Page and choose Newpage from the submenu, moving the box to the next page (see fig. 11.16).

Q&A adds a page-break marker in column 1 of the last line of the preceding page. The marker looks like a reversed double L.

To delete a page break, position the cursor on the page-break marker, and press the Del key.

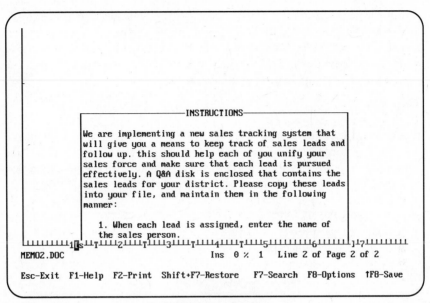

```
                    ─INSTRUCTIONS─
We are implementing a new sales tracking system that
will give you a means to keep track of sales leads and
follow up. this should help each of you unify your
sales force and make sure that each lead is pursued
effectively. A Q&A disk is enclosed that contains the
sales leads for your district. Please copy these leads
into your file, and maintain them in the following
manner:

    1. When each lead is assigned, enter the name of
    the sales person.
```

```
MEMO2.DOC                      Ins  0 %  1  Line 2 of Page 2 of 2

Esc-Exit  F1-Help  F2-Print  Shift+F7-Restore  F7-Search  F8-Options  ↑F8-Save
```

Fig. 11.16.   *The new page with the text at the top.*

Moving the Cursor to Another Page

You can use Ctrl-F7, the GoTo key, to move to another page in your document or to move to a specific line on a page. When you press Ctrl-F7, a box is displayed, as shown in figure 11.17. The box prompts you to enter the number of the page you want to display; type the number, and press Enter. Next, enter the line number, and press F10. The cursor moves to the location you specified.

Pressing F5 copies the current page and line number into the GoTo box. You can use this feature as a page marker; when you move to a different location and press Ctrl-F7, the cursor position recorded when you pressed F5 is displayed.

You also can use the Options menu to move to a different page. Press F8 (Options), press O (Other Options), and choose Go to Page/Line from the Other Options submenu.

Using Headers and Footers

For reports, letters, and memos that are longer than a page, or for other types of long manuscripts, Q&A's header and footer capabilities offer the options of automatically entering titles, dates, page numbers, and so forth at the top or bottom of each page. A simple footer, for example, can be just a page number. Business letters of more than one page often have an identification header that starts on the second page. The header can include the addressee's name, the page number, and the date, as in the following example:

Mr. Robert Woods — 2 — June 15, 1991

You can add, edit, or delete headers, footers, or both at any point in the document. You can set their starting page with the Write menu's Define Page option. When added, headers and footers appear on every page, beginning with their starting page.

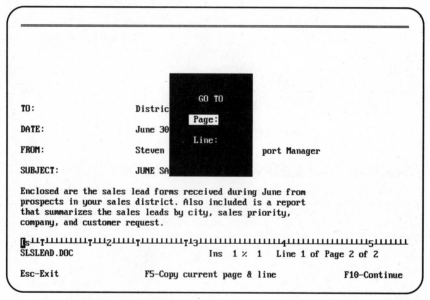

Fig. 11.17. *The GoTo box.*

Adding Headers and Footers

The header at the top of the second page of the sales memo displays the memo's subject and date. The footer at the bottom of the second page is the page number—for example, Page 2. If you haven't already added the header and footer as described in Chapter 9, perform the following procedure:

1. Press F8 (Options).

2. Select Lay Out Page from the Options menu.

3. Choose Edit Header from the Lay Out Page submenu. Q&A displays the top of the page (see fig. 11.18). Notice that the cursor is in the header and that a double line separates the header from the rest of the page. Notice also that the key assignment line indicates that the Text Enhancements and Fonts menu and the Options menu are available for editing the header.

4. Type the information to be included in the header. Remember that the top edge of the paper is indicated by the top border lines above the header.

```
 June Sales Leads
 June 30, 1991



 TO:                     District Sales Managers

 DATE:                   June 30, 1991

 FROM:                   Steven Hill, Marketing Support Manager

 SUBJECT:                JUNE SALES LEADS

 Enclosed are the sales lead forms received during June from
 prospects in your sales district. Also included is a report
 that summarizes the sales leads by city, sales priority,
 company, and customer request.
 [sᴸᴸᵀᴸᴸᴸᴸᴸᴸᴸᴸᴸᴸᴸᵀᴸᴸᴸᴸ2ᴸᴸᴸᴸᵀᴸᴸᴸᴸᴸᴸᴸᵀᴸ3ᴸᴸᴸᴸᴸᴸᴸᴸᴸᴸᴸᴸᴸᴸᴸᴸᴸᴸᴸᴸ4ᴸᴸᴸᴸᴸᴸᴸᴸᴸᴸᴸᴸᴸᴸᴸᴸᴸᴸ5ᴸᴸᴸᴸᴸᴸ
 SLSLEAD.DOC                           Ins  1 %  14  Line 2 Header


 F1-Help           Shift+F6-Enhance        F8-Options         F10-Exit Header
```

Fig. 11.18.   *The header editing area.*

To format the header, use the Enhance and Options menus. The Options menu offers the Lay Out Page, Align Text, Block Operations, and other Options submenus from which you can choose commands to format headers and footers. The Text Enhancements and Fonts menu offers Boldface, Underline, Italic, Subscript, and Superscript type. You also can enter print codes directly in the text (discussed in Chapter 13). After you create the header, press F10 to return to Type/Edit mode.

The procedure for adding a footer is the same as for adding a header, except that you select Edit Footer from the Lay Out Page submenu on the Optons menu. Type *Page #* as the footer text for the sales lead memo. (The # sign indicates that you want Q&A to use automatic page numbering. See "Inserting Page Numbers in Headers or Footers" for more information.)

To edit a header or footer, you select Edit Header or Edit Footer from the Layout Page menu of the Options menu and then use the program's normal text-editing features.

Setting the Header and Footer Starting Points

You set the starting point for a header and footer by using two options in the Define Page screen:

> Begin Header/Footer on Page #
> Begin Page Numbering with Page #

When you set one, you ordinarily set the other as well. For example, because the memo's header begins on page 2, the footer containing the page number also begins on page 2.

To set the header and footer starting points, follow these steps:

1. From the Type/Edit screen, press Ctrl-F6; or press the Esc key and select the Define Page command from the Write menu. Q&A displays the Define Page screen.

2. Using the Tab or down-arrow key, move the cursor to the Begin Header/Footer on Page # option.

3. Type the number of the page on which you want the header or footer to start (2 in this example), and press Enter.

4. Move the cursor to the Begin Page Numbering with Page # option.

5. Type the number of the page on which you want the page numbering to start (2 in this example), and press Enter.

6. Press F10 to return to the Type/Edit screen and the memo. Notice that the header and footer begin on page 2 rather than page 1. Notice also that the page number on page 2 correctly states `Page 2`.

Inserting Page Numbers in Headers and Footers

Q&A Write can number your pages automatically. For example, the memo's footer reads `Page #`. Q&A Write reads the pound sign (#) as "Put the page number here." The page number appears wherever you enter the pound sign in a header or footer. If you want a header or footer to show a pound sign followed by the page number, enter ##. This format is printed on page 7, for example, as #7.

Adding Date and Time to Headers and Footers

Headers and footers often include the date and time. Q&A uses the computer's current date and time; that is, the time and date you set when you turned on the computer. To include the date or time in a header or footer, use the following format:

```
*@DATE(n)*
*@TIME(n)*
```

The *n* is the display format number for the date and time. Twenty different formats are available for dates, and three formats for time. The following list shows all the available date and time formats

@DATE(1)	Sep 2, 1991	@DATE(11)	September 2, 1991
@DATE(2)	2 Sep 1991	@DATE(12)	2 September 1991
@DATE(3)	9/2/91	@DATE(13)	9-2-91
@DATE(4)	2/9/91	@DATE(14)	2-9-91
@DATE(5)	9/2/1991	@DATE(15)	09-02-91
@DATE(6)	2/9/1991	@DATE(16)	09-02-1991
@DATE(7)	09/02/91	@DATE(17)	02.09.91
@DATE(8)	02/09/91	@DATE(18)	02.09.1991
@DATE(9)	09/02/1991	@DATE(19)	1991-09-02
@DATE(10)	02/09/1991	@DATE(20)	1991/09/02
@TIME(1)	11:39 am	@TIME(3)	11.39
@TIME(2)	11:39		

Although dates and times are used often within headers and footers, you can use these features anywhere in the document. If you are creating a form letter, for example, you can save considerable time by having Q&A insert the date and time for you.

Customizing Global Options in Q&A Write

Q&A Write has values preset for a wide range of global settings that affect the editing of your document and its appearance on-screen and in printouts. These values include tab settings, page formats, header/footer settings, and print options. By changing these settings, you can customize the Write word processor to meet your own preferences and needs.

To change Write's global settings, select Utilities from the Write menu. Next, select Set Global Options from the Write Utilities menu, calling up the Global Options menu. This menu includes four commands:

> E - Set Editing Options
> P - Change Print Defaults
> D - Change Page Defaults
> I - Change Import Defaults

From the Global Options menu, you can elect to change editing, printing, page, and import settings. The global options determine how Write is configured when you first load it. Of course, you can make changes inside Write for special treatment of any document, but you should establish global options so that Write is set up the way you want to use the program most of the time.

Remember that none of the changes from the Global Options menu is retroactive. They apply only to newly created documents. Each document retains its own formatting specifications when it is saved.

Setting Editing Options

To set the editing defaults, select Set Editing Options from the Global Options menu. The Editing Options screen appears, as shown in figure 11.19.

Use the Default Editing Mode option to determine whether you will use Insert or Overtype mode when you edit the document. The setting you choose depends on your personal preference. People often use Insert mode to keep them from accidentally typing over text they have entered.

The Default Export Type setting is used to export files in ASCII format. The two options represent the types of ASCII files: with carriage returns or without. The ASCII with CR option places a carriage return/line feed at the end of every line. You select this setting for exporting tables and charts, or for use in another editing system that does not support wordwrap. The ASCII without CR option places carriage return/line feed combinations only at paragraph breaks. Lines within paragraphs do not end in a carriage return, so another text-processing package can perform its own wordwrap on the text. (For more information on exporting data to ASCII files, see Chapter 20.)

Another global option is the Automatic Backups selection. When you select Yes, a backup of your document is created each time you save the file. Before you can use this feature, you must have saved the file one time so that Q&A has a file name to work with. For example, with this option, if you have an existing document named LET1.DOC, and you edit and save it to disk, your disk contains two files: LET1.DOC and LET1.BAK. This duplication is a major safety feature of Q&A: in case of data loss, you can rename the BAK file rather than have to re-create your entire document.

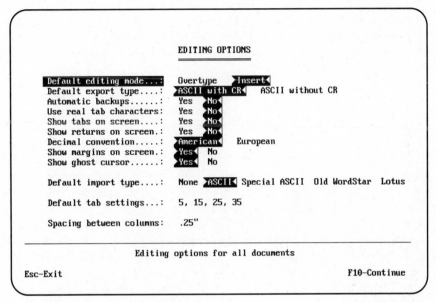

```
                         EDITING OPTIONS


         Default editing mode...:  Overtype    Insert
         Default export type....:  ASCII with CR    ASCII without CR
         Automatic backups......:  Yes   No
         Use real tab characters:  Yes   No
         Show tabs on screen....:  Yes   No
         Show returns on screen.:  Yes   No
         Decimal convention.....:  American    European
         Show margins on screen.:  Yes   No
         Show ghost cursor......:  Yes   No

         Default import type....:  None  ASCII  Special ASCII  Old WordStar  Lotus

         Default tab settings...:  5, 15, 25, 35

         Spacing between columns:  .25"

                     Editing options for all documents

    Esc-Exit                                          F10-Continue
```

Fig. 11.19. *The Editing Options screen.*

With the Use Real Tab Characters option, you can tell Q&A whether to insert spaces or real tab characters when you press Tab at the editing screen. Real tabs conform to most other word processor formats and are recommended if you plan to convert documents for use with WordPerfect, Microsoft Word, and other programs.

With the Show Tabs on Screen option set to Yes, Q&A inserts an arrow each time you press Tab in a document. This feature is useful to distinguish between a single tab and five spaces, for example.

The Show Returns on Screen option tells Q&A to insert a paragraph symbol each time you press the Enter key to insert a carriage return in the editing screen.

With the Decimal Convention option, you can choose the American or European decimal system; the only difference is the decimal indicator. The American style uses the period as the indicator (for example, 1.2), whereas the

European style uses the comma (for example, 1,2). You need to use this feature when you are setting decimal tabs or using row/column arithmetic.

If you set Show Margins On Screen to No, Q&A does not display left, right, top, and bottom margins, leaving you more room for editing text. If you accept the Yes default, two brackets appear on the ruler line, indicating the right and left margins, and a screen border indicates page edges.

The Show Ghost Cursor option displays on the ruler line a cursor that corresponds to the cursor on the Type/Edit screen. The *ghost cursor* is like a shadow of the main cursor and helps you locate the exact typing position in the document by character position.

The Default Import Type option enables you to set a standard format for documents from other word processor formats that you plan to edit with Q&A. If you set the default import type to None, when you choose a "foreign" document with the Q&A Write menu's Get option, Q&A displays the Import Document menu and asks you to choose a format. If you set the default import type to one of the other listed choices, Q&A automatically performs the specified conversion whenever you try to Get a document whose format Q&A doesn't recognize. You should use this option with care because if you choose WordStar as the default, for example, Q&A performs a WordStar conversion on any unrecognized file formats that you retrieve. If you plan to use documents from several other word processors, a safer approach is to choose None for the Default Import Type. You also can import documents in WordPerfect, Microsoft Word, and other formats from the Import a Document menu, described in Chapter 12.

With the Default Tab Settings option, you can assign a ruler line location to each tab. For example, if you want to set tabs at 5-character intervals beginning at the 25th character position, and set a decimal tab at position 50, you type the following:

    25, 30, 35, 40, 45, 50D

Because Write can print more than one column of text on a page, the Editing Options screen has an option, Spacing between Columns, that enables you to set the amount of space between columns. You can enter the setting in inches (.25"), centimeters (.95cm), or ruler line increments (7). These settings indicate how columns will print if you specify multiple column printing from the Print Options screen for a specific document. The default is one column, but you can specify up to eight columns. (You display the Print Options screen by pressing F2 (Print) in Type/Edit mode.)

After you have made all the appropriate changes on the Editing Options screen, press F10 to save the settings. These global settings then apply to all new documents created in Write. If you don't want to save the settings, press Esc to return to the Global Options menu.

Changing Print Defaults

From the Global Options menu (accessed by choosing Set Global Options from the Write Utilities menu), you also can change global print settings. When you select Change Print Defaults, the Print Options screen is displayed. This screen is the same Print Options screen you see when you print an individual document. The difference is that these settings are global in nature. (See Chapter 13 for more information on setting print options.)

After you make any necessary changes, press F10. The new settings then apply to all new documents created in Write. If you want to abandon the changes, press Esc on the Print Options screen to return to the Global Options menu.

Changing Page Defaults

Change Page Defaults is the third command on Write's Global Options menu. When you select this command, the Define Page screen appears. The screen is the same one displayed when you press Ctrl-F6 (Define Pg) in Type/Edit mode. When you enter the screen through the Global Options menu, however, any changes apply to all new documents rather than just the document currently on-screen.

You can choose the defaults for the left, right, top, and bottom margins and can specify page length and width for new documents from this screen. The length and width settings indicate the paper size in characters or inches. To define margins in inches, use whole or fractional numbers followed by the inch sign ("). If you use character columns or number of lines, you must use whole numbers.

The left and right margins are shown as the brackets on the ruler line, and the top and bottom margins appear on-screen as equal signs (=). Other defaults include the characters per inch setting, header and footer designation, and page numbering system.

After you make the changes and save the settings, all new documents have the same defaults. You can modify the defaults if necessary, which makes creating several different documents from one Write document an easy task. (See Chapter 10 for more information on the Define Page screen.)

The last item on the Global Options menu, Change Import Defaults, tells Q&A how to format documents when you import them from other programs. Choosing this menu item displays the Define Page for Imported Documents screen, which is the same as the Define Page screen discussed in the section on "Formatting the Page" in Chapter 10. When you change the settings for margins, page dimensions, and characters per inch, Q&A applies your settings to documents imported from ASCII, WordStar, and Lotus. For more information on importing documents, see Chapter 20.

Using WordStar Control Characters in Q&A Write

If you have used WordStar, you will feel at home with Q&A. Q&A Write incorporates the WordStar control characters listed in tables 11.1 and 11.2. You can add other WordStar commands by defining a macro and assigning it to the WordStar control-key combination. (For more information about macros, see Chapter 19.)

Table 11.1
Using WordStar Cursor-Movement Keys in Q&A

Key Combination	Function
Ctrl-A	Move to previous word
Ctrl-S	Move to previous character
Ctrl-D	Move to next character
Ctrl-F	Move to next word
Ctrl-E	Move up one line
Ctrl-X	Move down one line
Ctrl-R	Move to first character of preceding screen (page up)
Ctrl-C	Move to first character of next screen (page down)
Ctrl-I	Tab
Ctrl-M	Enter

Table 11.2
Using WordStar Editing Keys in Q&A

Key Combination	Function
Ctrl-G	Delete character at cursor
Ctrl-T	Delete to end of word
Ctrl-N	Insert line
Ctrl-H	Backspace
Ctrl-Y	Delete line
Ctrl-V	Turn Insert mode on/off

Using Q&A's Math Functions

If your document includes numbers, such as costs of individual items, travel expenses, quantities, and the like, you may need to use Q&A to perform calculations. With Q&A, you can total, average, count, multiply, or divide a row or column of numbers. You can perform calculations on numbers you type directly into a Write document or on numbers that you import into a document from another program, such as 1-2-3 or Symphony.

To calculate a row or column of numbers, follow these steps:

1. Position the cursor after the last number in the row you want calculated, or at the end of the last number in the column you want calculated.

2. Press Alt-F9. Q&A highlights the column and displays the Calculation menu, which includes five math functions: Total, Average, Count, Multiply, and Divide.

Note: You also can display the Calculation menu from the Options menu. Press F8 (Options), O (Other Options), and C (Calculate).

3. Select the operation you want.

4. Move the cursor to the screen position where the result should be inserted, and press F10. Q&A conducts the calculation and places the result at the cursor location.

Q&A is capable of performing calculations on rows or columns that contain only numbers (no text) as well as on rows or columns that have text and numbers together (see figs. 11.20 and 11.21).

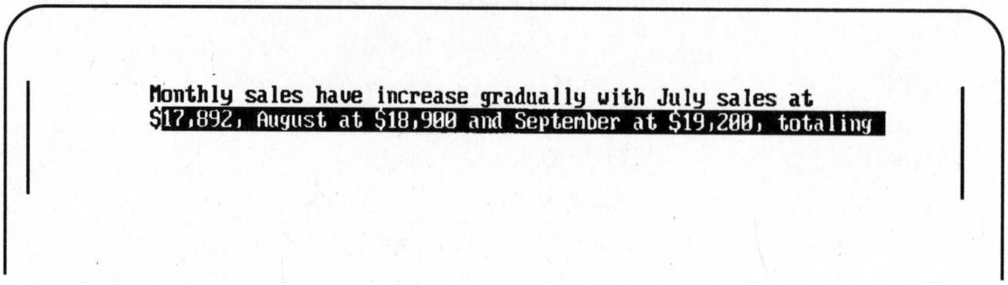

```
Monthly sales have increase gradually with July sales at
$17,892, August at $18,900 and September at $19,200, totaling
```

Fig. 11.20.   *Calculating numbers interspersed with text.*

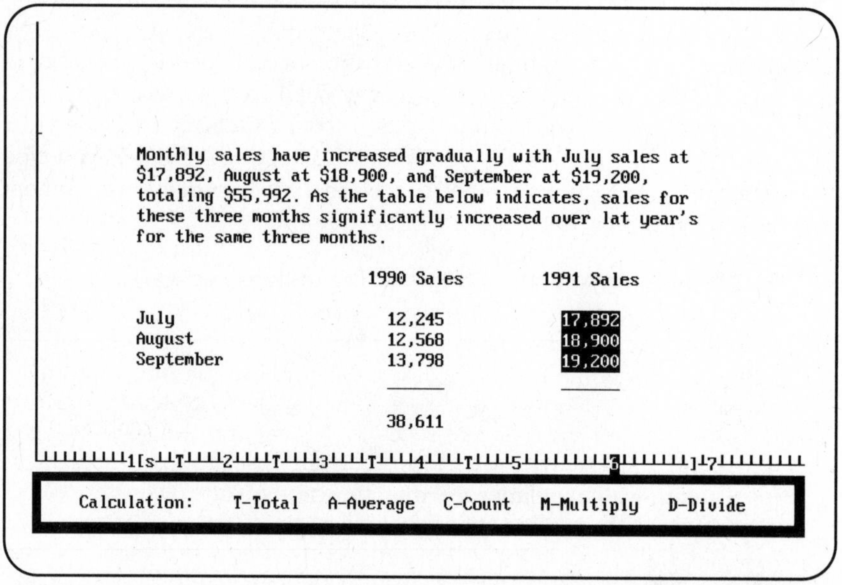

```
Monthly sales have increased gradually with July sales at
$17,892, August at $18,900, and September at $19,200,
totaling $55,992. As the table below indicates, sales for
these three months significantly increased over lat year's
for the same three months.

                            1990 Sales         1991 Sales

        July                12,245             17,892
        August              12,568             18,900
        September           13,798             19,200
                            _____
                            38,611

Calculation:    T-Total    A-Average    C-Count    M-Multiply    D-Divide
```

Fig. 11.21.   *Calculating columns of numbers.*

If you change any of the numbers on which you have performed a calculation, you need to recalculate the values by repeating the Alt-F9 operation. Q&A Write does not recalculate automatically.

Using Apple Macintosh Documents with Write

With Q&A Version 3.0 and later versions, Symantec has addressed the growing trend toward heterogeneous computer environments. Rarely do all users in a business have the same machines and operating systems. For example, some people depend on the IBM PC or a clone for the variety of software or for compatibility across a broad range of applications. Other people use an Apple Macintosh for its excellent graphics support or user-friendly interface.

Whatever the reason, users increasingly need to be able to share information among both similar and dissimilar machines. To answer this need, Q&A is compatible with a number of IBM PC-based networks, as well as Apple's AppleShare file server software. AppleShare support enables you to attach an IBM PC running Q&A to an AppleShare file server and share files across the network with other PCs or Apple machines.

To use Q&A with an AppleShare file server, you need a special interface card for your PC. Your Apple dealer can supply more information. After the hardware link is working, you can store Q&A programs and files on the AppleShare file server. You can run programs on your PC from the server and store Q&A Write or File data on the server, where other PC-based Q&A users can share the data and where Apple users can access files you have stored in an Apple-compatible format.

Q&A currently does not run directly on Apple machines, but Apple users can access Microsoft Word, WordPerfect, and other word processing programs. As a Q&A user, you can save Q&A text files in Macintosh ASCII format for access by an Apple software program.

To export files to ASCII format, select Utilities from the Write menu and then choose Export to ASCII. Q&A then displays the ASCII Export menu, which includes three commands. The Standard ASCII command includes a carriage return/line feed combination at the end of every line. The Document ASCII command includes carriage returns and line feeds only at paragraph breaks. This command is designed for use with other text-processing software that can handle wordwrap. The third command, Macintosh ASCII, exports files with the Macintosh carriage-return character, which is different from the one used by PC DOS or MS-DOS computers.

Chapter Summary

This chapter has demonstrated text enhancements and formatting. After reading this chapter and Chapter 10, you should be able to use the word processing capabilities of Q&A Write to produce an edited and formatted document, ready to be printed.

Q&A Write compares favorably with other word processors in most of its functions and outshines the others in at least one function—a direct link to the mailing lists and other data in Q&A File. This integration helps you to produce personalized mailings, reports with information from databases, and dozens of other mail-merge projects. The next chapter thoroughly explains how you can become the fastest "mail merger" in your office.

12

Merging Documents with Q&A Write

You often begin your work by using only one document at a time. As the various segments of your work become related, however, you may need to combine the information from files originally created in Q&A and those created with other software programs. You may want to pull blocks of text from one document and insert them into another, add one document to another, or merge File data into a Write document. Q&A's power and flexibility can help you perform these operations.

This chapter explains how to move text from an existing Write document to a newly created Write document, how to use Q&A's mail-merge capability to merge File data into a Write document, and how to import text from other programs and insert the text into a Write document.

Moving Text from an Existing Write Document to a New Write Text File

Write's built-in capability to move blocks of text out of an existing document and into a newly created document can be used in many ways. You can extract from a memo pieces of information that you want to use again, for example. Or you can save from a long document only what you need, thus reducing disk storage space.

To move text out of a document and into a new text file, you use the Alt-F5 command with the text-block selection process explained in Chapter 10. Note that this operation not only moves text to a new text file, but also removes that text from the current document.

Suppose that you want to export the second paragraph in figure 12.1 to another file so that you can copy the paragraph into other documents.

```
FROM:                    Steven Hill, Marketing Support Manager

SUBJECT:                 JUNE SALES LEADS

Enclosed are the sales lead forms received during June from
prospects in your sales district. Also included is a report
that summarizes the sales leads by city, sales priority,
company, and customer request.

                    INSTRUCTIONS

We are implementing a new sales tracking system that will
give you a means to keep track of sales leads and follow up.
This should help each of you to unify your sales force and
make sure each lead is pursued effectively. A Q&A disk is
enclosed that contains the sales leads for your district.
Please copy these leads into your file and maintain them
in the following manner:

     1. When each lead is assigned, enter the name of the
        sales person.
SLSLEAD.DOC                        Ins  2 %  1   Line 25 of Page 2 of 2

Esc-Exit  F1-Help  F2-Print  Shift+F7-Restore   F7-Search  F8-Options  ↑F8-Save
```

Fig. 12.1.   *Preparing to move text to a new document.*

The procedure for moving a block of text on-screen to another file consists of marking the block that you want to move and then indicating the file name to which you want to move the block. First, move the cursor to the beginning of the text you want to move. Press Alt-F5 to begin the move operation. When Q&A prompts you to highlight the block you want to export, move the cursor to the end of the block (see fig. 12.2). (To highlight a block quickly, use the procedures described in the section on "Deleting, Moving, Copying, and Printing Blocks of Text" in Chapter 10.)

Another method is to use the Options menu to move a text block to a file. Rather than press Alt-F5, press F8 (Options), press B (Block Operations), and choose Move to File.

Use the arrow keys to highlight the text to move. Next, press F10 to indicate where you want the block moved. When the prompt Move to appears, you can enter a file name—either to create a new file for saving the block or to use an existing file. If you use the name of an existing file, all text currently in the file is overwritten by the new block. If an existing file is going to be overwritten, Q&A alerts you and asks for confirmation to proceed with the operation. After you indicate the text file to which Q&A should move the block, Q&A removes the block from the document on-screen and saves it to the file.

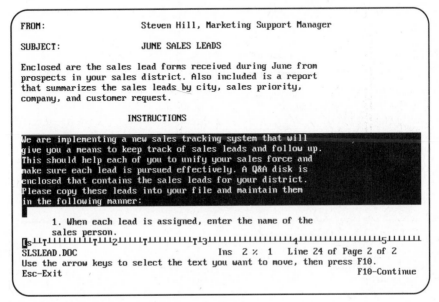

```
FROM:               Steven Hill, Marketing Support Manager

SUBJECT:            JUNE SALES LEADS

Enclosed are the sales lead forms received during June from
prospects in your sales district. Also included is a report
that summarizes the sales leads by city, sales priority,
company, and customer request.

                    INSTRUCTIONS
We are implementing a new sales tracking system that will
give you a means to keep track of sales leads and follow up.
This should help each of you to unify your sales force and
make sure each lead is pursued effectively. A Q&A disk is
enclosed that contains the sales leads for your district.
Please copy these leads into your file and maintain them
in the following manner:

     1. When each lead is assigned, enter the name of the
        sales person.
[s⌐⌐⊥T⊥⊥⊥⊥⊥⊥⊥⊥⊥T⊥2⊥⊥⊥⊥T⊥⊥⊥⊥⊥⊥⊥⊥⊥T⊥3⊥⊥⊥⊥⊥⊥⊥⊥⊥⊥⊥⊥⊥⊥⊥⊥⊥⊥4⊥⊥⊥⊥⊥⊥⊥⊥⊥⊥⊥⊥⊥⊥5⊥⊥⊥⊥⊥
SLSLEAD.DOC                        Ins  2 %  1   Line 24 of Page 2 of 2
Use the arrow keys to select the text you want to move, then press F10.
Esc-Exit                                                    F10-Continue
```

Fig. 12.2.   *Highlighting the text to be moved.*

Merging Q&A File Data into a Write Document

Mail merge, an automated process in which Q&A File and Write are closely integrated, is an excellent example of Q&A's "appropriate integration" of database and word processor. In the *mail-merge* operation, Q&A inserts data from a File database into a Write document and prints the document. Few programs perform mail-merge operations as effortlessly as Q&A.

With mail merge, you can produce forms and automatically fill the forms with appropriate information. Such forms include contracts and other legal documents; personnel records; form letters; and tax, accounting, and business forms.

Before you can perform a merge operation, you must have a Q&A File database from which to retrieve data. Merging the File data into a Write document is a two-step process. First, using Write, you create a merge document (such as a letter or form) to which you add formatting instructions for the merged data. Wherever information is to be merged into the document, an asterisk precedes and follows the name of a database field. You then specify the proper print options and print the document. (Note that during the initial document design and preparation, you do not need to specify which database File will use during the merge. That information is supplied when the Write document is printed.)

When you instruct Write to print with a merge operation, Q&A notes the database from which the merge information will be retrieved, looks through the document for merge specifications that indicate which fields to use in the merge, and retrieves that information from the database. Q&A then inserts the information into the document and prints the document with the merged information.

Figures 12.3 and 12.4 show the Write document and the File form involved in a mail merge. Figure 12.3 shows a contract form before the merge.

```
                  COPYRIGHT ASSESSMENT

     The "Software" shall mean the computer program
currently referred to as *Software*, version *version*.
The "Developer" is *Developer*. The "Publisher" is
*Publisher*.

     For valuable consideration, the Developer,
*Developer*, hereby assigns, sells, transfers, sets over,
and conveys to the Publisher, *Publisher*, all right,
title, and interest in and to *software*, version
*version*, including the undivided copyrights, trade
secret rights, and other proprietary rights, therein now
known or hereafter created throughout the world, and
further, including any and all claims, demands, and causes
of action, for infringement or otherwise, of the same,
past, present, and future, and all of the proceeds from
the foregoing accrued and unpaid and hereafter accruing.

[s       2     3     4     5     6     ]7
COPYRITE.DOC                      Ins  0 %  18  Line 18 of Page 1 of 1

Esc-Exit F1-Help F2-Print Shift+F7-Restore  F7-Search F8-Options ↑F8-Save
```

Fig. 12.3. *A Write document with merge specifications.*

The merge operation is based on field names in a File database. By enclosing field names in asterisks, you tell Write to go to a File database, look for the named field, and substitute the information found there for the field label in the

Write document. These File specifications in a Write document form the *merge spec*. The merge spec tells Q&A Write which fields to use from the linked database and where to place the fields in the document.

The example in figure 12.3 uses field labels from the CONTRACT.DTF database shown in figure 12.4. Write searches the CONTRACT.DTF database for the field label Software, for example, and inserts Autobook where the merge spec *Software* appears. Write finds the field label Version in the same record and substitutes 1.0 where the merge spec *version* appears in the Write document.

In addition to using mail merge with legal documents, you can use the feature to produce personalized mailings by inserting names, addresses, and other information into a form letter. With Q&A's mail-merge operation, you can address a single letter to one person or hundreds of letters to hundreds of people.

Figure 12.5 shows an example of a mail-merge letter from the Sales Lead Tracking System database. For this letter, data has been merged from the Sales Lead database form shown in figure 12.6.

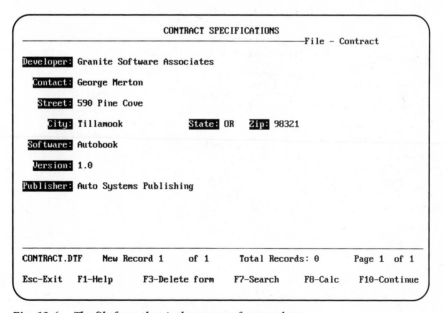

Fig. 12.4. *The file form that is the source of merge data.*

Turner Philips
General Manager
Nashville Medical Technology
552 Thompson Lane
Nashville, TN 37204

Dear Mr. Philips:

Thank you for your interest in Titan Technology products. I
have enclosed our sales catalog, along with flyers announcing
our current sale items.

If you have any questions or would like to see a demonstration
of our products, contact Mr. Gubin at our Cincinnati office.
To place an order, call 1-800-456-1234.

We appreciate your interest in Titan Technology and look
forward to working with you in the future.

Fig. 12.5. *A personalized letter with merged file data.*

```
              TITAN TECHNOLOGY SALES LEAD TRACKING SYSTEM
================================================= File Name -- SlsLead
LastName: Philips                      FirstName: Turner
Title: General Manager
Company: Nashville Medical Tech        Telephone: (615) 492-1935
Address1: 552 Thompson Lane
Address2:
City: Nashville                        State: TN      Zip: 37204
   No. of Labs: 7                      Annual Revenue: $375,000.00
   Current Customer: N                 Company Priority: 1
─────────────────────────────LEAD INFORMATION─────────────────────────
   Product Interest: 2000
   Request For: Info                   Lead Source: Adv
   Months to Purchase: 2               Product Priority: 1
─────────────────────────────SALES ACTION─────────────────────────────
   Sales Priority: 1.0                 Date Entered: Sep 27, 1990
   Sales Dist.: Cincinnati             Sales Manager: Aarons
   Salesman: Gubin                     Phone: (   )   -
   Status:


──────────────────────────────────────────────────────────────────────
SLSLEAD.DTF    Retrieved form 2    of --     Total Forms: 6     Page 1  of 1

Esc-Exit   F1-Help   Alt+F6-Table   F7-Search   F8-Calc   F9-Go back   F10-Continue
```

Fig. 12.6. *The file form from which merged data was retrieved.*

Creating and Formatting a Merge Document

A merge spec can be located on a line of its own, within a paragraph, or wherever you want it.

You can see by comparing figures 12.5 and 12.7 that the length of the merged database information varies, depending on the data found in the specified file.

```
*Firstname* *Lastname*
*Title*
*Company*
*Address*
*City*, *St* *Zip*

Dear Mr. *Lastname*:

Thank you for your interest in Titan Technology products. I
have enclosed our sales catalog, along with flyers announcing
our current sale items.

If you have any questions or would like to see a demonstration
of our products, contact Mr. *Salesman* at our *Sales Dist.*
office. To place an order, call 1-800-456-1234.

We appreciate your interest in Titan Technology and look
forward to working with you in the future.

[s⌊⌊T⌊⌊⌊⌊⌊⌊⌊⌊⌊T⌊⌊2⌊⌊⌊⌊⌊T⌊⌊⌊⌊⌊⌊⌊⌊T₃⌊⌊⌊⌊⌊⌊⌊⌊⌊⌊⌊⌊⌊⌊⌊4⌊⌊⌊⌊⌊⌊⌊⌊⌊⌊⌊⌊⌊⌊5⌊⌊⌊⌊⌊
TITAN.DOC                            Ins  0 %  43  Line 18 of Page 1 of 1

Esc-Exit  F1-Help  F2-Print  Shift+F7-Restore   F7-Search  F8-Options  ↑F8-Save
```

Fig. 12.7.   *The form letter with the merge specs.*

The entire first name found in the file is inserted at the specified location, a space is entered, and then the entire last name is inserted. The name Joe Smith requires less space in the merged Write document than the name Franklyn McCormick.

To prepare a merge document, type the text of the document as you normally would. To insert variable data, move the cursor to the position where you want the data to print. At the Data File Name prompt, type the name of the database from which you want to draw the data. Press Enter to display the field names list, then move the cursor to the name of a field and press Enter. Q&A inserts a correctly formatted field name code in the document. You now can press Alt-F7 to redisplay the field names list and insert other field codes. You also can display the List Fields box by pressing F8 (Options), O (Other Options), and L (List Fields).

Suppose that you want to create a merge document like the letter in figure 12.7. Begin by using Write to create and edit a document without merge specifications or by using an existing Write document retrieved with the Get option. Following the format in figure 12.7, add the merge specifications by selecting field names from the field names box as described in the preceding paragraph, or by typing an asterisk, the field label, and a second asterisk wherever you want Q&A to insert data. Note the following examples:

Name
Part No.

When you finish the merge specifications, press Shift-F1 to make sure that the spelling in your document is correct. Save the document, perhaps using a special extension such as MRG.

As you will see in the examples that follow, database information that is merged into a document begins at the left asterisk and fills as many spaces as the information has characters. After the database information has been printed, printing of the document resumes in the first space to the right of the final asterisk. Note that the asterisks do not occupy spaces in the printout.

For example, the salutation with a merge spec

Dear *First Name*:

prints as

Dear Jeff:

The sentence with a merge spec

Thank you for your order of *Quantity* *Part*s and the payment in advance.

prints as

Thank you for your order of 2,500 bowling balls and the payment in advance.

Certain situations call for different formats, which you can control by using text and tabular formatting.

Using a Text Format

If your database data has been entered on more than one line but you want the data to appear on one line in the merge document, use the Text (T) command in the merge spec at the end of the field name. If you don't add the T, Q&A will wordwrap the text to the following line(s).

For example, suppose that the database field is on two lines:

> Address: 195 Greenbush St.
> Minot, ND 58301

You can use the Text command to force the two lines into one line. The sentence with this merge spec

> Your address is listed as *Address(T)*.

prints as

> Your address is listed as 195 Greenbush St. Minot, ND 58301.

Note that the space between asterisks expands to fit the text being merged. By using a text format merge, you force the data fields into a wordwrap document.

Using a Tabular Format

The widely used tabular format is invaluable for creating columns, formatting documents that will be printed on preprinted forms, and dozens of other needs.

To create a document field in which the text appears flush left or flush right, Q&A mail merge uses the Left-Justify (L) command and Right-Justify (R) command with a pair of asterisks. In this format, the asterisks set the document's field length.

In the following examples, notice that when the Left- and Right-Justify commands are used, the space between the asterisks no longer is flexible. Instead, the space becomes a set width, determined by your merge spec.

You can create a document field and position merged data on the field's left margin by combining the Left-Justify command and a pair of asterisks.

For example, the merge specs

> *LastName(L)   * *FirstName(L) *
> *Position(L)   * *Date Hired(L) *

print as

> Finklebinder   Jerome
> Light-bulb tester 6/17/59

The data in the LastName field is merged in a flush-left format within the document field, starting at the position of the first asterisk. Note that space is available for 20 characters between the asterisks in the first document field (the LastName field). When the merge data (the name, in this case) has fewer characters than the document field has spaces, Q&A fills with blank spaces the space between the end of the data and the second asterisk. If the merge data has more characters than the document field has spaces, however, the characters overrun the field and are lost. Q&A truncates File data to fit into the space you specify in the Write tabular merge spec. Be sure, therefore, to make document fields wide enough for the data they will hold.

The left-justify tabular format has many uses. For example, you can use this format to create a merge document that automatically fills a form with data (see figs. 12.8 and 12.9). As you can see in figures 12.8 and 12.9, the asterisks are spaced to provide room for the form's information.

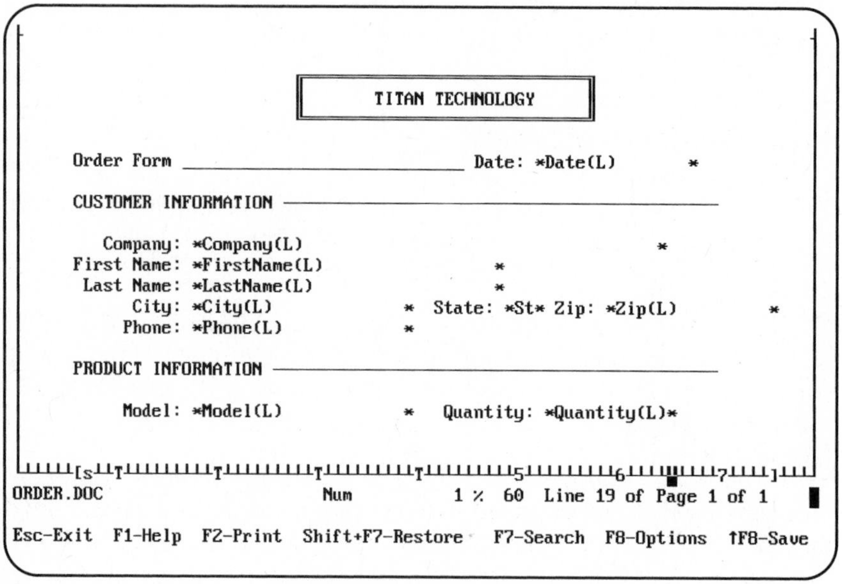

Fig. 12.8. *Creating a document with left-justified tabular format.*

When you use the Right-Justify command, the right-justify tabular format creates a document field between asterisks and positions the information at the right side of the field.

For example, the merge specs

```
   *Company(R)      * *Amount Due(R)    *
   *Credit Code(R)  * *Date Due(R)      *
```

print as

```
        Burns Medical      $55,142.00
                  5A           10/1/86
```

```
================================
|        TITAN TECHNOLOGY        |
================================

Order Form _____      Date: July 5, 1991

CUSTOMER INFORMATION -----------------------------------------

   Company: Northern Supply Company
First Name: Jack
 Last Name: Wilson
      City: West Fargo          State: ND    Zip: 52832
     Phone: 701-292-3006

PRODUCT INFORMATION ------------------------------------------

   Model: 1500                  Quantity: 5
```

Fig. 12.9.   *The printed document with left-justified format.*

The data in the fields is merged in a flush-right format that ends at the final asterisk's position.

Note that the first document field (the Company field) has space for 20 characters between the asterisks. If the merge data has fewer characters than the document field has spaces, Q&A fills with blank spaces the space between the beginning of the data and the initial asterisk. If the merge data has more characters than the document field has spaces, however, the extra characters are truncated.

The Order Confirmation letter in figure 12.10 shows how the right-justify tabular format is entered into the merge document specs. Data from the ORDERS file (see fig. 12.11) is merged with the document to produce the printed letter (see fig. 12.12).

You can place information from more than one Q&A File database in each copy of the document. Programming a merge document with XLOOKUP statements is discussed later in this chapter, in the section on "Using Programming

Statements in the Retrieve Spec." You may want to use this procedure to print monthly statements in which a number of transactions has occurred against a single client record, or to detail items in a bill of materials list.

```
            *Address*
            *City*, *St* *Zip*

                                    Re: Order Confirmation

            Dear *FirstName*:

            Thank you for your order! This letter confirms your order
            and verifies the delivery date.

                Model:              *Model(R)*        *
                Quantity            *Quantity(R)*     *
                Unit Price:         *Unit Price(R)*        *
                Total Cost:         *Total Cost(R)*        *
                Shipping:           *Shipping(R)*          *
                Sales Tax:          *Sales Tax(R)*         *
                Total:              *Total(R)*             *

                Delivery:      *Date of Delivery(R)* *

            If you have any questions about your order, please contact
CONFIRM.DOC                         Ins  0 %  20  Line 19 of Page 1 of 1

Esc-Exit  F1-Help  F2-Print  Shift+F7-Restore   F7-Search  F8-Options  ↑F8-Save
```

Fig. 12.10.   Creating a document with right-justified tabular format.

```
                            File Name - ORDERS
    _____

    Last Name: Wilson                   Date: July 7, 1991
    First Name: Jack
    Company: Northern Supply Company    Address: 322 Second St.
    City: West Fargo                    Phone: 701-292-3006
    St: ND                              Zip: 52832

    Model: 1500                         Total Cost: $25000.00
    Quantity: 5                         Shipping: $237.47
    Unit Price: $5000.00                Sales Tax: $1250.00
                                        Total: $26487.47

    Delivery: Aug. 10, 1991



    _____
    ORDERS.DTF    Retrieved form 1   of --   Total Forms: 1   Page 1  of 1

    Esc-Exit   F1-Help   Alt+F6-Table   F7-Search   F8-Calc   F10-Continue
                            FIGURE 12-11
```

Fig. 12.11.   The file form that is the source of merge data.

```
322 Second St.
West Fargo, ND 52832

                                         RE: Order Confirmation

Dear Jack:

Thank you for your order.   This letter confirms your order and
verifies the delivery date.

     Model:                    1500
     Quantity:                    5
     Unit Price:             $5000.00
     Total Cost:            $25000.00
     Shipping:                $237.47
     Sales Tax:              $1250.00
     Total:                 $26487.47

     Delivery:          Aug. 10, 1991

If you have any questions about your order, please contact
```

Fig. 12.12.   The printed document with right-justified format.

Printing a Merge Document

After you create and format a merge document, you instruct Q&A to print the document. First, you set the print options, including the name of the database file from which the data will be retrieved. Next, using the Identifier Spec screen, you match the database field labels with the document's merge specifications. Note that if your merge fields and database fields use the same names, the Identifier Spec is unnecessary and Q&A skips this step. You then fill in the Retrieve Spec to determine the database forms from which the data will be retrieved.

To help you through this three-step merge-printing process, the following paragraphs again use the Order Confirmation letter as an example.

Setting the Print Options

The first step in printing a merge document is to set the print options. You set options to determine how many copies will be printed and how long the printed document will be. (If you want to print only page 9, for example, indicate 9 as the From Page and the To Page options on the Print Options screen.) You establish whether the document will be single- or double-spaced and whether the text will be justified. You even can set an option to print an envelope. By setting the Print To option, you direct printing to a specific printer or to disk. You can set the print offset, the printer control codes, and the type of paper feed.

To set the print options for a merge document, begin by pressing F2 from the merge document. Q&A displays the Print Options screen. Set the print options as you normally would to print the document. Next, move the cursor to the Name of Merge File option and enter the name of the Q&A File database from which the merge data is to be retrieved. Complete the procedure by pressing F10.

Q&A displays the Identifier Spec screen if differences exist in your merge document field names and those used in the database itself.

Using the Identifier Spec

The purpose of the Identifier Spec screen is to help you match the document merge specs with the database field labels. If all document merge specs match their database field labels, the Identifier Spec screen does not appear. You can press F10 at the Print Options screen to proceed to the Retrieve Spec screen.

If the merge specs and the field labels are different, you must match them so that Q&A can do the merge. For example, in the Order Confirmation letter, the labels and the specs differ:

Document merge spec: Date of Delivery
Database field label: Delivery

To match the label and the spec in this example, type *Date of Delivery* in the Identifier Spec's Delivery field.

The way you fill in the Identifier Spec depends on whether you know which database field labels need substitute names. If you know which field labels do not match the merge specs, move the cursor to the appropriate database field, enter the substitute merge spec, and press F10. If you enter the substitute specs incorrectly or incompletely, Q&A displays the Identifier Spec warning screen.

Also, if you don't know which merge specs do not match the field labels, press F10 before you enter anything in the Identifier Spec screen. Q&A displays the Identifier Spec warning screen, which lists the merge specs that don't match the database field labels. (In this example, the spec "Date of Delivery" does not match.)

To match specs and labels after such a warning, press Esc and then enter the substitute merge spec into the Write document. (Substitute *Delivery* for *Date of Delivery*, for example.) Press F10 to continue. If you press F10 without entering the substitute merge spec, that merge spec is not merged when you print the document.

Under most circumstances, the Write document merge specs should use the same field labels that appear in the linked database file. You may want to write generic documents, however, that can refer to more than one file and therefore to different field labels. In this case, choose a field label in the merge document that describes the type of data that will be substituted; then use the Identifier Spec screen to make the link just before you print the document.

Using the Retrieve Spec

Use the Retrieve Spec to specify which forms are to be merged with the document. Fill out the spec as you would any Retrieve Spec in Q&A File. Remember that you can get help by pressing the F1 (Help) key. (If you need a review of how to fill out a Retrieve Spec, see Chapter 6.) You may want to specify an entire database or only one form. You also can retrieve data from more than one database file, as described in the next section, "Using Programming Statements in the Retrieve Spec."

Because the Order Confirmation letter will be sent only to Mr. Turner Philips at Nashville Medical Labs, you need to retrieve only the Philips form. To do so, enter *Philips* in the Last Name field of the Retrieve Spec (see fig. 12.13).

You can give the Retrieve Spec a name and use it again later. Press Shift-F8 and type a name at the prompt; then press F10 to return to the Retrieve Spec screen. To view a list of stored specs, press Alt-F8. To insert one of the named specs into the Retrieve Spec screen, highlight the spec and press Enter.

If you want to sort forms before the merge print begins, press F8. Q&A displays the Sort Spec screen. If you use the Sort Spec to sort forms alphabetically before you print them, the documents print in alphabetical order. (For more information on the Sort Spec, see Chapter 6.) If the mailing is large, you may want to sort by ZIP code instead, to help prepare the documents for the office.

Press F10 to continue the printing process. Q&A confirms the merge-print operation, displaying the name of the document and the number of database forms to be merged. If you want to start printing, press Enter; if not, press the Esc key.

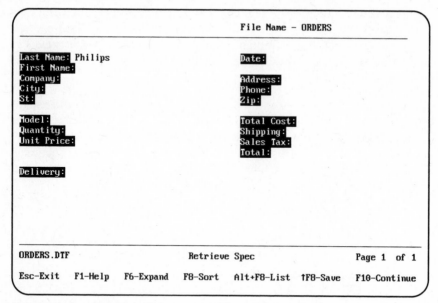

Fig. 12.13. *Specifying a retrieval on the Retrieve Spec screen.*

You have many ways in which you can use Q&A Write's capability to insert Write text files and Write-compatible files into a Write document. For example, you can create a separate report from portions of other reports, insert boilerplate paragraphs into contracts, and import tables and charts from other programs.

Using Programming Statements in the Retrieve Spec

Beginning with Q&A Version 4.0, you can calculate data pulled from a File database before Write inserts the data in a mail-merge document. You also can retrieve information into mail-merged text from more than one database file. Detailed information on using programming and calculations in the Retrieve Spec is given in Chapter 6, in the section on "Retrieving and Updating Forms."

To use calculations in the Retrieve Spec, enter the calculation in the appropriate field. You can use any valid calculation or programming expression, but you cannot use programming statements such as IF...THEN. Programming functions that you cannot use in the Retrieve Spec include @NUMBER, @TOTAL, @AVERAGE, @COUNT, @MAXIMUM, @MINIMUM, @VAR, @STD, @MSG, and @DITTO.

Suppose that you want to retrieve records for which net sales is greater than $10,000. In the NetSales field, type

NetSales: >=10000

To insert data from a database file other than the mail-merge file you specify in the Name of Merge File field on the Print Spec, use the @XLOOKUP function. Note that the external file must be indexed and linked with the file specified at the Name of Merge File field, in accordance with the rules for the @XLOOKUP statement as explained in Chapter 6.

If you want to insert names of regional sales representatives from an external file called SALESREP.DTF, for example, enter the following statement in place of the Name field in the target file:

Name: ={@XLOOKUP("SALESREP.DTF","IDNo","ID","Name")}

IDNo is the key field in the primary file, ID is the key field in the external file SALESREP, and Name is the field from which data will be extracted in the external file.

Using Programming Expressions in a Merge Document

You can enter programming expressions in your merge documents rather than in the Retrieve Spec. More instructions for using programming functions are given in Chapter 6. The basic form for entering programming statements in text to be merged is

program { <expression> }

in which you type the word *program*, followed by one or more programming expressions enclosed in curly braces. The statement may be no longer than 80 characters. As explained in Chapter 6, you can use field numbers or field names in a programming expression.

You can insert an @XLOOKUP statement in the body of your text to look up sales rep names, as described in the previous section. Or you can print sequential numbers in your mail-merged letters, beginning with 1000:

Your ID number is *program {@NUMBER(1000)}*.

Importing Files To Insert into Write Documents

The format of a document or file determines how it is inserted. Q&A Write automatically inserts other Write files and text files created with PFS: Write or IBM's Writing Assistant. Files from WordStar ASCII files or 1-2-3 and Symphony files, however, go through Q&A's reformatting procedure before being imported to Write.

Inserting Q&A Write-Compatible Files

You use the same process to import into a Write document other Write files or files from PFS: Write or the IBM Writing Assistant program.

Suppose that you want to incorporate a PFS: Write file into the middle of a document you are creating with Q&A Write. Begin by positioning the cursor where you want the text from the source file (PFS, in this case) to begin. Press F8 to access the Options menu, then press D (Documents) and I (Insert a Document). When Q&A prompts you for the name of the file that you want to insert into your present text, type the file name and press Enter. (If the file you want to import is stored in the default directory, press Enter immediately after selecting Insert a Document to display a complete list of files. If the file is not in the default directory, you must specify a path name so that Q&A can find the file.) After you type the name and press Enter, the new text appears in your current document.

Inserting Files from Other Software Packages

When you want to insert a file other than a Q&A Write, a PFS: Write, or an IBM Writing Assistant file, you use the same initial procedure required for those types of files (position the cursor, press F8, press D, press I, type the file name, and press Enter). The procedure changes, however, after you type the name of the file to insert. Because the format is different from the format for Write, PFS, and IBM Assistant files, Q&A displays the Import Document window shown in figure 12.14, with four options: ASCII, Special ASCII, Old WordStar, and Lotus 1-2-3 or Symphony.

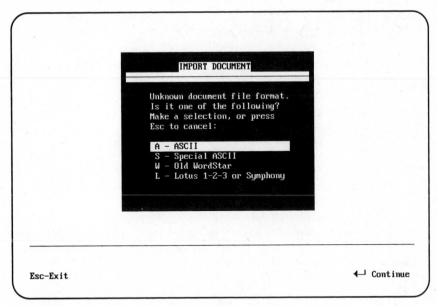

Fig. 12.14.   *The Import Document window.*

If the file you want to insert is in one of the four listed formats, choose the appropriate format and Q&A automatically reformats the file and inserts it into your Write document, as explained in the next sections.

You also can change the default import type so that Q&A Write doesn't display the list of four file formats whenever you retrieve or insert a file of the default type, but instead converts the file automatically. To change the default, choose Utilities, Global Options, and Set Editing Options from the Write menu. In the Default Import Type field, choose None, ASCII, Special ASCII, Old WordStar, or Lotus. Be careful when choosing a default import type because Q&A automatically converts files of all unrecognized types to the default format.

If the file to import is too big, Q&A displays the message `!Problem! Not enough memory to complete your request.` (For more information, see Appendix F.) Press Enter to continue.

Inserting WordStar Files

Because of Q&A's unique file format, WordStar files (and those of most other word processors) are not compatible with Write. To insert a WordStar file into a Write document, you must choose Old WordStar from the Import Document window (see fig. 12.14) by pressing W and then Enter. Write reformats the WordStar file, making the file compatible with Q&A. You then can edit the former WordStar document as if it were a Write document. If you need to keep this document in its original WordStar format, make a copy before using this Q&A reformat feature.

Inserting ASCII Files without Wordwrap

Choose option A (ASCII) from the Import Document window when you do not want wordwrap in the reformatted document. You will use this option frequently for such files as database reports (including Q&A Report files), spreadsheet tables, columnar data, and software program listings. Because the reformatted documents and files retain a carriage return at the end of every line, the arrangement of text does not change. To choose the ASCII option, press A and then Enter.

Inserting ASCII Files with Wordwrap

Use option S (Special ASCII) from the Import Document window to insert files in which you want to retain wordwrap. This option removes the carriage return from the end of a line if the following line contains text; the carriage return remains on a line that is followed by a blank line. Option S retains the original form of an ASCII document that has one or more blank lines between paragraphs. To select the Special ASCII option, press S and then Enter.

To see how option S affects a document with tabular data, compare the text samples in figures 12.15 and 12.16. Figure 12.15 shows the original ASCII document with tabular data that is maintained with carriage returns at the end of each line. After the file is imported into Write with the Special ASCII option (see fig. 12.16), the carriage returns have been removed and the tabular format has been lost.

The Special ASCII format is useful if you want to format data that contains only text and you want Write to be able to conduct its own formatting. But if the original ASCII file contains information that should be presented in Write without changes, use the standard ASCII format instead.

```
make sure each lead is pursued effectively. A Q&A disk is
enclosed that contains the sales leads for your district.
Please copy these leads into your file and maintain them
in the following manner:

      1. When each lead is assigned, enter the name of the
      sales person.
      2. Enter the date when the first sales contact was
         made with the sales lead.

Monthly sales have increased gradually:

         1990 Sales           1991 Sales

July        12,245            17,892
August      12,568            18,900
September   13,798            19,200

            _____            _____

            38,611

[s⌊⌊T⌊⌊⌊⌊⌊⌊⌊⌊⌊T⌊⌊2⌊⌊⌊⌊⌊T⌊⌊⌊⌊⌊⌊⌊⌊⌊⌊T⌊3⌊██⌊⌊⌊⌊⌊⌊⌊⌊⌊⌊⌊⌊⌊4⌊⌊⌊⌊⌊⌊⌊⌊⌊⌊⌊⌊5⌊⌊⌊⌊⌊
SLSLEAD.DOC                    Ins  2 %  40  Line 36 of Page 2 of 2

Esc-Exit  F1-Help  F2-Print  Shift+F7-Restore    F7-Search  F8-Options  ↑F8-Save
```

Fig. 12.15. *Tabular text in an ASCII file.*

```
make sure each lead is pursued effectively. A Q&A disk is
enclosed that contains the sales leads for your district.
Please copy these leads into your file and maintain them
in the following manner:

      1. When each lead is assigned, enter the name of the
      sales person.
      2. Enter the date when the first sales contact was
         made with the sales lead.

Monthly sales have increased gradually:

         1990 Sales           1991 Sales

July        12,245            17,892  August
12,568            18,900September    13,798
19,200 _____              _____  38,611




[s⌊⌊T⌊⌊⌊⌊⌊⌊⌊⌊⌊T⌊⌊2⌊⌊⌊⌊⌊T⌊⌊⌊⌊⌊⌊⌊⌊⌊█⌊3⌊⌊⌊⌊⌊⌊⌊⌊⌊⌊⌊⌊⌊⌊⌊4⌊⌊⌊⌊⌊⌊⌊⌊⌊⌊⌊⌊5⌊⌊⌊⌊⌊
SLSLEAD.DOC                    Ins  2 %  35  Line 37 of Page 2 of 2

Esc-Exit  F1-Help  F2-Print  Shift+F7-Restore    F7-Search  F8-Options  ↑F8-Save
```

Fig. 12.16. *Imported ASCII text after using the Special ASCII option.*

Inserting 1-2-3 and Symphony Files

The fourth option available for inserting files into a Write document enables you to import 1-2-3 and Symphony worksheet files. This option particularly benefits those of you who use 1-2-3 or Symphony for creating financial spreadsheets and want to import some or all of the numeric data into a Q&A document. Inserting 1-2-3 and Symphony files is similar to inserting ASCII or WordStar files. One exception, however, is that when you import 1-2-3 and Symphony files, you are not limited to inserting only the complete file; you can insert any part of the 1-2-3 or Symphony worksheet file.

Suppose that you want to insert the January and February travel expenses from a 1-2-3 worksheet containing expenses for the entire year (see fig. 12.17). To insert the information you need, you must import the appropriate range of the columns and rows from the worksheet in figure 12.17.

To insert these columns into a Q&A Write document, begin by moving the cursor to the location in your Write document where you want the first column inserted. Then press F8 (Options), D (Documents), and I (Insert a Document).

When the prompt box appears and asks for the file name of the worksheet you want to insert, type the file name or press Enter for a complete list of available file names. Remember that when you press Enter for a list of files, Q&A returns the files from the default drive and path; if your 1-2-3 or Symphony worksheet file is located in another drive and path, change the drive and path in the prompt box before pressing Enter.

After you type the worksheet file name (or select the worksheet file from the list) and press Enter, Q&A displays the Import Document window, which indicates that the file format is unknown and asks you to select one of the conversion selections listed. Select the fourth option, Lotus 1-2-3 or Symphony, to insert your worksheet or part of a worksheet.

After you select Lotus 1-2-3 or Symphony, Q&A displays a Define Range screen, which enables you to indicate specific columns and rows or a range name for the area of the worksheet you want to insert (see fig. 12.18). Notice that the third line of text in figure 12.18 indicates the complete data area of the worksheet from which you want to insert information: from column A, row 1, to column R, row 55. If you want to insert all data from the worksheet, press F10. If you want to import only part of the worksheet, you can indicate the columns and rows or the range name of the area. In working with spreadsheets, use range names for any area you are likely to reference often. This process reduces the chance of errors when you specify the ranges manually during calculation, merge, or other operations.

```
A16: [W1] '                                                        READY

     A   B    C         D         E  F  G  H  I   J     K    L    M
16  |18-Jan-91|Shipping          |         |  |   10.06 |  10.06 |
17  |         |January Travel    |         |  |  389.05 | 389.05 |
18  |         |       Word Perfect|        |  |         |        |
19  |         |       Datability |         |  |         |        |
20  |         |       Boston (DEC)|         |  |         |        |
21  |28-Jan-91|January Travel    |         |  | 1100.01 |1100.01 |
22  |         |       NYC-Ungermann|       |  |         |        |
23  |         |       D.C.-Comnet |        |  |         |        |
24  |19-Feb-91|February Travel   |         |  |  843.28 | 843.28 |
25  |         |       Dallas:Usenix|       |  |         |        |
26  |         |       NYC:Dexpo East|      |  |         |        |
27  |         |Boston: VAXstation 80|      |  |   43.56 |  43.56 |
28  |04-Mar-91|NYC + Ship + Tele |         |  |  253.71 | 253.71 |
29  |         |Boston: Vax  8000 |         |  |         |        |
30  |         |D.C. OSI/ANSI     |         |  |  137.30 | 137.30 |
31  |31-Mar-91|Interface + Telephone|      |  |  573.37 | 573.37 |
32  |09-Apr-91|Boston: Digital   |         |  |  825.35 | 825.35 |
33  |29-Apr-91|Boston: VAX 6200  |         |  |  495.66 | 495.66 |
34  |29-Apr-91|Boston: Ancona+eln|         |  |  356.97 | 356.97 |
35  |16-May-91|Atlanta, Bos, Mob |         |  |  791.93 | 791.93 |
28-Feb-91  01:24 PM      UNDO                             NUM
```

Fig. 12.17. *Information on a 1-2-3 worksheet.*

To insert the merge range by name, don't fill in the Column and Row fields. Instead, move the cursor to the prompt for the name of the range, and type the name. If you are unsure of the range name, you can press the PgDn and PgUp keys to select the range name from available ranges in the spreadsheet.

In the example, the merge range occupies cells A16 through M27. Press F10 to complete the procedure; Q&A imports the remaining columns of data (see fig. 12.19). Note that the 1-2-3 file uses a date-formatting function (@DATE(91,1,18)). The date fields are formatted in 1-2-3 to be displayed in the form 18-Jan-91, but Q&A interprets the dates in the form 1/18/91.

After you insert data from a 1-2-3 or Symphony worksheet into your Write document, you can use all the Write commands and keys for editing or changing data. In particular, you can use Write's math calculation capability to total, average, count, multiply, and divide the numbers originally inserted from 1-2-3 or Symphony.

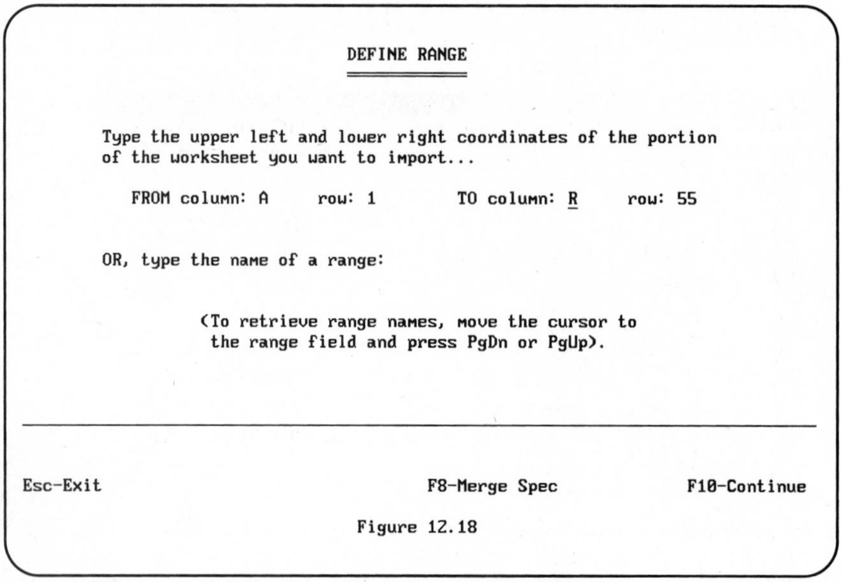

```
                            DEFINE RANGE
                            ============


        Type the upper left and lower right coordinates of the portion
        of the worksheet you want to import...

            FROM column: A     row: 1       TO column: R     row: 55


        OR, type the name of a range:


                   (To retrieve range names, move the cursor to
                    the range field and press PgDn or PgUp).




        _____



    Esc-Exit                         F8-Merge Spec            F10-Continue

                              Figure 12.18
```

Fig. 12.18. *The Define Range screen for choosing 1-2-3 data.*

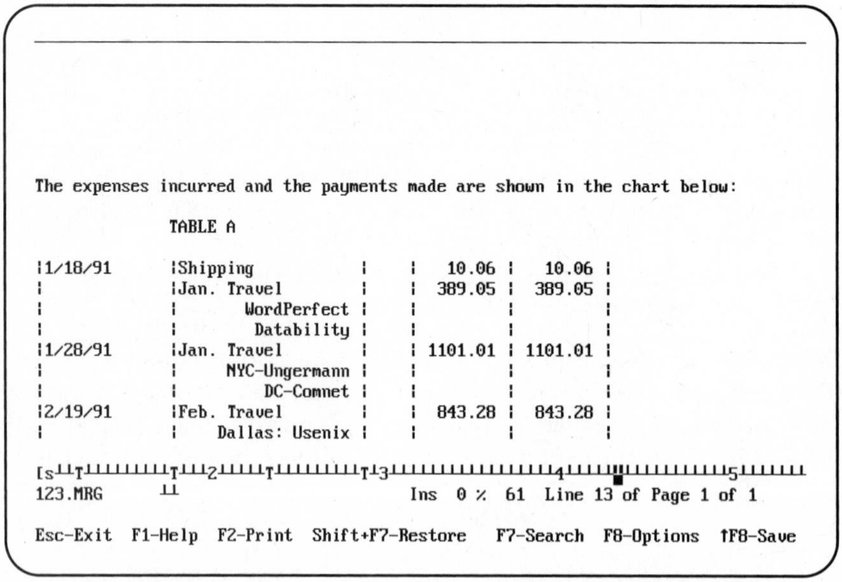

```
    The expenses incurred and the payments made are shown in the chart below:

                    TABLE A

    |1/18/91       |Shipping          |   |   10.06 |   10.06 |
    |              |Jan. Travel       |   |  389.05 |  389.05 |
    |              |        WordPerfect|  |         |         |
    |              |         Datability|  |         |         |
    |1/28/91       |Jan. Travel       |   | 1101.01 | 1101.01 |
    |              |       NYC-Ungermann|  |        |         |
    |              |         DC-Comnet |   |         |         |
    |2/19/91       |Feb. Travel       |   |  843.28 |  843.28 |
    |              |     Dallas: Usenix|  |         |         |

    [s__T_____T__2_____T_____T_3_____4_____5_____
    123.MRG    __                    Ins  0 %  61  Line 13 of Page 1 of 1

    Esc-Exit  F1-Help  F2-Print  Shift+F7-Restore   F7-Search  F8-Options  ↑F8-Save
```

Fig. 12.19. *Data from a 1-2-3 worksheet inserted into a Write document.*

Inserting Other Word Processor Files

Beginning with Version 4.0 of Q&A Write, you can import and export documents created with the following programs: DCA, WordStar (Versions 3.3 through 5.5), WordPerfect (Versions 5.0 and 5.1), Microsoft Word (Versions 3.0 through 5.0), MultiMate 3.3, MultiMate Advantage (3.6 and 3.7), and Professional Write (1.0 through 2.1). To import a document in one of these formats, follow these steps:

1. From the Write menu, choose Utilities.

2. From the Write Utilities menu, choose Import a Document.

3. From the Write Import menu, choose the format of the document to be imported.

Write converts the document and displays the text in the editing screen.

Chapter Summary

The capability to merge files from other modules or other programs is an important feature of Q&A Write. As your database system becomes more complex, you will need to move data from one module to another and create documents by using data from existing documents or files. If you have been using other word processing programs, you can import the files to Q&A Write so that you don't have to enter the data again.

In this chapter, you have learned how to move text from an existing Write document to a new Write document, how to use Q&A's mail-merge capability to merge File data into a Write document, and how to import and insert other documents into Write. The next chapter provides additional detail on printing Write documents.

13

Printing a Write Document

O ne of Q&A's most impressive features is the capacity to retrieve, organize, and print data. Each of the Q&A modules has the capability of producing printouts. Whether you want a record from File, a letter from Write, a listing of survey results from Report, or a compiled columnar list from the Intelligent Assistant, Q&A makes printing easy.

Unlike other popular programs, Q&A has a print feature that does not apply "across the board." Instead of having one print procedure that applies to all features of the program, Q&A provides each module with its own procedure, complete with different menus and specification screens. Each Q&A module has separate print options, so you don't have to leave the Main menu of any module in order to print. Although this feature may seem confusing at first, the logical structure of the separate print procedures helps you catch on quickly. This chapter introduces you to the print features in the Write module of Q&A.

Printing from Write

When you're ready to make a printed copy of a document you have created with Write, you have several options. One option is to print the document as soon as you have entered it, without leaving Type/Edit mode. Simple reports are easy to print with Q&A, such as interoffice memos and other short correspondence (see fig. 13.1). If you want a more elaborate printout, Q&A also offers the easy-to-use Print Options settings and accepts printer control codes for text enhancement (see fig. 13.2).

391

```
TO:             District Sales Managers

DATE:           June 30, 1991

FROM:           Steven Hill, Marketing Support Manager

SUBJECT:        JUNE SALES LEADS

Enclosed are the sales lead forms received during June from
prospects in your sales district.  Also included is a report that
summarizes the sales leads by city, sales priority, company, and
customer request.

We are implementing a new sales tracking system that will give
you a means to keep track of sales leads and follow up. This
should help each of you unify your sales force and make sure that
each lead is pursued effectively. A Q&A disk is enclosed that
contains the sales leads for your district. Please copy these
leads into your file, and maintain them in the following manner:

   1.   When each lead is assigned, enter the name of the Sales
        Person.
   2.   Enter the date when the first sales contact was made with
        the sales lead.
   3.   Record the date of the demonstration.
   4.   Enter the status of the sale after the demonstration in
        one of the following forms:


            Sale (Model Number)       a sale was made

            Postpone                  the purchase decision was
                                      delayed

            Competitor (select one)   the prospect bought from a
                                      competitor
            Brock
            Med Sci
            Am Lab

            Other

At the end of the month, please send me a copy of this report and
the updated forms (on disk).  I will then prepare an analysis of
your district's sales activity and the effectiveness. We will be
discussing this new system more fully at our next district
meeting.
```

Fig. 13.1.   A plain memo printed with Q&A Write.

```
TO:            District Sales Managers

DATE:          June 30, 1991

FROM:          Steven Hill, Marketing Support Manager

SUBJECT:       JUNE SALES LEADS

Enclosed are the sales lead forms received during June from
prospects in your sales district.  Also included is a report that
summarizes the sales leads by city, sales priority, company, and
customer request.

We are implementing a new sales tracking system that will give
you a means to keep track of sales leads and follow up. This
should help each of you unify your sales force and make sure that
each lead is pursued effectively. A Q&A disk is enclosed that
contains the sales leads for your district. Please copy these
leads into your file, and maintain them in the following manner:

     1.  When each lead is assigned, enter the name of the Sales
         Person.
     2.  Enter the date when the first sales contact was made with
         the sales lead.
     3.  Record the date of the demonstration.
     4.  Enter the status of the sale after the demonstration in
         one of the following forms:

              Sale (Model Number)       a sale was made

              Postpone                  the purchase decision was
                                        delayed

              Competitor (select one)   the prospect bought from a
                                        competitor
              Brock
              Med Sci
              Am Lab

              Other

At the end of the month, please send me a copy of this report and
the updated forms (on disk).  I will then prepare an analysis of
your district's sales activity and the effectiveness. We will be
discussing this new system more fully at our next district
meeting.
```

Fig. 13.2. *A memo with text enhancements and formatting features.*

Printing from the Type/Edit Screen

If you have just finished typing a document, you can order printing without leaving the Edit mode. For example, if your work is still on-screen, you can press F2 to print the document. The Print Options screen, which is discussed later in this chapter, then is displayed. If Q&A is installed for your printer and the Print Options settings are correct, you can bypass the menu by pressing F10. Your document is printed instantly.

Q&A users often forget that they can print any portion of a document quickly without displaying the Print Options screen. All you must do is press Ctrl-F2 and then highlight the block to be printed by using the cursor arrow keys. You also can print blocks of text from the Type/Edit screen by using the Options menu. Press F8 (Options), B (Block Operations), P (Print). After the block is marked, make sure that your printer is ready and press F10. The block is printed immediately.

If you don't like the way the document is being printed from the Type/Edit screen, press Esc to cancel the operation. Q&A returns you to the Type/Edit screen. Printing stops if you press F2, and the Print Options screen is displayed again. You then can modify the settings on the Options menu and press F10. The printing starts again from the beginning of the file. If your printer has a buffer that stores input from your computer, however, printing does not stop immediately when you press F2. If the buffer is large, you may want to turn off the printer and reset the top of the form when you cancel printing, to avoid printing large amounts of unwanted text.

Printing from the Write Menu

If you want to print a document from the Write menu, the document must be on the editing screen. To print the document, return to the Write menu, select the Print option, and press F10. Before you can print a file that you are not working on currently, you must load the file into memory by selecting the Get option from the Write menu.

Q&A displays the name of the most recently used file as the default in the document line. If you cannot remember the name of the file you want to print, press the space bar to clear the default name and press Enter. A list of available document files is displayed (see fig. 13.3).

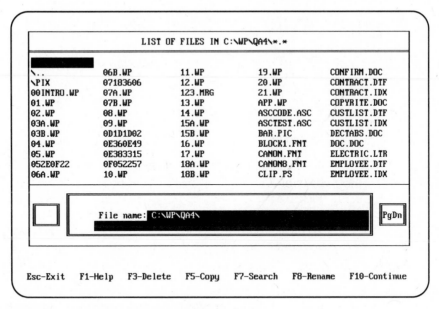

```
                    LIST OF FILES IN C:\WP\QA4\*.*

    \..            06B.WP       11.WP       19.WP       CONFIRM.DOC
    \PIX           07183606     12.WP       20.WP       CONTRACT.DTF
    00INTRO.WP     07A.WP       123.MRG     21.WP       CONTRACT.IDX
    01.WP          07B.WP       13.WP       APP.WP      COPYRITE.DOC
    02.WP          08.WP        14.WP       ASCCODE.ASC CUSTLIST.DTF
    03A.WP         09.WP        15A.WP      ASCTEST.ASC CUSTLIST.IDX
    03B.WP         0D1D1D02     15B.WP      BAR.PIC     DECTABS.DOC
    04.WP          0E360E49     16.WP       BLOCK1.FNT  DOC.DOC
    05.WP          0E383315     17.WP       CANON.FNT   ELECTRIC.LTR
    052E0F22       0F052257     18A.WP      CANON8.FNT  EMPLOYEE.DTF
    06A.WP         10.WP        18B.WP      CLIP.PS     EMPLOYEE.IDX


    ┌──┐   ┌──────────────────────────────────────────────┐ ┌────┐
    │  │   │ File name: C:\WP\QA4\                          │ │PgDn│
    │  │   │                                                │ └────┘
    └──┘   └──────────────────────────────────────────────┘

    Esc-Exit   F1-Help   F3-Delete   F5-Copy   F7-Search   F8-Rename   F10-Continue
```

Fig. 13.3. *Pressing Enter to see a list of your files.*

Use the cursor keys to move the highlighting to the file you want and press Enter. The file is displayed on the Type/Edit screen. You then can press F2 to print, as explained in the previous example.

Using the Print Options Screen

As you can see, you have the option of changing Q&A's defaults or accepting the defaults as they are. At times, however, you may not want to print every page of your document. You can change the default so that Q&A prints only the pages you want. In your office correspondence, you may be required to make three copies of every letter; you can set the default to take care of this task for you. If you find that you use a certain setting often, you may want to change that setting permanently. Even after you change a default permanently, you can modify the default at any time.

The Print Options screen gives you the chance to change the way your text is printed (see fig. 13.4). Before printing a document, you can arrange and enhance the printed text by adjusting line spacing, setting the justification, specifying the number of columns, and adding special print codes. You can control the printing by specifying the number of copies, printer ports, and merge files used. The changes you make at this point are good only during this session; when you leave the Write module, all your settings return to the Q&A default settings. You modify the default settings by specifying options on the Write Utilities menu. The following sections explain how you can use these features of Q&A to make your printouts more attractive.

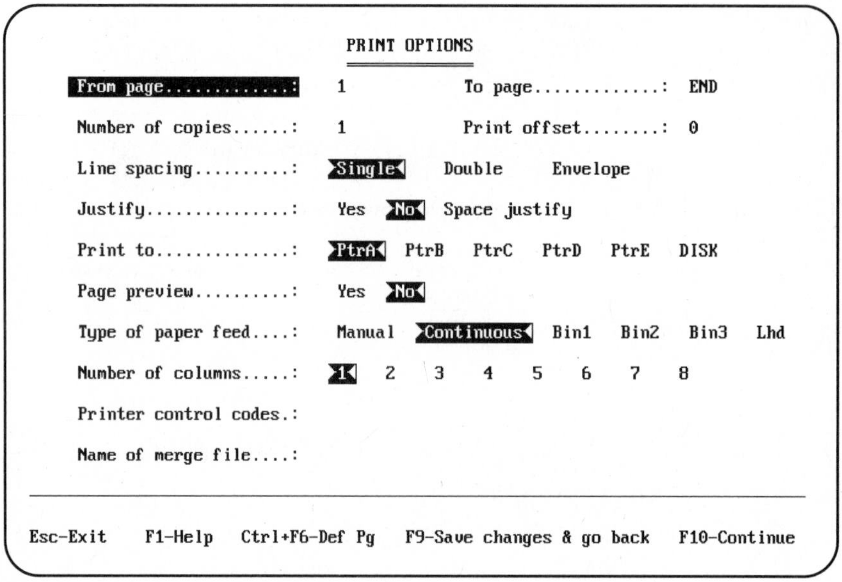

```
                        PRINT OPTIONS

     From page............:   1          To page............:  END

     Number of copies......:  1          Print offset........:  0

     Line spacing..........:  >Single<   Double     Envelope

     Justify...............:  Yes  >No<  Space justify

     Print to..............:  >PtrA<  PtrB   PtrC   PtrD   PtrE   DISK

     Page preview..........:  Yes  >No<

     Type of paper feed....:  Manual  >Continuous<  Bin1   Bin2   Bin3   Lhd

     Number of columns.....:  >1<  2   3   4   5   6   7   8

     Printer control codes.:

     Name of merge file....:


  Esc-Exit    F1-Help    Ctrl+F6-Def Pg    F9-Save changes & go back    F10-Continue
```

Fig. 13.4.   *Changing the default print options.*

Arranging the Text

Different kinds of printouts deserve different text arrangements. Although you double-space the first draft of your monthly report, for example, you may prefer single-spacing for the final draft. With the options on the Print Options screen, Q&A enables you to change the line spacing and justification of your text with just a few simple keystrokes. Remember, however, that the settings are good only for the current session.

Changing Line Spacing from the Print Options Screen

Three line-spacing options are available; select the option you want by typing the first letter of the option. Single- and double-spacing require no explanation, except the reminder that Q&A always shows you a document single-spaced on-screen. When the document is printed, the spacing you specified is provided.

The page designations on the Print Options screen do not change when you change the line spacing. For example, if you take a three-page, single-spaced document and select double-spaced printing, the number of pages in your printout actually is doubled, even though the number in the To Page option does not change to 6. Therefore, if you tell Q&A to print only the first page of the double-spaced document, the first two pages are printed.

The print options respond to a change in page length. If you shorten the page length by one-third, for example, the total number of pages indicated is decreased by a third.

Changing Line Spacing from within a Document

Line spacing also can be changed from within a document. You can change line spacing with a command that is similar to the commands for inserting characters and changing type styles (discussed later in this chapter). For example, if you want a single-spaced section in the middle of your double-spaced document, embed the following command in your file on a blank line just before the place you want the change to occur:

   LS 1

The LS stands for line spacing. You also can type *line spacing 1* if you find that phrase easier to remember. The command can be entered as uppercase or lowercase. To switch to triple-spacing, change the 1 in these examples to 3. Q&A recognizes any line spacing interval up to and including 9.

Remember that this command must appear on a blank line by itself because the command affects line spacing. Note also that Q&A obeys the command on that line, but the line containing the command is not printed—the line is eliminated entirely from the printout.

Changing Type/Edit Line Spacing

You can change the line spacing of your document in the Type/Edit screen, without affecting the way the document prints. You may, for example, find editing double-spaced text on-screen easier. You can choose single, double, or triple spacing from the Options menu. Press F8 (Options), A (Align Text), and press S (Single Space), D (Double Space), or T (Triple Space). This changes the way Write displays the entire document.

Setting Text Justification for a Complete Document

Most correspondence does not use justified text. A ragged right margin usually is preferred for business use. *Justified* means that blank space is inserted between words so that each line extends to the right margin. Although a justified right margin gives the printout a pleasing appearance, many people consider this format to be the sign of a printed form letter (see fig. 13.5).

Q&A's Print Options menu has three settings related to justification. Figure 13.5 shows a document printed with Space Justify selected. As you can see, as many as three spaces are between some words. This erratic spacing can make the paragraphs more difficult to read. Although the justification shows up on the printout, the Type/Edit screen does not show the extra spacing. If your printer supports justification with equal spaces between letters, your documents will look much better if you choose Yes at the Justify prompt on the Print Options menu. This tells Q&A to use your printer's microjustification (equal spacing) feature instead of inserting whole spaces between words. If you decide to use Q&A's justification feature, you may want to turn off the feature when you create a table—lining up the columns in a table is almost impossible when justification is turned on. To turn off justification, set the Justify option to No.

Like other popular word processing programs, Q&A supports microjustification. In a microjustified document, small spaces are inserted between the characters so that the spacing effect is less noticeable. To see whether your printer can support microjustification, check your printer manual.

```
TO:          District Sales Managers

DATE:        June 30, 1991

FROM:        Steven Hill, Marketing Support Manager

SUBJECT:     JUNE SALES LEADS

Enclosed  are  the  sales  lead  forms received  during  June from
prospects in your sales district.  Also included is a report that
summarizes the sales leads by  city, sales priority, company, and
customer request.

We are  implementing a new  sales tracking system  that will give
you a  means to  keep track  of sales  leads and  follow up. This
should help each of you unify your sales force and make sure that
each lead  is pursued  effectively. A  Q&A disk  is enclosed that
contains the  sales leads  for your  district. Please  copy these
leads into your file, and maintain them in the following manner:

   1.  When each lead  is assigned, enter the  name of the Sales
       Person.
   2.  Enter the date when the first sales contact was made with
       the sales lead.
   3.  Record the date of the demonstration.
   4.  Enter the status  of the sale  after the demonstration in
       one of the following forms:

            Sale (Model Number)       a sale was made

            Postpone                  the purchase  decision was
                                      delayed

            Competitor (select one)   the prospect bought from a
                                      competitor
            Brock
            Med Sci
            Am Lab

            Other

At the end of the month, please send me a copy of this report and
the updated forms (on disk).  I  will then prepare an analysis of
your district's sales activity and  the effectiveness. We will be
discussing  this  new  system more  fully  at  our  next district
meeting.
```

Fig. 13.5. *Erratic spacing caused by right justification.*

Setting Text Justification for Part of a Document

In some cases, you may want to justify only a section of the text within a document. With your file displayed in Type/Edit mode, instead of selecting justification from the menu, enter the following command just before the text you want to justify:

   Justify Yes

This command can be abbreviated as follows:

   JY Y

To end justification, move to the place you want the justification to stop and type the following:

   Justify No

The abbreviation for this command is as follows:

   JY N

Figure 13.6 shows the file in Type/Edit mode with the opening and closing justification commands. Figure 13.7 shows the printout. As you can see, the commands that appear on-screen do not appear on the printed letter.

```
DATE:        June 30, 1991

FROM:        Steven Hill, Marketing Support Manager

SUBJECT:     JUNE SALES LEADS

Enclosed are the sales lead forms received during June from
prospects in your sales district.  Also included is a report that
summarizes the sales leads by city, sales priority, company, and
customer request.
*Justify Yes*

We are implementing a new sales tracking system that will give
you a means to keep track of sales leads and follow up. This
should help each of you unify your sales force and make sure that
each lead is pursued effectively. A Q&A disk is enclosed that
contains the sales leads for your district. Please copy these
leads into your file, and maintain them in the following manner:
*Justify No*

     1.  When each lead is assigned, enter the name of the Sales
MEMO.DOC                      Ins  3 %  13  Line 21 of Page 1 of 1

Esc-Exit  F1-Help  F2-Print  Shift+F7-Restore   F7-Search  F8-Options  ↑F8-Save
```

Fig. 13.6. *A memo with open and close justification commands.*

```
TO:            District Sales Managers

DATE:          June 30, 1991

FROM:          Steven Hill, Marketing Support Manager

SUBJECT:       JUNE SALES LEADS

Enclosed are the sales lead forms received during June from
prospects in your sales district.  Also included is a report that
summarizes the sales leads by city, sales priority, company, and
customer request.

We are implementing a new sales tracking system that will give
you a means to keep track of sales leads and follow up.  This
should help each of you unify your sales force and make sure that
each lead is pursued effectively.  A Q&A disk is enclosed that
contains the sales leads for your district.  Please copy these
leads into your file, and maintain them in the following manner:

     1.   When each lead is assigned, enter the name of the Sales
          Person.
     2.   Enter the date when the first sales contact was made with
          the sales lead.
     3.   Record the date of the demonstration.
     4.   Enter the status of the sale after the demonstration in
          one of the following forms:

               Sale (Model Number)      a sale was made

               Postpone                 the purchase decision was
                                         delayed

               Competitor (select one)  the prospect bought from a
                                         competitor
               Brock
               Med Sci
               Am Lab

               Other

At the end of the month, please send me a copy of this report and
the updated forms (on disk).  I will then prepare an analysis of
your district's sales activity and the effectiveness. We will be
discussing this new system more fully at our next district
meeting.
```

Fig. 13.7. A memo printed with only the second paragraph justified.

Enhancing the Printout with Printer Control Codes

If you use Q&A Write for business applications, your company may expect certain stylistic conventions for memos and reports. With Q&A, you can stylize your documents with different type size and text enhancements by inserting printer codes in the body, header, or footer of a document. If your printer produces near-letter quality text when you use Double-strike mode, you can insert codes in your document so that the printing is done that way. You can also use Q&A to print in Condensed mode, if your printer supports that mode. (Check your printer manual to see which effects are supported by your printer and what the codes are for those effects.)

Q&A recognizes printer codes that are entered in ASCII code. For example, on an Epson printer, ESC 15 is the code for Condensed mode. The decimal equivalent of ESC is 27. To print a Q&A document in Condensed mode, therefore, you enter the following code at the Printer Control Codes prompt:

27, 15

Most printer manufacturers supply ASCII control-code tables with their documentation because ASCII codes commonly are used to send controls to a printer. Codes sometimes are shown as a combination of nonprintable control characters (such as ESC) and alphabetic characters (ESC "E", for example). Use the ASCII conversion chart in your printer documentation to make the necessary conversion or enter the control sequences in Q&A in the way your printer documentation suggests.

The Printer Control Codes prompt on the Print Options screen is helpful if you want to print an entire document in a different mode. But what if you want only a line or a few words printed in Condensed mode? Q&A enables you to insert printer control codes directly in your document so that you can enhance selective portions of your text.

Make sure that the document you want to enhance is loaded in the Type/Edit screen. To do this procedure, remember that you select Get from the Write menu and enter the file name. With the text on-screen, move to the place where you want the effect to start. You may want the code to begin in the middle of a word if only certain characters are to be affected.

Enter an asterisk (*) so Q&A knows that the characters which follow are a command. Type the word *Printer*—or just the letter *P*, if you prefer—and press the space bar. Next, enter the decimal ASCII-equivalent code for the effect you want and end the command with another asterisk. If you want to print expanded-width characters on an Epson printer, for example, you can enter the following code:

P 27,14

Move to the place where you want the enhancement to end and enter the same command. If you want to use multiple codes, separate the numbers with commas. The codes make the screen look cluttered, but don't worry; the codes do not appear on your printout.

When you insert printer control codes directly in your text, Q&A does not readjust the text for printing. If you insert the codes to print the company name in expanded type, for example, you need to center the title manually. When you insert the codes, the title is moved to the right, and when the memo is printed, the title appears on paper in the same place the title appears on-screen.

In figure 13.8, the code has been inserted in the first line of the memo so that the company name is printed in large letters. The ending code really is not necessary in this case because Epson's command for expanded printing is valid for only one line. After the coded line, the print type returns to normal. Figure 13.9 shows the printout of the memo.

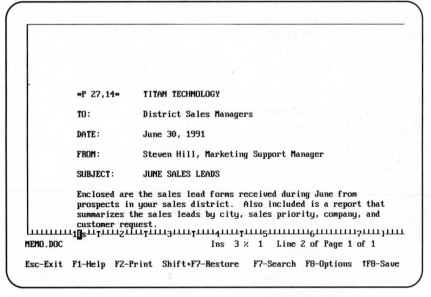

Fig. 13.8. *The printer code that produces expanded characters.*

```
            TITAN  TECHNOLOGY

TO:          District Sales Managers

DATE:        June 30, 1991

FROM:        Steven Hill, Marketing Support Manager

SUBJECT:     JUNE SALES LEADS

Enclosed are the sales lead forms received during June from
prospects in your sales district.  Also included is a report that
summarizes the sales leads by city, sales priority, company, and
customer request.

We are implementing a new sales tracking system that will give
you a means to keep track of sales leads and follow up.  This
should help each of you unify your sales force and make sure that
each lead is pursued effectively. A Q&A disk is enclosed that
contains the sales leads for your district. Please copy these
leads into your file, and maintain them in the following manner:

   1.  When each lead is assigned, enter the name of the Sales
       Person.
   2.  Enter the date when the first sales contact was made with
       the sales lead.
   3.  Record the date of the demonstration.
   4.  Enter the status of the sale after the demonstration in
       one of the following forms:


           Sale (Model Number)        a sale was made

           Postpone                   the purchase decision was
                                      delayed

           Competitor (select one)    the prospect bought from a
                                      competitor
           Brock
           Med Sci
           Am Lab

           Other

At the end of the month, please send me a copy of this report and
the updated forms (on disk).  I will then prepare an analysis of
your district's sales activity and the effectiveness. We will be
discussing this new system more fully at our next district
meeting.
```

Fig. 13.9.   Printout of text with expanded characters.

Using Special Character Codes

Most printers can print more characters than the characters that appear on the
keyboard. Q&A accepts special character codes that cause these characters to

be printed in your document. With a procedure similar to inserting printer control codes, you can print foreign money symbols, mathematical symbols, copyright notices, accent marks for foreign languages, and other special characters. If these characters are supported by your printer, you can insert the characters anywhere in a Q&A Write document (see your printer manual for the special character codes).

One problem with embedding printer and special character codes in your text is that the file as it appears on-screen may be difficult to read. Because word-wrap is affected, you also may have trouble visualizing how the document will look on paper. In Chapter 19, you will learn how to create macros that help you differentiate the codes from the text and keep track of the codes you use most often.

Viewing a Page Preview

If your computer's monitor supports graphics, you can view a formatted copy of your printed data on-screen. At the Write Print Options screen, set Page Preview to Yes and press F10 to display the page preview. Page Preview is available from Q&A's print specs in File, Write, Report, and also can be displayed from the Intelligent Assistant.

When the Page Preview screen appears, you can press the + and – keys to "zoom" in and out of enlarged and reduced views of the page. Press F1 (Help) for the complete list of options, which include viewing side-by-side pages as well as actual-size, half- and full-page views, scrolling up and down, and viewing next and previous pages. Press F2 to return to the Write Print Options screen.

Selecting Options for Printing

After you select the options for formatting and enhancing the text, you are ready to print the document. Similar to other popular word processors, Q&A enables you to print partial or complete documents and make multiple copies of the same document with one keystroke. Options are provided in the Print Options menu so that you can make your printer pause for paper change or start printing from a different point on the page. By selecting different printer ports for different print jobs, you can use more than one installed printer with Q&A.

Designating the Page Range for Printing

You may not always want to print a document from beginning to end. Suppose that you have modified pages 2 and 3 of a report; you can tell Q&A to print only those pages by specifying their page numbers in the From Page and To Page fields of the Print Options menu. If you enter a *2* at the From Page prompt and a *3* at the To Page prompt, printing starts at the beginning of page 2 and continues to the end of page 3. If you want to print one page only, that page number should appear in both the From Page and To Page positions. If you don't specify a page number, Q&A prints the document from start to finish.

Printing Multiple Copies

In some cases, you may need to print several copies of the same document. Perhaps you have a memo that should go to four different managers. You can enter a *4* at the Number of Copies prompt. When the document is printed, four copies are produced.

Using the Print Offset Option

The Print Offset option establishes the position from which the print head starts printing. The default value is zero, but you can change the setting by adjusting the left margin. To start the print head further to the left, enter a minus sign (–) before the number of characters. If you want the printing to begin three spaces to the left of the default setting, for example, enter *–3*. Entering a plus sign (+) and a number, or just a number, shifts the printing that number of characters to the right.

Selecting the Printer

You must specify which printer you are using before you can send any data to the printer. If you have installed more than one printer, you can tell Q&A which printer to use for each job by redirecting the output to a different printer port. When you move the cursor to PtrA, PtrB, and so on, Q&A displays at the bottom of the screen the name of the printer you've installed for that designation. (To learn how to install a printer, see Appendix A.) If you choose the Disk option, a standard ASCII file is created for exporting data to another software program. The file includes the same margins and page breaks as the Q&A file, and headers and footers are preserved.

Selecting Paper Feed

An important choice to make is the setting for the type of paper you use. Many computer users choose perforated paper rather than single-sheet paper, which enables users to print a document or report without having to insert sheets individually. To use this type of paper, select the Continuous option from the Type of Paper Feed field. If you plan to insert paper one sheet at a time, choose the Manual option.

The other four paper feed options (Bin1, Bin2, Bin3, and Lhd) are used when you have a sheet feeder on your printer. Each of the Bin settings corresponds to the bin of the sheet feeder from which the paper is taken. Lhd is used to specify that the first sheet is letterhead paper and the rest of the sheets are standard bond paper. Lhd causes the first sheet to be taken from Bin1 and the remaining pages from Bin2.

Printing Columns

Q&A has a word processing feature that few other programs have: the capability to print more than one column on a page. Up to eight columns, also called *newspaper columns*, can be printed on a page, depending on the width of your paper.

To print the text in a columnar format, move the cursor to the Number of Columns option and select the number of columns you want to print. You may want to set the Justify option to Yes so that your columns are displayed evenly. To check the results, use Page Preview.

Special Print Applications

At some time, you may want Q&A Write to do more than just print reports and memos. Suppose that you are sending a mailing to all customers in Santa Cruz, California. You could address all the envelopes by hand, or you could delegate the responsibility. Why not have Q&A do it for you? Q&A can even insert another Write document into the one you want to print or merge data from another file into your printout. This section discusses these special print applications available with Q&A Write.

Merging Spreadsheet and Graphics Files

When you are creating a report, you can enhance your document by adding parts of a worksheet or graph. Files from PFS:GRAPH or spreadsheets and graphs from 1-2-3 or Symphony can be incorporated into your Write document to help illustrate your discussion.

Specifying this feature is similar to specifying other merge features. Type the word *spreadsheet*, the name of the file to import, and the range of the worksheet you want to include. For example, each of the following lines can import graphs or spreadsheets into your Write document:

    spreadsheet budget, A1-H19

    ss budget, A1-H19

    ss c:\data\123\budget, A1-H19

    graph pie

As with other printer commands, these lines must be enclosed within asterisks. When you import a range from a worksheet, you have the option of typing the word *spreadsheet* or entering the letters *ss*. The file-name extension is not necessary. After the name of the file, type a comma and enter the range of the worksheet you want to import.

To import a graph, type *graph* and enter the graph name. If necessary, you can add the drive designation and path, but the file-name extension is unnecessary.

Using Other Printer Commands

You can embed any of the following commands in a Write document, and Q&A interprets the command as described:

Printer Command	Meaning
@DATE(n)	Inserts today's date; (n) is the data format number
@FILENAME	Inserts the name of the document you're printing
GRAPH Abbreviation: *G*	Inserts a Lotus or Symphony .PIC file, PFS: graph picture, or graph in BSAV format. Your printer must print graphics.
JOIN Abbreviation: *J*	Prints the named documents at the end of the current file

Printer Command	Meaning
JUSTIFY Abbreviation: *JYY* or *JYN*	Use *JUSTIFY Yes* to turn on microjustification and *JUSTIFY No* to turn microjustification off.
LINESPACING n Abbreviation: *LSn*	Changes line spacing at print time, in which n is an integer from 1-9 indicating the spacing. Can be used to change spacing for sections of the document. Toset spacing for an entire document, use the Options menu.
POSTFILE	Inserts a PostScript program
POSTSCRIPT	Embeds a PostScript code
PRINTER Abbreviation: *P*	Embeds a printer code in ASCII decimal format
PROGRAM Abbreviation: *PG*	Embeds a Q&A programming expression
QUEUE Abbreviation: *Q*	Prints a series of documents (used in a document containing only *QUEUE* commands)
QUEUEP	Continues pagination across queued documents
SPREADSHEET Abbreviation: *SS*	Inserts a Lotus spreadsheet. To insert a range, use *SPREADSHEET fs range*, in which fs is the file path and name and range is the range name or top left and bottom right cells.
STOP	Stops the printer until you press Enter
@TIME(n)	Inserts the time using time format n

Printing a Mail-Merge Document

You may want to merge data from another file instead of incorporating the entire file by using the Join command (discussed later in this chapter). For example, if you want to pull names and addresses from files stored in a Q&A database, you can use the program's merge capability.

If you are working on the document you want to print, you can start the merge process by pressing F2. You also can press P to choose the Print option from the Write menu. The Print Options menu then is displayed. After setting all the defaults you want to use, move to the Name of Merge File prompt. Type the name of the file you want to use with the Write document and press F10.

After you name the file to be merged and press F10, Q&A warns you if any field names in the merge don't match field names in the data file. You then can press F8 to display the Identifier Spec (see fig. 13.10). With this screen, you can identify the fields to be merged from the File database, using any names you want. The correct names are shown on the Identifier Spec screen, and you can type any substitute names you used in the document. Q&A then accepts those names as field merge specifications.

```
                    TITAN TECHNOLOGY SALES LEAD TRACKING SYSTEM
                                                    File Name -- SlsLead
LastName: █████████████████     FirstName:
Title:
Company:                        Telephone:
Address1:
Address2:
City:                           State:          Zip:
    No. of Labs:                Annual Revenue:
    Current Customer:           Company Priority:
LEAD INFORMATION──────────────────────────────────────────────────────

      If all the field names in your document match field labels in your
      database, press F10 to continue. If not, type the names as they appear
      in the document in the corresponding fields here, and press F10.

      If you are NOT SURE whether everything matches, press F10 anyway. Q&A
      will tell you which ones don't match and give you another opportunity
      to match them up.  If everything matches, Q&A will take you to the
      Retrieve Spec.  (Esc will cancel this message).

──────────────────────────────────────────────────────────────────────

SLSLEAD.DTF                   Identifier Spec                Page 1  of 1

Esc-Exit          F3-Clear Spec        F6-Expand field        F10-Continue
```

Fig. 13.10. *The Identifier Spec.*

Notice that the key assignment line at the bottom of the screen shows that you can use F6 to expand a field. This option appears on other Q&A screens and permits you to type instructions or specifications that are longer than the space available on-screen. Although the information on the display may be truncated, the entire entry in the field remains intact.

If you press F10 again, the Retrieve Spec screen is displayed, unless you have included field names in your merge document that don't match the fields in your database. In that case, you are confronted with a warning screen. You then can match the names by entering them on the Identifier Spec or you can press F10 to ignore the field names.

The Retrieve Spec is used in merge operations to select certain items of information. You can use the Retrieve Spec, for example, to select customers in Chicago who should receive a special mailing. For detailed instructions for using the Retrieve Spec, see Chapter 7.

Don't forget that you can press F1 to get a list of available retrieval specification symbols whenever the Retrieve Spec screen is displayed.

If you want to sort the forms before executing the merge, press F8 from the Retrieve Spec to display the Sort Spec screen (for more information on Sort Specs, see Chapter 6). To choose from a list of saved Retrieve Specs, press Alt-F8, and to give the current spec a name and save it, press Shift-F8. Press F10 to begin printing. If you make a mistake in filling out the Retrieve Spec screen, you may get the following warning message: No forms were found that meet your retrieve request. Do you want to check or change your request? If you select Yes, the Retrieve Spec is displayed again, and you can make any necessary changes.

Printing Mailing Labels

You have the option of using either Write or File to create and print mailing labels, but the Type/Edit screen in Write is easier to use. Q&A can print using most popular label formats, or you can customize any of the standard templates for a special label size.

To print mailing labels, follow these steps:

1. At the Write menu, choose Mailing Labels. Q&A displays a list of predefined label types (see fig. 13.11).

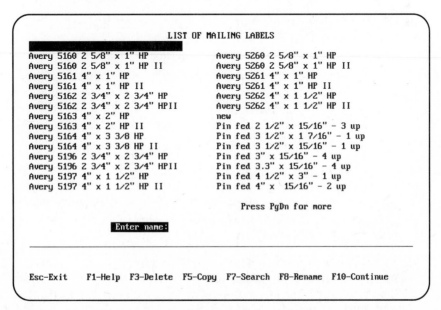

Fig. 13.11. *The List of Mailing Labels screen.*

2. Choose a label size that closely matches your labels. Highlight the label and press F5 (Copy).

3. At the prompt, type a name of up to 32 letters for your new label design. Press Enter.

4. Choose the new design from the list and press F10. Q&A displays the label template on the screen, with generic field labels. You can delete these labels and enter other field names or text.

5. Move the cursor into the on-screen label template and position the cursor where you want to begin entering field names.

6. Press Alt-F7. Q&A asks for the name of a File database. Type the name, or press Enter to choose from a list of files.

7. A box appears, listing the field names in the database. To add a field to the label, position the cursor on the name and press Enter. Press Alt-F7 again to redisplay the fields list and select other fields.

8. To change the dimensions of the label, press Ctrl-F6 to display the Define Label Screen. Press F1 (Help) for instructions on editing the label template.

9. Press F10 and then press Shift-F8 to save the new label definition.

Printing Multiple Copies of the Same Label

You sometimes may need to print the same text on many labels—return addresses, for example. To do so, follow these steps:

1. At the Write menu, choose Mailing Labels and choose a label type from the list that appears.

2. Press F5 (Copy), and give the label a new name.

3. Highlight the new label and press F10 to select it.

4. Enter field names or text on the label template, as described in the previous section. Press F2 to display the Mailing Label Print Options screen (see figure 13.12).

5. In the Number of Copies field, type the number of labels to print, then press F10 to print the labels.

```
                        MAILING LABEL PRINT OPTIONS
                        ═══════════════════════════

   Number of copies.......:    1          Print offset...........:    0

   Print to..............:    ▶PtrA◀  PtrB   PtrC   PtrD   PtrE   Disk

   Page preview...........:    Yes   ▶No◀

   Type of paper feed.....:    Manual   ▶Continuous◀  Bin1   Bin2   Bin3   Lhd

   Number of labels across:    1    2    ▶3◀   4    5    6    7    8
   Space between labels...:    1/8"
   Lines per label sheet..:    60
   Blank lines at top.....:    0
   Blank lines at bottom..:    0

   Printer control codes..:

   Name of Q&A merge file.:

   ─────────────────────────────────────────────────────────────────────
                    Print Options for Avery 5160 2 5/8" x 1" HP

   Esc-Exit      F1-Help           F9-Save changes & go back      F10-Continue
```

Fig. 13.12.   *The Mailing Label Print Options screen.*

Integrating Documents with the Join Command

Suppose that you are writing a business letter to a sales manager and you want to incorporate in the letter a copy of a one-page table you have stored in a separate file. You can insert one Write document into another by using the Join command. If you are using files in an ASCII format, you can insert documents produced by other programs, such as PFS:REPORT.

If the file you want to insert is in the current directory on the current drive, you can enter the following command at the point where you want the document added:

   *Join *file name**

You can abbreviate *Join* by typing *J*. If the file is on another drive (D, for example), you enter the following:

   *Join D:*file name**

Mass Printing with Queue

Printing can be one of the most time-consuming aspects of computing. Because this process can waste valuable time, you may want to save all your printing to do at one time. Using Q&A's Queue command, you can organize all the print jobs into one file that you can print later.

To use the Queue command to consolidate your printing tasks, create a Write document by choosing Type/Edit from the Write menu. Enter the Queue command as follows, with the names of the files you want printed:

queue letter1.doc

queue letter2.doc

queue letter3.doc

After you specify all the files you want to print, save the document under a name such as QUEUE.MRG and then print the document. The page settings in the QUEUE.MRG file don't matter because the page settings are taken from each document listed with the Queue command.

Nesting Fields

When you print a merge document, you can use nested fields to substitute different field names for different conditions. Suppose that the Title field in the Sales Lead database stores values such as President, Vice President, and Purchasing Agent. By using nested fields, you can send a letter to each of these people and change the third paragraph to include the correct title of each recipient.

To do this procedure, enter the following line in place of the third paragraph when you type the letter:

*join *Title**

Next, type each of the different paragraphs you want to insert at this point. Be sure to save each paragraph in a separate file named to match the title name (President, Vice President, etc.). When you merge-print your document, the paragraph that corresponds to the Title field is inserted in the correct place.

Printing Envelopes

A special printing option is available for envelopes. If you have a letter loaded in memory, you can have Q&A "pick up" the name and address from the letter. Simply choose Envelope in the Line Spacing field of the Print Options screen, and then select the rest of the print options as appropriate. After you choose the print settings, press F10. You then are prompted to insert the envelope in your printer.

Q&A prints at a predetermined position on the envelope, so inserting the envelope correctly is important. The envelope should be inserted in the printer so that the top edge is under the print head. Printing will start 10 lines down from that position and 3.5 inches from the left margin.

How does Q&A know where the address is on the letter? Q&A ignores the indented material and assumes that the first line of copy at the left margin is the name of the person to whom the letter is addressed and that the lines immediately following are the address. If you prefer to use a flush-left format, Q&A can handle that, too. The program checks to see whether the first line is a date or a name. If the first line ends in two or more digits, the line is assumed to contain a date. The program skips that line and finds the first line that isn't indented. Q&A assumes that this line is the first line of the address and that the blank line following the address marks its end.

Chapter Summary

Printing a document from Q&A Write is not a difficult process. Depending on the type of printout you want, you can print the on-screen document instantly by pressing F2, or tailor the printout by specifying print options from the Print Options screen.

Q&A's capacity to accept printer control codes enables you to change the print type in your document and to insert special character codes so that your printout can include any characters supported by your printer.

In the next chapter, you will learn how to use Q&A Report. To learn how to print from Q&A File, see Chapter 8. To learn how to print from Q&A Report, see Chapter 16.

Part IV

Using Q&A Report

Includes

Q&A Report Quick Start

Creating a Report

Printing a Report

14

Q&A Report Quick Start

Report is Q&A's module for converting your data in File into usable and easy-to-create printed output. In addition to producing hard copy of data in File, the Report module also can perform calculations and generate derived columns, headers, footers, lookup functions, and unique column headings. The reports generated in this module can follow the traditional columnar report format, rather than the free-form or coordinate styles available in File. You also can print cross-tab reports that summarize the data in your file. Just as in the other modules, information on designing and printing these reports is at your fingertips if you press F1 (Help).

You begin by designing a basic report. After going through the design steps and printing the report, you use some of the more advanced features to redesign the report.

Designing a Report

Access the Report module from the Q&A Main menu the same way you accessed the File module. To access the Report module, follow these steps:

1. Select Report from the Q&A Main menu.

    The Report menu appears (see fig. 14.1). This menu has four selections: Design/Redesign a Report, Print a Report, Set Global Options, and Rename/Delete/Copy.

419

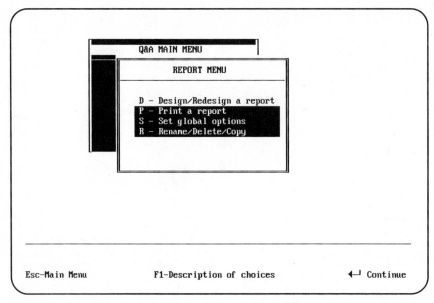

Fig. 14.1.   The Report menu.

2. Select Design/Redesign a Report from the Report menu. Q&A asks you for the name of the database in which you want the report compiled.

3. Type *house.dtf* or press the Enter key to view database names and choose HOUSE.DTF from that list.

If you are redesigning an existing report, at this point a menu listing all reports saved for the database HOUSE.DTF is displayed. You can select the report to redesign by using the arrow keys. For this example, name this new report Inventory.

4. Type the report name *Inventory* and press Enter.

5. Q&A now asks if you want to design a Columnar report or a Crosstab report. Press C to design a Columnar report.

A columnar report displays your data in a row format that you customize using the functions available in the Report module. Cross-tab reports summarize your data by showing the relationship between the data in one field and two other fields.

Retrieving Forms for Your Report

Next, you need to retrieve the forms for this report. You use the Retrieve Spec screen, which appears after you press C to select Columnar Report, to retrieve the forms.

1. Press F1 (How to retrieve) to review how to retrieve forms for the report.

   For this report, you need to retrieve all the forms in the database.

2. Press F10 to indicate that all forms are to be retrieved.

At the Retrieve Spec, you can press Alt-F8 to display a list of stored Retrieve Specs, then move the cursor to a named spec and press Enter to insert the spec into the current form. You also can fill out the spec and then press Shift-F8 to give the spec name and save the spec for later use.

Determining Columns and Sorting Order

Column/Sort Spec is the next screen that appears. You use this screen to determine which fields print in which columns and the sorting for each of those fields. This spec can become quite complex, depending on your requirements.

1. Press F1 (Info) to view the help screens (the screens are several pages long). Next, press Esc (Cancel) to return to the Column/Sort Spec.

2. Enter the following specifications in the appropriate fields:

Item: 3	Third column to print
Quantity: 2	Second column to print
Location: 1, AS	First column to print, in ascending order (A-Z)
Date of Purchase: 6	Sixth column to print
Amount of Purchase: 7	Seventh column to print
Serial Number: 5	Fifth column to print
Description: 4	Fourth column to print
Item Number: (blank)	This field will not be included.

Your Column/Sort Spec should look like figure14.2

3. Press F10 (Continue) to save the specifications in the Column/Sort Spec and continue to the next step.

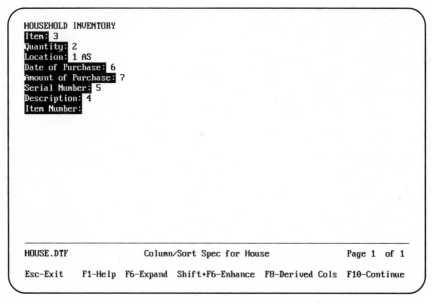

```
HOUSEHOLD INVENTORY
Item: 3
Quantity: 2
Location: 1 AS
Date of Purchase: 6
Amount of Purchase: 7
Serial Number: 5
Description: 4
Item Number:



HOUSE.DTF          Column/Sort Spec for House        Page 1 of 1

Esc-Exit    F1-Help  F6-Expand  Shift+F6-Enhance  F8-Derived Cols  F10-Continue
```

Fig. 14.2.   Entering specifications in the Column/Sort Spec.

Entering Print Options for Your Report

The Report Print Options screen appears next. Although similar to the File Print Options menu, this screen also enables you to print totals and justify text within the report. You use this screen to determine which printer to use, the type of paper, the printer offset, any external printer codes, totals to be included, and the text justification for the report. If your computer monitor is capable of displaying graphics, you can choose to preview the report on-screen, in a format that closely resembles the printed results. You should verify the settings in the Report Print Options screen and change the settings if necessary:

Print to: SCREEN
Page preview: No
Type of paper feed: Continuous
Print offset: 0 (To move the entire report five spaces to the right, enter 5.)
Printer control codes: (blank)
Print totals only: No

Justify report body: Left
Line spacing: Single
Allow split records: Yes

Compare your Report Print Options screen with figure 14.3.

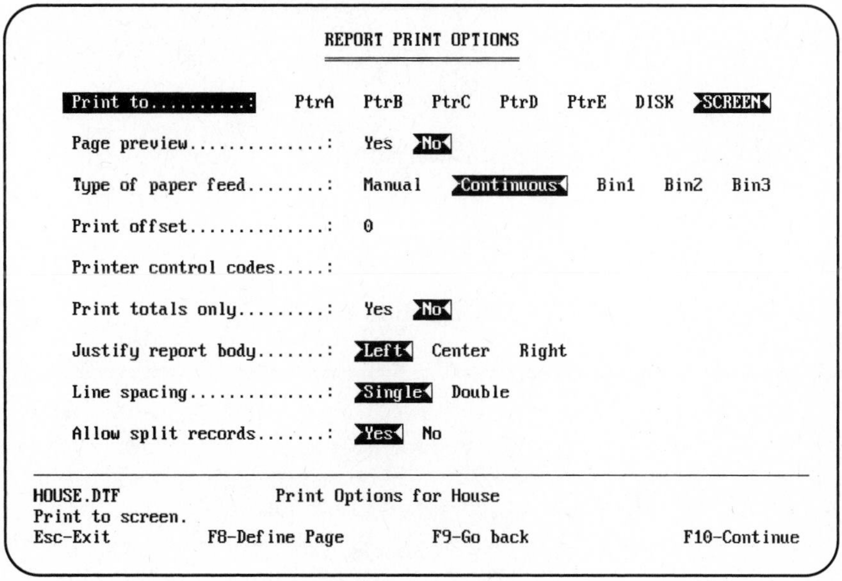

```
                        REPORT PRINT OPTIONS

      Print to..........:    PtrA   PtrB   PtrC   PtrD   PtrE   DISK  ▶SCREEN◀

      Page preview............:    Yes  ▶No◀

      Type of paper feed.......:   Manual  ▶Continuous◀  Bin1  Bin2  Bin3

      Print offset............:    0

      Printer control codes.....:

      Print totals only.........:   Yes  ▶No◀

      Justify report body.......:  ▶Left◀  Center   Right

      Line spacing.............:   ▶Single◀  Double

      Allow split records.......:  ▶Yes◀  No
      _____
HOUSE.DTF                Print Options for House
Print to screen.
Esc-Exit          F8-Define Page          F9-Go back          F10-Continue
```

Fig. 14.3.   *Verifying the print options.*

Defining the Page Options

Before printing the report, you need to be sure that the Define Page settings are sufficient to print the entire report. When you print several columns, you require extra space.

1. Press F8 (Define Page) to move to the Define Page screen.

The Define Page screen holds information about margins, page length, characters per inch, and any headers or footers to appear on the report. You change some of these settings to allow for the extra width of the report. You also set a header to display the current date at the top of the report and a footer to display the page number at the bottom of the report.

2. Check the parameters on the Define Page screen and change them if necessary to the following settings:

Page width: 240   Page length: 66

Left margin: 5   Right margin: 235

Top margin: 3   Bottom margin: 3

Characters per inch: 17

HEADER

1: Inventory Report As of @DATE(n)

FOOTER

1: Page #

Your screen now should look like figure 14.4.

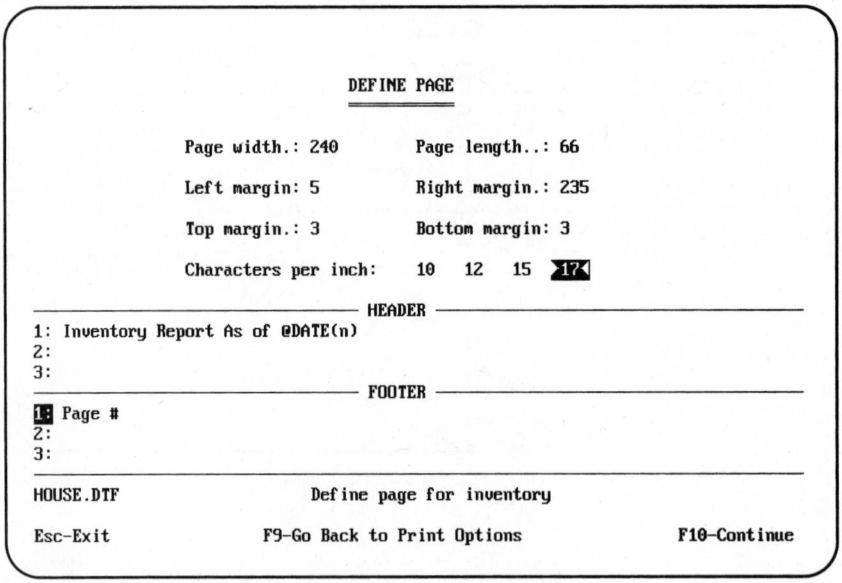

```
                            DEFINE PAGE
                            ═══════════

            Page width.: 240        Page length..: 66

            Left margin: 5          Right margin.: 235

            Top margin.: 3          Bottom margin: 3

            Characters per inch:    10   12   15  ▌17◀
─────────────────────────────── HEADER ──────────────────────────────
1: Inventory Report As of @DATE(n)
2:
3:
─────────────────────────────── FOOTER ──────────────────────────────
▌1▐ Page #
2:
3:
──────────────────────────────────────────────────────────────────────
HOUSE.DTF              Define page for inventory

Esc-Exit          F9-Go Back to Print Options          F10-Continue
```

Fig. 14.4.   Verifying the Define Page screen settings.

These parameters are chosen for specific reasons. The page width is 240 because that's the maximum width of a report. If you don't know the width needed, 240 is a good starting point. You then can decrease the width setting as needed. The right margin of 235 allows for a five-space margin if the entire width of 240 spaces is required. You are using 17 characters per inch to gain the benefit of condensed type. The width of the report is minimized using smaller characters (possibly minimized enough to fit on a sheet of 8 1/2-inch-by-11-inch paper if needed), thus making the report more compact but still readable. Because you are printing to the screen, however, you do not see a smaller type size on-screen.

The header will appear at the top of each printed page and will include the current date. Each page will be numbered at the bottom as specified in the footer. Because you are printing to the screen, however, headers and footers do not appear.

3. Press F10 to save your design and continue. A notice appears, informing you that your design has been saved and asking if you want to print the report.

4. Respond Yes and press Enter.

The final report is printed to your screen. Because your data is not identical to this HOUSE.DTF database, your field information will be different. The column headings and placement are shown in figure 14.5.

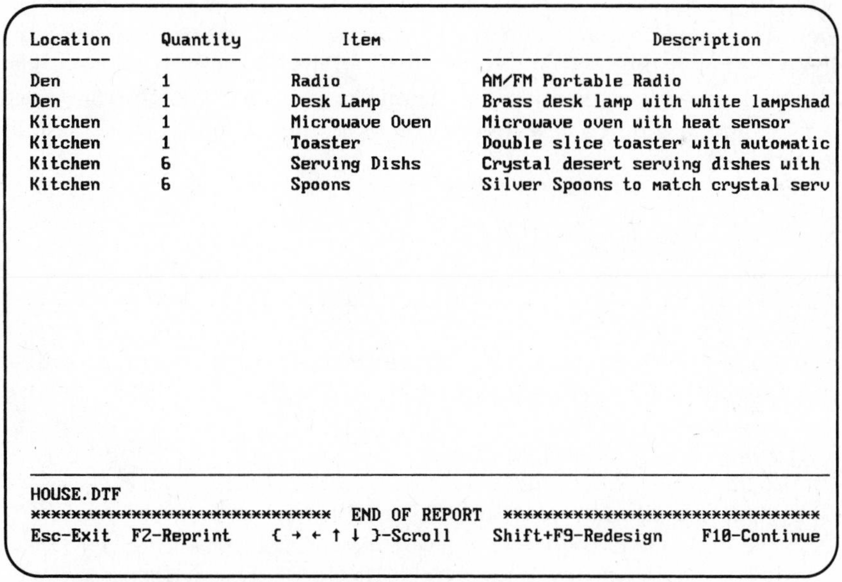

```
Location       Quantity         Item                     Description
--------       --------      ------------      ------------------------------------
Den            1             Radio             AM/FM Portable Radio
Den            1             Desk Lamp         Brass desk lamp with white lampshad
Kitchen        1             Microwave Oven    Microwave oven with heat sensor
Kitchen        1             Toaster           Double slice toaster with automatic
Kitchen        6             Serving Dishs     Crystal desert serving dishes with
Kitchen        6             Spoons            Silver Spoons to match crystal serv




                           
                           
                           
                           
                           
                           
_____
HOUSE.DTF
********************************* END OF REPORT ********************************
Esc-Exit   F2-Reprint    ( → ← ↑ ↓ )-Scroll    Shift+F9-Redesign   F10-Continue
```

Fig. 14.5.   Printing your report on-screen.

As you can see, not all the data is displayed on-screen. You requested several more columns than Location, Quantity, Item, and Description. The other columns are included in the report—they are to the right of the columns displayed. To view these "hidden" columns, use the scroll feature shown on the key assignment line.

5. Press and hold the right-arrow key to scroll across the rest of the report.

If you want to change something in the report, you can access the design screens again by pressing Shift-F9 (Redesign), or you can change settings on the Report Print Options screen by pressing F2 (Reprint).

Now that you know how to design a basic report, you are ready to learn some of the many ways to improve this report's appearance and have the report perform calculations for you.

Redesigning Your Report

When reports are saved, they stay with the database they reference until you delete the reports from memory. You can redesign saved reports at any time. One way to redesign a report is to select Design/Redesign a Report from the Report menu. Another way is to redesign a report after it appears on your screen. A good practice to follow is to use Print Preview or Print to Screen to view reports before printing them on paper. You then can see what the report looks like before producing a printed copy, and you can make changes quickly. You now can redesign the Inventory report by adjusting the Column/Sort Spec settings and by adding a new column that uses other columns in the report to make calculations.

Adding to the Column/Sort Spec Settings

You can add to the settings in this spec to format the report to be more concise and easier to read by performing the following steps:

1. Press Shift-F9 (Redesign).

   A message block appears at the bottom of the screen, giving you the option to change the Retrieve Spec, the Column/Sort Spec, Derived Columns, Print Spec, or the Define Page screen.

2. Select Column/Sort. Q&A returns you to that screen.

Your settings for this spec are saved. You will use these settings again and adjust them.

The Item field remains the same.

3. Change the Quantity field to display the following:

    2,F (JC)

    Each element of this program instructs Q&A to carry out a separate step:

2	Print this field in column 2.
F	A format is being specified.
JC	The field will be center-justified.

    The Location and Date of Purchase fields do not change.

4. Change the Amount of Purchase field as follows:

    7,ST,F(JR,C),H(12:Amount!of Purchase)

    Each element of this program gives an instruction to Q&A:

7	Seventh field to print
ST	This field will have subtotals.
F	A format is being specified.
JR	The field will be right-justified.
C	The field will have commas inserted.
H	This heading will be changed.
12	The heading will have twelve spaces.
Amount!	The first line of the heading is "Amount." The exclamation mark (!) indicates that the heading will split and be continued on the next line.
of Purchase	The second line of the heading is "of Purchase".

    The Serial Number field does not change.

5. Change the Description field as follows:

    4,H(40:)

    The elements in this program give Q&A three instructions:

4	Print the field in column 4.
H	The heading will be changed.
40	The heading will have 40 spaces.

The text of the heading doesn't change. Figure 14.6 shows the Column/Sort Spec.

If you use all the space in a field into which you are entering the column/sort criteria, you can expand the length of that field temporarily to contain additional sorting criteria by pressing F6 (Expand). Pressing F6 expands the area that accepts sorting or programming criteria to a maximum of 240 spaces.

Notice the following function key assignment at the bottom of the screen: Shift+F6-Enhance. You can apply character enhancements such as bold, italic, and underline to any part of a report and to any fonts that can be used with your printer. The Text Enhancements and Fonts menu are described in Chapter 15.

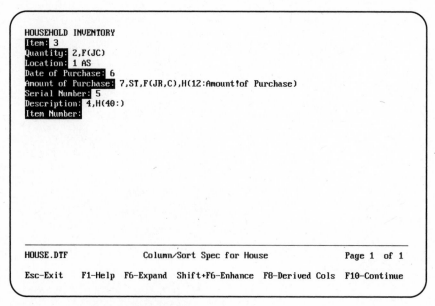

```
HOUSEHOLD INVENTORY
Item: 3
Quantity: 2,F(JC)
Location: 1 AS
Date of Purchase: 6
Amount of Purchase: 7,ST,F(JR,C),H(12:Amount!of Purchase)
Serial Number: 5
Description: 4,H(40:)
Item Number:




HOUSE.DTF            Column/Sort Spec for House          Page 1  of 1
Esc-Exit    F1-Help  F6-Expand  Shift+F6-Enhance  F8-Derived Cols  F10-Continue
```

Fig. 14.6.   *Revising the Column/Sort Spec.*

Using a Derived Column

A derived column is a column that does not exist in the database from which the Report module gets its data. The column is derived from data in other columns in the report and holds its own unique data. Many mathematical functions can be performed in a derived column, such as a total, average, count, minimum, and maximum.

The Inventory report would be more useful if you could determine the total value of all items in your household inventory. This number does not exist in any field, but you can calculate the number and display it in a derived column.

1. From the Column/Sort Spec, press F8 (Derived Columns) to display the Derived Columns screen.

    The Derived Columns screen consists of Heading, Formula, and Column Spec settings. Only four groups of settings are displayed on-screen, but up to 16 derived columns are available. In the bottom right of the screen you see Page 1 of 4 on the message line. This screen is four pages long, and you can enter additional derived column data by pressing the PgDn key.

2. In the first group of settings on the Derived Columns screen, enter the following data:

    Heading: Total Value!of Inventory   The first line of the heading will be "Total Value" and the second line will be "of Inventory".

    Formula: #7 + #8   The column will hold the totals of column #7 (Amount of Purchase) and column #8 (the derived Total column).

    Column Spec: 8,T   The derived column will be column #8, and calculations will be totaled at the end of the report.

Figure 14.7 shows the Derived Columns screen with this information entered.

3. Press F10 (Continue) to save the settings for the derived column.

4. Respond Yes when Q&A asks whether you want to print the report. You now are ready to print the report. The new report appears on-screen.

5. Use the arrow keys to scroll across the report, verifying the changes you made:

    •   Data in the Quantity column is centered.

    •   The Description column is narrower, with the descriptions wrapping to a second or third line if needed.

- The Amount of Purchase column heading is now two lines instead of one; the column is subtotaled, right-justified with commas, and twelve spaces wide.

- Total Value of Inventory is the last column, with subtotals *c* calculated as items are added and a grand total as the last figure in the column.

```
                            DERIVED COLUMNS


     Heading: Total Value! of Inventory
     Formula: #7 + #8
     Column Spec: 8,T

     Heading:
     Formula:
     Column Spec:

     Heading:
     Formula:
     Column Spec:

     Heading:
     Formula:
     Column Spec:


     HOUSE.DTF          Derived Columns for House              Page 1 of 4

     Esc-Exit        F1-Help      F9-Go back to Column/Sort Spec    F10-Continue
```

Fig. 14.7. Entering settings for the derived column.

Figures 14.8 and 14.9 show your Inventory report.

6. Press Esc to return to the Report menu.

Printing Your Report without Making Permanent Changes

You can print existing reports without going through all the steps you just completed. Reports saved in memory can be printed using the Print a Report command on the Report menu.

```
Location      Quantity         Item                    Description
---------     --------    ----------------    ------------------------------------
Den           1           Radio               AM/FM Portable Radio
Den           1           Desk Lamp           Brass desk lamp with white lampshad


Total:
Kitchen       1           Microwave Oven      Microwave oven with heat sensor
Kitchen       1           Toaster             Double slice toaster with automatic
Kitchen       6           Serving Dishs       Crystal desert serving dishes with
Kitchen       6           Spoons              Silver Spoons to match crystal serv




Total:
========      ========    ==============      ==================================
Total:


HOUSE.DTF
************************************ END OF REPORT ************************************
Esc-Exit  F2-Reprint    { → ← ↑ ↓ }-Scroll    Shift+F9-Redesign    F10-Continue
```

Fig. 14.8. The first screen of your final report.

```
mber      Date of Purchase    Amount of Purchase    Total Value of Inventory
----      ----------------    ------------------    ------------------------
          Sep 27,1990                   $79.95                      $79.95
          Jan 24,1991                   $49.95                     $287.01

                                    ------------
                                        $287.01
          Jun 4, 1990               $1,265.00                   $1,473.69
285       Jun 3, 1991                   $63.95                   $1,537.64
          Jun 9, 1991                    $0.00                   $1,537.64
          Jun 9, 1991                    $0.00                   $1,537.64


                                    ------------
                                      $1,329.83
====      ================    ==================    
                                                                $1,458.85



HOUSE.DTF
************************************ END OF REPORT ************************************
Esc-Exit  F2-Reprint    { → ← ↑ ↓ }-Scroll    Shift+F9-Redesign    F10-Continue
```

Fig. 14.9. The second screen of your final report.

1. Select Print a Report from the Report menu. The program asks for the name of the database that contains the report.

2. Enter the name of the database. Type the file name *house.dtf* and press Enter. If you are not sure of the name, press the Enter key, and a list of the databases appears for you to select from. A list of reports in the HOUSE.DTF database, including Inventory, is displayed.

3. Use the arrow keys to select the Inventory report, and press Enter.

   A menu appears asking whether you want to make any temporary changes. Notice that any changes are temporary and are not saved after you print the report. This feature is useful if you want to modify a report to meet a one-time requirement, yet want to keep the original report unchanged. If you choose to make temporary changes, Q&A takes you back through all the screens used to design or redesign a report and offers you the opportunity to change the screens. You do not make any temporary changes now.

4. Respond No on this menu and press Enter. The report as you designed it is printed on your screen (refer to figs. 14.8 and 14.9).

5. Press Esc until you are at the Report menu.

Setting Global Options

Global options are choices that affect column headings and widths, and format, print, and page definitions. These options apply automatically to all the current database's reports generated after these options are set. Reports created before you change any of these settings remain as designed originally and are not altered.

Select Set Global Options from the Report menu for the database HOUSE.DTF. The Global Options menu appears. Choose C for the Columnar Global Options screen. This menu includes the following four commands:

Set Column Headings/Widths
Set Format Options
Set Print Options
Set Page Options

With the first command, Set Column Headings/Widths, you can change headings and column widths for all the reports that reference HOUSE.DTF. Perhaps you want the Item field to be called "Object" on all reports and to be centered. This formatting is done from this screen. (The same format is used as with the Column/Sort Spec when you first designed the Inventory report.) Or maybe you want the Amount of Purchase field always to be printed as a two-line heading. You indicate this format in the appropriate field; all future reports will reflect this specification.

The second command, Set Format Options, provides four formatting features. You can set the number of spaces between columns to a definite number, instead of letting the spacing vary according to the page width. In your Inventory report, most of the spaces between columns are five or six. To condense a report, you can reduce these spaces to three or four. Printing reports that require identical values to be repeated also are indicated with this command. When the location of items was identical in the Inventory report, for example, the location was printed only once. For a report containing last names, however, you want to print all the last names, even identical ones. You also can use this command to fill blank values with zero—financial reports compiled from a database require zeros to be placed in all blank fields for effective calculation and presentation. The last item that can be changed is to skip column breaks. For large reports, for example, you can specify not to leave a blank line after each column break.

The third command, Set Print Options, controls the Report Print Options menu that appears when you print a report. You have worked with these items already. One other useful setting is the type of paper feed. Depending on your printer, you can use continuous paper or paper stored in bins, such as letterhead or second sheets to letterhead. This setting can be changed here. Another frequent change is the printer that is used. Large spreadsheets often are printed on a different printer than a printer used for letterhead. You can specify here the printer for a database that is used to generate wide reports.

The final selection, Set Page Options, displays the Define Page screen. You can specify consistent margins or characters-per-inch settings for a particular database, thus eliminating the need to check the Define Page screen when queuing (or arranging) reports to print. Most reports require page numbering, which you can preset here; pages then are numbered automatically on all reports or even dated with the current date.

Press Esc to accept the default settings until you return to the Q&A Main menu.

Chapter Summary

In this quick start, you learned how to design a report to extract information from a database. You now can sort information, print the information in the proper sequence, and generate and print new data in a derived column. You can redesign previously saved reports and make permanent changes to those reports, or print a temporary report while preserving your original design. By using global options, you can format and define all future reports and save valuable time by not editing standard formats each time you generate a report.

With the Report module, you can retrieve the data in the File module in a form beneficial to both you and your organization. In the next two chapters, you will learn much more about Q&A's Report module, including more on the possibilities for creating, formatting, and printing reports.

Creating a Report

After you create a database and enter data in the files, you need to organize the data into a report for your analysis and for others to review. Q&A Report can pull information from the forms in File and print reports in a variety of ways.

Q&A Report enables you to print database records selectively with user-specified column headings and sort order. You also can print cross-tab reports that summarize the data in useful ways. Additionally, you can compute information that is not stored in the database for inclusion on the report.

The Report module is one of three ways of retrieving information from a Q&A File database. The other two ways are retrieving and printing records with print facilities inside the File module and using the Intelligent Assistant. For information on using the print facilities in the File module, see Chapters 6 and 8.

You may prefer to use the Intelligent Assistant to produce ad hoc reports quickly and easily. The Intelligent Assistant's reporting features work best when you need a quick report that answers a specific question or one-time request. (For detailed information on using the IA to produce reports, see Chapters 17 and 18.)

When you need to design a report that will be used repeatedly, however, you will want to use the flexibility of Q&A Report, which enables you to customize column headings and widths, include derived columns, and add headers and footers. This chapter explains how to create and use this type of report.

Reports Available with Q&A Report

Q&A Report produces several varieties of columnar, detailed, summary, and cross-tab reports by using the data entered in File. If you used classic database design methods to build your files, you already have a good idea how you want the reports to appear. You can use the flexible design features in the Report module, however, to experiment with data presentation.

Figure 15.1 shows the Source of Leads report. The sales leads on this report are grouped by source: Advertising, Mailing, Phone, and Salesman. The rows of calculated subtotals show that Phone Sales produced the most leads during the reporting period. This information will be helpful in planning future sales promotions.

Source of Lead	Date Entered	State	Sales Priority	Product Interest	Request For	Status
Adv	Jun 15, 1988	MO	Hot	2500;1500	Demo	Sale; 2500
	Apr 16, 1988	CA	1.0	1500;2000	Demo	Postpone
	Jul 27, 1988	IN	2.0	2500	Salesman	Sale; 2500
	May 7, 1988	TN	1.0	2000	Info	Postpone
	Jul 1, 1988	AL	1.0	2500;1500	Demo	No Decision
Count:		5				
Mail	Jun 2, 1988	MI	1.5	2000;1000	Info	Postpone
	Jun 6, 1988	CO	Hot	1500;2000	Info	Sale
	Jul 27, 1988	IN	1.0	2000	Info	Follow up
Count:		3				
Phone	Jul 10, 1988	TN	1.0	2000;1200	Info	Sale; 1200
	Jul 15, 1988	SD	Hot	1200;2000	Info	Follow up
	May 15, 1988	GA	1.5	2000;2500	Salesman	No Decision
	Jul 29, 1988	CO	1.0	1000;1500	Salesman	Follow up
	Jul 27, 1988	IN	2.0	1000	Info	Follow up
	Jun 4, 1988	PA	1.0	1200;1500	Demo	Postpone
Count:		6				
Salesman	Jul 5, 1988	PA	1.5	1200;1500	Demo	Sale; 1500
	Apr 28, 1988	WA	2.0	1500;2500	Info	Sale; 1500
	Jun 5, 1988	MI	1.5	1000;2000	Salesman	Postpone
	Jul 20, 1988	PA	1.5	2000;1500	Salesman	Sale; 2000
Count:		4				

Fig. 15.1. *The Source of Leads report.*

The Sales District report, shown in figure 15.2, shows the leads divided according to sales districts. This type of report may be sent to the district sales managers. Subtotal, total, and average counts are included in this report.

```
                                                                    Sales
Sales Dist.        Company              City       Request For  Product Interest  Priority
-----------    ------------------   -----------   -----------  ----------------  --------
Atlanta        Mattis Medical Laboratories  Atlanta      Salesman     2000;2500         1.5
               ----------------------------
Count:                          1

Cincinnati     Nashville Medical Technology  Nashville   Info         2000              1.0
               ----------------------------
Count:                          1

Denver         Mountain Labs        Denver       Salesman     1000;1500         1.0
               Mountain Labs        Boulder      Info         1500;2000         Hot
               ----------------------------
Count:                          2

Detroit        University of Michigan  Detroit    Salesman     1000;2000         1.5
               ----------------------------
Count:                          1

Indiana        Central Laboratories              Info         2000              1.0
               Indiana Medical, Inc.            Info         1000              2.0
               Hoosier Clinics, Inc.           Salesman     2500              2.0
               ----------------------------
Count:                          3

Knoxville      Advanced Medical Associates  Knoxville  Info         2000;1200         1.0
               ----------------------------
Count:                          1

Los Angeles    Cherry Electronics, Inc.  San Francisco  Demo      1500;2000         1.0
               ----------------------------
Count:                          1

Michigan       Bay City Laboratories  Grand Rapids  Info        2000;1000         1.5
               ----------------------------
Count:                          1

Missouri       Independent Medical Labs  Independence  Demo      2500;1500         Hot
               ----------------------------
Count:                          1

Mobile         Hope Laboratories, Inc.  Mobile       Demo         2500;1500         1.0
               ----------------------------
Count:                          1

Philadelphia   Franklyn Lab Associates  Philadelphia   Demo       1200;1500         1.5
               Penn Medical Technology  King of Prussia  Demo     1200;1500         1.0
               Pike Pharmaceutical, Inc.  Reading      Salesman   2000;1500         1.5
               ----------------------------
Count:                          3

Seattle        Washington Medical Labs, Inc  Seattle   Info        1500;2500         2.0
               ----------------------------
Count:                          1
```

Fig. 15.2. *The Sales District report.*

The Sales Leads Revenue Per Lab report, shown in figure 15.3, is an analysis of the company's annual revenue. This report contains a special column (Revenue Per Lab) that is calculated for this report only. Marketing information of this type is helpful for long-range planning.

Company	No. of Labs	Annual Revenue	Revenue Per Lab	Sales Priority	Sales Dist.
Mountain Labs	3	$5378667.00	$1,792,889.00	Hot	Denver
Hope Laboratories, Inc.	2	$500000.00	$250,000.00	1.0	Mobile
Plaines Medical Associates	4	$750000.00	$187,500.00	Hot	South Dakota
Hoosier Clinics, Inc.	3	$100000.00	$33,333.33	2.0	Indiana
Central Laboratories	1	$50000.00	$50,000.00	1.0	Indiana
Indiana Medical, Inc.	4	$125000.00	$31,250.00	2.0	Indiana
Independent Medical Labs	3	$223500.00	$74,500.00	Hot	Missouri
Mountain Labs	2	$100210.00	$50,105.00	1.0	Denver
Advanced Medical Associates	3	$5300623.00	$1,766,874.33	1.0	Knoxville
Cherry Electronics, Inc.	20	$4000000.00	$200,000.00	1.0	Los Angeles
Nashville Medical Technology	7	$8000375.00	$1,142,910.71	1.0	Cincinnati
Franklyn Lab Associates	5	$6456000.00	$1,291,200.00	1.5	Philadelphia
Penn Medical Technology	3	$50000.00	$16,666.67	1.0	Philadelphia
Mattis Medical Laboratories	5	$1000210.00	$200,042.00	1.5	Atlanta
Washington Medical Labs, Inc	6	$200500.00	$33,416.67	2.0	Seattle
University of Michigan	3	$325000.00	$108,333.33	1.5	Detroit
Pike Pharmaceutical, Inc.	1	$210000.00	$210,000.00	1.5	Philadelphia
Bay City Laboratories	1	$150250.00	$150,250.00	1.5	Michigan

Fig. 15.3. The Sales Leads Revenue Per Lab report.

The Sales Analysis cross-tab report, shown in figure 15.4, provides a summary of the company's sales by district and lead source.

			Sales Dist.		
Lead Source	East	Midwest	South	West	This Year
Print	$45,000	$35,000	$15,000	$80,000	$175,000
Phone	$5,000	$9,000	$2,000	$3,000	$19,000
Radio	$50,000	$115,000	$95,000	$140,000	$400,000
TV	$500,000	$85,000	$100,000	$525,000	$1,210,000
This Year	$600,000	$244,000	$212,000	$748,000	$1,804,000

Fig. 15.4. The Sales Analysis cross-tab report.

You can produce many different reports from a single database. Each report can have its own format, calculations, and derived columns. This chapter explains how to design a report using the different capabilities of Q&A Report.

Designing a Columnar Report

Designing a columnar report with the Report module is relatively easy. You should follow this basic procedure:

1. Specify which data file or files Report will use.

2. Tell Report which records to print—the Retrieve Spec.

3. Choose the fields from each record to print.

4. Specify field and record order.

Although each of these basic steps may have several parts, if you remember the basics, the process is not difficult.

Think of a printed or on-screen report as a window into the database. After you store the data on disk that you want to analyze, you can look through the report window to view the data in many forms. This concept is particularly important if you are in a multiuser environment, because Q&A Report enables you to look at File information only at a suspended moment in time. All the reports you generate reflect how the database looks when you ask for the report. Other users may change information while your report is being prepared, but you won't see the changes unless you generate a later report. This capability enables Q&A to support simultaneous access by users.

To begin designing a report, select Report from the Q&A Main menu. The Report menu is displayed (see fig. 15.5). As you design your report, remember to use F1 (Help) to display instructions for each step.

Two procedures can be used in designing a report form: sequential and direct. The *sequential procedure* goes through the design process step-by-step; the *direct procedure* takes you straight to the step you want. This section focuses on the sequential method. Later, you learn how to use the direct method to make changes to the report design.

To begin the design process, select Design/Redesign a Report from the Report menu. The program prompts you for the name of the file that stores the data. Type the file name or press Enter to display a list of files. When you find the file name you want, press Enter. If you have designed reports previously, a list of report names is displayed.

To design a new report, respond to the prompt at the bottom of the screen by typing a report name of up to 20 characters. After you press Enter, Report responds by asking whether you want to design a columnar report or a cross-tab report. Press C to design a columnar report. Q&A displays the Retrieve Spec screen, and you are ready to begin retrieving information for your report.

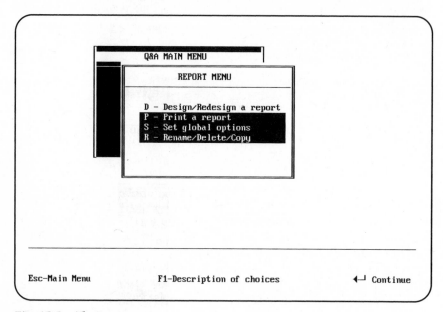

Fig. 15.5. *The Report menu.*

Retrieving File Information

The Retrieve Spec is used to specify the forms that are to be included in your report. If the report you are creating will use all the forms in the file, leave the Retrieve Spec blank and press F10 to continue.

When you want to use only a selected group of forms, you can specify the forms by entering retrieval operators on the Retrieve Spec. (For more information on using retrieval operators and specifying the forms you want to use, see Chapter 6.)

When you retrieve a group of forms, you can have the program search for either a piece of information or a range of information. If you want to retrieve all sales leads from the New York sales district, for example, enter *New York* in the Sales Dist. field (see fig. 15.6). If you want to retrieve all sales leads that have 1 to 10 labs, however, enter the range specification of 1..10 in the No. of Labs field. To retrieve a range in a text field, use the format >1..<10.

```
             TITAN TECHNOLOGY SALES LEAD TRACKING SYSTEM
============================================================== File Name -- SlsLead
LastName:                            FirstName:
Title:
Company:                             Telephone:
Address1:
Address2:
City:                                State:         Zip:
    No. of Labs:                     Annual Revenue:
    Current Customer:                Company Priority:
-----------------------------LEAD INFORMATION------------------------
    Product Interest:
    Request For:                     Lead Source:
    Months to Purchase:              Product Priority:
------------------------------SALES ACTION---------------------------
    Sales Priority:                  Date Entered:
    Sales Dist.: New York            Sales Manager:
    Salesman:                        Phone:
    Status:


-------------------------------------------------------------------------
SLSLEAD.DTF              Retrieve Spec for Sales Revenue      Page 1  of 1

Esc-Exit   F1-Help   F3-Clear  F6-Expand  Alt+F8-List  ↑F8-Save    F10-Continue
```

Fig. 15.6.   *Entering a retrieval spec.*

If you are not sure how information may have been entered with File, use Q&A's Sounds Like searching character, the tilde (~). Use the tilde at the beginning of a search spec when you are only guessing at the correct spelling or the correct choice among several possibilities.

Suppose that you want a list of the sales leads from the Hohenwald, Tennessee, office, and you suspect that different people have entered the office name in different ways. By specifying *~Hohenwald* in the Sales District field, you retrieve records with such diverse spellings as Hoenwald, Hoenwaldt, and Hoinwald.

Note: You can prevent this varied data entry problem by using lookup tables, external files, and custom help screens to enforce spelling compliance during data entry.

You can use the Tab key, Return, and the cursor-movement keys to move the cursor from field to field in report screens. If you need more space when entering a retrieval specification, you can press F6 to expand the field length. If you want to erase the Retrieve Spec without saving it, you can press Esc to return to the Report menu. When all necessary specifications have been entered, press F10 to continue. The Column/Sort Spec then is displayed.

After you fill in the Retrieve Spec, you can give it a name and save it for later use. Press Shift-F8 and type a name at the prompt. To retrieve a spec, press Alt-F8 and choose a stored spec from the list that appears.

Organizing Information for a Report

The simplest report you can create with the Report module consists of fields from your database file displayed in columnar form, but you can generate more complex reports. For example, you can create special columns—*derived columns*—that show the results of calculations using values from the original database forms. You also can create reports that are divided into categories based on information in keyword fields. The following sections teach you how to use features for organizing database information into a Q&A report.

Selecting Fields for Columns

The next step in designing a report involves selecting and ordering the fields by using the Column/Sort Spec screen (see fig. 15.7).

```
                TITAN TECHNOLOGY SALES LEAD TRACKING SYSTEM
   ════════════════════════════════════════════════════ File Name -- SlsLead
   LastName:                              FirstName:
   Title:
   Company: 1                             Telephone:
   Address1:
   Address2:
   City:                                  State:          Zip:
      No. of Labs: 5                      Annual Revenue: 10
      Current Customer:                   Company Priority:
   ─────────────────────────────LEAD INFORMATION─────────────────────
      Product Interest:
      Request For:                        Lead Source:
      Months to Purchase:                 Product Priority:
   ───────────────────────────────SALES ACTION───────────────────────
      Sales Priority: 15                  Date Entered:
      Sales Dist.: 20█████████            Sales Manager:
      Salesman:                           Phone:
      Status:


   SLSLEAD.DTF          Column/Sort Spec for Sales Revenue      Page 1  of 1

   Esc-Exit    F1-Help  F6-Expand  Shift+F6-Enhance  F8-Derived Cols  F10-Continue
```

Fig. 15.7. Selecting and ordering the file fields on the Column/Sort Spec screen.

When you organize a report, each field you select becomes a column in the report. You select the fields by numbering them, as shown in figure 15.7. Notice that the Column/Sort Spec in figure 15.7 does not show consecutive numbering. Numbering with increments larger than one enables columns to be added between the original columns without renumbering the fields. Figure 15.8 shows that the number you type in the field determines the column in which the field information will appear in the report. You can have up to 50 columns in a report.

Company	No. of Labs	Annual Revenue	Revenue Per Lab	Sales Priority	Sales Dist.
Mountain Labs	3	$5378667.00	$1,792,889.00	Hot	Denver
Hope Laboratories, Inc.	2	$500000.00	$250,000.00	1.0	Mobile
Plaines Medical Associates	4	$750000.00	$187,500.00	Hot	South Dakota
Hoosier Clinics, Inc.	3	$100000.00	$33,333.33	2.0	Indiana
Central Laboratories	1	$50000.00	$50,000.00	1.0	Indiana
Indiana Medical, Inc.	4	$125000.00	$31,250.00	2.0	Indiana
Independent Medical Labs	3	$223500.00	$74,500.00	Hot	Missouri
Mountain Labs	2	$100210.00	$50,105.00	1.0	Denver
Advanced Medical Associates	3	$5300623.00	$1,766,874.33	1.0	Knoxville
Cherry Electronics, Inc.	20	$4000000.00	$200,000.00	1.0	Los Angeles
Nashville Medical Technology	7	$8000375.00	$1,142,910.71	1.0	Cincinnati
Franklyn Lab Associates	5	$6456000.00	$1,291,200.00	1.5	Philadelphia
Penn Medical Technology	3	$50000.00	$16,666.67	1.0	Philadelphia
Mattis Medical Laboratories	5	$1000210.00	$200,042.00	1.5	Atlanta
Washington Medical Labs, Inc	6	$200500.00	$33,416.67	2.0	Seattle
University of Michigan	3	$325000.00	$108,333.33	1.5	Detroit
Pike Pharmaceutical, Inc.	1	$210000.00	$210,000.00	1.5	Philadelphia
Bay City Laboratories	1	$150250.00	$150,250.00	1.5	Michigan

Fig. 15.8. File fields as they appear in the report.

To organize fields in report columns, move the cursor to the field that you want to appear in the left column of the report, and type *1*. In figure 15.7, the Company field is designated as the left column. Continue entering numbers in the fields that you want to appear on the report. You may want to number the fields by increments of 10 in order to accommodate later insertions.

The number of columns you specify is not limited to the width of your printer's paper. With Q&A, you can set the page width up to 1,000 characters. Because most printers are limited to a width of 240 characters, a large report may be partitioned onto more than one page. Whenever the page width isn't enough for your report, you are prompted with the following menu just before the report prints:

C - Cancel Printing
T - Truncate report and continue
E - Edit options & reprint
S - Split report across pages

You select C to cancel the report so that you can redesign the report to fit on the page. The second option, Truncate, continues with the report, but any data that does not fit on the standard page width is dropped. You can choose E to make minor changes in the report design before trying to reprint. You can specify S to generate a report split across two or more pages.

Notice the function key label at the bottom of the page: Shift+F6-Enhance. Beginning with Release 4.0, you can enhance your reports with boldface, underline, italics, and any fonts available with your printer. Report enhancement will be described later in this chapter, in the section titled "Formatting Report Columns."

After you organize the fields into columns, you can add derived columns to the report. The following section explains derived columns and shows how you can use them.

Now that you have specified the columns for the report, you can print a simple report to check what you have done. Press F10 to display the Report Print Options menu. You can send the report to the screen or the printer.

Adding Derived Columns

Q&A Report has the capability of creating, or deriving, a column by performing calculations on the data in one or more existing columns in the report. As a result, your report can have columns displaying information that doesn't exist in the file itself. Each report can have up to 16 derived columns, which are calculated from file fields or from other derived columns.

In the report in figure 15.8, the Revenue Per Lab column is a derived column. To find the values in that column, Q&A divided the values in the Annual Revenue column by the numbers in the No. of Labs column.

To add a derived column to a report, press F8 from the Column/Sort Spec to display the Derived Columns screen (see fig. 15.9).

On the Derived Columns screen, type the heading, formula, and column location. The first item that appears on the Derived Columns screen is the Heading prompt. A column heading can be on one line only, but headings that have more than one word look better divided into two or three lines (three lines is the maximum). Use an exclamation mark to indicate where you want the heading to break. For example, the entry Order!Minus!Discount will print as the following:

```
Order
Minus
Discount
```

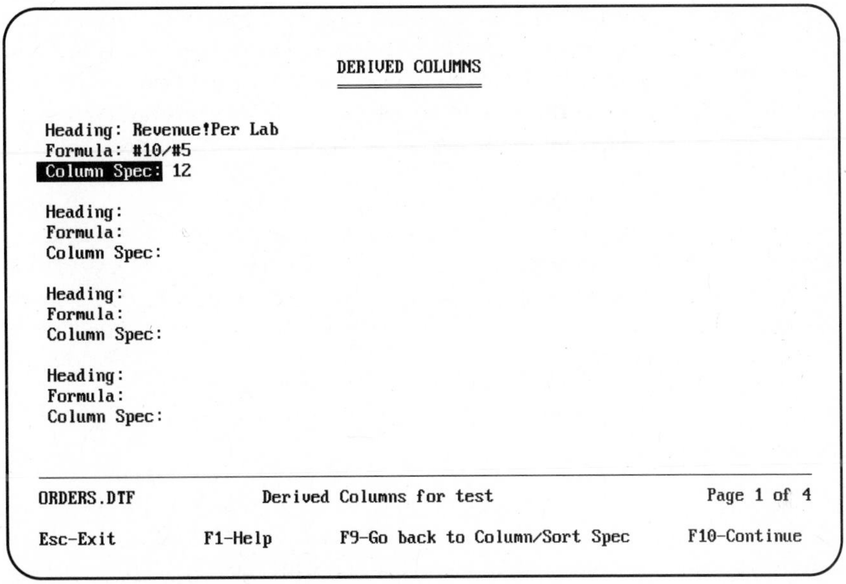

```
                           DERIVED COLUMNS
                           ==============

    Heading: Revenue!Per Lab
    Formula: #10/#5
    Column Spec: 12

    Heading:
    Formula:
    Column Spec:

    Heading:
    Formula:
    Column Spec:

    Heading:
    Formula:
    Column Spec:


    ORDERS.DTF           Derived Columns for test           Page 1 of 4

    Esc-Exit      F1-Help      F9-Go back to Column/Sort Spec   F10-Continue
```

Fig. 15.9. *Filling in the Derived Columns spec.*

The line below the Heading prompt is the Formula prompt. On this line, you enter the formula used to create the derived column (refer to fig. 15.8). A derived-column formula uses a combination of column numbers and arithmetic operators. The calculation order of the operators is as follows:

()   First
* /   Second
+ –   Third

The formulas for derived columns look like simple mathematical equations. For example, consider the following formulas:

Formula	Calculates
#4 + #5 – #7	Column 4 plus column 5 minus column 7
#1 / (#3 + #5)	Column 1 divided by the sum of columns 3 and 5
#2 + #3 + #5 + #6	The sum of columns 2, 3, 5, and 6

The example in figure 15.9 computes the revenue per lab by dividing the total annual revenue by the number of labs. The heading is split into two lines with the exclamation mark between Revenue and Per Lab.

At the Column Spec prompt, type a number that indicates where the derived column should be located. In this example, the derived column is the new fourth column; it is given a number (12) between the third column (10) and the current fourth column (15). When the Derived Columns screen is complete, press F10 to return to the Report Print Options screen, or press F9 to go to the Column/Sort Spec.

Use derived columns when you want to display information that is not stored in the database. You can save storage space and data entry time by calculating information you need rather than entering and storing the information with each record. You also can use constants as part of the derived column spec as well as references to columns.

Creating Self-Referencing Derived Columns

Derived columns can reference themselves in Q&A Report formulas to produce running totals, as shown in figures 15.10 and 15.11.

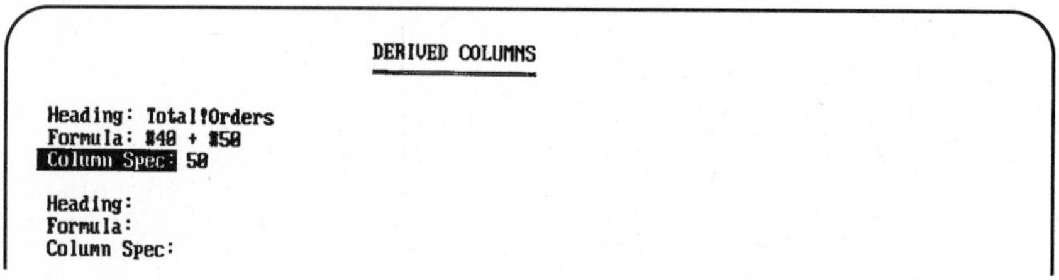

```
                          DERIVED COLUMNS
                          ─────────────────

     Heading: Total↑Orders
     Formula: #40 + #50
     Column Spec: 50

     Heading:
     Formula:
     Column Spec:
```

Fig. 15.10.   Creating a self-referencing column.

In figure 15.10, the formula in the derived Total Orders column adds column 40 (Total) to column 50 (derived Total Orders). You enter formulas like this the same way you enter formulas on a calculator: #40 + #50. The example in figure 15.11 shows how Report adds the number from the preceding row of the Total Orders derived column to the current row of the Total column and puts the result in the current row of the Total Orders column.

```
                                              TOTAL
                 Company            Model   Quantity   ORDERS
.......................................    .....    .........   ......
          Cherry Electronics       1500        13        13

          Mountain Labs                        10        23

          Northern Supply Company               5        28
                                                .........
                                   Total:       28

          Plaines Medical Services 2000        45        73

          Nashville Medical Technology         12        85

          Bay City Laboratory                   8        93

          Arizona Medical Services              6        99

          Independent Medical Laboratory        5       104

          Hope Laboratories                     2       106

          Washington Medical Labs               1       107
                                                .........
                                   Total:       79

          Pike Pharmaceutical Co.  2400        23       130

          Univ. of Michigan                     4       134

          Penn Medical Labs                     2       136

          Mattis Medical Labs                   1       137
                                                .........
                                   Total:       30
```

Fig. 15.11.   *Total Orders in a self-referencing column.*

Using Summary Functions in Derived Columns

You can use derived columns to compute summary information on data that appears in physical columns. Available summary functions are shown in table 15.1. Note that you can compute summaries for all items in a specified column, or only subsummaries by conducting the calculation after a break occurs in the same or another column. A break in a report occurs when the data in a sorted column changes. If your report is sorted by city, for example, a break occurs when the city changes.

Table 15.1
Derived Column Summary Functions

Function	Meaning
@TOTAL(x)	Total of values in column x
@AVERAGE(x)	Average of values in column x
@COUNT(x)	Count of values in column x (how many different values listed in report)
MINIMUM(x)	Minimum value of all values that appear in column x
MAXIMUM(x)	Maximum of all values that appear in column x
@TOTAL(x,y)	Subtotal of values in column x on a break in column y
@AVERAGE(x,y)	Subaverage of values in column x on a break in column y
@COUNT(x,y)	Subcount of values in column x on a break in column y
@MINIMUM(x,y)	Subminimum of values in column x on a break in column y
@MAXIMUM(x,y)	Submaximum of values in column x on break in column y

Using LOOKUP Functions in Derived Columns

Among Q&A's most powerful functions are LOOKUP and XLOOKUP, which enable you to use internal and external tables to store data associated with information in database forms. For example, you can store a short sales office ID code in the database and keep the office name and address in a File lookup table. This technique saves considerable storage space but gives you all the information on printed reports. You also can use the XLOOKUP function to store customer names and addresses in a separate File database for retrieval during report preparation. The LOOKUP functions in Report operate essentially the same as those for File. (See Chapter 7 for details on these functions.)

To use the LOOKUP function in Report, select F8 (Derived Cols) from the Column/Sort Spec screen and enter the appropriate function in the Formula position for the derived column. For example, to insert the company name in Report column 2 from an external file, you can use the following formula, assuming that the company ID is in field #1 in the primary file:

Heading: Company Name
Formula: @XLOOKUP("Company",#1,"Company ID","Company Name")
Column Spec: 2

Remember that to use external data files in this way, you must have matching data in the primary and external files; the linked fields in both files must be indexed (set for speed-up searches), and the key-field data must be unique.

Making a Keyword Report

A keyword report can be used to sort and format a report on one keyword field. Remember that a keyword field contains a variety of items separated by semicolons. When you specify a keyword report type, Q&A knows that it will be dealing with multiple entries in this field and can search for the terms you specify.

This capability enables you to categorize report sections according to types of data in a keyword field (see fig. 15.12). Files without keywords also can be sorted and formatted, but you have to enter all the specifications.

```
                    TITAN TECHNOLOGY SALES LEAD TRACKING SYSTEM
                    ═══════════════════════════════════════ File Name -- SlsLead
 LastName:                              FirstName:
 Title:
 Company:                              Telephone:
 Address1:
 Address2:
 City:                                 State:          Zip:
    No. of Labs:                       Annual Revenue:
    Current Customer:                  Company Priority:
 ───────────────────────────────────LEAD INFORMATION──────────────────────
    Product Interest: 1,K
    Request For:                       Lead Source: 10
    Months to Purchase:                Product Priority:
 ─────────────────────────────────SALES ACTION──────────────────────
    Sales Priority:                    Date Entered:
    Sales Dist.:                       Sales Manager:
    Salesman:                          Phone:
    Status:


 ─────────────────────────────────────────────────────────────────────
 SLSLEAD.DTF          Column/Sort Spec for Sales Revenue      Page 1 of 1

 Esc-Exit    F1-Help  F6-Expand  Shift+F6-Enhance  F8-Derived Cols  F10-Continue
```

Fig. 15.12.   The Product Interest keyword report.

You specify a keyword report on the Column/Sort Spec. In figure 15.12, the Product Interest field shows the keyword report code (K). Figure 15.13 shows that the keyword fields—product model numbers—are grouped automatically and sorted in ascending order.

```
                    Source
                    of Lead
Product Interest                        Company
.................   .......     ..........................
      1000          Phone       Mountain Labs
                    Mail        Bay City Laboratories
                    Salesman    University of Michigan
                    Phone       Indiana Medical, Inc.

      1200          Salesman    Franklyn Lab Associates
                    Phone       Penn Medical Technology
                    Phone       Advanced Medical Associates
                    Phone       Plaines Medical Associates

      1500          Salesman    Washington Medical Labs, Inc
                    Phone       Mountain Labs
                    Adv         Cherry Electronics, Inc.
                    Salesman    Franklyn Lab Associates
                    Adv         Hope Laboratories, Inc.
                    Phone       Penn Medical Technology
                    Adv         Independent Medical Labs
                    Salesman    Pike Pharmaceutical, Inc.
                    Mail        Mountain Labs

      2000          Salesman    University of Michigan
                    Salesman    Pike Pharmaceutical, Inc.
                    Mail        Bay City Laboratories
                    Phone       Mattis Medical Laboratories
                    Adv         Cherry Electronics, Inc.
                    Adv         Nashville Medical Technology
                    Mail        Mountain Labs
                    Phone       Advanced Medical Associates
                    Phone       Plaines Medical Associates
                    Mail        Central Laboratories

      2500          Adv         Hoosier Clinics, Inc.
                    Adv         Hope Laboratories, Inc.
                    Adv         Independent Medical Labs
                    Phone       Mattis Medical Laboratories
                    Salesman    Washington Medical Labs, Inc
```

Fig. 15.13.   Specifying the Product Interest keyword report.

To produce a keyword report, you must organize the file fields into report columns, as explained previously. When you specify the column order, however, assign the lowest number to the keyword field, making the keyword field the left column.

After the column specification, type the letter *K*. You then add other columns and specifications to complete the report.

If you want to retrieve information based on a single keyword, that keyword must be entered in the appropriate field of the Retrieve Spec. For example, if the Product Interest Report in figure 15.13 is to include only the sales leads that have expressed interest in model 1500, the Product Interest field of the Retrieve Spec appears as follows:

```
Product Interest: 1500
```

To retrieve information based on more than one keyword, several keywords must be entered in the appropriate field of the Retrieve Spec. For example, if the Product Interest Report is to include sales leads interested in model 1500 and model 2000, the Product Interest field of the Retrieve Spec appears as follows:

```
Product Interest: &1500;2000
```

The entry must begin with an ampersand (&), and the keywords must be separated by semicolons (;). Do not put any spaces between the semicolons and the keyword entries.

Formatting Report Columns

After you organize the file information into a columnar report, you need to add formatting instructions on the Column/Sort Spec. With Q&A Report, you can do the following:

- Sort up to 16 columns in ascending or descending order
- Format and enhance the contents of a column
- Remove column breaks
- Insert page breaks
- Repeat a category
- Make columns "invisible"

Sorting Information

Although a maximum of two or three sort columns is common among some competing products, up to 16 column sorts, in ascending or descending order, can be specified with Q&A Report.

To specify a sorting order, you can enter codes in the Column/Sort Spec or the Derived Columns screen. If you want the column to be sorted in ascending order, enter the code *AS*; for a descending sort, enter *DS*. Entering the code for an ascending sort in the Lead Source field results in the forms being sorted in ascending order according to the first letter of the entry (see fig. 15.14). Note that the primary sort is the Product Interest field, which is the keyword field.

```
                    TITAN TECHNOLOGY SALES LEAD TRACKING SYSTEM
                                              ══════ File Name -- SlsLead
  LastName:                        FirstName:
  Title:
  Company:                         Telephone:
  Address1:
  Address2:
  City:                            State:          Zip:
     No. of Labs:                  Annual Revenue:
     Current Customer:             Company Priority:
  ──────────────────────────────LEAD INFORMATION──────────────────────────
     Product Interest: 1,K
     Request For:                  Lead Source: 10,AS
     Months to Purchase:           Product Priority:
  ────────────────────────────────SALES ACTION───────────────────────────
     Sales Priority:               Date Entered:
     Sales Dist.:                  Sales Manager:
     Salesman:                     Phone:
     Status:


  ──────────────────────────────────────────────────────────────────────
  SLSLEAD.DTF          Column/Sort Spec for Product Interest     Page 1 of 1

  Esc-Exit    F1-Help  F6-Expand  Shift+F6-Enhance  F8-Derived Cols  F10-Continue
```

Fig. 15.14.   The result of the sort specifications.

If you want to sort a derived column, press F8 to display the Derived Column screen. Type the column number after the Column Spec prompt, press the space bar, and type the correct code.

When all the sorting codes are entered, you can press F10 to print the report, or you can add other formatting specifications, as explained in the following sections.

Formatting Column Contents

When a report is generated, Q&A's default format settings do a good job of formatting your data. For example, text appears left-justified, numbers are right-justified, and money is displayed in a currency format. The date and time appear as they are entered in the database.

Although the default settings are fine for basic formatting, you may want to make some changes when creating a custom report design. Table 15.2 shows all the options available for specifying column formats.

Table 15.2.
The Options for Specifying Column Format

Symbol	Command	Meaning
JR	Justify Right	All data in the column is aligned on the right. This is the default for numbers and money.
JL	Justify Left	All data in the column is aligned on the left. This is the default for text.
JC	Justify Center	All data in the column is centered.
U	Uppercase	All text in the column is uppercase.
C	Comma	Numbers print with commas. Money values print with commas and currency symbols by default.
WC	Without Comma	Money values print without commas.
Dn	Date format n	n is a number from 1 to 20, standing for 20 different date formats.
Hn	Hour format n	n is a number from 1 to 3, standing for 3 different time formats.
TR	Truncate	Truncate data that does not fit in the column width instead of continuing the data on the next line of the column.
M	Money	Treat a number as money.
Nn	Number format n	n is a number from 1 to 7, representing up to 7 decimal places to a number. If x is not specified, Q&A determines how many decimal places to use based on its default.
T	Text	Treat a number as text.

To specify column formats, type the word *Format* (or press F) in the correct field, and enter the code in parentheses. For example, to sort the first column in ascending order and display the values in uppercase letters centered in the column, you enter the following:

    1,AS,FORMAT(U,JC)

If you run out of room as you type the specifications, press F6 (Expand) to expand the field.

Using Text Enhancements and Fonts

You can enhance report column headings, calculations, and sub-calculations with boldfaced, underlined, super- or subscripted, strikeout, or italic text, and with any fonts that your printer supports. To apply a character enhancement, do the following:

1. At the Column/Sort Spec, move the cursor to the code that represents the text or calculations you want to enhance.

   For example, to enhance totals generated by the following codes, highlight the T:

      Salaries:1,DS,T

2. Press Shift-F6 to display the Text Enhancement and Fonts menu.

3. Press B, U, P, S, I, X, or R to apply bold, underline, superscript, subscript, italics, strikeout, or regular (Roman) text. Pressing R removes any enhancements already in place and returns the default regular (Roman) type.

4. To apply a font, press key 1 through 8.

5. Press F10 to return to the Column/Sort Spec.

Before you can use fonts, you must install them. To assign fonts to items 1 through 8 on the Text Enhancements and Fonts menu, do the following:

1. Press A at the Text Enhancements and Fonts menu. Q&A displays a Font Assignment screen.

2. With the cursor in the Font file-name prompt, press Enter to display the list of printers you've installed for use with Q&A.

3. Move the cursor to a printer name and press F10. Q&A returns you to the Font Assignments screen.

4. Move the cursor to an empty line in the Font 1...8 section, and press F6 to display the List of Available Font Descriptions for the selected printer. Highlight a font and press F10 to assign it to Font 1...8. Press F10 to return to the Column/Sort Spec.

You also can apply enhancements to the labels of summary fields such as TOTAL, AVERAGE, COUNT, and so on. You need to enter special codes in the fields on the Column/Sort Spec for which you intend to use a summary function. To enhance a summary label, enter one or more of the following codes and apply an enhancement or font to the code as described above:

Code	Function
TL	Enhances the TOTAL label
AL	Enhances the AVERAGE label
CL	Enhances the COUNT label
MINL	Enhances the MIN label
MAXL	Enhances the MAX label
STDL	Enhances the STD label
VARL	Enhances the VAR label
HS	Enhances heading separator lines. You can specify a separator in parentheses: HS(-). Q&A uses the character to separate the heading from the column.
SL	Enhances the separator line when using subcalculations and column breaks. Place the separator line in parentheses: SL(_)
DL	Enhances the separator line when printing subcalculations

Setting Column Headings and Widths

The last step before printing is adjusting the column headings and widths. When you first design a report, Q&A uses the field labels as headings and determines column width based on data width. Report also centers the headings and spaces the columns.

To make adjustments for the fields you want to change, enter the column width and heading specifications on the Column/Sort screen (or after the Heading prompt on the Derived Columns screen, if you're printing a derived column). Be sure to separate the column width and the heading by entering a colon (:). Even if you don't indicate a new heading, a colon must follow the column width. For example, suppose that the field you are specifying is to be the first column, sorted in ascending order, assigned a column width of 6, and titled Labs. To make these settings, you enter the following:

    1,AS,HEADING(6:Labs)

Figure 15.15 illustrates a report before changes are made. The field names are used as column headings, the column widths are adapted to data or heading width, and the forms are not sorted.

```
                              No. of    Current    Company     Source
             Company           Labs     Customer   Priority   of Lead
   ..........................  ......   .........  .........   ........
   Mountain Labs                 3       Y            1        Mail
   Hope Laboratories, Inc.       2       N            2        Adv
   Plaines Medical Associates    4       N            1        Phone
   Hoosier Clinics, Inc.         3       Y            3        Adv
   Central Laboratories          1       N            2        Mail
   Indiana Medical, Inc.         4       N            1        Phone
   Mountain Labs                 2       N            1        Phone
   Advanced Medical Associates   3       Y            2        Phone
   Cherry Electronics, Inc.     20       Y            1        Adv
   Nashville Medical Technology  7       N            1        Adv
   Franklyn Lab Associates       5       N            2        Salesman
   Penn Medical Technology       3       Y            1        Phone
   Mattis Medical Laboratories   5       Y            3        Phone
   Washington Medical Labs, Inc  6       Y            3        Salesman
   University of Michigan        3       Y            2        Salesman
   Pike Pharmaceutical, Inc.     1       Y            1        Salesman
   Bay City Laboratories         1       Y            1        Mail
   Independent Medical Labs      3       Y            2        Adv
```

Fig. 15.15. *A report before changes are made on the Column/Sort Spec screen.*

Figure 15.16 shows the report after changes have been made in the No. of Labs field. That field is now the first column with the heading Labs. The column width (6) is slightly larger than the heading width, and the forms are sorted in ascending order.

```
                                        Current    Company     Source
   Labs            Company              Customer   Priority    of Lead
   ......   ..............................  ........  .........  ........
     1      Bay City Laboratories          Y           1        Mail
            Pike Pharmaceutical, Inc.      Y           1        Salesman
            Central Laboratories           N           2        Mail

     2      Hope Laboratories, Inc.        N           2        Adv
            Mountain Labs                  N           1        Phone

     3      University of Michigan         Y           2        Salesman
            Penn Medical Technology        Y           1        Phone
            Mountain Labs                  Y           1        Mail
            Independent Medical Labs       Y           2        Adv
            Advanced Medical Associates    Y           2        Phone
            Hoosier Clinics, Inc.          Y           3        Adv

     4      Indiana Medical, Inc.          N           1        Phone
            Plaines Medical Associates     N           1        Phone

     5      Franklyn Lab Associates        N           2        Salesman
            Mattis Medical Laboratories    Y           3        Phone

     6      Washington Medical Labs, Inc   Y           3        Salesman

     7      Nashville Medical Technology   N           1        Adv

    20      Cherry Electronics, Inc.       Y           1        Adv
```

Fig. 15.16. *The report after changes are made.*

After you make all the changes to the Column/Sort Spec, press F10 to display the Report Print Options screen. If you press F10 again, Q&A saves your design and asks whether you want to print the report.

Indenting Multiple-Line Fields

When a field contains more than one line on a data form, you can set how far to indent the second and subsequent lines of data when the data prints in a report. This is called a *hanging indent*. After the column width setting, type a number to specify the desired indentation. (Note that to indent text, you must specify a column width.) These settings apply only to fields of more than one line on the original form. For example, the following codes set the width of column 3 at 3". If data in the column is wider than 3", the second and subsequent lines are indented 1".

   Part Description:3,H(3":1":Part!Description)

You also can tell Q&A whether to split long records across a page break or move the entire contents of the record to the next page. See Chapter 16 for more information on printing a report.

Removing Column Breaks

Q&A automatically inserts blank lines, called *column breaks,* when the value changes in a sorted column. For example, a blank line is inserted when the Company value in figure 15.13 changes. You can remove these column breaks by entering the cancel subcalculation code (CS).

Figure 15.17 shows the printout that results from placing the cancel subcalculation code in the Company field. Column breaks still appear in the Lead Source field. To eliminate these, add an additional CS code in the Lead Source field.

Inserting Page Breaks

To make your form easier to read, you can designate column breaks that cause a new page to be printed every time a column break occurs. Just enter the page-break code (P) in the appropriate field. This code causes a new page to be started when values in the field change. The header and the column headings are reprinted at the top of each page.

```
                      Source
                      of Lead      Company
  Product Interest    ........     ..........................
  ................
  1000                Mail         Bay City Laboratories

                      Phone        Indiana Medical, Inc.
                                   Mountain Labs

                      Salesman     University of Michigan

  1200                Phone        Advanced Medical Associates
                                   Penn Medical Technology
                                   Plaines Medical Associates

                      Salesman     Franklyn Lab Associates

  1500                Adv          Cherry Electronics, Inc.
                                   Hope Laboratories, Inc.
                                   Independent Medical Labs

                      Mail         Mountain Labs

                      Phone        Mountain Labs
                                   Penn Medical Technology

                      Salesman     Franklyn Lab Associates
                                   Pike Pharmaceutical, Inc.
                                   Washington Medical Labs, Inc

  2000                Adv          Cherry Electronics, Inc.
                                   Nashville Medical Technology

                      Mail         Bay City Laboratories
                                   Central Laboratories
                                   Mountain Labs

                      Phone        Advanced Medical Associates
                                   Mattis Medical Laboratories
                                   Plaines Medical Associates

                      Salesman     Pike Pharmaceutical, Inc.
                                   University of Michigan

  2500                Adv          Hoosier Clinics, Inc.
                                   Hope Laboratories, Inc.
                                   Independent Medical Labs

                      Phone        Mattis Medical Laboratories

                      Salesman     Washington Medical Labs, Inc
```

Fig. 15.17.   *A printout with fewer column breaks.*

Repeating Values

When a sorted column is displayed in report form, the value in the sorted column usually is displayed only once. In the example in figure 15.16, Q&A displays the value for the first entry only, even though the Product Interest model number 1500 applies to both companies. By entering the repeat value code (R) in the Column/Sort Spec, you can tell Q&A to print the value for each form.

```
                 TITAN TECHNOLOGY SALES LEAD TRACKING SYSTEM
                                                    File Name -- SlsLead
  LastName:                            FirstName:
  Title:
  Company: 20,CS                       Telephone:
  Address1:
  Address2:
  City:                                State:        Zip:
     No. of Labs:                      Annual Revenue:
     Current Customer:                 Company Priority:
                             LEAD INFORMATION
     Product Interest: 1,K,R
     Request For:                      Lead Source: 10,AS,R
     Months to Purchase:               Product Priority:
                              SALES ACTION
     Sales Priority:                   Date Entered:
     Sales Dist.:                      Sales Manager:
     Salesman:                         Phone:
     Status:


  SLSLEAD.DTF          Column/Sort Spec for Product Interest     Page 1  of 1

  Esc-Exit    F1-Help  F6-Expand  Shift+F6-Enhance  F8-Derived Cols  F10-Continue
```

Fig. 15. 18.   *Entering the repeat-values code.*

In figure 15.19, the repeat value code has been entered in the Product Interest and the Lead Source fields. Figure 15.18 shows the effect of the codes.

Making a Column Invisible

You may need to hide certain columns because they contain confidential information or because you need to reduce the width of a report. Even though these columns do not appear when displayed on-screen or when printed, you still can reference the columns in a formula that returns data in another column. These hidden, or invisible, columns can be used to produce a page break.

To create an invisible column, enter the code *I* in the appropriate field of the Column/Sort Spec. If the fields are numbered, type a comma before entering the code. Figure 15.20 shows the result of designating the Annual Revenue field as an invisible column. The field's contents are used in the Revenue per Lab derived-column formula, but do not appear in the printout.

```
                     Source
     Product Interest of Lead        Company
     ................ ........  ..........................
          1000         Mail      Bay City Laboratories

          1000         Phone     Indiana Medical, Inc.
          1000                   Mountain Labs

          1000         Salesman  University of Michigan

          1200         Phone     Advanced Medical Associates
          1200                   Penn Medical Technology
          1200                   Plaines Medical Associates

          1200         Salesman  Franklyn Lab Associates

          1500         Adv       Cherry Electronics, Inc.
          1500                   Hope Laboratories, Inc.
          1500                   Independent Medical Labs

          1500         Mail      Mountain Labs

          1500         Phone     Mountain Labs
          1500                   Penn Medical Technology

          1500         Salesman  Franklyn Lab Associates
          1500                   Pike Pharmaceutical, Inc.
          1500                   Washington Medical Labs, Inc

          2000         Adv       Cherry Electronics, Inc.
          2000                   Nashville Medical Technology

          2000         Mail      Bay City Laboratories
          2000                   Central Laboratories
          2000                   Mountain Labs

          2000         Phone     Advanced Medical Associates
          2000                   Mattis Medical Laboratories
          2000                   Plaines Medical Associates

          2000         Salesman  Pike Pharmaceutical, Inc.
          2000                   University of Michigan
```

Fig. 15.19. *Repeating values in a report.*

Company	No. of Labs	Revenue Per Lab	Sales Priority	Sales Dist.
Mountain Labs	3	$1,792,889.00	Hot	Denver
Hope Laboratories, Inc.	2	$250,000.00	1.0	Mobile
Plaines Medical Associates	4	$187,500.00	Hot	South Dakota
Hoosier Clinics, Inc.	3	$33,333.33	2.0	Indiana
Central Laboratories	1	$50,000.00	1.0	Indiana
Indiana Medical, Inc.	4	$31,250.00	2.0	Indiana
Mountain Labs	2	$50,105.00	1.0	Denver
Advanced Medical Associates	3	$1,766,874.33	1.0	Knoxville
Cherry Electronics, Inc.	20	$200,000.00	1.0	Los Angeles
Nashville Medical Technology	7	$1,142,910.71	1.0	Cincinnati
Franklyn Lab Associates	5	$1,291,200.00	1.5	Philadelphia
Penn Medical Technology	3	$16,666.67	1.0	Philadelphia
Mattis Medical Laboratories	5	$200,042.00	1.5	Atlanta
Washington Medical Labs, Inc	6	$33,416.67	2.0	Seattle
University of Michigan	3	$108,333.33	1.5	Detroit
Pike Pharmaceutical, Inc.	1	$210,000.00	1.5	Philadelphia
Bay City Laboratories	1	$150,250.00	1.5	Michigan
Independent Medical Labs	3	$74,500.00	Hot	Missouri

Fig. 15.20. *A report with an invisible column.*

Specifying Calculated Columns

Calculations on text and numerical columns can be produced automatically with Report. By specifying the correct codes on the Column/Sort Spec or the Derived Columns screen, you can do the following:

- Calculate all columns (text and numerical)
- Perform full-column and subcolumn calculations
- Perform more than one calculation on a column
- Combine calculations on various columns

To calculate a column, move the cursor to the correct field and type the calculation code (see table 15.3). Be sure to separate codes with a space or comma.

Table 15.3.
Calculation Operators

Code	Calculation
T	Totals numerical columns
A	Averages numerical columns
C	Counts numerical or text values
MIN	Finds minimum numerical values
MAX	Finds maximum numerical values
ST	Subtotals numerical columns
SA	Subaverages numerical columns
SC	Subcounts numerical and text values
SMIN	Finds subminimum values in numerical columns
SMAX	Finds submaximum values in numerical columns
SSTD	Finds standard deviation for column segment
SVAR	Finds variance for column segment

The last seven calculations are used to determine intermediate results. The answers for these calculations are displayed at column breaks.

Calculating the Entire Column

When you perform a calculation on a column, every entry in that column is affected. Figure 15.21 shows that when you enter the Total code (T) in the No. of Labs and Annual Revenue fields, the columns are added and the sum is displayed at the bottom of the column.

Product Interest	Company	No. of Labs	Annual Revenue	Revenue Per Lab
1000	University of Michigan	3	$325000.00	$108,333.33
	Bay City Laboratories	1	$150250.00	$150,250.00
	Mountain Labs	2	$100210.00	$50,105.00
	Indiana Medical, Inc.	4	$125000.00	$31,250.00
1200	Franklyn Lab Associates	5	$6456000.00	$1,291,200.00
	Advanced Medical Associates	3	$5300623.00	$1,766,874.33
	Penn Medical Technology	3	$50000.00	$16,666.67
	Plaines Medical Associates	4	$750000.00	$187,500.00
1500	Washington Medical Labs, Inc	6	$200500.00	$33,416.67
	Pike Pharmaceutical, Inc.	1	$210000.00	$210,000.00
	Penn Medical Technology	3	$50000.00	$16,666.67
	Independent Medical Labs	3	$223500.00	$74,500.00
	Franklyn Lab Associates	5	$6456000.00	$1,291,200.00
	Mountain Labs	3	$5378667.00	$1,792,889.00
	Cherry Electronics, Inc.	20	$4000000.00	$200,000.00
	Hope Laboratories, Inc.	2	$500000.00	$250,000.00
	Mountain Labs	2	$100210.00	$50,105.00
2000	Central Laboratories	1	$50000.00	$50,000.00
	Plaines Medical Associates	4	$750000.00	$187,500.00
	University of Michigan	3	$325000.00	$108,333.33
	Nashville Medical Technology	7	$8000375.00	$1,142,910.71
	Bay City Laboratories	1	$150250.00	$150,250.00
	Cherry Electronics, Inc.	20	$4000000.00	$200,000.00
	Mattis Medical Laboratories	5	$1000210.00	$200,042.00
	Advanced Medical Associates	3	$5300623.00	$1,766,874.33
	Mountain Labs	3	$5378667.00	$1,792,889.00
	Pike Pharmaceutical, Inc.	1	$210000.00	$210,000.00
2500	Independent Medical Labs	3	$223500.00	$74,500.00
	Washington Medical Labs, Inc	6	$200500.00	$33,416.67
	Hope Laboratories, Inc.	2	$500000.00	$250,000.00
	Hoosier Clinics, Inc.	3	$100000.00	$33,333.33
	Mattis Medical Laboratories	5	$1000210.00	$200,042.00
Total:		137	$57565295.00	

Fig. 15.21.   *Totals in entire-column calculations.*

Note that Report prints a double line under the columns, the name of the calculation (Total) in the left column, and the result of the calculation. The result is printed in the same format as the column.

You also have the option of mixing and matching calculations and columns. In figure 15.22, the columns and their calculations include the following:

Column	Calculation performed
Company	Count
No. of Lab	Total, Count, Average
Annual Revenue	Total, Average, Minimum, Maximum

Product Interest	Company	No. of Labs	Annual Revenue	Revenue Per Lab
················	·····························	······	···············	·············
1000	University of Michigan	3.00	$325000.00	$108,333.33
	Bay City Laboratories	1.00	$150250.00	$150,250.00
	Mountain Labs	2.00	$100210.00	$50,105.00
	Indiana Medical, Inc.	4.00	$125000.00	$31,250.00
1200	Franklyn Lab Associates	5.00	$6456000.00	$1,291,200.00
	Advanced Medical Associates	3.00	$5300623.00	$1,766,874.33
	Penn Medical Technology	3.00	$50000.00	$16,666.67
	Plaines Medical Associates	4.00	$750000.00	$187,500.00
1500	Washington Medical Labs, Inc	6.00	$200500.00	$33,416.67
	Pike Pharmaceutical, Inc.	1.00	$210000.00	$210,000.00
	Penn Medical Technology	3.00	$50000.00	$16,666.67
	Independent Medical Labs	3.00	$223500.00	$74,500.00
	Franklyn Lab Associates	5.00	$6456000.00	$1,291,200.00
	Mountain Labs	3.00	$5378667.00	$1,792,889.00
	Cherry Electronics, Inc.	20.00	$4000000.00	$200,000.00
	Hope Laboratories, Inc.	2.00	$500000.00	$250,000.00
	Mountain Labs	2.00	$100210.00	$50,105.00
2000	Central Laboratories	1.00	$50000.00	$50,000.00
	Plaines Medical Associates	4.00	$750000.00	$187,500.00
	University of Michigan	3.00	$325000.00	$108,333.33
	Nashville Medical Technology	7.00	$8000375.00	$1,142,910.71
	Bay City Laboratories	1.00	$150250.00	$150,250.00
	Cherry Electronics, Inc.	20.00	$4000000.00	$200,000.00
	Mattis Medical Laboratories	5.00	$1000210.00	$200,042.00
	Advanced Medical Associates	3.00	$5300623.00	$1,766,874.33
	Mountain Labs	3.00	$5378667.00	$1,792,889.00
	Pike Pharmaceutical, Inc.	1.00	$210000.00	$210,000.00
2500	Independent Medical Labs	3.00	$223500.00	$74,500.00
	Washington Medical Labs, Inc	6.00	$200500.00	$33,416.67
	Hope Laboratories, Inc.	2.00	$500000.00	$250,000.00
	Hoosier Clinics, Inc.	3.00	$100000.00	$33,333.33
	Mattis Medical Laboratories	5.00	$1000210.00	$200,042.00
================	=============================	======	==============	=============
Total:		137.00	$57565295.00	
Average:		4.28	$1798915.47	
Count:	32	32		
Maximum:			$8000375.00	
Minimum:			$50000.00	

Fig. 15.22. *A variety of entire-column calculations.*

Subcalculations in a Column

Report also produces subcalculations at the column breaks in a column. Enter your choice of the subcalculation codes listed in table 15.3.

The effect of a subcalculation is different from an entire column calculation, as in figures 15.23 and 15.24. The subcount calculations appear at every column break; the calculation name is repeated in the left column, and a line is drawn in the columns with a subcalculation.

```
              TITAN TECHNOLOGY SALES LEAD TRACKING SYSTEM
         ═══════════════════════════════════════ File Name -- SlsLead
  LastName:                          FirstName:
  Title:
  Company: 20,C,SC
  Address1:                          Telephone:
  Address2:
  City:                              State:        Zip:
     No. of Labs: 20,T,C,A→          Annual Revenue: 30,T,A,MAX,MIN
     Current Customer:               Company Priority:
                       ─LEAD INFORMATION─
```

Fig. 15.23.   *Entering subcalculaton codes.*

| | | No. of | | Revenue |
Product Interest	Company	Labs	Annual Revenue	Per Lab
1000	University of Michigan	3.00	$325000.00	$108,333.33
	Bay City Laboratories	1.00	$150250.00	$150,250.00
	Mountain Labs	2.00	$100210.00	$50,105.00
	Indiana Medical, Inc.	4.00	$125000.00	$31,250.00
Count:		4	4	
1200	Franklyn Lab Associates	5.00	$6456000.00	$1,291,200.00
	Advanced Medical Associates	3.00	$5300623.00	$1,766,874.33
	Penn Medical Technology	3.00	$50000.00	$16,666.67
	Plaines Medical Associates	4.00	$750000.00	$187,500.00
Count:		4	4	
1500	Washington Medical Labs, Inc	6.00	$200500.00	$33,416.67
	Pike Pharmaceutical, Inc.	1.00	$210000.00	$210,000.00
	Penn Medical Technology	3.00	$50000.00	$16,666.67
	Independent Medical Labs	3.00	$223500.00	$74,500.00
	Franklyn Lab Associates	5.00	$6456000.00	$1,291,200.00
	Mountain Labs	3.00	$5378667.00	$1,792,889.00
	Cherry Electronics, Inc.	20.00	$4000000.00	$200,000.00
	Hope Laboratories, Inc.	2.00	$500000.00	$250,000.00
	Mountain Labs	2.00	$100210.00	$50,105.00
Count:		9	9	
2000	Central Laboratories	1.00	$50000.00	$50,000.00
	Plaines Medical Associates	4.00	$750000.00	$187,500.00
	University of Michigan	3.00	$325000.00	$108,333.33
	Nashville Medical Technology	7.00	$8000375.00	$1,142,910.71
	Bay City Laboratories	1.00	$150250.00	$150,250.00
	Cherry Electronics, Inc.	20.00	$4000000.00	$200,000.00
	Mattis Medical Laboratories	5.00	$1000210.00	$200,042.00
	Advanced Medical Associates	3.00	$5300623.00	$1,766,874.33
	Mountain Labs	3.00	$5378667.00	$1,792,889.00
	Pike Pharmaceutical, Inc.	1.00	$210000.00	$210,000.00
Count:		10	10	
2500	Independent Medical Labs	3.00	$223500.00	$74,500.00
	Washington Medical Labs, Inc	6.00	$200500.00	$33,416.67
	Hope Laboratories, Inc.	2.00	$500000.00	$250,000.00
	Hoosier Clinics, Inc.	3.00	$100000.00	$33,333.33
	Mattis Medical Laboratories	5.00	$1000210.00	$200,042.00
Count:		5	5	
Total:		137.00	$57565295.00	
Average:		4.28	$1798915.47	
Count:	32	32		
Maximum:			$8000375.00	
Minimum:			$50000.00	

Fig. 15.24.   *A variety of subcalculations.*

Canceling Subcalculations

In some report designs, a subcalculation code can create too many column breaks and cause too many subcalculations (see fig. 15.25). This happens when a sorted column creates breaks every time the value in the column changes.

To eliminate this problem and make the form easier to read, cancel the subcalculation in the sorted column by entering the cancel subcalculation code (CS) in the Column/Sort Spec (see figs. 15.26 and 15.27).

Breaking on Year, Month, or Day

If you want to organize your report by year, month, or day, you can use Q&A Report to divide the pages. To do this, you enter the following codes:

Code	Meaning
YB	Yearly Break
MB	Monthly Break
DB	Daily Break

If you want a field to be displayed in the second column, sorted in descending order and divided by month and year, for example, you enter the following:

2,DS,MB,YB

These levels of break control also function with @ functions such as @TOTAL. For additional detail, see "Using Summary Functions in Derived Columns," earlier in this chapter (see also table 15.1).

Breaking on Alphabetic Change

You also can create a break when the first character of a sorted field changes. Unlike a break on field value, the alphabetic break occurs on only one letter. This feature is useful for printing lists such as telephone directories, bibliographies, or indexes.

To achieve an alphabetic break, insert the code AB in the appropriate field in the Column/Sort Spec screen. If field 1 is the last name field in a file, for example, you can cause a break whenever the first letter in the last names changes. Enter the following code:

1,AB

```
                       Source
                       of Lead         Company
        Product Interest
        ................    ........    ...........................
        1000           Mail        Bay City Laboratories
                                   ...........................
                       Count:                              1

                       Phone       Indiana Medical, Inc.

                                   Mountain Labs
                                   ...........................
                       Count:                              2

                       Salesman    University of Michigan
                                   ...........................
                       Count:                              1


                                   ...........................
        Count:                                             4

        1200           Phone       Advanced Medical Associates

                                   Penn Medical Technology

                                   Plaines Medical Associates
                                   ...........................
                       Count:                              3

                       Salesman    Franklyn Lab Associates
                                   ...........................
                       Count:                              1


                                   ...........................
        Count:                                             4

        1500           Adv         Cherry Electronics, Inc.

                                   Hope Laboratories, Inc.

                                   Independent Medical Labs
                                   ...........................
                       Count:                              3

                       Mail        Mountain Labs
                                   ...........................
                       Count:                              1

                       Phone       Mountain Labs

                                   Penn Medical Technology
                                   ...........................
                       Count:                              2

                       Salesman    Franklyn Lab Associates
```

Fig. 15.25. A subcalculation on a sorted column.

```
         TITAN TECHNOLOGY SALES LEAD TRACKING SYSTEM
                                        File Name -- SlsLead
LastName:                       FirstName:
Title:
Company: 10,C,SC,AS,CS          Telephone:
Address1:
Address2:
City:                           State:        Zip:
  No. of Labs: 20,T,C,A→        Annual Revenue: 30,T,A,MAX,MIN
  Current Customer:             Company Priority:
                      LEAD INFORMATION
```

Fig. 15.26. *Entering the cancel subcalculation code.*

```
                        Source
                        of Lead      Company
Product Interest
................      ........    ..............................
1000                    Mail      Bay City Laboratories
                        Phone     Indiana Medical, Inc.
                                  Mountain Labs
                        Salesman  University of Michigan
                                  ..............................
Count:                                                        4

1200                    Phone     Advanced Medical Associates
                                  Penn Medical Technology
                                  Plaines Medical Associates
                        Salesman  Franklyn Lab Associates
                                  ..............................
Count:                                                        4

1500                    Adv       Cherry Electronics, Inc.
                                  Hope Laboratories, Inc.
                                  Independent Medical Labs
                        Mail      Mountain Labs
                        Phone.    Mountain Labs
                                  Penn Medical Technology
                        Salesman  Franklyn Lab Associates
                                  Pike Pharmaceutical, Inc.
                                  Washington Medical Labs, Inc
                                  ..............................
Count:                                                        9

2000                    Adv       Cherry Electronics, Inc.
                                  Nashville Medical Technology
                        Mail      Bay City Laboratories
                                  Central Laboratories
                                  Mountain Labs
                        Phone     Advanced Medical Associates
                                  Mattis Medical Laboratories
                                  Plaines Medical Associates
                        Salesman  Pike Pharmaceutical, Inc.
                                  University of Michigan
                                  ..............................
Count:                                                       10

2500                    Adv       Hoosier Clinics, Inc.
                                  Hope Laboratories, Inc.
                                  Independent Medical Labs
                        Phone     Mattis Medical Laboratories
                        Salesman  Washington Medical Labs, Inc
                                  ..............................
Count:                                                        5
```

Fig. 15.27. *A canceled subcalculation on a sorted column.*

Redesigning a Report

To edit the original design of an existing report, select Design/Redesign a Report from the Report menu, and enter the name of the file you want to edit. (If you don't remember the name, you can press Enter and select the file from the list of data files displayed.) Follow the basic procedure for designing a report, as explained in the previous sections.

Setting Columnar Global Options

Up to this point, you have designed the report by entering specifications on a blank screen. If you use some of the same settings repeatedly, you can make them the default value to avoid entering the settings every time you enter report specifications. These default values are called *global options*.

Choose Set Global Options from the Report menu and press C at the Global Options Screen to display the Columnar Global Options menu. From this menu, you can set all default options except the options on the Retrieve Spec.

Setting Global Default Column Widths and Headings

The first global default you can set is column widths and headings. Choose C from the Columnar Global Options menu to display the Column Headings/ Width Spec screen.

The Column Headings/Width Spec is similar to the Column/Sort Spec. You can move from field to field on this Spec screen to enter the column width and column heading, separated by a colon (:), but you don't need to enclose the width and heading in parentheses or enter the word *heading*.

After you enter changes, press F10, and the Columnar Global Options screen is displayed. The new settings apply to all reports in the database, including reports generated by the Intelligent Assistant.

Setting Global Format Options

To set the global format options for all report designs, select Set Format Options from the Columnar Global Options screen. The screen in figure 15.28 is displayed.

Use the up- and down-arrow keys to move through the options and the right- and left-arrow keys to set each choice. You can specify the number of spaces (up to 9) to be inserted between columns, or you can keep the variable setting so that Q&A makes the determination. The default value is 5 spaces, but the program may choose fewer if the area is limited.

Other settings on this screen are for repeating values, printing blank values, and inserting blank space between column breaks.

As explained previously, if a value is repeated in a column, Q&A prints only the value's first occurrence. With the global default options, however, you can have the program print the repeated values. Select Yes in the Default to Repeating Values field on the Repeat Global Format Options screen.

If a number or money field has no data, the Report module is preset to enter a zero (0) in that position. If you prefer a blank to a zero, select Leave Blank on the Action on Blank Value line.

You can elect not to skip a line after a column break by choosing Don't Skip Line on the Action on Column Break line. The default is set to skip one line at each column break.

Setting Global Page Options

Your printer and the paper you use have particular characteristics that you need to specify. If you repeatedly use the same paper size, you can set a default value for your page settings. To do this, choose D for Set Page Options at the Columnar Global Options menu and make selections on the Define Page screen (see fig. 15.29).

Page width is the number of characters that can fit on one page of paper; page length is the number of lines on the page. The standard page length is 66 lines. You also can set the left and right margins for printing.

Although the number of lines allowed for top and bottom margins is fixed at three (three lines for the header and three lines for the footer), you can increase the margins. The Characters per Inch setting controls the number of printed characters per inch by determining the size of the characters. The choice you make for this option depends on your database and the reports you intend to produce.

Setting Global Print Options

Before you print the report, press P to choose Set Print Options from the Columnar Global Options menu. You can use the Report Print Options screen to specify printer settings (see fig. 15.30). You need to specify the printer port and type of paper feed you will use. If you want to have the report printed to the screen as a default, you can specify this by selecting SCREEN after the Print To option. You can choose to display a print preview of the report by default, and you also can specify printer offset and set printer control codes. The Print Totals Only option on this screen enables you to print the entire report or the calculated totals only. The last three options tell Q&A how to justify the report body, whether to use single or double line spacing, and whether to split long records across a page break or move them to the next page.

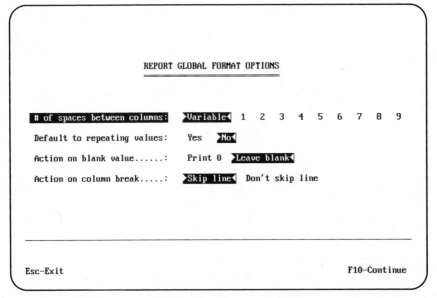

Fig. 15.28. The Report Global Format Options screen.

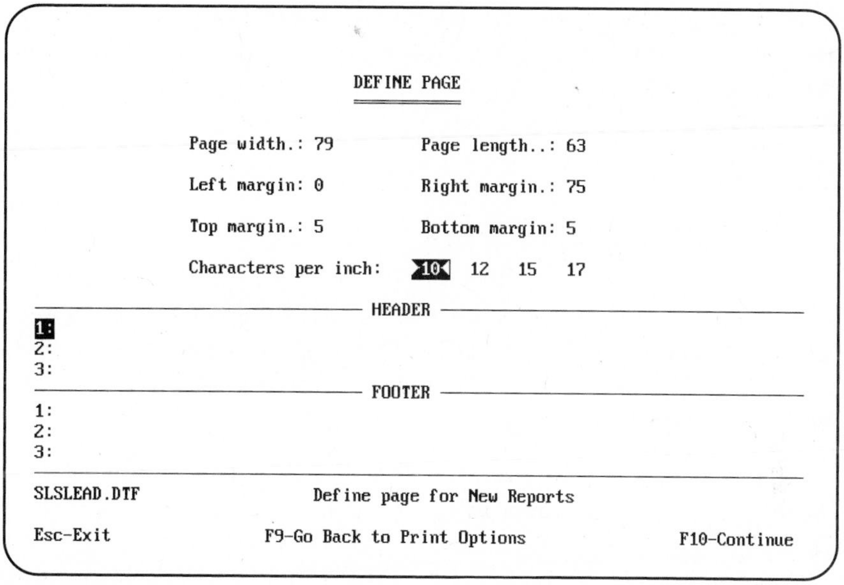

```
                          DEFINE PAGE
                          ==========

           Page width.: 79        Page length..: 63

           Left margin: 0         Right margin.: 75

           Top margin.: 5         Bottom margin: 5

           Characters per inch:    ▓10▓  12   15   17
  ───────────────────────── HEADER ─────────────────────────
 ▓1▓
  2:
  3:
  ───────────────────────── FOOTER ─────────────────────────
  1:
  2:
  3:
  ──────────────────────────────────────────────────────────
  SLSLEAD.DTF              Define page for New Reports

  Esc-Exit            F9-Go Back to Print Options        F10-Continue
```

Fig. 15.29.   *The Define Page screen.*

If you use more than one printer, be sure to set the printer option to match the printer you use most often. Figure 15.30, for example, shows the printer setting as LPT2. With this option, Q&A sends report output to the LPT2 printer unless you override the global setting temporarily when printing a specific report, or permanently by changing the appropriate global option.

You can set up your printer for special fonts or printing modes by inserting the proper codes on the Printer Control Codes line. See Chapter 16 for details on printing your report after it has been defined.

Renaming, Deleting, and Copying a Report

The Rename/Delete/Copy option in the Report menu can be used to manipulate existing reports. Rename changes only the report's name; Delete erases the report, and Copy duplicates the report. You can use Copy to create a report that is similar to an existing one. Just copy the report, then redesign and rename the report.

To rename a report, select Rename/Delete/Copy from the Report menu. When the File Name prompt is displayed, enter the name of the file or select the name from the list of data files. The following options are displayed:

R - Rename a Report
D - Delete a Report
C - Copy a Report

After you select Rename a Report, enter the name of the report you want to rename. At the Rename To prompt, press enter to see a list of the reports you have designed for the selected file, or enter a new name of up to 20 characters. Report returns you to the Rename/Delete/Copy menu after you press Enter.

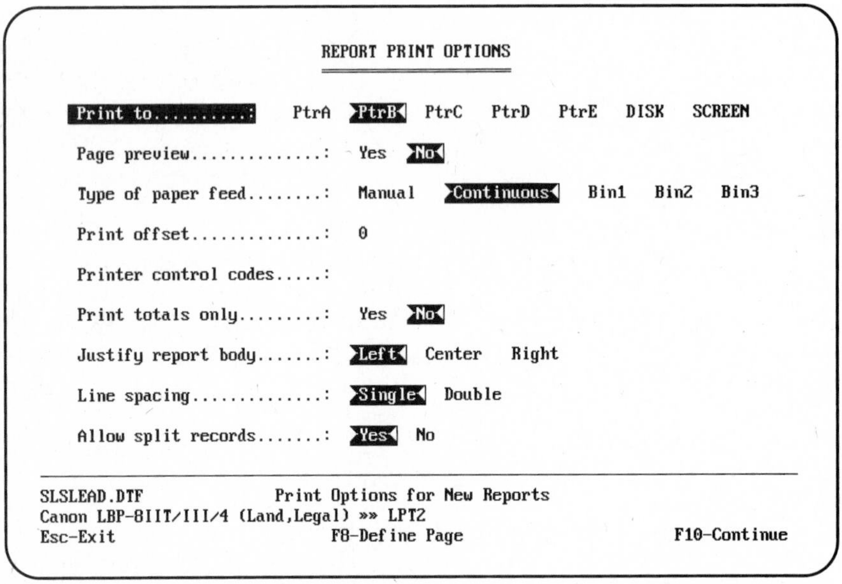

```
                      REPORT PRINT OPTIONS


   Print to.........:    PtrA  >PtrB<  PtrC   PtrD   PtrE   DISK   SCREEN

   Page preview.............:   Yes  >No<

   Type of paper feed........:   Manual  >Continuous<   Bin1   Bin2   Bin3

   Print offset..............:   0

   Printer control codes.....:

   Print totals only.........:   Yes  >No<

   Justify report body.......:  >Left<  Center   Right

   Line spacing..............:  >Single<  Double

   Allow split records.......:  >Yes<  No

   SLSLEAD.DTF           Print Options for New Reports
   Canon LBP-8IIT/III/4 (Land,Legal) »» LPT2
   Esc-Exit              F8-Define Page              F10-Continue
```

Fig. 15.30.   The Report Print Options screen.

To delete a report, select the appropriate option, enter the name of the report, and press Enter. Q&A displays a warning message that asks you to confirm the operation. If you press Y, the report is deleted; if you press N, the operation is canceled.

Copying a report is similar. Select Copy a Report, and enter the name of the report you want to copy at the Copy From prompt. At the Copy To prompt, enter the name of the new report.

After you press Enter, you are returned to the Rename/Delete/Copy menu.

Cross-Tab versus Columnar Reports

Standard, columnar reports provide a certain amount of insight into your business by displaying totals, subtotals, and calculated fields based on your data. But cross-tab reports help you look more deeply into the relationships contained in your database files.

Every cross-tab report draws data from three fields in a database. A visual example makes this easier to understand. Figure 15.31 shows how the relationships between three fields are displayed in a cross-tab report.

In the Titan Technology sales lead tracking system used throughout this chapter, suppose that you want to review the relationship between data in the Sales Dist., Lead Source, and Annual Revenue fields. A cross-tab report based on these fields displays sales district data in columns and lead source data in rows. In the report, sales and leads are related on the basis of annual revenue.

Q&A totals the annual revenue figures for forms with *Print* in the Lead Source field and *East* in the district field, then moves on to the next district. When all the districts are totaled for advertising lead source, the report goes on to the next row and calculates cross-tab data for the next lead source, *Phone*. A cross-tab report sheds light on the results of advertising expenditures in each sales district..

| Lead Source | Sales Dist. | | | | |
	East	Midwest	South	West	This Year
Print	$45,000	$35,000	$15,000	$80,000	$175,000
Phone	$5,000	$9,000	$2,000	$3,000	$19,000
Radio	$50,000	$115,000	$95,000	$140,000	$400,000
TV	$500,000	$85,000	$100,000	$525,000	$1,210,000
This Year	$600,000	$244,000	$212,000	$748,000	$1,804,000

Fig. 15.31.   *Sample cross-tab report*

Designing a Cross-Tab Report

To design a cross-tab report, first choose three fields in your database for which you want to examine subtle relationships. Cross-tab reports may contain calculations, a derived column and/or many derived fields, and may make use of text enhancements and fonts.

To design a cross-tab report, follow this procedure:

1. Choose Report at the Main menu, then Design/Redesign Report at the Report menu. Q&A asks for a file name.

2. Type the name of a file, or press Shift-F4 to delete the field and press Enter to select a file from the list of data files.

   As with columnar reports, cross-tab report names may contain up to 30 characters. Because columnar and cross-tab reports are not distinguished in the List of Reports in Database, you should give your cross-tab reports distinctive names—for example, "Xtab district sales by lead source."

3. If you enter a new report name, Q&A asks whether you want to create a columnar or cross-tab report. Choose X to select Crosstab Report (see fig. 15.32).

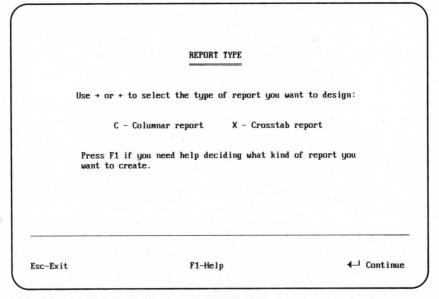

```
                        REPORT TYPE


        Use → or ← to select the type of report you want to design:


            C - Columnar report      X - Crosstab report


        Press F1 if you need help deciding what kind of report you
        want to create.




  _____


   Esc-Exit                  F1-Help                 ↵ Continue
```

Fig. 15.32. *Choose Columnar or Crosstab Report screen.*

4. The Retrieve Spec appears. This is the same Retrieve Spec used in the File module. Press F1 (Help) to display a list of retrieval codes.

    After filling in the Retrieve Spec, you can name the Spec and save it for later use by pressing Shift-F8 and typing a name at the prompt. To recall a stored Retrieve Spec, press Alt-F8, highlight a file's name, and press Enter.

5. Press F10 to display the Crosstab Spec.

The Crosstab Spec tells Q&A which columns to display in the report (see fig. 15.33). In the Crosstab Spec, you also can specify calculated and derived fields, field groupings to make the printout more readable, and character and label enhancements and fonts.

```
                    TITAN TECHNOLOGY SALES LEAD TRACKING SYSTEM
 ================================================================ File Name -- SlsLead
 LastName:                              FirstName:
 Title:
 Company: ROW                           Telephone:
 Address1:
 Address2:
 City:                                  State:            Zip:
    No. of Labs:                        Annual Revenue: SUM
    Current Customer:                   Company Priority:
 ────────────────────────────────LEAD INFORMATION────────────────────────
    Product Interest:
    Request For:                        Lead Source:
    Months to Purchase:                 Product Priority:
 ────────────────────────────────SALES ACTION───────────────────────────
    Sales Priority:                     Date Entered:
    Sales Dist.: COL                    Sales Manager:
    Salesman:                           Phone:
    Status:


 ───────────────────────────────────────────────────────────────────────
 SLSLEAD.DTF              Crosstab Spec for (NEW)              Page 1  of 1

 Esc-Exit   F1-Help   F6-Expand   F7-Groups   F8-Derived fields   F10-Continue
```

Fig. 15.33. *The Crosstab Spec.*

In the Crosstab Spec, you must specify a column field, a row field, and a summary field. You can optionally specify a summary calculation, formatting instructions, alternate headings, and a scale factor (to display thousands as 1,2,3, and so on, for example). A cross-tab report may contain just one row, column, and summary field, including one derived field.

Type the following cross-tab codes into the fields to be included in the report:

COL	Specifies column field
ROW	Specifies row field
SUM	Specifies summary field

Note that you can name the same field as a summary and row or column field. Type *COL,SUM* or *ROW,SUM* in the field. You also can suppress the display of the summary column, summary row, or both, by typing *NS* in the ROW or COL fields, separated from the other codes by a comma.

If you're using a key field as part of a cross-tab report, you should specify the key field as the row field because Q&A automatically groups the data in a key field, but only if the key field is named as a row.

Using Calculations in a Cross-Tab Report

Q&A can perform calculations on data before displaying the data in a cross-tab report. You can have columns that contain total, average, minimum, maximum, count, standard deviation, and variance. Even if you don't specify any of these summary calculations, however, Q&A uses the following defaults in a cross-tab report:

Data type	Default calculation
Text	Count
Number	Total
Money	Total
Keyword	Count
Date	Count
Hours	Count
Yes/No	Count

The following codes are used to specify summary calculations:

Code	Command	Meaning
T	Total	Prints total of cell values
A	Average	Prints average of cell values
C	Count	Prints count of values in cell
MIN	Minimum	Prints the minimum value in a cell

Code	Command	Meaning
MAX	Maximum	Prints the maximum value in a cell
STD	Standard	Prints the standard deviation from deviation the mean value of the values in the cells
VAR	Variance	Prints the variance of the values in the cells

You can specify more than one summary calculation for the summary field, as shown in Figure 15.34. For example, SUMMARY,C,A displays a count and average in the summary area of the report.

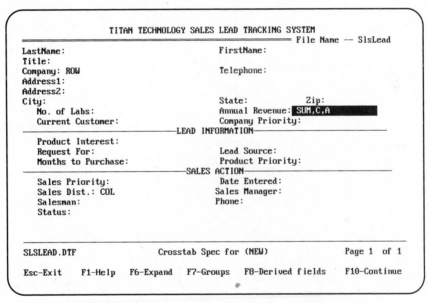

```
                    TITAN TECHNOLOGY SALES LEAD TRACKING SYSTEM
                    ═══════════════════════════════════════════ File Name -- SlsLead
LastName:                                FirstName:
Title:
Company: ROW                            Telephone:
Address1:
Address2:
City:                                   State:        Zip:
    No. of Labs:                        Annual Revenue: SUM,C,A
    Current Customer:                   Company Priority:
                              ─LEAD INFORMATION─
    Product Interest:
    Request For:                        Lead Source:
    Months to Purchase:                 Product Priority:
                              ─SALES ACTION─
    Sales Priority:                     Date Entered:
    Sales Dist.: COL                    Sales Manager:
    Salesman:                           Phone:
    Status:



SLSLEAD.DTF              Crosstab Spec for (NEW)              Page 1  of 1

Esc-Exit    F1-Help    F6-Expand   F7-Groups   F8-Derived fields   F10-Continue
```

Fig. 15.34. *Calculation codes in the SUMMARY field of a cross-tab report.*

Note that there is no Sort Spec for cross-tab reports. However, Q&A sorts row and column titles in ascending order by default. To change the sort order of headings, type a sort code in the row or column field. The code AS forces an ascending sort; DS forces a descending sort.

When the codes in a field become too long for the space available, press F6 to continue typing in the 240-character Expand Field line at the bottom of the screen.

Formatting Cross-Tab Reports

Cross-tab reports use the same formatting codes as columnar reports. Follow these steps to change the default formatting of a cross-tab report:

1. At the Crosstab Spec, move the cursor to the field whose row, column, or summary values you want to format.

2. Move the cursor to the end of the field. Type a comma, followed by the letter F. In parentheses, type any formatting codes for the field.

You can include more than one formatting code, separated by commas. For example, the codes

    SepDate: ROW,F(D6,U,JC)

tell Q&A to format separation date data values with date format number 6 (dd/mm/yy), and to print dates in uppercase and centered.

Enhancing Headings

As with columnar reports, you can customize the titles that Q&A displays in a cross-tab report. To apply character enhancements and fonts, enter the following special codes in the appropriate fields of the Crosstab Spec.

Code	Meaning
TL	Enhances the TOTAL label
AL	Enhances the AVERAGE label
CL	Enhances the COUNT label
MINL	Enhances the MIN label
MAXL	Enhances the MAX label
STDL	Enhances the STD label
VARL	Enhances the VAR label
H	Enhances the heading of the column, row, or summary field selected
SH	Enhances the subheading of the column or row field. This heading is derived from data; you cannot change the text of this heading.

HS   Enhances heading separator lines. To specify a separator character, place it in parentheses: HS(-). Q&A uses the character to separate the heading from the column.

SL   Enhances the separator line when using subcalculations and breaks. To specify a separator character, place it in parentheses: SL(+-+).

DL   Enhances the separator line when printing subcalculations.

At the end of a field that contains a T (total) code, for example, type a comma, enter the code *TL*, and then apply the boldface enhancement to the TL code, as described earlier in the section titled "Using Text Enhancement and Fonts."

Setting a Scale Factor

Large numbers can be scaled up or down in a cross-tab report to make them more readable. For example, you can display millions in units of one million; 1,000,000 therefore becomes 1, and so on. To enter a scaling factor, at the Crosstab Spec move the cursor to a row, column, or summary field. Move the cursor to the end of the field, type a comma, and then type *SCALE(n),* in which *n* is the number of units for the scale. For example, to represent 100,000 as 100, 200,000 as 200, and so on, type the following:

SCALE(1000)

Derived Fields in Cross-Tab Reports

Data for columns, rows, or summary in a cross-tab report may be derived from calculations on database fields that aren't included in the report. A cross-tab report may contain 1-3 derived fields. Unlike columnar reports, you may not have invisible columns in a cross-tab report.

To create a derived field, you either must number the fields on which calculations are based or refer to them by their field names. Field numbers must be entered on the Crosstab Spec before you use the Derived Fields Spec. Field numbers have no effect on the order in which columns will be displayed on the report, or on the sort order.

After numbering the fields or deciding to refer to fields by their field labels, perform the following steps:

1. At the Crosstab Spec, Press F8 to display the Derived Fields Spec (see fig. 15.35).

2. Move the cursor to the Heading field of the first field item.

3. Type the heading for the derived field.

4. Move the cursor to the Formula field and enter the formula for the derived field.

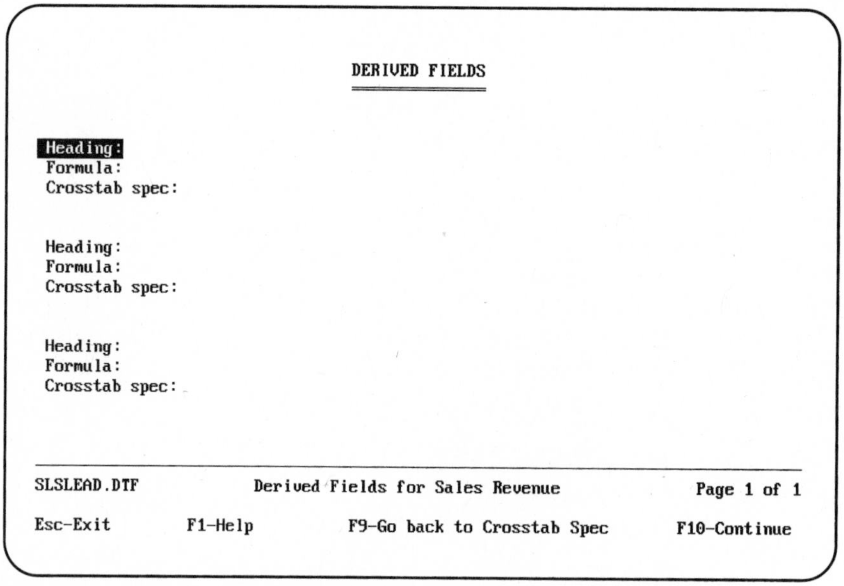

```
                          DERIUED FIELDS
                          ==============


  Heading:
  Formula:
  Crosstab spec:


  Heading:
  Formula:
  Crosstab spec:


  Heading:
  Formula:
  Crosstab spec:
  _____

  SLSLEAD.DTF        Derived Fields for Sales Revenue        Page 1 of 1

  Esc-Exit       F1-Help        F9-Go back to Crosstab Spec    F10-Continue
```

Fig. 15.35.   The Derived Fields Spec.

Remember, you can reference fields in the form that are not included in the Crosstab Spec. To refer to the fields, use field numbers or field names.

In the Formula field of the Derived Field Spec, you may use any of Q&A's LOOKUP commands to retrieve data from the lookup table or from an external file. You can enter the following, for example:

@XLOOKUP("Parts","PartID","PartID","Description")

This statement matches records in the source and target files based on PartID and retrieves a part description into the target Description field.

5. Move the cursor to the Crosstab Spec field and type *ROW*, *COL*, or *SUM*. This tells Q&A which part of the cross-tab report will be the derived field. Figure 15.36 shows the filled-in Derived Fields Spec.

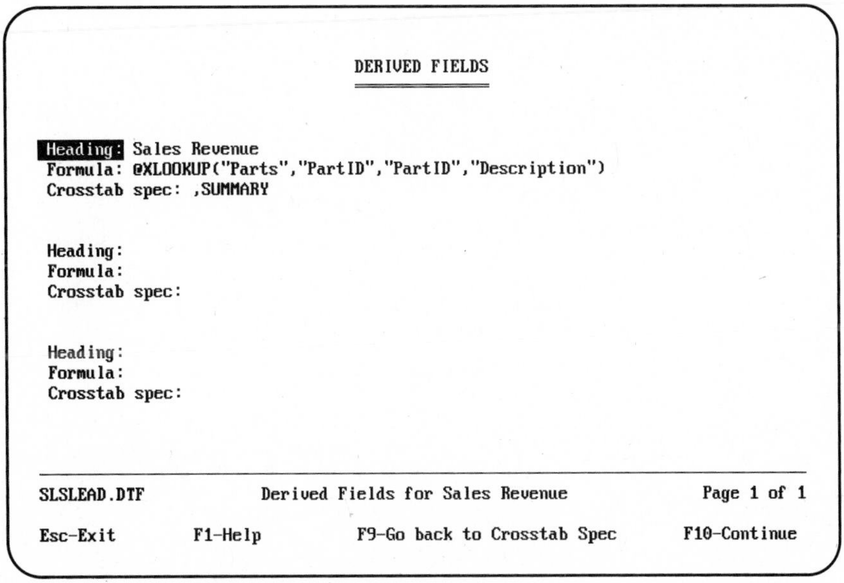

```
                        DERIVED FIELDS


 Heading: Sales Revenue
 Formula: @XLOOKUP("Parts","PartID","PartID","Description")
 Crosstab spec: ,SUMMARY


 Heading:
 Formula:
 Crosstab spec:


 Heading:
 Formula:
 Crosstab spec:


 SLSLEAD.DTF          Derived Fields for Sales Revenue        Page 1 of 1

 Esc-Exit      F1-Help        F9-Go back to Crosstab Spec     F10-Continue
```

Fig. 15.36. The completed Derived Field Spec.

6. Enter a Heading, Formula, and Crosstab Spec entry for each derived column, and then press F9 to return to the Crosstab Spec.

Grouping Report Data

Q&A normally groups the data in a cross-tab report using the field labels as row and column titles. You also can use Q&A's predefined groupings as an alternative way to group your data; or you can specify arbitrary ranges of your own. For example, groupings would be helpful if a file contained 365 daily attendance figures—resulting in a report with 365 titles, each with a single entry! Grouping the daily data by monthly range would be better, resulting in a shorter, more readable report.

To fill in the Grouping Spec, follow these steps:

1. Press F7 at the Crosstab Spec to display the Grouping Spec.

   The Grouping Spec has two columns, for Row and Column groupings.

2. Enter groupings for rows and columns. Press F1 (Help) to display five screens of instructions and examples for filling in the Grouping Spec.

In the Column grouping column, for example, you can enter the following:

```
<=10,000
>10,000..<20,000
>20,000..<30,000
>30,000..<40,000
>40,000..<50,000
>=50,000
```

This results in a report with column headings for each range and one row for each month of the year. If you specify groups that overlap, the report "double counts" fields for which the groupings overlap (for example, part numbers >1000 and >2000). The Grouping Spec has four pages, with space for up to 40 groupings of rows and columns.

3. When you finish filling in the Grouping Spec, press F9 to return to the Crosstab Spec.

Using Q&A's Built-In Groupings

Q&A enables you to use the following predefined groupings in the Crosstab Grouping Spec:

Grouping codes	Explanation
@ALL	Includes each unique field value as a row or column heading. (This is the default.)
@RANGE(x,y,z)	Groups data in a set of specified ranges, in which x is the starting number, y is the size of the interval, and z is the number of intervals. Example: @RANGE(0,5000,20)
@INTERVAL(x)	Groups data in predefined intervals, in which Q&A determines the ranges automatically, and x is the desired number of ranges. Example: @INTERVAL(10)
@DAY	Groups data by days of the year. (This is the same as using @ALL.)

Grouping codes	Explanation
@DOW	Groups data by day of the week. This produces a maximum of seven groupings.
@DOM	Groups data by day of the month. This produces a maximum of 31 groupings.
@MONTH	Groups data by month. This may produce 13 or more groups if the data extends over periods longer than a year.
@MOY	Groups data by month of the year. This produces a maximum of 12 groupings.
@YEAR	Groups data by year. This produces as many groupings as there are years in the retrieved forms.
@ALPHA	Groups data alphabetically, from a to z.

Specifying an Explicit Grouping

You may express groupings using the same comparisons that are available in the Retrieve Spec, such as the following:

>1000..<=2000   Groups data in the range 1001-2000

The complete list of grouping characters is shown on the Help screen accessed by pressing F1 twice at the Grouping Spec.

Enhancing Groupings

Enhancing groupings with fonts and character enhancements (boldface, underlining, and so on) is similar to enhancing headings, discussed earlier in this chapter. From the Grouping Spec, press Shift-F6, choose the enhancement you want, and select the grouping. When the report is printed, items that fall into the row or column grouping will be enhanced.

Chapter Summary

This chapter has explained how you can create a basic report and enhance it by adding column headings and widths, derived columns, and headers and footers. You also have learned how to produce cross-tab reports that summarize data in a variety of ways. The next chapter introduces you to printing from the Report module.

16

Printing a Report

Printing a report is a natural extension of the report design process. To print a report from a database that you created in the File module, you design the report specifications and send the output to the printer.

With a single exception—the Number setting on the Crosstab Print Options screen—the process of printing a report is essentially the same for printing columnar and cross-tab reports. The Number setting is discussed in "Using Print Options in Report," later in this chapter.

The print section of Report provides several options, including one to make temporary modifications to the report specifications before you print the report. If you want to modify the print settings for your report permanently, make changes from the Design/Redesign option of the Report menu. You do not have to leave the Design option screen before you print the report. This chapter briefly discusses making permanent changes to the print settings. For a more detailed explanation, see Chapter 15.

Printing from the Report Menu

If you have designed a report for your data files and you do not want to make any changes, you can print the report by selecting Print from the Report menu (see fig. 16.1). This routine selects print specifications to generate a report. If you want to make temporary changes to a report, choose the Retrieve and Column/Sort Specs within the Print option. The following sections discuss both report types; any differences are noted.

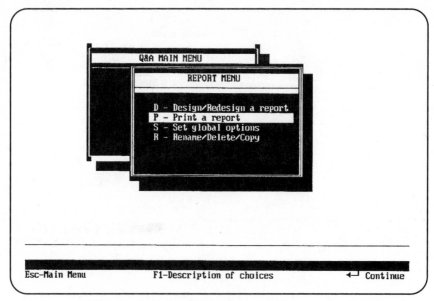

Fig. 16.1.   *Choosing the Print a Report option.*

Printing a Report

After you create a database to store and organize information, you can combine the information in printed reports. You can use the Report module of Q&A to arrange and print your data. You can specify the records to be used in the report by using the Retrieve Spec. With the Column/Sort Spec, you can tell Q&A how you want the data to be organized. Chapter 15 provides details on designing a report.

If you do not want to make any changes to the report before you print it, the print procedure from Report is simple. From the Q&A Main menu, select Report and then select Print a Report. Q&A prompts you to select a database and the report you want to print. After you make the selections, Q&A asks whether you want to make changes (see fig. 16.2). When you select No, the report prints.

Making Temporary Changes to a Report

You occasionally may want to make temporary changes to a report, print the report, and then return the specifications to their original settings. If you change a cross-tab report, the option screens differ from a columnar report. These differences are discussed in Chapter 15.

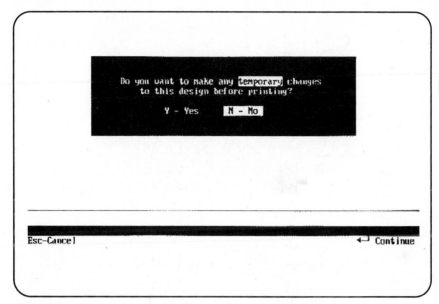

Fig. 16.2. *The screen prompt in Report for temporary changes.*

To make temporary changes to a report, select Print a Report from the Report menu. After you select the database (LEAD.DTF) and the report name, Q&A asks whether you want to make temporary changes. In this case, select Yes.

Using the Retrieve Spec

The Retrieve Spec displays when you choose to make temporary changes. You can reselect the forms to be pulled from the database. Suppose that you want to print a report of the sales prospects in Boston that have an annual revenue over $2,000,000. On the Retrieve Spec screen, you enter *Boston* in the City field and *>=2,000,000* in the Annual Revenue field (see fig. 16.3). When you press F10, the Column/Sort Spec displays. If you are redesigning a cross-tab report, Q&A displays the Crosstab Spec, which is discussed in detail in Chapter 15 and summarized below.

Using the Column/Sort Spec

The Column/Sort Spec tells Q&A which fields you want to print as columns on the report. At the same time, you can determine the sorting order for the records and specify which numeric fields you want to count, total, subtotal, or average. You also can change the column headings or column widths, or justify the data within the column.

```
              TITAN TECHNOLOGY SALES LEAD TRACKING SYSTEM
                                          File Name -- SlsLead
  LastName:                      FirstName:
  Title:
  Company:                       Telephone:
  Address1:
  Address2:
  City: Boston                   State:         Zip:
     No. of Labs:                Annual Revenue: >=2000000
     Current Customer:           Company Priority:
  LEAD INFORMATION───────────────────────────────────────────
     Product Interest:
     Request For:                Lead Source:
     Months to Purchase:         Product Priority:
  SALES ACTION───────────────────────DATES──────────────────
     Sales Priority:             Date Entered:
     Sales Dist.:                Date Info Sent:
     Salesman:                   Sales Contact:
     Status:                     Demo Date:


  ──────────────────────────────────────────────────────────
  SLSLEAD.DTF            Retrieve Spec for Sales Revenue    Page 1  of 1

  Esc-Exit   F1-Help   F3-Clear  F6-Expand  Alt+F8-List  ↑F8-Save   F10-Continue
```

Fig. 16.3.   *Using the Retrieve Spec.*

If you press F1 when the Column/Sort Spec is displayed, you see a brief reminder of how to fill out the screen. If you press F1 again, a detailed Help screen shows (see fig. 16.4). Press PgDn to display three more pages of information.

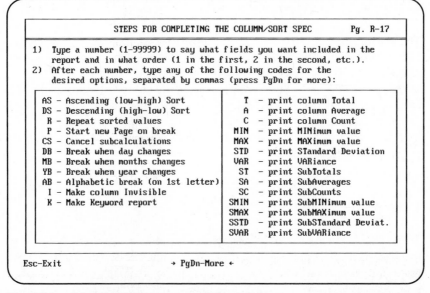

```
              STEPS FOR COMPLETING THE COLUMN/SORT SPEC      Pg. R-17

  1)  Type a number (1-99999) to say what fields you want included in the
      report and in what order (1 in the first, 2 in the second, etc.).
  2)  After each number, type any of the following codes for the
      desired options, separated by commas (press PgDn for more):

    AS - Ascending (low-high) Sort       T  - print column Total
    DS - Descending (high-low) Sort      A  - print column Average
     R - Repeat sorted values            C  - print column Count
     P - Start new Page on break       MIN  - print MINimum value
    CS - Cancel subcalculations        MAX  - print MAXimum value
    DB - Break when day changes        STD  - print STandard Deviation
    MB - Break when months changes     VAR  - print VARiance
    YB - Break when year changes        ST  - print SubTotals
    AB - Alphabetic break (on 1st letter) SA - print SubAverages
     I - Make column Invisible          SC  - print SubCounts
     K - Make Keyword report          SMIN  - print SubMINimum value
                                      SMAX  - print SubMAXimum value
                                      SSTD  - print SubSTandard Deviat.
                                      SVAR  - print SubVARiance

  Esc-Exit                  → PgDn-More ←
```

Fig. 16.4.   *A detailed Help screen available in Report.*

Decide the order in which you want the columns to be printed, and enter corresponding numbers in the fields. To make the company name appear in different widths in the first column and annual revenue appear in the second column, for example, make the entries as shown in figure 16.5.

```
                    TITAN TECHNOLOGY SALES LEAD TRACKING SYSTEM
                                               ═══════ File Name -- SlsLead
     LastName:                        FirstName:
     Title:
     Company: 1                       Telephone:
     Address1:
     Address2:
     City:                            State:        Zip:
        No. of Labs:                  Annual Revenue: 2
        Current Customer:             Company Priority:
     ─────────────────────────LEAD INFORMATION──────────────
        Product Interest:
        Request For:                  Lead Source:
        Months to Purchase:           Product Priority:
     ────────────────────────SALES ACTION──────────────
        Sales Priority:               Date Entered:
        Sales Dist.:                  Sales Manager:
        Salesman:                     Phone:
        Status:


     SLSLEAD.DTF        Column/Sort Spec for Sales Revenue      Page 1  of 1

     Esc-Exit    F1-Help  F6-Expand  Shift+F6-Enhance  F8-Derived Cols  F10-Continue
```

Fig. 16.5. *Specifying the order of columns to be printed.*

You can arrange the data in ascending (AS) or descending (DS) order. If you enter an incorrect letter code in any field, the warning Not a valid Column/ Sort Spec is displayed (see fig. 16.6). Before you can continue, you must correct the error by changing the letter code.

Using the Crosstab Spec

If you temporarily redesign a cross-tab report, press F10 at the Retrieve Spec to bring up the Crosstab Spec.

At the Crosstab Spec, you tell Q&A which data to display in columns, rows, and summary areas of a cross-tab report. You may specify summary calculations, derived columns, formatting options, alternate headings, data groupings, and a scale factor for repetitive field data. For more information, see Chapter 15.

Press F1 (Help) at the Crosstab Spec to display a help screen of sort and calculation codes for use with the Crosstab Spec. At the help screen, you may press PgDn repeatedly to review four additional screens of help.

```
              TITAN TECHNOLOGY SALES LEAD TRACKING SYSTEM
                                         File Name -- SlsLead
   LastName:                      FirstName:
   Title:
   Company: 1AA                   Telephone:

     Not a valid Column/Sort Spec.  F1 for help, or see pg. R-10 of your manual.

     No. of Labs:                   Annual Revenue:
     Current Customer:              Company Priority:
   LEAD INFORMATION────────────────────────────────────────
     Product Interest:
     Request For:                   Lead Source:
     Months to Purchase:            Product Priority:
   SALES ACTION───────────────────────DATES─────────────────
     Sales Priority:                Date Entered:
     Sales Dist.:                   Date Info Sent:
     Salesman:                      Sales Contact:
     Status:                          Demo Date:


   SLSLEAD.DTF         Column/Sort Spec for Sales Revenue      Page 1  of 1

   Esc-Exit    F1-Help  F6-Expand  Shift+F6-Enhance  F8-Derived Cols  F10-Continue
```

Fig. 16.6. *A Column/Sort Spec screen with an error message.*

Decide which three fields you wish to include in the cross-tab report, and type *ROW*, *COL*, and *SUM* in the appropriate columns, as described in Chapter 15. If you want to include the fields Lead Source, Sales Dist., and Annual Revenue, for example, type the appropriate code in each field, as shown in figure 16.7.

```
              TITAN TECHNOLOGY SALES LEAD TRACKING SYSTEM
                                         File Name -- SlsLead
   LastName:                      FirstName:
   Title:
   Company:                       Telephone:
   Address1:
   Address2:
   City:                          State:        Zip:
     No. of Labs:                 Annual Revenue: SUM
     Current Customer:            Company Priority:
   LEAD INFORMATION────────────────────────────────────────
     Product Interest:
     Request For:                 Lead Source: ROW
     Months to Purchase:          Product Priority:
   SALES ACTION───────────────────────DATES─────────────────
     Sales Priority:              Date Entered:
     Sales Dist.: COL             Date Info Sent:
     Salesman:                    Sales Contact:
     Status:                        Demo Date:


   SLSLEAD.DTF         Crosstab Spec for Sales Revenue        Page 1  of 1

   Esc-Exit    F1-Help  F6-Expand  F7-Groups  F8-Derived fields  F10-Continue
```

Fig. 16.7. *Filled-in Crosstab Spec showing fields Lead Source, Sales Dist., and Annual Revenue with ROW, COL, and SUM inserted, respectively.*

Press F10 to exit the Crosstab Spec and display the Crosstab Print Options screen, which is described in detail in Chapter 15 and summarized later, under "Using Print Options in a Report."

Using the Derived Columns Menu for Columnar Reports

In some cases, you may need to produce a column that is not included in a field of your database. If you have defined fields to store the number of sick days allotted and the number of sick days used for each employee, for example, you may want a field on the report that shows the number of remaining sick days. A Derived Column can do this for you.

To design a derived column, press F8 from the Columns/Sort menu to display the Derived Columns menu. You can change column widths or split column headings into more than one line by using an exclamation point to indicate a line break.

The Derived Columns menu has context-sensitive help that you can call up by pressing F1. When one of these Help screens is superimposed on the Derived Columns menu, you can use the arrow keys to move the cursor so that you can see a different Help screen appropriate for the adjacent line on the menu (see fig. 16.8). If you move the cursor from Formula to Heading, for example, a Help screen on headings displays.

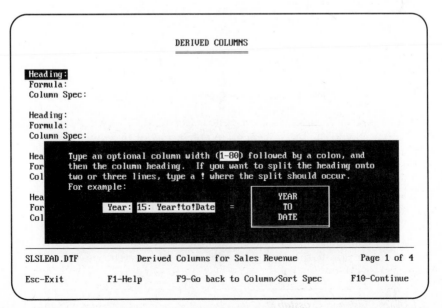

Fig. 16.8. *A Help screen superimposed on the Derived Columns screen.*

Using Print Options in Report

When you press F10 from the Column/Sort Spec or the Derived Columns menu, the Print Options screen displays. On this version of the menu, you have the option to print only totals if you want to create a summary report (see fig. 16.9).

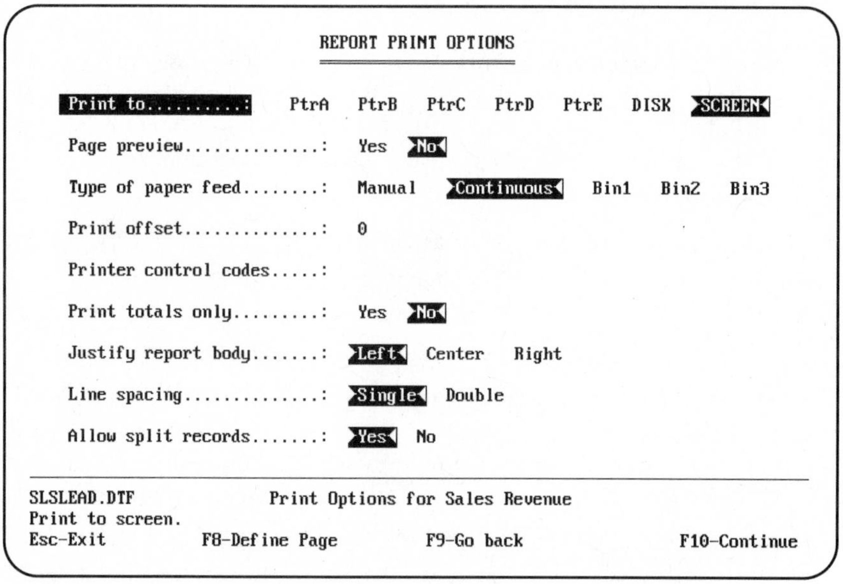

```
                        REPORT PRINT OPTIONS


      Print to.........:   PtrA   PtrB   PtrC   PtrD   PtrE   DISK  ▶SCREEN◀

      Page preview.............:   Yes  ▶No◀

      Type of paper feed........:  Manual  ▶Continuous◀   Bin1   Bin2   Bin3

      Print offset..............:   0

      Printer control codes.....:

      Print totals only.........:   Yes  ▶No◀

      Justify report body.......:  ▶Left◀  Center   Right

      Line spacing..............:  ▶Single◀  Double

      Allow split records.......:  ▶Yes◀  No


 SLSLEAD.DTF              Print Options for Sales Revenue
 Print to screen.
 Esc-Exit          F8-Define Page          F9-Go back          F10-Continue
```

Fig. 16.9.   *The Print Options screen in Report has a Totals option.*

With the options on this screen, you also can decide how you want the report justified on the page. If your page width is set at 132 characters, for example, and your report is only 100 characters wide, you can print the text centered or right-justified instead of printing the report on the left side of the page.

You can press F8 to access the Define Page menu. The following section explains how you can use this menu to enhance your printout.

Selecting Print Options for a Cross-Tab Report

The Print Options screen for cross-tab reports is similar to the Print Options screen for columnar reports, except that the Show Results As option enables you to decide how to display numbers in cross-tab calculations. The available options follow:

Numbers. Displays results as numbers (the default).

% Total. Displays results as a percentage of the total value for all summary field values from all records retrieved.

% Row. Displays results as a percentage of the TOTAL or COUNT for the row, based on all records retrieved.

% Column. Displays results as a percentage of the TOTAL or COUNT for the column, based on all records retrieved.

Normal. Displays results as an amount above or below the average, in which the average is represented as 100.

Using the Define Page Menu

Report's Define Page menu enables you to arrange the text on your printout. By entering headers and footers and changing page length and margins, you can vary the way your report is printed. By widening the margins of your report, you can print more information on one page. Q&A automatically divides wide reports to more than one page.

After you finish making temporary changes, press F10 to begin printing. While the report is printing, you can press F2 to cancel the operation and bring up the Print Options screen. You then can make additional changes, if necessary. When you press F10 again, the printing is restarted from the beginning of the file.

Making Permanent Changes to a Report

If you want to make permanent modifications to the print specifications for your report, use the Design/Redesign option of the Report menu. When you choose this option, you see the Retrieve and Column/Sort Specs, where you can make your adjustments. After the Specs are filled, the Print Options screen is displayed, and you are asked whether you want to print the saved report. For more information on creating Print Specs for Report, see Chapter 15.

Printing a New Report

The procedures for printing a new report and designing a report are similar. If you want to create a temporary report, select Print a Report from the Report menu. When the list of report names is displayed, press Enter to show the screens you enter when you design a report. The name NEW appears on the status line so that you know the report is temporary (see fig. 16.10). After the report is printed, you return to the Report menu. The temporary report is not saved.

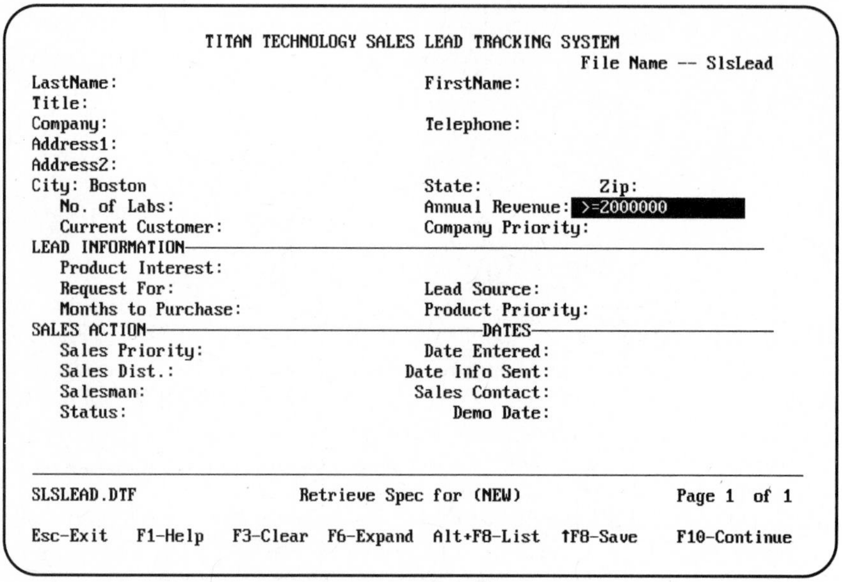

```
                    TITAN TECHNOLOGY SALES LEAD TRACKING SYSTEM
                                               File Name -- SlsLead
        LastName:                         FirstName:
        Title:
        Company:                          Telephone:
        Address1:
        Address2:
        City: Boston                      State:        Zip:
           No. of Labs:                   Annual Revenue:[>=2000000       ]
           Current Customer:              Company Priority:
        LEAD INFORMATION───────────────────────────────────────────────
           Product Interest:
           Request For:                   Lead Source:
           Months to Purchase:            Product Priority:
        SALES ACTION──────────────────────────DATES──────────────────────
           Sales Priority:                Date Entered:
           Sales Dist.:                   Date Info Sent:
           Salesman:                      Sales Contact:
           Status:                        Demo Date:


        ─────────────────────────────────────────────────────────────────
        SLSLEAD.DTF            Retrieve Spec for (NEW)          Page 1 of 1

        Esc-Exit   F1-Help   F3-Clear  F6-Expand  Alt+F8-List  ↑F8-Save   F10-Continue
```

Fig. 16.10. *The Temporary Report screen.*

Checking the Report before Printing

If you want to see how your report will look before the report prints, choose Screen at the Print To prompt of the Print Options screen. If your computer monitor can display graphics, you also can set Page Preview to Yes to display an image of the report similar to the final, printed results.

If you choose Print to Screen, the report shows on-screen (without headers and footers) one screen at a time. You can use the cursor keys to scroll the report. The End key shows the right edge of the report; the Home key shows the left edge. The PgUp and PgDn keys move to the previous or next screen, respectively. Pressing Enter or F10 also moves to the next screen.

If you choose Print Preview, the report is displayed as a graphic image. You can scroll between pages of the report with the PgUp and PgDn keys, or display the report in enlarged or reduced format. Press F1 (Help) at the Print Preview screen to display a list of viewing commands. Press F2 to return to the Print Options screen. Press F10 or Esc to return to the Report menu.

When you are satisfied with the report, print the report by specifying the printer port on the Print Options screen. As the report prints, however, you can press Shift-F9 to make changes. A direct access window enables you to go directly to the spec that you need to change (see fig. 16.11). After making the changes, press F10; the report starts printing from the beginning of the file.

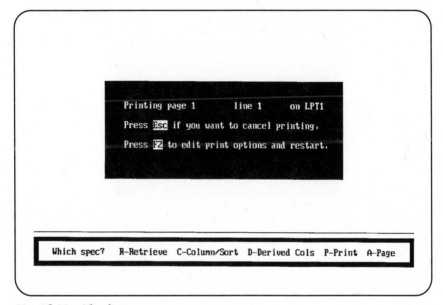

```
        Printing page 1          line 1          on LPT1

        Press Esc if you want to cancel printing.

        Press F2 to edit print options and restart.
```

```
   Which spec?   R-Retrieve  C-Column/Sort  D-Derived Cols  P-Print  A-Page
```

Fig. 16.11. The direct access screen.

Handling Column Overruns

If the report is too wide for your page, a warning message shows before the report prints. You can ignore the warning and proceed; Q&A truncates the data beyond the edge of the page. Instead of losing that part of your printout, you can return to the Print Options screen and correct the problem or cancel printing altogether.

Selecting Fonts

In Chapter 8, you learned how to select laser printer fonts when printing from the File module. Q&A Report provides the same capabilities. By selecting Report's Print Options screen, you can enter PostScript file names or direct printer commands in the Printer Control Codes field. For a discussion of this procedure, see Chapter 8.

If you are sending a PostScript control file to the printer, enter the full path name and file name. If you are sending direct printer control commands, precede the sequence with an exclamation mark (!). Choose codes appropriate to your printer, using the following format:

!Font Points (Ln In Sn)

The exclamation point at the beginning of the line separates the printer command line from a PostScript command file name. Font is the name of any font your printer recognizes. Points is the font size in 1/72-inch intervals. For Points=4, the font is four points high, or 4/72 of an inch. The range of possible values for Points depends on your printer.

The parameters in parentheses are optional. The parameters can set the following options:

Ln: Sets the number of points between lines. The default value for Ln is 12, which provides the standard 6 lines per inch (72/12=6).

In: Controls accented characters in the IBM character set. If you accept the default (I1), Q&A matches the IBM character set where it can. If your printer does not support PostScript fonts, set n=0.

Sn: Selects the symbol table. Q&A matches the IBM character set as closely as possible. Standard PostScript characters are switched with others to match the IBM set. To disable this feature, set Sn=S0.

Q&A does not accept font commands for defined printers that do not support fonts, or for undefined printers. Even if you have defined a font-supporting printer, you must have that printer selected as the current printer on the Print Options screen. Otherwise, an error occurs when you try to enter font commands on the Printer Control Codes line.

Chapter Summary

Printing from Report is simple. Although the Report module can perform complex tasks, by the time you are ready to print your information, the hard work is over.

In this chapter, you have learned how to use the Report menu to select reports to print and how to modify existing reports before printing them. By printing from the Report module of Q&A, you can tailor your reports to display data in a variety of ways. You can permanently modify the print settings for your report by using the Design/Redesign option of the Report menu. You also can print with Report by making temporary changes to the Print Spec. After you have defined a Print Spec in File, you can select Print from the Report menu.

Part V

Using Q&A's Intelligent Assistant and Query Guide

Includes

**Understanding the Intelligent Assistant
and Query Guide**

**Using the Intelligent Assistant
and Query Guide**

17

Understanding the Intelligent Assistant and Query Guide

I f you use Q&A Write, File, and Report, you have three powerful, easy-to-use tools for your small-business or departmental word processing, data-management, and reporting needs. Although you will benefit from your investment in Q&A by using only the File and Report modules, you will not be taking advantage of two other features that make Q&A far more powerful and easier to use than other programs that have integrated word processing and database capabilities. Q&A's Intelligent Assistant (also referred to as the IA) and Query Guide (QG) are the features that set the program apart from most other microcomputer applications programs available today.

The Intelligent Assistant uses sophisticated artificial-intelligence technology to help you communicate with Q&A by using your own language rather than the command menu system in File and Report. You can use English phrases and sentences to query a database that you created with File. You also can produce columnar or cross-tab reports, edit records, and add new records. Plain-English sentences even can be used to perform mathematical calculations or to ask for the date and time.

The Query Guide helps you build a query statement for the Intelligent Assistant by prompting you with menus and data-entry screens at each step of the process. The Query Guide is simpler to use than the Intelligent Assistant because you don't need to spend time teaching the Query Guide about terms you will use when performing data retrievals. The Query Guide is limited to Q&A's built-in retrieval "vocabulary," but still can help you to manage your data in extremely sophisticated ways.

When you begin using the Intelligent Assistant and Query Guide, you will discover how they simplify and reduce the time you spend on many of your data-management and reporting applications. Before you can use the IA/QG successfully, however, you need to learn the basics, experiment with their capabilities, and devise your own method for handling data-management and reporting needs.

In this and the following chapters, you will learn to experiment with and develop applications for the IA/QG. Chapter 17 gives you a conceptual introduction to these modules and describes their general capabilities. You are encouraged to experiment as soon as you have learned the basics of Q&A File and have created your own database. Chapter 18 provides more details on using the IA's data-management and report capabilities.

What Is the Intelligent Assistant?

The IA is a language processor or interpreter that has a built-in vocabulary of about 600 words. You can teach the IA new words, and the IA can learn new words that it finds in your database. With the Intelligent Assistant, you no longer have to communicate with Q&A through its own language (the command menu system in File and Report). Using the Intelligent Assistant is similar to asking a human assistant to locate, organize, change, analyze, or report information. If you had a file cabinet full of sales leads and you wanted the leads for your company's Los Angeles office, for example, you might ask your secretary or assistant, "Please bring me the file of Los Angeles sales leads." With the Intelligent Assistant, you make this request by typing *Display the Los Angeles forms.*

Q&A then displays all sales leads for the Los Angeles office. If you want to change a phone number in your database, you might ask your assistant, "Please change the phone number on Blackson's sales lead form." With the Intelligent Assistant, you simply type the following: *Change Blackson's phone number to 363-886-3980.*

The English words, phrases, or sentences replace the sequence of command operations that would be executed if you used the File or Report modules without the Intelligent Assistant.

To answer your requests, the IA depends on built-in knowledge and information it learns from your databases. Before you teach the IA about a database, the IA already knows the following:

- Time of day

- Current date

- How to conduct mathematical calculations

- Approximately 600 words

After you teach the IA about your database, the IA also knows the following:

- Database field names

- Field contents and data types

- Field descriptions (which field contains locations, for example)

- Relationships between fields (the first-name and last-name fields combine to form a complete name, for example)

- Synonyms for field names and contents

- Additional vocabulary words that you teach the IA

What Is the Query Guide?

The Query Guide is a system of menus that assist you at every step of retrieving information from your database. The Query Guide is similar to the Intelligent Assistant, but instead of interpreting plain-English phrases that you give the QG, the Query Guide asks you what you would like to do next and displays lists that suggest possible alternatives.

In the beginning, using the Query Guide probably will be quicker because you will not have to teach the QG about search terms or phrases. You also do not have to become familiar with the phrases that QG can understand, as you do when you begin using the Intelligent Assistant. Later, you may find the Intelligent Assistant quicker; after you have learned to speak its "language," IA enables you to perform complex queries in plain English.

After you have used both modules for awhile, you may find yourself using the Intelligent Assistant to perform report and retrieval functions with which you're familiar. But when you're not quite sure of the phrasing of a request, the Query Guide provides help by listing your options at each step of the way.

From the SLSLEAD database, you may want to display the records in which the ZIP code is between 90000 and 92999, the Current Customer is "Yes," and the Annual Revenue is greater than $5,000,000.

When using File, you have to type the following retrieval information in the appropriate fields of the Retrieve Spec:

Zip: >=90000..<=92999
Annual Revenue: >=5000000
Current Customer: ="Y"

You can enter the same query in the Intelligent Assistant by typing:

Show me the records where Zip is between 89999 and 93000, Annual Revenue is greater than 5000000, and Current Customer is "Yes"

If you're a newcomer to Q&A, you may not feel comfortable filling in the Retrieve Spec or using the IA. However, you probably will feel right at home when you use the Query Guide for the first time. To enter the above query with the QG, you simply select menu items and enter numbers when prompted. Specifically, at the Q&A Main Menu, you select Assistant, then Query Guide. From that point on, the Query Guide guides you in building an Intelligent Assistant retrieval. Figure 17.1 shows the first Query Guide options screen.

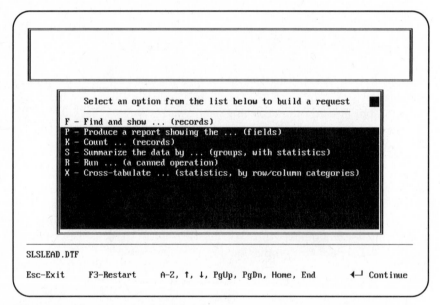

```
    Select an option from the list below to build a request   ■

F - Find and show ... (records)
P - Produce a report showing the ... (fields)
K - Count ... (records)
S - Summarize the data by ... (groups, with statistics)
R - Run ... (a canned operation)
X - Cross-tabulate ... (statistics, by row/column categories)




SLSLEAD.DTF

Esc-Exit     F3-Restart     A-Z, ↑, ↓, PgUp, PgDn, Home, End     ↵ Continue
```

Fig. 17.1. *The Query Guide retrieval screen.*

When you choose Find and Show ... (Records), Q&A enters Find and show in the Intelligent Assistant query box at the top of the screen. Subsequent menus help you fill in the IA query box with a perfectly formatted, error-free request.

Is the Intelligent Assistant/Query Guide for Advanced Users Only?

The Intelligent Assistant/Query Guide is not only for advanced users. If you know how to use File to create a form and enter data in a database, you're ready to begin experimenting with Q&A's IA/QG. One of the best ways to sharpen your skills with the IA/QG is to begin experimenting right away. By testing the capabilities of the Intelligent Assistant/Query Guide, you quickly discover the powerful, easy-to-use qualities of this Q&A feature.

Just as you must give a new employee time to become familiar with your habits, you must allow the IA/QG to "get to know" how to respond to your requests. The rest of this chapter helps you learn to experiment with the IA/QG so that you can begin to use it for your own applications.

How To Experiment with the Intelligent Assistant

Even before you begin, the Intelligent Assistant already has a limited amount of information. By using the Teach Me about Your Database option (hereafter referred to as the Teach option) on the Assistant menu (see fig. 17.2), you can teach the IA more about the English commands and the methods you will use to request information.

If you want to bypass this option, you can move directly to the Ask Me To Do Something option (hereafter referred to as the Ask option) and request an action from Q&A. You can use the Intelligent Assistant for simple searching, sorting, changing, and reporting tasks. Because you will learn faster by experimenting immediately, try using the Ask option right away. The first time you use this option, the IA takes time to learn from your database the basic information that the IA needs in order to make retrievals.

Because all the file records you are working with must be scanned the first time you use the IA, this initial procedure takes longer when many records are in the database. If you plan to use the IA with a particular data file, do this start-up procedure before you have many records entered.

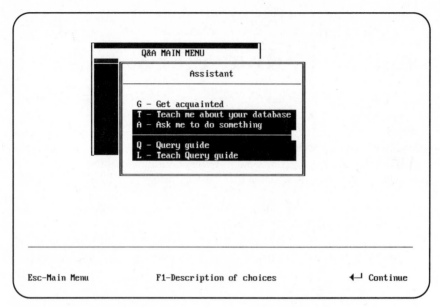

```
                  ┌─────────────────────────────┐
                  │        Q&A MAIN MENU         │
                  │    ┌──────────────────────────┐
                  │    │        Assistant          │
                  │    │                           │
                  │    │  G - Get acquainted       │
                  │    │  T - Teach me about your database│
                  │    │  A - Ask me to do something│
                  │    │                           │
                  │    │  Q - Query guide          │
                  │    │  L - Teach Query guide    │
                  │    │                           │
                  │    └──────────────────────────┘
                  └─────────────────────────────┘

 Esc-Main Menu          F1-Description of choices        ◄┘ Continue
```

Fig. 17.2.   The Assistant menu.

Even when you move directly to the Ask option without teaching Q&A about your database, the IA is capable of performing a number of simple operations on the forms available in your database. You must, however, phrase all your requests by using words that are found in the IA's built-in vocabulary or that come from the field names and values in your database. Even before you use the Teach option, for example, you can have the IA display telephone numbers from records with a field labeled "Phone." At the IA prompt, type the following: *Show me the phone numbers.*

Experimenting with the Intelligent Assistant in this manner helps you to discover the range of requests and responses allowed by the program. When you try to make more complicated requests, however, you will see how much help the Intelligent Assistant needs. A request for a sophisticated summary report, for example, may require much more information than is available in the built-in vocabulary and database words. For complex applications, using the Teach option is necessary to use the Intelligent Assistant. If you don't plan to use the IA often but you need help building a complex query, use the Query Guide.

When you use the Ask option from the Assistant menu, the information can be displayed in the form it was entered originally (see fig. 17.3). You also have the option of requesting a summary report of the information on-screen (see fig 17.4). How the information is displayed depends on how you ask the question and what you have told the IA about displaying the information it finds.

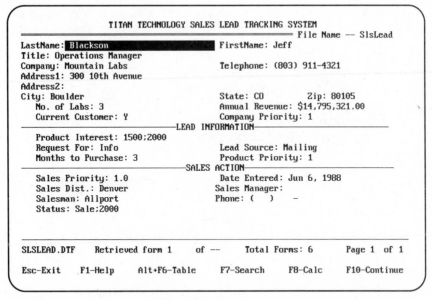

```
                TITAN TECHNOLOGY SALES LEAD TRACKING SYSTEM
═══════════════════════════════════════════════════ File Name -- SlsLead
LastName: Blackson                    FirstName: Jeff
Title: Operations Manager
Company: Mountain Labs              Telephone: (803) 911-4321
Address1: 300 10th Avenue
Address2:
City: Boulder                        State: CO      Zip: 80105
  No. of Labs: 3                     Annual Revenue: $14,795,321.00
  Current Customer: Y                Company Priority: 1
─────────────────────────────LEAD INFORMATION───────────────────────
  Product Interest: 1500;2000
  Request For: Info                  Lead Source: Mailing
  Months to Purchase: 3              Product Priority: 1
─────────────────────────────SALES ACTION───────────────────────────
  Sales Priority: 1.0                Date Entered: Jun 6, 1988
  Sales Dist.: Denver                Sales Manager:
  Salesman: Allport                  Phone: (   )   --
  Status: Sale;2000



SLSLEAD.DTF     Retrieved form 1     of --     Total Forms: 6     Page 1 of 1

Esc-Exit    F1-Help    Alt+F6-Table    F7-Search    F8-Calc    F10-Continue
```

Fig. 17.3. *Information in forms displayed by the Intelligent Assistant.*

```
Display the company, annual revenue, product interest, sorted according to
sales priority


Sales Priority            Company            Annual Revenue    Product
──────────────        ────────────────     ───────────────   ─────────
                      Advanced Medical Associates   $5,300,623.00    2000;120
                      Mountain Labs                   $100,210.00    1000;150

1.5                   Mattis Medical Technology    $1,000,210.00    2000;250
                      University of Michigan         $325,000.00    1000;200
                      Pike Pharmaceutical, Inc.      $210,000.00    2000;150
                      Bay City Laboratories          $150,250.00    2000;100
                      Franklyn Lab Associates      $6,456,000.00    1200;150

2.0                   Washington Medical Labs, Inc.  $200,500.00    1500;250

HOT                   Independent Medical Labs       $223,500.00    2500;150
                      Plaines Medical Associates     $750,000.00    1200;200

SLSLEAD.DTF                                                              █
*****************************  END OF REPORT  *********************************
Esc-Exit      F2-Reprint      { → ← ↓ ↑ PgUp PgDn }-Scroll      F10-Continue
```

Fig. 17.4. *Summary reports displayed by the Intelligent Assistant.*

Teaching the IA about your database involves defining which fields will be used in reports. When these fields are specified, a request such as *Show me the phone numbers* produces a columnar report that includes these fields.

Suppose that you are more specific and use the term *form* in your request: *Display forms where city=Boulder.* You then get a full-screen display of the record.

As you read through the rest of this chapter, you can experiment with the Intelligent Assistant by following these steps:

1. Create a simple practice database by using Q&A's File module. You can duplicate the database example used throughout this chapter or create your own.

2. Make sure that you make a backup of the database file by using either the Copy command from Q&A's File menu or the DOS COPY command (see Chapter 6 for directions on copying).

3. Enter the Intelligent Assistant module by selecting Assistant from Q&A's Main menu.

4. Select the Get Acquainted option from the Assistant menu.

5. Select the Ask Me To Do Something option from the Assistant menu, and indicate the file name for the database you want the IA to use.

   The Intelligent Assistant takes time to analyze your database. This may take quite a while if your database contains a large number of records.

6. When the Intelligent Assistant prompt screen appears, experiment by entering sample queries similar to those presented in the examples that follow.

Guidelines for Using the Intelligent Assistant

Whether you are just beginning to experiment with the IA or are using the IA regularly for your applications, the following guidelines will help you learn about and avoid problems with your Intelligent Assistant:

• Keep a current backup copy of your database file (DTF). Otherwise, if your computer is turned off or accidentally loses power while you're using the IA, you may not be able to access your database file.

- Pay close attention to the Intelligent Assistant's prompts. After you enter a request, if the prompts displayed indicate that the IA is unable to complete the task, don't proceed with the operation.

- Leave the Intelligent Assistant by pressing Esc from the Assistant menu to return to the Q&A Main menu.

How To Experiment with the Query Guide

Even though using the Query Guide is much simpler than using the Intelligent Assistant, you can build extremely sophisticated queries with the Query Guide. However, using the QG takes more time. IA queries can be specified as quickly as you can type a sentence. With the Query Guide, you're always restricted to prompts, menus, and submenus.

The Query Guide can perform the following Q&A operations:

- Retrieve records from your database

- Design, display, and print columnar and cross-tab reports

- Count records that meet certain criteria in a database

- Print information using print specs and stored reports

The Query Guide does have limitations. For example, the Query Guide cannot perform retrievals with XLOOKUP or other programming statements. But the QG saves time when you're not sure whether to formulate your request using File or the Intelligent Assistant.

Teaching the Query Guide

Setting up the QG is easier than customizing the Intelligent Assistant. The first time you use the QG, Q&A automatically learns about the field names in your file. You need only to tell the QG which text and key fields, if any, you will use when searching for data. After the QG records this information, the QG can display actual field data for you to select from in response to QG prompts.

To teach the Query Guide about the database you want to search, follow these steps:

1. At the Assistant menu, choose L-Teach Query Guide. Q&A asks for the name of a database. Type a name, or press Shift-F4 to clear the prompt, and press Enter to select from a list. You may teach the Query Guide about text or keyword fields only, and these may hold no more than one line of data.

2. If you have never used the Query Guide with your database, and you choose Q-Query Guide at the Assistant menu, Q&A asks if at this point you would like to teach the Query Guide to recognize field names and values from your database. Press Y to start the learning process, or press N to proceed and use the Query Guide without teaching it about field names and values.

3. Q&A displays a copy of your database form in the Query Guide Teach screen shown in Figure 17.5 and enters the letter Q in each text or keyword field.

```
                  TITAN TECHNOLOGY SALES LEAD TRACKING SYSTEM
═══════════════════════════════════════════════════ File Name -- SlsLead
LastName: Q                        FirstName:
Title:
Company: Q                         Telephone:
Address1:
Address2:
City: Q                            State: Q        Zip: Q
   No. of Labs:                    Annual Revenue:
   Current Customer:               Company Priority:
                          ──LEAD INFORMATION──
      ┌─────────────────────────────────────────────────────────┐
      │ Type "Q" in each text or keyword field that you wish to index │
      │ for use by the Query Guide.  For example, if you wish to have  │
      │ access to a scrollable list of cities in your database while in │
      │ the Query Guide, type a "Q" in the "City" field.              │
      │                                                                │
      │ SUGGESTION: Start by pressing F5 to mark all fields indexable by the │
      │ query guide with "Q"s.  Then, remove the "Q"s from those fields that │
      │ you do not wish to index.                                      │
      └─────────────────────────────────────────────────────────┘

SLSLEAD.DTF                    Query Guide Teach               Page 1  of 1

Esc-Exit    F1-Help      F3-Clear spec      F5-Select all      F10-Continue
```

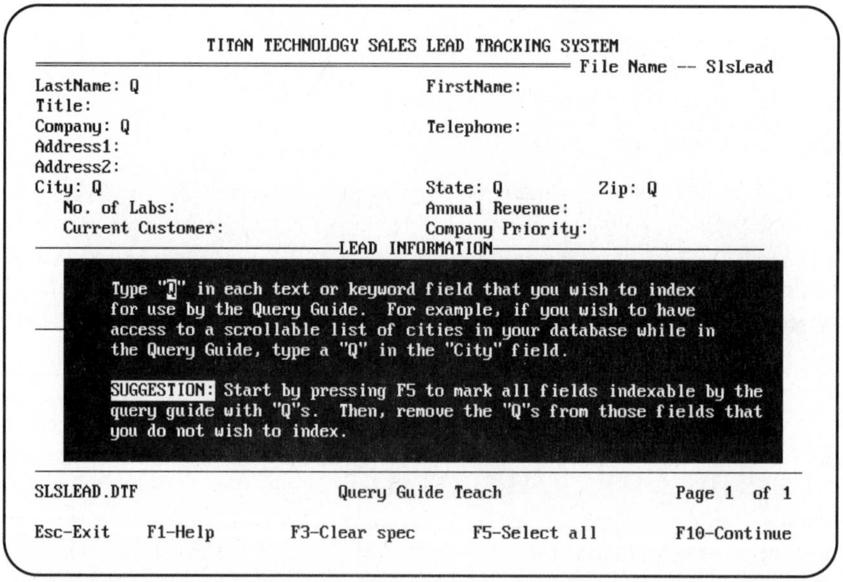

Fig. 17.5. *The Query Guide Teach screen.*

You cannot teach the QG about numerical or date fields. This restriction is a prudent feature of Q&A's design, because many different dates and numbers may be in such fields. Specifying data by searching through hundreds of numbers or dates with the cursor doesn't make much sense.

4. Move the cursor to each text or keyword field that you will not use with the QG and erase the Q that Q&A entered. To clear all fields, press F3. You then can move the cursor to selected fields and enter a *Q* manually.

   You can press F5 to enter a *Q* in every text and keyword field. You later can redisplay this screen and remove unneeded items.

5. Press F10 to exit the Query Guide Teach screen.

Q&A displays the Assistant menu, which was shown in figure 17.2.

You now can use the Query Guide to fill an Intelligent Assistant task statement. While you work with the Query Guide, you can back up to a previous screen at any point by pressing Esc. Q&A erases the most recently added phrase from the statement in the task box. Press Esc again and Q&A backs up another screen and erases the next element from the task statement. You can keep pressing Esc to back up to the first Query Guide screen.

File versus the Intelligent Assistant

When you compare using File alone with using File with the Intelligent Assistant, you quickly see the IA's power. Suppose that you want to ask the IA to display all sales leads for the Los Angeles office. The procedures you follow to complete this task using the Intelligent Assistant and using File are quite different.

Steps for Using File To Query a Database

Data-management capabilities are available through Q&A File even if you are not using the Intelligent Assistant. When you use File alone, however, even simple database searches or sorts can involve many steps. If you want to use File to search a sales lead database for the leads in the Los Angeles office, you first select the Search/Update option from the File menu. Q&A then displays the Retrieve Spec screen (see fig. 17.6).

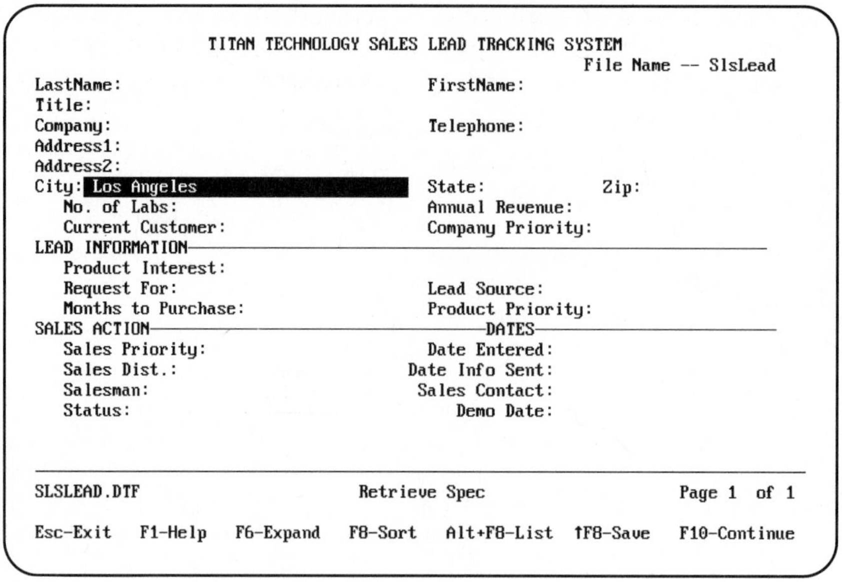

```
                   TITAN TECHNOLOGY SALES LEAD TRACKING SYSTEM
                                               File Name -- SlsLead
     LastName:                      FirstName:
     Title:
     Company:                       Telephone:
     Address1:
     Address2:
     City: Los Angeles              State:          Zip:
        No. of Labs:                Annual Revenue:
        Current Customer:           Company Priority:
     LEAD INFORMATION─────────────────────────────────────────
        Product Interest:
        Request For:                Lead Source:
        Months to Purchase:         Product Priority:
     SALES ACTION─────────────────────DATES────────────────────
        Sales Priority:             Date Entered:
        Sales Dist.:                Date Info Sent:
        Salesman:                   Sales Contact:
        Status:                     Demo Date:


     ────────────────────────────────────────────────────────
     SLSLEAD.DTF                 Retrieve Spec            Page 1  of 1

     Esc-Exit   F1-Help   F6-Expand   F8-Sort   Alt+F8-List  ↑F8-Save   F10-Continue
```

Fig. 17.6.   *The Retrieve Spec screen.*

To display all records for the Los Angeles sales district, move the cursor to the Sales Dist. field and type *Los Angeles.* With this specification entered as the data search, you are asking Q&A to display all Los Angeles records. When you press F10-Continue, the first record with *Los Angeles* entered in the Sales Dist. field is displayed. Each time you press F10, the next record that matches the search is displayed (see fig. 17.7).

Steps for Using the Intelligent Assistant To Query a Database

You also can use the Intelligent Assistant to complete the search for sales leads from the Los Angeles office. Begin by selecting the IA from the Q&A Main menu. When the Assistant menu is displayed, choose the Ask option from the list. When Q&A asks you to indicate the file containing the data you want to search, type the file name. The request window appears, and you can type a simple sentence such as: *Display the Los Angeles forms.*

When you press Enter, the Intelligent Assistant analyzes your sentence. A simple sentence such as *Display the Los Angeles forms* is easy for the Intelligent Assistant to understand because the sentence contains words that come from the IA's built-in vocabulary or are defined in your database. In addition, the IA can process the request because the IA understands the plural of *form* and makes assumptions about your request—assumptions that are based on knowledge of your database and databases in general.

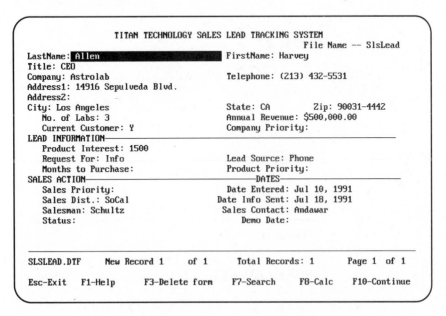

Fig. 17.7. *The first retrieved form that meets the search criteria.*

After successfully analyzing the sentence, the Intelligent Assistant displays the prompt shown in figure 17.8 before proceeding.

Notice that the prompt tells you how the Intelligent Assistant has analyzed your sentence and gives you an opportunity to cancel the request if you find the analysis wrong. In the example, however, the Intelligent Assistant has analyzed the sentence correctly; you want the IA to select and view the forms on which the sales district is Los Angeles.

By pressing Enter, you direct the Intelligent Assistant to display sales leads for the Los Angeles sales district. Because Los Angeles is a value in only one field, the IA assumes that you want the search to be conducted on that field. The IA displays the same initial form that is displayed when you manually request the Los Angeles leads by using the Search/Update command, the Retrieve Spec, and the function keys in the File module.

After the Intelligent Assistant displays the first record that meets the Los Angeles sales-district criterion, you can press F10-Continue to display other records for

Los Angeles sales leads. When you have reviewed all records that meet the criterion, you can display the records again or you can press Esc to return to the IA. When the Intelligent Assistant screen is displayed, you can enter other questions for sorting or searching for information in your database.

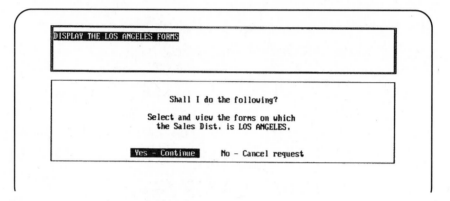

```
┌──────────────────────────────────────────────────────────┐
│ DISPLAY THE LOS ANGELES FORMS                              │
│                                                            │
│                                                            │
│   ┌────────────────────────────────────────────────────┐  │
│   │                                                      │  │
│   │             Shall I do the following?                │  │
│   │                                                      │  │
│   │        Select and view the forms on which            │  │
│   │         the Sales Dist. is LOS ANGELES.              │  │
│   │                                                      │  │
│   │      ███Yes - Continue███   No - Cancel request      │  │
│   └────────────────────────────────────────────────────┘  │
└──────────────────────────────────────────────────────────┘
```

Fig. 17.8. *The IA interpreting your request and asking for confirmation.*

One of the Intelligent Assistant's most sophisticated features is its capacity to modify the database. For example, you can ask the IA to change the telephone number on one of your forms:

    Change Blackson's telephone number to 363-886-3980

After you press Enter, the Intelligent Assistant analyzes your request, asks you to confirm its interpretation, and searches the forms in the database for the specified record. When the IA displays the forms you want to change, you press Shift-F10 to change the data and save the modifications.

File versus the Query Guide

When you use File to recall information from your database, you must type selection criteria in the Retrieval Spec, as described in the previous section, "Steps for Using File To Query a Database." Before you can fill in the Retrieve Spec, you must be familiar with Q&A's search terms and know how to format retrieval statements. When you use the Query Guide, you never need to look up the proper wording of a search element, because Q&A presents most of the possible entries in menus at each step of the way.

The Query Guide does have limitations. For example, you cannot specify data retrievals using LOOKUP or other programming statements, as you can with File or the Intelligent Assistant. Don't underestimate the Query Guide, however. QG is capable of handling most data retrieval chores offered by Q&A, including such complex queries as:

Cross-tabulate all statistics for Accrued Vacation by Department and decreasing Classification from the records where Accrued Vacation is greater than 4 and the Salary is at least 50000

The Query Guide works like an interactive tutor. After you become familiar with Q&A's search "language," you then can use the Retrieve Spec in Q&A File to perform retrievals more quickly. You also can teach the Intelligent Assistant a set of search terms to reduce entering database queries to a matter of typing them as simple English statements. The Query Guide always will be useful, however, when you're not sure of the correct terminology for a database search.

Steps for Using the Query Guide To Query a Database

Using the Query Guide is very similar to using the Intelligent Assistant, except that the QG builds a correctly formatted request statement for you. At the Main menu, select Assistant, then press Q at the Assistant menu to run the Query Guide. The last option on the screen, L-Teach Query guide, sets up the Query Guide so that the QG can display lists of text or keyword data from your database as selections for completing query guide statements. (This option is discussed in Chapter 18.) Q&A displays the Select an Option screen (see fig. 17.9).

Move the cursor to the first option, F - Find and Show ... (records). Press Enter. Q&A displays the records selection screen (see fig. 17.10). Move the cursor to the option, W - The Records Where ... (constraints are met). Notice that as you proceed from one screen to the next, Q&A adds your latest query restriction to the Intelligent Assistant query box displayed in the upper part of the screen. In effect, you are using the Query Guide to operate the Intelligent Assistant by entering preedited statements in the IA query screen.

Press Enter. Q&A displays the Select a Field screen (see fig. 17.11). In the list of field names, move the cursor to Zip by pressing Z. Press Enter to display the Select a Constraint screen (see fig. 17.12).

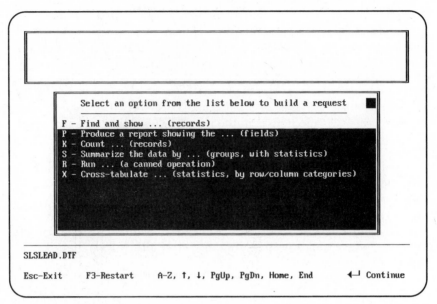

Fig. 17.9. *The initial Select an Option screen.*

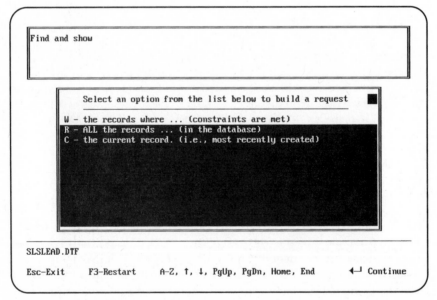

Fig. 17.10. *The records selection screen.*

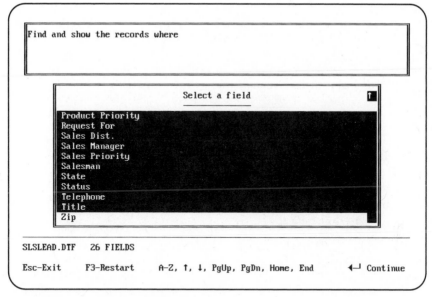

Fig. 17.11. *The Select a Field screen.*

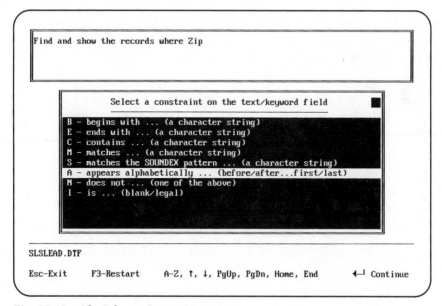

Fig. 17.12. *The Select a Constraint screen.*

The Intelligent Assistant query box at the top of the display now should read:

```
Find and show the records where Zip
```

Subsequent screens display the following questions, which you can answer by pointing to one of the listed field names or by typing your responses in a blank screen.

Query Guide screen item	User response
W - the records where ...	Zip
A - appears alphabetically ...	
A - after ...	89999
A - and the ...	Zip
A - appears alphabetically ...	
B - before ...	93001

At this point, the statement in the IA query box reads:

```
Show me the records where Zip appears alphabetically
after "89999" and Zip appears alphabetically before
"93001"
```

Choose the following menu item to execute the query statement:

. - . [execute the command]   . (runs the completed query)

At any point while building a Query Guide statement, you can go back one screen at a time by pressing Esc, or you can erase the query and start again by pressing F3 (Restart). As you back up through your query, Q&A erases the parts of the query statement that were entered at each screen.

The Query Guide is nearly as complex as Q&A itself with literally thousands of pathways through its prompts and menus. Describing all the possible QG requests, therefore, would require reviewing most of Q&A's features. This chapter is confined to building another complex retrieval. Using SLSLEAD, the following example constructs and executes the following statement:

Cross-tabulate the total and the count of values for Annual Revenue by Lead Source and Sales Dist. from ALL the records

To execute the preceding statement, follow these steps:

1. At the Query Guide Select an Option screen, press X to choose Cross-tabulate ... (statistics, by row/column categories). Q&A displays the Select Statistics screen, shown in figure 17.13.

   Notice that Q&A has entered the first element of the search in the dialog box at the top of the screen: Cross-tabulate.

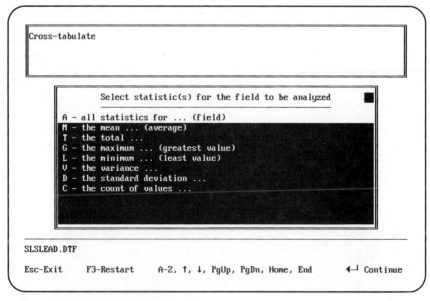

Fig. 17.13. *The Select Statistics screen.*

2. Press T to choose T - the Total .... Q&A displays the screen shown in figure 17.14.

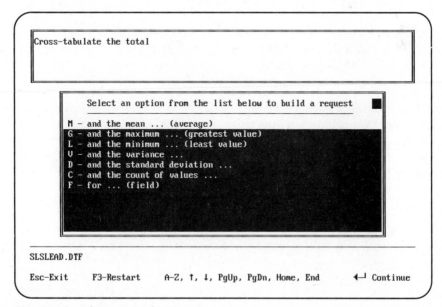

Fig. 17.14. *The statistical options screen.*

3. Choose C - and the Count of Values .... Q&A adds this element to the statement in the dialog box and displays the screen shown in figure 17.15.

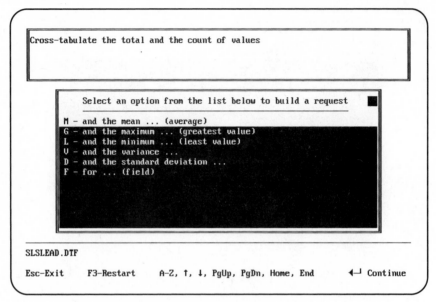

```
Cross-tabulate the total and the count of values



        Select an option from the list below to build a request   ■
   M - and the mean ... (average)
   G - and the maximum ... (greatest value)
   L - and the minimum ... (least value)
   V - and the variance ...
   D - and the standard deviation ...
   F - for ... (field)




SLSLEAD.DTF

Esc-Exit    F3-Restart    A-Z, ↑, ↓, PgUp, PgDn, Home, End    ←┘ Continue
```

Fig. 17.15. *The second statistical options screen.*

Because Q&A knows about the field names in your database, it displays a list of the field names (see fig. 17.16).

4. Press the first letter of a field name to move the cursor quickly to the field's name in the list, and press Enter to add the field name to the request statement in the dialog box. Q&A now displays the Select Sort Direction screen (see fig. 17.17).

5. Choose B - By ... (increasing values from the field) to sort row heading in ascending order. Q&A displays the Select a Row Title screen (see fig. 17.18).

6. Type *Le* to move the cursor to Lead Source, and press Enter to insert Lead Source in the request. Q&A displays another Select Sort Direction screen, for left-to-right column headings. Press A to select And ... (increasing values from the field). Q&A displays the Select a Column Title screen (see fig. 17.19).

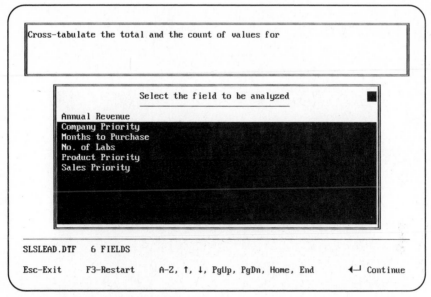

Fig. 17.16. *The field selection screen.*

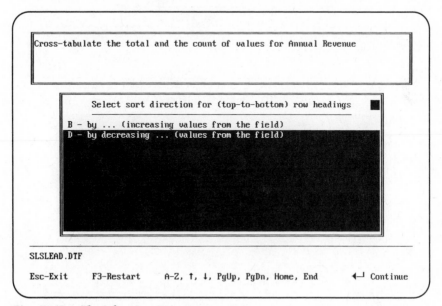

Fig. 17.17. *The Select Sort Direction screen.*

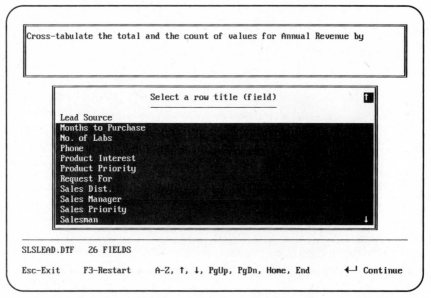

Fig. 17.18. The Select a Row Title screen.

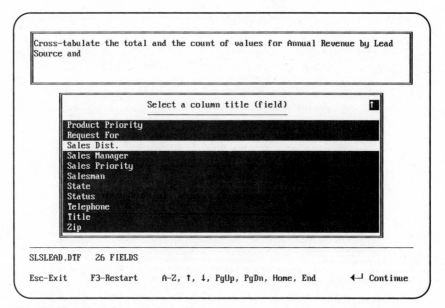

Fig. 17.19. The Select a Column Title screen.

7. Press S to choose Sales Dist., and press Enter. Q&A displays the option screen shown in figure 17.20.

8. Press R to select ALL records from the database.

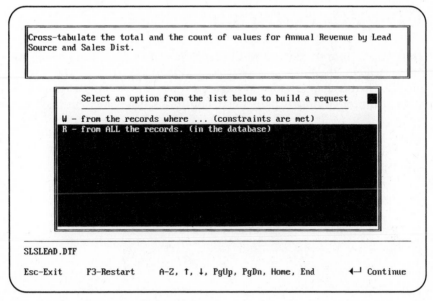

```
Cross-tabulate the total and the count of values for Annual Revenue by Lead
Source and Sales Dist.


        Select an option from the list below to build a request  ■
    ──────────────────────────────────────────────────────────────
    W - from the records where ... (constraints are met)
    R - from ALL the records. (in the database)




SLSLEAD.DTF

Esc-Exit    F3-Restart    A-Z, ↑, ↓, PgUp, PgDn, Home, End    ←┘ Continue
```

Fig. 17.20.   *The record selection screen.*

Q&A now displays the completed statement and immediately executes the request. The cross-tab report is displayed on the screen. Figure 17.21 shows the leftmost columns of the report. To view other sections of the report, you can scroll the screen vertically and horizontally using the PgUp, PgDn, and arrow keys.

```
Cross-tabulate the total and the count of values for Annual Revenue by Lead
Source and Sales Dist. from ALL the records.



                                         Sales Dist.
                        ─────────────────────────────────────────────────────
Lead Source                 Nevada        NorCal      Northeast        SoCal
───────────────────── ───  ──────────  ─────────────  ─────────────  ───────────
Adv                    Tot    $0.00        $0.00     $15,000,000.00  $5,000,000.00
                       Cnt      0            0             1              1
Phone                  Tot $14,000.00      $0.00         $0.00         $500,000.00
                       Cnt      1            0             0              4
Sales Call             Tot    $0.00    $14,000,000.00     $0.00         $0.00
                       Cnt      0            1             0              0
===================== ==== ==========  ============= ============== ===========
Total Annual Revenue   Tot $14,000.00  $14,000,000.00 $15,000,000.00 $5,500,000.00
                       Cnt      1            1             1              2


SLSLEAD.DTF

Esc-Exit  F2-Reprint    { → ← ↑ ↓ }-Scroll    Shift+F9-Redesign    F10-Continue
```

Fig. 17.21.   *The completed QG cross-tab report showing the leftmost columns.*

Chapter Summary

This chapter introduced you to the capabilities of Q&A's natural-language query facilities: the Intelligent Assistant and the Query Guide. The material provided in this chapter will help you get acquainted with IA/QG features and guide you through initial experiments using the Intelligent Assistant and Query Guide.

The next chapter offers additional help and more detailed information on applying the IA to your needs.

18

Using the
Intelligent Assistant
and Query Guide

C hapter 17 introduced the Intelligent Assistant and Query Guide and encouraged you to learn to use these unique Q&A features through experimentation. Chapter 17 also explained the range of capabilities and the manner in which the IA and QG process your requests.

In Chapter 17, you learned what the Intelligent Assistant can do before you expand its knowledge of your database and applications. In Chapter 18, you learn how to use the IA most effectively by applying the Intelligent Assistant to your particular database and applications. This chapter presents the following topics:

- Getting started with the IA

- Expanding the IA's knowledge

- Planning your requests

- Preparing the IA with Teach me about your database

- Entering requests

- Updating the IA's knowledge

- Using macros to automate the IA

In this chapter, you also learn about the kinds of database retrievals you can perform with the Query Guide. You learn how to tell the Query Guide about your database so that QG can display actual field data at prompts where you enter text or key field values.

Getting Started with the Intelligent Assistant

The Intelligent Assistant module is available through Q&A's Main menu. You select Assistant in the same way you select File, Report, or Write. After you choose the Assistant option, Q&A displays the Assistant menu. This menu provides five selections: Get Acquainted, Teach Me about Your Database (referred to here as Teach), Ask Me To Do Something (referred to as Ask), Query Guide, and Teach Query Guide. The Get Acquainted option provides a brief summary of the Intelligent Assistant's capabilities and makes recommendations on using the Intelligent Assistant. Use the Teach option to expand the Intelligent Assistant's vocabulary and to teach relationships to the IA so that the IA can process your requests. Selecting the Ask option displays the prompt screen, in which you enter your requests. The Query Guide and Teach Query Guide options are discussed later in this chapter.

When you first select the Teach or the Ask option, the Intelligent Assistant asks for the name of the database file to use. If you press Enter at this prompt, Q&A displays a list of database (DTF) files from the default data drive or path (see fig. 18.1). If the database file you want is listed, move the cursor to that name and press Enter. If your file is on another drive or path, type the new drive or path name, and press Enter. Q&A then displays the new list of DTF files.

The first time you use the Intelligent Assistant with your database, the IA analyzes the database before proceeding with the Teach or the Ask option. This analysis is necessary so that the IA can learn the field names, field type specifications, and information in each database form. After the Intelligent Assistant has analyzed your database, you can continue using the Teach or Ask option, as explained in the rest of this chapter.

The Q&A documentation recommends that you begin using the Intelligent Assistant by working through the lessons available with the Teach option. This book recommends, however, that you learn about the IA's capabilities through experimentation. This hands-on method gives you an immediate grasp of the IA's capabilities and helps you use the IA to meet your particular needs. Experimenting with the IA has one drawback: experimentation can cause the

IA to use disk space that may not be required after you learn how you will use this feature. You may want to create a temporary Q&A system for use while you learn about the IA, especially if you are operating on a network. Later, you can delete the temporary files and implement the required IA features in your working Q&A system.

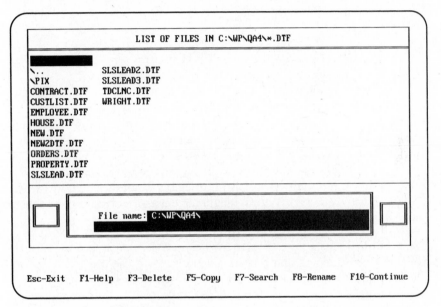

```
                    LIST OF FILES IN C:\WP\QA4\*.DTF

   \..              SLSLEAD2.DTF
   \PIX             SLSLEAD3.DTF
   CONTRACT.DTF     TDCLNC.DTF
   CUSTLIST.DTF     WRIGHT.DTF
   EMPLOYEE.DTF
   HOUSE.DTF
   NEW.DTF
   NEW2DTF.DTF
   ORDERS.DTF
   PROPERTY.DTF
   SLSLEAD.DTF



        File name: C:\WP\QA4\


   Esc-Exit   F1-Help   F3-Delete   F5-Copy   F7-Search   F8-Rename   F10-Continue
```

Fig. 18.1. *A list of the DTF files.*

After you have experimented with the Intelligent Assistant enough to be comfortable with its features and operation, use the IA for your daily data-management needs by following these basic steps:

1. Use a piece of paper or Q&A Write to make a list of requests you might enter.

2. Analyze your requests to determine what kind of assistance the IA needs so that it can understand your requests. Remember that you can teach the IA synonyms for field names, combine fields and give the combination a new name, and add words to the IA vocabulary. By studying the types of requests you are likely to give the IA, you can determine how to configure the IA for your application.

3. Prepare the IA for your requests by using some or all of the lessons available in the Teach option. The sample requests you have prepared can help you teach the IA what it needs to know to handle your application.

4. Enter requests for the IA to process.

5. Add to the Intelligent Assistant's knowledge as your needs grow. Remember to update the Intelligent Assistant's vocabulary and to teach the IA about the relationships between your requests and the database to which your requests refer.

Why Use the Teach Option?

You can use the Intelligent Assistant without expanding its built-in vocabulary or teaching it specific information about your database. Chapter 17 shows, for example, that as long as your questions contain words from the Intelligent Assistant's built-in vocabulary and the field names and values in your database, you can enter a wide range of requests. If a request contains a word the Intelligent Assistant doesn't recognize, however, the IA stops processing the request and prompts you to supply information about the unknown word. Depending on the word's context, the Intelligent Assistant may not be able to process the request.

The best way to make sure that the Intelligent Assistant can process most of your data management and reporting requests is to use the Teach option. Although you can forego that step and still use the IA to answer simple requests and produce reports, for more complicated tasks you need to teach the IA to recognize words that are unique to your database. When you use the Teach option to expand the Intelligent Assistant's information bank, you gain the following three important benefits:

- You can substitute alternative field names so that you can enter the same request many different ways. For example, in the sales lead database, many field names consist of two or more words, such as the No. of Labs, Annual Revenue, and Sales Manager fields (see fig. 18.2). To make queries easier, you can change these names to Labs, Revenue, and Manager and then use such questions as the following:

  Which leads have more than 10 labs?

  Who is the manager in the Philadelphia district?

  Which leads have revenue over $500,000?

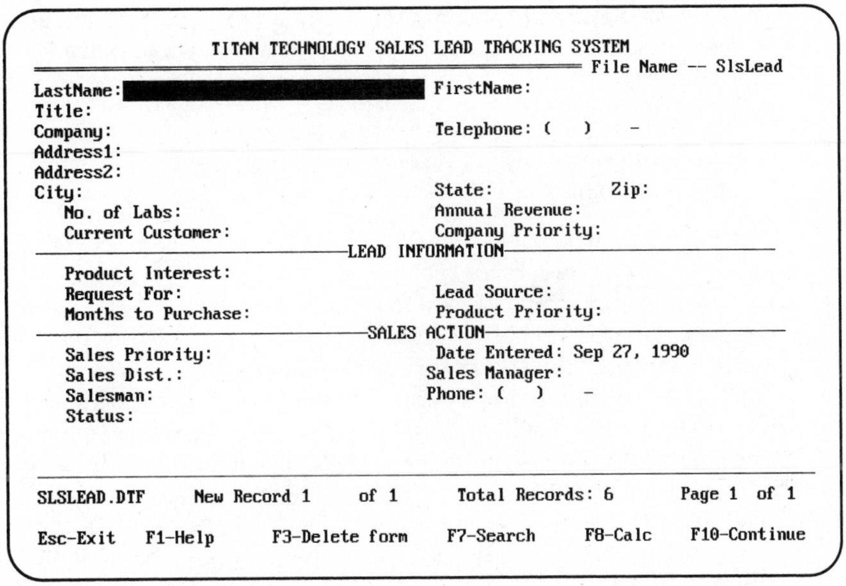

```
┌─────────────────────────────────────────────────────────────────┐
│              TITAN TECHNOLOGY SALES LEAD TRACKING SYSTEM          │
│  ═══════════════════════════════════════ File Name -- SlsLead    │
│  LastName:█████████████████████    FirstName:                    │
│  Title:                                                           │
│  Company:                          Telephone: (   )   -           │
│  Address1:                                                        │
│  Address2:                                                        │
│  City:                             State:        Zip:             │
│     No. of Labs:                   Annual Revenue:                │
│     Current Customer:              Company Priority:              │
│  ──────────────────────────LEAD INFORMATION──────────────────────│
│     Product Interest:                                             │
│     Request For:                   Lead Source:                   │
│     Months to Purchase:            Product Priority:              │
│  ──────────────────────────SALES ACTION──────────────────────────│
│     Sales Priority:                Date Entered: Sep 27, 1990     │
│     Sales Dist.:                   Sales Manager:                 │
│     Salesman:                      Phone: (   )   -               │
│     Status:                                                       │
│                                                                   │
│  ───────────────────────────────────────────────────────────     │
│  SLSLEAD.DTF    New Record 1     of 1    Total Records: 6    Page 1 of 1 │
│                                                                   │
│  Esc-Exit   F1-Help    F3-Delete form   F7-Search    F8-Calc   F10-Continue │
└─────────────────────────────────────────────────────────────────┘
```

Fig. 18.2. *The Sales Lead database.*

Without the Teach option, when you enter a request that includes only a part of a field name, such as *Labs* or *Revenue* in the preceding example, the Intelligent Assistant cannot process your request without help. The Intelligent Assistant doesn't understand that Labs is your alternative for No. of Labs, that Revenue refers to Annual Revenue, or that Manager means Sales Manager.

• Teaching the IA about your database makes querying, changing, and sorting easier for others who use your database to prepare reports. For example, you may ask your secretary to prepare a report listing annual revenues for all companies in the sales lead database. If you haven't taught the Intelligent Assistant the default field information to include in every report, the program responds to the request "List annual revenues" by displaying only a column of annual revenues but not the companies that earn those revenues. Teaching the IA alternative words for fields and values also makes other users' tasks much easier. When others query the IA, they don't have to use the same words that you used to design the database.

• The more the Intelligent Assistant knows about your database, the faster the IA can process your requests. Whenever the Intelligent

Assistant encounters an ambiguous word or a word not included in the IA's vocabulary, processing stops. This delay can waste valuable time. Suppose that you ask the IA the following question before you have used the Teach option:

> Which companies requesting demonstrations on the 1500 are not current customers?

The Intelligent Assistant pauses three times before it can process this request. First, the IA asks for clarification of the verb *requesting* because this word does not exist in either the Intelligent Assistant's built-in vocabulary or in the words available in your database (see fig. 18.3). Second, the IA asks for clarification of *demonstrations*. Although the database stores information indicating which sales leads have asked for product demonstrations, this information is entered in abbreviated form—as demo. Third, the Intelligent Assistant asks you to clarify the use of the number 1500 (see fig. 18.4). Because the IA recognizes 1500 as a number and also as a value in the Product Interest field, the IA needs to know how you have used the number in your request.

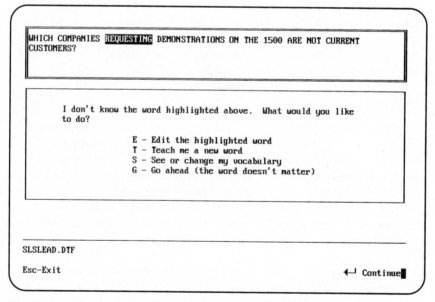

```
WHICH COMPANIES REQUESTING DEMONSTRATIONS ON THE 1500 ARE NOT CURRENT
CUSTOMERS?



        I don't know the word highlighted above.  What would you like
        to do?

                    E - Edit the highlighted word
                    T - Teach me a new word
                    S - See or change my vocabulary
                    G - Go ahead (the word doesn't matter)




SLSLEAD.DTF

Esc-Exit                                                  ↵ Continue
```

Fig. 18.3. *The IA asking for clarification of an unknown word.*

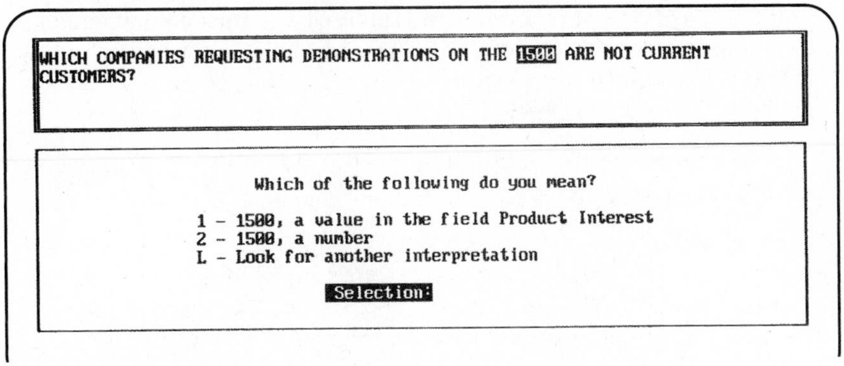

Fig. 18.4.   *The IA asking for clarification of an ambiguous term.*

Methods for Teaching the IA about Your Database

One of the Intelligent Assistant's most impressive features is its flexibility to fit different personal habits. If you like to plan an activity thoroughly before you begin, the Intelligent Assistant enables you to plot your requests carefully. You then can use these requests and the Teach option to prepare the Intelligent Assistant before you begin querying the database.

If you don't want to plan your requests before you enter them, you can teach the Intelligent Assistant interactively. Even if you bypass the Teach option and go directly to entering requests that contain vocabulary the IA doesn't understand, you can add the terms and relationships after the IA begins processing. When the Intelligent Assistant comes to something it cannot process, IA stops and asks for help, which gives you a chance to expand the IA's vocabulary. After you add the new terms to the IA's vocabulary, the IA continues to process your requests and stores the new terms for use in future requests. As you continue to enter questions, you gradually increase the Intelligent Assistant's vocabulary.

A third method for using the Intelligent Assistant combines the first two methods. You probably will find this method the most effective. Begin by planning how you want to use the Intelligent Assistant, and then teach the IA about your database. As you continue to enter questions, add to the information in the Intelligent Assistant's vocabulary by responding to problems that occur when the IA doesn't understand a part of your request.

When you select Teach Me about Your Database from the Assistant menu, the IA responds with a Basic Lessons menu that includes six choices:

- Learn Values for Assistant

- What this database is about

- Which fields identify a form

- Which fields contain locations

- Alternate field names

- Advanced lessons

One of these options is Advanced Lessons; selecting that option displays another five selections:

- What fields contain people's names

- Units of measure

- Advanced vocabulary: adjectives

- Advanced vocabulary: verbs

- Exit lessons

You therefore have a total of eleven Teach possibilities. Ten choices are for expanding the IA's information, and a final option is for exiting back to the Main menu. You may not need to use all ten options, but you should select those that best prepare the Intelligent Assistant for your requests. The time you spend working through the lessons on these menus will increase the capability and efficiency of the Intelligent Assistant.

Planning Your Requests

Before you begin the ten lessons, develop a list of as many questions as you can. Think of the questions you will use most often when instructing the Intelligent Assistant to query or sort your database, change or delete information, or provide summary reports.

Creating a List of Requests

The Intelligent Assistant is prepared to respond to simple requests for displaying information in your database. The IA also can perform more complex tasks, such as calculating values, presenting summary reports of information, and changing forms and data in the database.

Begin by determining the types of information your database contains. Next, consider exactly what information you want to retrieve, how you or others will want information displayed, and what information and forms you may want to change. Think of the kinds of requests you may enter concerning the different types of information. You may want to begin by writing down questions related to each field.

When you write your list of questions, make the list as comprehensive as possible. Consider the following three elements:

- *What task do you want to accomplish?* Do you want to retrieve data or a whole form, create a report, sort forms or data, or change data?

- *What type of information do you want?* Do you want information about people or places? Do you want to perform calculations? Do you want answers to yes/no questions?

- *How do you want the information displayed?* Do you want one column of information displayed? Do you want a predefined report?

Depending on the complexity of your database, you may want to retrieve many types of information. If you're using the IA with the sales lead database, for example, you may want to enter the following requests about sales leads:

How many sales leads are located in Pennsylvania?

How many sales leads are current customers?

Show all sales leads with annual revenue greater than $1,000,000.

You can enter more specific requests relating to values stored in the fields, such as the following:

Who is the Atlanta sales manager?

What is the address of Hope Laboratories?

How many labs does Hope Laboratories operate?

What is Hope Laboratories' annual revenue?

As you write down possible requests, consider not only the types of information you want, but also the operations you may want the IA to perform with the information in your database. Consider, for example, requests for changing, adding, and sorting information. You may want to make the following requests for changing information in the sales lead database:

Change Hope Laboratories' sales priority to 1.0.

Delete 2600 on the Hope Laboratories form.

Enter 5/3/88 for the Hope Laboratories Demo Date.

Consider requests that ask for types of reports. Notice in the following examples that the first three requests ask for a new report, but the last example asks the IA to display an existing report that was created in the Report module.

Display sales leads where revenue <5,000,000 >1,500,000.

List companies' sales priority = 1.5.

Show sales leads for the Los Angeles district office.

Show the sales priority report.

Decide whether you want the Intelligent Assistant to sum or calculate values in the databases by using the following requests:

How many sales leads are located in PA?

How many sales leads are current customers?

What is the total annual revenue for all sales leads in the LA sales district?

After you generate a working set of requests, you need to analyze and revise them so that the Intelligent Assistant can process your requests as quickly as possible. The next section discusses how to write requests that the IA can understand.

Revising Your List of Requests

Although the Intelligent Assistant's flexibility allows for various types of questions, you can save time and avoid problems by putting requests in the simplest form possible. You may want to keep a printed set of your often-used requests for querying, sorting, and changing the form and data in the database. When you design these requests, keep in mind the following guidelines:

- *Use the shortest form possible.* Use direct requests rather than complex questions, and use math symbols to simplify requests. You can replace a question such as "Which sales leads are not current customers?" with a request such as "List current customers = N." Notice that the latter request uses a command rather than a question and math symbols rather than full English syntax. (See Chapter 17 for more information on using math symbols in requests.)

- *Check for any ambiguities and revise to ensure the correct interpretation.* Suppose that the sales lead database contains the value Los Angeles in both the City and Sales District fields. If you enter a request such as *List all Los Angeles sales leads*, the IA cannot process this request without asking you to indicate whether Los Angeles refers to all sales lead companies with Los Angeles addresses or all sales leads that fall under the Los Angeles sales district. To ensure that the Intelligent Assistant interprets this request correctly, you can enter *List sales leads where city = Los Angeles.*

Preparing the IA for Your Requests

Creating a "working set" of requests helps you understand how best to use the Teach option. If you analyze the set of questions you have generated, you can determine what words you need to teach the Intelligent Assistant and how to control report output when you ask the IA to display information in column form. As mentioned previously, the IA Teach option includes two sets of lessons: Basic and Advanced. The lessons fit in the following categories:

- Providing synonyms for your database and its fields (Basic Lessons 2 and 5)

- Teaching the IA concepts related to fields (Basic Lessons 3 and 4; Advanced Lessons 1 and 2)

- Relating verbs and adjectives to the fields in your database (Advanced Lessons 3 and 4)

- Telling the IA what to include when you make requests for specific information rather than complete forms (Basic Lesson 3)

To select an option from the Basic Lessons menu or the Advanced Lessons menu, type the number or move the cursor to the selection, and press Enter. Many options display help screens that explain how you can use that particular option. For many selections, the Intelligent Assistant prompts you to enter numbers, words, phrases, and abbreviations that expand the IA's vocabulary and indicate relationships between information and fields in your database.

Using Cursor-Movement and Editing Keys in the Lesson Screens

Whenever you are asked to enter numbers, words, phrases, or abbreviations, use the keys in table 18.1 to move the cursor and edit or delete entries. (Remember, if you are already familiar with WordStar, the keys you use for editing and moving the cursor in WordStar also can be used in Q&A.)

Table 18.1
Cursor-Movement and Editing Keys Used in the IA Lesson Screens

Key	Function
↑	Moves cursor to preceding blank
↓	Moves cursor to next blank
→	Moves cursor to next character
←	Moves cursor to preceding character
Ctrl- →	Moves cursor to next word
Ctrl- ←	Moves cursor to preceding word
Tab	Moves cursor to next blank
Shift-Tab	Moves cursor to preceding blank
Home	Moves cursor to beginning of text entry
End	Moves cursor to end of text entry
Del	Deletes character at cursor location
Backspace	Deletes preceding character

Preparing the IA for Your Vocabulary

Lesson 1 tells the Intelligent Assistant about the database—what terms you are using to make a request. Lessons 2 and 5 on the Basic Lessons menu shown in figure 18.5 prepare the Intelligent Assistant for the range of requests you enter about your database. Lesson 2, What This Database Is About, helps the IA process requests that refer to the subject of your database. Lesson 5, Alternate Field Names, prepares the IA for the alternate words and phrases you use to refer to specific fields. The following sections explain these lessons as they relate to the sample sales lead database.

Teaching the IA about the Database

When you select the second option on the Basic Lessons menu, the Intelligent Assistant prompts you to list all words, phrases, abbreviations, and acronyms that you may use in your requests. After you have listed all possible words and word combinations, press F10 to save the words (see fig. 18.6).

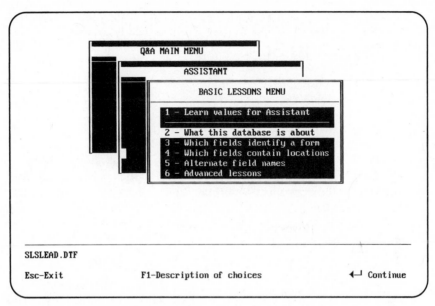

Fig. 18.5. *The Basic Lessons menu.*

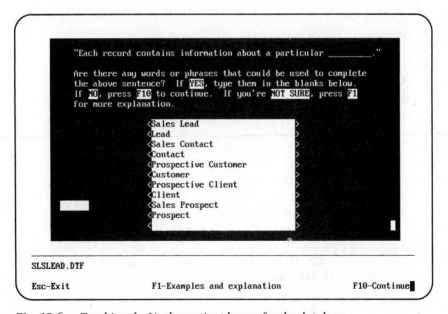

Fig. 18.6. *Teaching the IA alternative phrases for the database.*

In the Sales Lead database, you probably will often use the phrase *sales lead*. For example, you may enter the following requests and questions:

Display all sales leads for the New York office.

Which sales leads are current customers?

How many sales leads have annual revenue greater than $2,000,000?

IA requests probably will contain the sales lead phrase more often than other phrases, but you also will want to use other words and phrases. Figure 18.6 shows a list of 10 words and phrases that you can enter as alternatives to the primary phrase. For example, the IA can respond to such requests as "Which leads are interested in product 1500?" or "Which sales prospects would like product demos?" The Intelligent Assistant is able to recognize that *lead* and *sales prospect* are synonymous with *sales lead*, and IA then can respond correctly to your requests.

If you provide many synonyms in the What This Database Is About lesson, the Intelligent Assistant can process your requests more quickly with less action from you. Generating a comprehensive list saves time and effort for you and anyone else who uses your database.

Entering Alternative Field Names

You can use the fifth option, or lesson, in the Basic Lessons menu to teach the IA a wide range of synonyms for field names. When you select the Alternate Field Names lesson, the Intelligent Assistant displays a new screen so that you can enter up to nine alternative field names (see fig. 18.7). The alternative names can be words, phrases, or abbreviations. The original field name is shown as the first entry in the prompt box.

When displaying a columnar report in response to your requests, the IA uses the original field names unless you change the entry by using the Alternate field names option (see fig. 18.8). If you want the Company field name to be displayed in capital letters, for example, select Alternate Field names from the Basic Lessons menu, press F8 three times to move the highlight to the company field, move the cursor to the first entry in the Alternate Field Names prompt, and change the entry in the prompt box to all capital letters.

```
                    TITAN TECHNOLOGY SALES LEAD TRACKING SYSTEM
                                              File Name -- SlsLead
   LastName:▓▓▓▓▓▓▓▓▓▓▓▓▓▓▓▓▓▓▓▓ FirstName:
   Title:
   Company:                         Telephone:
   Address1:
   Address2:
   City:                            State:        Zip:
     No. of Labs:                   Annual Revenue:
     Current Customer:              Company Priority:
                          ─LEAD INFORMATION─
         ┌──────────────────────────────────────────────────────┐
         │  In the blanks below, type whatever names you will use to refer │
         │  to the field shown highlighted, then press ▓F8▓ to type names for │
         │  the next field.  When you are finished, press ▓F10▓. │
         │                                                         │
         │   <LastName          >     <Surname           >        │
         │   <Last Name          >     <              >            │
         │   <              >     <              >                 │
         │   <              >     <              >                 │
         │   <              >     <              >                 │
         └──────────────────────────────────────────────────────┘

   SLSLEAD.DTF                                       Page 1   of 1

   Esc-Exit     F6-Select previous field    F8-Select next field    F10-Continue▓
```

Fig. 18.7. *Entering synonyms for field names.*

```
   ┌──────────────────────────────────────────────────────────────┐
   │ Display the Company and Annual Revenue where Sales District is equal to │
   │ Knoxville                                                      │
   │                                                                │
   └──────────────────────────────────────────────────────────────┘

           Company                 Annual Revenue
   ─────────────────────      ──────────────────
   Advanced Medical Associates        $5300623.00
```

Fig. 18.8. *The column heads supplied by database field names.*

You can provide synonyms for all fields on your form. If you want to enter synonyms for succeeding fields, press F8; for previous fields, press F6. Keep in mind, however, that Q&A does not accept the same alternative field name in different fields. For example, the sales lead database contains three field names that use the word *priority*: Company Priority, Product Priority, and Sales Priority. If you decide to enter the single word *priority* as an alternative, you can use priority with only one field name. If you try to use the same synonym for more than one field, you see the prompt, Sorry. This word/phrase is already used. It must be unique.

When you enter alternative field names, consider all the possible terms that you may use in requests. Suppose, for example, that you want to enter alternative names for the Sales Dist. field in the sales lead database. Figure 18.9 shows the alternatives entered to cover the range of requests that refer to the Sales Dist. field.

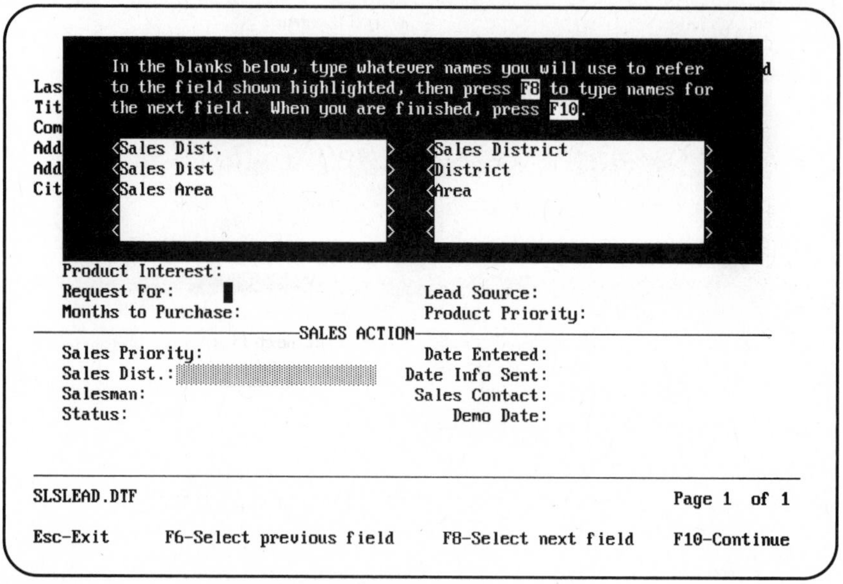

Fig. 18.9. *Alternative field names for Sales Dist.*

Notice in figure 18.9 that each alternative is typed in the prompt box connected with the Sales Dist. field. After you enter these alternatives, you can ask questions such as the following:

What sales district handles sales leads for Oklahoma City?

In which district is Hope Laboratories located?

Who is the sales manager for the Los Angeles area?

When you teach the Intelligent Assistant alternative field names, keep in mind the following suggestions for generating your list of names:

- *Consider both abbreviations and long forms of existing field names.* In the sales lead database, for example, the field name abbreviates the word *district* as *Dist.*, so you need to include the full form (sales district), if you want to use that form in any requests.

- *Include special symbols or acronyms if someone else will use these in requests.* Figure 18.10, for example, shows the alternative field names for the No. of Labs field from the Sales Lead database. Alternative names for this particular field name include the full form, the abbreviated form, and the number symbol (#).

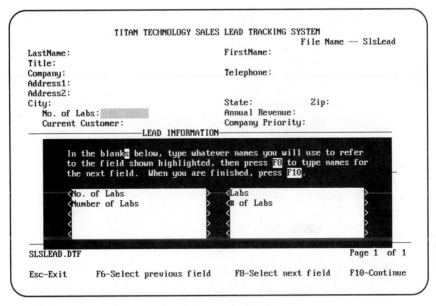

Fig. 18.10.   *Alternative field names for No. of Labs.*

With these alternatives, the Intelligent Assistant is prepared to process such requests as the following:

How many labs does Hope Laboratories operate?

Show the # of labs at Washington Medical.

When you finish entering synonyms, press F10 to return to the Basic Lessons menu.

Teaching the IA To Relate Fields to Names, Locations, and Units of Measure

Unlike humans, whose language is built on complex relationships between information and concepts, the Intelligent Assistant needs your help to make connections between a few basic concepts and the information in your database. Humans take for granted the fact that a question such as "Where is Hope Laboratories?" requires an answer specifying a location. Humans know that "Who sold the model 1500 to Washington Medical Labs?" requires a person's name in response. And "How many months are there before so-and-so needs delivery on the 2400?" presupposes that you understand months as a unit of time before you can answer. The IA, however, cannot process these simple requests without your assistance. Several lessons help you teach the IA about people's names (Advanced Lesson 1), locations (Basic Lesson 4), and units of measure (Advanced Lesson 2).

Identifying Name Fields

If your database includes fields that store the names of individuals—prospective customers, current customers, clients, employees, and consultants—you probably will want to make requests for these names. The sales lead database, for example, has five fields that contain either full names or parts of names. The first three fields contain parts of the full name for each sales contact; another field is the name of the district sales manager; and still another field contains the name of the salesperson who followed up on the sales lead. Before the IA can respond to a request such as "Who is the lab director at Hope Laboratories?" you must teach the IA to recognize which fields in the sales lead database contain people's names. To do so, choose option 1, What Fields Contain People's Names, from the Advanced Lessons menu shown in figure 18.11.

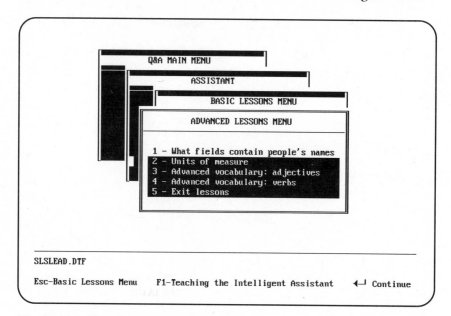

Fig. 18.11. *The Advanced Lessons menu.*

When you select this option, the IA displays a prompt asking you to press F1 if any fields contain a person's name. When you press F1, the Intelligent Assistant directs you to number each field that contains a name (see fig. 18.12).

To tell the Intelligent Assistant which fields are parts of a single name and should be combined into one composite name, enter the same number in each field, followed by a single-letter code to indicate whether the field contains the last name (L), first name (F), middle name (M), or title (T). If a field contains the whole name, use W. Notice in figure 18.12 that 1L, 1F, and 1T are the codes to identify each part of the name for each sales lead. The code 2W identifies the whole name for the sales manager. You can program the IA to recognize up to nine separate names in each record.

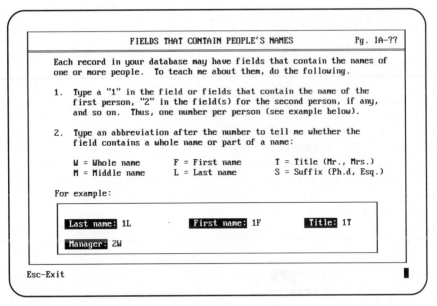

```
┌─────────────────────────────────────────────────────────────────┐
│           FIELDS THAT CONTAIN PEOPLE'S NAMES          Pg. IA-??   │
├─────────────────────────────────────────────────────────────────┤
│   Each record in your database may have fields that contain the   │
│   names of one or more people.  To teach me about them, do the    │
│   following.                                                      │
│                                                                   │
│   1.  Type a "1" in the field or fields that contain the name of  │
│       the first person, "2" in the field(s) for the second        │
│       person, if any, and so on.  Thus, one number per person     │
│       (see example below).                                        │
│                                                                   │
│   2.  Type an abbreviation after the number to tell me whether    │
│       the field contains a whole name or part of a name:          │
│                                                                   │
│       W = Whole name    F = First name   T = Title (Mr., Mrs.)    │
│       M = Middle name   L = Last name    S = Suffix (Ph.d, Esq.)  │
│                                                                   │
│   For example:                                                    │
│   ┌─────────────────────────────────────────────────────────┐   │
│   │ Last name: 1L        First name: 1F       Title: 1T      │   │
│   │ Manager: 2W                                              │   │
│   └─────────────────────────────────────────────────────────┘   │
│                                                                   │
│ Esc-Exit                                                       ▋  │
└─────────────────────────────────────────────────────────────────┘
```

Fig. 18.12.   *Numbering fields that refer to people's names.*

Specifying Location Fields

If you have in your database fields that store address, city, or state information, you need to teach the Intelligent Assistant that these fields refer to locations. For example, to help the Intelligent Assistant process a question such as "Where is Hope Laboratories?" use the fourth option from the Basic Lessons menu, Which Fields Contain Locations, to identify the Address, City, State, and ZIP fields as location fields. Otherwise, the IA may ask a question such as the one shown in figure 18.13. If you identify Address1, City, State, and Zip as locations, they appear in the report, even if you do not tell the IA these fields help identify a form (see #3 from the Basic Lessons menu).

To identify fields that refer to locations, select option 4 from the Basic Lessons menu. The Intelligent Assistant then asks you to number each field in the order you want the items to appear in the IA's response. Figure 18.14 illustrates the numbers for each location field in the sales lead database. As you can see, the location fields have been numbered so that they will appear as displayed on the original sales lead form.

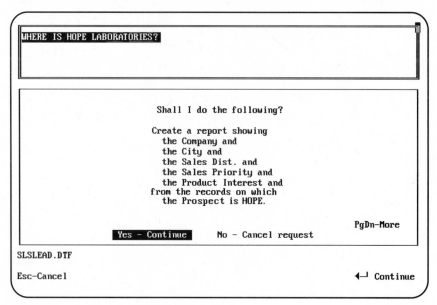

Fig. 18.13.   Before defining location fields.

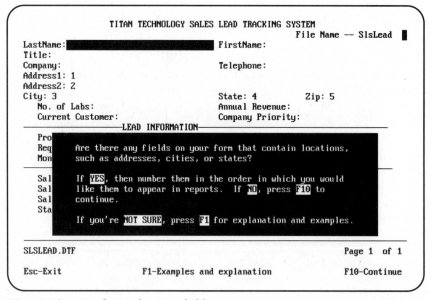

Fig. 18.14.   Numbering location fields.

You can limit the IA's response to complex location questions by teaching the Intelligent Assistant to interpret as one address terms or phrases from two or more fields. For example, suppose that you want to ask the following question:

What is Hope Laboratories' address?

Before the IA can respond correctly by displaying the address, city, state, and ZIP code, you must teach the Intelligent Assistant how to interpret the word *address*. Select the Ask Me To Do Something option from the Intelligent Assistant menu. When the request box appears, type the following sentence:

Define address as address1, city, state, and ZIP.

After you type the sentence and press Enter, the Intelligent Assistant asks for confirmation, then saves your definition of address. From that point on, whenever you use address in your requests, the IA displays the information from the Address1, City, State, and Zip fields.

Identifying Units of Measure Fields

You also can help the Intelligent Assistant answer questions that relate to units of measure. For example, the Months to Purchase field in the sales lead database has the word *months* in the field name, but Q&A doesn't know what value constitutes a month. Until you teach this concept to the Intelligent Assistant, the IA will be unable to answer questions such as the following:

How many months are there before Arizona Medical Services needs to purchase the 2400?

How many companies need to purchase the 2400 in 2 months?

Before the Intelligent Assistant can understand that the values entered in the Months to Purchase field are monthly units, you need to use Advanced Lesson 2, Units of Measure, to identify the units of measure for all numeric fields.

When you select this option, the Intelligent Assistant asks you to indicate the particular unit for the highlighted field. Q&A displays a screen that explains how to specify the units of measure for the field (see fig. 18.15). In the sales lead database, for example, you can enter *months* as the unit of measure in the Months to Purchase field. If you want to change the selected field, press F8 or F6 to move the cursor. After you have identified the measurement types for the fields, press F10 to save the information.

```
                 TITAN TECHNOLOGY SALES LEAD TRACKING SYSTEM
                                              File Name -- SlsLead
   LastName:                      FirstName:
   Title:
   Company:                       Telephone:
   Address1:
   Address2:
   City:                          State:          Zip:
     No. of Labs:##########       Annual Revenue:
     Current Customer:            Company Priority:################
                    ──────LEAD INFORMATION──────
```

Is the field shown highlighted measured in some kind of unit?
If YES, type the unit in the blank below. If NO, press F8 to
select any other number fields that have units, or F10 to
continue to the next lesson. If you're NOT SURE, press F1 for
examples and explanation.

Unit of measure: ▮▮▮▮▮▮▮▮▮▮▮▮>

Example units: mpg, inches, yards, tons, cups.

```
SLSLEAD.DTF                                       Page 1   of 1

Esc-Exit       F6-Select previous field     F8-Select next field   F10-Continue
```

Fig. 18.15.   *Defining units of measure.*

Teaching the IA Adjectives and Verbs

Initially, the Intelligent Assistant's vocabulary is smaller than a young child's. (See "Checking and Changing Vocabulary," later in this chapter, for a partial list of the built-in vocabulary.) You can scan the IA vocabulary at any time by pressing F6 when you are in the IA module of Q&A. The more sophisticated your sentence structure and vocabulary, the more difficulty the IA has processing your requests. In Chapter 17, you learned that the IA can process simple requests easily—if the requests include only words and phrases from your database or from the IA's built-in vocabulary. For example, the IA can respond to the following requests about the sales lead database:

What is Blackson's phone number?

Display forms with demo dates between 7/1/88 and 9/1/88.

What company has the greatest annual revenue?

Display the Los Angeles forms.

If you analyze each request, you find that all words come from either the field names and data in the sales lead database or from words in the IA's vocabulary. In these examples, the words taken from the built-in vocabulary include the following:

what	is
display	forms
with	between
and	has
the	greatest

Compared to your vocabulary, the Intelligent Assistant is limited in its range of adjectives and verbs. When you use adjectives and verbs that are new to the IA, the IA asks for your help in relating the words to the information in your database. Advanced lessons 3 and 4 help you teach the IA how to connect the special adjectives and verbs in your requests with the information in your database.

Entering Special Adjectives

Chapter 17 explains that the IA's built-in vocabulary includes adjectives used in searching and sorting operations. Therefore, the Intelligent Assistant can interpret phrases with words like greatest, highest, least, fewest, and so on (see table 18.2). If you use adjectives that refer to a degree not included in the IA's vocabulary, you need to add these words to the IA's knowledge.

Table 18.2
Adjectives in the Built-In Vocabulary

above	below	under
big	bigger	biggest
early	earlier	earliest
few	fewer	fewest
great	greater	greatest
high	higher	highest
large	larger	largest
late	later	latest
little	littler	littlest
long	longer	longest
low	lower	lowest
many	more	most
maximum	minimum	
much	less	least
small	smaller	smallest
top	bottom	

For example, if you want to be able to ask the IA a question such as "Who is the most successful sales lead?" and receive a report on which sales lead has the highest annual revenue, you first must teach the Intelligent Assistant that *successful* is an adjective referring to the Annual Revenue field. After you establish that relationship, the IA can process your request.

To teach the IA the special adjectives you plan to use in your requests, select lesson 3, Advanced Vocabulary: Adjectives, from the Advanced Lessons menu. Highlight the field to which the adjectives will relate by pressing F6 for the preceding field and F8 for the next field. When you select this lesson, the Intelligent Assistant displays a screen that explains the purpose and method for using the lesson (see fig. 18.16). Below the explanation are blanks on which you enter pairs or single adjectives to convey high or low values. For the sales lead database, for example, you can enter the following adjectives:

High value	Low value
rich	poor
successful	unsuccessful
prosperous	struggling
hot	

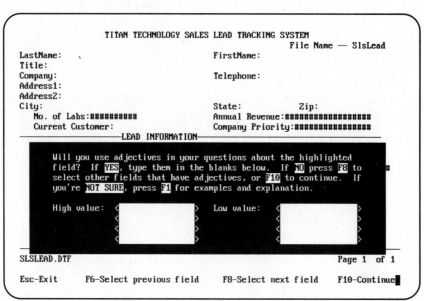

Fig. 18.16.   *Entering adjectives that relate to your database.*

You can enter adjectives in one or both columns; you don't need to provide pairs of adjectives in every case. For example, you can enter the adjective *hot* so that you can use the query "Which lead is the hottest?" but you do not have to supply an opposite. You don't need to enter the *est* form of the adjective when you enter the word in the prompt box; Q&A understands that automatically.

You can enter adjectives for every field in your database. If you want to use the same adjective to refer to more than one field, however, you must enter the adjective for each field. When you use the same adjective to refer to more than one field, you have to specify the field in your requests. If you don't make the field reference clear, the IA assumes that you mean the first field that contains the adjective. For example, if you use the adjective *hot* to refer to both the Annual Revenue and Sales Priority fields, you must phrase your questions so that the IA knows to which field *hot* refers. The following queries make the relationship obvious:

Which company has the hottest annual revenue?

Which company is the hottest sales priority?

The Intelligent Assistant can respond easily to a request for the highest or lowest value in a field. If you ask the Intelligent Assistant to determine whether a range of values is high or low, however, the IA can interpret high or low values only as they relate to an average value. If you ask "Which companies are prosperous?", for example, the Intelligent Assistant interprets your request as "Which companies have above the average annual revenue?" Figure 18.17 shows how the IA confirms your request.

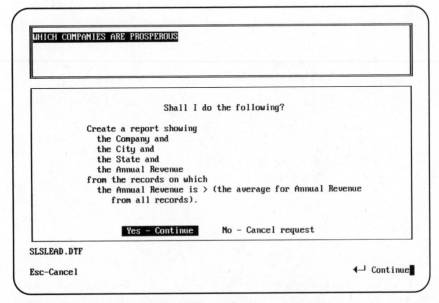

```
WHICH COMPANIES ARE PROSPEROUS



                              Shall I do the following?

                    Create a report showing
                        the Company and
                        the City and
                        the State and
                        the Annual Revenue
                    from the records on which
                        the Annual Revenue is > (the average for Annual Revenue
                            from all records).


                        Yes - Continue        No - Cancel request

   SLSLEAD.DTF

   Esc-Cancel                                                    ←┘ Continue
```

Fig. 18.17.   *Interpreting high and low values.*

Entering Special Verbs

The built-in vocabulary of the Intelligent Assistant contains verbs that you can use to specify operations for displaying, sorting, searching, calculating, or changing data (see table 18.3). In addition, the IA includes a number of other verbs that are used often in requests. When you enter a verb that the Intelligent Assistant does not recognize, however, the IA needs you to define the word and its relationship to the field the word references.

Table 18.3
Verbs in the IA's Built-in Vocabulary

add	define	find	print	set
blank	delete	get	remove	show
change	display	increase	replace	sum
count	divide	list	report	total
create	enter	make	run	
decrease	erase	multiply	search	

For example, the Intelligent Assistant has trouble responding to the following requests:

How many labs does Hope Laboratories administer?

Display all companies that administer 2 or more labs.

Before the IA can process these requests, you need to use the fourth option from the Advanced Lessons menu, Advanced Vocabulary: Verbs, to define the word *administer* and show its relationship to the No. of Labs field.

When you select this lesson, the Intelligent Assistant asks you to enter the verbs you will use to refer to the fields in your database. Figure 18.18 shows that several verbs have been entered for the No. of Labs field. The Intelligent Assistant then can process questions such as the following:

How many labs does Washington Medical Labs direct?

Does Hope Laboratories control 3 labs?

Although you can enter verbs for any field in your database, you cannot enter the same verb in more than one field. Move to the field you want by pressing F8 for the next field and F6 for the preceding field. When you have finished entering verbs for the fields, press F10 to save the entries.

```
                    TITAN TECHNOLOGY SALES LEAD TRACKING SYSTEM        ▮
                                              File Name -- SlsLead
    LastName:                         FirstName:
    Title:
    Company:                          Telephone:
    Address1:
    Address2:
    City:                             State:         Zip:
      No. of Labs: ▓▓▓▓▓▓▓▓▓          Annual Revenue:
      Current Customer:               Company Priority:
    ─────────────────────LEAD INFORMATION─────────────────────────────
    ╔═════════════════════════════════════════════════════════════════╗
    ║  If you need help, press F1.  If not, type verbs you wish to use  ║
    ║  with the field shown highlighted, then press F8 to teach me verbs ║
    ║  for the next field, if desired.  Press F10 when done.            ║
    ║  ┌─────────────────────────┐  ┌────────────────────────────┐     ║
    ║  <Operate                  >  <Direct                      >      ║
    ║  <Control                  >  <Own                         >      ║
    ║  <Administer                >  <                           >      ║
    ║  <                          >  <                           >      ║
    ║  <                          >  <                           >      ║
    ╚═════════════════════════════════════════════════════════════════╝
    SLSLEAD.DTF                                          Page 1  of 1

    Esc-Exit      F6-Select previous field      F8-Select next field      F10-Continue
```

Fig. 18.18. *Examples of verbs used in the No. of Labs field.*

If you plan to use any irregular verbs (verbs that do not have regular endings such as -s, -es, -en, -ed, or -ing), you must enter all forms of the verb. For example, the verb *sell* plus its irregular past tense form of *sold* must be entered in reference to the Salesman field. This entry allows you to ask the IA a question such as "Who sold the 2400 to Hope Laboratories?"

Controlling the Display of Columnar Reports

The Intelligent Assistant responds to your requests by displaying complete forms or by listing the results in columnar format (see fig. 18.19). When you ask the IA to "Display all forms for sales leads in the Mobile sales district," however, the IA displays each form (see fig. 18.20). If you ask the IA to answer "Which companies are in PA?", however, the IA produces a single-column list of those companies (see fig. 18.21). No other information is displayed unless you specify that the IA should include certain fields each time it displays a columnar report.

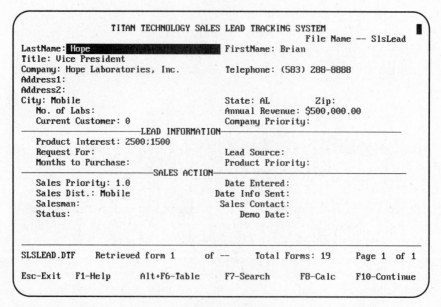

```
┌─────────────────────────────────────────────────────────────────────┐
│ ┌───────────────────────────────────────────────────────────────┐   │
│ │Display companies, current customer field, co. priority, and product│ │
│ │interest.                                                       │   │
│ │                                                                │   │
│ │                                                                │   │
│ └───────────────────────────────────────────────────────────────┘   │
│                                                                       │
│              Company              Current Customer   Company Priority   Prod │
│        ─────────────────────    ──────────────────   ──────────────    ──── │
│     Mountain Labs                      Y                      1         1500 │
│     Hope Laboratories, Inc.                                            2500 │
│     Bay City Laboratories                                             2000 │
│     Penn Medical Technology            Y                               2000 │
│     Mattis Medical Technology                                         2500 │
│     Washington Medical Labs, Inc.                                     1500 │
│     Franklyn Lab Associates            N                               1200 │
│     University of Michigan                                            1000 │
│     Independent Medical Labs                                          2500 │
│     Plaines Medical Associates                                        1200 │
│     Mountain Labs                                                     1000 │
│     Pike Pharmaceutical, Inc.          Y                               2000 │
│     Advanced Medical Associates        Y                               2000 │
│     ───────────────────────────────────────────────────────────────────── │
│     SLSLEAD.DTF                                                            │
│     ***************************** END OF REPORT *************************** │
│     Esc-Exit      F2-Reprint      { → ← ↓ ↑ PgUp PgDn }-Scroll   F10-Continue■ │
└─────────────────────────────────────────────────────────────────────┘
```

Fig. 18.19.   *A columnar report in the Intelligent Assistant.*

```
┌─────────────────────────────────────────────────────────────────────┐
│              TITAN TECHNOLOGY SALES LEAD TRACKING SYSTEM          ■   │
│                                              File Name -- SlsLead     │
│  LastName:[Hope                    ]  FirstName: Brian                │
│  Title: Vice President                                                │
│  Company: Hope Laboratories, Inc.     Telephone: (583) 288-8888       │
│  Address1:                                                            │
│  Address2:                                                            │
│  City: Mobile                         State: AL      Zip:             │
│     No. of Labs:                      Annual Revenue: $500,000.00      │
│     Current Customer: 0               Company Priority:               │
│  ─────────────────────LEAD INFORMATION─────────────────────────      │
│     Product Interest: 2500;1500                                       │
│     Request For:                      Lead Source:                    │
│     Months to Purchase:               Product Priority:               │
│  ─────────────────────SALES ACTION─────────────────────              │
│     Sales Priority: 1.0               Date Entered:                   │
│     Sales Dist.: Mobile               Date Info Sent:                 │
│     Salesman:                         Sales Contact:                  │
│     Status:                           Demo Date:                      │
│                                                                       │
│  ───────────────────────────────────────────────────────────────     │
│  SLSLEAD.DTF    Retrieved form 1     of --    Total Forms: 19    Page 1 of 1 │
│                                                                       │
│  Esc-Exit   F1-Help     Alt+F6-Table    F7-Search    F8-Calc    F10-Continue │
└─────────────────────────────────────────────────────────────────────┘
```

Fig. 18.20.   *The IA displaying a form as a response.*

```
Which companies are in PA




        Company
----------------------
Franklyn Lab Associates
```

Fig. 18.21.   *The IA displaying a single column.*

To specify which fields you want the IA to display in all columnar reports, select
the third option, Which Fields Identify a Form, from the Basic Lessons menu.
On the screen that appears, you can specify the order of the fields in the
columnar report. For example, suppose that you want the Intelligent Assistant
to display the name and title of the sales lead, the company name, and the
telephone number each time a columnar report is produced. To indicate that
you want those fields included, number the fields in the order you want them
to appear. In figure 18.22, for reports generated from the sales lead database,
the LastName field has been numbered as 1, FirstName as 2, Title as 3, Company
as 4, and Telephone as 5.

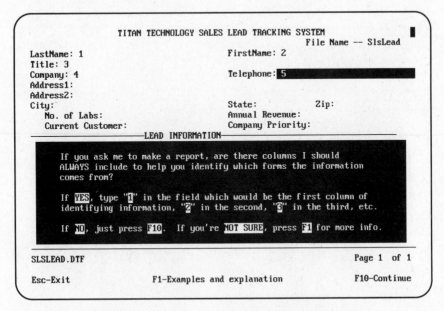

Fig. 18.22.   *Numbering the fields you want included in every report.*

To save your settings, press F10. From that point on, each time you produce a columnar report, the IA includes those fields. For example, if you later ask the IA to list all companies that have a 1.5 sales priority, the IA produces a list of companies, including the name of the contact at the company and the telephone number (see fig. 18.23). Unless you tell the Intelligent Assistant not to include this information (by using the Which Fields Identify a Form option), the IA includes these fields every time it creates a summary report in response to a request.

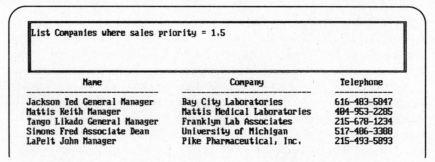

```
List Companies where sales priority = 1.5



                Name                      Company              Telephone
            ---------------          -----------------      -------------
Jackson Ted General Manager       Bay City Laboratories       616-483-5847
Mattis Keith Manager              Mattis Medical Laboratories 404-953-2285
Tango Likado General Manager      Franklyn Lab Associates     215-678-1234
Simons Fred Associate Dean        University of Michigan      517-486-3388
LaPelt John Manager               Pike Pharmaceutical, Inc.   215-493-5893
```

Fig. 18.23. *All columns specified in lesson 1 are displayed in reports.*

Figure 18.23 shows that the Intelligent Assistant returns under the Name column the last name, first name, and title of the company contact. You can produce this result by using Advanced Lesson 1 to direct the Intelligent Assistant to combine the LastName, FirstName, and Title fields. If these fields are not combined, the report displays with each of those fields as a separate column (see fig. 18.24).

```
List companies where sales priority = 1.5



LastName    FirstName      Title              Company
--------    ---------   --------------     -----------------
Jackson     Ted         General Manager    Bay City Laboratories        6
Mattis      Keith       Manager            Mattis Medical Laboratories  4
Tango       Likado      General Manager    Franklyn Lab Associates      2
Simons      Fred        Associate Dean     University of Michigan       5
LaPelt      John        Manager            Pike Pharmaceutical, Inc.    2
```

Fig. 18.24. *Each field listed in a column.*

Displaying Additional Columns

You can add columns to summary reports—without changing the information—through Basic Lesson 3. Suppose that you decide to display the sales district in addition to the name, company, and telephone number. You can enter the following request:

List all 1.5 sales priorities and display sales districts.

The Intelligent Assistant understands from this request that you want an additional column displayed in the report. Figure 18.25 shows that the IA asks for confirmation before proceeding with the request.

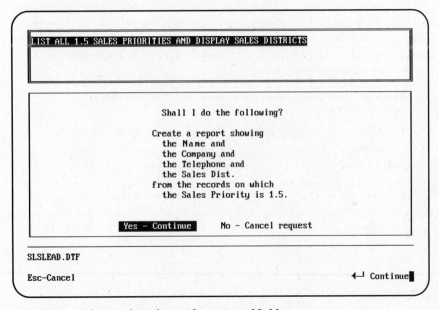

```
┌──────────────────────────────────────────────────────────────────┐
│ ┌────────────────────────────────────────────────────────────┐   │
│ │LIST ALL 1.5 SALES PRIORITIES AND DISPLAY SALES DISTRICTS│    │   │
│ │                                                              │   │
│ │                                                              │   │
│ └────────────────────────────────────────────────────────────┘   │
│ ┌────────────────────────────────────────────────────────────┐   │
│ │            Shall I do the following?                         │   │
│ │                                                              │   │
│ │      Create a report showing                                 │   │
│ │          the Name and                                        │   │
│ │          the Company and                                     │   │
│ │          the Telephone and                                   │   │
│ │          the Sales Dist.                                     │   │
│ │      from the records on which                               │   │
│ │          the Sales Priority is 1.5.                          │   │
│ │                                                              │   │
│ │        Yes - Continue      No - Cancel request               │   │
│ └────────────────────────────────────────────────────────────┘   │
│ ─────────────────────────────────────────────────────────────    │
│ SLSLEAD.DTF                                                        │
│                                                                    │
│ Esc-Cancel                                            ←┘ Continue  │
└──────────────────────────────────────────────────────────────────┘
```

Fig. 18.25. *The IA asking for confirmation of fields.*

Restricting Columns

The Intelligent Assistant can "hide" columns of information that you don't want to appear in a summary report. To suppress the column display, you simply add one of three acronyms at the end of your request. The acronyms used to hide columns are listed in table 18.4.

Table 18.4
Suppressing Columns of Information in IA Reports

Acronym	Meaning	Purpose
WNIC	With No Identification Columns	Suppress columns listed in basic lesson 2
WNRC	With No Restriction Columns	Suppress restriction columns
WNEC	With No Extra Columns	Suppress extra columns

You can suppress the display of the columns you specified in Basic Lesson 3 (Which Fields Identify a Form) so that only the columns affected by your request are displayed. For example, if you want the Intelligent Assistant to display only Company and Annual Revenue columns when you request a report of all companies with annual revenue between $500,000 and $1,000,000, you can enter the following request:

List companies with annual revenues between 500000 and
1000000. WNIC

The IA asks for confirmation that you want only companies and revenues displayed. Figure 18.26 shows the Intelligent Assistant's response to your request.

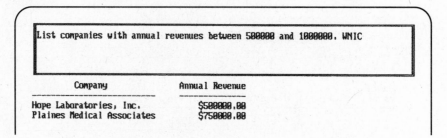

Fig. 18.26.   Using WNIC in a request.

The IA has assumed that you want the revenues for each company displayed. The column that shows the revenues, called the restrict column, is the column that defines the limits of your request. If the information in the restrict column is confidential, you can suppress it by entering WNRC (with no restriction columns) at the end of your request, such as in the following example:

List companies with annual revenues between 500000 and
1000000. WNRC

The result of this request, shown in figure 18.27, includes all columns of information originally set in Basic Lesson 3. The Annual Revenue field, however, is not included.

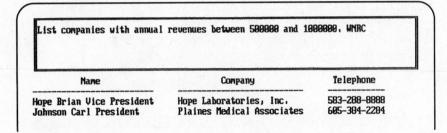

Fig. 18.27. *Omitting the restriction column with WNRC.*

Using the acronym WNEC (with no extra columns), you can tell the Intelligent Assistant to display only the columns you specify in your request. For example, you can have the IA display only the companies that have an income between $500,000 and $1,000,000 by entering the following request:

> List companies with annual revenues between 500000 and
> 1000000. WNEC

The results of this request appear in figure 18.28.

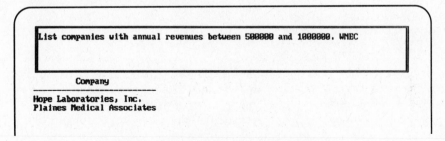

Fig. 18.28. *Using WNEC to display only requested columns.*

Entering Requests to the Intelligent Assistant

After you enhance the knowledge of the Intelligent Assistant by going through the lessons in the Basic Lessons and Advanced Lessons menus, the IA should be able to respond to most of your requests. IA is much easier to use than File or Report for querying, adding, changing, or reporting information. With the IA, you don't have to use function keys or menu screens to enter your requests. You type the question, and the IA can interpret and carry out your request. If the IA has trouble, it supplies a prompt or a warning.

In addition to describing the special features of the IA menu, screens, and cursor-movement and editing keys, this section gives examples of the range of the IA's capabilities and offers some tips for using the IA to meet your data-management needs.

Using the Ask Option To Enter Requests

When you want to ask the Intelligent Assistant to process a request, select the Ask Me To Do Something option from the Assistant menu. Before your first request can be analyzed, the IA must analyze your database. That process may take a few minutes, depending on the size of your database and the hardware you use. After IA has analyzed your database, you can enter requests in the box at the top of the screen.

The center of the screen is reserved for messages and prompts that help you use the Intelligent Assistant. The bottom of the screen shows the file name of your database and lists explanations of the special keys.

Keys Used for Entering Requests

Many of the editing keys available in Write can be used with the Intelligent Assistant. If you're familiar with the keys used to move the cursor and edit text, then entering, deleting, and changing information in the request box is easy. (For more information on the keys used in Write, see Chapters 9 and 10.)

Similar to Write, the IA enables you to use Overwrite or Insert mode for entering characters. You also can use the WordStar key combinations for moving the cursor and editing text. You can use the following keys in the IA to move the cursor:

Key	Moves the cursor
→ or Ctrl-D	One character to the right
← or Ctrl-S	One character to the left
↑ or Ctrl-E	Up one line
↓ or Ctrl-X	Down one line
Home	To the beginning of the line
End	To the end of the line
Ctrl- → or Ctrl-F	One word right
Ctrl- ← or Ctrl-A	One word left

Use the following keys to delete characters, words, or lines:

Key	Deletes
Del	Character at cursor position
Backspace	One character to the left
Ctrl-G	Character at cursor position
F4	Word to the right
Ctrl-Y	Line at cursor position

The Intelligent Assistant screens display the special uses of keys when you are entering and processing requests. When you are entering requests, for example, the special keys include Esc, F1, F6, F8, and Enter. If you press Esc after entering all or part of a request, you are returned immediately to the Assistant menu. Use F1 when you need to display a help screen about entering a prompt. F6 shows a menu that displays the different portions of the Intelligent Assistant's vocabulary. A menu of options for teaching the IA information about your database is displayed when you press F8. Pressing Enter tells the Intelligent Assistant to begin processing your request.

Tips for Entering Requests

As you know, you can use the Intelligent Assistant to search, sort, change, add, and calculate data. The IA can create new forms, produce reports, and delete existing forms. The IA also can respond to requests regarding the date and time and can operate as a calculator for simple equations. This section lists tips for using the Intelligent Assistant to your best advantage.

- *When you ask the IA to change information in a text field, enclose the new entry in quotation marks.* Suppose that you want to change the value in the Sales Manager field for all Atlanta sales leads. You enter the following request:

    Change sales manager to *Jim Stevens* in all forms where sales district = Atlanta.

    Only text fields require that the new information be enclosed in quotation marks; you can specify number, date, and time fields in the usual way. For example, in the request "Change the sales priority to 1.0 for the University of Michigan," the numeric value needs no quotation marks.

- *Save yourself time and keystrokes by using follow-up questions.* Instead of typing a new request every time you query the Intelligent

Assistant, you can use phrases that refer to a previous request. If you last requested the IA to list all 1.5 sales priorities, your next request can be "Change these to 2.0 sales priorities."

• *Use math symbols to simplify your requests.* Although you probably will want to use English phrases in most of your requests, you can use math symbols to reduce your typing time and help the IA process faster. For example, compare the different versions of these next two requests:

> Display annual revenues that are greater than $3,000,000. Annual revenue >$3,000,000.

> Display sales leads entered between 4/15/88 and 7/1/88. Display leads for date entered >4/15/88 and <7/1/88.

The shorter versions not only include math symbols but also have been written with as few words as possible. The shorter your request, the quicker the IA can respond.

• *Use the word "define" in the request box to teach the IA new synonyms.* In addition to teaching the IA new words by using the Teach option, you can enter synonyms with requests such as the following:

> Define address as company, address1, city, state, and ZIP.

After you enter this request, the Intelligent Assistant displays the Company, Address1, City, State, and ZIP fields whenever you ask for "address."

• *To have the IA display a yes/no field in a columnar report, include the word "field" in your request.* For example, the Current Customer field in the sales lead database is a yes/no field. To ask the IA to display leads from Philadelphia and to indicate whether they are current customers, type the following request:

> Show sales leads from the Philadelphia sales district and the current customers field.

After processing this request, the Intelligent Assistant responds with the report shown in figure 18.29.

```
┌─────────────────────────────────────────────────────────────────┐
│ Show sales leads from the Philadelphia sales district and the current │
│ customers field.                                                  │
│                                                                   │
│                                                                   │
│                                                                   │
└─────────────────────────────────────────────────────────────────┘

                        Company           Telephone      Current Customer
                   ─────────────────   ──────────────   ────────────────
   f technician    Penn Medical Technology   215-594-2241      Y
   ager            Franklyn Lab Associates   215-678-1234      N
                   Pike Pharmaceutical, Inc.  215-493-5893      Y
```

Fig. 18.29.   *Displaying Yes and No fields.*

Updating the IA's Knowledge of Your Database

As you enter requests to the IA, you probably will need to add to the information you originally specified with the Teach option. Instead of returning to the Teach option, however, you can add to the IA's vocabulary and help the IA process requests while you're working with the Ask option on the request screen. By pressing F1, you can display a help screen that lists the function keys available for reviewing and adding vocabulary.

The Intelligent Assistant provides two options for updating information. First, you can use the F6 and F8 function keys when entering a request. Second, you can update the IA when the IA is unable to process a request because of an unknown or ambiguous term.

Checking and Changing Vocabulary

If you begin to enter a request in the request box and suspect that the IA may have difficulty processing a word or phrase, press the F6 function key. When you press F6, the IA displays a menu of options for checking the built-in vocabulary, adding synonyms to field names, and adding synonyms that you have created by using the word *define*.

Selecting Built-in Words displays a list of the IA's vocabulary. Scroll through the list by pressing PgDn (see fig. 18.30). When you choose Field Names, the IA displays a series of screens in which you can enter the synonyms. For example, if you want to add the synonym *home office* to the Sales Dist. field, you can do so at this point. Choosing the third option, Synonyms, displays a list of the synonyms that you have created with the word *define*.

```
                         BUILT-IN VOCABULARY


A              ANY          BELOW       COME          DECREASE      ENTRY
ABOUT          ANYONE       BEST        COMMENCING    DEFINE        EQUAL
ABOVE          APPEAR       BETTER      CONCERN       DEFINITION    ERASE
ACCORDING      APRIL        BETWEEN     CONSTRAINT    DELETE        EVERY
ADD            ARE          BIG         CONTAIN       DESCENDING    EVERYBODY
AFTER          AS           BLANK       COULD         DETAIL        EVERYTHING
AGAIN          ASCENDING    BOTH        COUNT         DEVIATION     EXCEED
AGAINST        ASSIGN       BOTTOM      CREATE        DIFFERENCE    EXCLUDE
AGO            AT           BREAK       CROSSTAB      DISPLAY       EXCLUSIVE
ALL            AUGUST       BUT         CROSSTABULATE DIVIDE        EXIST
ALONG          AVERAGE      BY          CURRENT       DO            F
ALPHABETICAL   AWAY         CALCULATE   CUT           DURING        FALSE
ALSO           B            CAME        DAILY         EACH          FEBRUARY
AM             BE           CAN         DATA          EARLY         FETCH
AMONG          BEEN         CHANGE      DATABASE      EITHER        FEW
AN             BEFORE       CHRISTEN    DATE          EMPTY         FIELD
AND            BEGIN        CHRISTMAS   DAY           END           FILE
ANNUAL         BEING        COLUMN      DECEMBER      ENTER         FILL



Esc-Exit                     PgDn-View More Definitions              ▮
```

Fig. 18.30.   The Intelligent Assistant's built-in vocabulary.

Using the F8 Key To Add Information

When you enter a request, press F8 if you want to change or add to information you entered with the Teach option. When you press F8, a menu appears and shows options for changing or adding synonyms or preparing the IA for verbs you are using in your request (see fig. 18.31).

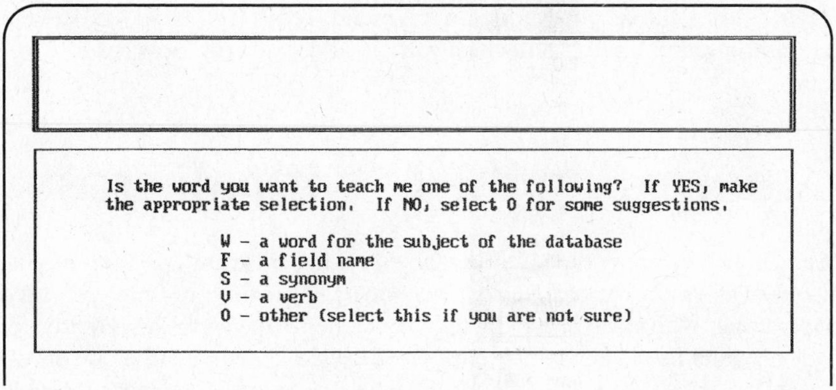

```
Is the word you want to teach me one of the following?  If YES, make
the appropriate selection.  If NO, select O for some suggestions.

                W - a word for the subject of the database
                F - a field name
                S - a synonym
                V - a verb
                O - other (select this if you are not sure)
```

Fig. 18.31.   *The menu for changing or adding synonyms or teaching verbs.*

Helping the IA Interpret a Word

Whenever the Intelligent Assistant has problems with a word in your request,
the IA pauses and displays a menu that gives you a chance to add to or change
vocabulary. Suppose, for example, that in a request you use the phrase *home
office* to refer to the Sales Dist. field in the sales lead database. If you do not
prepare the IA for that phrase, the IA indicates that it is having trouble
processing one or both of the words (see fig. 18.32).

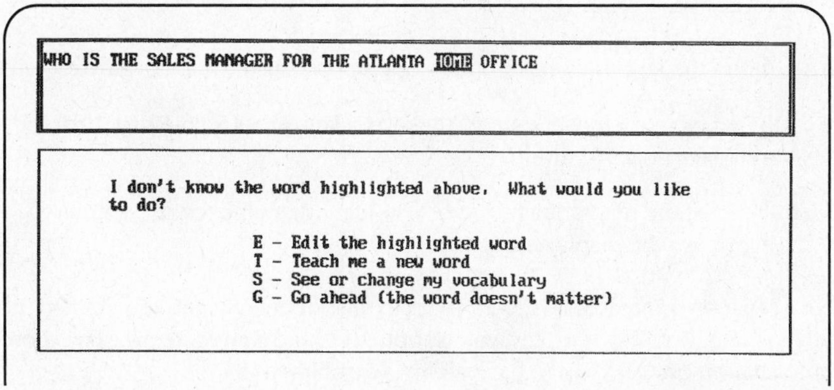

```
WHO IS THE SALES MANAGER FOR THE ATLANTA HOME OFFICE



        I don't know the word highlighted above.  What would you like
        to do?

                    E - Edit the highlighted word
                    T - Teach me a new word
                    S - See or change my vocabulary
                    G - Go ahead (the word doesn't matter)
```

Fig. 18.32.   *The warning displayed when the IA has trouble processing a word.*

If you choose the second option on this menu, Teach Me a New Word, the IA
displays another menu from which you can add synonyms or verbs.

Automating the IA with Macros

Similar to the macro capability available in other business applications programs, Q&A's macro capability enables you to automate your frequently used
operations. With macros, you can record a sequence of keystrokes required for
any program function and play back those keystrokes by pressing one or two
keys. If you often enter the same request when you use the Intelligent Assistant,
you can save yourself time and effort by automating the operation with a Q&A
macro.

Suppose that you enter the same request every week, asking the Intelligent
Assistant to create a report of weekly sales. To automate the process, you can
create a macro to make the request for you. Creating a macro for automating
requests entered in the Intelligent Assistant involves the following steps:

1. Select the screen in which you want the macro to begin. For
   example, if you want the macro to begin running at the Q&A Main
   menu, display that screen.

2. Press Shift-F2 to access Q&A's Macro menu.

3. Select the Define Macro option.

4. Press the keys that make up the operation you want to automate.

5. When you are finished entering keystrokes, press Shift-F2 to turn
   off Macro Record mode.

6. To save the macro for future use, enter a file name, or press Enter
   to accept the displayed file name.

You can test your macro by moving back to the screen in which you defined the
macro and pressing the key you supplied as the macro name. For more
information on Q&A's macro capability, see Chapter 19.

Chapter Summary

Q&A's Intelligent Assistant and Query Guide are the program features that make Q&A easier to learn and use than many other database products. In this chapter, you learned to build on the knowledge of the IA so that the IA can respond to your data-management needs according to the specific features of your database. You also learned how to customize the Query Guide so that it displays actual text or key data from your database file when prompting you to enter data field information. By following the methods and tips explained in this chapter and continuing to experiment on your own, you will find that using the Intelligent Assistant and the Query Guide streamlines your data-entry and processing tasks.

Part VI

Advanced Q&A Applications

Includes

Creating and Using Q&A Macros and Custom Menus

Importing and Exporting Data in Q&A

Networking: Using Q&A in a Multiuser Environment

19

Creating and Using
Q&A Macros and
Custom Menus

Many business applications programs on the market include macro capabilities. When first introduced in early versions of 1-2-3, macro capability was thought to be only for advanced users. Q&A, however, like many recent programs, provides macro capabilities even beginners can use.

This chapter introduces you to Q&A macros and describes how to create and use macros to save time when you use File, Write, Report, and the Intelligent Assistant. The chapter also explains how you can create custom macro menus from which you can select and run your macros.

What Are Macros and Custom Menus?

Q&A macros are special programs storing series of commands or text entries that "play back" with one keystroke. You can use macros in any Q&A module—File, Write, Report, and the Intelligent Assistant—to duplicate command sequences and data-entry procedures that are repeated frequently. If you often use the same temporary margin or tab settings while working in Write, for example, you can create a macro to enter these settings automatically.

After you begin using macros, you will discover how much time they save. Q&A macros can save you from having to look up special printer codes for print enhancements—for example, you can store the codes and play the macro any time you need to enter the codes. You also can create macros to save a text file, enter special print settings, and automatically print the file. Macros are ideal for inserting frequently used paragraphs, sentences, or phrases in your documents. Macros also can reassign the keys on your keyboard.

With Q&A Version 4.0, you can name your macros and list them in a menu, with descriptions that tell what each macro does. You then can run your macros by choosing them from the menu. Q&A enables you to create menus that can extend or even replace the program's existing menus. With macro menus, you can customize Q&A so that a new user needs never see one of Q&A's "ordinary" menus. By pressing a key at a macro menu, even a beginner can perform complex tasks such as printing monthly payroll reports or billing labels.

Learning the Basics of Creating Macros

Two methods are available to create Q&A macros. First, you can have Q&A automatically record a series of keystrokes as you enter them. To use the recording method, you direct Q&A to store a set of keystrokes as a macro program. All you do is tell Q&A when to begin recording keystrokes, when to stop, and what name to assign the recorded keystrokes. Second, you can create macros by typing each one. To use the interactive method, you must open a text file, type the special commands that represent each keystroke, and indicate where the macro begins and ends.

You may want to use the interactive method when trying out a new macro because this method enables you to see the definition as you enter the command sequence. You also need to use the interactive method when editing a macro created with the recording method (see the "Editing Macros" section of this chapter).

In most cases, however, a macro is easier to create with the recording method. When you record a macro, you don't have to leave the current document, and all Q&A's normal keystrokes are available for defining the macro. When you have completed the sequence, you simply turn off the recording feature; no programming is involved.

Defining Macros in Record Mode

You have three ways to name your recorded macro: with an invocation key such as Alt-A or Ctrl-B, with a plain-English name such as Print Reports, or with both. You learn how to name macros in the next section. If you choose a single-key identifier such as Alt-A, you can run your macro by pressing the identifier key without having to select the macro from a menu. (You also can run such a macro from a list of macros if you prefer.) If you choose a plain-English name for your macro, you can run the macro only from a list of macros that Q&A displays when you press Alt-F2 to display the Macro Names list from any point in Q&A. You also can press Shift-F2 to display the Macro menu, then choose R-Run Macro to display the Macro Names list. In either case, Q&A gives you the opportunity to enter a description for the macro on the Macro Names list (see fig. 19.1).

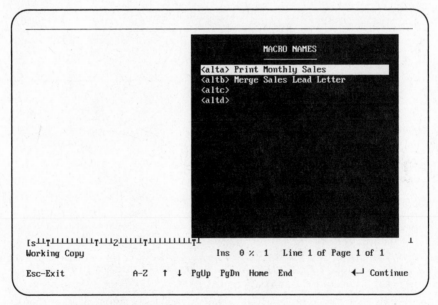

Fig. 19.1. *The Macro Names list.*

By combining Ctrl or Alt with a letter, you have more than 80 possible macro identifier keys from which to choose. Table 19.1 lists the keys and combinations already used by Q&A for Write, File, Report, and Intelligent Assistant operations. When you define macros, use identifier keys other than those listed in the table unless you want to override a key's Q&A assignment. If, for example, you name a macro Ctrl-F for use within the Write module, you disable Write's regular use of Ctrl-F for moving the cursor from one word to the next.

Table 19.1
Key Combinations Used by Q&A
(Not available for macro names)

Ctrl-A	Ctrl-Bksp	F1	Shift-F1	Del
Ctrl-C	Ctrl-PrtSc	F2	Shift-F2	End
Ctrl-D	Ctrl-F2	F3	Shift-F3	Home
Ctrl-E	Ctrl-F5	F4	Shift-F4	Ins
Ctrl-F	Ctrl-F6	F5	Shift-F5	PgDn
Ctrl-G	Ctrl-F7	F6	Shift-F6	PgUp
Ctrl-H	Ctrl-F8	F7	Shift-F7	↓
Ctrl-I	Ctrl-[	F8	Shift-F8	←
Ctrl-M	Ctrl-Home	F9	Shift-F9	→
Ctrl-R	Ctrl-PgDn	F10	Shift-F10	↑
Ctrl-S	Ctrl-PgUp		Shift-Bksp	Bksp
Ctrl-T	Alt-F2		Shift-Esc	Esc
Ctrl-V	Alt-F5		Shift-Enter	Enter
Ctrl-W	Alt-F8		Shift-TabTab	
Ctrl-Y	Alt-F9			
Ctrl-Z				

Recording Macros

Q&A makes recording macros easy. Follow these steps:

1. Press Shift-F2 to display the Macro menu (see fig. 19.2).

2. Select Define Macro from the menu. Q&A prompts you for a macro name.

3. If you want to use a macro identifier key, press that key combination (for example, Alt-A). If you try to define the same key twice, or enter a name already used by Q&A, an error message is displayed at the bottom of the Q&A screen and a prompt asks whether you want to redefine the key. Press Y in response to the prompt if you want to use that existing key combination.

   If you want to use a plain-English macro name, press Enter without typing an identifier key. When you finish recording, Q&A will enable you to give the macro a name and description.

4. Type any keystrokes you want to record. Q&A displays a flashing square at the bottom of the screen to remind you that macro recording is turned on.

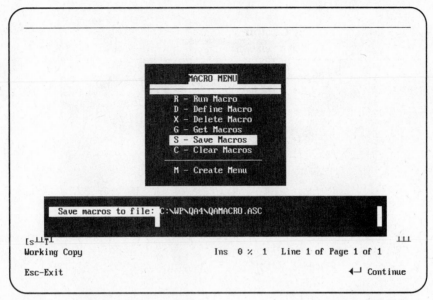

```
                    ┌─────────────────────┐
                    │     MACRO MENU      │
                    │─────────────────────│
                    │  R - Run Macro      │
                    │  D - Define Macro   │
                    │  X - Delete Macro   │
                    │  G - Get Macros     │
                    │  S - Save Macros    │
                    │  C - Clear Macros   │
                    │                     │
                    │  M - Create Menu    │
                    └─────────────────────┘

  ┌──────────────────────────────────────────────────────────────┐
  │ Save macros to file: C:\WP\QA4\QAMACRO.ASC                   ▌ │
  └──────────────────────────────────────────────────────────────┘
[s⊥⊥ₜ⊥                                                            ⊥⊥⊥
Working Copy                      Ins   0 %  1   Line 1 of Page 1 of 1

Esc-Exit                                                  ←┘ Continue
```

Fig. 19.2. *The Macro menu.*

You can record any Q&A function, but you cannot start recording a second macro while you are recording a macro. (You can "nest" macros, however, by typing the identifier keys of existing macros as you record.)

If you want the macro to pause for input during playback—for example, while you type a response at a Q&A prompt—press Alt-F2. Type the required text at the prompt, and press Alt-F2 to end the pause. When you play back the macro, Q&A pauses until you finish typing and press Enter

5. Press Shift-F2 to turn off macro recording. Q&A displays the Macro Options box (see fig. 19.3).

6. At the Macro Description field on the Macro Options box, Q&A displays a code for the macro identifier key, if you entered one. At this point you have three options:

   • Accept the code.

   • Move the cursor to the right of the identifier code, enter a space, and type a description for the macro. (The macro's identifier and description can total up to 31 characters.)

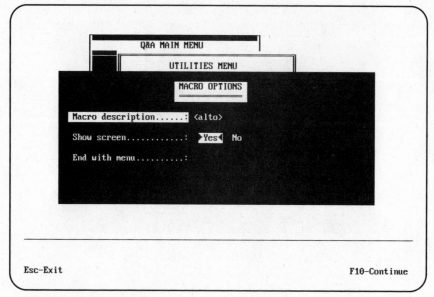

Fig. 19.3. *The Macro Options box.*

- Move the cursor to the left end of the line and type over the code as you enter a name and/or description for the macro. The identifier key remains in effect (you can still invoke the macro either from the menu or by pressing its identifier key).

7. At the Show Screen field, tell Q&A whether you want screens to be displayed when you run the macro. If you choose No, the macro will run faster.

8. At the End with Menu field, you can type the name of a custom or Q&A menu that you want to display immediately after the macro runs. For example, you can have a macro run a spell check and then display the Write Print Options menu. Assigning macros to custom menus is described in this chapter's section "Creating Custom Menus."

   You can press Alt-F7 to display a list of existing custom menus for the current macro file. To enter a menu's name at the prompt, highlight the name with the cursor and then press Enter.

9. Press F10. Q&A displays the name of the currently loaded macro file; the default macro file name is QAMACRO.ASC.

10. Press Enter to accept the default, or type a new macro file name and press Enter. A macro file is a DOS file and macro file names must conform to DOS file-naming conventions.

You can press Esc rather than F10 at the Macro Options menu to avoid saving the macro, but when you turn your computer off or get another macro file, all macros currently in memory are lost. You can save the macros in memory at any point by pressing Shift-F2 to display the Macro menu and then choosing Save Macros.

Playing Back and Changing Recorded Macros

To play back a macro you have created, you can use one of three methods:

- Press the macro's invocation key from anywhere in Q&A.

- Press Alt-F2 from any Q&A screen to display the Macro Names list; then highlight the macro on the list, and press Enter.

- Press Shift-F2 to display the Macro menu, choose Run Macro, and select the macro from the list that Q&A displays (see fig. 19.4).

```
              Q&A MACROS CURRENTLY DEFINED

       Alt-P      Enters File Print Settings
       Alt-S      Sort file by Sales District
       Alt-L      Enters Los Angeles Sales District Data
       Alt-N      Enters New York Sales District Data
       Alt-C      Enters Chicago Sales District Data




[s⊥⊥T⊥⊥⊥⊥2⊥⊥⊥⊥T⊥⊥⊥⊥3⊥⊥⊥⊥T⊥⊥⊥4⊥⊥⊥T⊥⊥⊥⊥5⊥⊥⊥⊥⊥⊥⊥⊥6⊥⊥█⊥⊥⊥]⊥7⊥⊥⊥⊥⊥⊥⊥⊥⊥⊥⊥⊥⊥⊥⊥⊥⊥
Working Copy                          0 %  54  Line 7 of Page 1 of 1

Esc-Exit  F1-Help  F2-Print  Shift+F7-Restore   F7-Search  F8-Options  ↑F8-Save
```

Fig. 19.4.   Running a macro from a list.

If the macro doesn't work properly, press Esc to stop execution. Then, to redefine the macro, press Shift-F2 and select Define Macro from the Macro menu. Press the same identifier key you used to define the macro the first time, and Q&A tells you that the key is already defined. Press Y to redefine the key; then record a revised or new macro to the identifier. Press Shift-F2 again when you have recorded the keystrokes.

Saving Recorded Macros

When you create a recorded macro, you can choose to save the macro only for the current work session or to save the macro for later use. If you use a macro to perform a calculation on a field for a one-time application, you don't need to save the macro. If you create a macro to perform a recurring function, such as inserting a heading on personal letters, you need to save the macro to disk. Macros created with the recording method are stored in RAM.

To save macros, press Shift-F2 to display the Macro menu, and press S to select Save Macros. Enter a macro file name in response to the prompt that Q&A displays at the bottom of the screen (see fig. 19.5). You can use any name that follows DOS conventions—up to eight characters with an optional three-character extension. The default file to which Q&A saves your macros is QAMACRO.ASC. You may save macros with other file names, but you have to load those files each time you want to use those macros because Q&A automatically loads the file called QAMACRO.ASC whenever you start the program. To load a different macro file, press Shift-F2 to display the Macro menu, press G to select Get Macros, type the name of the macro file you want to load, and press Enter to continue.

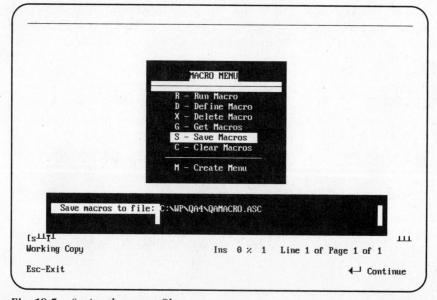

Fig. 19.5. *Saving the macro file.*

To edit macros later, you can access the macro file from the Write module. Procedures for importing a macro file to Write are included in this chapter under "Editing Macros."

Don't save new macros to a macro file until a previous version of the file, if any, has been loaded in RAM. Suppose that you have already saved several macros in a file and want to save a new macro you have just created. If the macro file isn't loaded in RAM, and you save the new macro with the same file name, Q&A replaces the old macro file with the new file. To save your macros without losing any valuable information, heed these precautions:

- Load the file into memory before you record any macros.

- Resave the file after you add new macros.

- Back up your macro files by saving copies with different names (Q&A does not make automatic backups). If you inadvertently overwrite the original file, you then can use a copy.

- Save macro files with names that are easy to identify (with an ASC or MAC extension, for example).

Clearing Recorded Macros from Memory

After you have saved the macros to disk, you can choose Clear Macros from the Macro menu to remove all macros from RAM. This command does not affect macros that have been saved to disk. To clear all macros from memory, press Shift-F2 to display the Macro menu, and press C to select Clear Macros. If you want to use macros after using Clear Macros, you must load a macro file as described in the preceding section.

The Clear Macros command returns all your macro keys and key combinations to their original functions. Don't use Clear Macros until you know which macros will be deleted, because no warning is displayed before macros are erased.

Clearing macros from RAM enables you to work on another set of macros or return the keyboard to its normal state. This capability is useful if you have defined a set of macros for a single application or database and want to use another database or define new macros.

You can create and save to disk any number of macro sets as long as you use different file names.

Defining Macros in Interactive Mode

The interactive method of creating macros takes place within Q&A Write. To write macros, you type each command sequence in a format that can be read by Q&A. Interactive mode can be helpful when you are creating a complex macro; seeing each command on the screen sometimes helps you enter the keystrokes in the correct sequence.

Creating macros in the interactive mode is like programming in a simple language. If you have programming experience, you will learn how to program Q&A macros easily. If you have never written a program in another language, you may have to spend a little extra time grasping the concept, but it is relatively simple.

(You also can build custom menus interactively, as described later in this chapter in "Creating Custom Menus.")

Writing Interactive Macros

Unlike recorded macros, interactive macros must be entered in a specific format. Q&A creates a command file for you when you record macros, but with the interactive mode, *you* create the command file. Each macro begins with the code <begdef>, which stands for begin definition. The identifier key is entered next, followed by the keystrokes in the macro. Each keystroke is enclosed within less-than and greater-than signs and typed in lowercase letters. Text that is to appear literally should not be enclosed. The code <enddef> tells Q&A to end the definition.

If you want to create a macro that moves the cursor to the Company field in the sales lead database, for example, you type the following:

```
<begdef><alta><home><home><enter><enter><enter><enddef>
*
```

The <begdef> code tells Q&A that a macro follows. The <alta> code tells Q&A that Alt-A is the identifier. The commands that follow (<home> and <enter>) define the actual macro. Q&A now knows that when Alt-A is pressed, the cursor must be moved to the Home position (upper left corner of the screen), and then to the Company field by a series of three Enter keystrokes. The <enddef> tells Q&A that the macro has ended, and the asterisk on the line below the macro is used to separate macros in a file.

Every Q&A macro has the same structure, although not all these components are mandatory:

<begdef><keystroke ID> ¦ <nokey><name>"Macro
Name"<vidon> ¦ <vidoff>recorded keystrokes...<call>"Menu
Name"<wait><keyname><enddef>

The following chart describes these Q&A macro elements:

Component	Function
<begdef>	Indicates start of a macro
<keystroke ID> ¦ <nokey>	If no macro invocation key exists, Q&A inserts <nokey> here during interactive macro recording. While writing macros, you can type a <nokey> code or enter the invocation key, such as <alta>.
<name>	The macro's name. The name follows the <name> code and is enclosed in double quotation marks (not angle brackets). This name is the one that appears in Q&A's list of macros when you choose Run Macro from the Macro menu. If the macro has no name, nothing is entered here.
<vidon> ¦ <vidoff>	Tells Q&A whether or not to display screens while a macro runs. If you don't enter either code, Q&A assumes <vidon>.
recorded keystrokes...	The keystrokes that the macro plays back
<call>	Followed by a menu name, <call> tells Q&A to display the named menu that follows the code.
"Menu Name"	The name of the menu invoked with <call>. The menu name is enclosed in double quotation marks.
<wait>	An optional code that tells Q&A to pause while the user types text. Macro play back resumes when the user presses Enter or <keyname>, as described subsequently.
<keyname>	An optional code used with <wait> to tell Q&A to end a pause when the user presses the key named in <keyname>.
<enddef>	Ends the macro

When you write macros interactively, keep the following rules in mind:

- An asterisk (*) must separate a macro from the preceding macro in the macro file. The first macro in the file is not preceded by an asterisk.

- Less-than and greater-than signs (angle brackets) are used to enclose each element of the macro. Do not insert spaces between elements.

- Let Q&A wordwrap the macro codes. Do not press Enter at the end of a line.

Also, when you write and edit interactive macros, you must enter the following special keys and key combinations in the specific format indicated:

Key combination	Q&A macro format
Alt-A	<alta>
Alt-5	<alt5>
Alt-F2	<altf2>
Backspace	<bks>
Ctrl-Home	<ctrlhom>
Ctrl-PgUp	<ctrlpgu>
Ctrl-Enter	<ctrlent>
↓	<dn>
↑	<up>
Escape	<esc>
Ins	<ins>
←	<lft>
→	<rgt>
Enter	<enter>
Shift-F1	<capsf1>
Shift-Tab	<capstab>
Tab	<tab>

All the keys accessible to you during macro preparation are not shown in this table, but you enter them in the same way. For example, you can enter all function keys as normal, shifted, or with the Alt key by following the F1 and F2 examples given in the table. F10 is entered in a macro as <f10>, for example, and Alt-F10 is <altf10>. When in doubt about how to enter command keystrokes, try what appears logical, and Q&A tells you if you need to try another combination.

If you cannot figure out how to construct a key sequence in the interactive mode, temporarily save the macro: call up the Macro menu with Shift-F2, select Define Macro, and enter the keystrokes you want to add to your interactive macro. Save the RAM-resident macro to a temporary file. Then you can load this file into Write and examine how Q&A constructed the sequence. Either merge this file directly into the interactive macro or type the sequence.

Saving Interactive Macros

Saving macro files you have created with the interactive method takes two steps. First, you must save the macro as a Q&A Write document. Second, you must convert this Write text file to an ASCII file. Q&A can read the macro file only in ASCII format.

To save a macro file as a Write text file and convert it to an ASCII file, take the following steps. After you have finished typing all commands for the macro, press Shift-F8 to save the file as a text file. When you want to use the macros from within a module, press Shift-F2 to access the Macro menu. Then select Get Macros, and enter the macro file name at the prompt (be sure to include the path). Q&A loads the macros you created in Write.

Remember, you can have as many macro files as you want, but you can *use* only macros that have been loaded into RAM.

To play back a macro, use the steps described in the earlier section, "Playing Back and Changing Recorded Macros." In review, you may play back a macro by pressing its invocation key; by pressing Alt-F2 and selecting the macro from the Macro Names list; or by pressing Shift-F2 to display the Macro menu, pressing R to select Run Macro, and selecting a macro from the Macro Names list.

Editing Macros

If you make a spelling error while recording an elaborate sequence of text and commands, you can use the Backspace key to erase the error before you save the macro. Each time you use the macro, however, it repeats the same steps, including the error and correction.

You can use the interactive mode to edit the macros you create, but you must save the macro file to disk before editing. If you don't save the current file, any changes you make during your work session are lost.

In the Write module, use the Get command to load the macro file for editing with standard Write procedures. When the Import Document menu appears, choose ASCII. The file is then converted into Q&A format and can be edited.

For example, if you mistakenly type *credentails* in the macro sequence, use the Backspace key to remove characters and type the correct ending for the word. Q&A records the macro as follows:

<begdef><altu>credentails<bks><bks><bks><bks>ials<enddef>

Note that Q&A records the Backspace keystroke as <bks> in a macro. The correct ending, *ials*, appears before the ending of the definition.

To remove extra keystrokes in the recorded macro, erase those you don't need. After editing, the correct macro should read as follows:

<begdef><altu>credentials<enddef>

Using the Interactive Method To Solve Recorded Macro Problems

If your recorded macro does not work, you can use the interactive method to fix the problem. Suppose that the final command in a macro instructs Q&A to exit to DOS. You cannot save that macro, because the final command deposits you at the DOS prompt before you can select Save Macros.

Solve the problem by ending the recorded definition before the last command and selecting the Save Macros option. Then enter the macro file through Q&A Write, find the macro, and add

X<enter>

before the end of the definition (<enddef>). Save the file as explained in the section "Saving Interactive Macros." Now you have in your file a macro that exits Q&A from the Main menu as the final step.

The interactive method also is helpful when you need to create a series of similar macros. To keep from having to enter the same keystrokes repeatedly, you can use Write's block-copying capabilities to copy the keystrokes to each macro.

Reloading Your Macro Files

You can create as many macro files as you have room for on your disk. To retrieve the file you want to use, press Shift-F2 for the Macro menu and then G for Get Macros. Enter the macro file name at the prompt. The macro file is then loaded in RAM and ready to use.

Creating Custom Menus

In addition to the three methods already discussed (pressing the invocation key; pressing Shift-F2, choosing Run Macro, and choosing the macro; and pressing Alt-F2 and choosing the macro), you can run a macro from a custom menu of your own design.

To create a custom menu, follow these steps:

1. Press Shift-F2 to display the Macro menu.

2. Choose Create Menu. Q&A displays the Macro Names list with a list of existing custom menus, as shown in figure 19.6.

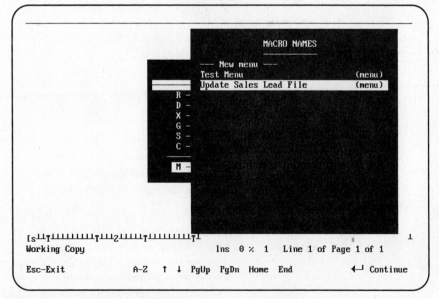

Fig. 19.6.   The custom menus list.

3. To create a new menu, choose New Menu. To edit an existing menu, choose its name from the list. Q&A displays the Macro Menu Options screen shown in figure 19.7.

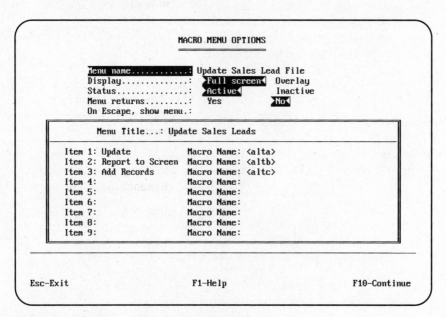

Fig. 19.7.   *The Macro Menu Options screen.*

4. Complete the fields as indicated in the following chart:

Field	Description
Menu Name	Type the name you plan to use to call the menu with macros and from other menus.
Display	Choose Full Screen to display the menu in a blank screen. Choose Overlay to display the menu in a box over the current Q&A screen.
Status	Choosing Active tells Q&A to display the menu when you play back a macro that calls the menu to the screen. If you choose Inactive, the menu can be called from a macro but is not displayed. This is useful, for example, when a macro prompts the user to press a key. The user's keystroke selects an item from a hidden menu.

Field	Description
Menu Returns	Choose Yes to redisplay the menu after a menu item finishes running.
On Escape, Show Menu	Type the name of a menu to display when the user presses Esc at this menu.
Menu Title	Type the title that you want to display at the top of the menu. This name need not be the same as the menu name you gave at the top of the screen, which is used to call the menu.
Items 1 through 9	Type the text that you want to display next to each menu item.
Macro Name	Type the name or key identifier of the macro that will be run by each menu item. To choose a macro from the current macro file, press Alt-F7, highlight a macro, and press Enter.

5. When you're finished with the Macro Menu Options screen, press F10. Q&A saves the menu automatically.

Naming and Calling Menus

Be careful when naming macros and menus. If you name a custom menu "File Menu," for example, Q&A replaces the Q&A File menu with your custom menu. If you name a macro "File Menu," whenever you choose File from the Main menu, Q&A runs your macro. This can be useful for creating custom applications as described in the next section. For example, you can create a menu that replaces the Q&A Report menu and lists such items as the following:

M - Print monthly statements
C - Cash flow report
Q - Quarterly contact list printout

Some Q&A menus have duplicate names—for example, the Global Options menus have identical names in Write, Report, and File Print. If you need to call one of these Q&A menus with a macro or custom menu, use the following names:

Menu	Name to use in macro or custom menu
Rename/Delete/Copy (File)	File, Print, Rename/Delete/Copy
Rename/Delete/Copy (Report)	Report, Rename/Delete/Copy
Print Global Options	File, Print, Global Options
Report Global Options	Report, Global Options
Columnar Global Options	Report, Global Options, Columnar Global Options
Crosstab Global Options	Report, Global Options, Crosstab Global Options
Write Global Options	Write, Utilities, Global Options
Assistant Menu	Assistant Menu (use this name, not a customized name you have assigned the Intelligent Assistant)

Creating and Editing Menus Interactively

Custom menus that you create are stored in the currently loaded Q&A macro file when you save them. Just as you can create and edit macros interactively, as described previously, you can build and revise menus by editing the macro file.

A menu has the following macro structure:

<begdef><nokey><name>"Menu Name"<vidon><menu>"Menu Title:Item1/Item1macro,Item2/Item2macro...Itemn/Itemnmacro/"<enddef>

The following chart explains these codes:

Component	Function
<begdef>	Begins the menu
<nokey>	Every menu must have a <nokey> code in this position.
<name>	Menu name follows (see "Menu Name"). Every menu must have a name.
"Menu Name"	The menu name, consisting of up to 31 characters and enclosed in double quotation marks. (You may not use quotation marks within the name itself.) This name is the one that Q&A uses

Component	Function
	to call the menu from a macro, and may not be the same as "Menu Title," which is described subsequently.
\<menu\>	Indicates that the menu structure follows
"Menu Title: Item1..."	The title of the menu and the list of choices that appear in the menu, with the macros that each choice invokes

Keep the following rules in mind when creating a custom menu:

- The menu structure is enclosed in quotes but may not contain quotes.

- You may specify up to 9 menu choices with 255 characters total.

- You may not use spaces or carriage returns within the menu structure codes.

- A colon separates the menu title from the choices and their associated macros.

- Separate each choice from its macro with a slash.

- Use commas to separate menu choices.

Building a Custom Application

Building a customized Q&A application is a simple process, involving two steps:

1. Write macros for the functions that you want to assign to menus.

2. Using Q&A's automated menu-creation process, assign your macros to menus that supplement or replace Q&A's menus.

Suppose that you want to replace the Report menu with a customized menu from which the user can print monthly reports. First, you need to write a macro that prints each monthly report. You can use pauses as described previously in this chapter to enable the user to indicate retrieval specifications, adjust the Print Spec, and so on while the macro runs.

After the macros have been written and tested, you create a custom menu. You can tell Q&A that when a report finishes printing, it should redisplay the custom menu, display a Q&A menu, or run a macro that exits Q&A. These processes were described previously in the section "Creating Custom Menus."

Protecting Macro Files and Applications

You may want to protect your macros and custom applications so that other users cannot tamper with them. When Q&A protects a macro file or application, the user can only run the macros. Protected macro/application files cannot be edited, nor can a user get, create, delete, save, or clear macros while the protected file is loaded.

To protect a macro file or an application, follow these steps:

1. From the Q&A Main menu, choose File.

2. From the File menu, choose Design File. Q&A displays the Design menu.

3. From the Design menu, choose Customize Application. Q&A displays the Customize Application menu.

4. Choose Protect Macro File. Q&A displays the Protect Macro box.

5. Enter the name of the macro file you want to protect.

6. Type a new name for the protected macro file.

Be careful. If you type the name of the old macro file, Q&A overwrites it with the new, protected version, and you will not be able to edit it again.

To load the protected file, press Shift-F2 to display the Macro menu, and choose Get Macros.

Using Autostart Macros

Q&A automatically loads QAMACRO.ASC at start-up. If you want a macro file to load automatically when you start Q&A, name the file QAMACRO.ASC. When the program is booted, Q&A searches for that macro file. Only one macro file, however, can be in memory at a time.

If you want to use another macro file, you have to choose the Get Macros command from the Macro menu to load the file after the system is booted and the autoloading macros are finished executing.

To have Q&A load a different macro file at start-up, type the following line at the DOS prompt to load Q&A:

    QA -AL<*macro filename*>

To make a file other than QAMACRO.ASC the permanent default start-up macro file, type the following line at the DOS prompt:

QA -AD<*macro filename*>

Note: You *must* include a space between QA and the -AL or -AD code.

Exploring Advanced Macro Techniques

The macros you create can be used in every module of Q&A. You will discover many time-saving applications for macros, whether you define them by interactive recording or write them in the Q&A Write Editing screen. This section explains some of the advanced techniques that add to Q&A's macro capability.

Nesting Macros within Macros

Suppose that you created a macro to type the name of your regional manager, Jonathan T. McGillicuddy, and you assigned the macro to Alt-N. Now you want to create another macro to type his name and address. This macro will be named Alt-A.

When you record the new macro, you can press Alt-N rather than type the name again to enter the old macro as part of the new macro's definition. Then you can add the other information to complete the macro. In interactive mode, these macros appear as follows:

<begdef><altn>Jonathan T. McGillicuddy <enter><enddef>
*

<begdef><alta><altn>, Regional Manager<enter>
Titan Technologies<enter>1234 Main Street<enter>
Lumberyard, PA 12534<enter><enddef>
*

Q&A accepts up to five levels of macros within macros. Only one level was used in the preceding example.

Using Other Word Processors To Create Q&A Macros

You can create Q&A macro files in any word processing program that can generate, read, and save files in ASCII format. For example, you can write Q&A macros with WordPerfect, using the Text In/Out function (Ctrl-F5) to import and export macro files in ASCII format.

Examining Sample Macro Applications

Q&A macros can make your work easier in any of the program's modules. This section offers a few ideas for macro applications and may inspire you to create additional macros.

All macros in this section have been designed to start from the Q&A Main menu, but you can write macros that begin at any point within Q&A. If you record a macro from within a module, however, remember in which module it originates; otherwise, the series of keystrokes and menu selections may be wrong.

Querying the Intelligent Assistant

The following macro accesses the Intelligent Assistant, enters the name of the sales lead database (SLSLEAD.DTF), activates the file, and asks the Intelligent Assistant for a current list of companies in the database:

```
<begdef><alts><name>"RUN IA"<vidoff>a<enter>aslslead.dtf
<enter> Show me the companies in the database.<enter>y<enter>
<enddef>
*
```

The <begdef> code tells Q&A that you are starting a new macro. Alt-S is the identifier key (the one you use to start the macro). The <name> code followed by "RUN IA" tells Q&A what name to display when it lists macros. The <vidoff> code tells Q&A to suppress screen display during playback. The first letter *a* and the Enter keystrokes select the Intelligent Assistant from the Main menu. The second letter *a* selects the Ask option from the Intelligent Assistant menu; *slslead.dtf* tells Q&A the name of the database. The query *Show me the companies in the database.* causes Q&A to display a report of the specified data. The remaining entries in the macro are responses to prompts about the query.

If you plan to use a macro repeatedly, you should type the file name you want to access with the macro rather than use the arrow keys to highlight the file name. The arrow keys work when you define the macro, but if you add a database file, the macro may access the wrong file.

You can use the same macro to ask the Intelligent Assistant questions. Rather than include the name of the database file and query in the macro, you can insert a <wait> code so that the program waits for input. The macro appears as follows:

```
<begdef><alts><name>"RUN IA"<vidoff>a<enter><wait>
<enter>Show me the companies in the database.<enter>y<enter>
<enddef>
*
```

Printing Reports

Macros, like the following example, enable you to print a report by pressing only one key:

```
<begdef><altr><name>"Report Printout"<vidoff>r<enter>
psales.dtf<enter>salesrep<enter><enter><enddef>
*
```

After the begin definition code, Alt-R is specified as the identifier key and "Report Printout" as the name. <vidoff> tells Q&A to suppress menu display during playback, *r* tells Q&A to select Report from the Main menu, and *p* tells Q&A to print a file. *sales.dtf* is the name of the database, and *salesrep* is the name of the report. The remaining Enter keystrokes finish the process.

The following macro uses the Intelligent Assistant to create a report from the sales lead database. The macro tells Q&A to select sales leads from the Indiana district and to print a report of the findings:

```
<begdef><altf8><name>"IA IN Sales Report"<vidoff>aaslslead
<enter>List Indiana companies<enter><f2><home><f8><tab>
<tab><tab><tab><tab><tab>Sales Leads in the Indiana
District<f10><enddef>
```

This macro is more complicated than the previous ones. The first letter *a* selects the Intelligent Assistant. The second letter *a* selects "Ask me to do something" on the Assistant menu. The database file *slslead* is specified. The macro then tells the IA to *List Indiana companies* and answers the prompt with an Enter keystroke.

The report then is displayed (see fig. 19.8) and sent to the printer. The <f2> code tells Q&A to print the retrieved records. <home> moves the cursor to PtrA at the Print to: prompt. The <f8> code displays the Print Options screen, and the <tab> keystrokes move the cursor into the Header box, where header text is entered: "Sales Leads in the Indiana District." The <f10> keystroke sends the report to the printer (see fig. 19.9). The concluding Esc keystrokes return you to the Main menu.

```
list Indiana companies


         Company
--------------------------
Hoosier Clinics, Inc,
Central Laboratories
Indiana Medical, Inc,
```

Fig. 19.8.   A report generated by a macro.

```
Sales Leads in the Indiana District

        Company
---------------------
Hoosier Clinics, Inc.
Central Laboratories
Indiana Medical, Inc.
```

Fig. 19.9.   The printed result generated by the macro.

Creating Company Memos

You can automate the process of writing memos by creating a macro to enter the information that appears on all memos so that you have to enter only the actual text. You can create a blank memo form within Write and call up the form by using the macro. Figure 19.10 shows an example of a blank memo form created in Write. (For more information on creating Write documents, see Chapters 9 through 13.)

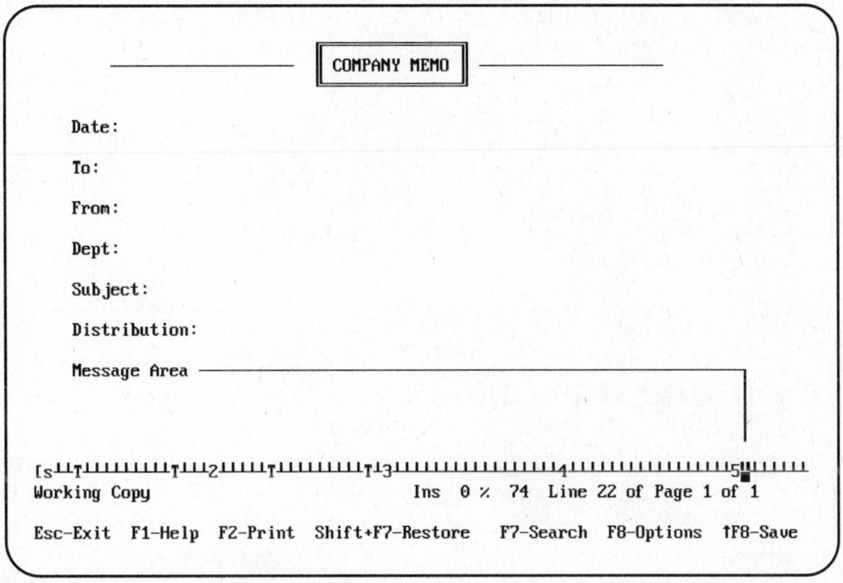

```
COMPANY MEMO

Date:

To:

From:

Dept:

Subject:

Distribution:

Message Area

[s       1       2       3       4       5
Working Copy                    Ins  0 %  74  Line 22 of Page 1 of 1

Esc-Exit  F1-Help  F2-Print  Shift+F7-Restore  F7-Search  F8-Options  ↑F8-Save
```

Fig. 19.10.   A sample memo form.

The following macro finds and loads the blank memo file:

<begdef><altw><name>"Memo Form"<vidoff>w<enter>
gcomemo<enter><enddef>
*

The macro identifier is Alt-W (for Write), and the letter *w* followed by <enter> selects the Write module from the Main menu. (If you have configured Q&A for single keystroke operation, you need to remove the <enter> command after the *w*.) The *g* selects the Get command from the Write menu, and *comemo* is the file name for the company memo form.

After you create the form in Write, position the cursor at the beginning of the first field before saving the form. This way, when you use the macro, the cursor is positioned in the first field, and you can start typing immediately.

Adding Forms to a Database

If you have a database that is used often, you may want to use the following macro to enter all menu selections and to position the cursor on the first blank field of a new record:

```
<begdef><altf><name>"Add to DB"<vidoff>f<enter>aslslead.dtf
<enter><enddef>
*
```

This macro can save you considerable time by choosing the options from the Q&A menu system for you. The *f* selects File at the Main menu, and the *a* selects Add Data at the File menu. Remember, if you have configured Q&A for single keystroke operation, you need to remove the <enter> command after the *f* that selects the File module.

Importing Information

If your business uses another software program to keep track of company finances, you probably frequently need to import data from that program to use in Q&A. The following macro accesses the Utilities module, imports a Lotus worksheet, and converts the worksheet into a Q&A database.

```
<begdef><altd><name>"Lotus Import"<vidoff>u<enter>i<enter>
ldata.wk1<enter>weekly.dtf<enter><F10><enddef>
*
```

This macro sets Alt-D as the identifier key and calls up the Utilities menu. The letter *i* selects the Import option, and *l* selects Lotus as the program from which to import the file. The name of the Lotus file (*data.wk1*) is followed by the receiving Q&A file (*weekly.dtf*). The F10 keystroke initiates the transfer.

Chapter Summary

Macros can save time and effort when you are performing repetitive data-entry or data-management tasks. This chapter has explained both the recording and interactive methods of creating macros, described how to create custom menus from which your macros can be called, explored some macro techniques, and provided some sample macro applications that you can modify to suit your own needs.

The next chapter shows you how to use Q&A's import/export capability to transfer data to and from other popular programs.

20

Importing and Exporting Data in Q&A

T his chapter deals with more technical aspects of file operations: importing and exporting data. If you have used other software programs in the past, or if you use additional programs to help you with your record keeping, finances, and word processing, you probably will need to transfer data in and out of Q&A.

Importing Data into Q&A

With the Q&A Utilities module, you can import information from most other software programs. Depending on what other programs you are using, the procedure may be simple or complex.

Before you learn how to import data by using the Utilities module, however, you should know that you can import text files into the Write module without using Utilities at all. A *text file* is a letter, a bulletin, a report—any document that is not a database or spreadsheet file. The following section covers importing text files; the next covers importing databases. The text file shown in figure 20.1 is an excerpt from Titan Technology's annual report.

593

```
        Titan Technology Report 1991              page 1



            Titan Technology: A History

    Titan Technology was created in early 1974 to answer a
    fast-growing need in the medical supply business.  Owners
    Bob Lancaster and Dan Evans, working in Bob's unheated
    garage in Chicago, Illinois, packed and shipped their
    first order on February 23,1974.

    Since that time, Titan Technology has become a leader in
    the medical sales industry.  With over 20,000 customers
    annually, Titan Technology has developed into one of the
    world's most prosperous wholesale medical supply houses.
```

Fig. 20.1.   *A sample text file.*

Importing Text Files

To import a text file into Write, first copy the file to the directory in which you
store your Q&A word processing files. Next, use the Get command from the
Write menu to select the file. You also can use the Options menu: press F8
(Options), D (Document), and G (Get a Document).

The program displays the Import Document menu to alert you that the file is
not a standard Q&A file. (This menu is different from the Import menu accessed
through Write Utilities, which can be used to import non-Q&A file formats such
as WordPerfect, Microsoft Word, and WordStar.) You then indicate whether to
import the file as an ASCII file (without wordwrap), a special ASCII file (with
wordwrap), a WordStar file, or a 1-2-3 or Symphony file.

If the document is in WordStar format, the program converts the data to a Q&A
file as soon as you press W. You must manually replace the WordStar dot
commands and some print-enhancement commands with the corresponding
Q&A commands. Print commands for boldface, underline, superscript, and
subscript features translate into Q&A without adjustment.

Figure 20.2 shows the original WordStar file. Notice the set of dot commands
at the top of the page. Two commands set the top and bottom margins, another
command specifies the header, and others set the page number and cancel the
bottom-of-page page number.

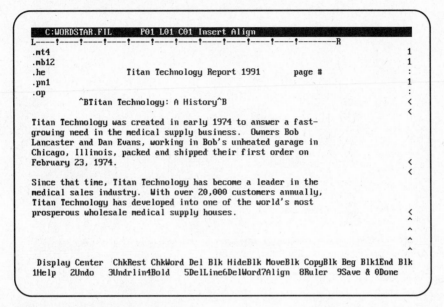

```
 C:WORDSTAR.FIL        P01 L01 C01 Insert Align
L----?----?----?----?----?----?----?----?----?----?--------R
.mt4                                                                        1
.mb12                                                                       1
.he                    Titan Technology Report 1991        page #           :
.pn1                                                                        1
.op                                                                         :
            ^BTitan Technology: A History^B                                 <
                                                                            <
Titan Technology was created in early 1974 to answer a fast-
growing need in the medical supply business.  Owners Bob
Lancaster and Dan Evans, working in Bob's unheated garage in
Chicago, Illinois, packed and shipped their first order on
February 23, 1974.                                                          <
                                                                            <
Since that time, Titan Technology has become a leader in the
medical sales industry.  With over 20,000 customers annually,
Titan Technology has developed into one of the world's most
prosperous wholesale medical supply houses.                                 <
                                                                            ^
                                                                            ^
                                                                            ^
                                                                            ^
  Display Center  ChkRest ChkWord Del Blk HideBlk MoveBlk CopyBlk Beg Blk1End Blk
  1Help   2Undo   3Undrlin4Bold   5DelLine6DelWord7Align  8Ruler  9Save & 0Done
```

Fig. 20.2.   *The WordStar file.*

Each of these specifications can be duplicated in Q&A, but you must use a different method. First, you must copy the WordStar file into the appropriate Q&A directory. Suppose that the Q&A word processing files are on the hard disk (drive C) in the QATEXT directory, and the WordStar files are in the WORDSTAR.FIL subdirectory of the WSDIR directory. To copy the files to the appropriate Q&A directory, you type the following:

    copy c:\wsdir\wordstar.fil\filename.ext c:\qatext

When you use the DOS COPY command and you plan to keep the name of the copied file, you don't have to specify the file name in the destination.

When the WordStar file is in the QATEXT directory, you can import the file by selecting the Get command from the Write menu or the Options Document submenu; the Import Document menu appears. Choose WordStar to tell Q&A that the unknown file is a WordStar document.

The file is translated into Q&A format and loaded onto the Type/Edit screen (see fig. 20.3). Notice that the document is slightly different from the original WordStar version. The margins are wider in Q&A, so fewer words appear on each line. The page-number designation has been carried over onto the next line and now appears in the middle of the dot commands.

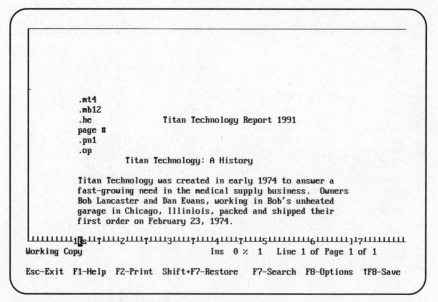

```
         .mt4
         .mb12
         .he              Titan Technology Report 1991
        page #
         .pn1
         .op
                     Titan Technology: A History

         Titan Technology was created in early 1974 to answer a
         fast-growing need in the medical supply business.  Owners
         Bob Lancaster and Dan Evans, working in Bob's unheated
         garage in Chicago, Illiniois, packed and shipped their
         first order on February 23, 1974.
```

```
Working Copy                              Ins  0 %  1    Line 1 of Page 1 of 1

Esc-Exit  F1-Help  F2-Print  Shift+F7-Restore   F7-Search  F8-Options  ↑F8-Save
```

Fig. 20.3. *A WordStar file as first imported into Q&A.*

Another difference is that the heading no longer is enclosed in the ^B symbols (WordStar's boldface codes). Q&A recognizes those codes and turns them into the Q&A equivalent for boldface. Although you cannot see the result in figure 20.3, Q&A displays the heading in letters that are brighter than the surrounding text, which indicates that the heading will appear in boldface on the printout.

You also may notice that the heading is not centered on the screen. WordStar codes cause the heading to be moved to the right, but when the file is printed, the heading appears centered on the page.

To fix this problem, press F8 (Options), and choose the Edit Header command from the Lay Out Page submenu. The cursor moves to the header box, which is displayed at the top of the screen (see fig. 20.4). You then can type the header you want and *Page #*. In WordStar and Q&A, the pound sign specifies automatic page numbering. You also can press F8, A (Align Text), and choose the Center Line command to center the header.

Press F10 when you have created the header. The header box disappears, but the header stays on-screen, and the pound sign has been replaced with the number *1*. After you delete the WordStar commands and the heading from the WordStar file, the importing process is complete.

Importing ASCII text files also is a simple process. ASCII, an acronym for American Standard Code for Information Interchange, is a standard numeric code used to translate binary zeros and ones into letters, numbers, punctuation symbols, and special characters. Most ASCII text files are in the "ASCII without wordwrap" format, which means that a carriage return is at the end of each line. In this case, all formatting and print enhancements must be implemented through Q&A. If you plan to make major changes to a document after it is imported, however, choose Special ASCII. In this form, all carriage returns are taken out unless the program encounters two carriage returns in a row, which indicates the end of a paragraph.

The last type of file that can be imported to Write with Get is a 1-2-3 or Symphony file. You can use Q&A Write, for example, to import data from 1-2-3 or Symphony for use in a document or mail-merge operation. You import data from these programs by specifying the ranges on the Define Range screen, which is discussed later in this chapter.

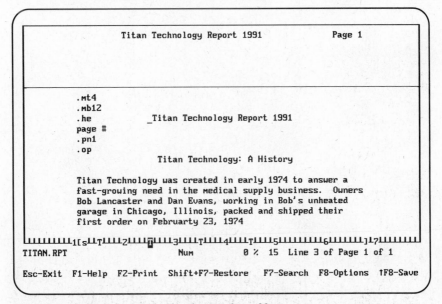

```
                    Titan Technology Report 1991           Page 1




        .mt4
        .mb12
        .he            _Titan Technology Report 1991
        page #
        .pn1
        .op

                    Titan Technology: A History

        Titan Technology was created in early 1974 to answer a
        fast-growing need in the medical supply business.  Owners
        Bob Lancaster and Dan Evans, working in Bob's unheated
        garage in Chicago, Illinois, packed and shipped their
        first order on Februarty 23, 1974
LLLLLLLLL1[s⌐⌐T⌐⌐⌐2⌐⌐⌐⌐⌐█⌐⌐⌐⌐3⌐⌐⌐⌐T⌐⌐⌐4⌐⌐⌐⌐T⌐⌐⌐5⌐⌐⌐⌐⌐⌐⌐⌐⌐6⌐⌐⌐⌐⌐⌐⌐]⌐7⌐⌐⌐⌐⌐⌐⌐
TITAN.RPT                      Num         0 % 15 Line 3 of Page 1 of 1

Esc-Exit  F1-Help  F2-Print  Shift+F7-Restore   F7-Search  F8-Options  ↑F8-Save
```

Fig. 20.4. *Typing the header for the WordStar file.*

Importing Other Word Processor Files

You also can import documents created with the following programs: DCA, WordStar (Versions 3.3 through 5.5), WordPerfect (Versions 5.0 and 5.1), Microsoft Word (Versions 3.0 through 5.5), MultiMate 3.3 and 4.0, MultiMate Advantage (3.6 and 3.7), and Professional Write (1.0 through 2.1). To import a document in one of these formats follow these steps:

1. From the Write menu, choose Utilities, then choose Import a
   Document at the Write Utilities menu.

2. At the Write Import menu, choose the format of the document to
   be imported. Write converts the document and displays the text
   in the editing screen.

Importing Files from PFS: Professional File and the IBM Filing Assistant

The File Utilities module is used to import database files into Q&A. Q&A
supports imported data from a variety of formats:

- PFS: Professional File

- IBM Filing Assistant

- 1-2-3 or Symphony

- DIF

- Fixed ASCII

- Standard ASCII

- dBASE II/III/IV

- Paradox Version 2.0 or 3.x

The general procedure for importing database files into Q&A is similar,
whatever the format. The specific steps vary, however, according to the kind of
file being imported. This discussion begins with a detailed explanation of
importing PFS: Professional File and the IBM Filing Assistant. The other formats
then are described in turn.

If the file you want to use was created with PFS: Professional File or the IBM
Filing Assistant, you can import the data and the entire database structure
directly. Q&A automatically creates a file structure to receive the data. You also
can import data into an existing Q&A file, and Q&A will append the new data
at the end of the file. In this chapter, the procedures explained for PFS:
Professional File apply also to the IBM Filing Assistant. Q&A handles both
products the same way.

The procedures used to import the different programs begin in a similar way.
With some data formats, however, before you import, you first must create a
Q&A file to receive the imported data.

Creating a Q&A Database To Receive Data

You begin the importing procedures at the Utilities menu. To import data, follow these steps:

1. Select Utilities from the File menu, and call up the Import menu by selecting Import Data.

2. Choose the type of file to import, and name the specific file.

   If you cannot remember the name, and the file is located in the default drive and path, press Enter; a list of file names is displayed. Use the cursor keys to highlight your selection, and press Enter. (If the file is in another drive and path, press Ctrl-Y to delete the default drive and path, and enter the correct drive and path.)

3. Type the name of the Q&A file that will receive the data.

From this point on, the procedure varies according to the kind of file that you're importing. The following sections explain each of the procedures.

When you import data from PFS: Professional File into Q&A, you must specify the name of the file that will receive the data. If the Q&A file doesn't exist, the file is created with the same structure as the PFS: Professional File original. Q&A also will duplicate report and print specifications that have been created for the file.

For example, if you are importing a PFS: Professional File database that has eight fields, the same eight fields appear in the Q&A database. The field lengths are the same, although you need to change the data type to match Q&A specifications (discussed later in this chapter). If the PFS: Professional File database has six reports structured to extract and print records for six regional offices, the same six reports are carried into Q&A. If special printer codes are included in the PFS: Professional File database, a Print Options screen is filled in automatically when the file is imported into Q&A.

What happens when you enter the name of a receiving file that is in use? Q&A adds the records from the imported file to the end of the existing records. (The restrictions for this procedure are covered later in this chapter.)

Remember that in the sections that follow, the procedures for PFS: Professional File and the IBM Filing Assistant are identical.

Importing the Data

To import a file from PFS: Professional File, first select the program from the Import menu of the Utilities module. Next, type the file name, or press Enter to display a list of PFS: Professional File database files. The list displayed does not contain files exclusively from PFS: Professional File; all files in the directory are listed (see fig. 20.5). Select the file by moving the cursor to the file you want and pressing Enter.

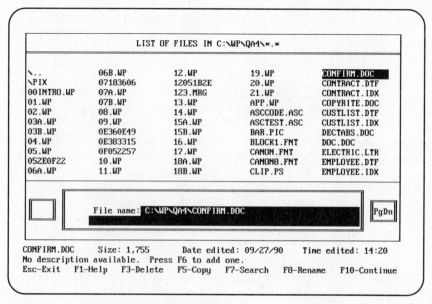

Fig. 20.5. *A listing of files in the current directory.*

The Import menu is displayed again. This display doesn't indicate that your entry didn't work; you have been returned to the Import menu so that you can enter the name of the new Q&A file to be created. The name of the file to be imported is displayed after the Import From: prompt, and you need to answer the prompt File Name:. The drive and directory identification—the path to the file—appears after the prompt. After you type the file name and press Enter, Q&A adds the DTF extension to the name.

Specifying Information Types

Q&A moves from the Import menu to the Format Spec after you enter the file name. Whether the receiving file is new or already existing, you must specify the information type for each field on the Format Spec screen. Each field name is displayed; if you have many fields in the database, you may have more than one screen of information. Press PgDn to display any additional screens.

Each field name is specified initially as a text field (T). This setting is the default, so Q&A assumes that all the fields you are importing are text fields, unless you specify otherwise on the Format Spec screen. The field types are as follows:

Code	Field type
T	Text
N	Number
M	Money
D	Date
H	Hours (time of day)
Y	Logical (requiring a yes/no answer)
K	Keywords

Figure 20.6 shows an example of the Format Spec screen for the SLSLEAD database file. Most of the fields shown on this screen have been specified as text fields. When you specify fields for the imported information, remember that a text field can contain letters, numbers, or both.

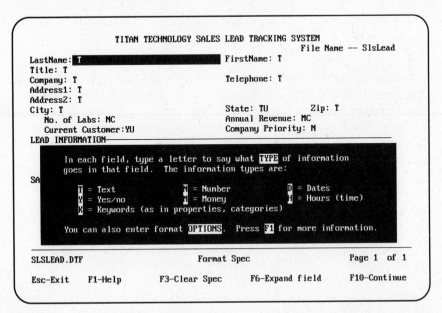

Fig. 20.6. The Format Spec for text fields.

The fields in the lower part of the Format Spec screen contain several different specifications (see fig. 20.7). The Sales Priority field has been coded to accept numeric values with one decimal place (N1); Sales District is a keyword field (K); and the Date Entered field contains the code for accepting date values (D).

```
   ┌──────────────────────────────────────────────────────────┐
   │ In each field, type a letter to say what TYPE of information │
La │ goes in that field.  The information types are:            │
Ti │                                                            │
Co │   T = Text           N = Number          D = Dates         │
Ad │   Y = Yes/no         M = Money           H = Hours (time)  │
Ad │   K = Keywords (as in properties, categories)              │
Ci │                                                            │
   │ You can also enter format OPTIONS.  Press F1 for more information. │
   └──────────────────────────────────────────────────────────┘
LEAD INFORMATION─────────────────────────────────────────────
   Product Interest: K
   Request For: K                    Lead Source: K
   Months to Purchase: N             Product Priority: N
SALES ACTION─────────────────────────DATES────────────
   Sales Priority: N1                Date Entered: D
   Sales Dist.: K                    Date Info Sent: T
   Salesman: T                       Sales Contact: T
   Status: T                         Demo Date: T


SLSLEAD.DTF                   Format Spec                 Page 1  of 1

Esc-Exit    F1-Help      F3-Clear Spec     F6-Expand field     F10-Continue
```

Fig. 20.7.   The Format Spec with other specifications.

For more information on entering character types, see Chapter 5. In that chapter, you also can review how to specify formatting options, such as justification of text, the use of commas in money fields, and the use of codes to convert text field values to uppercase letters. Remember that you always can display a help screen by pressing F1. When you have specified all information types, press F10 (Continue) to save the Format Spec.

Selecting and Ordering Fields

The next screen displayed is the Merge Spec. Use this screen to select and order the fields to be imported. If you press F10, all fields will be imported in their original order. The numbers you enter on the Merge Spec screen to indicate the order should be the field numbers from the imported file. The field names displayed are the ones from the new Q&A database.

Suppose that when you set up the new database to receive the PFS: Professional File information, for example, you need to change the order in which the information is displayed. The Title field may have been field #1 in the PFS: Professional File database, but Title is field #3 on the Titan Technology form. To show Q&A where to put the data, you enter a *1* in the Title field on the Merge Spec screen (see fig. 20.8). When you import the data, the contents of field #1 in the PFS: Professional File database are copied to field #3 in the Q&A database.

```
                    TITAN TECHNOLOGY SALES LEAD TRACKING SYSTEM
                                               File Name -- SlsLead
        LastName:                      FirstName:
        Title: 1
        Company:                       Telephone:
        Address1:
        Address2:
        City:                          State:          Zip:
           No. of Labs:                Annual Revenue:
           Current Customer:           Company Priority:
        LEAD INFORMATION
           Product Interest:
           Request For:                Lead Source:
           Months to Purchase:         Product Priority:
        SALES ACTION                         DATES
           Sales Priority:             Date Entered:
           Sales Dist.:             Date Info Sent:
           Salesman:                   Sales Contact:
           Status:                       Demo Date:


        SLSLEAD.DTF                 Merge Spec              Page 1   of 1

        Esc-Exit    F1-Help    F3-Clear    Alt+F8-List   Shift+F8-Save  F10-Continue
```

Fig. 20.8. *Changing the field order with Merge Spec.*

You also can use the Merge Spec screen to discard fields when you import information. For example, suppose that in the PFS: Professional File database you have fields that record the name and employee number of the data-entry operator, and you don't want those fields to appear on the Titan Technology form. If you don't enter the field numbers of those fields on the Merge Spec screen, the data from the fields will not be imported. Similarly, if the Q&A database has fields that you have not numbered, no data will be transferred to those fields.

After you have filled in the Merge Spec, press F10 to import the data into Q&A.

Special Conditions for Importing Data from PFS: Professional File

You should be aware of special conditions as you import files into Q&A from PFS: Professional File and the IBM Filing Assistant. If the PFS: Professional File database has fields that extend more than one line, you will have to use a different procedure. If you follow the previous procedure, all data beyond the first line will be lost in the transfer.

You also will have a problem with attachment fields from PFS: Professional File and the IBM Filing Assistant. A memo attached to records may be an attachment field, similar to a memo field in dBASE. Q&A cannot transfer attachment fields with the usual importing procedure; but there is a way to solve this problem.

The solution is the same for both programs. First, select the type of file from the Import menu, as you would in a normal import procedure. Then enter the names of the file to be imported and the new Q&A file.

Q&A starts to create the database, and the Format Spec is displayed. In this case, do not change the default settings for the information types (T); press Esc to return to the Main menu.

You then must go through the procedure for redesigning a file. Select File from the Main menu, and choose Design File from the File menu. At the Design menu, select Redesign a File, and enter the new file name at the prompt.

Q&A displays the new file's form design. Don't change the letter codes that Q&A has added after each field name; the codes are used by the program to maintain the structure of your database.

To solve the problem of multi-line fields, enter a greater-than symbol (>) where you want the field to end (see fig. 20.9). Because the lines are slightly longer in PFS: Professional File than in Q&A, add an extra line at the end of your Q&A multi-line fields to guard against data loss.

For attachment fields, press PgDn to display a new page in the form design. Type *Attachment:* at the top of the new screen. Move the cursor to the bottom right corner of the screen, and enter a greater-than symbol. When you press F10 (Continue), your modifications are saved, and you have added a full-page attachment field to your form.

After you press F10, the Format Spec is displayed again. Specify the information types for the fields; don't forget the attachment field on the next page. When you are finished, press F10.

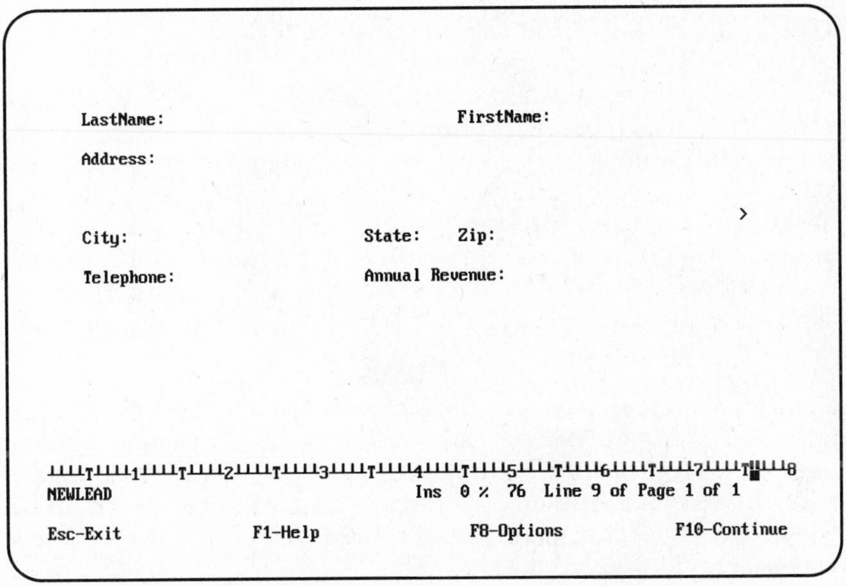

```
        LastName:                        FirstName:

        Address:


        City:                   State:   Zip:                         >

        Telephone:              Annual Revenue:




   |||||ᴛ|||||1|||||ᴛ|||||2|||||ᴛ|||||3|||||ᴛ|||||4|||||ᴛ|||||5|||||ᴛ|||||6|||||ᴛ|||||7|||||ᴛ|||||8
   NEWLEAD                                    Ins  0 %  76  Line 9 of Page 1 of 1

        Esc-Exit            F1-Help              F8-Options            F10-Continue
```

Fig. 20.9. Specifying a multi-line field.

Next, select Import Data from the Utilities menu, and enter the name of the file
you want to import. After you enter the name of the new Q&A file and press
Enter, the Merge Spec is displayed. If you don't need to change the selection
or order of the fields, you can skip this step by pressing F10. The file then is
imported into Q&A, with multi-line and attachment fields intact.

Importing data can give you some problems if you are using PFS: Professional
File or the IBM Filing Assistant. For example, you may have trouble importing
data into Q&A if you have:

- More than 10 pages in the original database

- More than 240 fields on one page

- More than 2,400 fields overall

- A zero-length field

- A page with no fields

You can take two approaches to these problems. You can reduce the number
of pages or fields, eliminate or expand the zero-length field, or remove the
empty page; or you can construct a Q&A database that has the same fields and
field lengths as the source database. The second method is used later in the
chapter to transfer data from other software programs to Q&A.

Importing a File from dBASE

The dBASE programs—dBASE II, dBASE III, dBASE III Plus, and dBASE IV—are some of the most popular database programs available. Because of the popularity of the programs, Q&A has added the ability, introduced with Q&A Version 4.0, to import dBASE files directly. When you tell Q&A to import a dBASE file, the program reads the form design of the dBASE file and creates a new Q&A file with the same form design. If you tell Q&A to import dBASE data into an existing Q&A file, the data is appended at the end of the existing Q&A file.

After specifying a file to be imported and the name of a new or existing Q&A file as described above, you see a Format Spec that reflects the form that Q&A has created from the dBASE file. Fill in any changed types of information, and press F10 to continue the importing process. If the Format Spec contains number, money, date, or time information, Q&A next displays the Global Format Spec; if the Format Spec does not contain number, money, date, or time information, Q&A displays the Merge Spec.

You can use the Merge Spec to specify which fields in the source database will be imported. Note that Q&A imports entire dBASE memo fields up to the maximum 32K length. After you make your specifications on the Merge Spec screen, press F10, and the data is imported into the new Q&A database file.

If an existing Q&A database name is used for the new database, only the Merge Spec screen is displayed. After you press F10, the imported data is added to the end of the existing Q&A database.

Importing a File from 1-2-3 or Symphony

If you created a Q&A database to receive the data, Q&A can import a Lotus 1-2-3 2.2 or a Symphony WKS or WK1 file without first converting the file to a PRN file. When you construct the database, remember that each row is a record in a Q&A database. A single column in a 1-2-3 database holds all the field contents for that database. When the data is merged into a Q&A data file, the first column in the 1-2-3 database file or range is transferred to the first Q&A field, the second column goes into the second Q&A field, and so on. Of course, you can use the Merge Spec screen to rearrange the order of these fields. Figure 20.10 shows a Q&A database that has been designed to receive a 1-2-3 file.

```
┌──────────────────────────────────────────────────────────────────┐
│                                                                    │
│              ┌───────────────── MARKETING DATABASE ──────────────┐ │
│                                                                    │
│           MARKET:                          MARKET TYPE:            │
│                                                                    │
│         Projected Sales:      Marginal Income:      G&A:           │
│         Sales Office:         Adv. Support:         Field:         │
│         Demos:                Trade Allowances:     Samples:       │
│         Coupons:              Point of Purchase:                   │
│                                                                    │
│                                                                    │
│         Total Expense:                                             │
│                                                                    │
│         Profit/Loss:                                               │
│                                                                    │
│                                                                    │
│                                                                    │
│   └┴┴┴┴┬┴┴┴┴┴1┴┴┴┴┬┴█┴┴2┴┴┴┴┬┴┴┴┴3┴┴┴┴┬┴┴┴┴4┴┴┴┴┬┴┴┴┴5┴┴┴┴┬┴┴┴┴6┴┴┴┴┬┴┴┴┴7┴┴┴┴┬┴┴┴┴8  │
│   123DATA                       Ins  0 %  17  Line 17 of Page 1 of 1  │
│                                                                    │
│   Esc-Exit            F1-Help           F8-Options        F10-Continue │
└──────────────────────────────────────────────────────────────────┘
```

Fig. 20.10. Designing a database to receive the 1-2-3 file.

If you don't provide enough fields in your Q&A database to accommodate the active cells in the worksheet rows, Q&A will discard the rightmost cells for which it has no fields. The other mismatch alternative is less disastrous; if you have more fields in the Q&A database than you have rows in the worksheet, some of the fields in the database will be empty.

Press F10 after you set up your fields; the Format Spec screen is displayed. Be careful when you format the fields for your database. Remember that all Lotus cells are fixed in length. A Q&A field, however, extends to the edge of the screen unless the field length is ended by another field label or by a greater-than symbol (>). Because of this consideration, you won't want to use right-justified fields in the Format Spec. Doing so can cause the value to be separated from the field label by almost the entire screen width.

Next, select Import Data from the Utilities menu. When the Import menu is displayed, select 123/Symphony. You will be asked for the name of the Lotus file you want to import; type your answer (be sure to include the complete path description). If you have copied the worksheet into Q&A, press Enter to display the list of 1-2-3 files in your current directory (see fig. 20.11). Highlight the file you want to use, and press Enter.

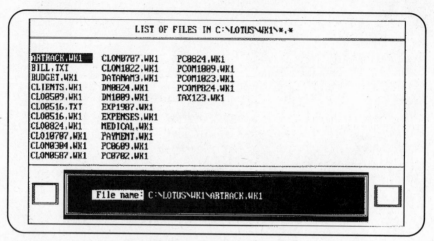

Fig. 20.11.   *Displaying Lotus file names.*

When you are prompted for the name of the Q&A database that will receive the information, type the name and press Enter. (You can redisplay the list of files by pressing Enter. Type the file name and press Enter.)

The Define Range screen then is displayed (see fig. 20.12). On this screen, you can specify a range from the Lotus worksheet to be imported. To do this, you either supply the cell coordinates or type the title of a named range that you created in the 1-2-3 file. If you want to import the entire worksheet, don't specify anything on this screen.

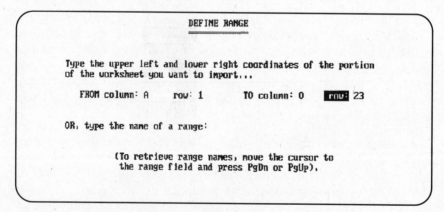

Fig. 20.12.   *Defining a 1-2-3 range to import.*

If you want to eliminate cells or alter the order of the cells you are importing, press F8 to display the Merge Spec. The procedure for filling in this screen is the same as the procedure explained previously.

Remember that a field in 1-2-3 is a column in each record and that columns in Lotus are identified by letters instead of numbers. For example, if the range you're importing begins at the 1-2-3 Home position, column A is the first column to be imported. Refer to column A as field #1 when you fill in the Merge Spec. Similarly, column D is field #4 on the Merge Spec screen (see fig. 20.13). If the range you want to import begins in column G of the worksheet, start numbering the fields at that point. That makes column G field #1, column H field #2, and so forth.

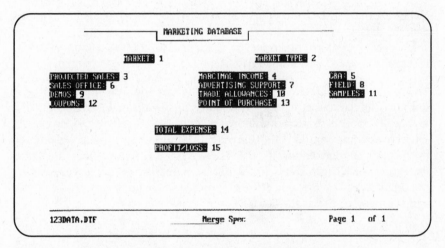

Fig. 20.13. *The Merge Spec for importing a 1-2-3 worksheet.*

Whether you use the Define Range and Merge Spec screens or not, press F10 when you are ready to import the worksheet. Each form is displayed on-screen as the data is imported. When the process is complete, you have a functioning Q&A database created from your 1-2-3 file.

Importing an ASCII or DIF File

Database files from other programs can be imported if the programs can export data to a standard ASCII or DIF file. As you know, ASCII is a numeric code used to represent characters. DIF, an acronym for Data Interchange Format, is another type of industry code used for exchanging data. Both types of files can be imported to a Q&A file after the Q&A database has been set up to receive the data.

The import procedure is similar to that described in previous sections of this chapter. To import an ASCII or DIF file, select the file type from the Import menu. Next, enter the name of the file to be imported and the Q&A file to receive the data. After you press Enter, the Merge Spec is displayed. You don't need to enter anything on this screen unless you want to change the order or selection of the imported fields. When you press F10, the importing process begins.

Make sure that the database you create in Q&A has enough fields to accommodate the data you are importing. Remember also that you don't have to create a new database before you import the data; you can add the data as additional records in an existing Q&A database if the field sizes are compatible.

The type of ASCII you choose depends on the way your text file looks. If your text file is similar to the one shown in figure 20.14, choose Fixed ASCII (SDF). If your file appears like the one shown in figure 20.15, select Standard ASCII. When you choose Standard ASCII, an ASCII Options screen appears, giving you the flexibility to decide how the data is saved on disk. In a standard ASCII file, the data for each field are enclosed in quotation marks, and fields are separated by commas. However, you can choose whether to use the quotation marks and which symbol to use as the field delimiter.

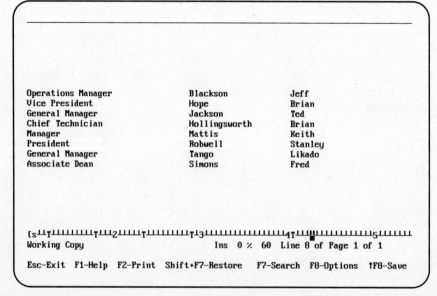

Fig. 20.14. *A fixed ASCII file.*

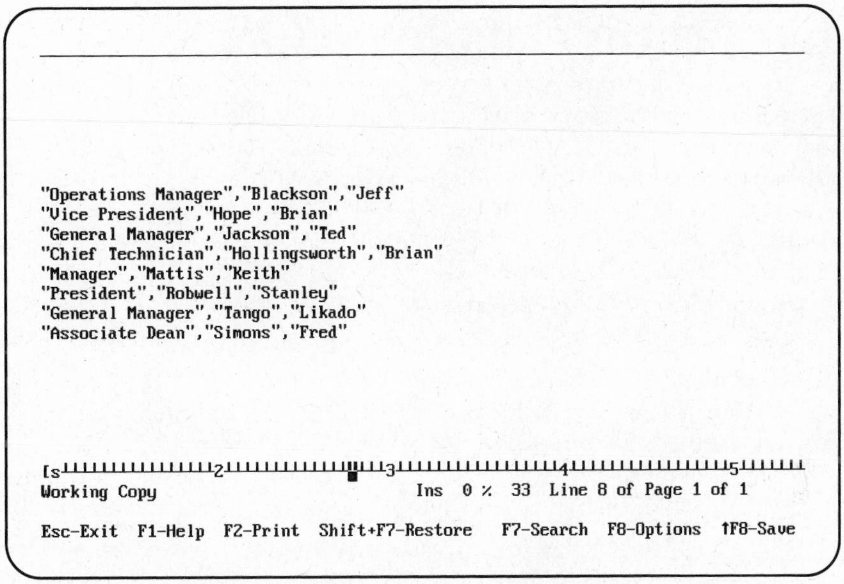

```
  "Operations Manager","Blackson","Jeff"
  "Vice President","Hope","Brian"
  "General Manager","Jackson","Ted"
  "Chief Technician","Hollingsworth","Brian"
  "Manager","Mattis","Keith"
  "President","Robwell","Stanley"
  "General Manager","Tango","Likado"
  "Associate Dean","Simons","Fred"




  [s⊥⊥⊥⊥⊥⊥⊥⊥⊥⊥⊥⊥⊥2⊥⊥⊥⊥⊥⊥⊥⊥⊥⊥⊥⊥⊥▐▌⊥⊥3⊥⊥⊥⊥⊥⊥⊥⊥⊥⊥⊥⊥⊥⊥4⊥⊥⊥⊥⊥⊥⊥⊥⊥⊥⊥⊥⊥⊥5⊥⊥⊥⊥⊥
  Working Copy                         Ins  0 %  33  Line 8 of Page 1 of 1

  Esc-Exit  F1-Help  F2-Print  Shift+F7-Restore   F7-Search  F8-Options  ↑F8-Save
```

Fig. 20.15. *A standard ASCII file.*

When a DIF file is generated by another program, the file usually is given a DIF extension. When you import a DIF file, you don't need to specify any special options, as you did with Standard ASCII.

Importing a Paradox Version 2.0 or 3.x File

You can import Paradox databases directly into Q&A, and Q&A will create a form design to receive the Paradox data. You also can import Paradox data into an existing Q&A file, and Q&A will append the data to the end of the file. If the file you want to import is in Paradox 1.0 format, you first must convert the file to Paradox 2.0 or 3.x format.

To start the import process, choose Import a File from the File Utilities menu, and at the File Import menu choose Paradox 2.0/3.x. After naming the file to be imported and the Q&A file to receive the data, Q&A asks you to remove password protection (if a password exists) from the Paradox file. If the file isn't password protected, Q&A displays a Format Spec created from the Paradox database. Fill in the Format, Global Format, and Merge Specs as described previously in the sections "Selecting and Ordering Fields" and "Specifying Information Types."

Exporting Data from Q&A

Up to this point, the chapter has covered importing data into Q&A. You also may need to export Q&A text files and databases to other programs. The following sections explain how to export data from Q&A.

Exporting Text Files

The beginning of this chapter explains how to import text files in the Write module. You also can use Write to export text files by creating a standard ASCII file. Two methods can be used to export data in the Write module, neither of which involves the main Q&A Utilities module. The Write exporting procedure is easy to use, and you can export a file with headers, footers, and margins by using the Print Options screen.

Before you export a file through the Write menu, you can load the file into memory by using the Get command from the Write menu. The document then is displayed on-screen. Press Esc to return to the Write menu.

Select Utilities from the Write menu, and select Export a Document from the Write Utilities menu. At the Write Export menu, you can choose one of nine export formats. If you select one of the first four options—ASCII, Document ASCII, Macintosh ASCII, or DCA—Q&A prompts you for a file name and then exports the file. If you choose any other option, Q&A asks for the version number of the program whose format you have chosen. The export options are as follows:

WordPerfect	5.0, 5.1
WordStar	3.3, 3.31, 3.45, 4.0, 5.0
Microsoft Word	3.0, 3.1, 4.0, 5.0
MultiMate	3.3, 4, Advantage 3.6, Advantage II 3.7
Professional Write	PFS: Write Version C, Professional Write 1.0, PFS:First Choice 1.0 and 2.0

Choose a format, press F10, type a name for the exported file, and press Enter. Q&A creates the new file in the chosen format.

To export ASCII data from Write by using the Print facility, use the Get command from the Write menu to load the file into memory. Then press F2 to print the document. The Print Options screen is displayed (see fig. 20.16). The Print to option is used to tell Q&A where to send the data.

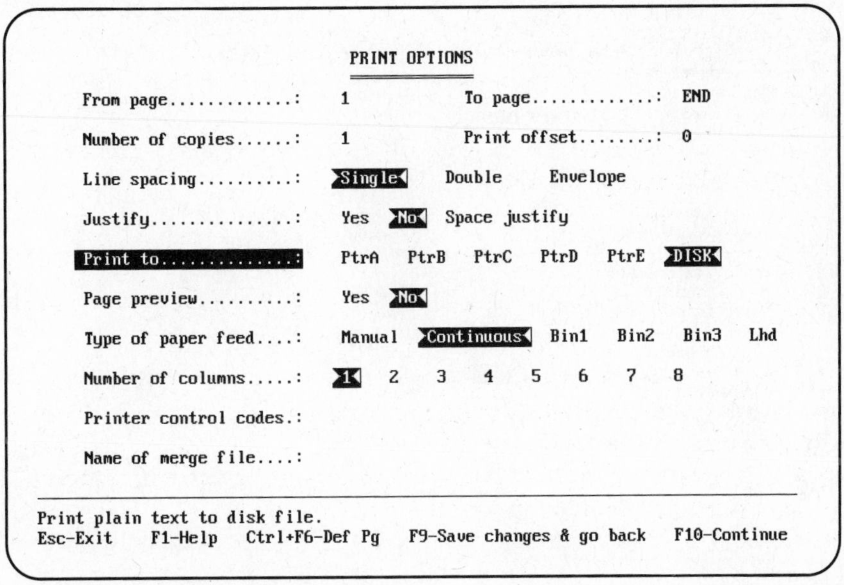

```
                           PRINT OPTIONS
                           _____

   From page............:   1            To page............:  END

   Number of copies......:  1           Print offset........:  0

   Line spacing..........:  ▶Single◀    Double    Envelope

   Justify...............:  Yes  ▶No◀   Space justify

   Print to..............:  PtrA  PtrB  PtrC  PtrD   PtrE  ▶DISK◀

   Page preview..........:  Yes  ▶No◀

   Type of paper feed....:  Manual  ▶Continuous◀  Bin1  Bin2  Bin3  Lhd

   Number of columns.....:  ▶1◀  2   3   4   5   6   7   8

   Printer control codes.:

   Name of merge file....:

  Print plain text to disk file.
  Esc-Exit    F1-Help    Ctrl+F6-Def Pg    F9-Save changes & go back    F10-Continue
```

Fig. 20.16.   *The Print Options screen.*

The various Ptr settings assign different printers, but you can use the DISK selection to create an ASCII file. After you choose DISK, press F10 to save the settings. Q&A then displays the Disk Print menu; choose IBM ASCII or Mac ASCII. If the file you are exporting has headers and footers, they are copied to the new file along with the original margin settings.

Exporting Database Files

Most database programs accept outside files in either ASCII or DIF format. With Q&A you can do more than simply export the data; you can select the forms and fields you want to export, and sort them in a particular order.

For this procedure, select Export Data from the File Utilities menu to display the Export menu. This menu has seven options, similar to the Import menu. When you select the file type and enter the source and destination file names, the Retrieve Spec is displayed (see fig. 20.17).

```
                TITAN TECHNOLOGY SALES LEAD TRACKING SYSTEM
══════════════════════════════════════════════════ File Name -- SlsLead
LastName:                              FirstName:
Title:
Company:                               Telephone:
Address1:
Address2:
City:                                  State:        Zip:
   No. of Labs:                        Annual Revenue:
   Current Customer:                   Company Priority:
─────────────────────────────LEAD INFORMATION─────
   Product Interest:
   Request For:                        Lead Source:
   Months to Purchase:                 Product Priority:
─────────────────────────────SALES ACTION─────
   Sales Priority:                     Date Entered:
   Sales Dist.: SOUTH CENTRAL          Sales Manager:
   Salesman:                           Phone:
   Status:


─────────────────────────────────────────────────────────────
SLSLEAD.DTF               Retrieve Spec              Page 1  of 1

Esc-Exit   F1-Help   F6-Expand   F8-Sort   Alt+F8-List  ↑F8-Save   F10-Continue
```

Fig. 20.17.   The Retrieve Spec.

You can use the Retrieve Spec screen to restrict the data to be exported. You also can press Shift-F8 to select a stored Retrieve Spec. If you want to export the file with no changes, press F10. Otherwise, enter the retrieve specifications here. After you enter the restrictions on the Retrieve Spec screen, your specifications filter out the forms you don't want to be included in the export process. If you are exporting to SDF format, you must fill in the Retrieve Spec to specify column positions and field lengths.

If you want to sort the file, press F8, and the Sort Spec screen appears. Enter any sorting specifications you want to make. You can press Shift-F8 to name and save the retrieve specifications, or you can press F10 to move on to the Merge Spec screen (unless you are exporting to SDF format).

On the Retrieve Spec screen, you specify the forms to be exported; on the Merge Spec screen, you set the field selection and order. (The Merge Spec is discussed in a previous section in this chapter.) After you enter the specifications, press F10.

Exporting to ASCII or DIF

If you are exporting to a DIF file or a standard ASCII file, the export procedure now is finished. If you are creating a standard ASCII file, however, you have one more step. The ASCII Options screen prompts you to specify whether the data in each field will be enclosed in quotation marks and which delimiter will be used to separate fields. You have four choices for the delimiter: carriage return, semicolon, comma, or space. The default delimiter is the comma. The decision you make depends on the program that is to receive the data. When you press F10, the ASCII file is created.

Exporting to dBASE

The procedures for exporting to dBASE II, dBASE III, dBASE III Plus, and dBASE IV are identical, although each program requires a different utility. Simply select one of the utilities, enter the name of the Q&A database, and type the name of the dBASE database. (Be sure not to enter the name of an existing file unless you want it to be overwritten by the exported Q&A file.)

Fill in the Retrieve and Merge Specs, and press F10, which creates the database. The database created in dBASE automatically takes on the field type and length characteristics of the Q&A database.

Chapter Summary

Because Q&A's import and export capabilities are so easy to use, Q&A can be used with many of the most popular spreadsheet, database, and word processing programs. If you have read this book up to this point, you now are familiar with all the Q&A operating features; you know how to use Q&A as a self-contained unit and in conjunction with many other programs. The next chapter explains how to use Q&A in a multiuser environment on a local area network.

Networking: Using Q&A in a Multiuser Environment

Microcomputer users increasingly are turning to networking and other methods for multiuser access to programs and data files. With Version 3.0, Q&A addressed this trend by adding multiuser support. Version 4.0 has added sophisticated features for data file access control. For example, Version 4.0 enables you to control which users may change data in certain fields of your database form.

This chapter introduces networking and networking concepts and explains how Q&A fits into that environment. The section, "Q&A on a Network," discusses how to set up Q&A and presents ideas for configuring Q&A databases for multiuser operation. The section "Q&A Network Setup," explains the differences between using Q&A in a single-user environment and on a network.

Network Concepts

Networks may be unfamiliar to many PC users who are accustomed to single-user systems. The following paragraphs explain computer networks, the benefits of a network, and how Q&A resides on a network.

What Is a Network?

A *local area network* (LAN) refers to the equipment and software that connects personal computers to each other and usually to a centrally located device called a *server*. The server can be another PC dedicated to server duties, or it can be a minicomputer or mainframe that functions as a server while conducting other duties.

A LAN uses coaxial cable, telephone wire, or another medium to connect personal computers through a plug-in circuit board. Driver software to support the additional hardware usually must be installed at each PC as well.

After the physical link is established, PC users can access each other's machine or the server to exchange database information, send and receive electronic mail, and share word processing files. When a minicomputer or mainframe is part of a network, personal computer users can share the same information and the facilities of the server. Hooking PCs to mainframes or minicomputers also gives users access to any available wide area network. A *wide area network* (WAN) connects computers over a long-distance network by using telephone cable, satellite links, or other systems.

Why Use a Network?

One reason for the early popularity of personal computers was that earlier computer users were linked to large machines controlled by data-center personnel. Installing or changing programs sometimes took weeks or months, however, if the change was even possible. Also, one user's needs had to coordinate with other users' needs.

Single-user personal computers gave users the freedom to install whatever software they wanted. Within relatively broad budget and procedural limitations, users could do about anything they wanted with their PCs. The refinement of personal computer hardware brought computing power to the people and eliminated what some people have called the "priesthood of computer control."

Within the past few years, however, a growing trend has been to bring PC users back together under some central arrangement that enables them to keep the benefits of personal computer hardware while regaining the strengths of central data and program storage. The local area network has made this change possible.

A LAN offers several advantages over stand-alone PCs. One benefit is that networking reduces disk swapping. A LAN also enables many people to work on database maintenance at the same time. Another benefit of a network is that, when properly configured, networking gives all users simultaneous access to the same versions of database information, word processing files, electronic mail, and programs. For many users, the cost of applications software alone can justify the expense and effort of establishing a network.

Most major software companies offer networked versions of their software so that only one copy of the programs need be installed. The software is stored at the central server, and those who need to use the software access the software there rather than from their individual computers. In this way, companies need to purchase only one copy of the software rather than copies for each user. Although multiuser software costs more than single-user software, the total cost of networked software to serve a large number of users frequently is much less than the cost of buying individual copies.

Networked users also can share printers. Although light-duty printers are available for a few hundred dollars, users increasingly demand high speed, letter quality, graphics, and even color. Laser printers with these capabilities can be expensive: one popular high-resolution color printer currently sells for nearly $25,000. For most companies, the only way users can access such an expensive device is to share the printer through a network server, which is much more efficient than carrying floppy disks to a central print station computer.

Disk storage also can be less expensive and more efficient on a network. Moving applications software and data to a central location eliminates most redundant storage requirements. Thus, users can use only floppy disk drives or relatively small hard disks. In fact, some network configurations support disk-free workstations, which further reduces the cost of each PC attached to the network.

In addition, central data storage makes maintaining backups easier. Instead of depending on individual users to back up their data regularly, a network management staff backs up the server disk. In this way, everyone's data is backed up at the same time. The manager can use high-speed, high-capacity tape devices, which frequently provide automatic, timed operations, because only one or two units are required, rather than a device for each user.

Network Terms

Networks institute a set of terms that are unfamiliar to many PC users. This section defines a few of the most common network terms.

One definition is especially important for Q&A users. Although network file sharing and multiuser file sharing have some differences, Symantec uses the term *multiuser* to mean networked users. Because Q&A is a microcomputer-based product and multiuser microcomputers are essentially all networked, this multiuser definition is a valid assumption, which this book also adopts.

Database administrator. A person charged with maintaining database files and programs. A database administrator's activities generally include backing up files, assigning access rights, installing software upgrades, and designing shared database structures.

File locking. A process that denies access to entire database files for more than one user at a time. The first user to access a given file secures all rights to the file. Subsequent users are locked out of the file until the first user releases the file.

Local area network, or LAN. Equipment and software that permits a group of computers to share files and programs. A LAN's operation usually is transparent to the users. The workstations are located relatively close to each other, such as in the same building or on the same campus.

Multiuser. Processes and procedures that can be conducted by more than one person simultaneously. Applications software, such as Q&A, can be established as multiuser programs. Databases and other files, when they can be shared by more than one person at a time, are said to be multiuser files.

Password. A group of characters used to uniquely identify a computer user. Passwords typically are entered when a user first accesses a program such as Q&A.

Record locking. A process that denies access to individual database records for more than one user at a time. The first user to access a given record secures modify privileges. Subsequent users are locked out of modify operations until the first user releases the record.

Security. A set of processes and procedures to ensure the integrity of computer information. Included are unique user IDs, user-level and group-level passwords, personal paths and directories, and individually assigned access and procedure rights.

Server. A central processing unit dedicated to disk, communications, or other shared operations. Disk server functions are the most common server operations of interest to networked Q&A users.

Wide area network, or WAN. Equipment and software that permits a group of computers to share files and programs. A WAN's operation is usually transparent to the users. A WAN is located over a large distance, such as in different cities or even different countries.

The User Versions of Q&A

You can use Q&A on a network for simultaneous multiuser access in the following ways:

- Shared files (single-user Q&A)
- Shared programs and files (multiuser Q&A)

If each user on a network has an individual copy of Q&A, database files still can be stored on the network server and shared among network users. However, these copies are of the single-user version of Q&A. To install a single copy of Q&A on a network server and have multiple users share the program, the single-user version of Q&A must be upgraded to a networked version (the Q&A Network Pack).

No fundamental differences exist between the single-user version of Q&A and the networked, multiuser version. The single-user software supports shared data access and even record locking to ensure that two or more users don't try to modify the same record at the same time.

The networked version of Q&A operates essentially the same as the single-user version. The multiuser version asks you to provide your identification (usually your name) and a password for some operations, and certain functions cannot be shared. Q&A will display messages to tell you when you are trying to perform an operation that another user is already doing. Also, printing is usually less immediate. (See the next section in this chapter for more details on the differences in operation.)

Q&A on a Network

After any Q&A multiuser software is installed and the data files are created, little fundamental difference exists between single-user access and multiuser access. However, several aspects of Q&A, such as printing and file access, operate somewhat differently on a network. The following paragraphs describe some differences you should be aware of when you use Q&A under multiuser access.

Data Access

With most LANs, the network server is accessed as one or more additional disk drives from the users' PCs. DOS sets aside drives A through E as local drives, so the first network drive is F.

To access Q&A files or programs from the network, set the appropriate drive default (probably F or above), and run Q&A as if it were on your local drive. Q&A and file access should function virtually the same in the network environment as they do on a single-user PC.

You occasionally may get a message saying that another user is performing the operation you want to perform. You also may notice that some operations are slower than they are in a single-user environment. Otherwise, accessing Q&A data on a network is the same as accessing Q&A on a single-user workstation.

Record Locking and File Locking Considerations

A law of physics states that no two objects can occupy the same space at the same time. In a sense, multiuser databases follow that law. Although many users can open a file simultaneously, they can modify individual records only one at a time. The first user to display a specific database record locks that record against modification by any other user.

If user A displays a sales lead record on-screen, for example, that user gains modification rights to that record. He can make changes in accordance with his access rights and save the modified record back to disk. While user A is displaying a record, the record is said to be *locked*.

If user B finds the same record while user A is modifying the record, Q&A shows user B the following message:

```
Form is being edited by another user. You can't make changes
at this time.
```

User B can view the information, but cannot change it. This restriction is necessary to ensure data integrity. If both users could modify the record simultaneously, the last user to use the record would overwrite previous changes. By controlling access so that only the first user to access a given record has rights to modify the record, all of user A's changes are retained. As soon as the first user writes his changes and moves on to another record, subsequent users then can call up that record for editing.

Most Q&A networked operations are open at any time to all users sharing a database. However, some networked operations can be performed by only one user at a time. Table 21.1 shows operations that are *single-user functions on a shared file*. Although multiple users can access the shared file, only one user at a time can perform each operation listed. For example, one user can design a Print Spec and another can assign passwords in the same file simultaneously, but two users cannot design a Print Spec at the same time.

Table 21.1
Single-User Functions on a Shared File

Module	Function
File	Design a Print Spec
	Assign passwords
	Assign user rights
	Use named specs
Report	Design a report
IA	Teach

Some operations are critical to database integrity and directly affect the view other users have of the database. These functions are considered *single-user functions on a locked file* and completely lock the file against access by any other user for any type of operation. The operations that lock the file are listed in table 21.2.

Table 21.2
Single-User Functions on a Locked File

Module	Function
File	Redesign a file
	Customize a file
	Copy/design forms
	Mass file update
	Posting
	Remove file forms
	Delete duplicate records
IA	Teach
	Mass file update
Utilities	Database recovery
	DOS commands

Network Messages

In addition to the normal Q&A messages, other messages and error reports may appear when you operate in a multiuser environment. A summary of networking messages is listed in table 21.3.

Table 21.3
Network Messages

Message	Meaning
This form is being edited by <network ID>. You can view it only.	You attempted to write to a record being written to by another user.
File in use by <network ID>.	You attempted to use a single-user command on a locked file while someone else was using the database.
This file is being used by <network ID>.	You attempted to use the database while another user was executing a single-user command.

Printing in a Multiuser Environment

A shared printer can serve only one user (one print job) at a time. Your network software handles competing requests for the printer by queuing print jobs in a RAM cache or on disk. When you send a job to a networked printer, you should see no difference between printing on a LAN and printing in a single-user environment, except that your printout may not be produced immediately. If another user is accessing the printer when you send a report to be printed, your report will move into the queue and print in turn as jobs ahead of yours are finished.

In addition, Q&A handles file contention during report preparation by making a copy ("snapshot") of the database at the time you request a report. In this way, you can access data for a printout without interfering with other users who may be modifying the data. Of course, your report will not reflect any changes made to the database after the report printout is started.

Q&A Write in a Multiuser Environment

If you installed a Network Pack, you can share the Write programs in a network. You can view or modify a Write document and then save the document to a network server, where another user can access the document. However, Write documents are essentially single-user files. Two or more users cannot have access to the same Write document simultaneously.

The Intelligent Assistant in a Multiuser Environment

You can use the IA in a shared environment as you normally do, except for the Teach option. Only one user at a time can access the Teach facilities of the IA.

Macros in a Multiuser Environment

You can use your macros on a network in the same manner as a single-user environment, with one exception. When the Q&A Main menu first is displayed, press F6 to call up the password box and enter your password. Q&A remembers your password and will not ask for the password during other operations. By entering your password first (before Q&A must ask for it), macros that access password-protected operations do not stop to ask for your password.

Q&A Network Setup

Regardless of which user version of Q&A a network has, one person usually is in charge of setting up Q&A on the LAN. Often, the network administrator installs all applications software, manages the network, and possibly performs other full-time duties.

Single-User versus Multiuser Q&A

You should consult your dealer and study your network's uses of Q&A to determine whether networked software is more economical and efficient than individual copies of the software for each of your users. Some of the factors to study when you consider a multiuser Q&A upgrade are the size of your user community, the type of hardware each user has, the size and number of databases that will be shared, and the cost of single-user Q&A copies versus a multiuser license to support all your users.

Remember that sharing multiuser Q&A on a network can slow down access by individual users because a server has a maximum processing speed. When multiple users share the server and its software, the number of required disks and CPU accesses increases, which reduces the performance to any individual user.

Cost is also a major consideration. Check with your dealer and compare the costs of single-user Q&A for each user and the cost of a multiuser license. If the costs are similar, you should consider purchasing single-user software to provide the fastest access time to each user. You still can store Q&A data files on the server to share among your users.

If you decide to purchase single-user copies of Q&A, however, each user should have a hard disk workstation. If most users do not have hard disks on their PCs, you probably should use the multiuser version of Q&A. Q&A can run from floppy disks, but doing so is inconvenient for all but the most simple applications. And the cost of adding hard disks to user workstations can be significant.

Keep in mind that if you choose single-user software and new versions are released, you must upgrade each user individually. If you have a large user population, this cost can be significant.

Networks that Q&A Supports

Q&A probably will work in a multiuser environment on any of the popular networks that run under MS-DOS or PC DOS Version 3.1 or later and the AppleShare network. Symantec specifically mentions support for the 3Plus network, the IBM PC Network, Token-Ring, and networks that use NetWare software. In fact, any network that adheres to the multiuser procedures of DOS—any network that uses the DOS SHARE program or implements the SHARE protocols—should work with Q&A. Symantec is expanding regularly the list of supported networks. If you have questions about Q&A support for your specific network, contact the network vendor or Symantec.

Q&A Network Pack

The Q&A Network Pack contains additional software that enables simultaneous, multiuser access to Q&A. Without the Network Pack, each Q&A user must have a separate copy of the single-user version of the software. If each user has a single-user copy of Q&A, you don't need the Network Pack. If you want networked users to share Q&A, then you need the Network Pack to enable the multiuser features.

The Network Pack is an enhancement to an existing copy of single-user Q&A. Each Network Pack increases the number of users by three. The first Pack enables four users to access the Q&A program simultaneously, a second Pack supports up to seven users (the original single user, three users on Network Pack one, and three users on Network Pack two), and a third Pack supports up to 10 users.

When you use the Network Pack, you install a single-user copy of Q&A on your network server and then install the network portion. This procedure modifies your installed Q&A so that it runs on a network only. After installing a networked version of the software, you no longer can use the single-user version on a separate PC without violating the terms of your software license.

Included with the Network Pack is the *Q&A Network Administrator's Guide*, which shows you how to configure Q&A programs for shared access and offers some instruction on network management. The guide is a valuable part of the

Network Pack, and you should read the guide thoroughly before setting up
Q&A for network operation.

Upgrading to Multiuser Q&A

You easily can upgrade single-user copies of Q&A to a networked version by
purchasing one or more Network Packs (see the preceding section). Ask your
Q&A dealer or Symantec for information on current costs and procedures for
making the upgrade. If you purchase Q&A as a networked package, you receive
one single-user copy and enough Network Packs to support the number of
users required for your network.

To set up your system for network access, you may have to alter your system
files by doing the following:

- Determine whether you need to use the DOS SHARE program. DOS
  SHARE turns on DOS-level file contention control. Some networks,
  such as those that use a NetWare or a 3Plus network, supply these
  sharing codes for you. Others, such as MS-Net and PC-Net, require
  that you load the SHARE program before using multiuser files. If your
  network requires you to load SHARE, simply add the SHARE command to your AUTOEXEC.BAT file.

- Make sure that your CONFIG.SYS file contains the statement
  FILES=20, or a larger number. This limit ensures that DOS is set up to
  handle Q&A file access.

For detailed instructions on installing Q&A and configuring the package for
your computer environment, see Appendix A. For information on installing a
Q&A Network Pack for shared program access, contact Symantec.

Multiuser Databases

Although no fundamental differences exist between the single-user version of
Q&A and the networked version, whoever creates a database—whether the
database administrator or someone else—must consider some operational
factors when setting up a database for multiuser operation. If you are creating
a database, you must establish access rights for each database and declare the

Sharing mode, for example. You also can assign passwords to each database to restrict user access.

True multiuser operation in Q&A is restricted to databases and the support programs for them. A database file can be controlled so that each user can access one record at a time, which will give many users simultaneous access to the database file. Networked users also can share word processing files, but only one person at a time can have access to a given file. The reason for this limitation is that controlling how more than one person uses and changes a text-based file is difficult or impossible. The multiuser instructions in this chapter, therefore, apply to database access only.

Designing Multiuser Databases

The basic concepts of designing a database are essentially the same for single-user and multiuser operation. However, some additional considerations may apply to some database applications.

In a typical Q&A installation, several data files store different kinds of information. You may have an inventory file, a customer file, one or more sales support files, some accounting or bookkeeping files, and personnel files, for example. After you design these files (using some of the techniques described in Chapters 4, 5, and 6), you may want to restrict access to some of these files—the general payroll files or the inventory information files, for example.

One way to control this level of access easily is to establish user classes or groups. At the most basic level, each member of a group can be assigned a group ID and password. This arrangement reduces the number of different access rights that the database administrator must track. However, this arrangement is less secure than an arrangement in which each user is assigned a separate ID and unique password. Such group assignments must be done at the network level.

Q&A supports only user-based access. Several users can share the same ID and password, but the idea of groups, with each user in the group assigned a unique ID and password, is not supported. Some networks, such as NetWare, permit simultaneous group and individual ID and password assignments. You can use the security features of your individual network to enhance Q&A's multiuser access control. Refer to your network configuration manual for more information on security techniques.

Specifying the Mode

Before multiple users can share a database file, the file must be configured for sharing. Select Assign Access Rights from the Main/File/Design/Secure menu sequence, which calls up the Security menu (see fig. 21.1). Choose Declare Sharing Mode to call up the screen for setting multiuser access for a file (see fig. 21.2). To turn on Sharing mode, specify Allow from the Declare Sharing Mode screen; to disable Sharing mode, select Disallow from the screen. Because you must declare which file you want to customize before the Customize menu is displayed, the operations on the Access menu apply to one file at a time.

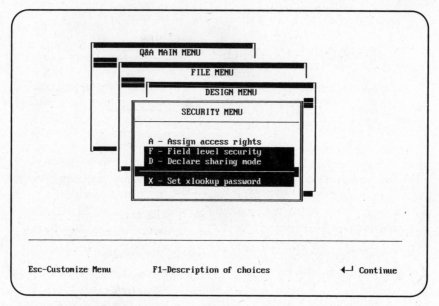

Fig. 21.1. *The Security menu.*

Q&A can handle file contention automatically by determining whether files are being stored on a server or a local PC. Additionally, if files are being stored on a network server, Q&A assumes that you want to share them. For some applications, forced Sharing or forced Non-Sharing mode is desirable. If you want to maintain a private, personal database, for example, you can prevent other users from accessing the database by disallowing sharing from the Declare Sharing Mode screen. Or you may want to force Sharing or Non-Sharing for some applications software.

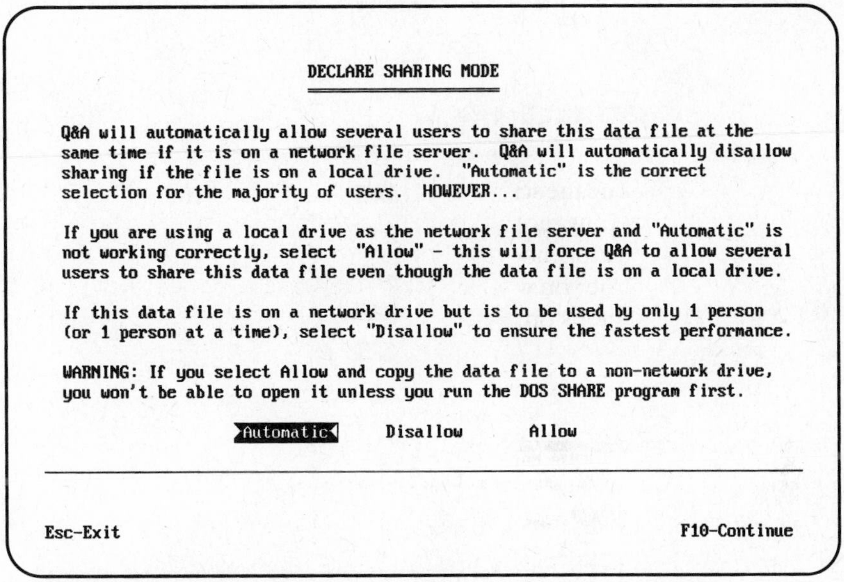

```
                        DECLARE SHARING MODE
                        ───────────────────

  Q&A will automatically allow several users to share this data file at the
  same time if it is on a network file server.  Q&A will automatically disallow
  sharing if the file is on a local drive.  "Automatic" is the correct
  selection for the majority of users.  HOWEVER...

  If you are using a local drive as the network file server and "Automatic" is
  not working correctly, select  "Allow" - this will force Q&A to allow several
  users to share this data file even though the data file is on a local drive.

  If this data file is on a network drive but is to be used by only 1 person
  (or 1 person at a time), select "Disallow" to ensure the fastest performance.

  WARNING: If you select Allow and copy the data file to a non-network drive,
  you won't be able to open it unless you run the DOS SHARE program first.

                    ▸Automatic◂    Disallow    Allow


  Esc-Exit                                                   F10-Continue
```

Fig. 21.2. The Declare Sharing Mode screen.

Specifying Access Rights and Passwords

One method of controlling access to network facilities is to assign each user a unique ID and password. Unless the ID and password are entered correctly, a user is denied access to specific network features, programs, or files.

If you want to restrict access to some of the files stored on a network server, choose Assign Access Rights from the Security menu (refer to fig. 21.1). Q&A displays the List of Users/Groups screen. Type a user ID or group name of up to 31 characters at the prompt. This is not the user's or group's password but rather an unrestricted name used for identification in Q&A lists and prompts related to network access functions.

Press F10, and Q&A displays the Access Control screen, where you can assign *user rights*, those functions that a user will be allowed to perform (see fig. 21.3). From this screen you also can assign user passwords. To designate yourself the database administrator, for example, you assign yourself the right to assign passwords and change design and program. Other users are assigned fewer rights: for example, only the setting Can Write Data? would be set to Yes.

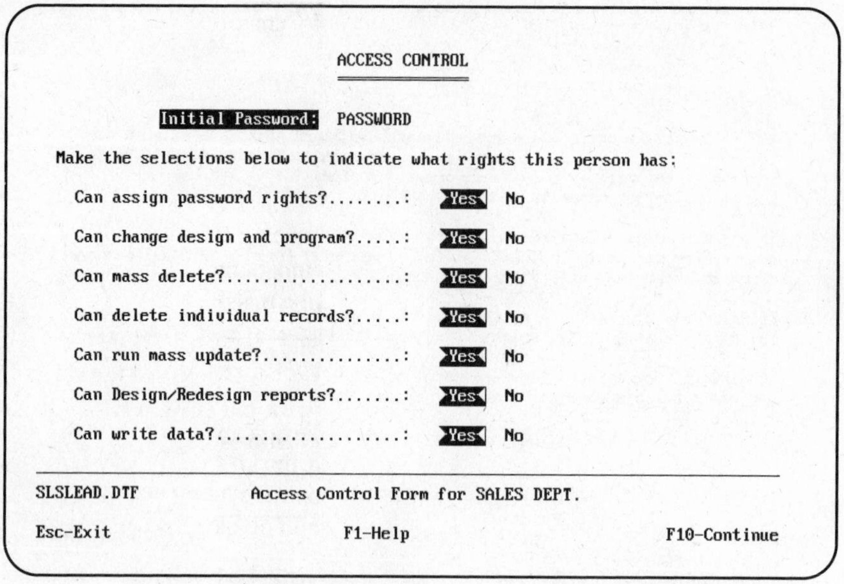

```
                              ACCESS CONTROL
                              ─────────────

                 Initial Password:  PASSWORD

        Make the selections below to indicate what rights this person has:

            Can assign password rights?........:    Yes   No

            Can change design and program?.....:     Yes   No

            Can mass delete?...................:      Yes   No

            Can delete individual records?.....:     Yes   No

            Can run mass update?...............:      Yes   No

            Can Design/Redesign reports?.......:      Yes   No

            Can write data?....................:      Yes   No
        ─────────────────────────────────────────────────────────────
        SLSLEAD.DTF         Access Control Form for SALES DEPT.

        Esc-Exit                    F1-Help                    F10-Continue
```

Fig. 21.3. *The Access Control screen.*

When you press F10 to exit the Access Control screen, Q&A saves your user ID and password and asks if you want to edit the Access Control screen for another user.

Field Level Security

Beginning with Q&A Version 4.0, you can assign access rights to certain fields on a database form. Before a user can enter data in a protected field, he or she must enter an access code. Other users (those not assigned to a field security spec as described below) may edit any field in the form.

Using the Field Security Spec

To assign access codes to individual fields in a file, you fill in the Field Security Spec by performing these steps:

1. From the File menu, choose Design File, then select Secure File. At the Security menu, choose the file that you want to secure.

2. Q&A displays the List of Field Security Specs screen. Select a spec from the list, or type the name of a new spec.

   Names for security specs can be up to 31 characters long. Create a descriptive name such as "View without personnel data," to design a security spec that selectively hides personnel information. The process of hiding fields is discussed below.

   Q&A displays the Field Security Spec, which consists of a copy of the database form. If this is a new Field Security Spec, Q&A enters a W code in each field, which indicates that users can presently read and write data in all fields.

3. Q&A overlays the form with a protection code description screen. To remove the overlay, press Esc.

4. Type one of the following access codes in each field:

Code	Meaning of Code
W	Read and Write. The user can view and change data.
R	Read Only. The user can see but not edit data.
N	No Access. The user cannot see or edit data. The field is hidden during Add and Search operations.

5. Press F10 to display the User Selection screen.

   In the User Selection screen, you tell Q&A which users or user groups are assigned the field security codes you just specified. In the two columns, type the names of users or groups. You also can press Alt-F7 and select users or groups from a list by highlighting names and pressing Enter.

6. Press F10 to leave the User Selection screen and end the field security selection process.

Setting XLOOKUP Passwords

If a user's ID and password are not valid for looking up data in an external file, you can allow the user password access to the external file for functions that use XLOOKUP to draw data from the external file. The special XLOOKUP password and ID will be valid for expressions that use XLOOKUP or @XLOOKUP.

To specify an XLOOKUP password, choose Set XLOOKUP Password from the Security menu. Type the user ID and password that will allow the user selective access to the external file.

Linking to an SQL Database

Q&A can retrieve data from databases that use *Standard Query Language* (SQL) protocols compatible with ORACLE Server and Gupta SQLBase. Your network workstation must be running the workstation component of the SQL software in order for Q&A to link with the database.

SQL databases use a slightly different terminology than Q&A's. In SQL parlance, for example, a field is referred to as a *column* and a record is called a *row*.

To import information from an SQL database, follow these steps:

1. From the file Utilities menu, choose Link-to-SQL. Q&A displays the SQL Import Menu, listing SQLBase and ORACLE.

   If you choose SQLBase, Q&A asks for a database name, user name, and password.

   If you choose ORACLE, Q&A prompts you for a user name, password, server name, and network protocol.

2. Enter the requested information and press F10.

   Q&A links to the SQL database and submits your user ID, password, etc. If no errors occur, Q&A asks for an SQL table (database) name and the name of the Q&A database that will receive the transferred records.

3. Type the name of the table and press Enter. You can press Enter to view a list of tables. Next, type the name of the Q&A database and press Enter, or press Enter to select from a list of Q&A files.

   If you are importing to an existing database, Q&A displays the Merge Spec. If you name a new database, Q&A can build the Q&A database for you and places the fields in the Merge Spec for you. You later can redesign the form and rearrange the fields.

4. Fill in the Merge and Retrieve Specs (see Chapter 20).

   When linking to an SQL database, you may not use the Retrieve Spec functions or MIN and MAX, but you can press F8 to create a Sort Spec.

5. Press F10 to start the import process.

Chapter Summary

This chapter introduces the concept of multiuser access to Q&A programs and data. You learned differences between single-user and multiuser Q&A operation and how to design and use the networked Q&A.

For detailed instructions on installing Q&A and configuring the package for your computer environment, see Appendix A. For information on installing a Q&A Network Pack for shared program access, contact Symantec.

Installing and Starting Q&A

The Q&A program requires the following hardware and software:

- IBM PC, IBM XT, IBM AT, IBM PS/2, or IBM-compatible computer

- PC DOS or MS-DOS, Version 2.1 or higher; DOS 3.1 required for network use; DOS 3.3 required for PS/2 model computers

- 512K of RAM recommended; 640K required for DOS 4.0 and network use; EMS required for linking to SQL

- 484K of RAM for computers using Q&A on a network

- A hard disk

- 80-column monochrome or color monitor

Preparing To Install the Q&A Program

When you have your hardware in place, you can begin the process of installing the Q&A program. While you use Q&A's menu-driven installation routine, you tailor Q&A to your computer system. This process involves specifying the printer to be used, selecting the type of display, installing the programs on floppies or your hard disk, and specifying the default drive and directory.

Before installing Q&A, check the CONFIG.SYS file in the root directory of your hard disk. This file should include the following statements, which ensure that Q&A can function properly:

```
FILES = 20
BUFFERS = 10
```

To view an existing CONFIG.SYS file, change to the root directory with the CD\ command. At the DOS prompt, type the following:

```
TYPE CONFIG.SYS
```

Press Enter. If a CONFIG.SYS file exists, text scrolls up the screen. If you do not see FILES and BUFFER statements, use any ASCII text editor to add these statements. Refer to your DOS manual for additional information on preparing CONFIG.SYS files.

If you do not have a CONFIG.SYS file, DOS responds with the following error message:

```
File Not Found
```

To create a new CONFIG.SYS file, use an ASCII editor or type the following command at the DOS root directory prompt:

```
COPY CON: CONFIG.SYS
```

Press Enter.

Next, type the following statements:

```
FILES = 20
BUFFERS = 10
```

Press Enter at the end of the FILES statement, but not at the end of the BUFFERS statement. Finally, press F6, or hold down the Ctrl key and press Z, and then press Enter.

Note: If your computer is short on memory, you can reduce the number of buffers to 2.

Installing Q&A on Your Hard Disk

Before you install Q&A, make backup copies of the original disks. The following installation instructions assume that you have made backup copies and that you are using these backup disks for the installation. Your DOS manual can help with the backup procedure.

Installation involves running the installation program on the first Q&A floppy disk, Installation Disk/Program Disk #1. The Install program transfers to your hard disk the programs needed to run Q&A. You cannot transfer these files using the DOS Copy command, because they are encoded in a space-saving archival format that must be decoded by the Install routine.

The Install program copies Q&A program files, then optionally installs printer drivers, tutorial files, and utilities. Install does not change your AUTOEXEC.BAT or CONFIG.SYS files. To run the installation routines, follow these steps:

1. Place the Q&A Installation Disk/Program Disk #1 in your computer's A drive and type the following:

   A:INSTALL

   Press Enter.

2. The Install program displays its first screen containing instructions for using the installation program to perform a first-time installation, upgrade an existing copy of Q&A, or copy selected program, printer font, sample database, or utility files. Press Alt-X to cancel the installation process at any point, or press Esc to back up to the previous screen.

   The Install program first asks you to choose your source and target drives from two menus. (Unless you're installing Q&A on a network, these drives normally are drives A and C.) Install then scans your hard disk for other copies of Q&A and displays a screen in which you can choose to install Q&A 4.0 in a new directory, C:\QA4, or overwrite or upgrade another copy of Q&A in an existing directory.

3. Install next asks if you want to perform a complete, first-time installation, or a selective installation of program, printer, tutorial, or utility files. Install then begins copying the files you specified.

Installing Printers and Fonts

Toward the end of the installation process, the Install program enables you to choose printer and font definition files to install. Q&A can support up to five printers and comes with an extensive library of printer and font definition files. If you're not sure which printer driver or set of fonts work with your printer, copy the most likely choices for your printer's brand. You then can experiment with the files and delete the ones that aren't needed.

Installing Tutorial Files

The Q&A manual includes a tutorial section, "Getting Started with Q&A." If you want to use the tutorial, you can install the required database and document files when the Install program asks if you would like to do so. You can wait until later to install tutorial files, if you want, by running the Install program again and choosing Selective Installation.

Installing Utility Files

Q&A comes with several utility files that you can install now. You also can wait until you need these files, and then install them by selecting Selective Installation with the Install program. The utility files are as follows:

Utility file	Use
QAFONT.EXE	Used to define new font definitions; recommended for advanced users only
QABACKUP.EXE	Used to back up large database on several floppies
FONTCONV.EXE	Converts Q&A 3.0 fonts for use with Q&A 4.0
HIMEM.SYS	An extended memory driver that enables you to increase the amount of memory available to Q&A on a network

Installing a Monitor

Q&A automatically configures itself to work with the most popular brands and models of computer monitors. If your monitor doesn't work properly, you may have to load Q&A with a special code at the DOS prompt. You need to do this only once; Q&A will remember the settings in future sessions. The following list gives the start-up options for various monitor types. You may have to try more than one code to get your monitor to work correctly.

Start-up option	Monitor type
QA -SCC	Color monitors
QA -SMC -A	Monochrome monitors
QA -SMM	Monochrome monitors
QA -A TV	Composite monitors, similar to sets; first try QA -SMC -A and QA -SMM

The following settings should work with the specified systems:

System/Display	Start-up option
NEC Multispeed	QA -ST
With monochrome monitor	QA -SMC ATT 6300
IBM PS/2 with monochrome monitor	QA -SMC -A
Toshiba 1100, 3100	QA -SMC
Zenith laptops	QA -A
Compaq with color monitor	QA -SCC
LCD display	QA -A or QA -ST

Installing a Printer

The Install program transfers printer and font files to your hard disk, but you must finish the printer installation with Q&A's Printer Selection screen. You can install as many as five printers. To install your printer, follow these steps:

1. At the Q&A Main menu, choose Utilities, then choose Install Printer. Q&A displays the Printer Selection Screen (see fig. A.1).

2. Highlight the first choice for your printer's port type (LPT, COM, or FILE), and press F10 to continue.

   Choose an LPT type if your printer has a parallel cable connection, COM if your printer has a serial connection, or FILE if you want to create a printer driver that saves documents or data in a disk file.

```
                        PRINTER SELECTION
                        ═════════════════

     A "Q&A PRINTER" is a combination of a PORT and a specific PRINTER MODEL
     and MODE (e.g. draft or letter).   Press F1 if you want more explanation.

     Highlight the Q&A PRINTER you want to install by pressing ↑ or ↓, then
     press ↵ .

     ┌─────────────────────┬────────┬─────────────────────────────────────┐
     │ Q&A PRINTER         │ PORT   │ PRINTER MODEL AND MODE              │
     ├─────────────────────┼────────┼─────────────────────────────────────┤
     │ ███████████████████ │ LPT1   │ Canon LBP-8IIT (A4, Portrait)       │
     │ Printer B (PtrB)    │ LPT2   │ Canon LBP-8IIT/III/4 (Land,Legal)   │
     │ Printer C (PtrC)    │ LPT3   │ Canon LBP-8IIT/III/4 (Env,Man)      │
     │ Printer D (PtrD)    │ FAX1   │ Intel Connection: Fine res/80 column│
     │ Printer E (PtrE)    │ COM2   │ Basic (Vanilla) Non-laser printer   │
     └─────────────────────┴────────┴─────────────────────────────────────┘

     ─────────────────────────────────────────────────────────────────────

     Esc-Exit                  F1-Help                          ↵ Continue
```

Fig. A.1. *The Printer Selection screen.*

3. Q&A displays the Port Selection screen (see fig. A.2).

```
                         PORT SELECTION
                         ══════════════

     Highlight the PORT you wish to assign to the Q&A PRINTER by pressing
     ↑ and ↓.  Press ↵ to select the highlighted PORT.

     ┌─────────────────────┬────────┬─────────────────────────────────────┐
     │ Q&A PRINTER         │ PORT   │ PRINTER MODEL AND MODE              │
     ├─────────────────────┼────────┼─────────────────────────────────────┤
     │ Printer A (PtrA)    │ ████   │ Canon LBP-8IIT (A4, Portrait)       │
     │                     │ LPT2   │                                     │
     │                     │ LPT3   │                                     │
     │                     │ COM1   │                                     │
     │                     │ COM2   │                                     │
     │                     │ FILE   │                                     │
     └─────────────────────┴────────┴─────────────────────────────────────┘

     ─────────────────────────────────────────────────────────────────────

     Esc-Exit      F1-Help      F8-Special Ports      F9-Go back  ↵ Continue
```

Fig. A.2. *The Port Selection screen.*

4. Highlight the port to which your printer is connected, then press F10 to continue.

   If you are using an Intel Connection board, you can choose it as a Q&A "printer" by pressing F8 to access the Special Port Options screen.

5. Q&A displays the List of Printer Manufacturers screen. Highlight your printer's brand name, and press Enter. Next, choose the printer's model from the List of *<brand name>* Printers screen.

   If you are having problems with communications between Q&A and your printer, press F8 to change the Special Printer Options screen. To set these options, you need to check your printer manual for information on required communications protocols. Press F10 to see more special printer options.

6. Press F10 to continue. Q&A asks if you want to install another printer. Press N to return to the Utilities menu or Y to return to the Printer Selection screen.

Installing Fonts

Q&A supplies font description files for many popular printers. To install these fonts for use with your printer, press Shift-F6 to display the Text Enhancements and Fonts menu at the Write Type/Edit screen. From the Text Enhancements and Fonts menu, choose A-Assign Fonts. When you make a font assignment, you tell Q&A to display the chosen font on the Text Enhancements and Fonts menu, which you can display from many Q&A screens by pressing Shift-F6. The process of assigning fonts is described in detail in the section "Using Fonts" in Chapter 11.

Note that you also can modify and create fonts by choosing Modify Font File from the Utilities menu. However, this is a complex process that should be undertaken only by advanced users.

Setting the Default Drive and Directory

Q&A selects default drives and directories to save document and database files as well as drives and directories where Q&A looks for its program files. You can set the drive and directory in the Set Default Directories option of the Utilities menu. You should set up separate subdirectories for your document and database files.

Why use a document subdirectory? Unless you change the directory, Q&A Write stores documents with the program files and the database files. This method doesn't cause a problem when you have only a few documents. As the number of documents increases, however, the list of files gets longer and longer. The tedious search through that list to find one document is time-consuming and unnecessary. You can avoid this problem by creating a subdirectory, thus creating a separate list of documents.

Why use a database subdirectory? Backing up database files is much easier if the files are in a separate subdirectory. You then need only one DOS command to copy everything in your database file directory to your backup disk.

To create subdirectories, use the DOS MD command (see your DOS manual). For example, to create QATEXT and QADATA subdirectories, type the following commands at the C> prompt, and press Enter after each command:

    MD\QATEXT
    MD\QADATA

To set the default drive and directory within Q&A, follow these steps by using drive C, the QATEXT subdirectory for documents, and the QADATA subdirectory for databases:

1. Select Set Global Defaults from the Utilities menu. Q&A displays the Set Global Defaults screen (see fig. A.3).

2. To set the default for the Q&A document files, type the following:

   C:\QATEXT

   Press Enter. C: sets the default drive to drive C. \QATEXT sets the subdirectory. You may select any convenient subdirectory that is compatible with DOS conventions.

3. To set the default for the Q&A database files, type the following and press Enter:

   C:\QADATA

4. Press F10 to return to the Utilities menu, or enter a setting for an alternate program, as explained in the following section.

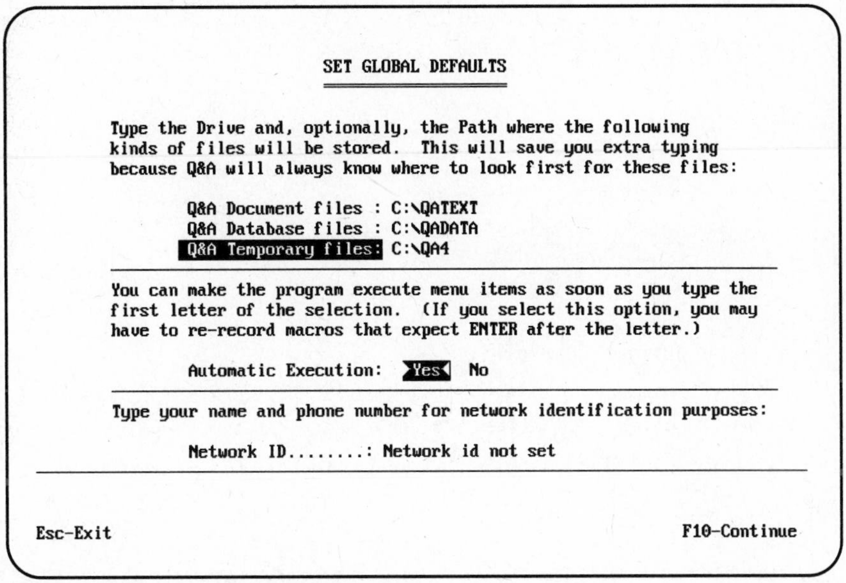

```
                          SET GLOBAL DEFAULTS

        Type the Drive and, optionally, the Path where the following
        kinds of files will be stored.  This will save you extra typing
        because Q&A will always know where to look first for these files:

              Q&A Document files : C:\QATEXT
              Q&A Database files : C:\QADATA
              Q&A Temporary files: C:\QA4

        You can make the program execute menu items as soon as you type the
        first letter of the selection.  (If you select this option, you may
        have to re-record macros that expect ENTER after the letter.)

              Automatic Execution:   Yes   No

        Type your name and phone number for network identification purposes:

              Network ID........: Network id not set


  Esc-Exit                                                    F10-Continue
```

Fig. A.3.   *The Set Global Defaults screen.*

Setting Alternate Programs

In addition to using the Set Global Defaults option from the Utilities menu for selecting the default drive and directory, you can use the Set Alternate Programs option to provide access to other programs from the Q&A Main menu. Use the Alternate Program selection to indicate the subdirectory where the alternate program is stored (see fig. A.4).

If you frequently use another software program, such as Lotus 1-2-3, you can enter the program as one of the default alternate programs. If you have installed 1-2-3 in a subdirectory called \123 on drive C, you can set the default alternate program by using the following procedure:

1. Select Set Alternate Programs from the Utilities menu.

2. To set Lotus 1-2-3 as a default alternate program, at the Alternate Program 1: prompt, type the following:

    C:\123\LOTUS.COM

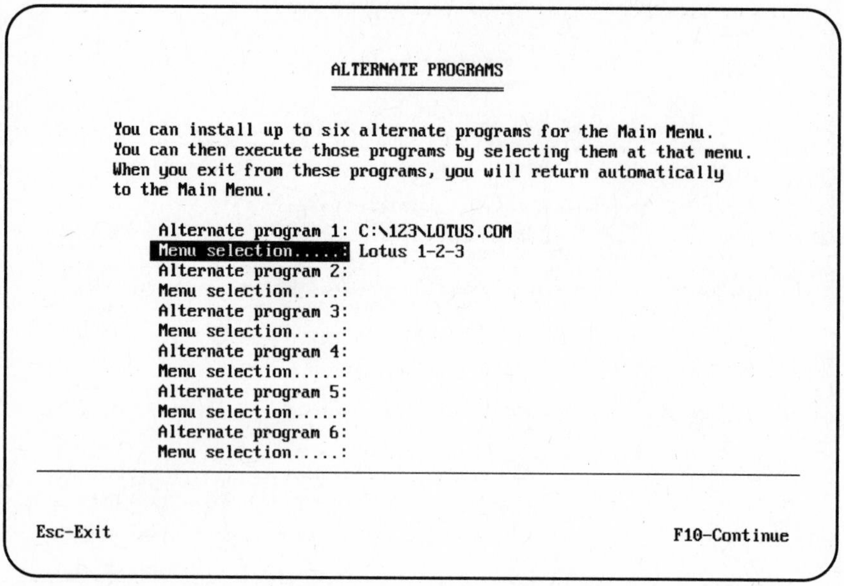

```
                    ALTERNATE PROGRAMS

      You can install up to six alternate programs for the Main Menu.
      You can then execute those programs by selecting them at that menu.
      When you exit from these programs, you will return automatically
      to the Main Menu.

            Alternate program 1: C:\123\LOTUS.COM
            Menu selection.....: Lotus 1-2-3
            Alternate program 2:
            Menu selection.....:
            Alternate program 3:
            Menu selection.....:
            Alternate program 4:
            Menu selection.....:
            Alternate program 5:
            Menu selection.....:
            Alternate program 6:
            Menu selection.....:



   Esc-Exit                                            F10-Continue
```

Fig. A.4.   The Alternate Program selection from the Set Default Directories screen.

3. To display Lotus 1-2-3 as a menu selection on Q&A's Main menu, type the following after Menu Selection:

   Lotus 1-2-3

4. Repeat these steps for up to five additional alternate programs.

After you enter settings in the Alternate Program and Menu Selection options and press F10, Q&A supplies additional menu items in its Main menu. Figure A.5, for example, shows Lotus 1-2-3, ProComm, and WordPerfect 5.1 as additional menu selections.

Q&A enables you to specify nearly any program name as an alternate selection, but if you select a name that begins with the same letter as a standard Q&A selection, your alternate selection replaces the Q&A default. For example, to install WordPerfect as the default word processor replacing Write, use WordPerfect as the program name. When you type *W* at the Main menu, you load WordPerfect rather than the Write module. You still can call up the Write module in this example by typing the number *3* at the Q&A Main menu, or you can specify another name for WordPerfect that does not conflict with Q&A's existing Write program name.

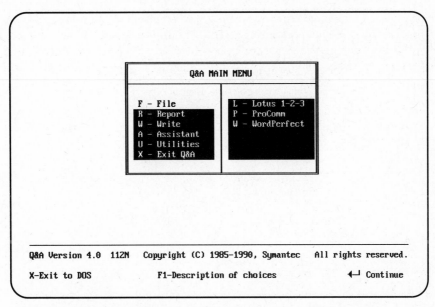

Fig. A.5. *Lotus 1-2-3, ProComm, and WordPerfect appearing as menu selections on Q&A's Main menu.*

Starting Q&A

After you install Q&A, you start the program by moving to the Q&A sub-directory with the DOS CD command (Change Directory). For example, type the following:

C> CD\QA4

To load Q&A, type *QA*, and press Enter at the DOS prompt.

Configuring Q&A for Multiuser Access

Version 3.0 and later of Q&A supports multiuser operation over local area networks in two ways: data files only or files and programs. You can share Q&A files over a network with the standard Q&A software as long as each network user has an individual copy of the program. To install a single copy of Q&A program files on a network server and have multiple users share the program, you must upgrade the single-user version of Q&A to a networked version. Contact Symantec for information on installing a Q&A Network Pack for shared program access.

To set up a database for multiuser access, use the Secure a File option on the Design menu (see Chapter 21). This option enables you to turn multiuser mode on or off and assign individual user rights.

Index

D

N

Computer Books From Que Mean PC Performance!

Spreadsheets

1-2-3 Database Techniques	$29.95
1-2-3 Graphics Techniques	$24.95
1-2-3 Macro Library, 3rd Edition	$39.95
1-2-3 Release 2.2 Business Applications	$39.95
1-2-3 Release 2.2 PC Tutor	$39.95
1-2-3 Release 2.2 QueCards	$19.95
1-2-3 Release 2.2 Quick Reference	$ 8.95
1-2-3 Release 2.2 QuickStart, 2nd Edition	$19.95
1-2-3 Release 2.2 Workbook and Disk	$29.95
1-2-3 Release 3 Business Applications	$39.95
1-2-3 Release 3 Workbook and Disk	$29.95
1-2-3 Release 3.1 Quick Reference	$ 8.95
1-2-3 Release 3.1 QuickStart, 2nd Edition	$19.95
1-2-3 Tips, Tricks, and Traps, 3rd Edition	$24.95
Excel Business Applications: IBM Version	$39.95
Excel Quick Reference	$ 8.95
Excel QuickStart	$19.95
Excel Tips, Tricks, and Traps	$22.95
Using 1-2-3/G	$29.95
Using 1-2-3, Special Edition	$27.95
Using 1-2-3 Release 2.2, Special Edition	$27.95
Using 1-2-3 Release 3.1, 2nd Edition	$29.95
Using Excel: IBM Version	$29.95
Using Lotus Spreadsheet for DeskMate	$22.95
Using Quattro Pro	$24.95
Using SuperCalc5, 2nd Edition	$29.95

Databases

dBASE III Plus Handbook, 2nd Edition	$24.95
dBASE III Plus Tips, Tricks, and Traps	$24.95
dBASE III Plus Workbook and Disk	$29.95
dBASE IV Applications Library, 2nd Edition	$39.95
dBASE IV Programming Techniques	$24.95
dBASE IV Quick Reference	$ 8.95
dBASE IV QuickStart	$19.95
dBASE IV Tips, Tricks,and Traps, 2nd Edition	$24.95
dBASE IV Workbook and Disk	$29.95
Using Clipper	$24.95
Using DataEase	$24.95
Using dBASE IV	$27.95
Using Paradox 3	$24.95
Using R:BASE	$29.95
Using Reflex, 2nd Edition	$24.95
Using SQL	$29.95

Business Applications

Allways Quick Reference	$ 8.95
Introduction to Business Software	$14.95
Introduction to Personal Computers	$19.95
Lotus Add-in Toolkit Guide	$29.95
Norton Utilities Quick Reference	$ 8.95
PC Tools Quick Reference, 2nd Edition	$ 8.95
Q&A Quick Reference	$ 8.95
Que's Computer User's Dictionary	$ 9.95
Que's Wizard Book	$ 9.95
Quicken Quick Reference	$ 8.95
SmartWare Tips, Tricks, and Traps 2nd Edition	$24.95
Using Computers in Business	$22.95
Using DacEasy, 2nd Edition	$24.95
Using Enable/OA	$29.95
Using Harvard Project Manager	$24.95
Using Managing Your Money, 2nd Edition	$19.95

Using Microsoft Works: IBM Version	$22.95
Using Norton Utilities	$24.95
Using PC Tools Deluxe	$24.95
Using Peachtree	$27.95
Using PFS: First Choice	$22.95
Using PROCOMM PLUS	$19.95
Using Q&A, 2nd Edition	$23.95
Using Quicken: IBM Version, 2nd Edition	$19.95
Using Smart	$22.95
Using SmartWare II	$29.95
Using Symphony, Special Edition	$29.95
Using Time Line	$24.95
Using TimeSlips	$24.95

CAD

AutoCAD Quick Reference	$ 8.95
AutoCAD Sourcebook 1991	$27.95
Using AutoCAD, 3rd Edition	$29.95
Using Generic CADD	$24.95

Word Processing

Microsoft Word 5 Quick Reference	$ 8.95
Using DisplayWrite 4, 2nd Edition	$24.95
Using LetterPerfect	$22.95
Using Microsoft Word 5.5: IBM Version, 2nd Edition	$24.95
Using MultiMate	$24.95
Using Professional Write	$22.95
Using Word for Windows	$24.95
Using WordPerfect 5	$27.95
Using WordPerfect 5.1, Special Edition	$27.95
Using WordStar, 3rd Edition	$27.95
WordPerfect PC Tutor	$39.95
WordPerfect Power Pack	$39.95
WordPerfect Quick Reference	$ 8.95
WordPerfect QuickStart	$19.95
WordPerfect 5 Workbook and Disk	$29.95
WordPerfect 5.1 Quick Reference	$ 8.95
WordPerfect 5.1 QuickStart	$19.95
WordPerfect 5.1 Tips, Tricks, and Traps	$24.95
WordPerfect 5.1 Workbook and Disk	$29.95

Hardware/Systems

DOS Tips, Tricks, and Traps	$24.95
DOS Workbook and Disk, 2nd Edition	$29.95
Fastback Quick Reference	$ 8.95
Hard Disk Quick Reference	$ 8.95
MS-DOS PC Tutor	$39.95
MS-DOS Power Pack	$39.95
MS-DOS Quick Reference	$ 8.95
MS-DOS QuickStart, 2nd Edition	$19.95
MS-DOS User's Guide, Special Edition	$29.95
Networking Personal Computers, 3rd Edition	$24.95
The Printer Bible	$29.95
Que's PC Buyer's Guide	$12.95
Understanding UNIX: A Conceptual Guide, 2nd Edition	$21.95
Upgrading and Repairing PCs	$29.95
Using DOS	$22.95
Using Microsoft Windows 3, 2nd Edition	$24.95
Using Novell NetWare	$29.95
Using OS/2	$29.95
Using PC DOS, 3rd Edition	$24.95
Using Prodigy	$19.95

Using UNIX	$2
Using Your Hard Disk	$2
Windows 3 Quick Reference	$

Desktop Publishing/Graphics

CorelDRAW Quick Reference	$
Harvard Graphics Quick Reference	$
Using Animator	$2
Using DrawPerfect	$2
Using Harvard Graphics, 2nd Edition	$2
Using Freelance Plus	$2
Using PageMaker: IBM Version, 2nd Edition	$2
Using PFS: First Publisher, 2nd Edition	$2
Using Ventura Publisher, 2nd Edition	$2

Macintosh/Apple II

AppleWorks QuickStart	$1
The Big Mac Book, 2nd Edition	$2
Excel QuickStart	$1
The Little Mac Book	$
Que's Macintosh Multimedia Handbook	$2
Using AppleWorks, 3rd Edition	$2
Using Excel: Macintosh Version	$2
Using FileMaker	$2
Using MacDraw	$2
Using MacroMind Director	$2
Using MacWrite	$2
Using Microsoft Word 4: Macintosh Version	$2
Using Microsoft Works: Macintosh Version, 2nd Edition	$2
Using PageMaker: Macinsoth Version, 2nd Edition	$2

Programming/Technical

Assembly Language Quick Reference	$ 8
C Programmer's Toolkit	$3
C Quick Reference	$ 8
DOS and BIOS Functions Quick Reference	$ 8
DOS Programmer's Reference, 2nd Edition	$29
Network Programming in C	$49
Oracle Programmer's Guide	$29
QuickBASIC Advanced Techniques	$24
Quick C Programmer's Guide	$29
Turbo Pascal Advanced Techniques	$24
Turbo Pascal Quick Reference	$ 8
UNIX Programmer's Quick Reference	$ 8
UNIX Programmer's Reference	$29
UNIX Shell Commands Quick Reference	$ 8
Using Assembly Language, 2nd Edition	$29
Using BASIC	$24
Using C	$29
Using QuickBASIC 4	$24
Using Turbo Pascal	$29

For More Information, Call Toll Free!

1-800-428-5331

All prices and titles subject to change without notice.
Non-U.S. prices may be higher. Printed in the U.S.A.

Find It Fast With Que's Quick References!

Que's Quick References are the compact, easy-to-use guides to essential application information. Written for all users, Quick References include vital command information under easy-to-find alphabetical listings. Quick References are a must for anyone who needs command information fast!

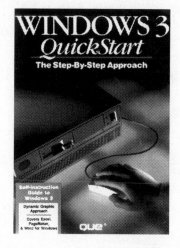